FIFTH EDITION

# Modern Real Estate Practice in Ohio

**FILLMORE W. GALATY**

**WELLINGTON J. ALLAWAY**

**ROBERT C. KYLE**

**THOMAS A. ENERVA, Consulting Editor**

**Dearborn**™
Real Estate Education

This publication is designed to provide accurate and authoritative information in regard to the subject matter covered. It is sold with the understanding that the publisher is not engaged in rendering legal, accounting, or other professional service. If legal advice or other expert assistance is required, the services of a competent professional person should be sought.

**Vice President:** Roy Lipner
**Publisher:** Evan Butterfield
**Development Editor:** David Cirillo
**Senior Managing Editor:** Ronald J. Liszkowski
**Typesetting:** Janet Schroeder
**Art Manager:** Lucy Jenkins

**Library of Congress Cataloging-in-Publication Data**

Galaty, Fillmore W.
    Modern real estate practice in Ohio / Fillmore W. Galaty, Wellington J. Allaway,
  Robert C. Kyle; consultling editor, Thomas A. Enerva.—5th ed.
        p. cm.
    Includes bibliographical references and index.
    ISBN 0-7931-4229-6
    1. Vendors and purchasers—Ohio.   2. Real estate business—Law and
legislation—Ohio.   I. Allaway, Wellington J.   II. Kyle, Robert C.   III. Title

  KFO126 .G35 2001
  346.77104'37—dc21                                              00-050881

# Contents

# 5 Agency 44

# 6 Real Estate License Laws 70

# 7 Listing Agreements and Buyer Representation 100

# Preface

**S**ince its first printing in 1990, *Modern Real Estate Practice in Ohio* has provided thousands of people with valuable real estate information, presented in a logical and accessible manner. Specifically tailored to Ohio real estate law and practice, *Modern Real Estate Practice in Ohio* sets the standard for contemporary information, whether the book is used to prepare for a state licensing examination, college or university program, or simply for personal knowledge.

This fifth edition has been revised to reflect recent trends and developments in the real estate industry, to note changes in a variety of laws, and to provide students with updated study aids. A new, more readable page design, created in consultation with education experts and graphic designers, actually works to improve students' comprehension by physically directing them to the most important materials for first-time reading, for reinforcement of basic ideas, and for study and review. New Ohio state icons have been added to the margins

**In Ohio...** to aid students in finding Ohio specific laws and practices. ◆

Margin notes direct readers' attention to important vocabulary terms, concepts, and study tips and serve as memory prompts for more efficient and effective studying. There are major revisions in the chapters on licensing law, agency, contracts, finance, and fair housing. The end-of-chapter questions reflect the style used for the state licensing examination questions, and the answer key now includes page references to reinforce learning so that students are better prepared for the licensing exam. The Instructor's Manual accompanying this text contains a conversion table to assist instructors in developing lectures and class assignments.

This text is only a tool. It is intended to introduce the reader to a variety of real estate concepts, theories, and specialties in practice. Instructors are encouraged to supplement the text material with classroom discussions, using practical examples and exhibits of forms and other documents common to the local area. The reader is encouraged to pursue further study through additional publications and discussions with industry practitioners. Education is a continuous process in which both reader and instructor are active participants.

The authors would particularly like to thank the Consulting Editor, Tony Enerva, J.D, of Chardon, Ohio, for his inspired input throughout the revision process. Mr. Enerva, who also served as the Consulting Editor for *Modern Real Estate Practice in Ohio,* 4th Edition, brings to the table a wealth of knowledge and real estate experience. He has coordinated and taught in the real estate program at Lakeland Community College in Kirtland, Ohio, since 1988. He also specializes in real estate matters as a management consultant. Mr. Enerva earned his J.D. from the University of Minnesota and his M.S. and B.A. from San Diego State University. He owes many thanks to his wife, Evelyn, and his three sons, Thomas, Samuel, and Joseph, whose patience and understanding made his work on this book possible.

The authors also offer special thanks to Rick Knowles from Capital Real Estate Training for his invaluable review of the new Math Appendix.

For their input in the development of this fifth edition of *Modern Real Estate Practice in Ohio,* the authors also wish to thank the following individuals:

Georgette Beres-Izworski, University of Akron
Joyce C. Collins, Jefferson Community College
Stephen J. Hummel, Ohio University-Chillicothe
Suzanne Murra, Owens Community College

# Introduction to the Real Estate Business

Real estate transactions are taking place all around you, all the time. When a commercial leasing company rents space in a mall or the owner of a building rents an apartment to a retired couple, it's a real estate transaction. If an appraiser gives an expert opinion of the value of farmland or a bank lends money to a professional corporation to purchase an office building, it's a real estate transaction. Most common of all, when an American family sells its old home and buys a new one, it takes part in the real estate industry. Consumers of real estate services include buyers and sellers of homes, tenants and landlords, investors, and developers. Nearly everyone, at some time, is involved in a real estate transaction.

All this adds up to really big business—complex transactions that involve billions of dollars every year in the United States alone. The services of millions of highly trained individuals are required: attorneys, bankers, trust company representatives, abstract and title insurance company agents, architects, surveyors, accountants, tax experts, and many others, in addition to buyers and sellers. All these people depend on the skills and knowledge of licensed real estate professionals.

## REAL ESTATE: A BUSINESS OF MANY SPECIALIZATIONS

Despite the size and complexity of the real estate business, many people think of it as being made up of only brokers and salespersons. Actually, the real estate industry encompasses much more. Appraisal, property management, financing, subdivision and development, counseling, and education are all separate businesses within the real estate field. To succeed in a complex industry, every real estate professional must have a basic knowledge of these specialties.

**Brokerage—Brokerage** is the business of bringing people together in a real estate transaction. A **broker** acts as a point of contact between two or more people in negotiating the sale, purchase, or rental of property. A broker may be the agent of the buyer, of the seller, or of both. The property may be residential, commercial, or industrial. A **sales agent** (the **salesperson)** is a licensee employed by or associated with the broker. The salesperson conducts brokerage activities on behalf of the broker. The broker, however, is ultimately responsible for the salesperson's acts. Brokerage is discussed in detail in Chapter 4.

**In Ohio...**    **Appraisal—Appraisal** is the process of estimating a property's market value, based on established methods and the appraiser's professional judgment. Although their training will give brokers some understanding of the valuation process, lenders generally require a professional appraisal, and property sold by court order requires an appraiser's expertise. Appraisers must have detailed knowledge of the methods of valuation. In Ohio, appraisers must be licensed or certified to engage in appraisal activities for any federally related transactions, which include most home mortgages and many commercial financing packages. Appraisal is covered in Chapter 19. ◆

**In Ohio...**    **Home inspection**—A home inspection is a visual examination of the components of a residential building, including (among other items) the plumbing system, electrical system, structural components, foundation, roof, and the heating and cooling system. Usually, a home inspection does not include environmental testing. Home inspections are becoming increasingly common. Home buyers often make their purchase offers conditioned on a satisfactory home inspection. Currently, home inspectors are not regulated in Ohio. However, legislation has been proposed that will regulate home inspectors and require their licensure. ◆

**Property management**—A **property manager** is a person hired to maintain and manage property on behalf of its owner. By hiring a property manager, the owner is relieved of such day-to-day management tasks as finding new tenants, collecting rents, altering or constructing new space for tenants, ordering repairs, and generally maintaining the property. The scope of the manager's work depends on the terms of the individual employment contract, known as a management agreement. Whatever tasks are specified, the basic responsibility of the property manager is to protect the owner's investment **In Ohio...** and maximize the owner's return on his or her investment. Property management, a licensed activity in Ohio, is discussed in Chapter 18. ◆

**Financing—Financing** is the business of providing the funds that make real estate transactions possible. Most transactions are financed by means of mortgage loans or trust deed loans secured by the property. Individuals involved in financing real estate may work in commercial banks, mortgage banking, and mortgage brokerage companies. A growing number of real estate brokerage firms affiliate with mortgage brokers to provide consumers with "one-stop-shopping" real estate services. Financing issues are examined in Chapters 15 and 16.

**Subdivision and development—Subdivision** is the splitting of a single property into smaller parcels. **Development** involves the construction of improvements on the land. These improvements may be either on-site or off-site. Off-site improvements, such as water lines and storm sewers, are made on public lands to serve the new development. On-site improvements, such as new homes or swimming pools, are made on individual parcels. While subdivision and development normally are related, they are independent processes that can occur separately. Subdivision and development are discussed further in Chapters 20 and 21.

**Counseling—Counseling** involves providing clients with competent independent advice based on sound professional judgment. A real estate counselor helps clients choose among the various alternatives involved in purchasing, using, or investing in property. A counselor's role is to furnish clients with the information needed to make informed decisions. Professional real estate counselors must have a high degree of industry expertise.

**In Ohio...** **Education—Real estate education** is available to both practitioners and consumers. Colleges and universities, private schools and trade organizations all conduct real estate courses and seminars, from the principles of a prelicensing program to the technical aspects of tax and exchange law. In Ohio, the state mandates continuing professional education for real estate brokers and agents, licensed or certified appraisers, and other professions as well. ◆

**In Ohio...** **Other areas—**Many other real estate career options are available. Practitioners will find that real estate specialists are needed in a variety of business settings. Lawyers who specialize in real estate are always in demand. Large corporations with extensive land holdings often have their own real estate and property tax departments. Local governments must staff zoning boards, building departments, and assessment offices. In Ohio, personal assistants to real estate agents are becoming popular as high producers require administrative and professional support. ◆

## PROFESSIONAL ORGANIZATIONS

**In Ohio...** Many trade organizations serve the real estate business. The largest is the National Association of REALTORS® **(NAR).** NAR is composed of state, regional, and local associations. NAR also sponsors various affiliated organizations that offer professional designations to brokers, salespersons, and others who complete required courses in areas of special interest. Members of the Ohio Association of REALTORS® **(OAR)** and affiliated local boards subscribe to a code of ethics and are entitled to be known as REALTORS® or REALTOR-ASSOCIATES®. ◆

 **WWWeb.Link**
www.realtor.com. The home site for the National Association of REALTORS®.
www.ohiorealtor.org. The home site for the Ohio Association of REALTORS®.

Among the other professional associations is the National Association of Real Estate Brokers **(NAREB),** whose members also subscribe to a code of ethics. Members of NAREB are known as Realtists. Other professional associations include the Appraisal Institute, the American Society of Appraisers **(ASA),** the National Association of Independent Fee Appraisers **(NAIFA)** and the Real Estate Educators Association **(REEA).** The growth in buyer brokerage, discussed in Chapter 5, led to the formation of organizations such as the Real Estate Buyer's Agent Council **(REBAC),** now associated with NAR, and the National Association of Exclusive Buyer's Agents **(NAEBA).** Other organizations include the Building Owners and Managers Association **(BOMA),** the Institute of Real Estate Management **(IREM),** the Commercial Investment Real Estate Institute **(CIREI),** and the American Society of Real Estate Counselors **(ASREC).**

## TYPES OF REAL PROPERTY

Just as there are areas of specialization within the real estate industry, there are different types of property in which to specialize. Real estate can be classified as:

- **residential**—all property used for single-family or multifamily housing, whether in urban, suburban, or rural areas;

---

**Five Categories of Real Property**

1. Residential
2. Commercial
3. Industrial
4. Agricultural
5. Special-purpose

---

- **commercial**—business property, including office space, shopping centers, stores, theaters, hotels, and parking facilities;
- **industrial**—warehouses, factories, land in industrial districts, and power plants;
- **agricultural**—farms, timberland, ranches, and orchards; or
- **special purpose**—churches, schools, cemeteries, and government-held lands.

The market for each of these types of property can be subdivided into the *sales market*, which involves the transfer of title and ownership rights, and the *rental market*, in which space is used temporarily by lease.

**In Practice**    Although it is possible for a single real estate firm or an individual real estate professional to perform all the services and handle all classes of property discussed in this chapter, this is rarely done. While such general services may be available in small towns, most firms and professionals specialize to some degree, especially in urban areas. Some licensees perform only one service for one type of property, such as residential sales or commercial leasing.

## THE REAL ESTATE MARKET

A **market** is a place where goods can be bought and sold. A market may be a specific place, like the village square. It may also be a vast, complex, worldwide economic system for moving goods and services around the globe. In either case, the function of a market is to provide a setting in which supply and demand can establish market value, making it advantageous for buyers and sellers to trade.

### Supply and Demand

When supply increases and demand remains stable, prices go down. When demand increases and supply remains stable, prices go up.

The operation of **supply and demand** in the market is how prices for goods and services are set. Essentially, *when supply increases and demand remains stable, prices go down; when demand increases and supply remains stable, prices go up.* Greater supply means producers need to attract more buyers, so they lower prices. Greater demand means producers can raise their prices because buyers compete for the product.

**FOR EXAMPLE** Here's how one broker describes market forces: "In my 17 years in real estate, I've seen supply and demand in action many times. When a car maker relocated its factory to my region a few years back, hundreds of people wanted to buy the few higher-bracket houses for sale at the time. Those sellers were able to ask ridiculously high prices for their properties, and two houses actually sold for more than the asking prices! On the other hand, when the naval base closed and 2,000 civilian jobs were transferred to other parts of the country, it seemed like every other house in town was for sale. We were practically giving houses away to the few people who were buying."

*Uniqueness* and *immobility* are the two characteristics of land that have the most impact on market value.

**Supply and demand in the real estate market.** Two characteristics of real estate govern the way the market reacts to the pressures of supply and demand: **uniqueness** and **immobility.** (See Chapter 2.) *Uniqueness* means that, no matter how identical they may appear, no two parcels of real estate are ever exactly alike; each occupies its own unique geographic location. *Immobility* refers to the fact that property cannot be relocated to satisfy demand where supply is low. Nor can buyers always relocate to areas with greater supply. For these reasons, real estate markets are local markets: each geographic area has different types of real estate and different conditions that drive prices. In these well-defined small areas, real estate offices can keep track of both what type of property is in demand and what parcels are available.

**In Practice**   Technological advances and market changes have widened the real estate professional's local market. No longer limited to a single small area, brokers and salespersons must track trends and conditions in a variety of different and sometimes distant local markets. Technology—including information networks and laptop PCs, cellular phones, fax machines, and a growing arsenal of other technologies—help real estate practitioners stay on top of their wide-ranging markets, as do Internet connections and web sites.

Because of real estate's uniqueness and immobility, the market generally adjusts slowly to the forces of supply and demand. Though a home offered for sale can be withdrawn in response to low demand and high supply, it is much more likely that oversupply will result in lower prices. When supply is low, on the other hand, a high demand may not be met immediately because development and construction are lengthy processes. As a result, development tends to occur in uneven spurts of activity.

Even when supply and demand can be forecast with some accuracy, natural disasters such as hurricanes and earthquakes can disrupt market trends. Similarly, sudden changes in financial markets or local events such as plant relocations or environmental factors can dramatically disrupt a seemingly stable market.

## Factors Affecting Supply

Factors that tend to affect the supply side of the real estate market's supply and demand balance include the **labor force, construction and material costs,** and **government controls and financial policies.**

**Labor force and construction costs.** A shortage of skilled labor or building materials or an increase in the cost of materials can decrease the amount of new construction. High transfer costs (such as taxes) and construction permit fees can also discourage development. Increased construction costs may be passed along to buyers and tenants in the form of higher prices and increased rents, which can further slow the market.

> Factors that affect the supply of real estate are
>
> - labor force,
> - construction costs,
> - government controls, and
> - government financial policies.

**Government controls and financial policies.** The government's monetary policy can have a substantial impact on the real estate market. The Federal Reserve Board establishes a **discount rate** of interest for the money it lends to commercial banks. That rate has a direct impact on the **interest rates** the banks in turn charge to borrowers. These interest rates play a significant part in people's ability to buy homes. Such government agencies as the Federal Housing Administration (FHA), the Government National Mortgage Association (GNMA), and the Federal Home Loan Mortgage Corporation (FHLMC) can affect the amount of money available to lenders for mortgage loans. (See Chapter 16.)

Virtually any government action has some effect on the real estate market. For instance, federal environmental regulations may increase or decrease the supply and value of land in a local market.

Real estate taxation is one of the primary sources of revenue for local governments. Policies on taxation of real estate can have either positive or negative effects. High taxes may deter investors. On the other hand, tax incentives can attract new businesses and industries. And, of course, along with these enterprises come increased employment and expanded residential real estate markets.

Local governments also can influence supply. Land-use controls, building codes, and zoning ordinances help shape the character of a community and control the use of land. Careful planning helps stabilize and even increase real estate values. The dedication of land to such amenities as forest preserves, schools, and parks also helps shape the market.

## Factors Affecting Demand

Factors that tend to affect the demand side of the real estate market include population, demographics, and employment and wage levels.

**Population.**  Shelter is a basic human need, so the demand for housing grows with the **population.** Although the total population of the country continues to rise (290 million in 2000), the demand for real estate increases faster in some areas than in others. In some locations, however, growth has ceased altogether or the population has declined. This may be due to economic changes (such as plant closings), social concerns (such as the quality of schools or a desire for more open space), or population changes (such as population shifts from colder to warmer climates). The result can be a drop in demand for real estate in one area, matched by an increased demand elsewhere.

> Factors that affect the demand for real estate are
>
> • population,
> • demographics, and
> • employment and wage levels.

**Demographics.**  **Demographics** is the study and description of a population. The population of a community is a major factor in determining the quantity and type of housing in that community. Family size, the ratio of adults to children, the ages of children, the number of retirees, family income, lifestyle, and the growing number of single-parent and "empty-nester" households are all demographic factors that contribute to the amount and type of housing needed.

**Employment and wage levels.** Decisions about whether to buy or rent and how much to spend on housing are closely related to income. When job opportunities are scarce or wage levels low, demand for real estate usually drops. The market might, in fact, be affected drastically by a single major employer moving in or shutting down. Licensees must be aware of the business plans of local employers, business cycles, and seasonal adjustments.

As we've seen, the real estate market depends on a variety of economic forces, such as interest rates and employment levels. To be successful, licensees must follow economic trends and anticipate where they will lead. How people use their income depends on consumer confidence. Consumer confidence is based not only on perceived job security but also on the availability of credit and the impact of inflation. General trends in the economy, such as the availability of mortgage money and the rate of inflation, will influence an individual's decision as to how to spend his or her income.

**KEY TERMS**

| | | |
|---|---|---|
| agricultural property | discount rate | property manager |
| appraisal | immobility | residential property |
| broker | industrial property | sales agent |
| brokerage | interest rate | salesperson |
| commercial property | labor force | special purpose |
| counseling | market | property |
| demand | NAR | subdivision |
| demographics | OAR | supply |
| development | population | uniqueness |

**SUMMARY**

- The industry provides many services, including:
  - real estate brokerage,
  - appraisal,
  - property management,
  - property development,
  - counseling,
  - property financing, and
  - education.
- Real property can be classified by its general use as:
  - residential,
  - commercial,
  - industrial,
  - agricultural, or
  - special purpose.
- A market is a place where goods and services can be bought and sold and where price levels can be established based on supply and demand.
- Because of its unique characteristics, real estate is relatively slow to adjust to the forces of supply and demand.
- The supply of and demand for real estate are affected by many factors, including:
  - changes in population and demographics,
  - wage and employment levels,
  - construction costs,
  - availability of labor, and
  - governmental monetary policy and controls.

**Real-Life Real Estate**

1. Since the real estate business is so broad, but is also so specialized, explain your choice(s) for the field you plan to concentrate on.
2. If the three most important factors in the value of real estate are location, location, and location, what are the next three most important considerations in real estate? Why?

# QUESTIONS

1. Commercial real estate includes all of the following *EXCEPT*
   a. office buildings for sale.
   b. apartments for rent.
   c. retail space for lease.
   d. fast-food restaurants for lease.

2. In general, when the supply of a certain commodity increases,
   a. prices tend to rise.
   b. prices tend to drop.
   c. demand tends to rise.
   d. demand tends to drop.

3. All of the following factors tend to affect supply *EXCEPT*
   a. the labor force.
   b. construction costs.
   c. government controls.
   d. demographics.

4. Factors that influence the demand for real estate include
   a. the number of real estate brokers in the area.
   b. the number of full-time real estate salespersons in the area.
   c. the wage levels and employment opportunities.
   d. the price of new homes being built in the area.

5. Property management, appraisal, financing, and development are all examples of
   a. factors affecting demand.
   b. specializations within the real estate industry.
   c. non–real estate professions.
   d. government regulation of the real estate industry.

6. A REALTOR® is
   a. a specially licensed real estate professional who acts as a point of contact between two or more people in negotiating the sale, purchase, or rental of property.
   b. any real estate broker or salesperson who assists buyers, sellers, landlords, or tenants in any real estate transaction.
   c. a member of the National Association of Real Estate Brokers who specializes in residential properties.
   d. a real estate licensee who is a member of the National Association of REALTORS®.

7. A major manufacturer of automobiles announces that it will relocate one of its factories, along with two thousand employees, to Smallville. What effect will this announcement likely have on Smallville's housing market?
   a. Houses are likely to become less expensive as a result of the announcement.
   b. Houses are likely to become more expensive as a result of the announcement.
   c. The announcement involves an issue of demographics, not a supply and demand issue; housing prices will stay the same.
   d. The announcement involves an industrial property; residential housing will not be affected.

8. *B* holds a real estate license and has several years of experience in the industry. However, *B* has "retired" from actively marketing properties. Now *B* helps clients choose among the various alternatives involved in purchasing, using, or investing in property. What is *B*'s profession?
   a. Real estate counselor
   b. Real estate appraiser
   c. Real estate educator
   d. REALTOR®

9. In general, when the demand for a certain commodity increases,
   a. prices tend to drop.
   b. prices tend to remain level.
   c. prices tend to rise.
   d. prices can no longer be established.

10. In an average market certain characteristics of goods sold will determine how quickly the forces of supply and demand will establish the goods' prices. Which of the following is *not* one of these characteristics?
    a. Product mobility
    b. Product cost
    c. Buyer and seller mobility
    d. Product standardization

11. In general terms, a *market* refers to which of the following?
    a. A process by which the price of any given product will always tend to rise
    b. The amount of goods available at a given price
    c. The quality of goods available to the public
    d. A forum where price levels are established

12. The demand for real estate in a particular community is *not* affected by
    a. population.
    b. wage levels.
    c. employment.
    d. construction costs.

13. The real estate market is considered local in character for all the following reasons *EXCEPT* that
    a. land is fixed, or immobile.
    b. most people generally are not mobile enough to take advantage of available real estate in distant areas.
    c. local controls can have a significant impact on the market.
    d. most people are generally mobile and take advantage of available real estate in distant areas.

14. Property that is part of the industrial market includes
    a. office buildings for lease.
    b. single-family homes.
    c. churches.
    d. factories.

15. Compared to typical markets, the real estate market
    a. is national in scope.
    b. is always stable and is not affected by supply or demand.
    c. does not affect any other industry but its own.
    d. is local in nature.

# Real Property and the Law

## LAND, REAL ESTATE AND REAL PROPERTY

The words *land, real estate,* and *real property* are often used interchangeably. To most people, they mean the same thing. Strictly speaking, however, the terms refer to different aspects of the same idea. To fully understand the nature of real estate and the laws that affect it, licensees must be aware of these subtle yet important differences in meaning.

**Land**    **Land** is defined as *the earth's surface extending downward to the center of the earth and upward to infinity, including permanent natural objects such as trees and water.* (See Figure 2.1.)

*Land,* then, means not only the surface of the earth but also the underlying soil. It refers to things that are *naturally* attached to the land, such as boulders and plants. It includes the minerals and substances that lie far below the earth's surface. Land even includes the air above the earth, all the way up into space. These are known respectively as the *subsurface* and the *airspace.*

**Real Estate**    **Real estate** is defined as *land at, above, and below the earth's surface, plus all things permanently attached to it, whether natural or artificial.* (See Figure 2.1.)

The term *real estate* is similar to the term *land,* but it means much more. *Real estate* includes not only the natural components of the land, but also all man-made improvements. An **improvement** is any artificial (man-made) thing attached to land, such as a building or a fence. The term *improvement,* as used in the real estate industry, refers to *any* addition to the land, most commonly a home or building. The word is neutral. It doesn't matter whether the artificial attachment makes the property better looking or more useful; the land is still said to be *improved.* Land also may be improved by streets, utilities, sewers, and other additions that make it suitable for building.

**Real Property**    **Real property** is defined as *the interests, benefits, and rights that are automatically included in the ownership of land and real estate.* (See Figure 2.1.)

The term *real property* is the broadest of all. It includes both *land* and *real estate.* Real property includes the surface, subsurface, and airspace, any improvements and the *bundle of legal rights*—the legal rights of ownership

**Figure 2.1    Land, Real Estate, and Real Property**

**Land**
Earth's surface to the center
of the earth and the airspace
above the land, including the
trees and water

*Example - oil, Rock, water*

**Real Estate**
Land plus permanent
man-made additions

*Example - House*

**Real Property**
Real estate plus "bundle
of legal rights"

that attach to ownership of a parcel of real estate (discussed later in this chapter). Real property includes the surface rights, subsurface rights, and air rights, all of which can be owned by different individuals.

Real property is often coupled with the word **appurtenance.** An appurtenance is anything associated with the property, although not necessarily a part of it. Typical appurtenances include parking spaces in multiunit buildings, easements, water rights, and other improvements. An appurtenance is connected to the property, and ownership of the appurtenance normally transfers with the real property itself.

---

**In Practice**    When people talk about buying or selling homes, office buildings, and land, they usually call these things real estate. For all practical purposes, the term is synonymous with *real property* as defined here. Thus, in everyday usage, *real estate* includes the legal rights of ownership specified in the definition of real property. Sometimes people use the term *realty* also.

---

**Subsurface and air rights.** The right to use the surface of the earth is referred to as a **surface right.** However, real property ownership can also include **subsurface rights,** which are the rights to the natural resources lying below the earth's surface. Although it may be difficult to imagine, the two rights are distinct: an owner may transfer his or her surface rights without transferring the subsurface rights.

**F**OR EXAMPLE  Abernathy sells the rights to any oil and gas found beneath her farm to an oil company. Later, Abernathy sells the remaining interests (the surface, air, and limited subsurface rights) to Baker, reserving the rights to any coal that may be found in the land. Baker sells the remaining land to Carleton, but Baker retains the farmhouse, stable, and pasture. After these sales, four parties have ownership interests in the same real estate parcel:

(1) the oil company owns all the oil and gas;
(2) Abernathy owns all the coal;
(3) Baker owns the farmhouse, stable, and pasture; and
(4) Carleton owns the remaining real estate rights.

The rights to use the air above the land, provided the rights have not been preempted by law, may be sold or leased independently. **Air rights** can be an important part of real estate, particularly in large cities, where air rights over railroads must be purchased to construct office buildings such as the Met Life Building in New York City and the Prudential Building in Chicago. To construct such a building, the developer must purchase not only the air rights but also numerous small portions of the land's surface for the building's foundation supports.

Before air travel was common, a property's air rights were considered to be unlimited, extending upward into the farthest reaches of outer space. Today, however, the courts permit reasonable interference with these rights, such as that necessary for aircraft (and presumably spacecraft), as long as the owner's right to use and occupy the land is not unduly lessened. Governments and airport authorities often purchase adjacent air rights to provide approach patterns for air traffic.

With the continuing development of solar power, air rights—and, more specifically, light or solar rights—are being closely examined by the courts. A new tall building that blocks sunlight from a smaller, existing building may be held to be interfering with the smaller building's right to sunlight, particularly if the smaller building is solar powered.

## REAL PROPERTY AND PERSONAL PROPERTY

**Personal property,** sometimes called *personalty*, is *all property that does not fit the definition of real property.* That is, if it's not real property, it's personal property.

*On Test* ── An important distinction between the two is that personal property is *movable.* Items of personal property, also referred to as **chattels,** include such tangibles as chairs, tables, clothing, money, bonds and bank accounts. Trade fixtures, discussed later, are included in this category.

**Mobile Homes**   The distinction between real and personal property is not always obvious. A mobile home, for example, is generally considered personal property, even though its mobility may be limited to a single trip to a mobile-home park. A mobile home may, however, be considered real property if it becomes permanently affixed to the land. (Manufactured or modular homes are those assembled at a factory and then installed on the site. They are also considered personal property until they are affixed to the land.) Real estate licensees should be familiar with local laws before attempting to sell mobile homes.

**Trees and Crops**   Trees and crops generally fall into one of two classes. Trees, perennial shrubbery, and grasses that do not require annual cultivation are considered real estate. Annual plantings or crops of wheat, corn, vegetables, and fruit, known as *emblements,* are generally considered personal property. As long as

The term used in the law for plants that do not require annual cultivation (such as trees and shrubbery) is *fructus naturales* (fruits of nature); emblements are known in the law as *fructus industriales* (fruits of industry).

an annual crop is growing, it will be transferred as part of the real property unless other provisions are made in the sales contract. That is, a farmer won't have to dig up growing corn plants and haul them away unless the sales contract says so: the young corn remains on the land. The farmer may come back and harvest the corn when it's ready. The former owner or tenant is entitled to harvest the crops that result from his or her labor.

An item of real property can become personal property by **severance.** For example, a growing tree is real estate until the owner cuts it down, literally severing it from the property. Similarly, an apple becomes personal property once it is picked from a tree, and a wheat crop becomes personal property once it is harvested.

It is also possible to change personal property into real property. If, for example, a landowner buys cement, stones and sand, mixes them into concrete, and constructs a sidewalk across his or her land, the landowner has converted personal property (cement, stones, and sand) into real property (a sidewalk). This process is called *annexation.*

Licensees need to know the distinction between real and personal property for many reasons. These are important issues that may arise when the property is transferred from one owner to another. Real property is conveyed by deed, while personal property is conveyed by a **bill of sale.** Transfers of real property are discussed in Chapter 13.   *On Test*

## Fixtures

In considering the differences between real and personal property, it is necessary to distinguish between a *fixture* and *personal property.*

A **fixture** is *personal property that has been so affixed to land or a building that, by law, it becomes part of the real estate.* Examples of fixtures are heating systems, elevator equipment in highrise buildings, radiators, kitchen cabinets, light fixtures, and plumbing. Almost any item that has been added as a *permanent part* of a building is considered a fixture.

During the course of time, the same materials may be both real and personal property, depending on their use and location.

**Legal tests of a fixture.**  Courts use four basic tests to determine whether an item is a fixture (real property) or personal property:

**Legal Tests of a Fixture:**

1. Intent
2. Method of annexation
3. Adaptation to real estate
4. Agreement

1. *Intent:* Did the person who installed the item intend for it to remain permanently on the property or for it to be removable in the future?
2. *Method of annexation:* How permanent is the method of attachment? Can the item be removed without causing damage to the surrounding property?
3. *Adaptation to real estate:* Is the item being used as real property or personal property?
4. *Agreement:* Have the parties contractually agreed on whether the item is real or personal property?

Although these tests may seem simple, court decisions have been inconsistent. Property that appears to be permanently affixed has sometimes been ruled to be personal property, while property that seems removable has been ruled a fixture. It is important that an owner and agent clarify what is included and excluded with the sale of the real estate at the very beginning of the sales process.

**In Practice**     At the time a property is listed, the seller and listing agent should discuss which items will be included in the sale. The written sales contract between the buyer and the seller should specifically list all articles that are being included in the sale, particularly if any doubt exists as to whether they are personal property or fixtures (for instance, built-in bookcases, chandeliers, ceiling fans, or exotic shrubbery). It is important to remember that writing the included items into the contract will avoid misunderstanding between the parties that could result in the collapse of the transaction and expensive lawsuits.

**Constructive annexation.** At times, an item is considered to be a fixture—and thus real property—because it is constructively annexed to the real property. While it is not physically attached to the property, it is a part of the real property because it *belongs to* or was *made for* the property. For example, the key to the front door and storm windows specifically made for the property may both be considered part of the real property, even though they are not physically attached to it. This is referred to as *constructive annexation.*

**Trade fixtures.** A special category of fixtures includes property used in the course of business. An article owned by a tenant and attached to a rented space or building or used in conducting a business is a **trade fixture,** or a *chattel fixture.* Some examples of trade fixtures would be bowling alleys, store shelves, bars, and restaurant equipment. Agricultural fixtures, such as chicken coops and toolsheds, are also included in this category. Trade fixtures must be removed on or before the last day the property is rented. The tenant is responsible for any damage caused by the removal of a fixture. Trade fixtures that are not removed become the real property of the landlord. Acquiring the property in this way is known as **accession.**

**F**OR EXAMPLE Paul's Pizza leases space in a small shopping center. Paul bolted a large iron oven to the floor of the unit. When Paul's Pizza goes out of business or relocates, Paul will be able to take his pizza oven with him if he can repair the bolt-holes in the floor; the oven is a trade fixture. On the other hand, if the pizza oven was brought into the restaurant in pieces, welded together and set in concrete, Paul might not be able to remove it without causing structural damage. In that case, the oven might become a fixture and thus real property.

Trade fixtures differ from other fixtures in these ways:

- Fixtures belong to the owner of the real estate, but trade fixtures are usually owned and installed by a tenant for the tenant's use.
- Fixtures are considered a permanent part of a building, but trade fixtures are removable. Trade fixtures may be attached to a building so they appear to be fixtures.
- Legally, fixtures are real property, so they are included in any sale or mortgage. Trade fixtures, however, are considered personal property and are not included in the sale or mortgage of real estate, except by special **In Ohio...**     agreement. (Legal interest in trade fixtures are recorded by filing a UCC1 security agreement with the Ohio Secretary of State's Office.) ◆

## CHARACTERISTICS OF REAL ESTATE

Real estate possesses seven basic characteristics that define its nature and affect its use. These characteristics fall into two broad categories—*economic* characteristics and *physical* characteristics.

**Economic Characteristics**

The economic characteristics of land affect its investment value. They are scarcity, improvements, permanence of investment, and area preference.

| Economic Characteristics of Real Estate |
| --- |
| 1. Scarcity |
| 2. Improvements |
| 3. Permanence of investment |
| 4. Area preference |

**Scarcity.** We usually do not consider land a rare commodity, but only about a quarter of the earth's surface is dry land; the rest is water. The total supply of land, then, is not limitless. While a considerable amount of land remains unused or uninhabited, the supply in a given location or of a particular quality is generally considered to be finite.

**Improvements.** Building an improvement on one parcel of land can affect the land's value and use as well as that of neighboring tracts and whole communities. For example, constructing a new shopping center or selecting a site for a nuclear power plant or toxic waste dump can dramatically change the value of land in a large area.

**Permanence of investment.** The capital and labor used to build an improvement represent a large fixed investment. Although even a well-built structure can be razed to make way for a newer building, improvements such as drainage, electricity, water, and sewerage remain. The return on such capital investments tends to be long term and relatively stable.

**Area preference.** This economic characteristic, sometimes called *situs*, does not refer to a geographic location, but rather to people's preferences for given areas. It is the unique quality of these preferences that results in different property values for similar units. *Area preference is the most important economic characteristic of land.*

**F**OR EXAMPLE A river runs through Bedford Falls, dividing the town more or less in half. On the north side of the river, known as North Town, houses sell for an average of $150,000. On the south side of the river, known as Southbank, identical houses sell for more than $200,000. The only difference is that homebuyers think that Southbank is a better neighborhood, even though no obvious difference exists between the two equally pleasant sides of town.

**Physical Characteristics**

Land has certain physical characteristics: **immobility, indestructibility** and **uniqueness.**

**Immobility.** It is true that some of the substances of land are removable (for instance, timber and minerals) and topography can be changed, but *the geographic location of any given parcel of land can never be changed.* It is fixed.

**Indestructibility.** Land is also *indestructible.* This permanence of land, coupled with the long-term nature of improvements, tends to stabilize investments in real estate.

The fact that land is indestructible does not, however, change the fact that the improvements on land depreciate and can become obsolete, which may dramatically reduce the property's value. This gradual depreciation should

| **Physical Characteristics of Real Estate** |
| --- |
| 1. Immobility |
| 2. Indestructibility |
| 3. Uniqueness |

not be confused with the knowledge that the *economic desirability* of a given location can change.

**Uniqueness.**  No two parcels of land are ever exactly the same. Although they may be substantially similar, all parcels differ geographically because each parcel has its own location. The characteristics of each measurable unit of property, no matter how small, differ from those of every other unit. An individual parcel has no substitute because each is unique. The uniqueness of land is also referred to as its **heterogeneity** or **nonhomogeneity.**

## OWNERSHIP OF REAL PROPERTY

Traditionally, real property is described as a **bundle of legal rights.** In other words, a purchaser of real estate actually buys the rights of ownership held by the seller. These rights include the

- right of possession,
- right to control the property within the framework of the law,
- right of enjoyment (that is, to use the property in any legal manner),
- right of exclusion (to keep others from entering or using the property), and
- right of disposition (to sell, will, transfer, or otherwise dispose of or encumber the property).

The concept of a bundle of rights comes from old English law. In the middle ages, a seller transferred property by giving the purchaser a handful of earth or a bundle of bound sticks from a tree on the property. The purchaser, who accepted the bundle, then owned the tree from which the sticks came and the land to which the tree was attached. Because the rights of ownership (like the sticks) can be separated and individually transferred, the sticks became symbolic of those rights. (See Figure 2.2.)

## LAWS AFFECTING REAL ESTATE

| **Real Estate Laws** |
| --- |
| • Contract law |
| • General property law |
| • Agency law |
| • Real estate license law |
| • Federal regulations |
| • Federal, state and local tax laws |
| • Zoning and land use laws |
| • Federal and state fair housing laws |
| • Federal, state and local environmental regulations |

*[handwritten note in margin: Need to know. So you don't get in to trouble]*

The unique nature of real estate has given rise to an equally unique set of laws and rights. Even the simplest real estate transaction involves a body of complex laws. Licensees must have a clear and accurate understanding of the laws that affect real estate.

The specific areas important to the real estate practitioner include the *law of contracts*, the *general property law*, the *law of agency* and *real estate license law*, and federal and state fair housing laws. All of these will be discussed in this text. Federal regulations (such as environmental laws), as well as federal, state, and local tax laws, also play an important role in real estate transactions. State and local land-use and zoning laws have a significant effect on the practice of real estate, too.

Obviously, a real estate practitioner can't be an expert in all areas of real estate law. However, licensees should know and understand some basic principles. Perhaps most important is the ability to recognize problems that should be referred to a competent attorney. Only attorneys are trained and licensed to prepare documents defining or transferring rights in property and to give advice on matters of law. *Under no circumstances may a broker or salesperson*

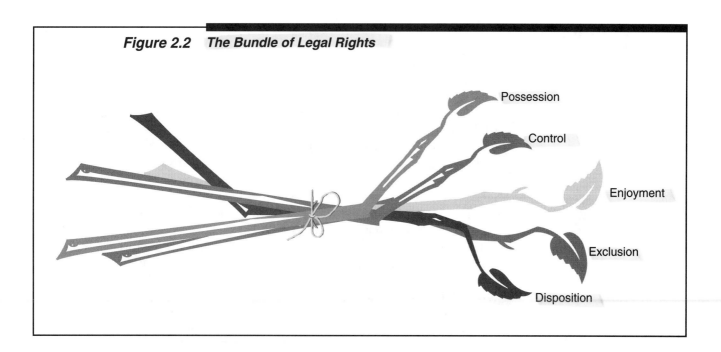

**Figure 2.2  The Bundle of Legal Rights**

Possession

Control

Enjoyment

Exclusion

Disposition

*act as an attorney unless he or she is also a licensed attorney representing a client in that capacity. (It is a misdemeanor to practice law without a license.)*

All phases of a real estate transaction should be handled with extreme care. Carelessness in handling the negotiations and documents connected with a real estate sale can lead to disputes and expensive legal actions. The result can be a financial loss, a loss of goodwill in the community, a loss of business or, in some cases, the loss or suspension of a real estate license.

**Real estate license laws.**  Because brokers and salespersons are involved with other people's real estate and money, the need for regulation of their activities has long been recognized. The purpose of real estate license laws is to protect the public from fraud, dishonesty and incompetence in real estate transactions. All 50 states, the District of Columbia, and all Canadian provinces have passed laws that require real estate brokers and salespersons to be licensed. Although state license laws are similar in many respects, they differ in some details, such as the amount and type of prelicense education required. Chapter 6 describes more fully the license laws and the required standards for Ohio under Ohio Revised Code.

In all states, applicants must meet specific personal and educational qualifications. In addition, they must pass an examination to ensure at least a minimum level of competency. To qualify for license renewal, licensees must follow certain standards of business conduct. Many states, including Ohio, **In Ohio...** also require licensees to complete continuing education courses. ◆

It is extremely important that anyone planning to become a licensed real estate professional be fully aware of his or her state's specific license laws, licensure requirements and rules and regulations governing the conduct of real estate agents in the state. When a licensee's practice is likely to extend into other states, he or she must be aware of these laws and regulations as well.

## KEY TERMS

| | | |
|---|---|---|
| accession | fixture | real estate |
| air rights | heterogeneity | real property |
| appurtenance | immobility | scarcity |
| bill of sale | improvement | severance |
| bundle of legal rights | indestructibility | subsurface rights |
| chattel | land | surface rights |
| constructive annexation | nonhomogeneity | trade fixture |
| emblements | personal property | uniqueness |

## SUMMARY

- Land includes the earth's surface, the mineral deposits under the earth, and the air above it.
- The term real estate further expands the definition of land to include all natural and man-made improvements attached to the land. The term *real property* describes real estate plus the bundle of legal rights associated with its ownership.
- The various rights to the same parcel of real estate may be owned and controlled by different parties, one owning the surface rights, one owning the air rights, and one owning the subsurface rights.
- All property that does not fit the definition of real estate is classified as personal property, or chattels.
  - When articles of personal property are affixed to land, they may become fixtures and as such are considered part of the real estate.
  - However, personal property attached to real estate by a tenant for business purposes is classified as a trade fixture (or chattel), and remains personal property.
- The economic characteristics of land include scarcity, improvements, permanence of investment, and area preference. Physically, land is immobile, indestructible, and unique.
- Every U.S. state and Canadian province has some type of licensing requirement for real estate brokers and salespersons. Students must become familiar with the real estate laws and licensing requirements not only of their own states but of other states into which their practice may extend as well.

## Real-Life Real Estate

1. The number and complexity of laws affecting real estate transactions requires practitioners in every specialty area to maintain in-depth understanding of current legal obligations. How will you ensure that you are fully prepared to represent your client's interests and preserve your professional reputation?
2. The legal principles behind the bundle of rights and legal tests for fixtures are complicated and confusing to most buyers and sellers. How will you help them understand their respective rights and responsibilities regarding these matters?

# QUESTIONS

1. Real estate includes all the following *EXCEPT*
   a. trees.
   b. air rights.
   c. annual crops.
   d. mineral rights.

2. *H* owns a building in a commercial area of town. *T* rents space in the building and operates a bookstore. In *T*'s bookstore, large tables are fastened to the walls, where customers are encouraged to sit and read. Shelves create aisles from the front of the store to the back. The shelves are bolted to both the ceiling and the floor. Which of the following best characterizes the contents of *T*'s bookstore?
   a. The shelves and tables are trade fixtures and will be sold when *H* sells the building.
   b. The shelves and tables are trade fixtures and must be removed before *T*'s lease expires.
   c. Because *T* is a tenant, the shelves and tables are fixtures and may not be removed except with *H*'s permission.
   d. Because the shelves and tables are attached to the building, they are treated the same as other fixtures.

3. The term *nonhomogeneity* refers to
   a. scarcity.
   b. immobility.
   c. uniqueness.
   d. indestructibility.

4. Bowling alleys, store shelves, and restaurant equipment are examples of which of the following?
   a. Real property
   b. Real estate
   c. Trade fixtures
   d. General fixtures

5. The bundle of legal rights includes all of the following *EXCEPT* the right to
   a. exclude someone from the property.
   b. enjoy the property within the framework of the law.
   c. sell or otherwise convey the property.
   d. use the property for any purpose, legal or otherwise.

6. *O* inherited Rolling Hills from his uncle. The first thing *O* did with the vacant property was to remove all the topsoil, which he sold to a landscaping company. *O* then removed a thick layer of limestone, and sold it to a construction company. Finally, *O* dug forty feet into the bedrock and sold it for gravel. When *O* died, he left Rolling Hills to his daughter, *P*. Which of the following statements is true?
   a. *P* inherits nothing, because Rolling Hills no longer exists.
   b. *P* inherits a large hole in the ground, but it is still Rolling Hills, down to the center of the earth.
   c. *P* owns the gravel, limestone, and topsoil, no matter where it is.
   d. *O*'s estate must restore Rolling Hills to its original condition.

7. A buyer and seller of a home are debating whether a certain item is real or personal property. The buyer says it is real property and should convey along with the house; the seller says it is personal property and may be conveyed separately through a bill of sale. In determining whether an item is real or personal property, a court would consider all the following *EXCEPT* the
   a. cost of the item when it was purchased.
   b. method of its attachment to other real property.
   c. intention of the person who installed the item that it become a permanent part of the property.
   d. manner in which the item is actually used with other real property.

8. All of the following are economic characteristics of real estate *EXCEPT*
   a. indestructibility.
   b. improvements.
   c. area preferences.
   d. scarcity.

9. Which of the following describes the act by which real property can be converted into personal property?
   a. Severance
   b. Accession
   c. Conversion
   d. Separation

10. When the buyer moved into a newly purchased home, the buyer discovered that the seller had taken the electric lighting fixtures that were installed over the vanity in the bathroom. The seller had not indicated that the fixtures would be removed. Which of the following is true?
    a. Lighting fixtures are normally considered to be real estate.
    b. The lighting fixtures belong to the seller because he installed them.
    c. These lighting fixtures are considered trade fixtures.
    d. Original lighting fixtures are real property, but replacement fixtures would be personal property.

11. A buyer purchased a parcel of land and sold the rights to minerals located in the ground to an exploration company. This means that the buyer now owns all of the following rights to this property *EXCEPT* certain
    a. air rights.
    b. surface rights.
    c. subsurface rights.
    d. occupancy rights.

12. *J* is building a new enclosed front porch on her home. A truckload of lumber has been left on *J*'s driveway for use in building the porch. At this point, the lumber is considered what kind of property?
    a. A fixture, because it will be permanently affixed to existing real property
    b. Personal property
    c. A chattel that is real property
    d. A trade or chattel fixture

13. Intent of the parties, method of annexation, adaptation to real estate, and agreement between the parties are the legal tests for determining whether an item is
    a. a trade fixture or personal property.
    b. real property or real estate.
    c. a fixture or personal property.
    d. an improvement.

14. Parking spaces in multiunit buildings, water rights, and other improvements are classified as
    a. trade fixtures.
    b. emblements.
    c. subsurface rights.
    d. appurtenances.

15. *Y* purchases Greenacre, a parcel of natural forest. *Y* immediately cuts down all the trees and constructs a large shed out of old sheets of rusted tin. *Y* uses the shed to store turpentine, varnish, and industrial waste products. Which of the following statements is true?
    a. *Y*'s action constitutes improvement of the property.
    b. *Y*'s shed is personal property.
    c. If *Y* is in the business of storing toxic substances, *Y*'s shed is a trade fixture.
    d. Altering the property in order to construct a shed is not included in the bundle of legal rights.

# CHAPTER 3

# Concepts of Home Ownership

## HOME OWNERSHIP

People buy their own homes for emotional as well as financial reasons. To many, home ownership is a sign of financial stability. It is an investment that can appreciate in value and provide federal and state income tax deductions. Home ownership also offers benefits that may be less tangible but are no less valuable: pride, security, and a sense of belonging to the community.

In the past, most homes were single-family dwellings bought by married couples with small children. Today, however, social, demographic, and economic changes have altered the residential real estate market considerably. For example, many real estate buyers today are single men and women. Many are *empty nesters* (married couples whose children have moved away from home). Others are unmarried couples or married couples who choose not to have children. Still others may be friends or relatives who plan to co-own a home together, in the same way they might share an apartment lease. In short, there are nearly as many different *kinds* of homeownership as there are people who own homes.

**Types of Housing** As our society evolves, the needs of its homebuyers become more specialized. The following paragraphs describe the types of housing currently available to meet these needs. Some housing types are not only innovative uses of real estate but also incorporate a variety of ownership concepts. Notice as you read how the different forms of housing respond to the demands of a diverse marketplace.

*Apartment complexes* are groups of apartment buildings with any number of units in each building. The buildings may be lowrise or highrise, and the amenities may include parking, security, clubhouses, swimming pools, tennis courts, and even golf courses.

The *condominium* is a popular form of residential ownership, particularly for people who want the security of owning property without the care and maintenance a house demands. It is also a popular ownership option in areas where property values make single-unit ownership inaccessible to many people. Condominium owners share ownership of common facilities such as

**21**

halls, elevators, swimming pools, clubhouses, tennis courts, and surrounding grounds. Management and maintenance of building exteriors and common facilities are provided by the governing association and outside contractors, with expenses paid out of monthly assessments charged to owners. The condominium form of ownership is discussed in detail in Chapter 9.

A *cooperative* also has units that share common walls and facilities within a larger building. The owners, however, do not actually *own* the units. Instead, they buy shares of stock in the corporation that holds title to the building. Owners receive *proprietary leases* that entitle them to occupy particular units. Like condominium unit owners, cooperative unit owners pay their share of the building's expenses. Cooperatives are discussed further in Chapter 9.

*Planned unit developments* (PUDs), sometimes called *master-planned communities,* merge such diverse land uses as housing, recreation, and commercial units into one self-contained development. PUDs are planned under special zoning ordinances. These ordinances permit maximum use of open space by reducing lot sizes and street areas. Owners do not have direct ownership interest in the common areas. A community association is formed to maintain these areas, with fees collected from the owners.

*Retirement communities,* many of them in temperate climates, are often structured as PUDs. They may provide shopping, recreational opportunities, and health care facilities in addition to residential units.

*Highrise developments,* sometimes called *mixed-use developments* (MUDs), combine office space, stores, theaters, and apartment units in a single vertical community. MUDs usually are self-contained and offer laundry facilities, restaurants, food stores, valet shops, beauty parlors, barbershops, swimming pools, and other attractive and convenient features.

*Converted-use properties* are factories, warehouses, office buildings, hotels, schools, churches, and other structures that have been converted to residential use. Developers often find renovation of such properties more aesthetically and economically appealing than demolishing a perfectly sound structure to build something new. An abandoned warehouse may be transformed into luxury loft condominium units, a closed hotel may reopen as an apartment building, and an old factory may be recycled into a profitable shopping mall.

*Manufactured housing* (also known as *mobile homes*) once was considered useful only as a temporary residence or for travel. Now, however, these units are more often permanent principal residences or stationary vacation homes. Relatively low cost, coupled with the increased living space available in the newer models, has made such homes an attractive option for many people. Increased sales have resulted in growing numbers of "housing parks" in some communities. These parks offer complete residential environments with permanent community facilities as well as semipermanent foundations and hookups for gas, water, and electricity.

**In Ohio...**    In Ohio, it is not necessary to have a real estate license to sell new or used *movable* mobile homes, which are considered personal, rather than real, property. However, a license is needed to sell permanently located mobile homes. ◆

*Modular homes* also are gaining popularity as the price of newly constructed homes rises. Each room is preassembled at a factory, driven to the building site on a truck, then lowered onto its foundation by a crane. Later, workers finish the structure and connect plumbing and wiring. Entire developments can be built at a fraction of the time and cost of conventional construction.

Through *time-shares,* multiple purchasers share ownership of a single property, usually a vacation home. Each owner is entitled to use the property for a certain period of time each year, usually a specific week. In addition to the purchase price, each owner pays an annual maintenance fee.

**In Ohio...** In Ohio, strict rules govern the marketing, sale, and transfer of time-share properties. The time-share estate is discussed in detail in Chapter 9, and state licensing requirements for "foreign" real estate dealers are discussed in Chapter 6. ◆

## HOUSING AFFORDABILITY

Housing affordability has become a major issue. Home ownership has declined severely among the young and low-income to moderate-income purchasers, especially first-time buyers. Real estate prices have risen, making it difficult for many potential buyers to save the down payment and closing costs needed for a conventional loan. Because more homeowners mean more business opportunities, real estate and related industry groups have a vital interest in ensuring affordable housing for all segments of the population. Congress, state legislatures, and local governments have been working to increase the availability of affordable housing.

Certainly not everyone wants to own a home. Home ownership involves substantial commitment and responsibility, and the flexibility of renting suits some individuals' needs. People whose work requires frequent moves or whose financial position is uncertain particularly benefit from renting. Renting also provides more leisure time by freeing tenants from management and maintenance.

Those who choose home ownership must evaluate many factors before they make a final decision to purchase a particular property. The purchasing decision must be weighed carefully in light of each individual's financial circumstances.

**Mortgage Terms** Liberalized mortgage terms and payment plans offer many people the option of purchasing a home. Low-down-payment mortgage loans are available under programs sponsored by the Federal Housing Administration (FHA) and the Department of Veterans Affairs (VA), discussed further in Chapter 16.

An increasing number of creative mortgage loan programs are being offered by various government agencies and private lenders. Adjustable-rate loans, whose lower initial interest rate makes it possible for many buyers to qualify for a mortgage loan, are now common. Specific programs may offer lower closing costs or deferred interest or principal payments for purchasers in targeted neighborhoods or for first-time buyers. Many innovative loans are tailored to suit the younger buyer, who may need a low interest rate to qualify, but whose income is expected to increase in coming years.

## Economic Qualification

Home ownership involves many expenses, including utilities (such as electricity, natural gas, and water), trash removal, sewer charges, and maintenance and repairs. Owners also must pay real estate taxes and buy homeowner's insurance, and they must repay the mortgage loan with interest.

---

**Memory Tip**

The basic costs of owning a home—mortgage **P**rincipal and **I**nterest, **T**axes and **I**nsurance, can be remembered by the acronym **PITI.**

---

To determine whether a prospective buyer can afford a certain purchase, lenders traditionally have used a ratio calculation: The monthly cost of buying and maintaining a home (mortgage payments—both principal and interest—plus taxes and insurance impounds) should not exceed 28 percent of gross (pretax) monthly income. The payments on all debts should not exceed 36 percent of monthly income. Expenses such as homeowner's insurance premiums, utilities, and routine medical care are not included in the 36 percent figure. Other factors used by the lender include the borrower's credit history, number of dependents, and net worth.

**F**OR EXAMPLE  A prospective homebuyer wants to know how much house he or she can afford to buy. The buyer has a gross monthly income of $3,000. The buyer's allowable housing expense may be calculated as follows:

$3,000 gross monthly income × 28% = $840 total housing expense allowed

$3,000 gross monthly income × 36% = $1,080 total housing and other debt expense allowed

These formulas allow for other debts of 8 percent of gross monthly income—the difference between the 36 percent and 28 percent figures. If actual debts exceed the amount allowed and the borrower is unable to reduce them, the monthly payment would have to be lowered proportionately because the debts and housing payment combined cannot exceed 36 percent of gross monthly income. However, lower debts would not result in a higher allowable housing payment; rather, it would be considered a positive compensating factor for approval of the loan.

## Investment Considerations

Purchasing a home offers several financial advantages to a buyer. First, if the property's value increases, a sale could bring in more money than the owner paid—a long-term capital gain. Second, as the total mortgage debt is reduced through monthly payments, the owner's actual ownership interest in the property increases. This increasing ownership interest is called **equity** and represents the paid-off share of the property, held free of any mortgage. A tenant accumulates nothing except a good credit rating by paying the rent on time; a homeowner's mortgage payments build equity and so increase his or her net worth. Equity builds even further when the property's value rises. The third financial advantage of homeownership is the tax deductions available to homeowners but not to renters.

---

Current market value –
Property debt = Equity

---

## Tax Benefits

To encourage home ownership, the federal government allows homeowners certain income tax advantages. Homeowners may deduct from their income some or all of the mortgage interest paid as well as real estate taxes and certain other expenses. They may even defer or eliminate tax on the profit received from selling the home. Tax considerations may be an important part of any decision to purchase a home. (See Figure 3.1.)

**Tax deductions.**  Homeowners may deduct from their gross income

- mortgage interest payments on most first and second homes,
- real estate taxes *(but not* interest paid on overdue taxes),
- certain loan origination fees,

---

| **Figure 3.1** | *Homeowners' Tax Benefits* |
| --- | --- |

**Income Tax Deductions**

- Loan interest on first and second homes, subject to limitation
- Loan origination fees
- Some loan discount points — 1% of Loan Amount
- Loan prepayment penalties —
- Real estate taxes —

**Deferment of Tax on Profit**

- Tax on $250,000 ($500,000 if married) of profit (gain) on sale is excluded

---

- loan discount points (paid by the buyer) and
- loan prepayment penalties.

When a homeowner fixes up his or her property in preparation for its sale, the homeowner may deduct certain expenses from his or her gain.

The cost of materials such as paint, carpeting, wallpaper, and of other repairs may be deducted if the expense meets specific IRS requirements.

**Capital gain.**  **Capital gain** is the *profit* realized from the sale or exchange of an asset, including real property. To stimulate investment, Congress at various times has allowed part of a taxpayer's capital gain to be free from income tax. Rules differ for rental, business, and commercial property.

**Exclusion of tax on capital gain.**  Until May 1997, all or part of the gain on the sale of a principal residence was exempt from immediate taxation if another residence was bought and occupied within 24 months (before or after) of the sale of the old residence. This "roll-over" provision has been replaced with a permanent exclusion of tax on gain from the sale of a residence. Under current tax law, if a taxpayer sells a principal residence, up to $250,000 ($500,000 if the taxpayer is married and both spouses are filing a joint return) of gain may be excluded from taxation if, during the five-year period before the sale, the taxpayer both owned the home and lived in it as a principal residence for at least two years.

The two years of use and ownership do not have to be contiguous, and short temporary absences for vacations (even if the taxpayer rents out the property during the absences) may be included in the two-year period. Furthermore, a taxpayer can meet both the ownership and use tests during different two-year periods, as long as both two-year periods occur in the previous five-year period.

**FOR EXAMPLE**  *T* lived in a rented apartment. A few years later, in 1996, the apartment building was converted into a condominium, and *T* purchased her apartment unit. Eighteen months later, *T* became ill and moved into her daughter's home. She rented out her condominium unit. Seven months later, she sold her apartment. Her use period began when she started renting the apartment and ended when she moved into her daughter's home several years later. Her ownership period began when she purchased the apartment in 1996 and ended when she sold it 25 months later. *T* qualified for the exemption.

This exclusion of gain is available for only one home sale every two years. If a taxpayer sells two homes within a two-year period, only one is eligible for exclusion.

Any gain in excess of the $250,000 or $500,000 limit is taxed as capital gain.

Note that the new exclusion of gain also replaces the one-time exclusion of gain for taxpayers age 55 or older.

---

**In Practice**    The Internal Revenue Service, a certified public accountant, a tax attorney or some other tax specialist should be consulted for further information on any income tax issue. IRS regulations, as well as both federal and state tax laws and policies, are subject to frequent revision and official interpretation. A real estate licensee should never attempt to give tax or legal advice to clients or customers.

---

# HOMEOWNER'S INSURANCE

A home is frequently the biggest investment many people ever make. Most homeowners see the wisdom in protecting such an important investment by insuring it. Lenders usually require that a homeowner obtain insurance when the debt is secured by the property. While owners can purchase individual policies that insure against destruction of property by fire or windstorm, injury to others, and theft of personal property, most buy packaged homeowner's insurance policies to cover all these risks. (Note that the premiums for homeowner's insurance are not tax deductible if the home is your principal residence.)

**Coverage and Claims**    The most common homeowner's policy is called a *basic form.* It provides property coverage against

- fire and lightning,
- glass breakage,
- windstorm and hail,
- explosion,
- riot and civil commotion,
- damage by aircraft,
- damage from vehicles,
- damage from smoke,
- vandalism and malicious mischief,
- theft, and
- loss of property removed from the premises when it is endangered by fire or other perils.

A *broad-form* policy is also available. It covers

- falling objects;
- damage due to the weight of ice, snow, or sleet;
- collapse of all or part of the building;
- bursting, cracking, burning, or bulging of a steam or hot water heating system or of appliances used to heat water;
- accidental discharge, leakage, or overflow of water or steam from within a plumbing, a heating, or an air-conditioning system;
- freezing of plumbing, heating, and air-conditioning systems and domestic appliances; and
- injury to electrical appliances, devices, fixtures, and wiring from short circuits or other accidentally generated currents.

### Determining Minimum Coverage

A homeowner's dwelling has a replacement cost of $100,000 and is insured for 80 percent of replacement cost. The home is severely damaged by fire. The estimated cost to repair the damaged portion of the dwelling is $71,000.

Replacement cost of dwelling: $100,000 × .80 = $80,000

Minimum coverage required on the dwelling: $80,000.

Thus, if the homeowner carries at least $80,000 insurance on the home, the claim against the insurance company can be for the full $71,000.

Further insurance is available from policies that cover almost all possible perils. Special apartment and condominium policies generally provide fire and windstorm, theft, and public **liability coverage** for injuries or losses sustained within the unit. However, they usually do not cover losses or damages to the structure. The basic structure is insured by either the landlord or the condominium owners' association.

Most homeowner's insurance policies contain a **coinsurance clause.** This provision usually requires that the owner maintain insurance coverage equal to at least 80 percent of the **replacement cost** of the dwelling (not including the price of the land). An owner who has this type of policy may make a claim for the full cost of the repair or replacement of the damaged property without deduction for depreciation.

If the homeowner carries less than 80 percent of the full replacement cost, however, the claim will be handled in one of two ways. Either the loss will be settled for the actual cash value (replacement cost less depreciation) or it will be prorated by dividing the percentage of replacement cost actually covered by the policy by the minimum coverage requirement (usually 80 percent).

## FEDERAL FLOOD INSURANCE PROGRAM

 **WWWeb.Link**
www.fema.gov. The official site of the Federal Emergency Management Agency. It provides maps of flood zones and other disaster-prone areas, such as earthquake zones.

The National Flood Insurance Act of 1968 was enacted by Congress to help owners of property in flood-prone areas by subsidizing flood insurance and by taking land-use and land-control measures to improve future management for floodplain areas. The Federal Emergency Management Agency (FEMA) administers the flood program. The Army Corps of Engineers has prepared maps that identify specific flood-prone areas throughout the country. (FEMA maps usually can be found at the building/zoning department or county planning department.) Owners in flood-prone areas must obtain flood insurance to finance property with federal or federally related mortgage loans. If they do not obtain the insurance (either they don't want it or they don't qualify because their communities have not properly entered the program), they are not eligible for this financial assistance.

In designated areas, **flood insurance** is required on all types of buildings—residential, commercial, industrial, and agricultural—for either the value of the property or the amount of the mortgage loan, subject to the maximum limits available. Policies are written annually and can be purchased from any licensed property insurance broker, the National Flood Insurance Program, or the designated servicing companies in each state. However, if a borrower can produce a survey showing that the lowest part of the building is located above the 100-year flood mark, the borrower may be exempted from the flood insurance requirement, even if the property is in a flood-prone area.

## KEY TERMS

| | | |
|---|---|---|
| capital gain | homeowner's | modular home |
| coinsurance clause | insurance policy | (manufactured housing) |
| condominium | liability coverage | PITI |
| equity | mobile home | ratio calculation |
| flood insurance | | replacement cost |

## SUMMARY

- Current trends in home ownership include single-family homes, apartment complexes, condominiums, cooperatives, planned unit developments, retirement communities, highrise developments, converted-use properties, modular homes, manufactured housing, and time-shares.
- Prospective buyers should be aware of both the advantages and disadvantages of home ownership.
  - A disadvantage is the cost of ownership, both the initial price and the continuing expenses.
  - An advantage is financial security, pride of ownership, and income tax benefits.
- There are two primary income tax benefits available to homeowners:
  - mortgage interest payments (with certain limitations) and property taxes may be deducted on federal income tax returns, and
  - income tax on up to $250,000 (or $500,000 if married) of the gain from a sale may be excluded from taxation.
- To protect their investment in real estate, most homeowners purchase insurance.
  - A standard homeowner's insurance policy covers fire, theft, and liability and can be extended to cover many types of less common risks.
  - Another type of insurance, which covers personal property only, is available to people who live in apartments and condominiums.
  - Many homeowner's policies contain a coinsurance clause that requires that the policyholder maintain insurance in an amount equal to 80 percent of the replacement cost of the home. If this percentage is not met, the policyholder may not be reimbursed for the full repair costs if a loss occurs.
  - In addition to homeowner's insurance, the federal government requires flood insurance for people living in flood-prone areas who wish to obtain federally regulated or federally insured mortgage loans.

## Real-Life Real Estate

1. Home ownership is the *American Dream,* but what are the some of the obligations that come with attaining that dream?
2. What would be the impact of the loss of the tax benefits related to home ownership?

# QUESTIONS

1. The real cost of owning a home includes certain costs or expenses that many people tend to overlook. All of the following are costs or expenses of owning a home *EXCEPT*
   a. interest paid on borrowed capital.
   b. homeowner's insurance.
   c. maintenance and repairs.
   d. taxes on personal property.

2. When a person buys a house using a mortgage loan, the difference between the amount owed on the property and its market value represents the homeowner's
   a. tax basis.
   b. equity.
   c. replacement cost.
   d. capital gain.

3. A building that is remodeled into residential units and is no longer used for the purpose for which it was originally built is an example of
   a. a converted-use property.
   b. urban homesteading.
   c. a planned unit development.
   d. a modular home.

4. A highrise development that includes office space, stores, theaters, and apartment units is an example of which of the following?
   a. Planned unit development
   b. Mixed-use development
   c. Converted-use property
   d. Special cluster zoning

5. *V*, age 38, sells his home of eight years and realizes a $25,000 gain from the sale. The profit from the sale of *V*'s home may be
   a. taxed at a lower rate because of his age.
   b. excluded from taxation if *V* meets the use and ownership requirements.
   c. reduced by the amount of mortgage interest paid over the life of the ownership.
   d. eliminated by claiming the once-in-a-lifetime exclusion.

6. *F*, age 62, sells the home she has owned and occupied for the last 15 years and realizes a $52,000 gain from the sale. The profit from the sale of *F*'s home may be
   a. eliminated by claiming the once-in-a-lifetime exclusion.
   b. deducted if *F* purchases another home of equal or greater value within 24 months.
   c. reduced by the amount of mortgage interest paid over the life of the ownership.
   d. excluded from taxation under the new tax laws.

7. A typical homeowner's insurance policy covers all of the following *EXCEPT*
   a. the cost of medical expenses for a person injured in the policyholder's home.
   b. theft.
   c. vandalism.
   d. flood damage.

8. The profit a homeowner receives from the sale of his or her residence
   a. is the homeowner's tax basis.
   b. may be excluded from taxation if the homeowner meets certain use and ownership requirements.
   c. is always considered taxable gain for tax purposes.
   d. reduces the taxable gain on the sale of his or her next residence.

9. All of the following are deductible from a homeowner's gross income *EXCEPT*
   a. mortgage interest payments on a principal residence.
   b. real estate taxes (except for interest on overdue taxes).
   c. the gain realized from the sale or exchange of a principal residence.
   d. loan discount points.

10. Which of the following best expresses the concept of equity?
    a. Current market value – Capital gain
    b. Current market value – Property debt
    c. Current market value – Cost of land
    d. Replacement cost – Depreciation

11. *M* incurs the following expenses: (1) $9,500 in interest on a mortgage loan on *M*'s residence; (2) $800 in real estate taxes plus a $450 late payment penalty; and (3) a $1,000 loan origination fee paid in the course of purchasing *M*'s home. How much may be deducted from *M*'s gross income?
    a. $9,800          c. $11,300
    b. $10,500         d. $11,750

# CHAPTER 4

# Real Estate Brokerage

## THE HISTORY OF BROKERAGE

The nature of real estate brokerage services, particularly those provided in residential sales transactions, has changed significantly in recent years. Through the 1950s, real estate brokerage firms were primarily one-office, minimally staffed, family-run operations. The broker listed an owner's property for sale and found a buyer without assistance from other brokerage companies. The sale was eventually negotiated and closed. It was relatively clear that the broker represented the seller's interests. The common-law doctrine of *caveat emptor* ("let the buyer beware") was the rule; buyers were pretty much on their own, although few were aware of that fact.

In the 1960s, however, the way buyers and sellers were brought together in real estate transactions began to change. Brokers started to share information about properties they listed, resulting in two or more brokers cooperating to sell a property. The brokers formalized this exchange of information by creating *multiple-listing services (MLSs)*. The MLS expedited sales by increasing a single property's exposure to a greater number of potential buyers. Because it resulted in more sales, the MLS quickly became a widely used industry service.

While this arrangement benefited sellers, buyers came to question whether their interests were being protected. They began to demand not only accurate, factual information but also objective advice, particularly in the face of increasingly complex real estate transactions. Buyers view the real estate licensee as the expert on whom they can rely for guidance. In short, buyers now seek not only protection but representation as well.

## REAL ESTATE LICENSE LAWS

A state's real estate licensing laws and regulations serve as a framework for brokerage operations by defining the authority and responsibility of brokers and salespeople and by addressing many aspects of the day-to-day business operations. For example, the laws require that the firm have a definite, regular place of business. They also govern the placement of business signs and set requirements for establishing and maintaining branch offices. The laws dictate proper accounting and advertising procedures, correct handling of non–interest-bearing trust or special accounts, and the specific manner of execution and retention of documents involved in real estate transactions.

## REAL ESTATE BROKERAGE

**Brokerage** is simply the business of bringing parties together. Mortgage brokers match lenders with borrowers; stockbrokers bring together investors and corporations; customs brokers help importers navigate through complex customs procedures. A **real estate broker** is defined as a person licensed to buy, sell, exchange, or lease real property for others and to charge a fee for these services.

A brokerage business may take many forms. It may be a *sole proprietorship* (a single-owner company), a *corporation,* or a *partnership with another broker*, or a *limited liability company (LLC).* The office may be independent or part of a regional or national franchise. The business may consist of a single office or multiple branches. The broker's office may be located in a downtown highrise, a suburban shopping center, or the broker's home. A typical real estate brokerage may specialize in one kind of transaction or service or may offer an array of services.

**In Ohio...** No matter what form the brokerage business takes, however, the real estate broker faces the same challenges as an entrepreneur in any other industry. In addition to mastering the complexities of real estate transactions, the broker must be able to handle the day-to-day details of running a business. He or she must set effective policies for every aspect of the brokerage operation: maintaining space and equipment, hiring employees and salespersons, determining compensation, directing staff and sales activities, and implementing procedures to follow in carrying out his or her duties. Ohio's real estate license laws and regulations govern many of the broker's business activities, so broker's must also be familiar with every aspect of the real estate law. ◆

---

**In Practice**      At each step in a real estate transaction, a broker would be wise to advise the parties to secure legal counsel to protect their interests (even though the parties may fail to take this advice). *Although real estate brokers and salespersons may bring buyers and sellers together, and in most states may fill in preprinted blank purchase agreement forms, only an attorney may offer legal advice or prepare legal documents. Licensees who are not attorneys are prohibited from practicing law.*

---

**Real Estate Assistants and Technologies**

Real estate brokers find it all too easy to get bogged down with paperwork, telephone calls, meetings, schedules, office management, and the numerous small but vital details of running a business. While all these things are important, they keep the broker from the real focus of his or her job and what he or she does best—brokerage. In recent years, two developments have begun to lighten the broker's load: real estate assistants and real estate technologies.

A *real estate assistant* (also known as a personal assistant or *professional assistant*) is a combination office manager, marketer, organizer, and facilitator with a fundamental understanding of the real estate industry. An assistant may or may not have a real estate license.

**In Ohio...** In Ohio, an assistant may perform duties ranging from clerical and secretarial functions to office management, telemarketing, market strategy development, and direct contact with clients and customers. A licensed assistant can set up and host open houses and assist in all aspects of a real estate transaction. ◆

In addition to assistants, a wide range of technologies is available to help a real estate licensee do his or her job more efficiently and effectively. Computers are a necessary ingredient in any modern real estate brokerage. Multiple-listing services and mortgage information are accessible online via services such as America Online and Prodigy or directly through the Internet. Numerous software packages have been designed specifically for real estate professionals, and generic word-processing and spreadsheet software is available. Some of these programs help real estate brokers and salespersons with such office management tasks as billing, accounting and timekeeping. Other software assists with marketing and advertising properties and services. If approved by the Division of Real Estate (DRE), continuing education requirements can be met through the use of specially designed continuing education software. Real estate web sites, home pages, and computer networks help licensees keep in touch, and some cable and satellite television channels are dedicated solely to real estate programming for both consumers and professionals.

Real estate brokers and salespersons can carry laptop computers with portable modems that link them with their offices, an MLS, or mortgage company from virtually anywhere. Portable fax machines, pagers, and cellular phones make licensees available to their offices and clients 24 hours a day. Voicemail systems can track caller response to advertisements and give callers information about specific properties when the broker or salesperson is unavailable. Yard signs are available that broadcast details about a property on an AM radio band, so drivers passing by can tune in for tempting information.

All this technology is a great boon to practitioners, but real estate brokers and salespersons must make careful decisions about which technologies best suit their needs. Furthermore, they must keep up with the rapidly changing world of high-tech real estate tools to remain competitive.

**In Practice**   Home listings are becoming available to the general public on the Internet through such web sites as REALTORS (http://www.realtor.com) CyberHomes (http://www.cyber-homes.com) and *Real-Net* (http://www.realnet.com). By accessing these services, potential buyers can preview photographs of properties and narrow their searches by price range, number of bedrooms, amenities, neighborhood, or school district.

## Broker-Salesperson Relationship

Although brokerage firms vary widely in size, few brokers today perform their duties without the assistance of salespersons. Consequently, much of the business's success hinges on the broker-salesperson relationship.

A *real estate salesperson* is any person licensed to perform real estate activities on behalf of a licensed real estate broker. The broker is fully responsible for the actions performed in the course of the real estate business by all persons licensed under the broker. In turn, all of a salesperson's activities must be performed in the name of the supervising broker. The salesperson can carry out *only* those responsibilities assigned by the broker with whom he or she is licensed and can receive compensation *only* from that broker. As an agent of the broker, the salesperson has no authority to make contracts with or receive compensation from any other party. The broker is liable for the acts of the salesperson within the scope of the employment agreement.

**Independent contractor versus employee.** The employment agreement between a broker and a salesperson should define the nature, obligations, and responsibilities of the relationship. Essentially, the salesperson may be either an *employee* or an *independent contractor*.

**In Ohio...**   Ohio license law generally treats the salesperson as the employee of the broker in regard to the broker's liability for the salesperson's actions, regardless of whether the salesperson is considered to be an employee or an independent contractor for income tax purposes. Whether a salesperson is treated as an employee or an independent contractor affects the structure of the salesperson's responsibilities and the broker's liability to pay and withhold taxes from the salesperson's earnings. ◆

A broker can exercise certain *controls* over salespersons who are employees. The broker may require that an **employee** follow rules governing such matters as working hours, office routine, attendance at sales meetings, assignment of sales quotas, and adherence to dress codes. As an employer, a broker is required by the federal government to withhold Social Security tax and income tax from wages paid to employees. The broker is also required to pay unemployment compensation tax on wages paid to one or more employees, as defined by state and federal laws. In addition, employees might receive benefits such as health insurance, profit-sharing plans, and worker's compensation.

A broker's relationship with a salesperson who is an **independent contractor** is very different. As the name implies, an independent contractor operates more independently than an employee, and a broker may not exercise the same degree of control over the salesperson's activities. While the broker may control what the independent contractor does, the broker cannot dictate how to do it. The broker cannot *require* that the independent contractor keep specific office hours or attend sales meetings. Independent contractors are responsible for paying their own income and Social Security taxes, and they receive nothing from brokers that could be construed as an employee benefit, such as health insurance or paid vacation time. As a rule, independent contractors use their own materials and equipment. The written agreement between the broker and the salesperson should make these requirements clear. (See Figure 4.1.)

The Internal Revenue Service often investigates the independent contractor/employee situation in real estate offices. Under the latest Internal Revenue Service publication, there are several factors considered when determining whether a worker is an independent contractor or an employee. All evidence of control and independence in the business relationship will be considered. This evidence falls into three categories - behavioral control, financial control, and the type of relationship.

**Behavioral control** includes facts that show whether the business has a right to direct and control how the work is done, through instructions, training, or other means.

**Financial control** includes facts that show whether the employer or business has a right to control the business aspects of the worker's job. This includes:

| **Figure 4.1    Employee or Independent Contractor? IRS Considerations** | | |
|---|---|---|
| **FACTORS INDICATING CONTROL**<br><br>*Note: These factors are only <u>possible indicators</u> of a worker's status. Each case must be determined on its own facts, based on all the information.* | **EMPLOYEE** | **INDEPENDENT CONTRACTOR** |
| Is the worker required to comply with **employer instructions** about when, where, and how work is to be performed? | Yes | No |
| Is the worker required to undergo **training?** | Yes | No |
| Does the worker hire, supervise, and pay **others** to perform work for which he or she is responsible? | No | Yes |
| Must the worker's job be performed during **certain set hours?** | Yes | No |
| Must the worker devote **full time** to the job? | Yes | No |
| Must the work be performed **on the employer's property?** | Yes | No |
| Must tasks be performed in a **certain order** set by the employer? | Yes | No |
| Is the individual required to submit **regular written or oral reports** to the employer? | Yes | No |
| Is **payment** by the **hour, week** or **month?** | Yes | No |
| Is **payment** in a **lump sum?** | No | Yes |
| Are the worker's **business and travel expenses** paid by the employer? | Yes | No |
| Does the employer furnish the **tools and materials** required for the job? | Yes | No |
| Does the worker rent his or her own **office or working space?** | No | Yes |
| Will the worker realize a **profit or loss** as a result of his or her services? | No | Yes |
| Does the individual work for **more than one firm** at a time? | No | Yes |
| Does the worker make his or her services **available to the general public?** | No | Yes |
| Does the employer have the **right to fire** the worker? | Yes | No |
| Does the worker have the **right to quit** the job at any time, whether or not a particular task is complete? | Yes | No |

- The extent to which the worker has unreimbursed business expenses,
- The extent of the worker's investment in the business,
- How the business pays the worker; and
- The extent to which the worker can realize a profit or incur a loss.

Facts related to **type of relationship** include:

- Written contracts describing the relationship the parties intended to create,
- The extent to which the worker is available to perform services for other, similar businesses,
- Whether the business provides the worker with employee-type benefits, such as insurance, a pension plan, vacation pay, or sick pay, and
- The permanency of the relationship.

---

**In Practice**     A broker should have a standardized employment agreement drafted and reviewed by an attorney to ensure its compliance with federal law. The broker should also be aware that written agreements carry little weight with an IRS auditor if the actions of the parties contradict the provisions of the contract. Specific legal and tax questions regarding independent contractors should be referred to a competent attorney or accountant.

---

**Broker's Compensation**     The broker's compensation is specified in the contract with the principal (the buyer or seller for whom the broker is working). License laws may stipulate that a written agreement (either a listing agreement or a buyer representation agreement) must establish the compensation to be paid. Compensation can be in the form of a **commission** or brokerage fee (computed as a percentage of the total sales price), a flat fee, or an hourly rate.

**In Ohio...**     In Ohio, *the amount of a broker's commission is negotiable in every case.* Attempting, however subtly, to impose uniform commission rates is a clear violation of state and federal antitrust laws (discussed later in this chapter). A broker may, however, set the minimum rate acceptable for that broker's firm. The important point is for broker and client to agree on a rate before the agency relationship is established. ◆

A commission is usually considered earned when the work for which the broker was hired has been accomplished. Most sales commissions are payable when the sale is consummated by *delivery of the seller's deed.* This provision is generally included in the written agreement. When the written agreement specifies no time for the payment of the broker's commission, the commission is usually earned when

- a completed sales contract has been executed by a ready, willing and able buyer;
- the contract has been accepted and executed by the seller; and
- copies of the contract are in the possession of all parties.

To be entitled to a sales commission, an individual must be

- a licensed broker/agent,
- the procuring cause of the sale and
- employed by the buyer or seller under a valid contract.

...onsidered the **procuring cause of sale,** the broker must have started ...ed a chain of events that resulted in the sale. A broker who causes or ...tes such an action without a contract or without having been promised ...nt is a volunteer and may not legally claim compensation. Many other ...affect a broker's status as a procuring cause. For instance, if the agent ...ns the transaction, he or she may not be able to return and claim to ...een the procuring cause. In all cases, the key is determining *who really ...e property.* Procuring cause disputes between brokers are often settled ...h an arbitration hearing conducted by the local board or association. ...es between a broker and a client are more rare, but they may have to ...lved in court.

...seller accepts an offer from a ready, willing, and able buyer, the selling ...is entitled to a commission. A **ready, willing, and able buyer** is one ...ed to buy on the seller's terms and ready to take positive steps toward ...nmation of the transaction.* Courts may prevent the broker from receiv-...ommission if the broker knew the buyer was unable to perform. If the ...ction is *not* consummated, the broker may still be entitled to a commis-...the seller

...ad a change of mind and refused to sell,
...as a spouse who refused to sign the deed,
...ad a title with uncorrected defects,
...ommitted fraud with respect to the transaction,
...as unable to deliver possession within a reasonable time,
- insisted on terms not in the listing (for example, the right to restrict the use of the property), or
- had a mutual agreement with the buyer to cancel the transaction.

In general, then, a *broker is due a commission if a sale is not consummated because of the principal's default.*

**In Ohio...**  In Ohio, it is illegal for a broker to pay a commission to anyone other than the salesperson licensed with the broker or another broker. Fees, commissions, or other compensation cannot be paid to unlicensed persons for services that require a real estate license. "Other compensation" includes tangible gifts, such as a new television, or other premiums, such as a vacation. This is not to be confused with referral fees paid between brokers for leads. Referral fees, including interstate referrals, are legal as long as both individuals are licensed. ◆

Note that a buyer's broker may have different compensation arrangements. Many buyer's brokers work under representation agreements that state that if the buyer purchases a property submitted to the multiple listing service, the buyer's broker will split the commission with the listing broker. However, if the buyer ends up purchasing a property that was for sale by owner, the buyer will owe his or her broker compensation, either a flat fee or a percentage of the sale's price.

**Salesperson's Compensation**

**In Ohio...**  The amount of compensation a salesperson receives is set by mutual agreement between the broker and the salesperson. A broker may agree to pay a fixed salary or a share of the commissions from transactions originated by a salesperson (this is the most common form of compensation in Ohio). ◆ In some cases, a salesperson may draw from an account against earned shares of commissions. Some brokers require that salespersons pay all or part of the expenses of advertising listed properties as well as other overhead costs.

Test. Yes

*[Handwritten marginal notes:]*
3,000 - gross monthly income
3,000 - gross monthly income × 36% = 1,080.00 total Housing + other debt expense allowed.
3,000 × 28% = 840.00 total Housing expense

Some companies have *graduated commission* splits based on a salesperson's achieving specified production goals. For instance, a broker might agree to split commissions 50/50 up to a $25,000 salesperson's share; 60/40 for shares from $25,000 to $30,000; and so on. Commission splits as generous as 80/20 or 90/10 are possible, however, particularly for high producers.

Other firms have adopted a *100 percent commission plan.* Salespersons in these offices pay a monthly service charge to their brokers to cover the costs of office space, telephones, and supervision in return for keeping 100 percent of the commissions from the sales they negotiate. The 100 percent commission salesperson pays all of his or her own expenses.

However the salesperson's compensation is structured, only the employing broker can pay it. In cooperating transactions, the commission must first be received by the employing broker and then paid to the salesperson.

### Sharing Commissions

A commission might be shared by many people: the listing broker, the listing salesperson, the selling broker, and the selling salesperson. Drawing a diagram can help you determine which person is entitled to receive what amount of the total commission.

For example, salesperson Emerson, while working for broker Hewitt, took a listing on a $73,000 house at a six percent commission rate. Salesperson Tomlinson, while working for broker Ming, found the buyer for the property. If the property sold for the listed price, the listing broker and the selling broker shared the commission equally and the selling broker kept 45 percent of what he received. How much did salesperson Tomlinson receive? (If the broker retained 45 percent of the total commission he received, his salesperson would receive the balance: 100% – 45% = 55%.)

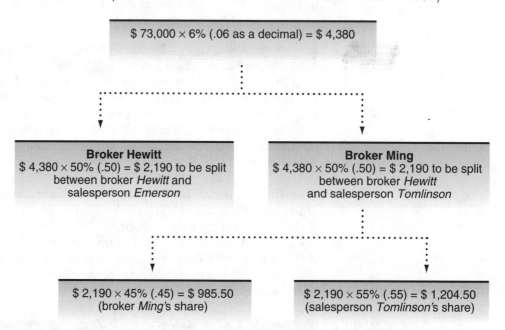

**Transactional Brokerage**    A **transactional broker** (also referred to as a *nonagent, facilitator, coordinator,* or *contract broker*) is not an agent of either party. A transactional broker's job is simply to help both the buyer and the seller with the necessary paperwork and formalities involved in transferring ownership of real property. The buyer

**In Ohio...** and the seller negotiate the sale without representation. Transactional brokers are not permitted under Ohio law. ◆

The transactional broker is expected to treat all parties honestly and competently, to locate qualified buyers or suitable properties, to help the parties arrive at mutually acceptable terms, and to assist in the closing of the transaction. Transactional brokers are equally responsible to both parties and must disclose known defects in a property. However, they may not negotiate on behalf of either the buyer or the seller, and they must not disclose confidential information to either party.

# ANTITRUST LAWS

The real estate industry is subject to federal and Ohio **antitrust laws.** These laws prohibit monopolies as well as any contracts, combinations and conspiracies that unreasonably restrain trade—that is, acts that interfere with the free flow of goods and services in a competitive marketplace. The most common antitrust violations are price fixing, group boycotting, allocation of customers or markets, and tie-in agreements.

**Price Fixing**

*Price fixing* is the practice of setting prices for products or services rather than letting competition in the open market establish those prices. In real estate, price fixing occurs when competing brokers agree to set sales commissions, fees, or management rates. *Price fixing is illegal.* Brokers must independently determine commission rates or fees for their own firms only. These decisions must be based on a broker's business judgment and revenue requirements without input from other brokers.

---

Antitrust violations include

- price fixing,
- group boycotting,
- allocation of customers,
- allocation of markets, and
- tie-in agreements.

---

Multiple-listing organizations, Boards of REALTORS® and other professional organizations may not set fees or commission splits. Nor can they deny membership to brokers based on the fees the brokers charge. Either practice could lead the public to believe that the industry not only sanctions the unethical practice of withholding cooperation from certain brokers but also encourages the illegal practice of restricting open-market competition.

The broker's challenge is to avoid even the impression of price fixing. Hinting to prospective clients that there is a "going rate" of commission or a "normal" fee implies that rates are, in fact, standardized. The broker must make it clear to clients that the rate stated is only what his or her firm charges.

**Group Boycotting**

*Group boycotting* occurs when two or more businesses conspire against another business or agree to withhold their patronage to reduce competition. Group boycotting is illegal under the antitrust laws.

**F**OR EXAMPLE *V* and *N*, the only real estate brokers in Potterville, agree that there are too many apartment-finder services in town. They decide to refer all prospective tenants to the service operated by *V*'s niece rather than handing out a list of all providers, as they have done in the past. As a result, *V*'s niece runs the only apartment-finder service in Potterville by the end of the year.

**Allocation of Customers or Markets**

*Allocation of customers or markets* involves an agreement among brokers to divide their markets and refrain from competing for each other's business. Allocations may be made on a geographic basis, with brokers agreeing to specific territories within which they will operate exclusively. The division may also occur by markets, such as by price range or category of housing. These agreements result in reduced competition and narrow markets.

**Tie-in Agreements**

Finally, *tie-in agreements* (also known as *tying agreements*) are agreements to sell one product only if the buyer purchases another product as well. The sale of the first (desired) product is "tied" to the purchase of a second (less desirable) product.

> **FOR EXAMPLE** *D,* a real estate broker, owns a vacant lot in a popular area of town. *B,* a builder, wants to buy the lot and build three new homes on it. *D* refuses to sell the lot to the builder unless *B* agrees to list the improved lot with *D* so that *D* can sell the homes. This sort of list-back arrangement violates antitrust laws.

**Penalties**
*Test*

The penalties for violating antitrust laws are severe. For instance, under the federal Sherman Antitrust Act, people who fix prices or allocate markets may be subject to a maximum $100,000 fine and three years in prison. For corporations, the penalty may be as high as $1 million. In a civil suit, a person who has suffered a loss because of the antitrust activities of a guilty party may recover triple the value of the actual damages plus attorney's fees and costs.

---

**KEY TERMS**

| | | |
|---|---|---|
| antitrust laws | independent contractor | real estate broker |
| brokerage | MLS | real estate |
| caveat emptor | price fixing | salesperson |
| commission | procuring cause of sale | tie-in agreements |
| employee | ready, willing, and | transactional broker |
| group boycotting | able buyer | |

---

**SUMMARY**

- Real estate license laws and regulations govern the professional conduct of brokers and salespersons. License laws are enacted to protect the public by ensuring a standard of competence and professionalism in the real estate industry.
- Real estate brokerage is the act of bringing together, for a fee or commission, people who wish to buy, sell, exchange, or lease real estate.
  - Real estate assistants and technologies are changing the way that brokerage offices are managed and operated.
- The broker's compensation in a real estate sale may take the form of a commission, a flat fee, or an hourly rate. The broker is considered to have earned a commission when he or she procures a ready, willing, and able buyer for a seller or find a home for a buyer.
- A broker may hire salespersons to assist in this work. The salesperson works on the broker's behalf as either an employee or an independent contractor.
- Federal and state antitrust laws prohibit brokers from conspiring to fix prices, engage in boycotts, allocate customers or markets, or establish tie-in agreements.

---

**Real-Life Real Estate**

1. Real estate brokers have a lot to think and worry about. Attracting and keeping good salespeople is a major challenge. How does the independent contractor relationship help or hurt staff retention?
2. "Procuring cause" is one of the primary causes of disputes among brokers and salespeople. What can brokers do to minimize this problem?

# QUESTIONS

1. Which of the following statements best explains the meaning of this sentence: "To recover a commission for brokerage services, a broker must be employed as the agent of the seller"?
   a. The broker must work in a real estate office.
   b. The seller must have made an express or implied agreement to pay a commission to the broker for selling the property.
   c. The broker must have asked the seller the price of the property and then found a ready, willing and able buyer.
   d. The broker must have a salesperson employed in the office.

2. A licensee who is paid in a lump sum and who works for multiple firms at the same time is probably a(n)
   a. transactional broker.
   b. buyer's agent.
   c. independent contractor.
   d. employee.

3. *M* is a licensed real estate salesperson. *M*'s written contract with broker *G* specifies that *M* is not an employee. In the last year, just under half of *M*'s income from real estate transactions came from sales commissions. The remainder was based on an hourly wage paid by *G*. Using these facts, it is likely that the IRS would classify *M* as which of the following for federal income tax purposes?
   a. Self-employed
   b. Employee
   c. Independent contractor
   d. Part-time real estate salesperson

4. While in the employ of a real estate broker, a salesperson has the authority to:
   a. list properties in his or her own name.
   b. assume responsibilities assigned by the broker.
   c. accept a commission from another broker.
   d. advertise property on his or her own behalf.

5. A real estate broker learns that her neighbor wishes to sell his house. The broker knows the property well and is able to persuade a buyer to make an offer for the property. The broker then asks the neighbor if the broker can present an offer from the prospective buyer, and the neighbor agrees. At this point, which of the following statements is true?
   a. The neighbor is not obligated to pay the broker a commission.
   b. The buyer is obligated to pay the broker for locating the property.
   c. The neighbor is obligated to pay the broker a commission.
   d. The broker may not be considered the procuring cause without a written contract.

6. A broker would have the right to dictate which of the following to an independent contractor?
   a. Number of hours the person would have to work
   b. Work schedule the person would have to follow
   c. Minimum acceptable dress code for the office
   d. Commission rate the person would earn

7. *V* and *W* were found guilty of conspiring with each other to allocate real estate brokerage markets. *P* suffered a $90,000 loss because of *V* and *W*'s activities. If *P* brings a civil suit against *V* and *W*, what can *P* expect to recover?
   a. Nothing; a civil suit cannot be brought for damages resulting from antitrust activities
   b. Only $90,000—the amount of actual damages P suffered
   c. Actual damages plus attorney's fees and costs
   d. $270,000 plus attorney's fees and costs

8. *B* and *C* are both salespersons who work for NMN Realty. One afternoon, they agree to divide their town into a northern region and a southern region. *B* will handle listings in the northern region, and *C* will handle listings in the southern region. Which of the following statements is true regarding this agreement?
   a. The agreement between *B* and *C* does not violate antitrust laws.
   b. The agreement between *B* and *C* constitutes illegal price fixing.
   c. *B* and *C* have violated the Sherman Antitrust Act, and are liable for triple damages.
   d. *B* and *C* are guilty of group boycotting with regard to other salespersons in their office.

9. A state has recently updated its *Rules and Regulations for the Real Estate Profession*. Assuming this state is like all other states and provinces, which of the following statements is true regarding this publication?
   a. The rules and regulations are state laws enacted by the legislature.
   b. The rules and regulations are a set of administrative rules adopted by the state Real Estate Commission and do not have the same force and effect as the statutory license law.
   c. The rules and regulations are a set of administrative rules adopted by the state Real Estate Commission that define the statutory license law and have the same force and effect as the license law itself.
   d. The rules and regulations create a suggested level of competence and behavior, but are not enforceable against real estate licensees.

10. *R* is a real estate salesperson associated with broker *B*. After a particularly challenging transaction finally closes, the client gives *R* a check for $500 "for all your extra work." Which of the following statements is accurate?
   a. While such compensation is irregular, it is appropriate for R to accept the check.
   b. *R* may receive compensation only from *B*.
   c. *R* should accept the check and deposit it immediately in a special escrow account.
   d. *B* is entitled to a share of the check.

11. A broker has established the following office policy: "All listings taken by any salesperson associated with this real estate brokerage must include compensation based on a seven percent commission. No lower commission rate is acceptable." If the broker attempts to impose this uniform commission requirement, which of the following statements is true?
   a. A homeowner may sue the broker for violating the antitrust law's prohibition against price fixing.
   b. The salespersons associated with the brokerage will not be bound by the requirement and may negotiate any commission rate they choose.
   c. The broker must present the uniform commission policy to the local professional association for approval.
   d. The broker may, as a matter of office policy, legally set the minimum commission rate acceptable for the firm.

12. GHI Realty has adopted a 100 percent commission plan. The monthly desk rent required of sales associates is $900, payable on the last day of the month. In August, a sales associate closed an $89,500 sale with a six percent commission and a $125,000 sale with a 5.5 percent commission. The salesperson's additional expenses for the month were $1,265. How much of her total monthly income did the salesperson keep?
   a. $10,080     c. $11,345
   b. $10,980     d. $12,245

13. Salesperson *M*, while working for broker *U*, took a listing on a house that sold for $129,985. The commission rate was eight percent. Salesperson *Y*, while working for broker *V*, found the buyer. Broker *U* received 60 percent of the commission on the sale; broker *V* received 40 percent. If broker *U* kept 30 percent of what he or she received, and paid M the remainder, how much did *M* earn on this sale?
   a. $1,247.86     c. $4,367.50
   b. $2,911.66     d. $6,239.28

14. On the sale of any property, a salesperson's compensation is based on the total commission paid to the broker. The salesperson receives 30 percent of the first $2,500, 15 percent of any amount between $2,500 and $7,500, and five percent of any amount exceeding $7,500. If a property sells for $234,500 and the broker's commission rate is 6.5 percent, what is the salesperson's total compensation?
    a. $1,887.13
    b. $4,609.13
    c. $6,626.67
    d. $7,621.25

15. G and H are competing real estate brokers. They meet for lunch and decide that D, a property developer, is gaining too much influence in the local market. G and H decide to try to drive D out. G happens to own a parcel of land that is key to the success of D's new subdivision, Alphabet Acres. H, on the other hand, owns 17 acres of polluted swamp next to an oil refinery. When D offers to buy G's property, G responds that the property is for sale only if D buys H's swamp at the same time. This puts D in an awkward position. Without G's property, Alphabet Acres will fail. Unfortunately, D doesn't have enough cash to pay the price H demands for the swamp. Rather than risk bankruptcy, D leaves town. This scenario is an example of which of the following violations of the antitrust laws?
    a. Group boycotting and allocation of markets
    b. Price fixing and tie-in agreements
    c. Tie-in agreements only
    d. Allocation of customers and price fixing

# CHAPTER 5

# Agency

## REAL ESTATE AGENCY IN OHIO

The relationship between a real estate licensee and the parties involved in a real estate transaction is not a simple one. In addition to the parties' assumptions and expectations, the licensee is subject to a wide range of legal and ethical requirements designed to protect the seller, the buyer, and the transaction itself. **Agency** is the word used to describe that special fiduciary relationship between a real estate licensee and the person he or she represents. (A **fiduciary relationship** is a relationship of trust and confidence.) Agency is governed by two kinds of law: *common law* (the rules of a society established by tradition and court decisions) and *statutory law* (the laws, rules, and regulations enacted by legislatures and other governing bodies).

**The History of Agency**

The basic framework of the law that governs the legal responsibilities of the broker to the people he or she represents is known as the *common-law law of agency.* The fundamentals of agency law have remained largely unchanged for hundreds of years. However, the *application* of the law has changed dramatically, particularly in residential transactions and especially in recent years. As states enact legislation that defines and governs the broker-client relationship, brokers are reevaluating their services. They must determine whether they will represent the seller, the buyer, or both in a transaction. They must also decide how they will cooperate with other brokers, depending on which party each broker represents. In short, the brokerage business is undergoing many changes as brokers focus on ways to enhance their services to buyers and sellers.

Even as the laws change, however, the underlying assumptions that govern the agency relationship remain intact. The principal-agent relationship evolved from the master-servant relationship under English common law. In that relationship, the servant owed absolute loyalty to the master. This loyalty superseded the servant's personal interests as well as any loyalty the servant might owe to others. In a modern-day agency relationship, the agent owes the principal similar loyalty. As masters used the services of servants to accomplish what they could not or did not want to do for themselves, principals use the services of agents. The agent is regarded as an expert on whom the principal can rely for specialized professional advice and to carry out the principal's instructions.

# LAW OF AGENCY

The law of agency defines the rights and duties of the **principal** and the **agent.** It applies to a variety of business transactions. In real estate transactions, contract law and real estate licensing laws—in addition to the law of agency—interpret the relationship between licensees and their clients. The law of agency is a common-law concept; it may be (and increasingly is) superseded by state statute.

**In Ohio...** In Ohio, the state legislature has adopted a statutory law of agency that creates uniform standards and enforcement mechanisms to regulate the relationships, duties, and responsibilities of real estate agents. The law establishes disclosure requirements for the permitted types of agency: primary, dual, and subagency. Licensees should consult with the Ohio Real Estate Commission regarding the availability of the mandatory forms. ◆

**Definitions** Real estate brokers and salespersons are commonly called agents. For instance, a homebuyer may casually refer to her "real estate agent." Legally, however, the term refers to strictly defined legal relationships. The buyer's real estate agent we just mentioned may actually represent the seller, not the buyer at all.

**In Ohio...** In Ohio, the following terms have specific definitions:

- *Agency* and *agency relationship* mean a relationship in which a licensee represents another person in a real estate transaction.
- *Agency agreement* means a contract between a licensee and a client in which the client promises to pay the broker a valuable consideration, or agrees that the licensee may receive a valuable consideration from another, for performing an act that requires a real estate license under the law.
- *Agent* and *real estate agent* mean a person licensed to represent another in a real estate transaction.
- *Affiliated licensee* means a licensed real estate broker or a real estate salesperson who is affiliated with a brokerage.
- *Client* means a person who has entered into an agency relationship with a licensee.
- *Confidential information* means all information that a client directs to be kept confidential or that if disclosed would have an adverse effect on the client's position in the real estate transaction (except to the extent the agent is required by law to disclose such information) and all information that is required by law to be kept confidential.
- *Dual agency relationship* means a brokerage, licensee, or management level licensee who represents both the purchaser and the seller as clients in the same transaction.
- *In-company transaction* means a real estate transaction in which the purchaser and seller are both represented by the same brokerage.
- *Management level licensee* means a licensee who is employed by or affiliated with a real estate broker and who has supervisory responsibility over other licensees employed by or affiliated with that real estate broker.
- *Subagency* and *subagency relationship* mean an agency relationship in which a licensee acts for another licensee in performing duties for the client of that licensee.
- *Timely* means as soon as possible under the particular circumstances. ◆

> An agent works *for* the client and *with* the *customer*.

There is a distinction between the level of services an agent provides to a client and those services the agent provides to a customer. The client is the principal to whom the agent gives *advice* and *counsel*. The agent is entrusted with certain *confidential information* and has *fiduciary responsibilities* (discussed in greater detail later) to the principal. In contrast, the *customer* is entitled to factual information and fair and honest dealings as a consumer, but does not receive advice and counsel or confidential information about the principal. The agent works *for* the principal and *with* the customer. Essentially, the agent is an advocate for the principal, not for the customer.

The relationship between the principal and agent must be *consensual;* that is, the principal *delegates* authority, and the agent consents to act. The parties must agree to form the relationship. An agent may be authorized by the principal to use the assistance of others, who become **subagents** of the principal.

Just as the agent owes certain duties to the principal, the principal has responsibilities to the agent. The principal's primary duties are to comply with the agency agreement and cooperate with the agent; that is, the principal must not hinder the agent and must deal with the agent in good faith. The principal also must compensate the agent according to the terms of the agency agreement.

## LIMITATIONS ON AN AGENT'S AUTHORITY

What an agent may do as the principal's representative depends solely on what the principal authorizes the agent to do.

A **universal agent** is a person empowered to do anything the principal could do personally. The universal agent's authority to act on behalf of the principal is virtually unlimited.

> A general agent represents the principal *generally;* a special agent represents the principal only for *special occasions,* such as the sale of a house.

A **general agent** may represent the principal in a broad range of matters related to a particular business or activity. The general agent may, for example, bind the principal to any contract within the scope of the agent's authority. This type of agency can be created by a general power of attorney, which makes the agent an attorney-in-fact. A real estate broker typically does not have this scope of authority as an agent in a real estate transaction.

A **special agent** is authorized to represent the principal in *one specific act or business transaction only, under detailed instructions.* A real estate broker is usually a special agent. If hired by a seller, the broker is limited to finding a ready, willing, and able buyer for the property. A special agent for a buyer would have the limited responsibility of finding a property that fits the buyer's criteria. As a special agent, the broker may not bind the principal to any contract. A *special power of attorney* is another means of authorizing an agent to carry out only a specified act or acts.

**F**OR EXAMPLE You are very busy with an important project, so you give your colleague $5 and ask him to buy your lunch. Your colleague is your *general agent:* you have limited his scope of activity to a particular business (buying your lunch) and established the amount that may be spent (up to $5). Still, he has broad discretion in selecting what you will eat and where he will buy it. However, if you had told your colleague, "Please buy me a Number 3 salad at Lettuce Eat Lettuce," you would have further limited his authority to a very specific task. Your colleague, therefore, would have been your *special agent.*

**Creation of Agency**

An agency relationship may be based on a formal agreement between the parties (an **express agency**), or it may result from the parties' behavior (an **implied agency**).

**Express agency.** The principal and agent may enter into a contract, or an **express agreement,** in which the parties formally express their intention to establish an agency and state its terms and conditions. The agreement may be either oral or written. An agency relationship between a seller and a broker is generally created by a written employment contract, commonly referred to as a **listing agreement,** which authorizes the broker to find a buyer or tenant for the owner's property.

**In Ohio...**

Although a written listing agreement is usually preferred, Ohio considers an oral agreement binding. An express agency relationship between a buyer and a broker is created by a **buyer agency agreement.** Similar to a listing agreement, it stipulates the activities and responsibilities the buyer expects from the broker in finding the appropriate property for purchase or rent.

In Ohio, the written agency agreement must contain an expiration date, a statement of the fair housing laws, the definition of "blockbusting" (stating that the practice is illegal), and a copy of the HUD logo. ◆

**Implied agency.** An agency may also be created by **implied agreement.** This occurs when the actions of the parties indicate that they have mutually consented to an agency. A person acts on behalf of another as agent; the other person, as principal, delegates the authority to act. The parties may not have consciously planned to create an agency relationship. Nonetheless, one can result *unintentionally, inadvertently* or *accidentally* by their actions.

**FOR EXAMPLE** *N* tells *B,* a real estate broker, that she is thinking about selling her home. *B* immediately contacts several prospective buyers. One of them makes an attractive offer without even seeing the property. *B* goes to *N*'s house and presents the offer, which *N* accepts. Although no formal agency agreement was entered into either orally or in writing, *B*'s actions *implied* to prospective buyers that *B* was acting as *N*'s agent. If *B* made any misrepresentations to the buyer, *N* may be held liable.

Even though licensees may be required to disclose whom they represent to the parties, customers may misunderstand the disclosure. Suppose a buyer asks a salesperson to show him some properties. He assumes from the beginning that the salesperson is acting as his agent. The salesperson discloses to the buyer that she is representing the seller, but the buyer misunderstands and continues to assume that the salesperson represents him. An implied agency with the buyer may result if the words and conduct of the salesperson do not dispel this assumption. If an implied agency with the buyer is created, the salesperson ends up in the difficult (and unlawful) position of representing both parties without their knowledge and consent. This is called *dual agency.* Dual agency, which will be discussed in greater detail later, may occur even though it was not intended.

**In Ohio...**

**Compensation.** Under Ohio law, the *source of compensation does not determine agency.* An agent does not necessarily represent the person who pays his or her commission. In fact, agency can exist even if no fee is involved (called a *gratuitous agency*). Buyers and sellers can agree between themselves as to how the agent will be compensated, regardless of which is the agent's principal. For instance, a seller could agree to pay a commission to the buyer's agent.

The written agency agreement should state how the agent is being compensated and explain all the alternatives available. ◆

**Termination of Agency**

An agency may be terminated for any of the following reasons:

- *Death* or *incapacity* of either party (notice of death is not necessary)
- *Destruction* or *condemnation* of the property
- *Expiration* of the terms of the agency
- *Mutual agreement* by all parties to the contract
- *Breach* by one of the parties, such as abandonment by the agent or revocation by the principal (in which case the breaching party might be liable for damages)
- By *operation of law,* as in bankruptcy of the principal (bankruptcy terminates the agency contract, and title to the property transfers to a court-appointed receiver)
- *Completion, performance* or *fulfillment* of the purpose for which the agency was created

An **agency coupled with an interest** is an agency relationship in which the agent is given an interest in the subject of the agency, such as the property being sold. An agency coupled with an interest cannot be revoked by the principal or be terminated on the principal's death.

**F**OR EXAMPLE  A broker agrees to provide the financing for a condominium building being constructed by a developer in exchange for the exclusive right to sell the units once the building is completed. The developer may not revoke the listing agreement once the broker has provided the financing because this is an agency coupled with an interest.

**Fiduciary Responsibilities**

The agency agreement usually authorizes the broker to act for the principal. The agent's **fiduciary relationship** of trust and confidence with the principal means that the broker owes the principal certain specific duties. These duties are not simply moral or ethical; they are the law—the common law of agency or the statutory law governing real estate transactions.

**In Ohio...**

Under both the common law of agency and Ohio state law, an agent owes the principal the duties of *care, obedience, accounting, loyalty* (including confidentiality), and *disclosure.* Figure 5.1 illustrates the differences between client and customer services provided to a buyer and seller. ◆

**Care.**  The agent must exercise a reasonable degree of care and due diligence while transacting the business entrusted to him or her by the principal. The principal expects the agent's skill and expertise in real estate matters to be superior to that of the average person. The most fundamental way in which the agent exercises care is to use that skill and knowledge in the principal's behalf. The agent should know all facts pertinent to the principal's affairs, such as the physical characteristics of the property being transferred and the type of financing being used.

If the agent represents the seller, care and skill include helping the seller arrive at an appropriate and realistic listing price, discovering and disclosing facts that affect the seller, and properly presenting the contracts that the seller signs. It also means making reasonable efforts to market the property, such as advertising and holding open houses, and helping the seller evaluate the terms and conditions of offers to purchase.

---

**Memory Tip**

The five common-law fiduciary duties may be remembered by the acronym COALD: **C**are, **O**bedience, **A**ccounting, **L**oyalty, and **D**isclosure.

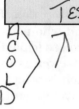

## Figure 5.1  Customer-Level versus Client-Level Service

### THE SELLING BROKER

*Customer-Level Service as Subagent*          *Client-Level Service as Buyer's Broker*

#### RESPONSIBILITIES

Be honest with buyer, but owe greater responsibility to seller, including duty of skill and care to promote and safeguard seller's best interests.

Be fair with seller, but owe greater responsibility to buyer, including duty of skill and care to promote and safeguard buyer's best interests.

#### EARNEST MONEY DEPOSIT

Collect amount sufficient to protect seller.

Suggest minimum amount, perhaps a note; put money in interest-bearing account; suggest that forfeiture of earnest money be sole remedy if buyer defaults.

#### SELLER FINANCING

Can discuss, but should not encourage, financing terms and contract provisions unfavorable to seller, such as (1) no due-on-sale clause, (2) no deficiency judgment (nonrecourse), (3) unsecured note. If a corporate buyer, suggest seller require personal guaranty.

Suggest terms in best interests of buyer, such as low down payment, deferred interest, long maturity dates, no due-on-sale clause, long grace period, nonrecourse.

#### DISCLOSURE

Disclose to seller pertinent facts (which might not be able to disclose if a buyer's broker), such as (1) buyer's willingness to offer higher price or better terms, (2) buyer's urgency to buy, (3) buyer's plans to resell at profit or resubdivide to increase value, (4) buyer is sister of broker.

Disclose to buyer pertinent facts (which might not be able to disclose if subagent of seller), such as (1) seller near bankruptcy or foreclosure, (2) property overpriced, (3) other properties available at better buys, (4) negative features such as poor traffic flow, (5) construction of chemical plant down street that may affect property value.

#### NONDISCLOSURE

Refrain from disclosing to buyer facts that may compromise seller's position (e.g., seller's pending divorce) unless under legal duty to disclose (e.g., zoning violation).

Refrain from disclosing to seller such facts regarding buyer's position as buyer has options on three adjoining parcels. No duty to disclose name of buyer or that broker is loaning buyer money to make down payment.

#### PROPERTY CONDITION

Suggest use of "as is" clause, if appropriate to protect seller (still must specify hidden defects).

Require that seller sign property condition statement, and confirm representations of condition; require soil and termite inspections, if appropriate; look for negative features and use them to negotiate better price and terms.

#### DOCUMENTS

Give buyer a copy of important documents, such as mortgage to be assumed, declaration of restrictions, title report, condominium bylaws, house rules.

Research and explain significant portions of important documents affecting transaction, such as prepayment penalties, subordination, right of first refusal; refer buyer to expert advisers when appropriate.

#### NEGOTIATION

Use negotiating strategy and bargaining talents in seller's best interests.

Use negotiating strategy and bargaining talents in buyer's best interests.

**Figure 5.1** *Customer-Level versus Client-Level Service (Continued)*

*Customer-Level Service as Subagent*          *Client-Level Service as Buyer's Broker*

### SHOWING

Show buyer properties in which broker's commission is protected, such as in-house or MLS-listed properties. Pick best times to show properties. Emphasize attributes and amenities.

Search for best properties for buyer to inspect, widening marketplace to "for sale by owner" properties, lender-owned (REO) properties, probate sales, unlisted properties. View properties at different times to find negative features, such as evening noise, afternoon sun, traffic congestion.

### PROPERTY GOALS

Find buyer the type of property buyer seeks; more concerned with *sale* of seller's property that fits buyer's stated objectives.

Counsel buyer as to developing accurate objectives; may find that buyer who wants apartment building might be better with duplex at half the price or that buyer looking for vacant lot would benefit more from investment in improved property.

### OFFERS

Can help prepare and transmit buyer's offer on behalf of seller; must reveal to seller that buyer has prepared two offers, in case first offer not accepted.

Help buyer prepare strongest offer; can suggest buyer prepare two offers and have broker submit lower offer first without revealing existence of second offer.

### POSSESSION DATES

Consider best date for seller in terms of moving out, notice to existing tenants, impact on insurance, risk of loss provision.

Consider best date for buyer in terms of moving in, storage, favorable risk of loss provision if fire destroys property before closing.

### DEFAULT

Discuss remedies upon default by either party. Point out to seller any attempt by buyer to limit liability (nonrecourse, deposit money is sole liquidated damages).

Suggest seller's remedy be limited to retention of deposit money; consider having seller pay buyer's expenses and cancellation charges if seller defaults.

### BIDDING

Can bid for own account against buyer customer, but disclose this to buyer and seller.

Cannot bid for own account against buyer client.

### EFFICIENCY

Don't expend much time and effort, as in an open listing, because in competition with the listing broker, seller, and other brokers to sell buyer a property before someone else does.

Work at an exclusive listing efficiency, realizing that broker's role is to assist buyer in locating and acquiring best property, not to sell buyer a particular property.

### APPRAISAL

Unless asked, no duty to disclose low appraisal or fact broker sold similar unit yesterday for $10,000 less.

Suggest independent appraisal be used to negotiate lower price offer; review seller's comparables from buyer's perspective.

### BONUS

Cannot agree to accept bonus from buyer for obtaining reduction in listed price.

Can receive incentive fee for negotiating reduction in listed price.

### TERMINATION

Easier to terminate subagency relationship (as when broker decides to bid on property).

Legal and ethical implications of agency relationship and certain duties may continue even after clearly documented termination.

**In Ohio...** An agent who represents the buyer is expected to help the buyer locate suitable property and evaluate property values, neighborhood and property conditions, financing alternatives, and offers and counteroffers with the buyer's interest in mind. ◆

An agent who does not work diligently to properly represent the interests of the principal could be found by a court to have been negligent. The agent is liable to the principal for any loss resulting from the agent's negligence or carelessness. The standard of care will vary from market to market and depends on the expected behavior for a particular type of transaction in a particular area.

---

**In Practice**    Because real estate licensees have, under the law, enormous exposure to liability, some brokers purchase what are known as **errors and omissions insurance policies** for their firms. Similar to malpractice insurance in the medical and legal fields, E&O policies cover liability for errors and negligence in the usual listing and selling activities of a real estate office. Individual salespersons also might be insured. Licensing laws in several states now require E&O insurance for brokers and, in some cases, for individual salespersons as well. However, no insurance policy will protect a licensee from litigation arising from criminal acts. Insurance companies normally exclude coverage for violation of civil rights laws as well.

---

**Obedience.** The fiduciary relationship obligates the agent to act in good faith at all times, obeying the principal's instructions in accordance with the contract. However, that obedience is not absolute. The agent may not obey instructions that are unlawful or unethical. Because illegal acts do not serve the principal's best interests, obeying such instructions violates the broker's duty of loyalty. On the other hand, an agent who exceeds the authority assigned in the contract will be liable for any losses that the principal suffers as a result.

**FOR EXAMPLE** A seller tells the listing agent, "I don't want you to show this house to any, you know, minorities." Because refusing to show a property to someone on the basis of race is illegal, the agent must not follow the seller's instructions.

**Accounting.** The agent must be able to report the status of all funds received from or on behalf of the principal in a timely manner.

**In Ohio...** Ohio real estate license laws require that a broker give accurate copies of all documents to all parties affected by them and keep copies on file for a specified period of time. Most license laws, including Ohio, also require that the broker deposit immediately, or within 24 to 48 hours, all funds entrusted to the broker (such as earnest money deposits) in a special trust, or escrow account. Commingling such monies with the broker's personal or general business funds is strictly illegal. ◆

**Loyalty.** The duty of loyalty requires that the agent place the principal's interests above those of all others, including the agent's own self-interest. The agent must be particularly sensitive to any possible conflicts of interest. *Confidentiality* about the principal's personal affairs is a key element of loyalty. An agent may not, for example, disclose the principal's financial condition. When the principal is the seller, the agent may not reveal such things as the principal's willingness to accept less than the listing price or his or her anxiousness to sell unless the principal has authorized the disclosure. If the principal is the buyer, the agent may not disclose, for instance, that the buyer will pay more than the offered price if necessary, or that the buyer is under a tight moving schedule, or any other fact that might harm the principal's bargaining position.

**In Ohio...** In Ohio, there are certain *exceptions to this rule of confidentiality*. Confidential information can be disclosed under four circumstances:

1. The client permits disclosure.
2. The disclosure is required by law or by court order (for instance, the law requires the agent to disclose material facts about the condition of the property itself).
3. The information becomes public from a source other than the licensee.
4. The information is necessary to prevent a crime the client intends to commit. ◆

The duty of loyalty also requires that the agent act without self-interest, unless with the principal's knowledge and consent.

**In Ohio...** Ohio forbids brokers or salespeople to buy property listed with them for their own accounts or for accounts in which they have a personal interest without first notifying the principal of such interest and receiving the principal's consent. In this situation, it is imperative that the agents disclose the fact that they are licensed and are buying the property for themselves. When selling property in which the agent has a personal interest, Ohio license law requires that a broker or licensee disclose this information, either verbally or in writing, to cooperating brokers and potential buyers. Unlawful, undisclosed dual agency (discussed later in the chapter) could result in rescission, monetary damages, forfeiture of commission, and/or loss or suspension of license. ◆

**Disclosure.** It is the agent's duty to keep the principal informed of all facts or information that could affect a transaction. Duty of disclosure includes relevant information or material facts that the agent knows or should have known.

**In Ohio...** Every Ohio real estate salesperson and broker is required to disclose to prospective sellers, purchasers and tenants which party he or she represents in a transaction. The purpose of this disclosure is to avoid possible undisclosed or unintended **dual agency** status or unintended or accidental agency. Residential lease or rental agreements for less than one year are exempt from the disclosure requirement. Ohio real estate license laws prohibit a broker from representing both the buyer and the seller in the same transaction—that is, acting as a dual agent—unless both give their informed written consent to this limited representation.

The *agency disclosure statement* must be provided to the prospective purchaser as soon as possible, and in no event later than the time an offer to purchase is prepared or submitted. The seller signs the form at the time the buyer's offer is presented, and the form must be kept in the broker's files for at least three years. (See Figure 5.6.) Agency disclosure statements are discussed in more detail later in this chapter. ◆

The agent is obligated to discover facts that a reasonable person would feel are important in choosing a course of action, regardless of whether they are favorable or unfavorable to the principal's position. The broker may be held liable for damages for failure to disclose such information. For example, an agent for the seller has a duty to disclose:

- all offers;
- the identity of the prospective purchasers, including the agent's relationship, if any, to them (such as a relative or the broker's being a participating purchaser);
- the ability of the purchaser to complete the sale or offer a higher price;
- any interest the broker has in the buyer (such as the buyer's asking the broker to manage the property after it is purchased); or
- the buyer's intention to resell the property for a profit.

An agent for the buyer must disclose deficiencies of a property as well as sales contract provisions and financing that do not suit the buyer's needs. The broker would suggest the lowest price that the buyer should pay based on comparable values, regardless of the listing price. The agent would disclose information about how long a property has been listed or why the seller is selling that would affect the buyer's ability to negotiate the lowest purchase price. If the agent were representing the seller, this information would violate the agent's fiduciary duty to the seller.

**In Ohio...**   **Additional statutory duties.** Ohio law also lists some agency duties that are not common-law duties, but are required by the Ohio Real Estate Commission (OREC). These include

- performing the terms of any written agency agreement;
- complying with all applicable state and federal laws, rules and regulations; and
- *advising* the client to obtain expert advice when necessary or appropriate (e.g., legal or accounting advice). ◆

## TYPES OF AGENCY RELATIONSHIPS

**In Ohio...**   In Ohio, a variety of agency relationships may be created.

- A *primary agency relationship* between the licensee and the seller
- A *primary agency relationship* between the licensee and the purchaser
- A *dual agency relationship* between the licensee and both the seller and the purchaser
- A *subagency relationship* between the licensee and the client of another licensee ◆

The distinction among these types of relationships is not always clear. When consumers feel their individual interests have not been adequately protected, licensees may face legal and ethical problems.

**In Ohio...**   Each Ohio brokerage is required to develop and maintain a written policy establishing the types of agency relationships that members of the brokerage are permitted to establish. (The written policy may be included in the written agency agreement.) For instance, the brokerage may choose as a matter of policy that dual agency is not allowed. Licensees must not only be aware of

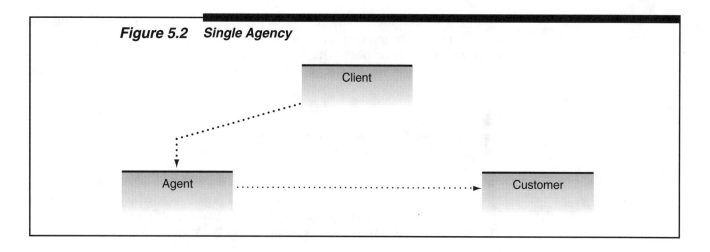

**Figure 5.2    Single Agency**

brokerage policies regarding types of agency relationship, they must follow them consistently. Procedures for ensuring the confidentiality of client information must also be implemented. At all times, the principal always controls the agency relationship. ◆

When an agency relationship is formed between a licensee and a client, both the licensee's brokerage and the management level licensees (managers) in the brokerage who have supervisory responsibilities are also the client's agents. Management-level licensees who have no supervisory duties over the licensee, however, are not agents of the client. No other licensees affiliated with the brokerage are the client's agents unless they assisted in establishing the agency relationship or are specifically appointed to represent the client. The client must consent to any appointment of other licensees.

**Single Agency**     The two primary agency relationships discussed above are often called *single agency relationships*. In single agency, the agent represents only one party in any single transaction. The agent owes fiduciary duties exclusively to one principal, who may be *either* the buyer *or* the seller (or the landlord or tenant) in a transaction. Any third party is a customer. (See Figure 5.2.)

**Seller as principal.**  If a seller contracts with a broker to market the seller's real estate, the broker becomes an *agent* of the seller; the seller is the *principal,* the broker's *client.* In single agency, a buyer who contacts the broker to review properties listed with the broker's firm is the broker's *customer.* Though obligated to deal fairly with all parties to a transaction and to comply with all aspects of the license law, the broker is strictly accountable only to the principal—in this case, the seller. The customer (in this case, the buyer) represents himself or herself and should follow the principal of *caveat emptor*—buyer beware.

**In Ohio...**     According to Ohio agency law, a licensee who is representing the seller is to promote the interest of the seller by:

- seeking a purchase offer at a price and with terms acceptable to the client;
- presenting any purchase offer to the client in a timely manner, even if the property is subject to a contract of sale, lease, or letter of intent to lease; and
- prior to presenting the seller an offer to purchase, providing the seller with a copy of any agency disclosure form signed by the purchaser (discussed on the following page). ◆

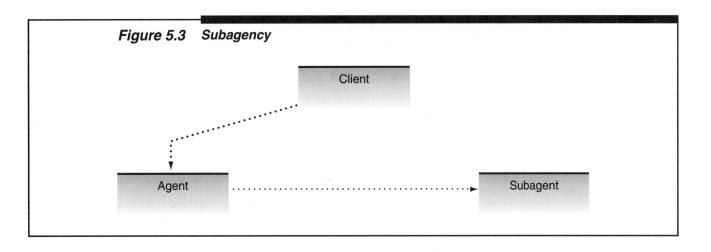

**Figure 5.3** *Subagency*

A licensee does not breach his or her duty to the seller by showing alternative properties to a prospective purchaser or by acting as an agent or subagent for other sellers. However, the seller's agent cannot extend an offer of subagency to other licensees or offer compensation to a broker who represents a buyer without the seller's knowledge and consent.

The listing contract usually authorizes the broker to use licensees employed by the broker as well as the services of other, cooperating brokers in marketing the seller's real estate. These cooperating brokers may assist the broker (agent) as **subagents** or may be the agents for other parties. It is important to note that not all cooperating brokers are subagents. A cooperating agent who enters into a buyer agency relationship will represent the buyer rather than the seller (as a subagent).

The relationship of a salesperson or an associate broker to an employing broker is also an agency. These licensees are thus agents of the broker in addition to being subagents of the principal.

**Subagency.** A subagency is created when one broker, usually the seller's agent, appoints other brokers (with the seller's permission) to help perform client-based functions on the principal's behalf. These *cooperating brokers* have the same fiduciary obligation to the seller as does the *listing broker*: helping produce a ready, willing, and able buyer for the property. The listing broker is liable for the conduct of all of the subagents and their salespersons. (See Figure 5.3.)

**F**OR EXAMPLE If you give your colleague $5 and ask him to buy your lunch, your colleague is your agent. If your colleague is busy, he may hand your money to a friend, along with your instructions. The friend is a *subagent*—an agent of your agent. Your colleague's friend is still responsible for buying *your* lunch in accordance with *your* instructions. The subagent, like the agent, is ultimately responsible to you, the principal.

A subagency arrangement may be created through an offer of cooperation and compensation made in a multiple-listing service (MLS). However, participation in an MLS by itself, does not necessarily create a subagency relationship. Because of widespread agency reforms, a cooperating broker cannot be presumed to be a subagent, and subagency relationships are becoming increasingly rare.

**Buyer as principal.** When a buyer contracts with a broker to locate property and represent his or her interests in a transaction, the buyer is the *principal*—the broker's client. The broker, as *agent,* is strictly accountable to the buyer. The seller is the customer.

In the past, it was simple: brokers always represented sellers, and buyers were expected to look out for themselves. With the widespread use of MLSs and subagency, a buyer often had the mistaken impression that the subagent was the buyer's agent, although the reality was that both agent and subagent represented the seller's interests.

Today, however, many residential brokers and salespersons are discovering opportunities of buyer representation. Some brokers and salespersons have become specialists in the emerging field of buyer brokerage, representing buyers exclusively.

Buyer agency has become increasingly popular because of the many services buyers can enjoy by having their own representation. Buyer agents typically:

- evaluate the specific wants and needs of the buyer;
- help the buyer determine the appropriate price range;
- preview and show buyers affordable properties that meet their criteria;
- investigate properties the buyer is interested in to identify any problems or potential problems before any offer is made;
- help the buyer structure an appropriate offer for the property;
- present the offer to the seller's agent;
- negotiate the best terms possible for the buyer;
- review and explain legal documents to the buyer;
- help the buyer secure the financing required to purchase the property; and
- provide the buyer with names of qualified vendors, such as attorneys, accountants, inspectors, and movers.

Real estate regulatory agencies across the country have developed rules and procedures to regulate **buyer's brokers,** and local real estate associations develop agency representation forms and other materials for them to use. Professional organizations offer assistance, certification, training, and networking opportunities for buyer's agents.

A buyer agency relationship is established in the same way as any other agency relationship: by contract or agreement. The buyer's agent may receive a flat fee or a share of the commission or both, depending on the terms of the agency agreement. It is important to determine the basis for compensation in the first meeting and enter into an agency agreement before the licensee shows the buyer any property. Buyer brokerage and buyer agency agreements are discussed in Chapter 7.

**In Ohio...** According to Ohio agency law, a licensee who is representing the buyer is to promote the interest of the buyer by

- seeking a property at a price and with purchase or lease terms acceptable to the purchaser and
- presenting any offer to purchase or lease to the seller or the seller's agent in a timely manner, even if the property is subject to a contract of sale, lease, or letter of intent to lease. ◆

Real estate licensees who represent buyers may have to expend extra effort to find an acceptable property for the buyer. For instance, they should not limit their search to those properties listed in the MLS. They should also research properties that are for sale by owner, contact other brokerage companies, investigate properties that are in the foreclosure process, and look into any other avenues for discovering properties, such as the Internet.

Once the buyer has found a property he or she may be interested in, a buyer's agent must take steps to protect the buyer's interest before an offer is made. The buyer's agent should always prepare a competitive market analysis for the buyer, so the buyer will know what the value of the property is before making an offer. The buyer's agent should also inform the buyer about any issues that may be unique to the property's neighborhood or community, such as future development, traffic congestion, or crime. The buyer's agent should make the buyer aware of various information about the property, such as:

- the shape and size of the lot,
- current zoning restrictions,
- any easements or other encumbrances that affect title or use of the property,
- the amount of current property taxes and other assessments,
- any factors that may affect resale values (including stigmas that have arisen because of the property's past),
- whether the property is in a flood plain, earthquake zone, or other dangerous area,
- the appreciation rates of other properties in the area, and
- information about the quality of local schools.

Buyer's agents should also recommend necessary inspections, such as soil test, pest inspections, and structural inspections. Buyer's agents should also make sure that the buyer receives and examines any property disclosure statements prepared by the seller.

**In Ohio...** Note that a buyer's agent does not breach any duty to the buyer by showing the same properties to other purchasers or by acting as an agent or subagent for other purchasers, except that any dual agency relationship must be properly disclosed. However, the buyer's agent cannot extend an offer of subagency to other licensees or accept compensation from a broker who represents a seller without the buyer's knowledge and consent. ◆

**Landlord as principal.** An owner may employ a broker to market, lease, maintain, or manage the owner's property. Such an arrangement is known as *property management*. The broker is made the agent of the property owner through a property management agreement. As in any other agency relationship, the broker has a fiduciary responsibility to the client-owner. Sometimes, an owner may employ a broker for the sole purpose of marketing the property to prospective tenants. In this case, the broker's responsibility is limited to finding suitable tenants for the owner's property. Property management is discussed further in Chapter 18.

**Dual agency.** *Dual agency* exists when one agent represents both the seller and the buyer in the same transaction. A dual agency relationship usually occurs when a buyer and seller are represented by different licensees in the same brokerage. Because both licensees are working on behalf of the same broker, a dual agency is created. (See Figure 5.4.)

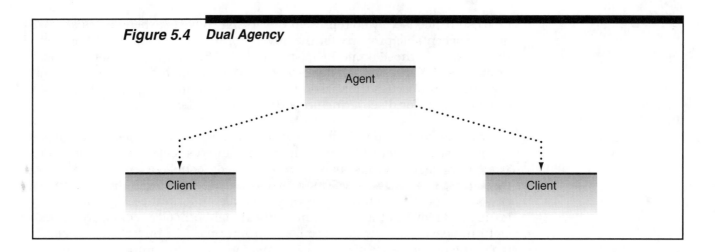

**Figure 5.4　Dual Agency**

**In Ohio...**　Dual agency is permitted under the Ohio law only with the knowledge and written consent of both parties. This means that the licensee must disclose to both parties all the relevant information that is necessary to enable each party to make an informed decision as to whether to consent to the dual agency relationship. Then both parties must sign and date a dual agency disclosure statement. (See Figure 5.5.)

According to state law, a brokerage cannot engage in a dual agency relationship unless

- the brokerage has established a procedure under which licensees, including management-level licenses, who represent one client will not have access to and will not obtain confidential information concerning another client of the brokerage involved in the dual agency transaction and
- the licensee who is an agent for each client fulfills the licensee's duties exclusively to that client. For example, the seller's agent must be loyal to the interests of his client, not the interests of the buyer. ◆

The required dual agency disclosure statement must generally describe the duties of an agent in a dual agency relationship. In addition, it must contain sections for the disclosure of other information, including (among other facts)

- a disclosure that the clients' interests are, or could be, different or adverse;
- a statement that a dual agent may not disclose to one client information intended to be kept confidential by the other;
- a disclosure of any material relationship between the brokerage and either client other than the subject transaction;
- a specification of the source of compensation; and
- a statement that the client's consent has been given voluntarily, that his or her signature indicates informed consent, and that the disclosure has been read and understood.

The disclosure statement must be provided to the parties in a timely manner as soon as it is determined that a dual agency relationship exists. The disclosure statement must be signed by the purchaser when an offer to purchase or lease is made, and then it must be initialed before the parties sign the offer. The initialed disclosure statement is then delivered, along with the offer, to the licensee who represents the seller. The seller's licensee then

### Figure 5.5 Sample Dual Agency Disclosure Statement

## DUAL AGENCY DISCLOSURE STATEMENT

Seller/Landlord(s):_____ Buyer/Tenant(s):_____
Seller/Landlord(s):_____ Buyer/Tenant(s):_____
Property Involved:_____

For purposes of this form, the term "seller " includes a landlord and the term "buyer" includes a tenant.

**DUAL AGENCY:** Ohio law permits a real estate agent and brokerage to represent both the seller and buyer in a real estate transaction **AS LONG AS THIS IS DISCLOSED TO BOTH PARTIES AND THEY BOTH AGREE. THIS IS KNOWN AS DUAL AGENCY.** As a dual agent, a real estate agent and brokerage represent two clients whose interests are, or at times could be, different or adverse. For this reason, the dual agent(s) may not be able to advocate on behalf of the client with the same skill and energy the dual agent may have if the agent represents only one client.

This statement discloses that _____
                                                    (Name of brokerage)
and its agent(s)_____
                           (Name of agent(s))
**WILL BE ACTING AS A DUAL AGENT IN THE CONTEMPLATED TRANSACTION INVOLVING THE NAMED PROPERTY.**

IT IS UNDERSTOOD AND AGREED BY THE PARTIES THAT **AS A DUAL AGENT**, THE AGENT AND BROKERAGE **SHALL:**
1. Treat both clients honestly;
2. Disclose latent, material defects to the purchaser, if known by the agent or brokerage;
3. Provide information regarding lenders, inspectors and other professionals, if requested;
4. Provide market information available from a property listing service or public records, if requested;
5. Prepare and present all offers and counteroffers at the direction of the parties;
6. Assist both parties in completing the steps necessary to fulfill the terms of any contract, if requested.

IT IS ALSO UNDERSTOOD AND AGREED BY THE PARTIES THAT **AS A DUAL AGENT**, THE AGENT AND BROKERAGE **SHALL NOT:**
1. Disclose information that is confidential, or that would have an adverse effect on one party's position in the transaction, unless such disclosure is authorized by the client or required by law;
2. Advocate or negotiate on behalf of either the buyer or seller;
3. Suggest or recommend specific terms, including price, to be offered, accepted, rejected or countered or disclose the terms or price a buyer is willing to offer or that a seller is willing to accept;
4. Engage in conduct that is contrary to the instructions of either party and may not act in a biased manner on behalf of one party.

**MATERIAL RELATIONSHIP:** Unless indicated below, neither the agent or the brokerage acting as a dual agent in this contemplated transaction has a material relationship with either buyer or seller. A material relationship would include, any personal, family or business relationship with one of the parties. (If such a relationship does exist, explain):_____
**COMPENSATION:** Unless indicated as follows, the brokerage will be compensated per the listing agreement:_____
**RESPONSIBILITIES OF THE PARTIES:** The duties of the agent and brokerage in a real estate transaction do not relieve the Buyer and Seller from the responsibility to protect their own interests. The Buyer and Seller are advised to carefully read all agreements to assure that they adequately express their understanding of the transaction. The agent and brokerage are qualified to advise on real estate matters. **IF LEGAL OR TAX ADVICE IS DESIRED, YOU SHOULD CONSULT THE APPROPRIATE PROFESSIONAL.**

#### FAIR HOUSING STATEMENT

It is illegal, pursuant to the Ohio Fair Housing Law, Division (H) of Section 4112.02 of the Revised Code and the Federal Fair Housing Law, 42 U.S.C.A. 3601, to refuse to sell, transfer, assign, rent, lease, sublease, or finance housing accommodations, refuse to negotiate for the sale or rental of housing accommodations, or otherwise deny or make unavailable housing accommodations because of race, color, religion, sex, familial status, ancestry, handicap, or national origin; or to so discriminate in advertising the sale or rental of housing, in the financing of housing, or in the provision of real estate brokerage services.

It is also illegal, for profit, to induce or attempt to induce a person to sell or rent a dwelling by representations regarding the entry into the neighborhood of a person or persons belonging to one of the protected classes.

> BY SIGNING BELOW, YOU ACKNOWLEDGE THAT YOU HAVE READ AND UNDERSTAND THIS FORM. YOU ARE GIVING YOUR VOLUNTARY, INFORMED CONSENT TO THIS DUAL AGENCY. IF YOU DO NOT AGREE TO THE AGENT AND/OR BROKERAGE ACTING AS A DUAL AGENT, YOU ARE NOT REQUIRED TO CONSENT TO THIS AGREEMENT AND YOU MAY EITHER REQUEST A SEPARATE AGENT IN THE BROKERAGE BE APPOINTED TO REPRESENT YOUR INTERESTS OR YOU MAY TERMINATE YOUR AGENCY RELATIONSHIP AND SEEK REPRESENTATION FROM ANOTHER BROKERAGE. IF YOU CHOOSE TO BE REPRESENTED BY ANOTHER BROKERAGE, HOWEVER, YOU MAY BE OBLIGATED TO PAY A COMMISSION TO THE ABOVE NAMED BROKERAGE. ANY QUESTIONS REGARDING POTENTIAL OBLIGATIONS SHOULD BE DIRECTED TO PERSONAL LEGAL COUNSEL.

_____    _____    _____    _____
Buyer/Tenant            Date        Seller/Landlord          Date

_____    _____    _____    _____
Buyer/Tenant            Date        Seller/Landlord          Date

_____    _____    _____    _____
Licensee                 Date        Licensee (if more than one)  Date

Any questions regarding the role or responsibilities of real estate brokers, brokerages, or agents in Ohio can be directed to an attorney or to: The Ohio Division of Real Estate at (614) 466-4100

**EQUAL HOUSING OPPORTUNITY**

12/96

presents the statement to the seller to sign, initial, and date the portion of the statement that indicates understanding and consent to the agency relationships. The statement must be presented to the seller before the offer to purchase or lease is presented.

## CUSTOMER-LEVEL SERVICES

> An agent owes a *customer* the duties of *reasonable care and skill; honest and fair dealing;* and *disclosure of known facts.*

Even though an agent's primary responsibility is to the principal, the agent also has duties to third parties. Any time a licensee works with a third party, or *customer,* the licensee is responsible for adhering to state and federal consumer protection laws as well as to the ethical requirements imposed by professional associations and state regulators. In addition, the licensee's duties to the customer include

- reasonable care and skill in performance,
- honest and fair dealing, and
- disclosure of all facts that the licensee knows or should reasonably be expected to know that materially affect the value or desirability of the property.

**In Ohio...**  Under Ohio law, an agent can assist a party who is not the agent's client in a real estate transaction. Permitted acts are limited to providing basic information and assisting in preparing or conveying offers or leases. ◆

As part of the recent trend toward public protection of purchasers, many states now have statutes requiring disclosure of property conditions to prospective buyers. Prepurchase structural inspections, termite infestation reports, or other protective documentation also may be used. The actual disclosures that sellers are required to make vary according to each state's law.

**In Ohio...**  In Ohio, an agent must disclose to any purchaser all material facts of which the agent has actual knowledge that pertain to the physical condition of the property and that the purchaser would not discover by a reasonably diligent inspection. This information includes material defects in the property, environmental contamination, and any other information that any statute or rule requires to be disclosed. Under state statute, the agent will be regarded as having actual knowledge of material facts if that agent acts with reckless disregard for the truth. Ohio laws regarding property disclosure statements are discussed in Chapter 7. ◆

**Environmental Hazards**  Disclosure of environmental health hazards, which can render properties unusable for the buyer's intended purpose, may be required. For instance, federal law requires the disclosure of lead-based paint hazards. Frequently, the buyer or the buyer's mortgage lender requests inspections or tests to determine the presence or level of risk.

**In Practice**    Licensees are urged to obtain advice from federal, state and local authorities responsible for environmental regulation whenever the following conditions may be present: toxic waste dumping; underground storage tanks; contaminated soil or water; nearby chemical or nuclear facilities; and health hazards such as radon, asbestos, and lead paint.

**Opinion versus Fact**

Brokers, salespersons and other staff members must always be careful about the statements they make. They must be sure that the customer understands whether the statement is an opinion or a fact. Statements of opinion are permissible only as long as they are offered *as opinions* and without any intention to deceive.

Statements of fact, however, must be accurate. Exaggeration of a property's benefits is called **puffing.** For instance, telling a buyer that a property has the best view in the city would be considered puffing. While puffing is legal, licensees must ensure that none of their statements can be interpreted as fraudulent. **Fraud** is the *intentional misrepresentation* of a material fact in such a way as to harm or take advantage of another person. That includes not only making false statements about a property but also intentionally concealing or failing to disclose important facts. In Ohio, fraud can be prosecuted criminally (as well as being the basis of a civil action.)

The misrepresentation or omission does not have to be intentional to result in broker liability. A **negligent misrepresentation** occurs when the broker *should have known* that a statement about a material fact was false. The fact that the broker may actually be ignorant about the issue is no excuse. If the buyer relies on the broker's statement, the broker is liable for any damages that result. Similarly, if a broker accidentally fails to perform some act—for instance, if he or she forgets to deliver a counteroffer—the broker may be liable for damages that result from such a negligent omission.

**F**OR EXAMPLE  1. While showing a potential buyer a very average-looking house, broker *Q* described even its plainest features as "charming" and "beautiful." Because the statements were obviously *Q*'s personal opinions, designed to encourage a positive feeling about the property (or puff it up), their truth or falsity is not an issue.

2. Broker *G* was asked by a potential buyer if a particular neighborhood was safe. Although *G* knew that the area was experiencing a skyrocketing rate of violent crime, *G* assured the buyer that no problem existed. *G* also neglected to inform the buyer that the lot next to the house the buyer was considering had been sold to a waste disposal company for use as a toxic dump. Both are examples of fraudulent misrepresentation.

If a contract to purchase real estate is obtained as a result of fraudulent misstatements, the contract may be disaffirmed or renounced by the purchaser. In such a case, the broker not only loses a commission but can be liable for damages if either party suffers loss because of the misrepresentation. If the licensee's misstatements were based on the owner's own inaccurate statements and the licensee had no independent duty to investigate their accuracy, the broker may be entitled to a commission, even if the buyer rescinds the sales contract.

**Latent Defects**

The seller has a duty to discover and disclose any known latent defects that threaten structural soundness or personal safety. A **latent defect** is a *hidden structural defect that would not be discovered by ordinary inspection.* Buyers have been able to either rescind the sales contract or receive damages when a seller fails to reveal known latent defects. For instance, sellers were found liable where a house was built over a ditch covered with decaying timber, where a buried drain tile caused water to accumulate, and where a driveway was built partly on adjoining property. The courts have also decided in favor of the buyer when the seller neglected to reveal violations of zoning or building codes.

In addition to the seller's duty to disclose latent defects, in some states the agent has an independent duty to conduct a reasonably competent and diligent inspection of the property.

**In Ohio...** However, in Ohio, an agent is not required to discover latent defects in the property. Nor are agents required to advise the purchaser on matters outside the scope of the knowledge required for real estate licensure or to verify the accuracy or completeness of statements made by the seller. There is an exception to this rule: if the agent is aware of information that should reasonably cause the agent to question the accuracy or completeness of the seller's statements, then the agent is required to verify the statements.

Note that the purchaser is still obligated to inspect the physical condition of the property. ◆

---

**In Practice**

**In Ohio...** Most agents in Ohio strongly recommend that the buyer obtain an independent home inspection when purchasing real property. ◆

---

**Stigmatized Properties** In recent years, questions have been raised about stigmatized properties— properties that society has branded undesirable because of events that occurred there. Typically, the stigma is a criminal event, such as homicide; illegal drug manufacturing or gang-related activity; or a tragedy such as suicide. However, properties even have been stigmatized by rumors that they are haunted. Because of the potential liability to a licensee for inadequately researching and disclosing material facts concerning a property's condition, licensees should seek competent counsel when dealing with a stigmatized property. Some states have laws regarding the disclosure of information about such properties, designed to protect sellers and local property values against a baseless psychological reaction. In other states, the licensee's responsibility may be difficult to define because the issue is not a physical defect, but merely a perception that a property is undesirable.

---

**In Practice** A disclosure that a property's previous owner or occupant died of AIDS or was HIV-positive constitutes illegal discrimination against the handicapped under the federal Fair Housing Act, discussed in Chapter 22.

---

## AGENCY DISCLOSURE LAW

It is easy for buyers to believe that the agent who shows them a property represents their interests in subsequent negotiations. This natural misunderstanding may arise out of the amount of time an agent typically spends with buyers and the professionally cordial relationship an agent properly seeks to build. A buyer may confide confidential financial information to the agent and feel that he or she is being represented in negotiations as well; however, if an agent represents the seller, the agent is obliged to pass on all relevant information and to represent only the seller's best interest.

**In Ohio...** To avoid problems with the issue of whom the agent represents, most states—including Ohio—have enacted or are planning to enact statutes that address some form of mandatory agency disclosure. (See Figure 5.6.) Whether the disclosure is on a separate written form or is part of a contract, whether it is made at first contact with a nonclient or customer or at some other time, is not the concern. Public policy demands a level playing field; nonclients or customers must somehow be informed that they are not being represented, and state real estate commissions are being charged with the responsibility of implementing that policy. ◆

## Contents of the Disclosure Statement

The *agency disclosure statement* to be read and signed by the parties explains the duties of a licensee in a real estate transaction, including

- the permissible agency relationships a licensee may establish under Ohio law and an explanation of the duties the licensee owes the client in each type of relationship.
- whether the brokerage may act as a dual agent and, if so, the possibility that different licensees affiliated with the brokerage might represent the separate interests of a purchaser or a seller in the same transaction. The disclosure statement contains an explanation that when different licensees affiliated with the same brokerage represent both the purchaser and seller in a transaction, each licensee represents only the interests of that licensee's client, but that the brokerage and the management level licensees in the brokerage are dual agents of both the seller and purchaser and have supervisory duties and limitations as dual agents. The disclosure also states that the broker will take steps to preserve the confidential information of the client.
- unless confidential, the names of all parties the licensee represents in the transaction.
- the fact that the signature of the client indicates the client consents to the agency relationship and that if the client does not understand the agency disclosure statement, the client should consult an attorney.

## Timing of the Disclosure Statement

A licensee who represents the seller must provide the agency disclosure statement to the seller prior to marketing or showing the seller's property.

A licensee working directly with a purchaser in a real estate transaction, whether as the purchaser's agent, the seller's agent, or the seller's subagent, will give the purchaser an agency *disclosure prior to the earliest of the following events:*

- Initiating a prequalification evaluation to determine whether the purchaser has the financial ability to purchase or lease the particular property
- Requesting specific financial information from the purchaser to determine the purchaser's ability to purchase or finance real estate in a particular price range
- Showing the property to the purchaser other than at an open house
- Discussing with the purchaser the making of an offer to purchase real property
- Submitting an offer to purchase or lease real property on behalf of the purchaser

If the earliest event described above is by telephone, the licensee must make a verbal disclosure of the nature of the agency relationship that the licensee has with both the seller and the purchaser. The licensee then will obtain the

**Figure 5.6** *Sample Disclosure of Agency Relationship Form*

## DISCLOSURE OF AGENCY RELATIONSHIP

The following agent _____, and _____
(name of agent)                                    (name of brokerage)
the brokerage with which the agent is affiliated, disclose the following concerning their agency relationship (CHECK APPROPRIATE BOX - ONLY ONE):
☐ They represent the seller as the seller's agent.
☐ They represent the buyer as a buyer's agent.

Disclosure of the potential future agency relationships that could be created: (CHECK APPROPRIATE BOX(ES) THAT APPLY):
☐ They represent the seller as a subagent.
☐ They represent the buyer as a subagent.
☐ The same agent who represents you could potentially represent the other party in a transaction involving you. The agent and brokerage would both be **DUAL AGENTS.** A management level licensee is a dual agent in an in-company transaction.
☐ A different agent in the same brokerage could potentially represent the other party in a transaction involving you. Each agent would represent the interest of their separate client. The brokerage would be a **DUAL AGENT.**

# C O N S E N T

> BY SIGNING THIS FORM YOU INDICATE YOUR CONSENT TO THE AGENCY RELATIONSHIP DISCLOSED ABOVE. BEFORE YOU CONSENT TO ANY AGENCY RELATIONSHIP, YOU SHOULD FULLY UNDERSTAND THE INFORMATION FOUND ON THE REVERSE SIDE OF THIS FORM. IF YOU DO NOT UNDERSTAND THE INFORMATION CONTAINED ANYWHERE IN THIS FORM, YOU SHOULD CONSULT AN ATTORNEY.

_____    _____    _____    _____
Buyer/Tenant          Date       Seller/Landlord      Date

_____    _____    _____    _____
Buyer/Tenant          Date       Seller/Landlord      Date

## TO BE COMPLETED ONLY IN AN IN-COMPANY TRANSACTION INVOLVING TWO AGENTS

Both buyer and seller **ACKNOWLEDGE AND AGREE** that in a contemplated transaction involving property located at _____, the buyer is represented by _____and the seller is represented by _____.

> YOU DO NOT HAVE TO CONSENT TO DUAL AGENCY. BEFORE YOU CONSENT TO ANY AGENCY RELATIONSHIP, YOU SHOULD FULLY UNDERSTAND THE INFORMATION FOUND ON THE REVERSE SIDE OF THIS FORM. IF YOU DO NOT UNDERSTAND THE INFORMATION CONTAINED ANYWHERE IN THIS FORM, YOU SHOULD CONSULT AN ATTORNEY.

By initialing below **BOTH PARTIES ACKNOWLEDGE AND AGREE** that they are aware that both agents are affiliated with the same brokerage; that each agent will represent the separate interest of their separate client, except if a management level licensee is one of the agents involved in the transaction; that it was previously disclosed that this could occur; and that **THEY CONSENT TO THE BROKERAGE ACTING AS A DUAL AGENT.**

Buyer/Tenant's initials: _____ Date _____

Seller/Landlord's initials: _____ Date _____

Any questions regarding the role or responsibilities of the brokerage or its agents in Ohio can be
Directed to an attorney or to:
Ohio Division of Real Estate
77 S. High Street 20th Floor
Columbus, Ohio 43266-0547
(614) 466-4100

12/96

---

**Figure 5.6    Sample Disclosure of Agency Relationship Form (Continued)**

# AGENCY DISCLOSURE STATEMENT

This disclosure form is being provided to help you make an informed choice regarding the type of relationship you wish to enter into with the real estate agent. It is also intended to help you understand the role of other agents who may be involved in your real estate transaction. For purposes of the form, the term "seller" includes a landlord and the term "buyer" includes a tenant.

When you enter into an agency relationship with a real estate agent, the real estate brokerage with whom the agent is affiliated also becomes your agent. Unless they are appointed to represent you, the other agents in the brokerage are not your agents and do not represent you.

## AGENCY RELATIONSHIPS PERMITTED IN OHIO

<u>**Seller's Agency**</u>:        In this type of relationship, the agent and the brokerage owe the seller the duties of loyalty, obedience, confidentiality, accounting, and reasonable skill and care in performing their duties, and any other duties contained in an agency agreement. The agent and brokerage are required to act solely on behalf of the seller's interest to seek the best price and terms for the seller. Finally, a seller's agent and brokerage also have a duty to disclose to the seller all material information obtained from the buyer or from any other source.

<u>**Subagency:**</u>    In this type of relationship, buyer's/sellers may authorize their agent and brokerage to offer subagency to other licensees/brokerages. A subagent also represents the client's interests and has all of the same duties as the client's agent, including a duty of loyalty and confidentiality and a duty to disclose all material facts to the client.

<u>**Buyer's Agency**</u>:        In this type of relationship, a buyer's agent and the brokerage owe the buyer the duties of loyalty, obedience, confidentiality, accounting, and reasonable skill and care in performing their duties and any other duties contained in an agency agreement. The agent and brokerage are required to act solely on behalf of the buyer's interests to seek the best price and terms for the buyer. Finally, a buyer's agent and brokerage also have a duty to disclose to the buyer all material information obtained from the seller or from any other source.

<u>**Disclosed Dual Agency**</u>:    In this type of relationship, one agent may represent both parties in a real estate transaction, **BUT ONLY IF BOTH PARTIES CONSENT**. Disclosed dual agency is most likely to occur when both the buyer and seller are represented by the same agent. **IF THIS HAPPENS, THE BUYER AND SELLER MUST SIGN A SEPARATE DUAL AGENCY DISCLOSURE STATEMENT** that describes the duties and obligations of the dual agent. A dual agent may not disclose any confidential information that would place one party at an advantage over the other party and may not disclose any of the following information without the informed consent of the party to whom the information pertains: **1)** that a buyer is willing to pay more than the price offered; **2)** that a seller is willing to accept less than the asking price; **3)** motivating factors of either party for buying or selling; **4)** that a party will agree to financing terms other than those offered; **5)** repairs or improvements a seller is willing to make as a condition of sale; and **6)** or any concession having an economic impact upon the transaction that either party is willing to make.

<u>**Permitted Agency Relationships in an In-Company Transaction**</u>: In an in-company transaction where the buyer and seller are both represented as clients by the same brokerage, the following applies: If only <u>one agent</u> is involved in the transaction, that agent represents both the buyer and the seller. The agent and the brokerage are dual agents and cannot disclose confidential information to either client. If <u>two agents</u> are involved in the transaction, you and the other party will be represented by the agent with whom you have each entered into an agency relationship. Each agent will represent the sole interest of his/her client and must not share confidential information with each other. The brokerage is a dual agent. The only exception is if a management level licensee is one of the agents involved in the transaction. In this case, the management level licensee and the brokerage represent both the buyer and seller as dual agents. **The brokerage's role, as a dual agent, is to do the following**:
- ▸    Objectively supervise the agents involved so they can each fulfill their duties, as outlined above, to each of their clients;
- ▸    Assist the parties, in an unbiased manner, to negotiate a contract;
- ▸    Assist the parties, in an unbiased manner, to fulfill the terms of any contract.

**As a dual agent, the brokerage cannot**:
- ▸    Advocate or negotiate on behalf of either the buyer or seller;
- ▸    Disclose confidential information to any party or any other employee or agent of the brokerage;
- ▸    Use confidential information of one party to benefit the other party to the transaction.

purchaser's signature and the date on an agency disclosure statement at the first meeting with the purchaser following verbal disclosure of the agency relationship.

**In Ohio...** A *buyer's agent* must disclose to the seller's agent (or to the seller if he or she is not represented) that the agent represents the buyer in the transaction. The disclosure must be made during the first contact the agent has with any employee or licensee of the brokerage with which the seller's agent is affiliated or during the first contact with the seller. If the seller is unrepresented, the buyer's agent must also disclose any intention of seeking compensation from the seller. ◆

If a purchaser or buyer refuses to sign an agency disclosure form, the licensee must note the following information on the bottom of the form:

- Party to whom the form was presented
- Date and time the form was presented
- Fact that the party declined to sign the form
- Reason for the refusal, if known

The licensee then must immediately inform his or her supervisor about the refusal. The brokerage must keep a copy of the disclosure form containing the required information for three years. The refusal to sign the disclosure statement cannot be used as a reason for a failure to present an offer to the refusing party.

Note that failure to properly disclose a licensee's agency status is a common cause for disciplinary action.

**Changing the Agency Relationship**

**In Ohio...** Sometimes, once the agency relationship has been disclosed, the licensee wants to represent another party to the transaction. To change the agency relationship after the agency disclosure has taken place, the party originally represented must consent, in writing, to the change in representation. The licensee must promptly notify all persons who had been notified of the original relationship. ◆

**Exceptions** The legislation's disclosure requirements do not apply in the following situations:

**In Ohio...**
- The rental or leasing of residential premises if the rental or lease agreement can be performed in one year or less
- The referral of a prospective buyer, tenant, seller, or landlord to another licensee
- Transactions involving the sale, lease, or exchange of foreign real estate
- Transactions involving the sale of a cemetery or interment right ◆

## POST-TRANSACTION OBLIGATIONS

**In Ohio...** Once all the licensee's duties have been performed or a contract has terminated or expired, a licensee owes no further duties to a client unless otherwise agreed to in writing. However, Ohio law does require that a licensee provide the client an accounting of all monies and property relating to the transaction and keep confidential information confidential. Certain exemptions to the confidentiality rule are provided, such as disclosing information by court order or to prevent a crime. ◆

## KEY TERMS

| | | |
|---|---|---|
| accounting | customer | latent defect |
| agency | diligence | listing agreement |
| agency coupled with | disclosure | loyalty |
|   an interest | dual agency | negligent |
| agency disclosure | express agency | misrepresentation |
|   statement | express agreement | obedience |
| agent | fiduciary relationship | principal |
| buyer agency | fraud | puffing |
|   agreement | general agent | special agent |
| buyer's broker | implied agency | subagent |
| care | implied agreement | universal agent |
| client | | |

## SUMMARY

- The law of agency governs the principal-agent relationship. Agency relationships may be expressed either by the words of the parties or by written agreement, or they may be implied by the parties' actions.
- In single agency relationships, the broker or agent represents one party, either the buyer or the seller, in the transaction.
  - If the agent elicits the assistance of other brokers who cooperate in the transaction, the other brokers may become subagents of the principal.
- Many states have adopted statutes that replace the common law of agency and that establish the responsibilities and duties of the parties. The common law agency duties include care, obedience, accounting, loyalty, and disclosure.
- Representing two opposing parties in the same transaction constitutes dual agency. Licensees must be careful not to create dual agency when none was intended.
  - Disclosed dual agency requires that both principals be informed of and consent to the broker's multiple representation.
- Many states have mandatory agency disclosure laws.
- The source of compensation for the client services does not determine which party is represented.
- Licensees have certain duties and obligations to their customers as well. Consumers are entitled to fair and honest dealings and to the information necessary for them to make informed decisions. This includes accurate information about the property. Some states have mandatory property disclosure laws.

## Real-Life Real Estate

1. Whether a salesperson represents the buyer or the seller in a real estate transaction has been a question that has always created confusion with the parties involved in the transaction. Discuss the evolution of the disclosure laws and explain how these laws fulfill their purpose.
2. Assume the role of a listing salesperson: Using the sample Ohio Agency Disclosure form, explain your relationship to a property owner.
3. Again, assume the role of a listing salesperson: Explain the agency relationships the owner may be exposed to as potential buyers view the property.
4. Assume the role of a selling agent: Describe the options the buyer has for representation.

# QUESTIONS

1. The term *fiduciary* refers to the
   a. sale of real property.
   b. person who gives someone else the legal power to act on his or her behalf.
   c. person who has legal power to act on behalf of another.
   d. principal-agent relationship.

2. The relationship between broker and seller is generally what type of agency?
   a. Special
   b. General
   c. Implied
   d. Universal

3. Which of the following statements is true of a real estate broker acting as the agent of the seller?
   a. The broker is obligated to render faithful service to the seller.
   b. The broker can disclose personal information to a buyer if it increases the likelihood of a sale.
   c. The broker can agree to a change in price without the seller's approval.
   d. The broker can accept a commission from the buyer without the seller's approval.

4. Y is a real estate broker. W lists a home with Y for $89,500. Later that same day, Q comes into Y's office and asks for general information about homes for sale in the $30,000 to $40,000 price range. Based on these facts, which of the following statements is true?
   a. Both W and Q are Y's customers.
   b. W is Y's client; Q is a customer.
   c. Y owes fiduciary duties to both W and Q.
   d. If Q asks Y to be Q's buyer representative, Y must decline because of the preexisting agreement with W.

5. In a dual agency situation, a broker may collect a commission from both the seller and the buyer if
   a. the broker holds a state license.
   b. the buyer and the seller are related by blood or marriage.
   c. both parties give their informed consent to the dual compensation.
   d. both parties are represented by attorneys.

6. Which of the following events will terminate an agency in a broker-seller relationship?
   a. The broker discovers that the market value of the property is such that he or she will not make an adequate commission.
   b. The owner declares personal bankruptcy.
   c. The owner abandons the property.
   d. The broker appoints other brokers to help sell the property.

7. Under the law of agency, a real estate broker owes all of the following duties to the principal *EXCEPT*
   a. care.
   b. obedience.
   c. disclosure.
   d. advertising.

8. A real estate broker hired by an owner to sell a parcel of real estate must comply with
   a. the common law of agency, even if a state agency statute exists that abrogates common law.
   b. dual agency requirements.
   c. the concept of caveat emptor.
   d. all lawful instructions of the owner.

9. Broker *A* is hired by a first-time buyer to help the buyer purchase a home. The buyer confides to *A* that being approved for a mortgage loan may be complicated by the fact that the buyer filed for bankruptcy two years ago. When the buyer offers to buy Mr. and Mrs. *T*'s home, what is *A*'s responsibility?
    a. *A* should discuss with the buyer *A*'s duty to disclose the buyer's financial situation to the local multiple-listing service.
    b. *A* has a duty of fair dealing toward Mr. and Mrs. *T* and must discuss the buyer's finances with them honestly, although in the best possible terms.
    c. *A* must politely refuse to answer any questions that would violate the duty of confidentiality.
    d. *A* has no responsibility toward Mr. and Mrs. *T* because *A* is the buyer's agent.

10. Broker *D* lists *K*'s residence. For various reasons, *K* must sell the house quickly. To expedite the sale, *D* tells a prospective purchaser that *K* will accept at least $5,000 less than the asking price for the property. Based on these facts, which of the following statements is true?
    a. *D* has not violated his agency responsibilities to *K*.
    b. *D* should have disclosed this information, regardless of its accuracy.
    c. The disclosure was improper, regardless of *D*'s motive.
    d. The relationship between *D* and *K* is referred to as a *general agency relationship*.

11. A buyer who is a client of the broker wants to purchase a house that the broker has listed for sale. Which of the following statements is true?
    a. If the listing salesperson and selling salesperson are two different people, there is no problem.
    b. The broker should refer the buyer to another broker to negotiate the sale.
    c. The seller and buyer must be informed of the situation and agree to the broker's representing both of them.
    d. The buyer should not have been shown a house listed by the broker.

12. What does the phrase "the law of agency is a common-law doctrine" mean?
    a. It is a legal doctrine that is not unusual.
    b. It is one of the rules of society enacted by legislatures and other governing bodies.
    c. It is a body of law established by tradition and court decisions.
    d. It may not be superseded by statutory law.

13. *B* is a real estate broker. *S* lists a home with *B* for $98,000. Later that week, *V* comes into *B*'s office and asks for general information about homes for sale in the $90,000 to $100,000 price range. Based on these facts, which of the following statements is true?
    a. Both *S* and *V* are *B*'s customers.
    b. *S* is *B*'s customer; *V* is a client.
    c. *V* is *B*'s customer; *S* is *B*'s client.
    d. If *V* asks *B* to present an offer to *S*, *B* must ask both parties to sign a disclosed dual agency agreement.

14. Broker *E* tells a prospective buyer, "This property has the most beautiful river view." In fact, the view includes the back of a shopping center. In a separate transaction, Broker *F* fails to mention to some enthusiastic potential buyers that a six-lane highway is planned for construction within ten feet of a house the buyers think is perfect. Based on these facts, which of the following statements is true?
    a. Broker *E* has committed fraud.
    b. Broker *F* has committed puffing.
    c. Both broker *E* and broker *F* are guilty of intentional misrepresentation.
    d. Broker *E* is merely puffing; broker *F* has misrepresented the property.

15. Under Ohio law, the Agency Disclosure Statement must be given to prospective purchasers/tenants
    a. before they are shown any properties.
    b. at an open house.
    c. at the closing table.
    d. before any offers to purchase or lease are prepared or presented.

# Real Estate License Laws

## REAL ESTATE LICENSE LAWS IN GENERAL

All states, the District of Columbia, and all Canadian provinces license and regulate the activities of real estate brokers and salespeople. Certain details of the laws vary from state to state, but the main provisions of many state laws are similar. In addition, uniform policies and standards in the fields of license law administration and enforcement are promoted by an organization of state license law officials known as **ARELLO,** the Association of Real Estate License Law Officials.

## PURPOSE OF LICENSE LAWS

The **real estate license laws** have been enacted to protect the public interest by establishing certain requirements for licensure and defining licensed activities and acceptable standards of conduct and practice for licensees. Although licensees may see these laws as those that regulate the real estate industry, their purpose is to serve the public interest by ensuring that the rights of purchasers, sellers, tenants, and owners are protected from unscrupulous practices. The laws are not meant to prevent licensees from conducting their businesses successfully. They are designed to ensure that the customers and clients are not disadvantaged by these business practices. Laws cannot legislate morality; they can, however, establish minimum levels of competency and standards of practice and prescribe disciplinary actions that can be taken against violators.

**Who Must Be Licensed** Generally, the state license laws stipulate that a person must be licensed as a real estate broker if he or she, *for another and for compensation or with the intent to collect compensation,* performs any of the following acts with regard to real property:

- Lists it for sale
- Sells it
- Rents or leases it
- Manages it
- Exchanges it
- Negotiates with or aids a person in obtaining for purchase, lease, or acquisition of an interest in real estate

- Deals in real estate options
- Offers to perform or negotiate one of these activities
- Represents that he or she engages in any of these activities

# THE OHIO REAL ESTATE LICENSE LAW*

The Ohio Real Estate License Law has been in effect since 1927. It provides for licensing prerequisites, postlicensing educational requirements, and complaint procedures governing the real estate profession. The license law, designated as Chapter 4735 of the Ohio Revised Code (**ORC**), also covers auctioneers who offer real estate for sale at auction. Real estate auctioneers are required to be licensed as both real estate brokers or salespersons and auctioneers.

In the definitions that follow, the term *real estate* includes leaseholds as well as any and every interest or estate in land situated in this state, whether corporeal or incorporeal, freehold or nonfreehold. It does not include cemetery interment rights or foreign real estate interests, although these areas are regulated also.

**Real Estate Broker (ORC Section 4735.01)**

A *real estate broker* is any person, partnership, association, limited liability company, limited liability partnership, or corporation, foreign or domestic, who performs (or attempts to perform) any of the following acts in exchange for or in expectation of a fee, commission, or other valuable consideration:

- Sells, exchanges, purchases, rents, or leases or negotiates the sale, exchange, purchase, rental, or leasing of any real estate
- Offers, attempts, or agrees to negotiate the sale, exchange, purchase, rental, or leasing of any real estate
- Lists or offers, attempts, or agrees to list, or auctions, or offers, attempts, or agrees to auction, any real estate
- Buys or offers to buy, sells or offers to sell, or otherwise deals in options on real estate
- Operates, manages, or rents, or offers, or attempts to operate, manage, or rent (other than as a custodian, caretaker, or janitor) any building or portions of buildings to the public as tenants
- Advertises or holds himself or herself out as being engaged in the business of selling, exchanging, purchasing, renting, or leasing real estate
- Directs or assists in procuring prospects or negotiating any transaction (other than mortgage financing) intended to result in the sale, exchange, leasing, or renting of any real estate
- Is employed by or on behalf of the owner of lots or parcels of real estate, whether at a fixed salary and/or on commission, to sell the lots or parcels in whole or in part, and who sells, exchanges or offers, attempts, or agrees to negotiate their sale or exchange
- Is engaged in the business of charging an advance fee or contracting for collection of a fee in connection with any contract to promote the sale, exchange, purchase, rental, or leasing of real estate in a publication issued for that purpose, or for referral of information concerning such real estate to brokers, or both (except for publishers of listings or compilation of sales of real estate by their owners)
- Collects rental information for the purpose of referring prospective tenants to rental units or the location of rental units, and who charges prospective tenants a fee for that service

* Because all the information in this chapter is Ohio specific, no **In Ohio...** icons will be used in it.

The Ohio Real Estate License Law provides that a licensed real estate broker may not pay a commission for acts covered by the license law to anyone who is not licensed.

## Real Estate Salesperson

A **real estate salesperson** is any person associated with a licensed real estate broker to do any of the acts permitted by the definition of a real estate broker, whether for or not for compensation.

A salesperson may conduct his or her business in association with only one licensed real estate broker. A salesperson has no independent status and must act at all times through his or her broker.

## Limited Real Estate Broker/Salesperson

A **limited real estate broker** engages exclusively in the sale of cemetery interment rights for a fee. A **limited real estate salesperson** is any person associated with a licensed real estate broker or licensed limited real estate broker whose license is limited to the sale of cemetery interment rights. Limited real estate licensees are not subject to any continuing education requirements (unless they also have a broker or salesperson license).

Note that licensed brokers and salespersons may *not* sell cemetery lots without having first obtained a limited real estate broker or salesperson license.

## Foreign Real Estate Dealer/Salesperson

A **foreign real estate dealer** includes any person, partnership, corporation, or association that, for a fee, commission, or other consideration, engages in the activities of a real estate broker with respect to foreign real estate (that is, real estate or an interest in real estate situated outside Ohio). A **foreign real estate salesperson** includes a person associated with a licensed foreign real estate dealer to do any of the acts permitted by definition of a foreign real estate dealer, for compensation or otherwise.

The regulation of foreign real estate dealers and salespersons is the responsibility of the Ohio Division of Real Estate. Foreign real estate licenses require separate and different applications and examinations.

## Auctioneers

To auction real property, the person conducting the auction must be licensed as both an auctioneer and a broker or salesperson. However, it is not necessary that the broker hold an auctioneer's license if the salesperson is so licensed.

## License Required (ORC Section 4735.02)

No person, partnership, association, or corporation may act as or advertise themselves as a real estate broker, real estate salesperson, limited real estate broker, limited real estate salesperson, or foreign real estate dealer or salesperson without first being licensed.

No real estate broker or salesperson may perform any service that constitutes the practice of law, unless he or she is a licensed attorney.

No partnership, association or corporation that holds a real estate license may employ as an officer, director, manager, or a principal employee any person who previously held any form of real estate license whose license was terminated and not reinstated.

## Exemptions

The terms *real estate broker, real estate salesperson* and *foreign real estate dealer* or *salesperson* do not apply to certain persons and entities who are exempt from the licensing provisions of the Ohio Real Estate License Law.

Specifically, persons, partnerships, associations, corporations, and their regular employees (as well as limited real estate brokers and salespersons), who perform acts that would otherwise require a real estate license, whether or not for a fee or commission, are exempt from the licensing requirements when their acts are performed

- with reference to their own real estate, or real estate acquired on their own account in the regular course of or incident to the management and investment of the property;
- as a receiver or trustee in bankruptcy, a guardian, executor, administrator, trustee, assignee, commissioner, or any person acting under court authority, as a public officer, or as executor, trustee, or other bona fide fiduciary under any trust agreement, deed of trust, will, or other instrument creating a bona fide fiduciary obligation;
- as a public officer while performing his or her official duties; or
- as an attorney-at-law in the performance of his or her legal duties.

### Ohio Real Estate Commission (ORC Sections 4735.03, .04, .05)

*Test*

The Ohio **Real Estate Commission** consists of five members who are appointed for five-year terms by the governor with the advice and consent of the Senate (see Figure 6.1). Four members must have been engaged as licensed real estate brokers in Ohio for ten years immediately preceding their appointment, and one member represents "the public." No more than three members may belong to any one political party.

The commission investigates complaints of licensing or regulatory violations, and may apply for court injunctions to stop violations and subpoena witnesses.

The commission's responsibilities include

- adopting Canons of Ethics for the real estate industry;
- reviewing, reversing, vacating, or modifying any order of the state superintendent of real estate upon an appeal by any party affected;
- administering the education and research special account and the recovery special account, and hearing appeals regarding claims;
- directing the superintendent on educational courses for salesperson and broker educational requirements;
- disseminating information relative to commission activities and decisions to licensees;
- notifying licensees of changes in state and federal civil rights laws pertaining to real estate, and making clear that civil rights violations subject licensees to disciplinary action; and
- publishing and distributing to public libraries and brokers booklets on housing and remedies available to dissatisfied clients.

### Division of Real Estate (ORC Section 4735.05)

Within the Ohio **Department of Commerce** is the **Division of Real Estate (DRE)**, which is under the control and supervision of the director of commerce. (See Figure 6.1.)

**WWWeb.Link**
www.com.state.oh.us/real. The home site for the Ohio Division of Real Estate.

**Superintendent of Real Estate.** The director of commerce is officially the executive officer of the Real Estate Commission, although he or she normally appoints a superintendent of real estate from among six persons—three whose

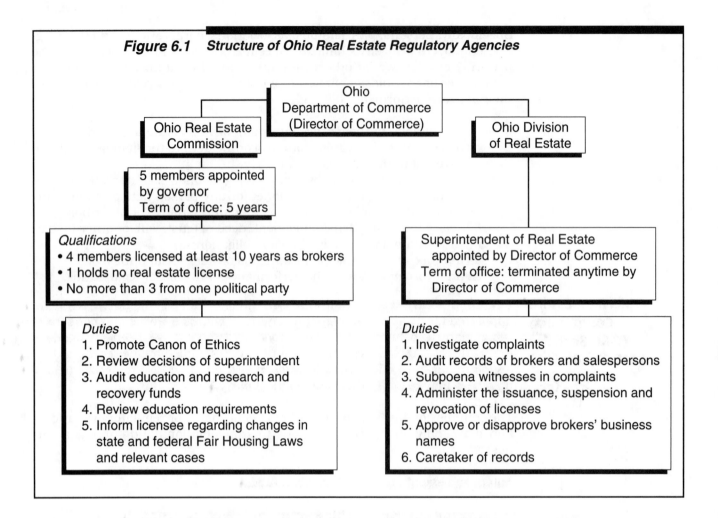

**Figure 6.1** **Structure of Ohio Real Estate Regulatory Agencies**

Ohio Department of Commerce (Director of Commerce)

Ohio Real Estate Commission

Ohio Division of Real Estate

5 members appointed by governor
Term of office: 5 years

*Qualifications*
- 4 members licensed at least 10 years as brokers
- 1 holds no real estate license
- No more than 3 from one political party

Superintendent of Real Estate appointed by Director of Commerce
Term of office: terminated anytime by Director of Commerce

*Duties*
1. Promote Canon of Ethics
2. Review decisions of superintendent
3. Audit education and research and recovery funds
4. Review education requirements
5. Inform licensee regarding changes in state and federal Fair Housing Laws and relevant cases

*Duties*
1. Investigate complaints
2. Audit records of brokers and salespersons
3. Subpoena witnesses in complaints
4. Administer the issuance, suspension and revocation of licenses
5. Approve or disapprove brokers' business names
6. Caretaker of records

names are submitted by the Ohio Real Estate Commission and three whose names are submitted by the Real Estate Appraiser Board. The superintendent of real estate is the administrator of the real estate license law and may issue any orders of the commission or any other orders necessary for carrying the law's provisions into effect.

In addition, the superintendent has the following duties:

- Investigate complaints concerning violations;
- Subpoena witnesses in connection with investigations;
- Apply for court injunctions to stop violations;
- Maintain a section of investigation and audit; and
- Recommend the appointment of ancillary trustees in the event of the death or revocation or suspension of a licensed broker (In such cases appointment would have to have the approval of the appropriate probate court.)

**Complaint procedure.** Anyone may file a complaint with the Ohio Division of Real Estate against a licensee. Ohio law provides for a voluntary, informal meeting of the licensee and the complaining party to try to reach a resolution of the complaint. If the parties do not agree to a meeting or fail to resolve their differences, the complaint is investigated by the Ohio Division of Real Estate.

After the investigation is complete, the complaint is either dismissed or scheduled for a formal hearing. The investigator's written report must be filed within 60 days of either the date of the complaint or the date of the informal meeting, if one was held. The hearing examiner's findings and recommendations must be reported to all parties within 25 business days after formal hearings conclude, and the commission's decision whether to suspend or revoke a licensee's license must be issued within 60 days of the hearing examiner's report or, in the case of a civil rights complaint, within 60 days of the filing of the complaint with the Ohio Civil Rights Commission.

If a license is suspended or revoked, the licensee has a right to appeal the decision to the common pleas court. An application to the commission to reverse, vacate, or modify an order must be filed within 15 days after the order is mailed to the party.

An investigation may be commenced against a licensee only if the complaint is filed within three years from the date of the alleged violation. After three years, an investigation is barred and no disciplinary action can be taken against the licensee as a result of the alleged violation.

All information obtained by investigators from licensees, complainants, or other persons and all reports, documents, and other work products that arise from that information or are prepared by division employees must be held in confidence.

**Application for Broker's License (ORC Section 4735.06)**

An application for a license as a real estate broker must be submitted to the superintendent of real estate on an official form, accompanied by a recent photograph, and sworn to by the applicant and notarized. (See Figure 6.2.) The application also must meet the following requirements:

- It must include the name of the person, partnership, association, or corporation making application and the location of the place of business for which the license is desired.
- It must include the names of three resident freeholders of the county in which the applicant resides or has a place of business. The freeholders must not be related to the applicant, and one of them must be his or her most recent broker.
- If the applicant will maintain more than one place of business within the state, he or she must apply for and obtain a duplicate license for each branch. Each branch is to be in the charge of a licensed broker or salesperson.
- If the applicant is a partnership or an association, the names of all members must be included; if a corporation, the names of the president and each of its officers must be included. All members or officers who are authorized to perform the function of a real estate broker as the agents of the partnership, association, or corporation must be personally licensed as real estate brokers.
- The application must be accompanied by a nonrefundable fee of $69. If the applicant fails the exam, an additional fee is required with each successive application; this fee covers the license, if it is issued.

Four dollars of each fee is paid to the treasurer of the state to be credited to the **real estate education and research fund.** The fund is used by the commission (1) to encourage education and research in real estate at any institution of higher education in the state or (2) to make loans not exceeding $500 to

### Figure 6.2   Application for Broker License

77 South High Street
Columbus, Ohio 43266-0547
(614) 466-4100

**STATE OF OHIO**
**DEPARTMENT OF COMMERCE**

615 Superior Ave. N.W.
Cleveland, Ohio 44113
(216) 787-3100

**BROKER APPLICATION**

| FOR DIVISION USE ONLY | | |
|---|---|---|
| Fiche No. | License Status | |
| File No. | Issue Date | |
| Type Code | License No. | |
| Broker No. | Fee No. | Amount |
| Ed. Code | Exam Date | |
| Ed. Exp. Date | Notice Sent | |
| County Code | E.C. | |

**IMPORTANT**

**ATTACH 2″ x 2″ PHOTO**

**TAKEN WITHIN**

**LAST 30 DAYS**

**FOR IDENTIFICATION**

**INSTRUCTIONS:**

1. This application is for broker examination only.
2. Applications must be typewritten (black ribbon only) and notarized. Photocopies of applications will not be accepted.
3. A check, certified check, or money order payable to the Ohio Division of Real Estate must accompany the application. The amount of the fee is $59. Do not send cash.
4. Submit with application a copy of transcript or certificate of required education.
5. See reverse side for explanation of forfeiture of fees.

1. Name of Applicant:   *Last*    *First*    *Initial*    Social Security No.:

2. Residence Address:   *Street*    *City*    *State*    *Zip Code*

3. Date of Birth:    Phone No.: *(Area Code)*    4. Original Licensure Date:    5. Last Year Licensed:    Attach statement describing any real estate experience other than sales.

6. Are there any unsatisfied judgments against you as a real estate sales associate?   ☐ Yes   ☐ No    If yes, attach explanation.

7. Have you ever been convicted of any unlawful conduct (excluding minor traffic violations)?   ☐ Yes   ☐ No    If yes, attach explanation.

8. Have you ever had a license refused, revoked, or suspended?   ☐ Yes   ☐ No    If yes, attach explanation.

9. Have any complaints been filed against you with the Ohio Real Estate Commission?   ☐ Yes   ☐ No    If yes, attach explanation.

10. Show number of real estate transactions in which you sold property for another in your capacity as a real estate sales associate.
A. Sales (Selling Agent) _____    B. Listings Sold _____    C. One-Year Leases: Residential _____   Commercial _____

11. In the past five years how many weeks have you worked as a real estate sales associate for an average of 30 hrs. per week?

12. Date of last broker examination if license not issued.

**FOR DIVISION USE ONLY:**

13. Doing Business As (DBA):    Phone No.: *(Area Code)*

14. Main Business Address:   *Street*    *City*    *State*    *County*    *Zip Code*

**STATE OF OHIO**

COUNTY OF _____   S.S.

_____ , being duly sworn, deposes and says that he/she is the person who has executed the foregoing application and that the statements made therein are true.

Signature of Applicant    Date:

Subscribed and sworn to before me this _____ day of _____ , 19 _____

_____ , Signature of Notary Public

Expiration date of notary commission must be affixed.

Approval of Superintendent    Date

COM 3578 (05/91)     R-1

**Figure 6.2    Application for Broker License (Continued)**

**FORFEITURE OF FEES**

**Rule 1301:5-1-05 Examinations:** (Under Section (B)

"If the applicant's failure to appear for the examination to which he is admitted is due to illness evidenced by a doctor's certificate received by the division within fifteen days after the date of such examination, he shall be admitted to the next scheduled examination without additional fee. No applicant shall be excused from taking the scheduled examination for any other reason than illness unless, in the superintendent's judgement, the applicant would suffer undue hardship thereby."

The above provision of the rules of the Ohio Division of Real Estate means that in the event you fail to appear for an examination once it has been scheduled, your examination fee is forfeited. The only exception is as stated in (B) above. Therefore, when you are scheduled for an examination, be sure that you will be able to appear for the examination at the time and place provided. Otherwise, your fee will be subject to forfeiture in the event you do not comply with the notice concerning the date and time of examination.

### COMPLETE THIS SECTION
### FOR BROKER'S APPLICATION

(Application must be accompanied by the recommendation of THREE RESIDENT FREEHOLDERS (property owners), not related to the applicant, of the county in which the applicant resides or has his place of business, at least one of whom is the most recent broker of the applicant. If most recent broker is a relative, use third freeholder and attach explanation.)

I hereby certify that I am a resident freeholder of _____ County, State of Ohio, and that the real estate I

own is located at _____
                 *(Street)*               *(City, Village or Township)*

_____ , and I hereby certify that the said _____
   *(County)*

applicant for a real estate broker's license is honest, truthful and of good reputation. I recommend that he/she be admitted to the examination provided
for in the Act, as amended, providing for the regulation, by license, of real estate or limited real estate brokers.

_____      _____
     *(Print Name of Freeholder)*               *(Signature of Freeholder)*

I hereby certify that I am a resident freeholder of _____ County, State of Ohio, and that the real estate I

own is located at _____
                 *(Street)*               *(City, Village or Township)*

_____ , and I hereby certify that the said _____
   *(County)*

applicant for a real estate broker's license is honest, truthful and of good reputation. I recommend that he/she be admitted to the examination provided
for in the Act, as amended, providing for the regulation, by license, of real estate or limited real estate brokers.

_____      _____
     *(Print Name of Freeholder)*               *(Signature of Freeholder)*

I hereby certify that I am a resident freeholder of _____ County, State of Ohio, and that the real estate I

own is located at _____
                 *(Street)*               *(City, Village or Township)*

_____ , and I hereby certify that the said _____
   *(County)*

applicant for a real estate broker's license is honest, truthful and of good reputation. I recommend that he/she be admitted to the examination provided
for in the Act, as amended, providing for the regulation, by license, of real estate or limited real estate brokers.

_____      _____
   *(Print Name of Broker/Freeholder)*          *(Signature of Freeholder — Present Broker)*

applicants for salesperson licenses to defray costs of satisfying the prelicense educational requirements. The loans must be repaid within three years, and total loans for the whole program may not exceed $10,000 in any one year.

**Examination of applicant for broker's license.** The applicant for a broker's license must produce evidence of having satisfied the character, educational, and experiential requirements.

*Character requirements.* The applicant must establish that he or she is at least 18 years old and honest, truthful, and of good reputation. No applicant may have been convicted of a felony or crime of moral turpitude or have been found to have violated any civil rights laws regarding real estate within the past two years. In addition, the applicant must not previously have violated any rules of the Ohio Division of Real Estate.

An individual who has been previously convicted of a felony or crime of moral turpitude, or who has violated civil rights laws or real estate rules of practice, may still apply for a license if he or she can produce evidence that the superintendent has disregarded the conviction or violation on the basis of the applicant's proof of good character and the unlikelihood of future incidents.

*Educational requirements.* Depending on when the applicant was originally licensed as a salesperson, he or she also must complete certain educational requirements to sit for the broker's examination.

Based on the date the applicant was licensed as a salesperson, the educational requirement for qualification to sit for the broker's examination is as follows:

- Salespersons licensed prior to January 2, 1972: no additional educational courses are required.
- Salespersons licensed on or after January 2, 1972, but prior to January 3, 1984: 30 hours in each of the following courses: Real Estate Principles and Practices, Real Estate Law, Real Estate Appraisal, and Real Estate Finance. (Applicants who are licensed attorneys are not required to take the Real Estate Law course.)
- Salespersons licensed on or after January 3, 1984, but prior to August 1, 2001: 30 hours (or three quarter-hours or its equivalent in semester hours) in each of the following courses: Real Estate Principles and Practices, Real Estate Law, Real Estate Appraisal, Real Estate Finance, Financial Management, Human Resources or Personnel Management, Applied Business Economics, and Business Law.

Applicants licensed on or after January 3, 1984, must also have completed a minimum of two years of college. The above courses may be included in the salesperson's two years of college.

*Experiential requirements.* To sit for the broker's examination, the applicant must have been licensed as a broker or salesperson for at least two years and for at least two of the five years preceding application must have worked for an average of at least 30 hours a week as a real estate salesperson. If the applicant was licensed in another state, these years can be counted.

In addition, the applicant must have completed 20 real estate transactions or have other acceptable equivalent experience. "Real estate transactions" are counted as follows:

- One sale of real property owned by another in which the applicant was the listing agent equals one-half transaction.
- One sale of real property owned by another in which the applicant was the selling agent equals one-half transaction.
- One lease of commercial or industrial property for a term of at least one year in which the applicant was the listing agent equals one-half transaction.
- One lease of commercial or industrial property for a term of at least one year in which the applicant was the procuring agent equals one-half transaction.
- One lease of residential property for a term of at least one year in which the applicant was the listing and/or procuring agent equals one-fourth transaction.

If leases constitute 16 or more of the transactions, the applicant also must have worked for three years in full-time property management.

Only those sales, listings, and leases that the applicant handled for another and through the broker or brokers with whom the applicant has been licensed can be accepted to meet the experiential requirement. Transactions involving the applicant's own property are not counted.

**Forfeiture of fees.** If an applicant fails to appear for the broker's examination due to illness that is evidenced by a physician's certificate, he or she will be admitted to the next examination without any additional fee. This physician's certificate must be received by the Division of Real Estate within 15 days after the date of the scheduled examination. No applicant shall be excused from taking the scheduled examination for any reason other than illness unless, in the superintendent's judgment, the applicant would suffer undue hardship if not excused.

*If the applicant fails to appear at the scheduled examination for any other reason, the application fee will be forfeited. A new application and fee will be required if the applicant wishes to reschedule.*

**Test results.** Test results are provided to the applicant immediately after the examination is completed. A score of 75 percent or higher is required to pass. If the applicant passed the examination, a pass letter is issued at the test site and the license will be sent to the licensee's broker within three working days.

If the applicant failed the real estate examination, a fail letter that includes a printout of areas that should be studied is issued at the test site. The applicant may apply to take it again. (There is no limit to the number of times an individual may retake the broker's examination.)

**Postlicensing and continuing education.** Within 12 months after becoming a licensed broker, an individual must successfully complete a ten-hour postlicensing course in real estate brokerage at an approved institution. If the new broker does not submit proof to the Division of Real Estate of having successfully completed this instruction within the allotted time, the broker's license automatically will be suspended. The new broker will have a grace period of one year following the suspension within which to complete the course.

As a broker, the individual will continue to be required to take 30 hours of continuing education. The completion date for this continuing education will be the same as it was when he or she was a salesperson.

**Application for License as Real Estate Salesperson (ORC Section 4735.09)**

An application for licensure as a real estate salesperson must be in writing on an official form, signed and sworn to by the applicant, and accompanied by a recent photograph. (See Figure 6.3.) The application must include a statement from the real estate broker with whom the applicant is or intends to be associated (commonly known as a *sponsoring broker*), certifying that the applicant

- is honest, truthful and of good reputation;
- has not been convicted of a felony or crime involving moral turpitude and has not been finally adjudged by a court to have violated any municipal, state, or federal civil rights law relevant to the protection of purchasers or sellers of real estate;
- has not violated any rules or regulations adopted by the Ohio Real Estate Commission;
- is at least 18 years of age;
- has received a high school diploma or its equivalent (in the case of applicants born after 1950); and
- has successfully completed (requirements as of August 1, 2001):
  a. 40 hours of classroom instruction in real estate practice;
  b. 40 hours of classroom instruction in Ohio real estate law, including state and federal civil rights law.
  c. 20 hours of classroom instruction in real estate appraisal; and
  d. 20 hours of classroom instruction in real estate finance.

An applicant for the sales examination may change sponsors while the application is pending (that is, awaiting completion of educational requirements). A letter from the original sponsoring broker indicating concurrence in the proposed transfer and a revised application indicating the new sponsor must be sent to the Ohio Division of Real Estate. No fee is required for change of sponsor if requested prior to the examination.

**Postlicensing requirement.** The new salesperson has one year after the issuance of a sales license to complete a ten-hour postlicensing course on current issues relating to consumers, real estate practice, ethics, and real estate law. If this ten-hour course is not completed within 12 months, the license will automatically be suspended with a one-year grace period in which to complete instruction.

*Note:* If the applicant for the sales exam has not been licensed formerly as a real estate broker or salesperson within the past four years, the prelicense courses must have been completed within the ten-year period immediately preceding the applicant's being seated for the exam.

Each application for the salesperson examination must be accompanied by a nonrefundable fee of $49, of which $4 is credited to the real estate education and research fund.

When the applicant passes the examination with a grade of 75 percent or better, the superintendent will issue a license. There is no limit to the times an applicant can retake the sales exam. However, the applicant must file an application and pay the fee each time the examination is taken.

The superintendent may waive the examination requirement when the applicant was previously licensed at some time within the two-year period immediately preceding the date of the current application. If a license is canceled by

### Figure 6.3    Application for Salesperson License

STATE OF OHIO
**DEPARTMENT OF COMMERCE**
**DIVISION OF REAL ESTATE**

77 South High Street, 20th Floor
Columbus, OH 43266-0547
(614) 466-4100

615 Superior Avenue, N.W.
Cleveland, OH 44113
(216) 787-3100

**SALES APPLICATION**

| FOR DIVISION USE ONLY | | |
|---|---|---|
| Fiche No. | License Status | |
| File No. | Issue Date | |
| Type Code | License No. | |
| Broker No. | Fee No. | Amount |
| Ed. Code | Exam Date | |
| Ed. Exp. Date | Notice Sent | |
| County Code | E.C. | |

**IMPORTANT**

**ATTACH 2" x 2" PHOTO**

**TAKEN WITHIN**

**LAST 30 DAYS**

**FOR IDENTIFICATION**

**INSTRUCTIONS:**
1. Incomplete applications will not be processed. Incomplete applications will be returned to you and accepted for processing when all required materials are submitted.
2. This application is for sales examination only.
3. Applications must be typewritten (black ribbon only) and notarized. Photocopies of applications will not be accepted.
4. A check, certified check, or money order payable to the Ohio Division of Real Estate must accompany the application. The fee is $49. Do not send cash.
5. Submit with application a copy of transcript or certificate of required education. Originals will not be returned.
6. See reverse for explanation of forfeiture of fees.

| | | | |
|---|---|---|---|
| 1. Name of Applicant:   *Last* | *First* | *Initial* | Social Security No.: |
| 2. Residence Address:   *Street* | *City*   *State* | *County*   *Zip Code* | |
| 3. Date of Birth: | Phone No.: *(Area Code)* | H.S. Graduate? | Year Graduated: |
| 4. Prospective Broker, Corporation, Partnership, or Association: | | | Broker File Number |
| 5. Doing Business As (DBA): | Phone No.: *(Area Code)* | | |
| 6. Main Business Address:  *Street* | *City*   *State* | *County*   *Zip Code* | |
| 7. Name of firm if previously licensed in Ohio: | | | |
| 8. Last Year Licensed (if applicable): | Date of last examination if license not issued: | | |

9. Are there any unsatisfied judgments against you?
   ☐ Yes  ☐ No  If yes, attach explanation.

10. Have you ever been convicted of any unlawful conduct (excluding minor traffic violations)?  ☐ Yes  ☐ No  If yes, attach explanation

11. Have you ever had a license refused, revoked, or suspended?
   ☐ Yes  ☐ No  If yes, attach explanation.

12. Have any complaints been filed against you with the Ohio Real Estate Commission?  ☐ Yes  ☐ No  If yes, attach explanation.

**Figure 6.3    Application for Salesperson License (Continued)**

STATE OF OHIO

COUNTY OF _____     S.S.

_____, being duly sworn, deposes and says that he/she is the person who has executed the foregoing application and that the statements made therein are true.

| Signature of Applicant | Date: |
|---|---|
| | |

Subscribed and sworn to before me this _____ day of _____, 19_____

_____ , Signature of Notary Public

Expiration date of notary commission must be affixed.

**THE FOLLOWING CERTIFICATION IS TO BE COMPLETED BY THE SPONSORING BROKER**

I hereby certify that, from the investigations made by me, I find that _____, applicant for a real estate sales license, is honest, truthful, and of good reputation. I have known him/her for _____ years and to the best of my knowledge he/she has not been convicted of a felony or crime involving moral turpitude nor has he/she been finally adjudged by a court to have violated any state or federal civil rights laws relevant to the protection of purchasers or sellers of real estate other than disclosed in the above application. I recommend that this applicant be admitted to the examination for a real estate sales license.

| Broker's Name – Please Type | Signature of Licensed Broker | |
|---|---|---|
| Approval of Superintendent | | Date |

COM 3568  (Rev. 05/93)                                                                                        R-2

**FORFEITURE OF FEES**

**Rule 1301:5-1-05 Examinations:  (Under Section (B))**

"If the applicant's failure to appear for the examination to which he is admitted is due to illness evidenced by a doctor's certificate sent to the commission prior to the date of such examination, he shall be admitted to the next scheduled examination without additional fee.  No applicant shall be excused from taking the scheduled examination for any other reason than illness unless, in the commission's judgement, the applicant would suffer undue hardship thereby."

The above provision of the rules of the Ohio Division of Real Estate means that in the event you fail to appear for an examination once it has been scheduled, your examination fee is forfeited.  The only exception is as stated in (B) above. Therefore, when you are scheduled for an examination, be sure that you will be able to appear for the examination at the time and place provided.  Otherwise, your fee will be subject to forfeiture in the event you do not comply with the notice concerning the date and time of examination.

**Ohio Revised Code Section 4735.09(B)**

"The application fee shall be retained by the superintendent if the applicant is admitted to the examination for the license or the examination requirement is waived, but, if an applicant is not so admitted and a waiver is not involved, one-half of the fee shall be retained by the superintendent to cover the expenses of processing the application and the other one-half shall be returned to the applicant.  A fee of forty-nine dollars shall be charged by the superintendent for each successive application made by the applicant."

The above provision of the real estate license laws means that in the event your application for a sales license is denied or withdrawn, one-half of your fee will be retained by the Division of Real Estate and the other one-half will be refunded to the applicant.

the Ohio Division of Real Estate, the former licensee has the right of reinstatement for a period of two years from the cancellation date. Reissuance of the license requires the submission of the prescribed form along with a fee of $49.

**Application for License as a Limited Real Estate Broker and Limited Real Estate Salesperson (ORC Section 4735.091)**

A person who wishes to sell only cemetery interment rights may become licensed as a limited real estate broker or limited real estate salesperson. These applications are made on special forms furnished by the superintendent. A limited real estate salesperson may be licensed with either a limited real estate broker or a real estate broker. A limited real estate broker's or salesperson's activities must not extend to matters other than cemetery interment rights, and the license must so indicate.

**Form of License (ORC Section 4735.11)**

The form and size of real estate licenses is determined by the Ohio Real Estate Commission. Each license bears the name and street address of the licensee, and a salesperson's license also shows the name of the real estate broker with whom he or she is associated. In the case of a corporate or partnership licensee, the license shows the names of each of its members or officers.

**Real Estate Recovery Special Account (ORC Section 4735.12)**

The **real estate recovery fund** was established in 1975 to replace the former requirement that Ohio brokers purchase an annual surety bond to cover court-ordered judgments against brokers or their salespeople. The fund is administered by the superintendent of real estate, and is required to maintain a $1 million minimum balance at all times. It is used to satisfy unpaid claims against a broker or salesperson who violated the real estate licensing law, resulting in financial loss to a person. (See Figure 6.4.)

Claims may be made in a court of common pleas by any injured individual who has a final court judgment for damages against a broker or salesperson, if the claimant has submitted evidence to the court that he or she has diligently pursued all other avenues to receive payment and has been unable to find or levy on sufficient assets of the debtor/broker to pay the court judgment in full. Claims must be filed within one year after the final court decision.

The law limits the amount of claims against any one salesperson or broker to $40,000. If that amount is not sufficient to meet the claims of multiple complainants, the $40,000 will be divided among them in proportion to the amount of their judgments. The court can order all claimants to join in one action.

The license of any salesperson or broker against whom claims from the recovery fund are paid will be automatically suspended. The license cannot be reinstated until the licensee has paid the full amount taken from the fund

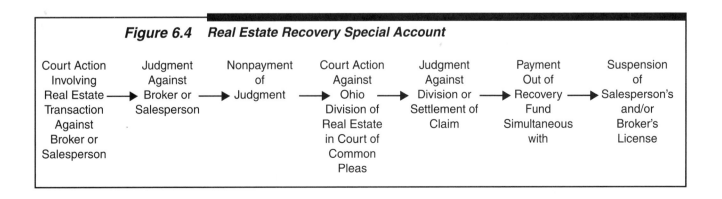

**Figure 6.4   Real Estate Recovery Special Account**

| Court Action Involving Real Estate Transaction Against Broker or Salesperson | Judgment Against Broker or Salesperson | Nonpayment of Judgment | Court Action Against Ohio Division of Real Estate in Court of Common Pleas | Judgment Against Division or Settlement of Claim | Payment Out of Recovery Fund Simultaneous with | Suspension of Salesperson's and/or Broker's License |
|---|---|---|---|---|---|---|

plus interest. A discharge in bankruptcy does not relieve the licensee of the suspension and requirements for reinstatement. Once a broker's license has been reinstated, the fund will again assume liability for the broker.

**Provisions as to Licenses (ORC Section 4735.13)**

The license of a real estate broker must be displayed prominently in the broker's place of business. A real estate salesperson's license is mailed to, and remains in the possession of, the broker with whom he or she is associated until either the license is canceled or the salesperson leaves the broker. (See Figure 6.5.) Although there is no requirement that salespeople's licenses be displayed, they must be kept available for public inspection. In case the broker's business location changes, the broker must notify the superintendent, who will issue a new license for the unexpired period without charge.

If a licensee is convicted of a felony or a crime involving moral turpitude, or is found guilty of having violated any municipal, state, or federal civil rights laws relevant to the protection of the purchasers or sellers of real estate, he or she must notify the superintendent within 15 days after such conviction. The superintendent then may revoke the individual's license. The Ohio Civil Rights Commission must be notified within 15 days by any court that convicts a licensee of a municipal civil rights law violation.

If a broker wishes to be associated with another broker as a salesperson, he or she must apply to the superintendent for authority to deposit the real estate broker's license with the superintendent and obtain a salesperson's license. This requires an application fee of $13 plus a fee of $25 for the salesperson's license. Four dollars of each fee is credited to the real estate education and research fund. A broker who intends to associate as a salesperson for another broker must give written notice to all salespeople with whom he or she is associated before November 1.

A real estate broker who wishes to become a member or officer of a partnership, association, or corporation that either is currently or intends to become a licensed real estate broker must notify the superintendent. A real estate broker who is a member or officer of a partnership, association, or corporation that is a licensed real estate broker may not act as a real estate broker other than as the agent of the partnership, association, or corporation, and no real estate salespeople may be associated with the broker.

**Inactive Status**

A real estate broker may choose to place his or her license on inactive status by depositing it with the Division of Real Estate for an indefinite period of time (with or without having obtained an active sales license). While a broker who has a license **"on deposit"** does not need to maintain a trust account, he or she must file a certificate of continuance each year.

A salesperson, on the other hand, cannot keep a license "on deposit." If a salesperson's license is sent to the Division of Real Estate, it is automatically canceled. It can, however, be reinstated for two years from the end of the last year in which it was active; that is, a license canceled on June 10, 1995, can be reinstated until December 31, 1997. A broker who sends a salesperson's license back to the Division of Real Estate for cancellation must, within ten days, send a notification letter to the salesperson, with a copy to the division.

Both brokers and salespersons may place their licenses on deposit with the Ohio Real Estate Commission in the event that they enter the armed forces. A fee of $7 is charged to cover the commission's expenses. The inactive status

### Figure 6.5   *Salesperson's License Transfer Application*

STATE OF OHIO
**DEPARTMENT OF COMMERCE**
**OHIO DIVISION OF REAL ESTATE**

77 South High Street
Columbus, OH 43266-0547
(614) 466-4100

615 Superior Ave. N.W.
Cleveland, OH 44113
(216) 787-3100

### SALES TRANSFER APPLICATION

| FOR DIVISION USE ONLY | | |
|---|---|---|
| Fiche No. | License Status | |
| File No. | Issue Date | |
| Type Code | License No. | |
| Broker No. | Fee No. | Amount |
| Ed. Code | | |
| Ed. Exp. Date | E.C. | |
| County Code | License Canceled | |
| Approved by | Date | |

Sales ..............................................$20.00

Limited Sales (Cemetery) ..........$20.00

**INSTRUCTIONS:**
1. **Incomplete applications will not be processed. Incomplete applications will be returned to you and accepted for processing when all required materials are submitted.**
2. **Applications must be typewritten (black ribbon only) and notarized. Photocopies of applications will not be accepted.**
3. **A check, certified check, or money order payable to the Ohio Division of Real Estate must accompany the application. The amount of the fee is $20.00. Cash will not be accepted.**
4. **Any previous license must be returned before a new license will be issued.**

| | | | | |
|---|---|---|---|---|
| 1. Name of Applicant: *Last* | *First* | *Initial* | Social Security No.: | |
| 2. Residence Address: *Street* | *City* | *State* | | *Zip Code* |
| 3. Date of Birth: | | Phone No.: *(Area Code)* | | |
| 4. Prospective Broker, Corporation, Partnership, or Association: | | | | |
| 5. Doing Business As (DBA): | | Phone No.: *(Area Code)* | | |
| 6. Main Business Address: *Street* | *City* | *State* | *County* | *Zip Code* |
| 7. Name of Previous Broker: | | | | |
| 8. Main Business Address of Previous Broker: *Street* | *City* | *State* | *County* | *Zip Code* |
| 9. Salesperson's File No.: | | Date of Separation: | | |

| | |
|---|---|
| 10. Are there any unsatisfied judgments against you as a real estate sales associate? ☐ Yes ☐ No If yes, attach explanation. | 11. Have you ever been convicted of any unlawful conduct (excluding minor traffic violations)? ☐ Yes ☐ No If yes, attach explanation. |
| 12. Have you ever had a license refused, revoked, or suspended? ☐ Yes ☐ No If yes, attach explanation. | 13. Have any complaints been filed against you with the Ohio Real Estate Commission? ☐ Yes ☐ No If yes, attach explanation. |

STATE OF OHIO

COUNTY OF_____ S.S.

_____, being duly sworn, deposes and says that he/she is the
person who has executed the foregoing application and that the statements made therein are true.

| Signature of Applicant | Date: |
|---|---|
| | |

Subscribed and sworn to before me this _____ day of _____, 19_____

_____, Signature of Notary Public
Expiration date of notary commission must be affixed.

### THE FOLLOWING CERTIFICATION IS TO BE COMPLETED BY THE SPONSORING BROKER

I hereby certify that, from the investigations made by me, I find that _____, applicant for a
real estate sales license, is honest, truthful, and of good reputation. I have known him/her for _____ years and he/she has not
been convicted of a felony or crime involving moral turpitude. He/She has not been finally adjudged by a court to have violated
any state or federal civil rights laws relevant to the protection of purchases or sellers of real estate other than disclosed in the above
application.

| Broker Name – Please type | Signature of Licensed Broker |
|---|---|
| | |

COM 3572 (Rev. 01/93)

is effective until six months after the licensee is discharged. A licensee whose license has been on deposit during his or her military duty is required to satisfy any outstanding continuing education requirements within one year of leaving the armed forces.

## Certificate of Continuation (ORC Section 4735.14)

Every license issued is valid without further recommendation or examination until revoked or suspended.

Each licensee must file a **certificate of continuation** before his or her birthday each year. The license of any licensee who fails to file a certificate of continuation prior to his or her birthday will be revoked. If, however, that broker can show good cause why a certificate was not filed, a 15-day extension may be obtained. An additional late penalty of 50 percent of the required fee is added.

## Continuing Education (ORC Section 4735.141)

Every three years, real estate licensees must submit proof of having satisfactorily completed 30 hours of approved continuing **real estate education.** (See Figure 6.6.) The deadline for submitting proof is the end of the month in which the broker or salesperson filed the certificate proving completion of the mandatory first-year postlicensing education requirement. The current minimum requirements are

- three hours on civil rights issues,
- three hours on core law and
- three hours on the Canons of Ethics.

If the 30-hour requirement is not met, the individual's license will be suspended. If the broker or salesperson fails to meet the continuing education requirements within 12 months from the date of suspension, his or her license will be revoked automatically. Revoked licenses that were issued prior to January 1, 1980, may be reinstated by satisfactory completion of continuing education requirements, usually 30 hours of Ohio real estate law certified for continuing education.

If a real estate broker's license is suspended for failure to comply with the mandatory continuing education, the licenses of any salespersons associated with the broker are suspended as well.

A licensee 70 years of age or older prior to June 13, 1999, must complete nine hours of continuing education over a three-year period. The nine hours must consist of three hours each in real estate law, civil rights, and ethics. This requirement will continue as long as the person is licensed or has reinstatement privileges. Any licensee who turned 70 after June 13, 1999, must complete the standard 30 hours of continuing education every three years.

## Fees (ORC Section 4735.15)

Other fees for licenses are as follows:

- $8 for a branch office license.
- $25 for the transfer of a broker's license into or out of a partnership or corporation or from one partnership or corporation to another.
- $20 for a real estate salesperson's license transfer.
- $49 for a certificate of continuation of a real estate broker. If the licensee is a partnership or corporation, the full fee is required for each member or officer who is a broker. A sliding fee schedule applies, depending on the number of salespeople associated with a broker.
- $39 for a certificate of continuation for a salesperson.

**Figure 6.6** **Continuing Education Compliance Form**

Ohio Department of Commerce
Division of Real Estate
77 South High Street, 20th Floor
Columbus, OH 43266-0547
(614) 466-4100

CONTINUING EDUCATION COMPLIANCE FORM                    R109

| NOTE: | THIS FORM MUST BE AN ORIGINAL TYPED IN BLACK INK, ANY COMPLIANCE FORM THAT IS NOT PROPERLY COMPLETED OR CONTAINS LESS THAN THE REQUIRED THIRTY HOURS OF CONTINUING EDUCATION WILL BE RETURNED. |

Name_____    Home Phone (___)_____

Home Address_____

City & State_____    Zip Code_____

License File No._____    Date of Birth_____

Broker Name_____    Broker Phone (___)_____

I certify that I am or will be 70 years of age or older during the next three year continuing education reporting period.

_____    _____    _____
Date of Birth                                        Signature                                        Date

| Requirements are: | 3 Hours of Civil Rights |
| | 3 Hours of Core Law |
| | 3 Hours of Canons of Ethics |
| | <u>21 Hours of other approved electives</u> |
| Total | 30 Hours of continuing education |

LIST EACH COURSE COMPLETED AND ENCLOSE A COPY OF ATTENDANCE CERTIFICATE
TO VERIFY DATE OF OFFERING AND STATE CERTIFICATION.

| Board, School, Company or Individual Course Offeror | Certification (Approval) Number | Course Title(s) | Date of Attendance | Hours |
|---|---|---|---|---|
| | | | | |

TOTAL HRS. _____

| NOTE: | RETURN THIS FORM <u>ONLY</u> AFTER YOU HAVE COMPLETED THE ENTIRE THIRTY HOURS OF CONTINUING EDUCATION TO: THE OHIO DIVISION OF REAL ESTATE 77 SOUTH HIGH STREET, 20TH FLOOR COLUMBUS, OH 43266-0547 |

I swear or affirm that the information hereon is, to the best of my knowledge, complete and accurate and that I did in fact attend the courses listed, for at least 90 percent of the time indicated.

_____    _____
Licensee's Signature                                        Date

ADDITIONAL SPACE IS PROVIDED ON THE BACK OF THIS FORM

All annual fees are paid to the treasurer of the state, and $4 of each fee is credited to the real estate education and research fund.

## Definite Place of Business, Advertising, and Registration of License (ORC Section 4735.16)

Every real estate broker must maintain a definite place of business in Ohio. The broker must display a sign in all his or her offices that plainly states that he or she is a real estate broker. In addition, the broker's office must prominently display an equal housing opportunity logo and a statement describing and pledging adherence to the fair housing laws. The statement must be displayed in the same immediate area as the real estate licenses. The wording and size of the statement are determined by the Real Estate Commission.

In all advertising, a real estate broker or salesperson must be identified by name, indicating that he or she is a real estate broker or salesperson. A real estate salesperson who advertises must also include the name of the broker with whom he or she is licensed, and the broker's name must be shown as prominently as the salesperson's. If the broker or salesperson is selling his or her own property, he or she still must identify himself or herself as a broker or salesperson.

Note that as of April, 2000, *a web site is considered advertising* and must comply with all of the rules that apply to other kinds of advertising. For example, the broker or brokerage name must be disclosed on the web site and on every page within the site that promotes real estate services.

Information on web sites that becomes outdated or expired must be updated within 14 days of the change. All web sites must indicate the date on which the web site was last updated. If a third party is responsible for maintaining the licensee's web site, the licensee must give the third party timely written notice of any updates. If the notice of the changes is provided in a timely manner, the licensee will not be in violation of this rule if the third party fails to update the information as requested.

Licensees cannot advertise property that he or she has not listed without the written consent of the owner or the owner's agent (i.e., the listing agent). When property listed by a broker is advertised on another broker's web site, the licensee must disclose the fact that he or she did not list the property and must include the name and telephone numbers of the listing broker and agent. This disclosure must be in a type size that is the same size or larger than the type size used to describe the property.

The broker or salesperson obtaining the signature of a party to an agency disclosure form, listing, or other agreement involved in a real estate transaction must immediately furnish the signing party with a true copy of the document.

## Trust Accounts

All brokers must maintain a trust bank account in a depository institution located in this state. The account must be a non-interest-bearing and it must be separate and distinct from any personal or business account of the broker. This account must be used for the deposit of all escrow funds, security deposits, and other money received by the broker in a fiduciary capacity.

All the deposit tickets and checks drawn on the trust account must bear the words "trust account" or "special account."

The name, account number, if any, and location of the depository must be submitted in writing to the superintendent.

A broker can deposit his own funds into the trust account only when they are clearly identified as the broker's funds and only under the following conditions:

1. If the financial institution in which the account is maintained requires a special minimum balance that must be maintained in order to keep the account open, the broker can maintain that amount in the account.
2. If the financial institution in which the account is maintained requires a service charge be paid for the account, the broker can maintain a reasonable amount to cover the service charge in the account.

If the broker fails to properly maintain a trust account, he or she may be subject to disciplinary action.

**Trust account records.** Every broker must keep a record of all trust funds received, including escrow funds, security deposits, and other funds received by the broker in a fiduciary capacity. The record will include the following information:

- Date funds received;
- Party from whom funds are received and the purpose of the funds;
- Amount received;
- Date funds are deposited into special or trust bank account;
- Check number and date funds are disbursed;
- Party to whom funds are disbursed and purpose of disbursement;
- Any other documents necessary and sufficient to verify and explain record entries and identify the current balance in the special or trust bank account.

**Property management trust accounts.** All brokerages who are engaged in property management must maintain a separate trust account (designated as **property management trust account),** for the deposit of security deposits, rents, and money received from the owner or on the owner's behalf for payment of expenses related to the management of property.

Security deposits received by a licensee must be deposited and maintained in the property management trust account unless the lease and property management agreement provide otherwise. Security deposits maintained in the property management trust account must be clearly identified and credited to each tenant.

The broker may exercise signatory authority for withdrawals from property management accounts maintained in the name of the property owner. The property management contract must specify the purposes for which the brokerage may make withdrawals from the owner's account and any dollar limits that exist on the amounts the brokerage may withdraw. Before making disbursements from a property management trust account, the real estate licensee must make sure that the account balance for that owner's property is sufficient to cover the disbursements.

The property management trust account may be interest-bearing. The interest will be payable on a pro rata basis to the owners of the properties on whose behalf the money is deposited into the trust account, unless otherwise agreed in writing. The interest must be paid or credited to the property owners on a regular basis (at least quarterly). Note that the property management trust account is not required to be interest-bearing.

A separate ledger sheet must be maintained for each owner of property managed by the brokerage identifying the following information:

- Name and/or address of the property;
- Parties to the transaction;
- Amount, date, and purpose of deposit(s);
- Party from whom deposits are received;
- Amount, date, check number, and purpose of disbursements;
- Party to whom disbursements are made;
- Running balance of funds on deposit for the particular owner of property;
- Amount of interest earned on behalf of the owner(s) of the property(ies), if any.

All brokers who engage in property management activities shall provide an accounting to each owner of property managed on a regular basis (at least quarterly).

**Rental Location Agents (ORC Section 4735.021)**

Anyone in the business of referring prospective tenants to landlords of rental units for a fee must be licensed as a real estate broker or a real estate salesperson acting in the name of a broker. A rental agent must provide each prospective tenant with a signed copy of a written contract that includes the following information:

- The manner in which the listings of rental units have been obtained
- A section providing for the refund of any fee in excess of $10 if the prospect does not find a rental property that meets his or her specifications within 60 days of the contract date
- A section providing for a full refund if the rentals listed by the agent are not current

Note that no prospect may be referred to a nonexistent address, nor may the prospect be referred to a property without the owner's consent. Any violation of this section of the license law is a first-degree misdemeanor and will be prosecuted under the Ohio criminal code.

**Nonresident Licensees (ORC Section 4735.17)**

A nonresident may obtain a license if he or she complies with all requirements for residents and also maintains an active place of business in Ohio. In addition, each nonresident applicant must file an irrevocable consent that lawsuits may be commenced against him or her in the proper court of any county in Ohio, and that the service of process or pleading on the Superintendent of Real Estate will be as binding as if it had been made on the applicant personally.

**Reciprocity of licenses.** The Ohio Real Estate Commission has entered into reciprocity agreements with several states (including Arkansas, Kentucky, Nebraska, Oklahoma, and Wyoming) whose educational and licensing requirements are similar to those in Ohio. Under such agreements, each state waives its real estate examination for qualified persons who are licensed in the other state. Such reciprocal agreements may be entered into by the Division of Real Estate only with states that have similar requirements and that also agree to waive their examination for Ohio licensees.

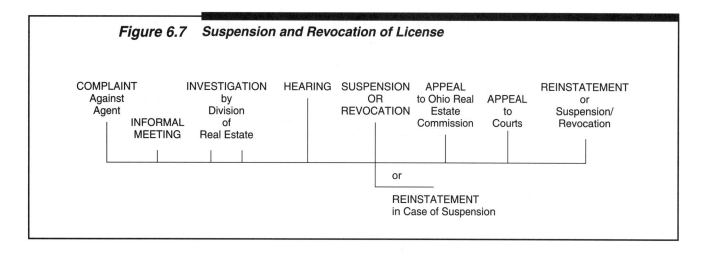

**Figure 6.7  Suspension and Revocation of License**

Ohio licensees interested in practicing real estate in another state may qualify for a license through reciprocity. Note, however, that under reciprocal agreements certain criteria—length of time licensed or residence, for example—still must be met before the examination may be waived. For up-to-date information, contact the Ohio Division of Real Estate (614/466-4100) and/or the real estate commission in the state in which you are interested.

**Suspension, Revocation or Refusal of Licenses (ORC Section 4735.18)**

The superintendent of real estate may investigate the conduct of any licensee at any time. If a verified written complaint is filed against a licensee, the superintendent must conduct an investigation. (See Figure 6.7.)

The superintendent will suspend or revoke any license or publicly reprimand, fine, and/or require additional continuing education whenever the licensee, in performing any act as a real estate broker or salesperson, or as a limited broker or salesperson, or in handling his or her own property, is found guilty of

- knowingly making any misrepresentation;
- making false promises with intent to influence, persuade, or induce;
- a continued course of making false promises or misrepresentations through agents, salespeople, advertising, or otherwise;
- acting for more than one party in a transaction without the knowledge or consent of all parties to the transaction; a licensee is considered to be the agent of the owner of real estate, unless there is an agreement to the contrary disclosed to all parties to the transaction;
- failing to account for or to remit within a reasonable time any money coming into the licensee's possession that belongs to others;
- engaging in dishonest or illegal dealing, gross negligence, incompetency, or misconduct;
- being found by a court to have violated any municipal or federal civil rights law relevant to the protection of purchasers or sellers of real estate;
- being found by a court to have engaged in any unlawful discriminatory practice, in his or her practice as a licensed real estate broker or salesperson, pertaining to the purchase or sale of real estate, if the parties were engaged in bona fide efforts to purchase, sell, or lease real estate;
- committing a second or subsequent violation of any unlawful discriminatory practice pertaining to the purchase or sale of real estate, or any second or subsequent violation of municipal or federal civil rights laws relevant to purchasing or selling real estate, whether or not there has been a final adjudication by a court, where the parties were engaged in

bona fide efforts to purchase, sell or lease real estate (for any second offense, the commission will impose a minimum two months' suspension or revoke the offender's license; for any subsequent offense, the offender's license will be revoked);

- procuring a license by fraud, misrepresentation, or deceit;
- willfully disregarding or violating any provisions of the license law;
- demanding a commission to which he or she is not entitled;
- paying a commission or fee to, or dividing a commission or fee with, anyone not licensed as a real estate broker or salesperson;
- falsely representing membership in any real estate professional association;
- accepting, giving, or charging any undisclosed commission, rebate, or direct profit on expenditures made for a principal;
- offering anything of value other than the consideration recited in the sales contract as an inducement to a person to enter into a contract for the purchase or sale of real estate;
- offering real estate or the improvements on real estate as a prize in a lottery or scheme of chance;
- acting in the dual capacity of real estate broker or salesperson and undisclosed principal in any transaction;
- guaranteeing or authorizing or permitting any person to guarantee future profits that may result from the resale of real property or cemetery interment rights;
- placing a sign on any property offering it for sale or for rent without the owner's consent or the consent of the owner's authorized agent;
- inducing any party to a contract of sale or lease to break his or her contract for the purpose of substituting in lieu of it a new contract with another principal;
- negotiating the sale, exchange, or lease of any real property directly with an owner or lessor knowing that a written contract exists granting exclusive agency to another real estate broker;
- offering real property for sale or for lease without the knowledge and consent of the owner or the authorized agent, or on any terms other than those authorized by the owner or the authorized agent;
- advertising in a misleading or inaccurate way, or in any way misrepresenting any properties, terms, values, policies, or services of the business conducted;
- knowingly withholding or inserting any statement that made an account or invoice materially inaccurate;
- publishing or circulating unjustified or unwarranted threats of legal proceedings to harass competitors or intimidate their customers;
- failing to keep complete and accurate records of all transactions for a period of three years from the date of the transaction, including copies of listing forms, earnest money receipts, offers to purchase, acceptances, and records of receipts and disbursements of all funds received, and any other relevant instruments or papers;
- failing to furnish all parties involved in a real estate transaction true copies of all listings and other agreements to which they are a party, at the time each party signs them;
- failing to maintain at all times a non–interest-bearing special or trust bank account, separate and distinct from any personal or other account, in which all escrow funds, security deposits, and other monies received by the broker in a fiduciary capacity must be deposited;
- failing to put definite expiration dates in all listing contracts;

- having an unsatisfied final judgment in any court of record arising out of his or her conduct as a licensed broker or salesperson;
- failing to render promptly upon demand a full and complete statement of the expenditures of funds advanced by or on behalf of a party to a real estate transaction;
- failing to render an accounting to and pay a real estate salesperson his or her earned share of a commission within a reasonable time of its receipt;
- failing to notify a real estate salesperson that the broker does not intend to list the salesperson on a continuation in business form;
- performing any service for another constituting the practice of law, as determined by any court of law;
- having been adjudicated incompetent for the purpose of holding a real estate broker's or salesperson's license, although a license that is revoked or suspended due to an adjudication of incompetency may be reinstated upon proof to the commission that the disability has been removed; or
- authorizing or permitting a person to act as a real estate broker or limited real estate broker, or a real estate salesperson or limited real estate salesperson, who has not been licensed to do so.

A license may be suspended or revoked as a result of the licensee's conviction of any type of felony or crime of moral turpitude (an act that violates moral standards of the community), regardless of whether it involved real estate activity. Like brokers, salespersons are also subject to disciplinary actions for failing to satisfy a judgment that arose out of conduct as a licensee. When a salesperson's license is suspended or revoked, the commission may also suspend or revoke the license of the broker with whom he or she is associated, if the commission finds that the broker had knowledge of the salesperson's unlawful actions. Similarly, foreign real estate dealers and salespersons are subject to the same standards as Ohioans, and the suspension or revocation of a foreign real estate salesperson's license may result in the suspension or revocation of the foreign real estate dealer with whom he or she is associated.

**Hearing required.** Under Section 119 of the Ohio Revised Code, persons whose licenses are to be revoked or suspended are entitled to a formal hearing. The statute provides for notices, service of summons and subpoenas, rules of evidence, administration of oaths, stenographic records, written reports, and the right of appeal to a court of common pleas.

# CANONS OF ETHICS

The Ohio Real Estate Commission has adopted **Canons of Ethics** for the real estate industry. All Ohio licensees are bound by the Canons of Ethics. In fact, failing to abide by the Canon of Ethics may be considered by the Division to be evidence of unprofessional behavior, giving rise to disciplinary action. REALTORS® that is, members of the National Association of REALTORS® (NAR) and affiliated local boards—are further bound by a separate NAR Code of Ethics.

The Ohio Canon of Ethics is reproduced in its entirety starting below.

**Canons of Ethics for the Real Estate Industry**

**ARTICLE 1.** Licensing as a real estate broker or salesperson indicates to the public at large that the individual so designated has special expertise in real estate matters and is subject to high standards of conduct in his business and personal affairs. The licensee should endeavor to maintain and establish high standards of professional conduct and integrity in his dealings with members of the public as well as with fellow licensees and, further, seek to avoid even the appearance of impropriety in his activities as a licensee.

**ARTICLE 2.** It is the duty of the Broker to protect the public against fraud, misrepresentation, or unethical practices in real estate transactions. He should endeavor to eliminate in his community, any practices which could be damaging to the public or to the integrity of the real estate profession.

**ARTICLE 2.1.** In all representations to the public, the licensee should strive to avoid advertisement or other dissemination of information which would mislead or tend to mislead the public.

**ARTICLE 2.2.** The licensee should not be a party to naming of a false consideration in any document, unless it be the naming of an obviously nominal consideration.

**ARTICLE 3.** The licensee should provide assistance wherever possible to the members and staff of the Real Estate Commission and Division of Real Estate in the enforcement of the licensing statutes and administrative rules and regulations adopted in accordance therewith.

**ARTICLE 3.1.** The licensee should be knowledgeable of the laws of Ohio pertinent to the conduct of his affairs in real estate and should keep informed of changes in the statutes of Ohio affecting his duties and responsibilities as a licensee.

**ARTICLE 3.2.** The licensee should comply with both the spirit and intent of the federal, state, and municipal civil rights laws relative to the protection of purchasers or sellers of real estate.

**ARTICLE 4.** A licensee should represent clients competently to the best of his abilities and should promote through his own conduct the advancement of professional education in the real estate industry.

**ARTICLE 5.** A licensee should endeavor to represent all clients with equal consideration and concern for their interest without regard to their race, color, age, sex, religion, handicap, national origin, or economic standing, being ever mindful of the public trust inherent in licensing by the Real Estate Commission.

**ARTICLE 5.1.** The licensee should keep himself informed as to matters affecting real estate in his community, state, and the nation, so that he may be able to contribute to public thinking on such matters including taxation, legislation, land use, city planning, and other questions affecting property interests.

**ARTICLE 5.2.** It is the duty of the licensee to be well informed on current market conditions in order to be in a position to advise his clients as to the fair market price and should not deliberately mislead the owner as to market value.

**ARTICLE 5.3.** The licensee should ascertain all material facts concerning every property for which he accepts the agency, so that he may fulfill his obligation to avoid error, exaggeration, misrepresentation, or concealment of material facts.

**ARTICLE 6.** The licensee should not engage in activities which constitute the unauthorized practice of law, and should recommend that title be examined and legal counsel be obtained.

**ARTICLE 7.** The licensee should keep in a special noninterest bearing bank account, separated from his own funds, monies coming into his hands in trust for other persons, such as escrows, trust funds, clients' monies, and other like items.

**ARTICLE 8.** The Broker in his advertising should be especially careful to present a true picture and should not advertise without disclosing his name or his firm name, nor permit his salesmen to use individual names or telephone numbers, unless the salesman's connection with the Broker is obvious in the advertisement.

**ARTICLE 9.** The licensee, for the protection of all parties with whom he deals, should see that financial obligations and commitments regarding real estate transactions are in writing, expressing the exact agreement of the parties; and that copies of such agreements, at the time they are executed, are placed in the hands of all parties involved.

**PART II.
Relations
to the Client**

**ARTICLE 10.** In accepting employment as an agent, the licensee pledges himself to protect and promote the interests of the client. This obligation of duty to the client is primary, but does not relieve the licensee from the obligation of dealing fairly with all parties to the transaction.

**ARTICLE 11.** In representing a client, a licensee should exercise independent professional judgment, avoiding wherever possible, employment by a principal whose interests are in conflict with those of the licensee or his business associates.

**ARTICLE 12.** Since the licensee is representing one or another party to a transaction, he should not accept compensation from more than one party without the full knowledge and consent of all parties to the transaction.

**ARTICLE 13.** The licensee should not acquire an interest in or buy for himself or any member of his immediate family, his firm or any member thereof, or a corporation in which he has an interest, property listed with him or his company or firm without making his true position known to the listing owner. In selling property owned by him, or in which he has some ownership interest, the exact facts should be revealed to the purchaser prior to an offer being made.

**ARTICLE 14.** When acting as an agent the licensee should not accept any commission, rebate, or profit on expenditures made for an owner/principal without the owner's/principal's knowledge and consent.

**ARTICLE 15.** The licensee should charge for his services only such fees as are fair and reasonable after discussion and negotiation with the client.

**ARTICLE 16.** When asked to make a formal appraisal of real property, the licensee should not render an opinion without careful and thorough analysis and interpretation of all factors affecting the value of the property. His counsel constitutes a professional service for which he should make a fair charge.

**ARTICLE 16.1.** The licensee should not undertake to provide professional services, make any appraisal, or render an opinion of value on any property where he has a present or contemplated interest unless such interest is specifically disclosed to all affected parties. Under no circumstances should he undertake to make a formal appraisal when his employment or fee is contingent upon the amount of his appraisal.

**ARTICLE 16.2.** The licensee should not undertake to make an appraisal that is outside the field of his experience unless he obtains the assistance of a licensee or appraiser familiar with such types of property, or unless the facts are fully disclosed to the client.

**ARTICLE 17.** The licensee should not advertise property without authority, and in any offering the price quoted should be that agreed upon with the owners as the offering price.

**ARTICLE 18.** In the event that more than one formal offer on a specific property is made, all written offers should be presented to the owner for his decision.

**PART III.
Relations to
Fellow-Licensees**

**ARTICLE 19.** The licensee should seek no unfair advantage over his fellow-licensees and should willingly share with them the lessons of his experience and study.

**ARTICLE 20.** When the licensee is charged with violating real estate license law, he should voluntarily place all pertinent facts before the Division of Real Estate and the Real Estate Commission for investigation and judgment.

**ARTICLE 21.** A licensee should respect the exclusive agency for another licensee until it has expired or until an owner, without solicitation, initiates a discussion with the licensee about terms upon which he might take a future listing or one commencing upon the expiration of any existing listing.

**ARTICLE 21.1.** A licensee should not solicit a listing that is currently listed with another broker, unless the listing broker, when asked, refuses to disclose the expiration and nature of the listing. In that event the licensee may contact the owner to secure such information and may discuss terms upon which he might take a future listing, or one commencing upon the expiration of any existing exclusive listing.

**ARTICLE 22.** The licensee should cooperate with other licensees on property listed, sharing commissions on an agreed basis. Negotiations concerning property listed exclusively with one broker should be carried on with the listing broker, not with the owner, except with the consent of the listing licensee.

**ARTICLE 23.** Signs giving notice of property for sale, rent, lease, or exchange should not be placed on any property by more than one licensee, and then only if authorized by the owner; unless the property is listed with and authorization by the owner is given to more than one licensee.

**KEY TERMS**

| | | |
|---|---|---|
| ARELLO | foreign real estate | real estate broker |
| Canons of Ethics | salesperson | Real Estate |
| certificate of | limited real estate | Commission |
| continuation | dealer | real estate education |
| continuing education | limited real estate | real estate education |
| Department of | salesperson | and research fund |
| Commerce | "on deposit" | real estate license laws |
| Division of Real Estate | pre-license | real estate recovery |
| earnest money | requirements | fund |
| foreign real estate | post-license | real estate salesperson |
| dealer | requirements | trust accounts |

**SUMMARY**

- The real estate license laws:
  - protect the public from dishonest brokers and salespeople,
  - prescribe certain licensing standards, and
  - maintain high standards in the real estate profession.
- State law:
  - stipulates who must be licensed and who is exempt from licensing,
  - sets forth certain operating standards to which brokers and salespersons must adhere,
  - creates certain licensing procedures and requirements,
  - imposes pre-licensing and post-licensing education requirements, and
  - sets forth the grounds and procedures for disciplinary action.
- The Canons of Ethics adopted by the Ohio Real Estate Commission binds licensees to strict rules of professional behavior.

**Real-Life
Real Estate**

1. A major segment of the Ohio license law concerns the educational requirements for obtaining and maintaining a license. Discuss the advantages and disadvantages (or costs vs. benefits) of ever-increasing educational mandates for salespeople and brokers.
2. Why do you suppose Ohio has licensing reciprocity with very few other states?
3. There are at least 37 ways to lose a license (suspension or revocation). Analyze the impact of suspension on the ability to continue to conduct business (particularly in a small-to-medium sized community).

# QUESTIONS

1. After a hearing, the Ohio Real Estate Commission may suspend or revoke the license of a licensee who
   a. has violated any of the provisions of the Ohio license law.
   b. is not a REALTOR®.
   c. is being sued in court.
   d. accepts an advance fee to promote the sale or lease of real estate.

2. In Ohio, to be engaged in a real estate brokerage business partnership or an association, all members of the partnership or association who are performing the functions of a real estate broker must
   a. be licensed brokers.
   b. be licensed brokers or licensed salespersons.
   c. be limited real estate dealers or limited real estate salespersons.
   d. have a majority of the partners with a broker's license, and the rest can hold a salesperson's license.

3. A person in the business of collecting and selling information on apartments available for rent
   a. is exempt from the Ohio Real Estate License Law.
   b. must hold an Ohio securities license.
   c. must hold an Ohio real estate license.
   d. must hold an Ohio vendor's license.

4. From the application and renewal fees for each real estate license
   a. $10 is put aside to further the cause of education and research of real estate at Ohio institutions of higher education.
   b. $4 is put aside to further the cause of education and research of real estate at Ohio institutions of higher education.
   c. $40 is put aside to replenish the real estate recovery special account.
   d. $10 is put aside to replenish the real estate recovery special account.

5. A licensee can have his or her Ohio real estate license revoked for
   a. placing a "for sale" sign on a property without the owner's consent.
   b. advertising in the local newspapers.
   c. belonging to a local trade association.
   d. buying a property he or she has listed after having disclosed to the seller, in writing, that he or she holds an Ohio real estate license.

6. An applicant who fails the Ohio broker or salesperson licensing exam
   a. may retake the exam as often as needed, without time limitation.
   b. may take the exam again only after completing a review course.
   c. must wait one full year before sitting for the exam again.
   d. must retake the exam within six months.

7. A salesperson may have his or her license suspended or revoked for
   a. advertising properties in another county.
   b. using a broker's separate account as a depository for monies received.
   c. paying a finder's fee to an unlicensed person.
   d. completing 30 hours of continuing education in one year.

8. A broker violates the Ohio Revised Code when he or she
   a. operates in his or her own name alone and at the same time as an active member or officer of a licensed partnership or corporation.
   b. associates with another broker as a salesperson.
   c. violates the Code of Ethics of the National Association of REALTORS®.
   d. deposits his or her license with the Ohio Division of Real Estate.

9. In Ohio the real estate license of a person who willingly disregards or violates any of the provisions of the Ohio Real Estate License Law
   a. will be suspended or revoked.
   b. may not be reissued for six months.
   c. will be suspended for six months.
   d. may be reinstated upon payment of a fine.

10. All Ohio real estate brokers must
    a. be bonded.
    b. display the licenses of their salespeople.
    c. post the equal housing poster in a prominent place in their office.
    d. be either Realtists or REALTORS®.

11. In Ohio, a real estate broker must
    a. list properties.
    b. include his or her name in advertisements of a client's property.
    c. belong to a local trade association.
    d. hold open houses.

12. A real estate licensee who is not an attorney and engages in any activity that constitutes the practice of law
    a. may charge a fee for preparing deeds.
    b. is in violation of the Ohio Real Estate License Law.
    c. may legally do so only in the area of real estate law.
    d. is not acting illegally.

13. Appointments to the Ohio Real Estate Commission are made by the
    a. director of commerce.
    b. superintendent of real estate.
    c. secretary of state.
    d. governor.

14. The Ohio Real Estate Commission is required by law to do all of the following *EXCEPT*
    a. promulgate a Code of Ethics for the real estate industry.
    b. promulgate a Canon of Ethics for the real estate industry.
    c. administer the education and research rotary fund and the recovery fund.
    d. direct the superintendent on content, scheduling, instruction, and offerings of real estate courses for salesperson and broker education requirements.

15. The superintendent of real estate is
    a. appointed by the director of commerce.
    b. appointed by the governor.
    c. elected at the general election.
    d. in the position for a five-year term.

16. In Ohio, if a written complaint against a licensee is filed, the complaint should be sent to whom?
    a. The governor
    b. The director of commerce
    c. The superintendent
    d. The Ohio Division of Real Estate

# 7

# Listing Agreements and Buyer Representation

## LISTING AGREEMENTS

**In Ohio...** A listing agreement is an employment contract rather than a real estate contract. It is a contract for the personal professional services of the broker, not for the transfer of real estate. In most states, the statute of frauds or the real estate license law requires that the listing be in writing to be enforceable in court. However, oral listings are permitted in Ohio. ◆

**In Practice**    Good business practice would dictate that real estate agents obtain written listing agreements and written buyer agency agreements.

As discussed in Chapter 5, a listing agreement creates a special agency relationship between the principal (the owner of the property) and the broker (the agent). As agent, the broker is authorized to represent the principal (and the principal's real estate) to third parties. That authorization includes obtaining and submitting offers for the property.

**In Ohio...** Under both the law of agency and Ohio license laws, only a broker can act as agent to list, sell, rent, or purchase another person's real estate and provide other services to a principal. A salesperson who performs these acts does so only in the name and under the supervision of the broker. ◆

Throughout this chapter, unless otherwise stated, the terms *broker, agent* and *firm* are intended to include both the broker and a salesperson working under the broker. However, the parties to a listing contract are the seller and the broker.

**Types of Listing Agreements**    Several types of listing agreements exist. The type of contract determines the specific rights and obligations of the parties. (See Figure 7.1.)

**Exclusive-right-to-sell listing.** In an **exclusive-right-to-sell listing,** one broker is appointed as the seller's sole agent. The broker is given the exclusive right, or authorization, to market the seller's property. If the property is sold while the listing is in effect, the seller must pay the broker a commission *regardless of who sells the property.* In other words, if the seller finds a buyer

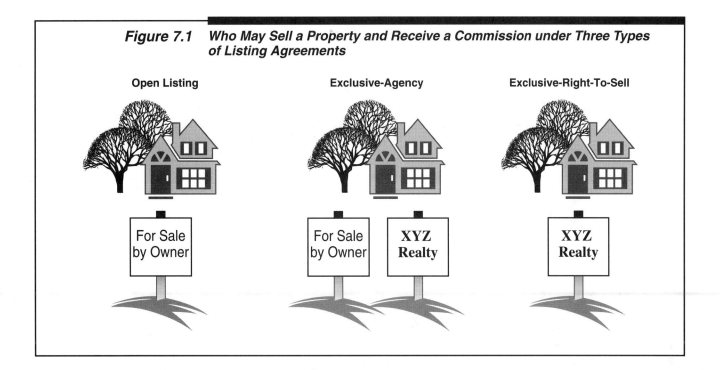

**Figure 7.1** *Who May Sell a Property and Receive a Commission under Three Types of Listing Agreements*

Open Listing

Exclusive-Agency

Exclusive-Right-To-Sell

For Sale by Owner

For Sale by Owner

XYZ Realty

XYZ Realty

---

> **Exclusive-right-to-sell listing:**
>
> One authorized agent-broker receives a commission regardless of who sells the property.

without the broker's assistance, the seller *still* must pay the broker a commission. Sellers benefit from this form of agreement because the broker feels more free to spend time and money actively marketing the property, making a timely and profitable sale more likely. From the broker's perspective, an exclusive-right-to-sell listing offers the greatest opportunity to receive a commission.

The exclusive right-to-sell listing is the one most commonly used in Ohio. (See Figure 7.2.)

> **Exclusive-agency listing:**
>
> - There is one authorized agent.
> - Broker receives a commission only if he or she is the procuring cause.
> - Seller retains the right to sell without obligation.

**Exclusive-agency listing.** In an **exclusive-agency listing,** one broker is authorized to act as the exclusive agent of the principal. However, *the seller retains the right to sell the property without obligation to the broker.* The seller is obligated to pay a commission to the broker only if the broker (or a subagent of the broker) has been the procuring cause of a sale. *Test -*

**Open listing.** In an **open listing** (also known in some areas as a *nonexclusive listing* or a *general listing*), the seller retains the right to employ any number of brokers as agents. The brokers can act simultaneously, and the seller is obligated to pay a commission to only that broker who successfully produces a ready, willing, and able buyer. If the seller personally sells the property *without the aid of any of the brokers,* the seller is not obligated to pay a commission. A listing contract that does not specifically provide otherwise ordinarily creates an open listing. An advertisement of property "for sale by owner" may indicate "brokers protected" or in some other way invite offers brought by brokers. Such an invitation does not, by itself, however, create a listing agreement.

> **Open listing:**
>
> - There are multiple agents.
> - Only selling agent is entitled to a commission.
> - Seller retains the right to sell independently without obligation.

Even the terms of an open listing must be negotiated, however. These negotiated terms should be in writing to protect the agent's ability to collect an agreed-on fee from the seller. Written terms may be in the form of a listing agreement (if the agent represents the seller) or a fee agreement (if the agent represents the buyer or the seller does not wish to be represented).

## Figure 7.2   *Exclusive-Right-To-Sell Listing*

**Exclusive Right to Sell Agreement**

1.  **SELLER**: Seller as owner or having the right and power to act for the owner of the following described property (the "Property") hereby authorizes Broker, _____, to offer for sale the Property at the price and terms stated below.

2.  **PROPERTY**:_____, Ohio _____
                    (Street Address)                           (Municipality)              (Zip)

    Perm. Parcel or Tax I.D. No._____ **Described As**_____.

3.  **PRICE**: $_____.

4.  **EXCLUSIVE RIGHT TO SELL**: In consideration of Broker's agreement to diligently work to secure a Purchaser for the Property, Seller hereby grants to Broker the sole and exclusive right to sell the Property from this date through midnight on _____199_____. (the "Exclusive Period"). In the event of sale or exchange of the Property at the price and terms stated, or such other price and terms as may be acceptable to Seller. Seller agrees to pay Broker a commission, on the full purchase or exchange price, of _____percent_____(%)
_____.

5.  **PROTECTION PERIOD**: Seller agrees to refer all real estate licensees, customers, or prospects who may come to Seller directly during the Exclusive Period or any extension thereof. In the event of any sale or exchange of the Property within six (6) months after the Exclusive Period (or any extension thereof) has expired, it is further agreed that Seller will pay the commission described above if the Purchaser had contact with Broker, or any real estate licensee regarding the purchase of the Property during the Exclusive Period (or any extension thereof), and Seller knew or had been advised in writing of such contact. However, Seller shall not be obligated to pay said commission if Seller enters into a written exclusive right to sell agreement with another real estate Broker during such six month Protection Period.

6.  **AUTHORIZATION TO MARKET**: Broker is authorized in its sole discretion, to place a for sale sign on the property, if permitted by law, to remove all other such signs, to place a lock box on the property, to have access to the property at all reasonable times for the purpose of showing it to prospective purchasers, to cooperate with other brokers and to use pictures of same for promotional purposes. The property shall be entered into the multiple listing service subject to the rules and regulations of that service.

7.  **FAIR HOUSING**: I have been given written information about fair housing laws. It is agreed that both the Broker and I will comply with all applicable Federal, State and Local Fair Housing Laws and that the Property will be offered without discrimination on the basis of race, color, religion, sex, ancestry, handicap, familial status or national origin.

8.  **SELLER'S PROPERTY DESCRIPTION**: I understand that the information which I provide to Broker as listing information will be used to advertise my property to the public and it is essential that this information be accurate. I HAVE REVIEWED THE MLS LISTING INPUT SHEET AND REPRESENT THAT THE INFORMATION CONTAINED IN IT IS TRUE AND ACCURATE TO THE BEST OF MY KNOWLEDGE. Though I am listing my property in its present physical condition ("as is" condition), I understand that I may be held responsible by a Purchaser for any latent or hidden, undisclosed defects in my property which are known to me but which are not disclosed to the Purchaser at time of sale. I have completed The "RESIDENTIAL PROPERTY DISCLOSURE FORM". I understand that the Disclosure and its contents will be shared with prospective Purchasers, and with any person or entity in connection with the actual or anticipated sale of this property. I further agree to disclose any additional items which may become known to me prior to recording of the deed. I understand that if prior to the acceptance of a purchase agreement, I do not provide said "RESIDENTIAL PROPERTY DISCLOSURE FORM", to the purchaser, then the purchaser may rescind the purchase agreement without penalty. _____

    I AM AWARE OF NO OTHER PROBLEMS OR DEFECTS IN THE PROPERTY, EXCEPT AS STATED WITHIN THE RESIDENTIAL PROPERTY DISCLOSURE FORM.

9.  **TITLE**: Title will be conveyed to the Purchaser or nominee by appropriate deed, with release of dower, if any, and Seller shall pay for a title search and one half (1/2) of the premium for an Owners Policy of the Title Insurance issued in the amount of the purchase price insuring title except for allowable exceptions appearing in the Purchase Agreement.

10. **APPURTENANT FIXTURES**: Items such as wall-to-wall carpeting, garage door openers, smoke detectors, built-in appliances, light fixtures, landscaping and many indoor and outdoor decorative items may legally be "fixtures" and if so they must remain with the property unless specifically excluded in the Purchase Agreement. Discuss this matter with your agent/Broker to avoid uncertainty regarding what you may take and what should remain with the property, and make specific provisions for these items in the Purchase Agreement. Excluded fixtures: _____

11. **HOME WARRANTY**: I agree ( ) to provide ( ) not to provide a limited home warranty program from _____at a charge of $_____plus options, if any. I acknowledge that the home warranty program is a limited warranty with a deductible. I acknowledge receipt of the application for such home warranty program.

12. **MUNICIPAL REQUIRED INSPECTIONS**: I agree to apply for and obtain any inspections and/or certificates required by law and shall place said document(s) in escrow. The responsibility for curing said violations shall be assumed by the ( ) seller, ( ) purchaser.

13. **FEES TO SUB AGENTS/ BUYER'S AGENTS AND DUAL AGENTS**: I understand and agree that _____shall also permit the property to be shown by purchaser's brokers, and at its sole discretion, may pay a part of the above commission to such buyer's brokers. _____is authorized at its sole discretion to determine with which brokers it will cooperate, and the amount of commission that it will offer cooperating brokers in the sale of the property. Seller acknowledges that the commission offered to such cooperating brokers may vary from broker to broker.

I understand and agree that other _____sales associates other than the listing sales associate may have represented the actual or prospective purchaser(s) of my property. I further understand and agree that if the property is sold through the efforts of a _____ sales associate who has represented the purchaser(s),_____, the listing sales associate, and the other _____ sales associate will be acting solely as dual agents (i.e., as agents both for me and for the purchaser(s)).

As a dual agent, the broker, _____, and its agents will represent both the Seller and Purchaser for the limited purpose of negotiating the sale or exchange of the property. In this limited capacity, I acknowledge that _____ and its agents will not disclose any confidential information received from either myself or Purchaser to the other party. I further understand that confidential information includes the possibility that the Seller will accept a price less than list price, that the Purchaser will pay a price greater than the price offered or any other information that could adversely affect either party's negotiating position.

Are there any pending lawsuits, Foreclosures, Divorce Actions, Probate or Tax Liens which could affect title to the property?     ❏ No     ❏ Yes
The word "I" in this agreement shall mean all sellers, jointly and severally, who have signed this agreement. I understand that this agreement does not guarantee the sale of my property. I hereby acknowledge receipt of a signed copy of this agreement.   (If seller is married both signatures are required)

ACCEPTED: _____         DATE:_____

DATE:_____     OWNER:_____

BY:_____     OWNER:_____

                                              ADDRESS:_____

OFFICE:_____

PHONE:_____     PHONE:_____

THIS AGREEMENT IS A LEGALLY BINDING CONTRACT. IF YOU HAVE ANY QUESTIONS OF LAW, CONSULT YOUR ATTORNEY.

## Special Listing Provisions

**Multiple listing.** A **multiple-listing clause** is often included in an exclusive listing. It is used by brokers who are members of **multiple-listing services (MLSs).** As discussed earlier, an MLS is a marketing organization whose broker members make their own exclusive listings available to other brokers and gain access to other brokers' listed properties as well.

An MLS offers advantages to both brokers and sellers. Brokers develop a sizable inventory of properties to be sold and are ensured a portion of the commission if they list real property or participate in the sale of another broker's listing. Sellers gain because the property is exposed to a larger market.

The contractual obligations among the member brokers of an MLS vary widely. Most MLSs require that a broker turn over new listings to the service within a specific, fairly short period of time after the broker obtains the listing. The length of time during which the listing broker can offer a property exclusively without notifying the other member brokers varies.

Under the provisions of most MLSs, a participating broker makes a unilateral offer of cooperation and compensation to other member brokers. The broker must have the written consent of the seller to include the property in an MLS. If a broker chooses to be an agent for the buyer of a property in the MLS, that broker must notify the listing broker before any communication with the seller takes place. All brokers must determine the appropriate way to proceed to protect their fiduciaries.

**In Ohio...** The selling agent is required by Ohio law to provide to the listing agent a signed and dated agency disclosure form as soon as practicable but in no event later than the presentation of the offer to the seller. Buyer's brokers and agency disclosures are discussed in Chapter 5. ◆

---

**In Practice**    Technology has enhanced the benefits of MLS membership. In addition to providing instant access to information about the status of listed properties, MLSs often offer a broad range of other useful information about mortgage loans, real estate taxes and assessments, municipalities, and school districts. They are equally helpful to the licensee who needs to make a competitive market analysis to determine the value of a particular property before suggesting an appropriate range of listing prices. Computer-assisted searches also help buyers select properties that best meet their needs.

---

In a *net listing*, the broker is entitled to any amount exceeding the seller's stated net; in an *option listing*, the broker has the right to purchase the property.

**Net listing.** A **net listing** provision specifies that the seller will receive a net amount of money from any sale, with the excess going to the listing broker as commission. The broker is free to offer the property at any price greater than that net amount. Because a net listing can create a conflict of interest between the broker's fiduciary responsibility to the seller and the broker's profit motive, however, net listings are illegal in many states and are discouraged in others. *[handwritten: No longer used in Ohio]*

Although not illegal in Ohio, this type of listing is not generally recommended. The question of fraud is frequently raised because of the uncertainty over the sales price set or received by the broker. The term *net amount* is often misunderstood and disputed. An agreement that is not spelled out very clearly and precisely may be considered unethical.

**F**OR EXAMPLE A seller explained her situation to her broker: "I want to sell my house, but I don't want to be bothered with percentages and bargaining and offers and counteroffers. I just need to walk out of this deal with $150,000 in my pocket. You sell the place for any price you want and keep anything over $150,000." The broker knows that comparable homes in the area are selling for more than $200,000. What should the broker do about this offer of a net listing?

**Option listing.** An **option listing** provision gives the broker the right to purchase the listed property. Use of an option listing may open the broker to charges of fraud unless the broker is scrupulous in fulfilling all obligations to the property owner. In some states, a broker who chooses to exercise such an option must first inform the property owner of the broker's profit in the transaction and secure in *writing* the owner's agreement to it.

## TERMINATION OF LISTING

A listing agreement is a personal service contract between a broker and a seller. Its success depends on the broker's personal, professional efforts. Because the broker's services are unique, he or she cannot turn over the listing to another broker without the principal's written consent. The property owner cannot force the broker to perform, but the broker's failure to work diligently toward fulfilling the contract's terms constitutes abandonment of the listing. In the event the listing is abandoned or revoked by the broker, the owner is entitled to sue the broker for damages.

Of course, the property owner also might fail to fulfill the terms of the agreement. A property owner who refuses to cooperate with the broker's reasonable requests, such as allowing the broker to show the property to prospective buyers, or who refuses to proceed with a complete sales contract could be liable for damages to the broker. If either party cancels the contract, he or she may be liable for damages to the other.

A listing agreement may be canceled for the following reasons:

- When the agreement's purpose is fulfilled, such as when a buyer or tenant is produced
- When the agreement's term expires without a successful transfer
- If the property is destroyed or its use is changed by some force outside the owner's control, such as a zoning change or condemnation by eminent domain (see Chapter 8)
- If title to the property is transferred by operation of law, as in the case of the owner's bankruptcy
- If the broker and seller mutually agree to end the listing or if one party ends it unilaterally (in which case he or she may be liable to the other party for damages)
- If either party dies or becomes incapacitated
- If either the broker or seller breaches the contract, the agreement is terminated and the breaching or canceling party may be liable to the other for damages

**Expiration of Listing Period**

**In Ohio...**

All listings must specify a definite period of time during which the broker is to be employed. *In Ohio, failing to specify a definite termination date in a listing is grounds for the suspension or revocation of a real estate license.* In fact, failing to include a definite termination date in a listing agreement is a common cause for disciplinary action in Ohio. ◆

Some listing agreements used to contain *automatic extension clauses.* These clauses provided for a base period of 90 days that "continues thereafter until terminated by either party hereto by 30 days' notice in writing." Extension clauses should be avoided. They are illegal in some states, and many listing contract forms specifically provide that there can be no automatic extensions of the agreement. Some courts have held that an extension clause actually creates an open listing rather than an exclusive-agency agreement.

Some listing contracts contain a *broker protection clause.* This clause provides that the property owner will pay the listing broker a commission if, within a specified number of days after the listing expires, the owner transfers the property to someone the broker originally introduced to the owner. This clause protects a broker who was the procuring cause from losing a commission because the transaction was completed after the listing expired. The time for such a clause usually parallels the terms of the listing agreement: a six-month listing may carry a broker protection clause of six months after the listing's expiration, for example. To protect their rights under this clause, brokers should keep a list of the prospects they have shown the property to. This list should then be given to the seller. To protect the owner and prevent any liability on the owner's part for two separate commissions, most of these clauses stipulate that they cannot be enforced if the property is relisted under a new contract either with the original listing broker or with another broker.

## THE LISTING PROCESS

Before signing a contract, the broker and seller must discuss a variety of issues. The seller's most critical concerns typically are the selling price of the property and the net amount the seller can expect to receive from the sale. The broker has several professional tools to provide information about a property's value and to calculate the proceeds from a sale.

Most sellers ask other questions as well: How quickly will the property sell? What services will the broker provide during the listing period? This is the broker's opportunity to explain the various types of listing agreements, the ramifications of different agency relationships, and the marketing services the broker provides. At the end of this process the seller should feel comfortable with his or her decision to list with the broker.

Similarly, before the listing agreement is finalized, the broker should be prepared to fulfill the fiduciary obligations the agreement imposes. The seller should have provided comprehensive information about both the property and his or her personal concerns. Based on this information, the broker can accept the listing with confidence that the seller's goals can be met in a profitable manner for both parties.

**Pricing the Property** While it is the responsibility of the broker or salesperson to advise and assist, *it is the seller who must determine the listing price for the property.* Because the average seller does not have the resources needed to make an informed decision about a reasonable listing price, real estate agents must be prepared to offer their knowledge, information, and expertise.

A salesperson can help the seller determine a listing price for the property by using a **competitive market analysis (CMA).** A buyer's agent should also

A *competitive market analysis* is an analysis of market activity among comparable properties; it is *not* the same as a formal appraisal.

**Market Value**

The most probable price property would bring in an arm's-length transaction under normal conditions on the open market.

prepare a CMA on a property before the buyer makes an offer on it. This is a comparison of the prices of properties recently sold, properties currently on the market, and properties that did not sell. The comparisons must be made with properties similar in location, size, age, style, and amenities to the seller's property. Although a CMA is not a formal appraisal, the salesperson uses many of the same methods and techniques an appraiser uses in arriving at a reasonable value range. (See Chapter 19.) If no adequate comparisons can be made, or if the property is unique in some way, the seller may prefer that a professional appraiser conduct a detailed, formal estimate of the property's value.

Whether a CMA or a formal appraisal is used, the figure sought is the property's market value. **Market value,** discussed in Chapter 19, is *the most probable price that a property would bring in a fair sale.* A CMA estimates market value as likely to fall within a range of values (for instance, $135,000 to $140,000). A CMA, however, should not be confused with a formal appraisal, which will indicate a specific value rather than a range.

While it is the property owner's privilege to set whatever listing price he or she chooses, a broker should consider rejecting any listing in which the price is substantially exaggerated or severely out of line with the indications of the CMA or appraisal. These tools provide the best indications of what a buyer will likely pay for the property. An unrealistic listing price will make it difficult for the broker to properly market the seller's property within the agreed-on listing period. Furthermore, a seller who is unreasonable about the property's value may prove uncooperative on other issues later on.

**Seller's Return**

The broker can easily calculate roughly how much the seller will net from a given sales price or what sales price will produce a desired net amount. The Math Concept on page 107 illustrates how the formulas are applied.

**In Practice**   When helping a seller determine an appropriate listing price, the broker must give an estimate of value as reasonable, conservative, and accurate as possible. Overpriced listings cost the broker time and money in wasted marketing and advertising and give sellers false hopes of riches to come. Ultimately, failing to move overpriced listings will cost the broker future business opportunities as well.

**Information Needed for Listing Agreements**

Once the real estate licensee and the owner agree on a listing price, the licensee must obtain specific, detailed information about the property. Obtaining as many facts as possible ensures that most contingencies can be anticipated. This is particularly important when the listing will be shared with other brokers through an MLS and the other licensees must rely on the information taken by the lister.

The information needed for a listing agreement generally includes

- the names and relationship, if any, of the owners;
- the street address and legal description of the property;
- the size, type, age, and construction of improvements;
- the number of rooms and their sizes;
- the dimensions of the lot;

- existing loans, including such information as the name and address of each lender, the type of loan, the loan number, the loan balance, the interest rate, the monthly payment and what it includes (principal, interest, real estate tax impounds, hazard insurance impounds, mortgage insurance premiums), whether the loan may be assumed by the
- buyer and under what circumstances and whether the loan may be prepaid without penalty;
- the possibility of seller financing;
- the amount of any outstanding special assessments and whether they will be paid by the seller or assumed by the buyer;
- the zoning classification of the property;
- the current (or most recent year's) property taxes;
- neighborhood amenities (for instance, schools, parks and recreational areas, churches, and public transportation);
- any real property to be removed from the premises by the seller and any personal property to be included in the sale for the buyer (both the listing contract and the subsequent purchase contract should be explicit on these points);
- any additional information that would make the property more appealing and marketable; and
- any required disclosures concerning agency representation and property conditions.

**MATH CONCEPTS**

**Calculating Sales Prices, Commissions, and Nets to Seller**

When a property sells, the sales price equals 100 percent of the money being transferred. Therefore, if a broker is to receive a 6 percent commission, 94 percent will remain for the seller's other expenses and equity. To calculate a commission using a sales price of $80,000 and a commission rate of 6 percent, multiply the sales price by the commission rate:

$$\$80,000 \times 6\% = \$80,000 \times .06 = \$4,800 \text{ commission}$$

To calculate a sales price using a commission of $4,550 and a commission rate of 7 percent, divide the commission by the commission rate:

$$\$4,550 \div 7\% = \$4,550 \div .07 = \$65,000 \text{ sales price}$$

To calculate a commission rate using a commission of $3,200 and a sales price of $64,000, divide the commission by the sales price:

$$\$3,200 \div \$64,000 = .05, \text{ or } 5\% \text{ commission rate}$$

To calculate the net to the seller using a sales price of $85,000 and a commission rate of 8 percent, multiply the sales price by 100 percent minus the commission rate:

$$\$85,000 \times (100\% - 8\%) = \$85,000 \times (1 - .08) = \$85,000 \times .92 = \$78,200$$

The same result could be achieved by calculating the commission ($85,000 × .08 = $6,800) and deducting it from the sales price ($85,000 − $6,800 = $78,200); however, this involves unnecessary extra calculations.

You may use this circle formula to help you with these calculations. In the circle, C is the commission amount, R is the rate and P is the price of the property. If you know two of the figures, you can determine the third.

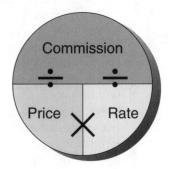

In Summary: Sales price × Commission rate = Commission

Commission ÷ Commission rate = Sales price

Commission ÷ Sales price = Commission rate

Sales price × (100% – Commission rate) = Net to seller

**Disclosures**

**In Ohio...**

Disclosure of agency relationships and property conditions has become the focus of consumer safeguards in the 1990s. As discussed in Chapter 5, Ohio law requires that agents disclose whose interest they legally represent, a particularly confusing issue when subagents are involved in the transaction. It is important that the seller be informed of the company's policies regarding cooperation with subagents and any potential for the property to be shown by an agent for the buyer. ◆

**Property Disclosure Form**

**In Ohio...**

Ohio law requires that sellers of residential property disclose *material matters relating to the physical condition of the property*. A completed property disclosure form must be provided to purchasers prior to closing, in order to clarify exactly what is being sold and what is being purchased. (See Figure 7.3.)

The form contains the following disclosures:

- The structural condition of the property, including the roof, foundation, walls, and floors
- The presence of hazardous materials or substances, including lead-based paint, asbestos, urea-formaldehyde foam insulation, and radon gas
- The source of water and the nature of the sewer system
- Any other material defects in the property that are known by the seller

In addition to specific disclosures regarding the property's condition, the disclosure statement must also include the following statements:

- That the form constitutes a statement of the conditions of the property and of information concerning the property actually known by the transferor
- That, unless the purchaser is advised in writing, the transferor has no greater knowledge of the property's condition, other than having lived at or owned the property, than that which could be obtained by the purchaser's careful inspection of the property

## Figure 7.3  *Residential Property Disclosure Form*

EFFECTIVE JULY 1993

### STATE OF OHIO
### DEPARTMENT OF COMMERCE

#### RESIDENTIAL PROPERTY DISCLOSURE FORM

**Pursuant to Ohio Revised Code Section 5302.30**
**TO BE COMPLETED BY OWNER** *(Please Print)*

Property Address: _____

_____

Owner's Name(s): _____

Date: _____ , 19 _____

Owner ☐ is ☐ is not occupying the property.          If owner is occupying the property, since what date _____

**Purpose of Disclosure Form:** This is a statement of the condition of the property and of information concerning the property actually known by the owner as required by Ohio Revised Code Section 5302.30. Unless otherwise advised in writing by the owner, the owner, other than having lived at or owning the property, possesses no greater knowledge than that which could be obtained by a careful inspection of the property by a potential purchaser. Unless otherwise advised, owner has not conducted any inspection of generally inaccessible areas of the property. THIS STATEMENT IS NOT A WARRANTY OF ANY KIND BY THE OWNER OR BY ANY AGENT OR SUBAGENT REPRESENTING THE OWNER OF THE PROPERTY. THIS STATEMENT IS NOT A SUBSTITUTE FOR ANY INSPECTIONS. POTENTIAL PURCHASERS ARE ENCOURAGED TO OBTAIN THEIR OWN PROFESSIONAL INSPECTION.

**Owner's Statement:** The representations contained on this form are made by the owner and are not the representations of the owner's agent or subagent. This form and the representations contained in it are provided by the owner exclusively to potential purchasers in a transfer made by the owner, and are not made to purchasers in any subsequent transfers. The information contained in this disclosure form does not limit the obligation of the owner to disclose an item of information that is required by any other statute or law to be disclosed in the transfer of residential real estate.

**Instructions to Owner:** (1) Answer ALL questions. (2) Identify any material matters in the property that are actually known. (3) Attach additional pages with your signature if additional space is needed. (4) Complete this form yourself. (5) If some items do not apply to your property, write NA (not applicable). If the item to be disclosed is not within your actual knowledge, indicate Unknown.

### THE FOLLOWING STATEMENTS OF THE OWNER
### ARE BASED ON OWNER'S ACTUAL KNOWLEDGE

**A)**  **WATER SUPPLY:** The source of water supply to the property is (check appropriate boxes):
☐ Public Water Service     ☐ Private Water Service     ☐ Well          ☐ Holding Tank
☐ Cistern                  ☐ Spring                    ☐ Pond          ☐ Unknown
☐ Other _____

If owner knows of any current leaks, backups or other material problems with the water supply system or quality of the water, please describe:

_____
_____
_____

**B)**  **SEWER SYSTEM:** The nature of the sanitary sewer system servicing the property is (check appropriate boxes):
☐ Public Sewer        ☐ Private Sewer        ☐ Septic Tank        ☐ Leach Field
☐ Aeration Tank       ☐ Filtration Bed       ☐ Unknown
☐ Other _____

If not a public or private sewer, date of last inspection _____

If owner knows of any current leaks, backups or other material problems with the sewer system servicing the property, please describe:

_____
_____
_____

**C)**  **ROOF:** Do you know of any current leaks or other material problems with the roof or rain gutters?     ☐ Yes     ☐ No
If "YES", please describe: _____

If owner knows of any leaks or other material problems with the roof or rain gutters since owning the property (but not longer than the past 5 years) please describe and indicate any repairs completed: _____

_____
_____

**D)**  **BASEMENT/CRAWL SPACE:** Do you know of any current water leakage, water accumulation, excess dampness or other defects with the basement/crawl space?     ☐ Yes     ☐ No
If "YES", please describe: _____

If owner knows of any repairs, alterations or modifications to the property or other attempts to control any water or dampness problems in the basement or crawl space since owning the property (but not longer than the past 5 years) please describe: _____

_____
_____

**E)**  **STRUCTURAL COMPONENTS (FOUNDATION, FLOORS, INTERIOR AND EXTERIOR WALLS):** Do you know of any movement, shifting, deterioration, material cracks (other than visible minor cracks or blemishes) or other material problems with the foundation, floors, or interior/exterior walls?     ☐ Yes     ☐ No
If "YES", please describe: _____

If you know of any repairs, alterations or modifications to control the cause or effect of any problem identified above, since owning the property (but not longer than the past 5 years) please describe: _____

_____
_____

**Figure 7.3　Residential Property Disclosure Form (Continued)**

F)　**MECHANICAL SYSTEMS:** Do you know of any current problems or defects with the mechanical systems? ☐

　　If "YES", please describe: _____

　　_____
　　_____
　　_____

　　For purposes of this section, mechanical systems include electrical, plumbing (pipes), central heating and air conditioning, sump pump, fireplace/chimney, lawn sprinkler, water softener, security system, central vacuum, or other mechanical systems that exist on the property.

G)　**WOOD BORING INSECTS/TERMITES:** Do you know of the presence of any wood boring insects/termites in or on the property or any existing damage to the property caused by wood boring insects/termites? ☐ Yes ☐ No

　　If "YES", please describe: _____

　　If owner knows of any inspection or treatment for wood boring insects/termites, since owning the property (but not longer than the past 5 years) please describe: _____
　　_____
　　_____
　　_____

H)　**PRESENCE OF HAZARDOUS MATERIALS:** Do you have actual knowledge of the presence of any of the below identified hazardous materials on the property?

|  |  | YES | NO | UNKNOWN |
|---|---|---|---|---|
| 1) | Lead-Based Paint | ☐ | ☐ | ☐ |
| 2) | Asbestos | ☐ | ☐ | ☐ |
| 3) | Urea-Formaldehyde Foam Insulation | ☐ | ☐ | ☐ |
| 4) | Radon Gas | ☐ | ☐ | ☐ |
|  | 4a) If YES, indicate level of Gas if known _____ | | | |
| 5) | Other toxic substances _____ | ☐ | ☐ | ☐ |

　　If the answer to any of the above questions is "YES", please describe: _____
　　_____
　　_____

I)　**DRAINAGE:** Do you know of any current flooding, drainage, settling or grading problems affecting the property? ☐ Yes ☐ No

　　If "YES", please describe: _____

　　If owner knows of any repairs, modifications or alterations to the property or other attempts to control any flooding, drainage, settling or grading problems since owning the property (but not longer than the past 5 years) please describe: _____
　　_____
　　_____

J)　**CODE VIOLATIONS:** Have you received notice of any building or housing code violations currently affecting the use of the property? ☐ Yes ☐ No

　　If "YES", please describe: _____

K)　**UNDERGROUND STORAGE TANKS/WELLS:** Do you know of any underground storage tanks, oil or natural gas wells (plugged or unplugged), or abandoned water wells on the property? ☐ Yes ☐ No

　　If "YES", please describe: _____

L)　**OTHER KNOWN MATERIAL DEFECTS:** The following are other known material defects currently in or on the property: _____
　　_____
　　_____

　　For purposes of this section, material defects would include any non-observable physical condition existing on the property that could be dangerous to anyone occupying the property or any non-observable physical condition that would inhibit a person's use of the property.

Owner represents that the statements contained in this form are made in good faith based on his/her actual knowledge as of the date signed by the Owner.

OWNER: _____　　DATE: _____

OWNER: _____　　DATE: _____

### RECEIPT AND ACKNOWLEDGMENT OF POTENTIAL PURCHASERS

Potential purchasers are advised that the owner has no obligation to update this form but may do so according to Revised Code Section 5302.30(G). Pursuant to Ohio Revised Code Section 5302.30(K), if this form is not provided to you prior to the time you enter into a purchase contract for the property, you may rescind the purchase contract by delivering a signed and dated document of rescission to Owner or Owner's agent, provided the document of rescission is delivered prior to all three of the following dates: 1) the date of closing; 2) 30 days after the Owner accepted your offer; and 3) within 3 business days following your receipt or your agent's receipt of this form or an amendment of this form.

I/WE ACKNOWLEDGE RECEIPT OF A COPY OF THIS DISCLOSURE FORM AND UNDERSTAND THAT THE STATEMENTS ARE MADE BASED ON THE OWNER'S ACTUAL KNOWLEDGE AS OF THE DATE SIGNED BY THE OWNER.

My/Our Signature below does not constitute approval of any disclosed condition as represented herein by the owner.

PURCHASER: _____　　DATE: _____

PURCHASER: _____　　DATE: _____

- That the disclosure statement is not a warranty of any kind by the transferor, or by any agent or subagent representing the transferor, and that the representations made in it are made by the transferor and not by his or her agent or subagent
- That the disclosure statement is not a substitute for any inspections
- That the purchaser is encouraged to obtain his or her own professional inspection of the property
- That the form and the representations contained in it are provided exclusively to the prospective purchaser in the present transaction, and are not made to transferees in any subsequent transfers

A buyer has the right to rescind a sales contract after he or she receives the disclosure statement within three business days following the date on which the disclosure form was received. The rescission must be made by a date either within 30 days of the seller's acceptance of the buyer's offer or the date of closing, whichever is earlier. If the contract is rescinded, the buyer is entitled to the return of his or her earnest money deposit. The right of rescission may be waived, and there is no right of rescission where the potential purchaser received a disclosure form prior to making an offer on the property. ◆

## THE LISTING CONTRACT FORM

A wide variety of listing contract forms are available. Some brokers draft their own contracts, some use forms prepared by the Ohio Association of REALTORS®. Some brokers use a separate information sheet (also known as a *profile* or *data sheet*) for recording property features. That sheet is wed to a second form containing the contractual obligations between the seller and the broker: listing price, duration of the agreement, signatures of the parties, and so forth. Other brokers use a single form. A sample listing agreement appears in Figure 7.2.

**Listing Agreement Issues**

Regardless of which standard form of listing agreement is used, the same considerations arise in most real estate transactions. This means that all listing contracts tend to require similar information. However, licensees should review the specific forms used in their areas, and refer to their states' laws for any specific requirements. Some of the considerations covered in a typical contract are discussed in the following paragraphs.

**The type of listing agreement.** The contract may be an exclusive-right-to-sell listing (the most common type), an exclusive-agency listing, or an open listing. The type of listing agreement determines the extent of a broker's authority to act on the principal's behalf. Most MLSs do not permit open listings to be posted in the system.

**The broker's authority and responsibilities.** The contract should specify whether the broker may place a sign on the property and advertise and market the property. Another major consideration is whether the broker is permitted to authorize subagents or buyer's brokers through an MLS. Will the contract allow the broker to show the property at reasonable times and upon reasonable notice to the seller? May the broker accept earnest money deposits on behalf of the seller, and what are the broker's responsibilities in holding the funds? Without the written consent of the seller, the broker cannot undertake any of these or other important activities.

**The names of all parties to the contract.** Anyone who has an ownership interest in the property must be identified and should sign the listing to validate it. If the property is owned under one of the forms of concurrent ownership discussed in Chapter 9, that fact should be clearly established. If one or more of the owners is married, it is wise to obtain the spouse's consent and signature on the contract to release the appropriate marital rights. If the property is in the possession of a tenant, that should be disclosed (along with the terms of the tenancy), and instructions should be included on how the property is to be shown to a prospective buyer.

**The brokerage firm.** The brokerage company name, the employing broker and, if appropriate, the salesperson taking the listing all must be identified.

**The listing price.** This is the proposed gross sales price. The seller's proceeds will be reduced by unpaid real estate taxes, special assessments, mortgage and trust deed debts, and any other outstanding obligations.

**Real property and personal property.** Any personal property that will be left with the real estate when it is sold must be explicitly identified. Similarly, any items of real property that the seller expects to remove at the time of the sale must be specified as well. Some of these items may later become points of negotiation when a ready, willing, and able buyer is found for the property. Typical items to consider include major appliances, swimming pool and spa equipment, fireplace accessories, storage sheds, window treatments, stacked firewood, and stored heating oil.

**Leased equipment.** Will any leased equipment—security systems, cable television boxes, water softeners, special antennas—be left with the property? If so, the seller is responsible for notifying the equipment's lessor of the change of property ownership.

**The description of the premises.** In addition to the street address, the legal description, lot size, and tax parcel number may be required for future insertion into a purchase offer.

**The proposed dates for the closing and the buyer's possession.** These dates should be based on an anticipated sale date. The listing agreement should allow adequate time for the paperwork involved (including the buyer's qualification for any financing) and the physical moves to be arranged by the seller and the buyer.

**The closing.** Details of the closing—such as a closing attorney, title company, or escrow company—should be considered even at this early stage. Will the designated party complete the settlement statements and disburse the funds? Will he or she file the proper forms, such as documents to be recorded, documents to be sent to the Internal Revenue Service, and documents to be submitted for registering foreign owners?

**The evidence of ownership.** The most commonly used proofs of title are a warranty deed and either a title insurance policy or an abstract and legal opinion.

**Encumbrances.** Which liens will be paid in full at the closing by the seller and which liens will be assumed by the buyer?

**Homeowner warranty program.** In some situations, it may be advisable to offer a homeowner warranty with the property. If so, the listing contract should answer these questions: What items does the warranty cover? Is the seller willing to pay for it? If not, will it be available to the buyer at the buyer's expense? What are the deductibles?

**The commission.** The circumstances under which a commission will be paid must be specifically stated: Is payment earned only on the sale of the property, or on any transfer of interest created by the broker? Will it be a percentage or a flat fee? When will it be paid? Will it be paid directly by the seller or by the party handling the closing?

**The termination of the contract.** A contract should provide some way for the parties to end it. Under what circumstances will the contract terminate? Can the seller arbitrarily refuse to sell or cooperate with the listing broker?

**The broker protection clause.** As previously discussed, brokers may be well advised to protect their interests against possible fraud or a reluctant buyer's change of heart. Under what circumstances will the broker be entitled to a commission after the agreement terminates? How long will the clause remain in effect?

**Warranties by the owner.** The owner is responsible for certain assurances and disclosures that are vital to the agent's ability to market the property successfully. Is the property suitable for its intended purpose? Does it comply with the appropriate zoning and building codes? Will it be transferred to the buyer in essentially the same condition as it was originally presented, considering repairs or alterations to be made as provided for in a purchase contract? Are there any known defects?

**Indemnification (hold harmless) wording.** The seller and the broker may agree to hold each other harmless (that is, not to sue one another) for any incorrect information supplied by one to the other. Indemnification may be offered regardless of whether the inaccuracies are intentional or unintentional.

**Nondiscrimination (equal opportunity) wording.** The seller must understand that the property will be shown and offered without regard to the race, color, creed or religious preference, national origin, family status, sex, sexual orientation, age, or handicap of the prospective buyer. Refer to federal, state, and local fair housing laws for protected classes (see Chapter 22).

**Antitrust wording.** The contract should indicate that all commissions have been negotiated between the seller and the broker. It is illegal for commissions to be set by any regulatory agency, trade association, or other industry organization.

**The signatures of the parties.** All parties identified in the contract must sign it, including all individuals who have a legal interest in the property.

**The date the contract is signed.** This date may differ from the date the contract actually becomes effective, particularly if a salesperson takes the listing, then must have his or her broker sign the contract to accept employment under its terms.

---

**In Practice**     Anyone who takes a listing should use only the appropriate documents provided by the broker. Most brokers are conscientious enough to use only documents that have been carefully drafted or reviewed by an attorney so that their construction and legal language comply with the appropriate federal, state, and local laws. Such contracts should also give consideration to local customs, such as closing dates and the proration of income and expenses, with which most real estate attorneys are familiar.

---

## BUYER AGENCY AGREEMENTS

Like a listing agreement, a **buyer agency agreement** is an employment contract. In this case, however, the broker is employed as the *buyer's* agent. The buyer, rather than the seller, is the principal. The purpose of the agreement is to find a suitable property. An agency agreement gives the buyer a degree of representation possible only in a fiduciary relationship. A buyer's broker must protect the buyer's interests at all points in the transaction. A typical buyer agency agreement appears in Figure 7.4.

**Types of Buyer Agency Agreements**

Three basic types of buyer agency agreements exist.

1. *Exclusive buyer agency agreement*—This is a completely exclusive agency agreement. The buyer is legally bound to compensate the agent whenever the buyer purchases a property of the type described in the contract. The broker is entitled to payment regardless of whether he or she locates the property. Even if the buyer finds the property independently, the agent is entitled to payment.
2. *Exclusive-agency buyer agency agreement*—Like an exclusive buyer agency agreement, this is an exclusive contract between the buyer and the agent. However, this agreement limits the broker's right to payment. The broker is entitled to payment only if he or she locates the property the buyer ultimately purchases. The buyer is free to find a suitable property without obligation to pay the agent.
3. *Open buyer agency agreement*—This agreement is a nonexclusive agency contract between a broker and a buyer. It permits the buyer to enter into similar agreements with an unlimited number of brokers. The buyer is obligated to compensate only the broker who locates the property the buyer ultimately purchases.

**Buyer Representation Issues**

A number of issues must be discussed by a broker and a buyer before they sign a buyer agency agreement. For instance, the licensee should make the same disclosures to the buyer that the licensee would make in a listing agreement. The licensee should explain the forms of agency available and the parties' rights and responsibilities under each type. The specific services provided to a buyer-client should be clearly explained. Compensation issues need to be addressed, as well. Buyer's agents may be compensated in the form of a flat fee for services, an hourly rate, or a percentage of the purchase price. The agent may require a *retainer fee* at the time the agreement is signed to cover initial expenses. The retainer is applied as a credit toward any fees due at the closing.

---

### Figure 7.4   *Sample Exclusive Buyer Agency Agreement*

## EXCLUSIVE AGENCY AGREEMENT TO LOCATE REAL PROPERTY

EQUAL HOUSING
OPPORTUNITY

### AGENCY AGREEMENT

The undersigned client, _____, hereby retains the undersigned Broker, _____, for a period commencing _____, 19____, through midnight, _____, 19____, for the purpose of locating real property of a nature outlined below and to negotiate terms and conditions for the acquisition or use of such real property acceptable to Client.  This agreement may be extended with written authorization of both parties prior to the above termination date.

### 1. RETAINER FEE
The Agent, _____ acknowledges receipt of a retainer fee in the amount of _____, which shall be subtracted from any compensation due under this agreement. The retainer is non-refundable and is earned when paid.

### 2. AGENT'S DUTIES
Broker/Agent shall use professional real estate knowledge and skills to represent the buyer client in a diligent and effective manner and to locate property which is available for purchase and suitable to the buyer.  Services may include but are not limited to: A) Meeting with buyer to establish objectives, desired time schedule, financial status and the type of property they desire to purchase; B) Review information provided by clients to determine acquisition strategies; C) Schedule and show prospective properties; D) Meet with client to discuss properties of interest and evaluate the desirability of any house, lot or neighborhood in terms of land values, appreciation rates, rental rates, physical condition, room layouts, operating expenses, taxes and maintenance considerations and any other issues of concern; E) Assist in the development of a purchase offer; F) Present and negotiate purchase offers on behalf of Client.  Note: The Agent may represent other buyers that have similar interests.

### 3. BUYER'S DUTIES
The Buyer Client shall: A) Work exclusively with the Agent during the term of this agreement; B) Comply with the reasonable requests of the Agent to supply any pertinent financial or personal data needed to fulfill the terms of this agreement; C) Be available during Agent's regular working hours to view properties; D) Compensate the agent as set forth below.

### 4. COMPENSATION
The Buyer Client shall pay a brokerage fee (less the retainer) of : (Check One) _____ a fee of _____ % of the negotiated purchase price, or _____ a flat fee of $ _____. The agreed compensation shall be due and payable to Broker if Client purchases any property, as described below, whether through the services of the Agent or otherwise. Any brokerage fee paid to Broker, _____, by the listing company or seller shall be credited against the compensation due under this agreement.  This agreement shall also apply to any property presented or described to Buyer Client by the Agent during the term hereof when a contract is entered into within days after this agreement expires unless the Buyer enters into a subsequent "Exclusive Agency Agreement To Locate Real Property with another real estate broker, in which event no additional compensation shall be due under this agreement.  Any obligation to pay the brokerage fee incurred under this agreement survives termination of this agreement.

### 5. CONFLICTING INTERESTS
Client understands and agrees that if Client elects to purchase or offer to purchase a property already listed with Broker, _____, a conflict of interest will result from the Broker having an agency relationship with both the seller and the buyer.  The undersigned Buyer Client also understands and agrees that Broker, _____, the listing associate and the associate representing the buyer will seek to be released from both agency relationships and instead function as facilitators for the purpose of consummating the transaction between buyer and seller.  In this and similar circumstances, Buyer Client agrees to sign a Consent To Release From Agency Relationship and Client understands that Broker, _____, will not disclose any confidential information received from either the buyer or the seller to the other party; confidential information includes the possibility that the seller will accept a price less than the listed price or that the buyer will pay a price greater than that offered or any other information that could adversely affect either party's negotiating position.

---

SOURCE: Attorney Anthony J. Aveni, Painesvillle, Ohio.

**Figure 7.4    Sample Exclusive Buyer Agency Agreement (Continued)**

## 6. EQUAL OPPORTUNITY

Properties shall be shown and made available to the buyer without regard to race, color, religion, sex, handicap, familial status or national origin as well as all classes protected by the laws of The United States, The State of Ohio and local jurisdictions.

## 7. OTHER

_____
_____
_____
_____

## 8. DESCRIPTION OF DESIRED PROPERTY

_____
_____
_____
_____
_____
_____
_____
_____
_____
_____
_____

## 9. ENTIRE AGREEMENT

This agreement, any exhibits and any addenda signed by both parties consitute the entire aggreement between the parties and supersede any other written or oral agreements between the parties. This agreement can only be modified in writing when signed by both parties.

NOTE: The Buyer should consult with the Agent before visiting any resale or new homes or contacting any other real estate agents that represent sellers; to avoid the possibility of confusion over the agency relationship and misunderstandings about liability for compensation.

Receipt of a copy of this agreement is hereby acknowledged

_____          _____
Results Agent                              Client

                                           _____
                                           Client

_____, 19 ____                  _____, 19 ____
Date                                       Date

As in any agency agreement, the source of compensation is not the factor that determines the relationship. A buyer's agent may be compensated by either the buyer or the seller. Issues of compensation are always negotiable.

Because the agency contract employs the agent to represent the buyer and locate a suitable property, the licensee must obtain detailed financial information from the buyer. In addition, the buyer's agent needs information about the buyer's specific requirements for a suitable property.

**In Practice**    Buyer agency, like any other kind of real estate agency, is increasingly subject to detailed provisions of state law. If a state has adopted an agency statute, it is highly likely that the rights, duties, and obligations of buyers' agents are specifically established.

## KEY TERMS

| | | |
|---|---|---|
| buyer agency agreement | exclusive right-to-sell listing | net listing |
| competitive market analysis (CMA) | listing agreement | open listing |
| disclosure | market value | option listing |
| exclusive-agency listing | multiple-listing clause | property disclosure |
| | multiple-listing service (MLS) | |

## SUMMARY

- To acquire an inventory of property to sell, brokers must obtain listings. Types of listings include:
  - exclusive-right-to-sell,
  - exclusive-agency,
  - and open listings.
- With an exclusive-right-to-sell listing, the seller employs only one broker and must pay that broker a commission regardless of whether it is the broker or the seller who finds a buyer, provided the buyer is found within the listing period.
- Under an exclusive-agency listing, the broker is given the exclusive right to represent the seller, but the seller can avoid paying the broker a commission by selling the property to someone not procured by the broker.
- With an open listing, the broker must find a ready, willing, and able buyer on the seller's terms before the property is sold by the seller or another broker to obtain a commission.
- A multiple-listing provision may appear in an exclusive-right-to-sell or an exclusive-agency listing. It gives the broker the additional authority and obligation to distribute the listing to other members of the broker's multiple-listing organization.
- A net listing, which is unethical in most areas, is based on the net price the seller will receive if the property is sold. The broker is free to offer the property for sale at the highest available price and will receive as commission any amount exceeding the seller's stipulated net.
- An option listing, which also must be handled with caution, gives the broker the option to purchase the listed property.

- A listing agreement may be terminated for the same reasons as any other agency relationship. All listings must have a definite termination date.
- Preprinted listing forms typically include such information as the type of listing agreement, the broker's authority and responsibility under the listing, the listing price, the duration of the listing, information about the property, terms for the payment of commission (including antitrust concerns and encumbrances) and the buyer's possession, and nondiscrimination laws.
  - Detailed information about the property may be included in the listing contract or on a separate property data sheet.
  - Disclosure of the broker's law of agency relationship and discussion of the broker's agency policies have become the focus of laws in many states.
  - The seller also may be expected to comply with mandatory disclosure of property conditions.
- A buyer agency agreement assures a buyer that his or her interests will be represented.
  - A buyer's broker is obligated to find a suitable property for the client, who is owed the traditional fiduciary duties.
  - Buyer agency may be regulated by state agency laws.

---

**Real-Life Real Estate**

1. As a potential listing agent, how will you persuade the property owner to engage in an exclusive-right-to-sell agreement when the other types of listings give the seller more freedom?
2. Why would an agent ever consider anything other than an exclusive-right-to-sell listing?
3. What are the main reasons for buyer representation?

Application #1: Obtain a copy of the listing agreement used by brokers in your area. Assume Sam and Sally Seller are relocating to Denver due to a job transfer. Complete the listing agreement using property information given to you by your instructor or based on a property you have access to, or create the property from your imagination.

# QUESTIONS

1. A listing taken by a real estate salesperson is an agreement between the seller and the
   a. broker.
   b. local multiple-listing service.
   c. salesperson.
   d. salesperson and broker together.

2. Which of the following is a similarity between an exclusive-agency listing and an exclusive-right-to-sell listing?
   a. Under both, the seller retains the right to sell the real estate without the broker's help and without paying the broker a commission.
   b. Under both, the seller authorizes only one particular salesperson to show the property.
   c. Both types of listings give the responsibility of representing the seller to one broker only.
   d. Both types of listings are open listings.

3. The listing agreement between broker *B* and seller *T* states that it expires May 2. All of the following events would terminate the listing *EXCEPT*
   a. the agreement is not renewed prior to May 2.
   b. B dies on April 29.
   c. on April 15, *T* tells *B* that *T* is dissatisfied with *B*'s marketing efforts.
   d. *T*'s house is destroyed by fire on April 25.

4. The seller has listed his property under an exclusive-agency listing with the broker. If the seller sells the property himself during the term of the listing to someone introduced to the property by the seller, he will owe the broker
   a. no commission.
   b. the full commission.
   c. a partial commission.
   d. only reimbursement for the broker's costs.

5. A broker sold a residence for $85,000 and received $5,950 as her commission in accordance with the terms of the listing. What was the broker's commission rate?
   a. 6 percent
   b. 7 percent
   c. 7.25 percent
   d. 7.5 percent

6. Under a listing agreement, the broker is entitled to sell the property for any price, as long as the seller receives $85,000. The broker may keep any amount over $85,000 as a commission. This type of listing is called a(n)
   a. exclusive-right-to-sell listing.
   b. exclusive-agency listing.
   c. open listing.
   d. net listing.

7. Which of the following is a similarity between an open listing and an exclusive-agency listing?
   a. Under both the seller avoids paying the broker a commission if the seller sells the property to someone the broker did not procure.
   b. Both grant a commission to any broker who procures a buyer for the seller's property.
   c. Under both the broker earns a commission regardless of who sells the property as long as it is sold within the listing period.
   d. Both grant an exclusive-right-to-sell to whatever broker procures a buyer for the seller's property.

8. The listed price for a property should be determined by
   a. the local MLS.
   b. the appraised value.
   c. the seller.
   d. the broker's CMA.

9. Which of the following statements is true of a listing contract?
   a. It is an employment contract for the personal and professional services of the broker.
   b. It obligates the seller to convey the property if the broker procures a ready, willing, and able buyer.
   c. It obligates the broker to work diligently for both the seller and the buyer.
   d. It automatically binds the owner, broker, and MLS to the agreed provisions.

10. *J*, a real estate broker, sold a property and received a 6½ percent commission. *J* gave the listing salesperson 30 percent of the commission, or $3,575. What was the selling price of the property?
    a. $55,000
    b. $95,775
    c. $152,580
    d. $183,333

11. A seller hired broker *N* under the terms of an open listing. While that listing was still in effect, the seller—without informing broker *N*—hired broker *F* under an exclusive-right-to-sell listing for the same property. If broker *N* produces a buyer for the property whose offer the seller accepts, then the seller must pay a
    a. full commission only to broker *N*.
    b. full commission only to broker *F*.
    c. full commission to both broker *N* and Broker *F*.
    d. half commission to both broker *N* and broker *F*.

12. Seller *G* listed her residence with broker *D*. Broker *D* brought an offer at full price and terms of the listing from buyers who are ready, willing, and able to pay cash for the property. However, seller *G* changed her mind and rejected the buyers' offer. In this situation seller *G*
    a. must sell her property.
    b. owes a commission to broker *D*.
    c. is liable to the buyers for specific performance.
    d. is liable to the buyers for compensatory damages.

13. Which of the following is true of an an open buyer agency agreement?
    a. The buyer may enter into agreements with multiple brokers and is obligated to pay only the broker who locates the property that the buyer ultimately purchases.
    b. While the buyer may enter into agreements with multiple brokers, he or she is under no obligation to pay the broker; the seller bears all brokerage expenses.
    c. Because multiple brokers may be involved, an open buyer agency agreement involves reduced fiduciary duties.
    d. The buyer may not look for or make offers on properties on his or her own.

14. Broker *N* and Buyer *B* enter into an exclusive-agency buyer agency agreement. This means
    a. *B* is obligated to compensate *N*, regardless of who locates the property ultimately purchased.
    b. *N* is entitled to payment only if *N*, or any broker acting under *N*'s authority, locates the property *B* ultimately purchases.
    c. *B* may enter into similar agreements with any number of other brokers.
    d. If *B* finds the property without any help from *N*, *B* must pay *N* a reduced compensation.

15. A competitive market analysis
    a. is the same as an appraisal.
    b. can help the seller price the property.
    c. by law must be completed for each listing taken.
    d. should not be retained in the property's listing file.

16. A property was listed with a broker who belonged to a multiple-listing service and was sold by another member broker for $53,500. The total commission was 6 percent of the sales price. The selling broker received 60 percent of the commission, and the listing broker received the balance. What was the listing broker's commission?
    a. $1,284
    b. $1,464
    c. $1,926
    d. $2,142

17. *S* signs a listing agreement with broker *K* to sell *S*'s home. The agreement states that *K* will receive a 7 percent commission. The home sells for $120,000. What is the net amount that *S* will receive from the sale?
    a. $36,000          c. $111,600
    b. $102,877         d. $120,000

18. A real estate broker and a seller enter into a listing agreement that contains the following language: "Seller will receive $100,000 from the sale of the subject property. Any amount greater than $100,000 will constitute Broker's sole and complete compensation." Which of the following statements is true regarding this agreement?
    a. This agreement is an example of an option listing.
    b. If the seller's home sells for exactly $100,000, the broker still will be entitled to receive the standard commission in the area.
    c. The broker may offer the property for any price over $100,000, but the agreement may be illegal.
    d. This type of listing is known as an open listing, because the selling price is left open.

19. All of the following would permit a listing agreement to be terminated *EXCEPT*
    a. destruction of the listed property.
    b. seller dissatisfaction with the wording of a newspaper advertisement.
    c. seller refusal to permit showings of the property during any time other than 6:00 AM to 7:30 AM.
    d. a breach by the broker.

20. Broker *G* enters into an agreement with a client. The agreement states: "In return for the compensation agreed upon, Broker will assist Client in locating and purchasing a suitable property. Broker will receive the agreed compensation regardless of whether Broker, Client, or some other party locates the property ultimately purchased by Client." What kind of agreement is this?
    a. Exclusive agency listing
    b. Exclusive-agency buyer agency agreement
    c. Exclusive buyer agency agreement
    d. Open buyer agency agreement

# CHAPTER 8

# Interests in Real Estate

## LIMITATIONS ON THE RIGHTS OF OWNERSHIP

As discussed in Chapter 2, an extensive bundle of legal rights goes along with owning real estate. However, many different interests in real estate can be acquired, and not all of them convey the entire bundle of legal rights to the owner. Licensees must take great care to ensure that prospective buyers understand exactly what interests a seller wishes to transfer.

Furthermore, ownership of real estate is not absolute. That is, a landowner's power to control his or her property is subject to other interests. Even the most complete ownership the law allows is limited by public and private restrictions. These are intended to ensure that one owner's use or enjoyment of his or her property does not interfere with others' use or enjoyment of their property or with the general welfare. Licensees should have a working knowledge of the restrictions that might limit current or future owners. A zoning ordinance that will not allow a physician's office to coexist with a residence, a condo association bylaw prohibiting resale without board approval, or an easement allowing the neighbors to use the private beach may not only burden today's purchaser but also deter a future buyer.

This chapter puts the various interests in real estate in perspective—what rights they confer and how use of the ownership may be limited.

## ESTATES IN LAND

An **estate in land** defines the degree, quantity, nature, and extent of an owner's interest in real property. Many types of estates exist. However, not all interests in real estate are *estates*. To be an estate in land, an interest must allow possession (either now or in the future) and must be measurable by duration. Lesser interests such as easements (discussed later in this chapter), which allow use but not possession, are not estates.

**F**OR EXAMPLE  *B* owns a movie theater. *B*'s ownership interest is an *estate* because *B* has the right to all the income from the theatre, the right to change the theater into a restaurant, the right to tear down the theater and build something else on the land,

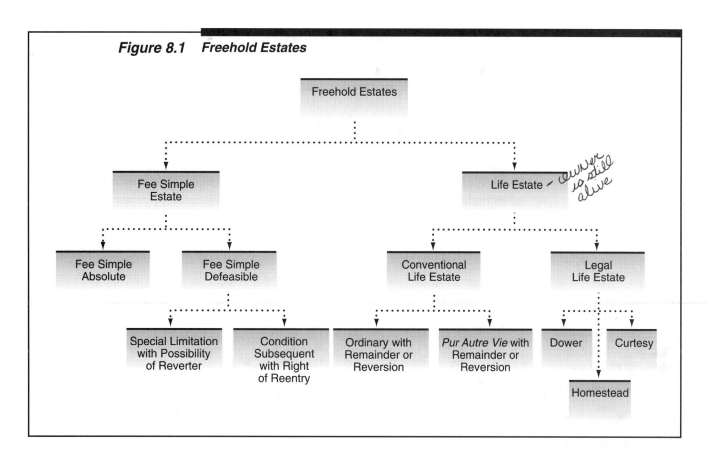

**Figure 8.1   Freehold Estates**

and the right to sell the theater to someone else—in short, the theater belongs to *B*. When *M* buys a ticket and sits down to watch a movie in *B*'s theater, *M* has an *interest* in the property, but it is *not* an estate. *M*'s interest is limited to the temporary use of a limited part of the theater.

Historically, estates in land have been classified as *freehold estates* and *leasehold estates*. The two types of estates are distinguished primarily by their duration.

**Freehold estates** last for an *indeterminable length of time*, such as for a lifetime or forever. They include fee simple (also called an *indefeasible fee*), defeasible fee, and life estates. The first two of these estates continue for an indefinite period and may be passed along to the owner's heirs. A life estate is based on the lifetime of a person and ends when that individual dies. Freehold estates are illustrated in Figure 8.1.

**Leasehold estates** last for a *fixed period of time*. They include estates for years and estates from period to period. Estates at will and estates at sufferance are also leaseholds, though by their operation they are not generally viewed as being for fixed terms. Leaseholds are discussed in Chapter 17, "Leases."

**Fee Simple Estate**

An estate in **fee simple** (or **fee simple absolute**) is the *highest interest in real estate recognized by law*. Fee simple ownership is absolute ownership: the holder is entitled to all rights to the property. It is limited only by public and private restrictions, such as zoning laws and restrictive covenants (discussed in Chapter 20). Because this estate is of unlimited duration, it is said to *run forever*. Upon the death of its owner, it passes to the owner's heirs or as provided by will. A fee simple estate is also referred to as an *estate of inheritance* or simply as *fee ownership*.

**Fee simple defeasible.** A **fee simple defeasible** (or *defeasible fee*) estate is a qualified estate—that is, it is subject to the occurrence or nonoccurrence of some specified event. Two types of defeasible estates exist: those subject to a condition subsequent and those qualified by a special limitation.

A fee simple estate may be qualified by a condition *subsequent*. This means that the new owner must *not* perform some action or activity. The former owner retains a *right of reentry* so that if the condition is broken, the former owner can retake possession of the property through legal action. Conditions in a deed are different from restrictions or covenants because of the grantor's right to reclaim ownership, a right that does not exist under private restrictions.

**F**OR EXAMPLE   A grant of land "on the condition that" there be no consumption of alcohol on the premises is a fee simple subject to a condition subsequent. If alcohol is consumed on the property, the former owner has the right to reacquire full ownership. It will be necessary, however, for the grantor (or the grantor's heirs or successors) to go to court to assert that right.

A fee simple estate also may be qualified by a *special limitation*. The estate ends *automatically* on the current owner's failure to comply with the limitation. The former owner retains a *possibility of reverter*. If the limitation is violated, the former owner (or his or her heirs or successors) reacquires full ownership, with no need to reenter the land or go to court. A fee simple with a special limitation is also called a **fee simple determinable** because it may end automatically. The language used to distinguish a special limitation—the words *so long as* or *while* or *during*—is the key to creating this estate.

The *right of entry* and *possibility of reverter* may never take effect. If they do, it will be only at some time in the future. Therefore, both of these rights are considered **future interests.**

**F**OR EXAMPLE   A grant of land from an owner to her church "so long as the land is used only for religious purposes" is a fee simple with a special limitation. If the church ever decides to use the land for a nonreligious purpose, title will revert to the previous owner (or her heirs or successors).

> Fee simple defeasible: "on the condition that"
>
> Fee simple determinable:
>
> "so long as"
>
> "while"
>
> "during"

## Life Estate

A *life estate* is a freehold estate *limited in duration to the life of the owner or the life of some other designated person or persons.*

**F**OR EXAMPLE   Brown, an elderly man, has a fee simple estate in his home and the surrounding acreage. Brown sells his property to a developer, Acme, but keeps a life estate for himself. As long as Brown is alive, he can live in his home and enjoy the surrounding property. However, once Brown dies the ownership of the property passes to the developer. In this way, Brown is assured of a home for as long as he lives.

There are two kinds of life estates: conventional life estates and legal life estates.

**Conventional life estate.** A **conventional life estate** is created by a property owner, either by deed or will. The owner of the life estate is called the *life tenant.* The life tenant has full enjoyment of the ownership for the duration of the life estate. However, when the life estate terminates, the ownership passes to a designated third party or returns to the previous owner. A life estate that is based on the life of the life tenant cannot be inherited.

**F**OR EXAMPLE  *A, who has a fee simple estate in Blackacre, conveys a life estate to P for P's lifetime. P is the life tenant. On P's death, the life estate terminates, and A once again owns Blackacre.*

A life estate also may be based on the lifetime of a person other than the life tenant. This is known as an **estate pur autre vie** ("for the life of another"). When a life estate is based on the life of someone other than the life tenant, it may be inherited. However, the estate that is inherited is limited in duration. Once the person on whom the life estate is based dies, the life estate is terminated.

A life estate pur autre vie is often created for a physically or mentally incapacitated person in the hope of providing an incentive for someone to care for him or her.

**F**OR EXAMPLE  *Anne conveys a life estate in Blackacre to Paula as the life tenant for the duration of the life of David, Anne's elderly relative. In return for the life estate, Paula is to care for David. Paula owns the life tenant, but the measuring life is David's. Upon David's death, the life estate ends. If Paula should die while David is still alive, Paula's heirs may inherit the life estate. However, when David dies, the heirs' estate ends.*

A life tenant is entitled to the rights of ownership. That is, the life tenant can enjoy both possession and the ordinary use and profits arising from ownership, just as if the individual were a fee owner. The ownership may be sold, mortgaged, or leased, but it is always subject to the limitation of the life estate.

A life tenant's ownership rights, however, are not absolute. The life tenant may not injure the property, such as by destroying a building or allowing it to deteriorate. In legal terms, this injury is known as waste. Those who will eventually own the property could seek an injunction against the life tenant or sue for damages.

Because the ownership will terminate on the death of the person against whose life the estate is measured, a purchaser, lessee, or lender can be affected. The life tenant can sell, lease, or mortgage only his or her interest— that is, ownership for a lifetime. Because the interest is obviously less desirable than a fee simple estate, the life tenant's rights are limited.

**Remainder and reversion.** The fee simple owner who creates a conventional life estate must plan for its future ownership. When the life estate ends, it is replaced by a fee simple estate. The future owner of the fee simple estate may be designated in one of two ways:

1. **Remainder interest:** The creator of the life estate may name a *remainderman* as the person to whom the property will pass when the life estate ends. (*Remainderman* is the legal term; neither the term *remainderperson* or *remainderwoman* is used.) (See Figure 8.2.)
2. **Reversionary interest:** The creator of the life estate may choose not to name a remainderman. In that case, the creator will recapture ownership when the life estate ends. The ownership is said to revert to the original owner. (See Figure 8.3.)

**F**OR EXAMPLE  *A conveys Blackacre to P for P's lifetime and designates R to be the remainderman. While P is still alive, R owns a remainder interest, which is a nonpossessory estate; that is, R does not possess the property, but has an interest in it*

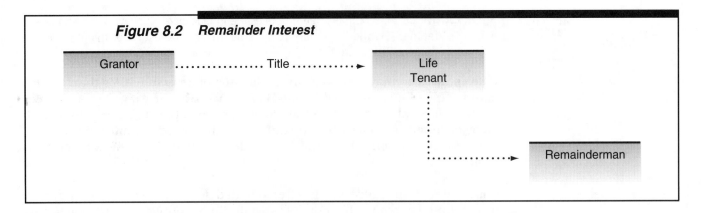

**Figure 8.2    Remainder Interest**

nonetheless. This is a *future interest* in the fee simple estate. When *P* dies, *R* automatically becomes the fee simple owner.

On the other hand, *A* may convey a life estate in Blackacre to *P* during *P*'s life. Upon *P*'s death, ownership of Blackacre reverts to *A*. *A* has retained a *reversionary* interest (also a nonpossessory estate). *A* has a *future interest* in the ownership and may reclaim the fee simple estate when *P* dies. If *A* dies before *P*, *A*'s heirs (or other individuals specified in *A*'s will) will assume ownership of Blackacre when *P* dies.

**Legal life estate.** The second type of life estate is a legal life estate. A *legal life estate* is not created voluntarily by an owner. Rather, it is a form of life estate established by state law. It becomes effective automatically when certain events occur. *Dower, curtesy* and *homestead* are the legal life estates currently used in some states.

In Ohio...     **Dower.** In Ohio, dower is the life estate that a wife or husband has in the real estate of the deceased spouse. In other states a husband's life estate in the real estate of his deceased wife is called *curtesy*. (Ohio does not recognize curtesy.)

Dower rights apply to all the real property owned by a married couple in Ohio, regardless of how or when the property came to be owned. (For instance, if the property was purchased by one spouse before the marriage, dower rights still apply to that property during the marriage.) A dower interest usually means that on the death of the owning spouse, the surviving spouse has a right to at least a one-third interest in the real property for the rest of his or her life. The purpose of dower is to give the surviving spouse a means of support when the other spouse dies. The surviving spouse has a right to demand and receive at least a one-third life estate in the real property, or its equivalent, even if the deceased spouse wills the real estate to others. (See Chapter 13.) ◆

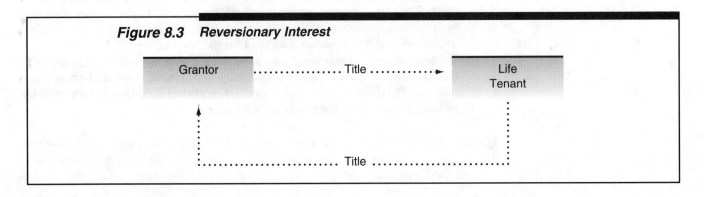

**Figure 8.3    Reversionary Interest**

**In Practice**

**In Ohio...**

Dower rights are extremely limited by Ohio law. If the property was owned at the time of death, the usual dower right of a surviving spouse terminates on the death of the spouse who was the owner of the real estate. The surviving spouse then inherits as an heir, in lieu of the expired dower. (See Chapter 13 regarding heirs.)

In Ohio, a spouse must join in the execution of a deed or mortgage by the owning spouse to a third party to release dower rights. If, during the lifetime of the owning spouse, the owner conveyed, mortgaged, or otherwise encumbered the real estate without the release of dower by the owner's spouse, upon the death of the owning spouse the surviving spouse will have dower. That is, the surviving spouse will have a life estate in one-third of the real estate. Statutory provisions are made for determining the dollar amount of the dower interest so that it may be settled from the proceeds of the sale of the real estate.

In Ohio, one spouse cannot convey his or her dower rights to the other spouse. Likewise, a spouse cannot convey dower to a third party unless the other spouse conveys the title to that third party. ◆

Generally the right of dower becomes effective only on the death of a spouse. During the lifetimes of the parties the dower right is *inchoate*, or incomplete—merely the possibility of an interest. For this reason the right of dower cannot be assigned or transferred to another party, and the owning spouse cannot cancel the right by selling the property. On the death of the owning spouse, the dower right becomes *consummate* (complete).

Dower interest is terminated by a divorce, whether in favor of or against a spouse. (In Chapter 9, see survivorship deed exception.)

**In Ohio...**    **Homestead exemptions.**  In Ohio, a husband and wife living together or a widow or a widower living with an unmarried daughter or unmarried minor son may hold a family homestead. A homestead is exempt from sale by judgment creditors for an amount not exceeding $5,000. Homestead means the home of the family, and the homestead must, in fact, be used and occupied as a home.

The right to the homestead exemption may be lost by failure to assert or claim it prior to the holding of a judicial sale to satisfy the claim of a judgment creditor. The homestead exemption also is waived if both husband and wife sign a mortgage in favor of a mortgagee.

Homeowners aged 65 years or older may apply for a *special homestead exemption* consisting of a reduction in the assessed valuation of the homestead for general real estate tax. This exemption is restricted to homeowners with limited total incomes. The homestead exemption applies to mobile homes, as well. ◆

**Fee Tail Estate**    A **fee tail estate** is recognized in Ohio. It is an estate that, instead of descending to the heirs as fee simple does, is limited to the "issue of the body" of the recipient—that is, the recipient's biological children. Fee tail is complicated, and the power of the owner to convey it is restricted. Questions regarding fee tail estate should be referred to legal counsel. ◆

**In Ohio...**

**F**OR EXAMPLE  D conveys Happy Acres "to B and the heirs of his body." While B is alive, he holds an estate tail, and upon B's death, the estate passes only to his biological daughter, not to his adopted son. However, *B*'s daughter inherits a fee simple estate without limitation. She may leave it to her natural and adoptive children alike.

# ENCUMBRANCES

An **encumbrance** is a claim, charge, or liability that attaches to real estate. Simply put, it is a right or an interest held by someone other than the fee owner of the property that affects title to real estate. An encumbrance may lessen the value or obstruct the use of the property, but it does not necessarily prevent a transfer of title.

Encumbrances may be divided into two general classifications:

1. *Liens* (usually monetary charges) and
2. *Encumbrances* such as restrictions, easements, and encroachments that affect the condition or use of the property.

## Liens

*A* **lien** *is a charge against property that provides security for a debt or an obligation of the property owner.* If the obligation is not repaid, the lienholder is entitled to have the debt satisfied from the proceeds of a court-ordered or forced sale of the debtor's property. Real estate taxes, mortgages and trust deeds, judgments, and mechanics' liens all represent possible liens against an owner's real estate. Liens are discussed in detail in Chapter 11.

## Restrictions

**Deed restrictions,** also referred to as *covenants, conditions, and restrictions, or CC&Rs,* are private agreements that affect the use of land. They may be imposed by an owner of real estate and included in the seller's deed to the buyer. Typically, however, restrictive covenants are imposed by a developer or subdivider to maintain specific standards in a subdivision. Such restrictive covenants are listed in the original development plans for the subdivision filed in the public record. Deed restrictions are discussed further in Chapter 20.

## Easements

*An* **easement** *is the right to use the land of another for a particular purpose.* An easement may exist in any portion of the real estate, including the airspace above or a right-of-way across the land.

An **appurtenant easement** is annexed to the ownership of one parcel and allows this owner the use of a neighbor's land. For an appurtenant easement to exist, two adjacent parcels of land must be owned by two different parties. The parcel over which the easement runs is known as the *servient tenement;* the neighboring parcel that benefits is known as the *dominant tenement.* (See Figures 8.4 and 8.5.)

An appurtenant easement is part of the dominant tenement, and if the dominant tenement is conveyed to another party, the easement transfers with the title. This type of easement is said to *run with the land.* It is an encumbrance on property and will transfer with the deed of the dominant tenement forever unless the holder of the dominant tenement somehow releases that right.

**FOR EXAMPLE** *K* and *L* own adjoining parcels of land near a lake. *K*'s property borders the lake, and *L*'s does not. *K* grants *L* an easement, established by a deed properly delivered and accepted. The easement gives *L* the right to cross *K*'s property to reach the lake. This is an easement appurtenant. When *K* sells the lakefront property to *M*, the easement is automatically included, even if *K*'s deed fails to mention it. *L*'s easement has become a limitation on the ownership rights of *K*'s land.

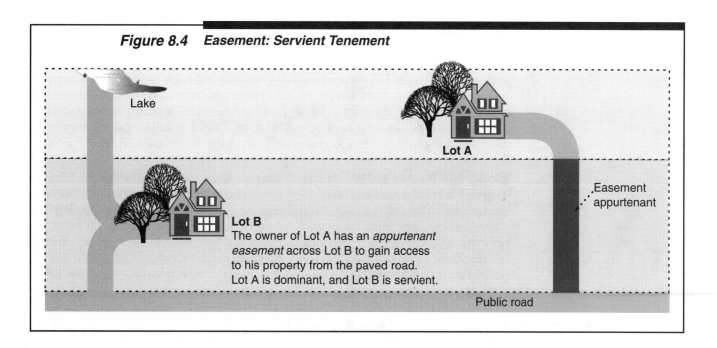

**Figure 8.4   Easement: Servient Tenement**

Lake

Lot A

Easement
appurtenant

**Lot B**
The owner of Lot A has an *appurtenant
easement* across Lot B to gain access
to his property from the paved road.
Lot A is dominant, and Lot B is servient.

Public road

**Creating an easement.** An easement is commonly created by a written agreement between the parties that establishes the easement right. It also may be created by the grantor in a deed of conveyance, where the grantor either *reserves* an easement over the sold land or *grants* the new owner an easement over the grantor's remaining land. An easement may be created by longtime *usage,* as in an easement by prescription; by necessity; and by implication (that is, the situation or the parties' actions *imply* that they intend to create an easement).

The creation of an easement always involves two separate parties, one of whom is the owner of the land over which the easement runs. It is impossible for the owner of a parcel of property to have an easement over his or her own land.

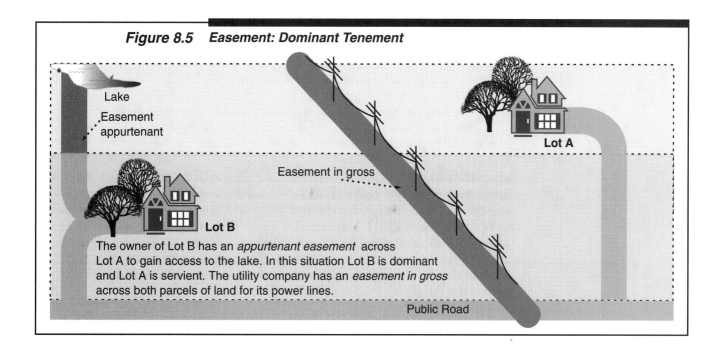

**Figure 8.5   Easement: Dominant Tenement**

Lake
Easement
appurtenant

Lot A

Easement in gross

**Lot B**
The owner of Lot B has an *appurtenant easement* across
Lot A to gain access to the lake. In this situation Lot B is dominant
and Lot A is servient. The utility company has an *easement in gross*
across both parcels of land for its power lines.

Public Road

**Party wall easement.**  A party wall can be an exterior wall of a building that straddles the boundary line between two lots or it can be a commonly shared partition wall between two connected properties. Each lot owner owns the half of the wall on his or her lot, and each has an appurtenant easement in the other half of the wall. A written party wall agreement must be used to create the easement rights. Expenses to build and maintain the wall are usually shared. A party driveway shared by and partly on the land of adjoining owners must also be created by written agreement, specifying responsibility for expenses.

**Easement by necessity.**  An appurtenant easement that arises when an owner sells part of his or her land that has no access to a street or public way except over the seller's remaining land is an **easement by necessity.** An easement by necessity is created by court order. Such an easement arises because all owners have the right to enter and exit their land—they cannot be landlocked. Remember, this form of easement is called an *easement by necessity;* it is not merely for convenience and is not imposed simply to validate a shortcut.

**In Ohio...**

*Test*

**Easement by prescription.**  When the claimant has made use of another's land for a certain period of time, as defined by state law, an **easement by prescription,** or a *prescriptive easement,* may be acquired. The prescriptive period in Ohio is 21 years. The claimant's use must have been continuous, exclusive, and without the owner's approval. The use must be visible, open, and notorious; that is, the owner must have been able to learn of it. ◆

The concept of *tacking* provides that successive periods of continuous occupation by different parties may be combined (tacked) to reach the required total number of years necessary to establish a claim for a prescriptive easement. To tack on one person's possession to that of another, the parties must have been *successors in interest,* such as an ancestor and his or her heir, a landlord and tenant, or a seller and buyer.

**F**OR EXAMPLE  *J*'s property is located in Ohio, where the prescriptive period is 21 years. For the past 22 years, *F* has driven his car across *J*'s front yard several times a day to reach his garage from a more comfortable angle. *F* has an easement by prescription.

For 25 years, *L* has driven across *J*'s front yard two or three times a year to reach her property when she's in a hurry. She does not have an easement by prescription because her use was not continuous.

For 15 years, *E* parked his car on *J*'s property, next to *J*'s garage. Six years ago, *E* sold his house to *N*, who also parked his car next to *J*'s garage. Last year, *N* acquired an easement by prescription through tacking.

*Test*

**Easement in gross.**  An **easement in gross** is an *individual* interest in or right to use someone else's land. For instance, a railroad's right-of-way is an easement in gross. So is the right-of-way for a pipeline or high-tension power line (utility easements). Commercial easements in gross may be assigned, conveyed, and inherited. However, personal easements in gross usually are not assignable. Generally, a personal easement in gross terminates on the death of the easement owner. An easement in gross is often confused with the similar personal right of license, discussed later in this chapter.

**Easement by condemnation.**  An **easement by condemnation** is acquired for a public purpose through the right of eminent domain. The owner of the servient tenement must be compensated for any loss in property value.

**Terminating an easement.**  An easement may be ended

- when the purpose for which the easement was created no longer exists;
- when the owner of either the dominant or the servient tenement becomes the owner of both—the properties are merged under one legal description (also known as *termination by merger*);
- by release of the right of easement to the owner of the servient tenement;
- by abandonment of the easement (the intention of the parties is the determining factor);
- by nonuse of a prescriptive easement;
- by adverse possession by the owner of the servient tenement;
- by destruction of the servient tenement, for instance, the demolition of a party wall;
- by lawsuit (an *action to quiet title*) against someone claiming an easement; or
- by excessive use, as when a residential use is converted to a commercial purpose.

Note that an easement may not *automatically* terminate for these reasons. Certain legal steps may be required.

**Licenses**   A **license** is a personal privilege to enter the land of another for a specific purpose. A license differs from an easement in that *it can be terminated or canceled by the licensor* (the person who granted the license). If a right to use another's property is given orally or informally, it generally is considered to be a license rather than a personal easement in gross. A license ends on the death of either party or the sale of the land by the licensor.

> ┌─────────────────────┐
> │ **Physical**
> │ **Encumbrances**
> │
> │ • Restrictions
> │ • Easements
> │ • Licenses
> │ • Encroachments
> └─────────────────────┘

**F**OR EXAMPLE   *P* asks *H* for permission to park a boat in *H*'s driveway. *H* says, "Sure, go ahead!" *P* has a license, but *H* may tell *P* to move the boat at any time. Similarly, a ticket to a theater or sporting event is a license: the holder is permitted to enter the facility and is entitled to a seat. But if the ticketholder becomes rowdy or abusive, he or she may be asked to leave.

**Encroachments**   An **encroachment** occurs when all or part of a structure (such as a building, fence, or driveway) illegally *extends beyond the land of its owner or beyond the*
**In Ohio...**   *legal building lines.* An encroachment usually is disclosed by either a physical inspection of the property or a spot survey. A spot survey shows the location of all improvements located on a property and whether they extend over the lot or building lines. As a rule, a spot survey is more accurate and reliable than a simple physical inspection. If a building encroaches on adjoining land, the neighbor may be able to either recover damages or secure removal of the portion of the building that encroaches. Encroachments that exceed Ohio's prescriptive period of 21 years, however, may give rise to easements by prescription. ◆

**In Practice**        Because an undisclosed encroachment could make a title unmarketable, an encroachment should be noted in a listing agreement and the sales contract. An encroachment is not disclosed by the usual title evidence provided in a real estate sale unless a survey is submitted while the title examination is being made.

# GOVERNMENT POWERS

Individual ownership rights are subject to certain powers, or rights, held by federal, state, and local governments. These limitations on the ownership of real estate are imposed for the general welfare of the community and, therefore, supersede the rights or interests of the individual. Government powers include the police power, the right of eminent domain, the power of taxation, and escheat.

## Police Power

Every state has the power to enact legislation to preserve order, protect the public health and safety, and promote the general welfare of its citizens. That authority is known as a state's **police power.** The state's authority is passed on to municipalities and counties through legislation called *enabling acts.*

---

**MEMORY TIP**

The four government powers can be remembered as PETE: *P*olice, *E*minent domain, *T*axation and *E*scheat.

---

Of course, what is identified as being "in the public interest" varies widely from state to state and region to region. Generally, however, a state's police power is used to enact environmental protection laws, zoning ordinances, and building codes. Regulations that govern the use, occupancy, size, location, and construction of real estate also fall within the police powers of a state. Police powers may be used to achieve a community's needs or goals. A city that deems growth to be desirable, for instance, may exercise its police powers to enact laws encouraging the purchase and improvement of land. On the other hand, an area that wishes to retain its current character may enact laws that discourage development and population growth.

Like the rights of ownership, the states' power to regulate land use is not absolute. The laws must be uniform and nondiscriminatory; that is, they may not operate to the advantage or disadvantage of any one particular owner or group of owners.

## Eminent Domain

**Eminent domain** is the right of the government to acquire privately owned real estate for public use. **Condemnation** is the process by which the government exercises this right, by either judicial or administrative proceedings. The proposed use must be for the public good, just compensation must be paid to the owner, and the rights of the property owner must be protected by due process of law. Public use has been defined very broadly by the courts to include not only public facilities but also property that is no longer fit for use and must be closed or destroyed.

---

*Eminent domain* is the government's *right* to seize property; *condemnation* is the way the right is *exercised.*

---

Generally, the states delegate their power of eminent domain to quasi-public bodies and publicly held companies responsible for various facets of public service. For instance, a public housing authority might take privately owned land to build low-income housing; the state's land-clearance commission or redevelopment authority could use the power of eminent domain to make way for urban renewal. If there were no other feasible way to do so, a railway, utility company or state highway department might acquire farmland to extend a railroad track, bring electricity to a remote new development or build a highway. Again, all are allowable as long as the purpose contributes to the public good.

Ideally, the public agency and the owner of the property in question agree on compensation through direct negotiation, and the government purchases the property for a price considered fair by the owner. In some cases, the owner may simply dedicate the property to the government as a site for a school, park or library, or another beneficial use. Sometimes, however, the owner's

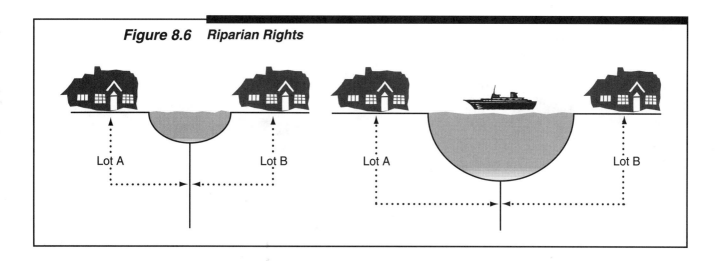

**Figure 8.6    Riparian Rights**

consent cannot be obtained. In those cases, the government agency can initiate condemnation proceedings to acquire the property.

**Taxation**    **Taxation** is a charge on real estate to raise funds to meet the public needs of a government. See Chapter 11 for more information on real estate taxes.

**Escheat**    Although escheat is not actually a limitation on ownership, it is an avenue by which the state may acquire privately owned real or personal property. State laws provide for ownership to transfer, or **escheat,** to the state when an owner dies leaving no heirs (as defined by the law) and no will that directs how the real estate is to be distributed. In some states, real property escheats to the county where the land is located; in others, it becomes the property of the state. Escheat is intended to prevent property from being ownerless or abandoned.

## WATER RIGHTS

> **MEMORY TIP**
>
> **R**iparian refers to **r**ivers, streams and similar waterways; **L**ittoral refers to **l**akes, oceans and similar bodies of water.

Whether for agricultural, recreational, or other purposes, waterfront real estate has always been desirable. Each state has strict laws that govern the ownership and use of water as well as the adjacent land. The laws vary among the states, but all are closely linked to climatic and topographical conditions. Where water is plentiful, for instance, many states rely on the simple parameters set by the common-law doctrines of riparian and littoral rights. Where water is more scarce, a state may control all but limited domestic use of water according to the doctrine of prior appropriation.

**Riparian Rights**    **Riparian rights** are common-law rights granted to owners of land along the course of a river, stream, or similar body of water. Although riparian rights are governed by laws that vary from state to state, they generally include the unrestricted right to use the water. As a rule, the only limitation on the owner's use is that it cannot interrupt or alter the flow of the water or contaminate it in any way.

**In Ohio...**    In addition, an owner of land that borders a nonnavigable waterway (that is, a body of water unsuitable for commercial boat traffic) owns the land under the water to the exact center of the waterway. In Ohio, land adjoining navigable rivers also usually is owned to the center of the riverbed. (See Figure 8.6.) Navigable waters are considered public highways over which the public has an easement or right to travel. ◆

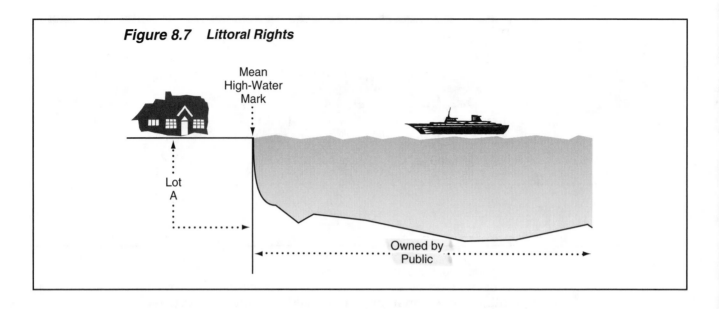

**Figure 8.7   Littoral Rights**

Mean
High-Water
Mark

Lot
A

Owned by
Public

**Littoral Rights**

Closely related to riparian rights are the **littoral rights** of owners whose land borders commercially navigable lakes, seas, and oceans. Owners with littoral rights enjoy unrestricted use of available waters, but own the land adjacent to the water only up to the mean (average) high-water mark. (See Figure 8.7). All land below this point is owned by the government.

Riparian and littoral rights are appurtenant (attached) to the land and cannot be retained when the property is sold. The right to use the water belongs to whoever owns the bordering land and cannot be retained by a former owner after the land is sold.

**Accretion, Erosion and Avulsion**

The amount of land an individual owns may be affected by the natural action of water. An owner is entitled to all land created through **accretion**—increases in the land resulting from the deposit of soil by the water's action. (Such deposits are called *alluvion* or *alluvium.*) If water recedes, new land is acquired by *reliction.*

On the other hand, an owner may lose land through **erosion.** Erosion is the gradual and imperceptible wearing away of the land by natural forces, such as wind, rain, and flowing water. Fortunately, erosion usually takes hundreds or even thousands of years to have any noticeable effect on a person's property. Flash floods or heavy winds, however, can increase the speed of erosion.

If erosion is a slow natural process, avulsion is its opposite. **Avulsion** is the sudden removal of soil by an act of nature. It is an event that causes the loss of land much less subtly than does erosion. An earthquake or a mudslide, for instance, can cause an individual's land holding to become much smaller very quickly.

**Doctrine of Prior Appropriation**

In states where water is scarce, ownership and use of water are often determined by the doctrine of **prior appropriation.** Under this doctrine, *the right to use any water, with the exception of limited domestic use, is controlled by the state rather than by the landowner adjacent to the water.*

To secure water rights in prior appropriation states, a landowner must demonstrate to a state agency that he or she plans a *beneficial* use for the water, such as crop irrigation. If the state's requirements are met, the landowner receives a permit to use a specified amount of water for the limited purpose of the beneficial use. Although statutes governing prior appropriation vary from state to state, the priority of water rights is usually determined by the oldest recorded permit date.

Once granted, water rights attach to the land of the permitholder. The permitholder may sell a water right to another party.

Issuance of a water permit does not grant access to the water source. All access rights-of-way over the land of another (easements) must be obtained from the property owner.

**KEY TERMS**

| | | |
|---|---|---|
| accretion | eminent domain | future interests |
| appurtenant easement | encroachment | homestead |
| avulsion | encumbrance | leasehold estate |
| condemnation | escheat | license |
| deed restrictions | estate in land | lien |
| easement | estate pur autre vie | life estate |
| easement by | fee simple | littoral rights |
|   condemnation | fee simple absolute | party wall |
| easement by necessity | fee simple defeasible | police power |
| easement by | fee simple | prior appropriation |
|   prescription |   determinable | riparian rights |
| easement in gross | freehold estate | taxation |

**SUMMARY**

- An estate is the degree, quantity, nature, and extent of interest a person holds in land.
  - Freehold estates are estates of indeterminate length.
  - Less-than-freehold estates are called *leasehold estates*, and they involve tenants.
- A freehold estate may be a fee simple estate or a life estate.
  - A fee simple estate can be absolute or defeasible on the happening of some event.
  - A life estate is limited in duration to the life of a named person. A conventional life estate is created by the owner of a fee estate; a legal life estate is created by law. Legal life estates include curtesy, dower, and homestead.
- Encumbrances against real estate can be:
  - liens,
  - deed restrictions,
  - easements,
  - licenses, or
  - encroachments.
- An easement is the right acquired by one person to use another's real estate. Easements are classified as interests in real estate but are not estates in land.
- There are two types of easements.
  - Appurtenant easements involve two separately owned tracts. The tract benefited is known as the *dominant tenement;* the tract subject to the easement is called the *servient tenement.*

- An easement in gross is a personal right, such as that granted to utility companies to maintain poles, wires, and pipelines.
- Easements may be created by agreement, express grant or reservation in a deed, necessity, prescription, or condemnation.
- An easement can be terminated when the purpose of the easement no longer exists, by merger of both interests, with an express intention to extinguish the easement by release, or by abandonment of the easement.
- A license is permission to enter another's property for a specific purpose. A license is usually created orally; it is temporary and can be revoked.
- An encroachment is an unauthorized use of another's real estate.
- An individual's ownership rights are subject to the powers held by government.
  - These powers include the police power, by which states can enact legislation such as environmental protection laws and zoning ordinances.
  - The government may acquire privately owned land for public use through the power of eminent domain.
  - Real estate taxes are imposed to raise government funds.
  - When a property becomes ownerless, ownership of the property may transfer, or escheat, to the state.
- Ownership of land encompasses not only the land itself but also the right to use the water on or adjacent to it.
  - Riparian rights: gives the owner of land adjacent to a nonnavigable stream ownership of the stream to its midpoint.
  - Littoral rights are held by owners of land bordering large lakes and oceans and include rights to the water and ownership of the land up to the mean high-water mark.
  - In states where water is scarce, water use is often decided by the doctrine of prior appropriation. Under prior appropriation, water belongs to the state, and it is allocated to users who have obtained permits.

---

### Real-Life Real Estate

1. Suppose you represent a government body that needs to acquire numerous residential and business properties in order to expand a road from two to four lanes. How will you present the information at the neighborhood association meeting?
2. A survey reveals that your neighbor's prize roses are five feet over on your property. Do you just start cutting them to give to your mother? Probably not. What kind of solution do you suggest?

**MATH CONCEPTS**

### Square or Rectangular Parcels

To compute the area of a square or rectangular parcel, use the following formula:

$$length \times width = area$$

Thus, the area of a rectangular lot that measures 200 feet long by 100 feet wide would be

$$200 \text{ feet} \times 100 \text{ feet} = 20,000 \text{ square feet}$$

*Area is always expressed in square units.* For example, one square foot equals 144 square inches; one square yard equals 9 square feet; one acre equals 43,560 square feet.

## Triangular Parcels

To compute the amount of surface in a triangular area, use the following formula:

$$\text{area} = \tfrac{1}{2} (\text{base} \times \text{height})$$

The *base* of a triangle is the bottom, the side on which the triangle rests. The *height* is an imaginary straight line extending from the point of the uppermost angle down and perpendicular to the base:

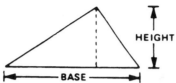

For example, if a triangular parcel has a base of 50 feet and a height of 30 feet, what will be its area?

$$\tfrac{1}{2} (50 \text{ feet} \times 30 \text{ feet}) = \text{area in square feet}$$
$$\tfrac{1}{2} (1,500 \text{ square feet}) = 750 \text{ square feet}$$

## Irregular Parcels

To compute the area of an irregular room or parcel of land, first divide the shape into regular rectangles, squares, or triangles. Then compute the area of each regular figure and add the results together to obtain the total area. For example, determine the area of this hallway:

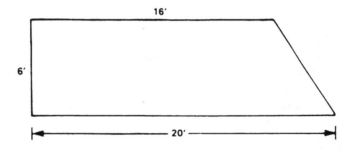

First, make a rectangle and a triangle by drawing a single line through the figure, as shown here:

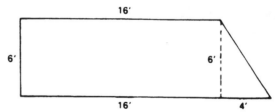

Compute the area of the rectangle:

$$\text{length} \times \text{width} = \text{area}$$
$$16 \text{ feet} \times 6 \text{ feet} = 96 \text{ square feet}$$

Next, compute the area of the triangle:

$$\text{area} = \tfrac{1}{2} (\text{base} \times \text{height})$$
$$4 \text{ feet} \times 6 \text{ feet} = 24 \text{ square feet}$$
$$\tfrac{1}{2} (24 \text{ square feet}) = 12 \text{ square feet}$$

Finally, add the two areas together:

$$96 + 12 = 108 \text{ square feet}$$

# QUESTIONS

1. The right of a government body to take ownership of real estate for public use is called
   a. escheat.
   b. eminent domain.
   c. condemnation.
   d. police power.

2. A purchaser of real estate learned that his ownership rights could continue forever and that no other person claims to be the owner or has any ownership control over the property. This person owns a
   a. fee simple interest.
   b. life estate.
   c. determinable fee estate.
   d. fee simple on condition.

3. J owned the fee simple title to a vacant lot adjacent to a hospital and was persuaded to make a gift of the lot. She wanted to have some control over its use, so her attorney prepared her deed to convey ownership of the lot to the hospital "so long as it is used for hospital purposes." After completion of the gift the hospital will own a
   a. fee simple absolute estate.
   b. license.
   c. fee simple determinable.
   d. leasehold estate.

4. After D had purchased his house and moved in, he discovered that his neighbor regularly used D's driveway to reach a garage located on the neighbor's property. D's attorney explained that ownership of the neighbor's real estate includes an easement over the driveway. D's property is properly called
   a. the dominant tenement.
   b. a freehold.
   c. a leasehold.
   d. the servient tenement.

5. A *license* is an example of a(n)
   a. easement.
   b. encroachment.
   c. temporary use right.
   d. restriction.

6. B is the owner of Blueacre. During her lifetime, B conveys a life estate in Blueacre to C. Under the terms of the grant, C's life estate will terminate when B's uncle dies. However, C dies shortly after moving to Blueacre, while B's uncle is still alive. C's will states, "I leave everything to D." Which of the following best describes the interests that the parties now hold?
   a. C possessed a life estate pur autre vie, measured by the life of B's uncle. D has the same interest as C had. D's interest in Blueacre will end when B's uncle dies. B has a reversionary interest in Blueacre.
   b. C possessed a life estate pur autre vie, measured by the life of B's uncle. D is the remainderman, and holds a nonpossessory estate until B's uncle dies. When B's uncle dies, Blueacre will escheat to the state.
   c. C possessed a determinable life estate in Blueacre. B's uncle is the measuring life. When C died, C's interest passed directly to D. When B's uncle dies, B may regain ownership of Blueacre only by suing D.
   d. B has a remainder interest in the conventional life estate granted to C. Because the grant was to C alone, the estate may not pass to D. When C died before B's uncle, the estate automatically ended and B now owns Blueacre in fee simple.

7. An Ohio homestead exemption
   a. can be ineffective if the husband and wife have a mortgage on the real estate the exemption is meant to protect.
   b. is a reduction of real estate taxes that is available to all persons age 65 or older.
   c. allows a person who dies in Ohio to be exempt from state inheritance tax.
   d. applies only to qualified people who own single-family homes. Those who own condominiums do not qualify.

8. If the owner of real estate does not take action against a trespasser before the statutory period has passed, the trespasser may acquire
   a. an easement by necessity.
   b. a license.
   c. title by eminent domain.
   d. an easement by prescription.

9. *M* wants to use water from a river that runs through his property to irrigate a potato field. In order to do so, *M* is required by his state's law to submit an application to the Department of Water Resources describing in detail the beneficial use he plans for the water. If the department approves *M*'s application, he will receive a permit to divert a limited amount of river water into his field. Based on these facts, it can be assumed that *M*'s state relies on which of the following rules of law?
   a. Common-law riparian rights
   b. Common-law littoral rights
   c. Doctrine of prior appropriation
   d. Doctrine of highest and best use

10. All of the following are powers of the government *EXCEPT*
    a. easement in gross.
    b. police power.
    c. eminent domain.
    d. taxation.

11. Property deeded to a town "for recreational purposes only" conveys a
    a. fee simple absolute.
    b. fee simple on condition precedent.
    c. leasehold interest.
    d. fee simple determinable.

12. *T* has the legal right to pass over the land owned by his neighbor. This is a(n):
    a. estate in land.
    b. easement.
    c. police power.
    d. encroachment.

13. All of the following are legal life estates *EXCEPT*
    a. leasehold.
    b. husband's curtesy.
    c. homestead.
    d. wife's dower.

14. A father conveys ownership of his residence to his daughter but reserves for himself a life estate in the residence. The interest the daughter owns during her father's lifetime is:
    a. pur autre vie.
    b. a remainder.
    c. a reversion.
    d. a leasehold.

15. *K* has fenced his property. The fence extends one foot over his lot line onto the property of a neighbor, *M*. The fence is an example of a(n):
    a. license.
    b. encroachment.
    c. easement by necessity.
    d. easement by prescription.

16. A homeowner may be allowed certain protection from judgments of creditors as a result of her state's
    a. littoral rights.
    b. curtesy rights.
    c. homestead rights.
    d. dower rights.

17. *K* has permission from *X* to hike on *X*'s property during the autumn months. *K* has
    a. an easement by necessity.
    b. an easement by condemnation.
    c. riparian rights.
    d. a license.

18. Encumbrances on real estate
    a. include easements and encroachments.
    b. make it impossible to sell the encumbered property.
    c. must all be removed before the title can be transferred.
    d. are of no monetary value to those who own them.

19. A tenant who rents an apartment from the owner of the property holds a(n)
    a. easement.
    b. license.
    c. freehold interest.
    d. leasehold interest.

20. Because a homeowner failed to pay her real estate taxes on time, the taxing authority imposed a claim against her property. This claim is known as a(n)
    a. deed restriction.
    b. lien.
    c. easement.
    d. appurtenant easement.

21. Dower rights are best defined as
    a. at least a three-quarter life estate interest a surviving spouse has in the real estate owned by his or her deceased spouse.
    b. at least a one-third life estate interest a surviving spouse has in the real estate owned by his or her deceased spouse.
    c. rights in a spouse's real estate that can never be extinguished, even by divorce.
    d. rights in a spouse's real estate that are extinguished on death.

22. When a fee simple estate in Ohio land is owed by the husband as sole owner, the deed of conveyance to the buyer
    a. need not be signed by the owner.
    b. need not be signed by the owner's wife.
    c. must be signed by the husband and wife and all their children.
    d. must be signed by both husband and wife.

23. To claim a special homestead real estate tax exemption, a homeowner must be
    a. age 65 or older and meet certain income requirements prescribed by law.
    b. a homeowner for at least ten years.
    c. a person who has reached the age of legal majority.
    d. a minor.

24. K's property has proven to be difficult to sell, and her salesperson has suggested that enclosing part of the backyard with a privacy fence might help the property sell faster. Fencing costs $6.95 per linear foot, and the lot is as illustrated below. How much will K's fence cost?

95'

42'6"

    a. $1,911.25          c. $1,615.88
    b. $1,654.10          d. $955.63

25. R has signed an agreement to purchase a condominium apartment from S. The contract stipulates that S replace a worn living room carpet. The carpet selected by R costs $16.95 per square yard, plus $2.50 per square yard for installation. If the living room dimensions are as illustrated, how much will S have to pay for the job?

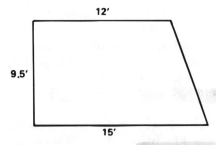

12'

9.5'

15'

    a. $241.54          c. $277.16
    b. $189.20          d. $2,494.46

# Forms of Real Estate Ownership

## FORMS OF OWNERSHIP

As we've seen, many different interests in land exist—fee simple, life estates, and easements, for instance. Licensees also need to understand how these interests in real property may be held. Brokers and salespersons must understand the fundamental types of ownership so they will know who must sign various documents. However, licensees should never give advice on how a buyer should take title and questions about forms of ownership always should be referred to an attorney.

Although the forms of ownership available are controlled by state laws, a fee simple estate may be held in three basic ways:

1. In **severalty,** where title is held by one individual
2. In **co-ownership,** where title is held by two or more individuals
3. In **trust,** where a third individual holds title for the benefit of another

## OWNERSHIP IN SEVERALTY

When title to real estate is owned by one individual, that individual is said to own the property *in severalty*. The term comes from the fact that this sole owner is "severed" or "cut off" from other owners. The severalty owner has sole rights to the ownership and sole discretion over the transfer of the ownership. When either a husband or wife owns property in severalty, state law may affect how ownership is held.

## CO-OWNERSHIP

When title to one parcel of real estate is held by two or more individuals, those parties are called *co-owners* or *concurrent owners*.

In Ohio...    Ohio recognizes various forms of co-ownership. Individuals may co-own property as tenants in common, survivorship tenants or tenants by the entirety, or they may co-own partnership property. Each of these forms of co-

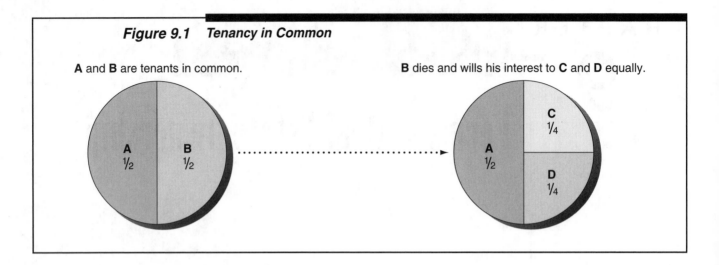

**Figure 9.1** **Tenancy in Common**

A and B are tenants in common.

B dies and wills his interest to C and D equally.

ownership will be discussed separately. It should be noted, however, that *joint tenancy is not recognized in Ohio.* ◆

## Tenancy in Common

A parcel of real estate may be owned by two or more people as tenants in common. In a **tenancy in common,** each tenant holds an *undivided fractional interest* in the property. A tenant in common may hold, say, a one-half or one-third interest in a property. The physical property, however, is not divided into a specific half or third. The co-owners have *unity of possession;* that is, they are entitled to possession of the whole property. It is the *ownership interest,* not the property, that is divided.

The deed creating a tenancy in common may or may not state the fractional interest held by each co-owner. If no fractions are stated, the tenants are presumed to hold equal shares. For example, if five people hold title, each would own an undivided one-fifth interest.

Tenants in common also hold their ownership interests in *severalty*. That is, because the co-owners own separate interests, each can sell, convey, mortgage, or transfer his or her interest without the consent of the other co-owners. However, no individual tenant may transfer the ownership of the entire property. When one co-owner dies, the tenant's undivided interest passes according to his or her will. (See Figure 9.1.)

When two or more people acquire title to real estate and the deed does not stipulate the form of the tenancy, the new owners are usually held to have acquired title as tenants in common.

### Forms of Co-ownership

1. Tenancy in common
2. Joint tenancy
3. Tenancy by the entirety
4. Community property

## Survivorship Tenancy

In Ohio...

Most states—Ohio is one exception—recognize some form of **joint tenancy,** which is an estate in land owned by two or more people. A valid joint tenancy requires four unities (as opposed to the one unity required for tenancy in common): unity in time, unity in possession, unity in title, and unity of interest. ◆

While there are many similarities between a tenancy in common and a joint tenancy, the distinguishing feature of joint tenancy is the *right of survivorship:* in a joint tenancy, the surviving joint tenant or tenants take over the interest of a deceased joint tenant.

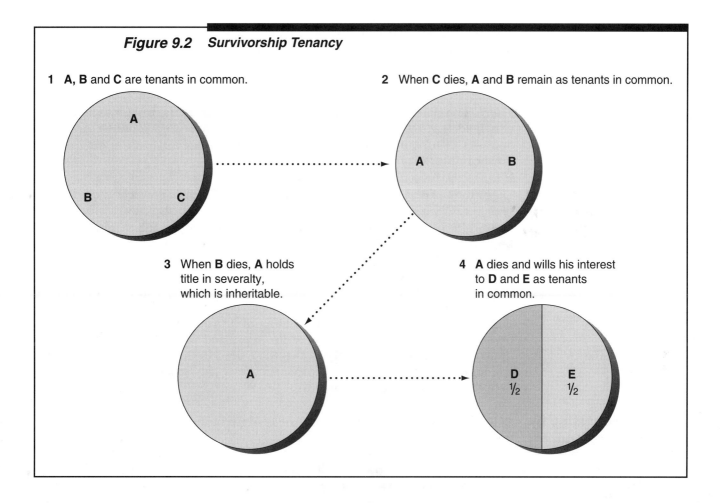

**Figure 9.2    Survivorship Tenancy**

**1   A, B** and **C** are tenants in common.

**2**   When **C** dies, **A** and **B** remain as tenants in common.

**3**   When **B** dies, **A** holds title in severalty, which is inheritable.

**4   A** dies and wills his interest to **D** and **E** as tenants in common.

**FOR EXAMPLE**  *C, D* and *E* own Tanacre as *tenants in common,* each with a one-third interest in the property. When *C* dies, his heirs assume his one-third interest.

*F, G* and *H* own Redacre as *joint tenants,* each with a one-third interest in the property. When *F* dies, *G* and *H* each take half of his one-third interest. When *H* dies, *G* will be the sole owner of Redacre.

**In Ohio...** *Test*  Remember: *Joint tenancy is not recognized in Ohio,* and a deed "to *A* and *B* as joint tenants" does not create a joint tenancy; *A* and *B* will take title as tenants in common. However, a deed may create a *survivorship tenancy* (described in Figure 9.2) if the intention to do so is clearly expressed, such as by the title "Survivorship Deed" and language such as "for their joint lives, remainder to the survivor of them." ◆

**In Ohio...**  **FOR EXAMPLE**  In Ohio, a conveyance "to Bob and Betty, and to the survivor of them, his or her heirs and assigns" clearly expresses the intent to create survivorship tenancy. In this case, when one owner dies, the survivor will take the entire fee ownership, subject only to possible state and federal estate taxes.

While joint tenancy is not available in Ohio, Ohioans do have the opportunity to create a form of survivorship tenancy called *tenants in common* with **right of survivorship.** This survivorship tenancy can be used when two or more persons are co-owners of real property. Co-owners, owning as tenants in common, may deed the property to themselves to create a survivorship tenancy on the death of one of the owners. The deceased owner's interest is not considered an asset of the probate estate, but title to the interest transfers by *contract* to the survivor or survivors. Although the deceased owner's interest is not subject to probate, it must be included for Ohio and federal estate tax purposes.

There is no dower in survivorship tenancy in Ohio. Thus, business associates can hold title to a parcel of real estate as survivorship tenants, and their spouses, if any, are not required to join in a conveyance in order to waive dower rights. ◆

**Termination of Co-Ownership by Partition Suit**

Co-owners of real estate may, by voluntary action and agreement, divide their real estate according to their interests. When division among co-owners cannot be agreed on voluntarily, it may be enforced by a suit for **partition,** filed in the county in which the land is located. Three property owners are appointed by the court as commissioners to divide the real estate into parts or, if this cannot be done, to make an appraisal of the value of the property. One or more of the co-owners may elect to purchase the property at the court-approved value or, if none of the co-owners elects to purchase, the court may order the sheriff to sell the property at a public auction. The property may not be sold for less than two-thirds of its appraised value. After the court has approved the sale, the sheriff will execute a deed to the purchaser on receiving the agreed payment. The sale proceeds, less the expenses of the sale, are delivered to the former co-owners.

**Ownership by Married Couples**

Some forms of ownership require the owners be legally married as a prerequisite to the tenancy.

**Tenancy by the entirety.** **Tenancy by the entirety** is a form of tenancy in which the owners are husband and wife.

**In Ohio...**

Although no longer available in Ohio, tenancies by the entirety could validly be created between 1972 and 1985. Those existing tenancies were "grandfathered" after the abolition of tenancy by the entirety, so this form of ownership still exists in some instances.

Each spouse has an equal, undivided interest in the property; each, in essence, owns the entire estate. During the owners' lives, title can be conveyed *only by a deed signed by both parties* (one party cannot convey a one-half interest). On the death of one spouse full title automatically passes to the surviving spouse—tenancy by the entirety is a *survivorship* estate. The transfer of the interest of the deceased spouse may be recorded by filing a certificate of death, an affidavit, or a certificate of transfer, as provided by law. ◆

Under early common law, a husband and wife were held to be "one flesh" in the eyes of the law—the wife's legal personality was merged with that of her husband's. As a result real estate owned by a husband and wife as tenants by the entireties is considered to be held by one indivisible legal unit. Divorce results in the parties becoming tenants in common. The old tenancy by the entireties title to property was generally not subject to a lien by a creditor of one of the owners, but the new "survivorship tenancy" does not provide this protection.

**Community property rights.** Community property laws are based on the idea that a husband and wife, rather than merging into one entity, are equal partners in the marriage. Any property acquired during a marriage is considered to be obtained by mutual effort. The states' community property laws vary widely. Essentially, however, they all recognize two kinds of property: separate property and community property.

**Separate property** is real or personal property that was owned solely by either spouse before the marriage. It also includes property acquired by gift or inheritance during the marriage, as well as any property purchased with separate funds during the marriage. Any income earned from a person's separate property remains part of his or her separate property. Separate property can be mortgaged or conveyed by the owning spouse without the signature of the nonowning spouse.

**In Ohio...**   **Community property** consists of all other property, both real and personal, acquired by either spouse during the marriage. Any conveyance or encumbrance of community property requires the signatures of *both* spouses. When one spouse dies, the survivor automatically owns one-half of the community property. The other half is distributed according to the deceased spouse's will. If the spouse dies without a will, the other half is inherited by the surviving spouse or by the decedent's other heirs, depending on state law. Community property does *not* provide an automatic right of survivorship, as joint tenancy does. Ohio is not a community property state. ◆

## TRUSTS

**In Ohio...**   In Ohio, title to real estate may be held in a trust. ◆ A **trust** is a device by which one person transfers ownership of property to someone else to hold or manage for the benefit of a third party. Perhaps a grandfather wishes to ensure the college education of his granddaughter, so he transfers his oil field to the grandchild's mother. He instructs the mother to use income from it to pay for the grandchild's college tuition. In this case, the grandfather is the *trustor*—the person who creates the trust. The granddaughter is the *beneficiary*—the person who benefits from the trust. The mother is the *trustee*—the party who holds legal title to the property and is entrusted with carrying out the trustor's instructions regarding the purpose of the trust. The trustee is a *fiduciary*, who acts in confidence or trust and has a special legal relationship with the beneficiary. The trustee's power and authority are limited by the terms of the trust agreement, will, or deed in trust. Real estate also may be held by a number of people in a real estate investment trust (or REIT), which will be discussed in Chapter 24.

**In Practice**     The legal and tax implications of setting up a trust are complex and vary widely from state to state. Attorneys and tax experts should always be consulted on the subject of trusts.

**Living and Testamentary Trusts**

**In Ohio...**   A property owner may provide for his or her own financial care or for that of the owner's family by establishing a trust. This trust may be created by agreement during the property owner's lifetime (a *living trust*) or established by will after the owner's death (a *testamentary trust*). In Ohio, title to real estate may be held by a trustee for the benefit of a beneficiary. This may be a trust established under a will or trust agreement. ◆

The person who creates the trust conveys real or personal property to a trustee (usually a corporate trustee), with the understanding that the trustee will assume certain duties. These duties may include the care and investment of the trust assets to produce an income. After paying the trust's operating expenses and trustee's fees, the income is paid to or used for the benefit of the beneficiary. The trust may continue for the beneficiary's lifetime or the assets may be distributed when the beneficiary reaches a certain age or when other conditions are met.

## OWNERSHIP OF REAL ESTATE BY BUSINESS ORGANIZATIONS

**In Ohio...**   A business organization is a legal entity that exists independently of its members. Ownership by a business organization makes it possible for many people to hold an interest in the same parcel of real estate. Investors may be organized to finance a real estate project in various ways. Some provide for the real estate to be owned by the entity; others provide for direct ownership by the investors. All of the following forms of business organization are recognized in Ohio. ◆

**Partnerships**   A **partnership** is *an association of two or more persons who carry on a business for profit as co-owners.* In a **general partnership,** all the partners participate in the operation and management of the business and share full liability for business losses and obligations. A **limited partnership,** on the other hand, consists of one or more general partners as well as limited partners. The business is run by the general partner or partners. The limited partners are not legally permitted to participate in the management of the business, and each can be held liable for business losses only to the extent of his or her investment. The limited partnership is a popular method of organizing investors because it permits investors with small amounts of capital to participate in large real estate projects with a minimum of personal risk.

**In Ohio...**   Most states, including Ohio, have adopted the *Uniform Partnership Act* (UPA), which permits real estate to be held in the partnership's name. ◆ The *Uniform Limited Partnership Act* (ULPA) also has been widely adopted. It establishes the legality of the limited partnership entity and provides that realty may be held in the limited partnership's name. Profits and losses are passed through the partnership to each partner, whose individual tax situation determines the tax consequences.

**In Ohio...**   Ohio law provides that real estate may be acquired, held, or conveyed by a general partnership or limited partnership. Every partnership transacting business in the state under a fictitious name must file a certificate stating the full names and places of residence of all partners. This certificate is to be filed with the recorder in the county of the partnership's principal place of business and in each county in which the partnership owns real estate. Without the filing of such a certificate, no conveyance of real property can be recorded to or from the partnership. Because of the complex nature of partnership matters, legal counsel should be consulted. ◆

General partnerships are dissolved and must be reorganized if one partner dies, withdraws, or goes bankrupt. In a limited partnership, however, the partnership agreement may provide for the continuation of the organization following the death or withdrawal of one of the partners.

**Corporations**   A **corporation** is a legal entity (an artificial person) created under the authority of the laws of the state from which it receives its charter. A corporation is managed and operated by its *board of directors.* The charter sets forth the powers of the corporation, including its right to buy and sell real estate (based on a resolution by the board of directors). Because the corporation is a legal entity, it can own real estate in *severalty.* Some corporations are permitted by their charters to purchase real estate for any purpose; others are limited to purchasing only the land necessary to fulfill the entities' corporate purposes.

As a legal entity, a corporation continues to exist until it is formally dissolved. The death of one of the officers or directors does not affect title to property owned by the corporation.

Individuals participate, or invest, in a corporation by purchasing stock. Because stock is *personal property,* shareholders do not have direct ownership interest in real estate owned by a corporation. Each shareholder's liability for the corporation's losses is usually limited to the amount of his or her investment.

One of the main disadvantages of corporate ownership of income property is that the profits are subject to *double taxation.* As a legal entity, a corporation must file an income tax return and pay tax on its profits. The portion of the remaining profits distributed to shareholders as dividends is taxed again as part of the shareholders' individual incomes.

An alternative form of business ownership that provides the benefit of a corporation as a legal entity but avoids double taxation is known as an *S corporation.* Only the shares of the profits that are passed to the shareholders are taxed. The profits of the S corporation are not taxed. However, S corporations are subject to strict requirements regulating their structure, membership, and operation. If the IRS determines that an S corporation has failed to comply with these detailed rules, the entity will be redefined as some other form of business organization, and its favorable tax treatment will be lost.

**Syndicates and**   Generally speaking, a **syndicate** is *two or more people or firms joined together*
**Joint Ventures**   *to make and operate a real estate investment.* A syndicate is not in itself a legal entity; however, it may be organized into a number of ownership forms, including co-ownership (tenancy in common, joint tenancy), partnership, trust, or corporation. A **joint venture** is a form of partnership in which *two or more people or firms carry out a single business project.* The joint venture is characterized by a time limitation resulting from the fact that the joint ventures do not intend to establish a permanent relationship.

**Limited**   The **limited liability company** (LLC) is a relatively recent form of business
**Liability**   organization. An LLC combines the most attractive features of limited part-
**Companies**   nerships and corporations. The members of an LLC enjoy the limited liability offered by a corporate form of ownership and the tax advantages of a partner-
**In Ohio...**   ship. In addition, the LLC offers flexible management structures without the complicated requirements of S corporations or the restrictions of limited partnerships. The structure and methods of establishing a new LLC or of converting an existing entity to the LLC form vary from state to state. ◆

## CONDOMINIUMS, COOPERATIVES AND TIME-SHARES

**In Ohio...** Not all forms of real property ownership involve land. Some, such as condominiums, involve ownership of enclosed space. Others, like cooperatives, involve personal property interests, and time-share ownership is a recurring, temporary interest in property. All three forms of these forms of ownership are recognized in Ohio. ◆

### Cooperative Ownership

*There is No Deed! Shares of stock*

In the usual **cooperative,** a corporation holds title to the land and building, and offers shares of stock to prospective tenants. The price the corporation sets for each apartment becomes the price of the stock. The purchaser becomes a shareholder in the corporation by virtue of stock ownership and receives a proprietary lease to the apartment for the life of the corporation. *The cooperative tenant/owners do not own real estate, as they do in a condominium, because stock is personal property.*

The cooperative building's real estate taxes are assessed against the corporation as owner. Generally, the mortgage is signed by the corporation, creating one lien on the entire parcel of real estate. Taxes, mortgage interest and principal, and operating and maintenance expenses on the property are shared by the tenant/shareholders in the form of monthly assessments.

Unlike in a condominium association, which has the authority to impose a lien on the title owned by one who defaulted on maintenance payments, the burden of any defaulted payment in a cooperative falls on the remaining shareholders. Each shareholder is affected by the financial ability of the others. For this reason, approval of prospective tenant/owners by the board of directors frequently involves financial evaluation. If the corporation is unable to make mortgage and tax payments because of shareholder defaults, the property might be sold by court order in a foreclosure suit. This would destroy the interests of all tenant/shareholders, including those who have paid their assessments.

**In Ohio...** Although an owner's interest in a cooperative is a personal property interest, Ohio brokers who participate in these transactions do not need a securities license. ◆

### Condominium Ownership

**In Ohio...**

*You have a deed. (interior is what you own)*

The **condominium** form of ownership has become increasingly popular in the United States. Condominium laws, often called *horizontal property acts*, have been enacted in every state, including Ohio. ◆

Under these laws, the owner of each unit holds a *fee simple title* to the unit. The individual unit owners also own a specified share of the undivided interest in the remainder of the building and land. These are known as the **common elements** (see Figure 9.3), and include such items as land, courtyards, lobbies, the exterior structure, hallways, elevators, stairways, and roof, as well as recreational facilities such as swimming pools, tennis courts, and golf courses. The individual unit owners own these common elements as *tenants in common*. State law usually provides, however, that unit owners do not have the right to partition that other tenants in common have.

Each unit and its percentage of interest in the common area is deemed to be a separate parcel for purposes of real estate assessment and taxation.

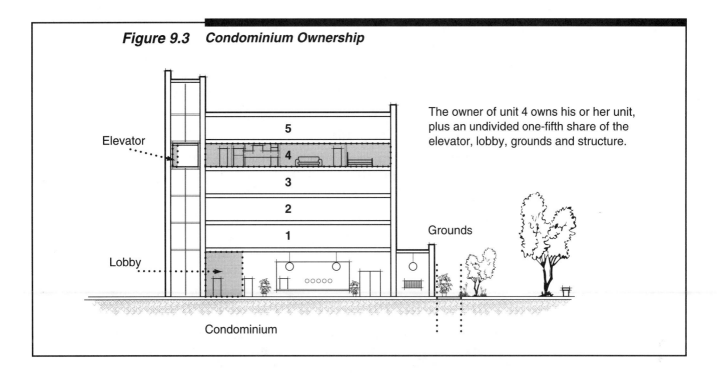

**Figure 9.3** *Condominium Ownership*

Elevator

5

4

The owner of unit 4 owns his or her unit, plus an undivided one-fifth share of the elevator, lobby, grounds and structure.

3

2

1

Grounds

Lobby

Condominium

**In Ohio...**

*Must Have a declaration*

**Creation of a condominium.** Under Ohio law, a condominium is created and established when the owners or developers of the property execute and record a declaration of its creation in the county where the property is located.

The declaration must contain a set of drawings of the property and a copy of the bylaws of the owners' association. The drawings must show the particulars of the building, including its layout and location as well as the dimensions of each unit and all common areas. ◆

**Operation and administration.** The condominium property generally is administered by an association of unit owners according to the bylaws set forth in the declaration. The association may be governed by a board of directors or other official entity, manage the property on its own, or engage a professional property manager to perform this function.

Acting through its board of directors or other officers, the association must enforce any rules it adopts regarding the operation and use of the property. The association is responsible for the maintenance, repair, cleaning, and sanitation of the common elements and structural portions of the property. It must also maintain fire and extended-coverage insurance as well as liability insurance for those portions of the property.

Expenses incurred in fulfilling the association's responsibilities are paid by the unit owners in the form of assessments collected by the owners' association. These fees are assessed to each unit owner and are due monthly, quarterly, semiannually, or annually, depending on the provisions of the bylaws. If the assessments are not paid, the association usually may seek a court-ordered judgment to have the property sold to cover the outstanding amount.

The board of managers must, unless otherwise provided for in the declarations, insure all unit owners with liability insurance, as well as provide for fire and extended coverage insurance on all buildings. The cost of this insurance is a common expense.

Unless the declaration provides otherwise, the unit owners, by an affirmative vote of all of them, may elect to remove the property from the provisions of the condominium act.

**In Ohio...**

**Sales and conversion.** Ohio law requires certain disclosures and other consumer protection measures in connection with the sale of residential condominium units. The creation of newly constructed, expandable, and conversion condominium properties is also strictly regulated.

In the case of a condominium conversion, the tenants must be given at least 120 days notice prior to being required to vacate the premises. All tenants must be offered an option, which they have 90 days to exercise, to purchase a condominium ownership interest. Any deposit or down payment in excess of $2,000 that is held for more than 90 days must earn at least four percent interest. All interest is credited to the purchasers' settlement at closing.

Developers must provide a one-year warranty covering structural, mechanical, and other elements of each unit and a two-year warranty covering the roof, structural components, mechanical, electrical and plumbing systems, and common servicing of the condominium structure. Developers selling new or conversion condominium developments are responsible for providing certain required disclosures, including

- the name and address of the condominium development; the name, address, and telephone number of the developer; and the name and address of the development manager or his or her agent;
- a general narrative description of the development;
- a general disclosure of the status of construction, zoning, site plan, and so on as applied to the development;
- the significant terms of any financing offered by or through the developer to the purchaser of the condominium ownership interest in the development;
- a description of warranties for structural elements and mechanical and other systems for each unit and for common areas and facilities;
- a two-year projection of annual expenditures necessary to operate and maintain the common areas and facilities and a like projection of the expenses attributed to each unit; and
- a report, in the case of a condominium conversion, by the developer stating age, condition, and the developer's opinion of the remaining useful life of the development's structural, mechanical, and supportive systems, including an estimate of repair and replacement costs projected over a five-year period. ◆

**In Ohio...**

**Ownership.** Once the property is established as a condominium, each unit becomes a separate parcel of real estate that is *owned in fee simple and may be held by one or more people in any type of ownership or tenancy recognized by Ohio law. It can be mortgaged like any other parcel of real estate.* ◆ A condominium unit can be sold or transferred to whomever the owner chooses, unless the condominium association provides for a "first right of refusal." In this case the owner must first offer the unit at the same price to the other owners in the condominium or the association before accepting an offer to purchase from the public.

Real estate taxes are assessed and collected on each unit as an individual property. Default in the payment of taxes or a mortgage loan by one unit owner may result in a foreclosure's sale of that owner's unit, but does not affect the ownership of the other unit owners.

**In Ohio...**

**Termination.** In Ohio, a building can be removed from condominium ownership under certain circumstances. Unless otherwise stated in the declaration, all unit owners must approve of the decision to remove the property from the condominium form of ownership. The unit owners then would become tenants in common, each owning an undivided interest in the entire property equal to their previous percentage of ownership in the common elements. ◆

**Time-Share Ownership**

**Time-share ownership** permits multiple purchasers to buy interests in real estate—usually in a resort property—with each purchaser receiving the right to use the facilities for a certain period of time. A time-share *estate* includes a real property interest in condominium ownership; a *time-share use* is a right by contract, under which the developer owns the real estate.

A time-share *estate* is a fee simple interest. The owner's occupancy and use of the property is limited to the contractual period purchased, such as during the 17th complete week, Sunday through Saturday, of each calendar year. The owner is assessed for maintenance and common area expenses based on the ratio of the ownership period to the total number of ownership periods in the property. Time-share estates theoretically never end, because of the real property interest. However, the physical life of the improvements is limited and must be looked at carefully when considering such a purchase.

The principal difference between a time-share *estate* and a time-share *use* lies in the interest transferred to an owner by the developer of the project. A time-share *use* consists of the right to occupy and use the facilities for a certain number of years—30 years is a common period. At the end of the time any rights in the property held by the owner terminate. In effect the developer has sold only a right of occupancy and use to the owner, not a fee simple interest.

**MATH CONCEPTS**

### Determining Volume

A condominium owner owns the airspace contained within the structural walls of the building. Such cubic space is measured as *volume*. Volume is used to describe the amount of space contained in any three-dimensional area. The formula for computing volume is

$$volume = length \times width \times height$$

Volume is always measured in *cubic units.* Cubic measurements of volume also are used to compute the construction costs per cubic foot of a building.

For example, the bedroom in a house is 12 feet long and 8 feet wide. Its ceiling height is also 8 feet. How many cubic feet does the room enclose?

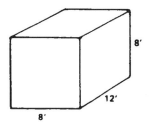

8 feet × 12 feet × 8 feet = 768 cubic feet

To compute the volume of a triangular space, such as the airspace in an A-frame house, use the following formula:

volume = ½(base × height × width)

For example, what is the volume of airspace in this house?

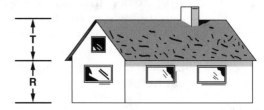

First, divide the house into two shapes: rectangular (R) and triangular (T).

Find the volume of T:

volume = ½(base × height × width)

½(25 feet × 10 feet × 40 feet) = ½(10,000 cubic feet) = 5,000 cubic feet

Find the volume of R:

volume = length × width × height

25 feet × 40 feet × 12 feet = 12,000 cubic feet

Add the volumes of T and R:

5,000 + 12,000 = 17,000 cubic feet of airspace in the house

## KEY TERMS

| | | |
|---|---|---|
| bylaws | joint tenancy | separate property |
| common elements | joint venture | severalty |
| community property | limited liability | syndicate |
| condominium |   company | tenancy by the entirety |
| cooperative | limited partnership | tenancy in common |
| co-ownership | partition | time-share ownership |
| corporation | partnership | trust |
| general partnership | right of survivorship | |

## SUMMARY

- Sole ownership, or ownership in severalty, means that title is held by one natural person or legal entity.
- Under co-ownership, title can be held concurrently by more than one person in several ways.
  - Under tenancy in common, each party holds a separate title but shares possession with other tenants. Individual owners may sell their interests. On the death of a tenant in common, his or her interest passes to the tenant's heirs or according to a will. When two or more parties hold title to real estate, they do so as tenants in common unless they express another intention.
  - Joint tenancy (not recognized in Ohio) indicates two or more owners with the right of survivorship. The intention of the parties to establish a joint tenancy with right of survivorship must be stated clearly. Ohio

does recognize a form of survivorship tenancy called tenants in common with right of survivorship.

- Tenancy by the entirety is actually a joint tenancy between husband and wife. It gives the couple the right of survivorship in all lands they acquired during marriage. During their lives, both must sign the deed for any title to pass to a purchaser.
- Community property rights exist only in certain states and pertain only to land owned by husband and wife. Usually, the property acquired by combined efforts during the marriage is community property, and each spouse owns one-half. Properties acquired by a spouse before the marriage and through inheritance or gifts during the marriage are considered separate property. Ohio is not a community property state.

- Real estate ownership may be held in trust. To create a trust, the trustor conveys title to the property to a trustee, who owns and manages the property.
- Various types of business organizations may own real estate.
  - A corporation is a legal entity and can hold title to real estate in severalty.
  - While a partnership is technically not a legal entity, the Uniform Partnership Act and the Uniform Limited Partnership Act, adopted by most states, recognize a partnership as an entity that can own property in the partnership's name.
  - A limited liability company (LLC) combines the limited liability offered by a corporate form and the tax advantages of a partnership without the complicated requirements of S corporations or the restrictions of limited partnerships.
  - A syndicate is an association of two or more people or firms that invest in real estate. Many syndicates are joint ventures assembled for only a single project. A syndicate may be organized as a co-ownership trust, corporation, or partnership.
- Cooperative ownership indicates title in one entity (a corporation or trust) that must pay taxes, mortgage interest and principal, and all operating expenses.
  - Reimbursement comes from shareholders through monthly assessments.
  - Shareholders have proprietary, long-term leases entitling them to occupy their apartments.
- Under condominium ownership, each owner-occupant holds fee simple title to a unit plus a share of the common elements.
  - Each unit owner receives an individual tax bill and may mortgage the unit.
  - Expenses for operating the building are collected by an owners' association through monthly assessments.
- Time-sharing enables multiple purchasers to own estates or use interests in real estate, with the right to use the property for a part of each year.

**Real-Life Real Estate**

1. You are a builder/developer. You are developing a property and trying to decide which form to use: condominium, cooperative, or time-share. Select one of these three and explain your choice.
2. You had a lot of success as a real estate salesperson and now you are starting your own real estate brokerage business. What form of ownership will make the most sense when you take title to your office building?

# QUESTIONS

1. A parcel of property was purchased by two friends, K and Z. The deed they received from the seller at the closing conveyed the property "to K and Z" without further explanation. K and Z took title as which of the following?
   a. Joint tenants
   b. Tenants in common
   c. Tenants by the entirety
   d. Community property owners

2. H owns one of 20 townhouses in the Luxor Lakes development. H owns the townhouse in fee simple, and a 5-percent ownership share of the parking facilities, recreation center, and grounds. What does H own?
   a. Cooperative          c. Time-share
   b. Condominium          d. Land trust

3. P conveys a vineyard in trust to R, with the instruction that any income derived from the vineyard is to be used for T's medical care. Which of the following statements most accurately describes the relationship of these parties?
   a. P is the trustee, R is the trustor and T is the beneficiary.
   b. P is the trustor, R is the trustee and T is the beneficiary.
   c. P is the beneficiary, R is the trustor and T is the trustee.
   d. P is the trustor, R is the beneficiary and T is the trustee.

4. D and S are married. Under the laws of their state, any real property that either owns at the time of their marriage remains separate property. Further, any real property acquired by either party during the marriage (except by gift or inheritance) belongs to both of them equally. This form of ownership is called
   a. a partnership.
   b. joint tenancy.
   c. tenancy by the entirety.
   d. community property.

5. E, J and Q were concurrent owners of a parcel of real estate. J died, and his interest passed according to his will to become part of his estate. J was a
   a. joint tenant.
   b. tenant in common.
   c. tenant by the entirety.
   d. severalty owner.

6. A legal arrangement under which the title to real property is held to protect the interests of a beneficiary is a
   a. trust.
   b. corporation.
   c. limited partnership.
   d. general partnership.

7. A condominium is created when
   a. the construction of the improvements is completed.
   b. the owner files a declaration in the public record.
   c. the condominium owners' association is established.
   d. all the unit owners file their documents in the public record.

8. O purchases an interest in a house in Beachfront. O is entitled to the right of possession only between July 10 and August 4 of each year. Which of the following is most likely the type of ownership O purchased?
   a. Cooperative          c. Time-share
   b. Condominium          d. Trust

9. Because a corporation is a legal entity (an artificial person), real estate owned by it is owned in
   a. trust.
   b. partnership.
   c. severalty.
   d. survivorship tenancy.

10. All of the following are forms of concurrent ownership *EXCEPT*
    a. tenancy by the entirety.
    b. community property.
    c. tenancy in common.
    d. severalty.

11. *T* and *R* are married and co-own Blueacre, with a right of survivorship. Theirs is most likely a(n)
    a. severalty ownership.
    b. community property.
    c. tenancy in common.
    d. estate by the entirety.

12. All of the following involve a fee simple interest *EXCEPT* a(n)
    a. ownership in severalty.
    b. tenancy for years.
    c. tenancy by the entirety.
    d. tenancy in common.

13. Goldacre is owned by *F, G* and *H* as tenants in common. When *G* dies, to whom will *G's* interest pass?
    a. F and H equally
    b. G's heirs
    c. The state, by the law of escheat
    d. F and H in joint tenancy

14. Which of the following best proves the ownership in a cooperative?
    a. Tax bill for the individual unit
    b. Existence of a reverter clause
    c. Shareholder's stock certificate
    d. Right of first refusal

15. *S* lives in the elegant Howell Tower. *S's* possessory interest is evidenced by a proprietary lease. What does *S* own?
    a. Condominium unit
    b. Cooperative unit
    c. Time-share
    d. Leasehold

16. *T* owns a fee simple interest in a lakefront cottage, along with 5 percent of the parking lot, laundry room, and boat house. *T* owns a
    a. membership camping interest.
    b. time-share estate.
    c. cooperative unit.
    d. condominium unit.

17. If property is held by two or more owners as survivorship tenants, the interest of a deceased cotenant will be passed to the
    a. surviving owner or owners.
    b. heirs of the deceased.
    c. state under the law of escheat.
    d. trust under which the property was owned.

18. Survivorship tenancy in Ohio is created only when
    a. a survivorship intent is clearly expressed in the deed.
    b. the parties to the deed are husband and wife.
    c. the parties to the deed are related.
    d. the parties to the deed are named as "joint tenants."

19. Partition in Ohio may be effected
    a. voluntarily.
    b. by a court order.
    c. by eminent domain.
    d. by escheat.

20. When a fee simple estate in a parcel of Ohio real estate is conveyed by a deed to two or more owners without designating the nature of their co-ownership, they are assumed to be
    a. tenants by the entireties.
    b. survivors.
    c. tenants in common.
    d. joint tenants.

21. Partnership in Ohio may be held in a
    a. fictitious name or a registered name.
    b. unregistered name.
    c. registered trademark.
    d. registered service mark.

22. Disclosure provisions of the condominium act do not apply to
    a. new condominiums.
    b. resale condominium units.
    c. expandable condominiums.
    d. newly converted condominiums.

23. Once a parcel of real estate is recorded under the condominium act, it
    a. can never be removed from the operation of the act.
    b. might be removed from the operation of the act but is probably better as a condominium.
    c. may be removed from the operation of the act by filing a declaration.
    d. may be removed from the operation of the act by consent of the owner(s).

24. Tenants presently occupying an apartment building that is to be converted to a condominium must be given
    a. 120 days' notice prior to being required to vacate the premises and a 90-day option to purchase the condominium interest.
    b. 30 days' notice to vacate.
    c. notice that they must purchase the condominium.
    d. no notice by the owners.

25. Ohio's condominium law requires which party to provide disclosure statements?
    a. The purchaser
    b. The property manager
    c. The occupant
    d. The real estate agent and the developer/seller

26. In connection with the sale of new or converted condominium developments in Ohio, the developer and real estate agent must disclose
    a. the significant terms of any financing offered by or through the developer to the purchaser and a five-year projection of annual expenses for operating and maintaining the common areas.
    b. the significant terms of any financing offered by or through the developer to the purchaser and a two-year projection of annual expenses for operating and maintaining the common areas.
    c. nothing.
    d. only the projection of annual expenses for operating and maintaining the common areas.

27. The Argyles are planning to construct a patio in their back yard. The area to be paved appears below. If the concrete is to be poured as a six-inch slab, how many cubic feet of concrete will be needed for the patio?

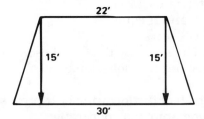

    a. 660 cubic feet
    b. 450 cubic feet
    c. 330 cubic feet
    d. 195 cubic feet

# Legal Descriptions

## DESCRIBING LAND

People often refer to real estate by its street address, such as "1234 Main Street." While that is usually enough for the average person to find a particular building, it is not precise enough to be used on documents affecting the ownership of land. Sales contracts, deeds, mortgages, and trust deeds, for instance, require a much more specific (or *legally sufficient*) description of property to be binding.

**In Ohio...** Courts have stated that a description is legally sufficient if it allows a competent surveyor to *locate* the parcel. In this context, however, locate means the surveyor must be able to define the exact boundaries of the property. Ohio courts have held that while a street address is sufficient to identify or locate a property, the street address alone is not a sufficient legal description. The street address "1234 Main Street" would not tell a surveyor how large the property is or where it begins and ends. Several alternative systems of identification have been developed that express a **legal description** of real estate. Note that the legal description in a deed or mortgage may be followed by the words "commonly known as" and the street address. ◆

## METHODS OF DESCRIBING REAL ESTATE

Three basic methods can be used to describe real estate:

1. Metes and bounds
2. Rectangular (or government) survey
3. Lot and block (recorded plat)

**In Ohio...** Although each method can be used independently, the methods may be combined in some situations. Some states use only one method; others use all three. Figure 10.1 shows the areas of the United States that use the rectangular survey system. In Ohio, land is described using all three methods. ◆

**Metes-and-Bounds Method** The **metes-and-bounds description** is the oldest type of legal description. It relies on a property's physical features to determine the boundaries and

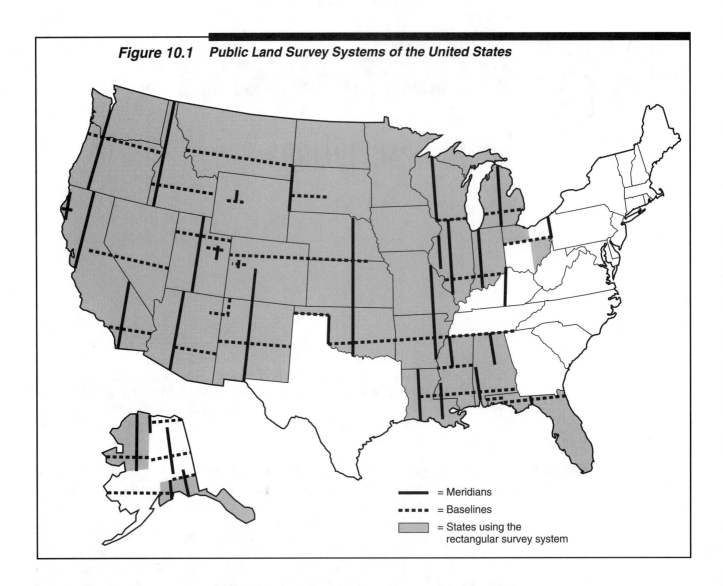

**Figure 10.1    Public Land Survey Systems of the United States**

— = Meridians
···· = Baselines
▨ = States using the rectangular survey system

measurements of the parcel. A metes-and-bounds description starts at a designated place on the parcel, called the **point of beginning (POB).** From there, the surveyor proceeds around the property's boundaries. The boundaries are recorded by referring to linear measurements, natural and artificial landmarks (called monuments), and directions. A metes-and-bounds description always ends back at the POB, so that the tract being described is completely enclosed.

**Monuments** are fixed objects used to identify the POB, the ends of boundary segments, or the location of intersecting boundaries. A monument may be a natural object, such as a stone, large tree, lake, or stream. It also may be a man-made object, like a street, highway, fence, canal, or markers (iron pins or concrete posts) placed by surveyors. Measurements often include the words *more or less* because the location of the monuments is more important than the distance stated in the wording. The actual distance between monuments takes precedence over any linear measurements in the description.

An example of a metes-and-bounds description of a parcel of land is pictured in Figure 10.2.

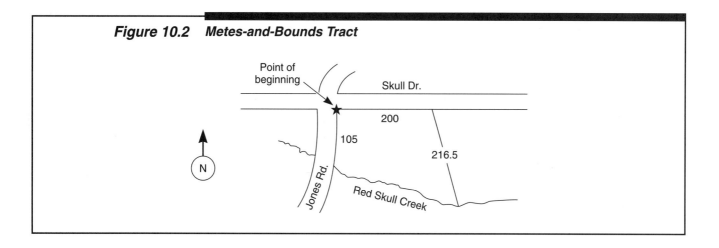

**Figure 10.2** *Metes-and-Bounds Tract*

A tract of land located in Red Skull, Ohio, described as follows: Beginning at the intersection of the east line of Jones Road and the south line of Skull Drive; then east along the south line of Skull Drive 200 feet; then south 15° east 216.5 feet, more or less, to the center thread of Red Skull Creek then northwesterly along the center line of said creek to its intersection with the east line of Jones Road; then north 105 feet, more or less, along the east line of Jones Road to the point of beginning.

When used to describe property within a town or city, a metes-and-bounds description may begin as follows:

Beginning at a point on the southerly side of Kent Street, 100 feet easterly from the corner formed by the intersection of the southerly side of Kent Street and the easterly side of Broadway; then. . .

In this description, the POB is given by reference to the corner intersection. *Again, the description must close by returning to the POB.*

Metes-and-bounds descriptions can be complex and should be handled with extreme care. When they include detailed compass directions or concave and convex lines, they can be difficult to understand. Natural deterioration or destruction of the monuments in a description can make boundaries difficult to identify. For instance, "Raney's oak" may have died long ago, and "Hunter's Rock" may no longer exist. Computer programs are available that convert the data of the compass directions and dimensions to a drawing that verifies that the description closes to the POB. Professional surveyors should be consulted for definitive interpretations of any legal description.

**In Ohio...**  Metes and bounds descriptions are commonly found in rural/agricultural areas in Ohio. ◆

**Rectangular (Government) Survey System**  The **rectangular survey system,** sometimes called the *government survey system,* was established by Congress in 1785 to standardize the description of land acquired by the newly formed federal government. The system is based on two sets of intersecting lines: principal meridians and base lines. The **principal meridians** run north and south, and the **base lines** run east and west. Both are located by reference to degrees of longitude and latitude. Each principal meridian has a name or number and is crossed by a base line. Each principal meridian and its corresponding base line are used to survey a definite area of land, indicated on the map by boundary lines.

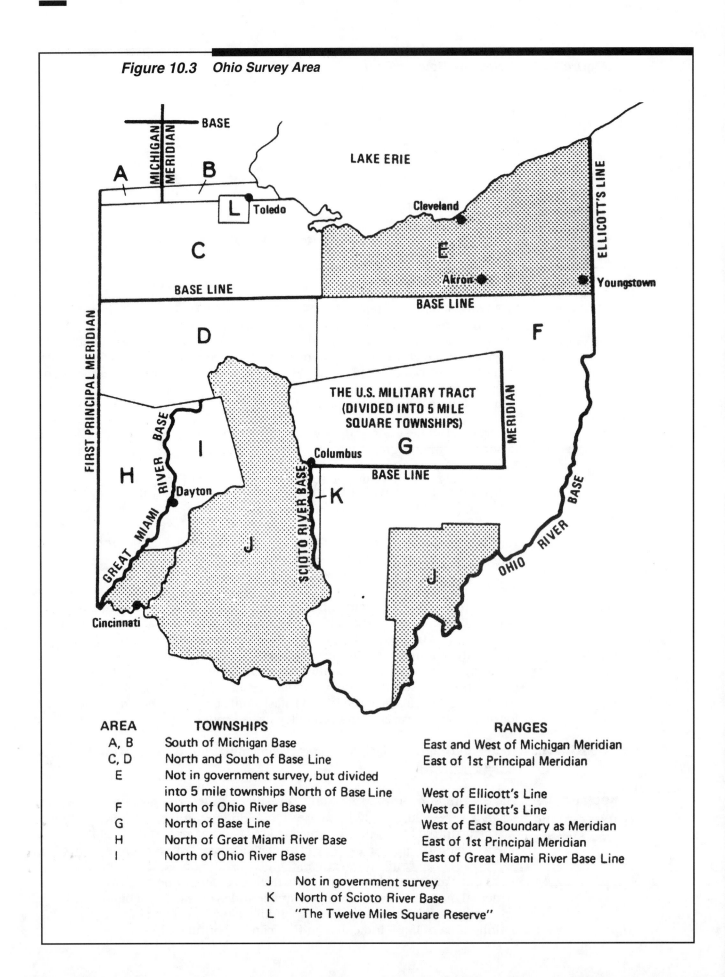

**Figure 10.3    Ohio Survey Area**

| AREA | TOWNSHIPS | RANGES |
|------|-----------|--------|
| A, B | South of Michigan Base | East and West of Michigan Meridian |
| C, D | North and South of Base Line | East of 1st Principal Meridian |
| E | Not in government survey, but divided into 5 mile townships North of Base Line | West of Ellicott's Line |
| F | North of Ohio River Base | West of Ellicott's Line |
| G | North of Base Line | West of East Boundary as Meridian |
| H | North of Great Miami River Base | East of 1st Principal Meridian |
| I | North of Ohio River Base | East of Great Miami River Base Line |

| | |
|---|---|
| J | Not in government survey |
| K | North of Scioto River Base |
| L | "The Twelve Miles Square Reserve" |

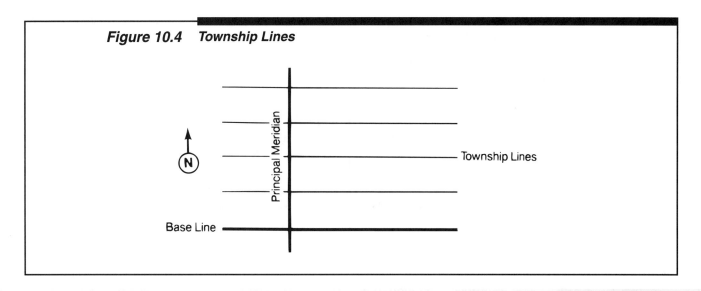

Figure 10.4    Township Lines

The map in Figure 10.3 indicates those portions of Ohio that are included in the rectangular survey system and those that are not. The eastern boundary of Ohio, Ellicott's line, was established in 1785 as the point of beginning of the rectangular survey system. ◆

Each principal meridian describes only specific areas of land by boundaries. No parcel of land is described by reference to more than one principal meridian. The meridian used may not necessarily be the nearest one.

Further divisions are used in the same way as monuments in the metes-and-bounds method. They are

- townships
- ranges
- sections and
- quarter-section lines.

The directions of township lines and range lines may be easily remembered by thinking of the words this way:

**T**ownship lines
**R**ange lines

**Township Tiers.** Lines running east and west, parallel to the base line and six miles apart, are referred to as **township lines.** They form strips of land called **township tiers.** (See Figure 10.4.) These township tiers are designated by consecutive numbers north or south of the base line. For instance, the strip of land between 6 and 12 miles north of a base line is Township 2 North.

**Ranges.** The land on either side of a principal meridian is divided into six-mile-wide strips by lines that run north and south, parallel to the meridian. These north-south strips of land are called ranges. (See Figure 10.5.) They are designated by consecutive numbers east or west of the principal meridian. For example, Range 3 East would be a strip of land between 12 and 18 miles east of its principal meridian.

**Township squares.** When the horizontal township lines and the vertical range lines intersect, they form squares. These township squares are the basic units of the rectangular survey system. (See Figure 10.6.) **Townships** are 6 miles square and contain 36 square miles (23,040 acres).

Note that although a township square is part of a township tier, the two terms *do not* refer to the same thing. In this discussion, the word *township* used by itself refers only to the township square.

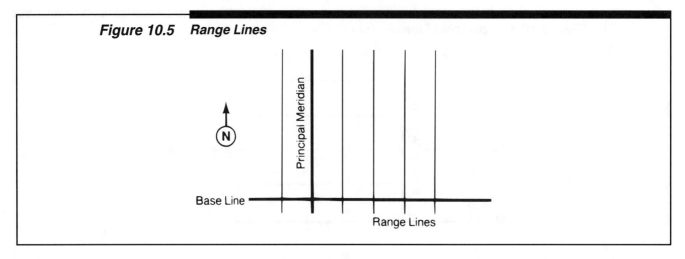

**Figure 10.5    Range Lines**

Each township is given a legal description. The township's description includes the following:

- Designation of the township strip in which the township is located
- Designation of the range strip
- Name or number of the principal meridian for that area

**F**OR EXAMPLE In Figure 10.6, the township marked with an x is described as Township 3 North, Range 4 East of the $n^{th}$ Principal Meridian. This township is the third strip, or tier, north of the base line, and it designates the township number and direction. The township is also located in the fourth range strip (those running north and south) east of the principal meridian. Finally, reference is made to the principal meridian because the land being described is within the boundary of land surveyed from that meridian. This description is abbreviated as *T3N, R4E 4th Principal Meridian.*

Townships are numbered the same way a field is plowed. (The word for such a system is *boustrophedonic*—literally, "turning like oxen pulling a plow.") Remember: right to left, left to right, right to left.

**Sections.** Each township contains 36 **sections.** Each section is one square mile, or 640 acres. Sections are numbered 1 through 36, as shown in Figure 10.7. Section 1 is always in the northeast, or upper right-hand, corner. The numbering proceeds right to left to the upper left-hand corner. From there, the numbers drop down to the next tier and continue from left to right, then back from right to left. By law, each section number 16 is set aside for school purposes. The sale or rental proceeds from this land were originally available for township school use. The schoolhouse was usually located in this section so it would be centrally located for all of the students in the township. As a result, Section 16 is always referred to as a *school section.*

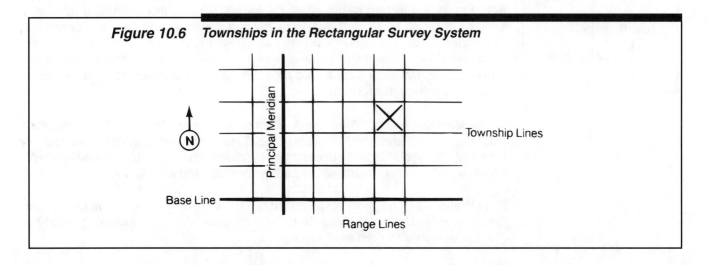

**Figure 10.6    Townships in the Rectangular Survey System**

**Figure 10.7    Sections in a Township**

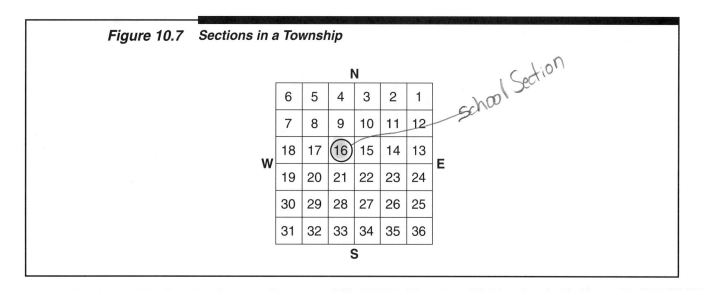

Sections (see Figure 10.8) are divided into *halves* (320 acres) and *quarters* (160 acres). In turn, each of those parts is further divided into halves and quarters. The southeast quarter of a section, which is a 160-acre tract, is abbreviated SE¼. The SE¼ of SE¼ of SE¼ of Section 1 would be a ten-acre square in the lower right-hand corner of Section 1.

The rectangular survey system sometimes uses a shorthand method in its descriptions. For instance, a comma may be used in place of the word *of:* SE¼, SE¼, SE¼, Section 1. It is possible to combine portions of a section, such as NE¼ of SW¼ and N½ of NW¼ of SE¼ of Section 1, which could also be written NE¼, SW¼; N½, NW¼, SE¼ of Section 1. A semicolon means *and.* Because of the word *and* in this description, the area is 60 acres.

**Figure 10.8    A Section**

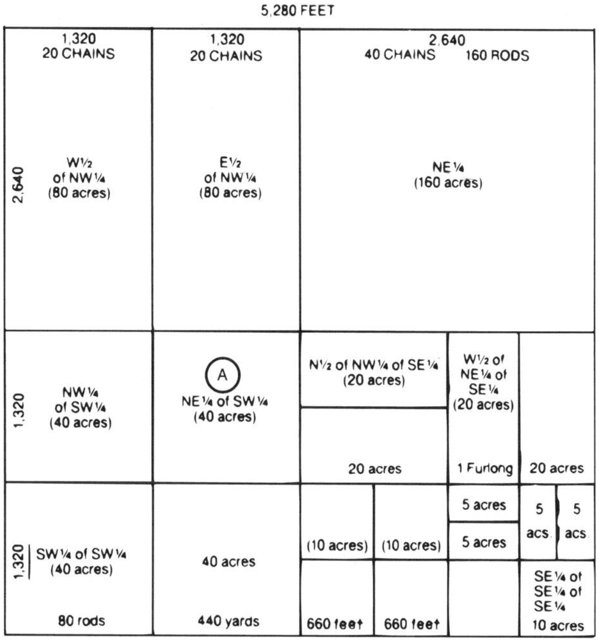

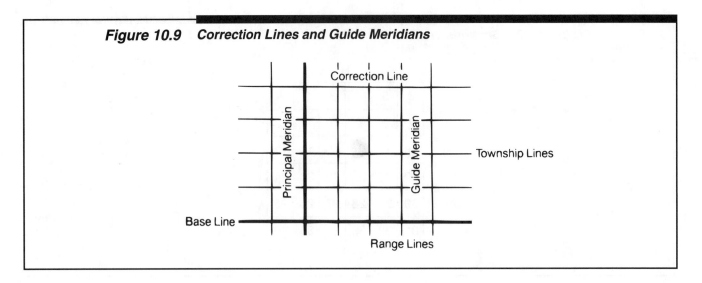

**Figure 10.9**    *Correction Lines and Guide Meridians*

**Correction lines.** Range lines are parallel only in theory. Because of the curvature of the earth, range lines gradually approach each other. If they are extended northward, they will eventually meet at the North Pole. The fact that the earth is not flat, combined with the crude instruments used in early days, means that few townships are exactly six-mile squares or contain exactly 36 square miles. The system compensates for this "round earth problem" with **correction lines.** (See Figure 10.9.) Every fourth township line, both north and south of the base line, is designated a correction line. On each correction line, the range lines are measured to the full distance of six miles apart. Guide meridians run north and south at 24-mile intervals from the principal meridian. A **government check** is the area bounded by two guide meridians and two correction lines—an area approximately 24 miles square.

Because most townships do not contain exactly 36 square miles, surveyors follow well-established rules of adjustment. These rules provide that any irregularity in a township must be adjusted in those sections adjacent to its north and west boundaries (Sections 1, 2, 3, 4, 5, 6, 7, 18, 19, 30, and 31). These are called fractional sections (discussed in the following paragraph). All other sections are exactly one square mile and are known as *standard sections.* These provisions for making corrections explain some of the variations in township and section acreage under the rectangular survey system of legal description.

**Fractional sections and government lots.** Undersized or oversized sections are classified as **fractional sections.** Fractional sections may occur for a number of reasons. In some areas, for instance, the rectangular survey may have been made by separate crews, and gaps less than a section wide remained when the surveys met. Other errors may have resulted from the physical difficulties encountered in the actual survey. For example, part of a section may be submerged in water.

Areas smaller than full quarter-sections were numbered and designated as government lots by surveyors. These lots can be created by the curvature of the earth; by land bordering or surrounding large bodies of water; or by artificial state borders. An overage or a shortage was corrected whenever possible by placing the government lots in the north or west portions of the fractional sections. For example, a government lot might be described as Government Lot 2 in the northwest quarter of fractional Section 18, Township 2 North, Range 4 East of the Salt Lake Meridian.

**Reading a rectangular survey description.** To determine the location and size of a property described in the rectangular or government survey style, start at the end and work backward to the beginning, *reading from right to left*. For example, consider the following description:

> The S½ of the NW¼ of the SE¼ of Section 11, Township 8 North, Range 6 West of the Fourth Principal Meridian.

To locate this tract of land from the citation alone, first search for the fourth principal meridian on a map of the United States. Then, on a regional map, find the township in which the property is located by counting six range strips west of the fourth principal meridian and eight townships north of its corresponding base line. After locating Section 11, divide the section into quarters. Then divide the SE¼ into quarters, and then the NW¼ of that into halves. The S½ of that NW¼ contains the property in question.

In computing the size of this tract of land, first determine that the SE¼ of the section contains 160 acres (640 acres divided by 4). The NW¼ of that quarter-section contains 40 acres (160 acres divided by 4), and the S½ of that quarter-section—the property in question—contains 20 acres (40 acres divided by 2).

In general, if a rectangular survey description does not use the conjunction and or a semicolon (indicating various parcels are combined), the *longer* the description, the *smaller* the tract of land it describes.

Legal descriptions should always include the name of the county and state in which the land is located because meridians often relate to more than one state and occasionally relate to two base lines. For example, the description "the southwest quarter of Section 10, Township 4 North, Range 1 West of the Fourth Principal Meridian" could refer to land in either Illinois or Wisconsin.

**Metes-and-bounds descriptions within the rectangular survey system.** Land in states that use the rectangular survey system also may require a metes-and-bounds description. This usually occurs in one of three situations: when describing an irregular tract; when a tract is too small to be described by quarter-sections; or when a tract does not follow the lot or block lines of a recorded subdivision or section, quarter-section lines or other fractional section lines. The following is an example of a combined metes-and-bounds and rectangular survey system description (see Figure 10.10):

> That part of the northwest quarter of Section 12, Township 10 North, Range 7 West of the Third Principal Meridian, bounded by a line described as follows: Commencing at the southeast corner of the northwest quarter of said Section 12 then north 500 feet; then west parallel with the south line of said section 1,000 feet; then south parallel with the east line of said section 500 feet to the south line of said northwest quarter; then east along said south line to the point of beginning.

**Lot-and-Block System**

In Ohio...

The third method of legal description is the **lot-and-block** (or *recorded plat*) **system.** This system uses lot-and-block numbers referred to in a **plat map** filed in the public records of the county where the land is located. In Ohio, the lot-and-block description is more common in cities and towns, particularly those areas with many subdivisions. ◆

A lot-and-block survey is performed in two steps. First, a large parcel of land is described either by a metes-and-bounds description or by rectangular

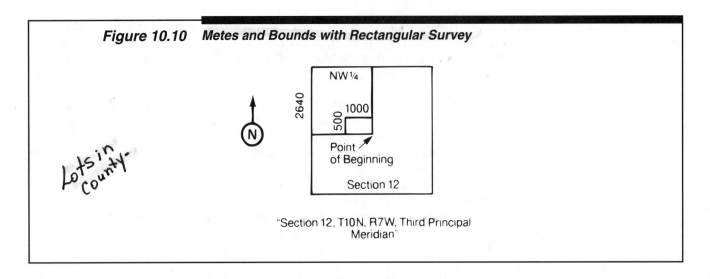

**Figure 10.10  Metes and Bounds with Rectangular Survey**

"Section 12, T10N, R7W, Third Principal Meridian"

survey. Once this large parcel is surveyed, it is broken into smaller parcels. As a result, a lot-and-block legal description always refers to a prior metes-and-bounds or rectangular survey description. For each parcel described under the lot-and-block system, the *lot* refers to the numerical designation of any particular parcel. The *block* refers to the name of the subdivision under which the map is recorded. The block reference is drawn from the early 1900s, when a city block was the most common type of subdivided property.

The lot-and-block system starts with the preparation of a subdivision plat by a licensed surveyor or an engineer. (See Figure 10.11.) On this plat, the land is divided into numbered or lettered lots and blocks, and streets or access roads for public use are indicated. Lot sizes and street details must be described completely and must comply with all local ordinances and requirements. When properly signed and approved, the subdivision plat is recorded in the county in which the land is located. The plat becomes part of the legal description. In describing a lot from a recorded subdivision plat, three identifiers are used:

1.  Lot and block number
2.  Name or number of the subdivision plat
3.  Name of the county and state

The following is an example of a lot-and-block description:

> Lot 7, Fertile Acres, located in a portion of the southeast quarter of Section 23, Township 7 North, Range 4 East of the Seward Principal Meridian in _____ County, Ohio.

Anyone who wants to locate this parcel would start with the map of the Seward principal meridian to identify the township and range reference. Then he or she would consult the township map of Township 7 North, Range 4 East, and the section map of Section 23. From there, he or she would look at the quarter-section map of the southeast quarter. The quarter-section map would refer to the plat map for the subdivision known as the second unit (second parcel subdivided) under the name of Happy Valley Estates.

Some subdivided lands are further divided by a later resubdivision. In the following example, one developer (Western View) purchased a large parcel from

**Figure 10.11** **Subdivision Plat Map -** *Lot + Block*

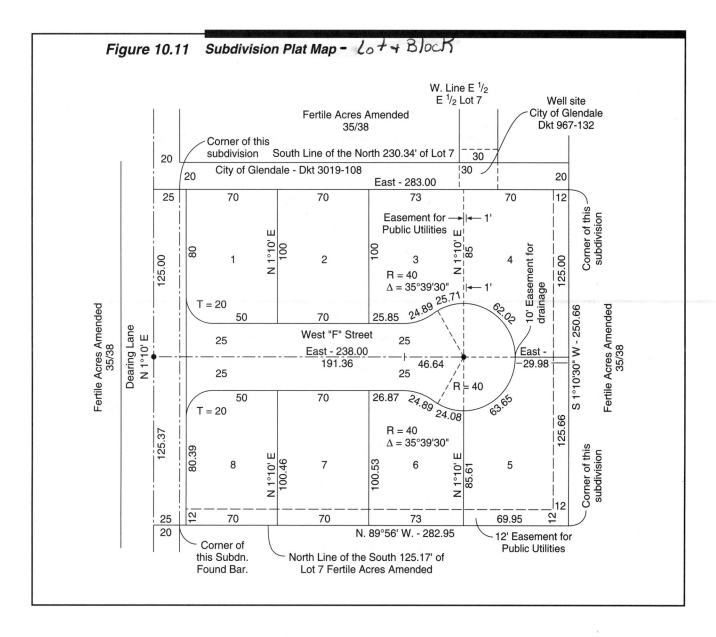

a second developer (Homewood). Western View then resubdivided the property into different-sized parcels:

> Lot 4, Western View Resubdivision of the Homewood Subdivision, located in a portion of west half of Section 19, Township 10 North, Range 13 East of the Black Hills Principal Meridian in County, Ohio.

**In Ohio...** **Ohio Plat Act.** The Ohio Plat Act provides that when an owner of a parcel of land shown as a unit on the last preceding tax roll divides it into two or more lots, any one of which is less than five acres, the owner must have the land surveyed and a plat prepared, acknowledged, and recorded in the office of the county recorder. A subdivider is required to place permanent markers to designate lot corners and lot lines. There are exceptions to this act, such as subdivision into more than five parcels among adjoining lot owners.

The act also provides that owners of adjoining land may agree to a common property line. If this agreement is reduced to writing and sufficiently described, acknowledged, and recorded, the line becomes established as the common boundary. ◆

## PREPARING A SURVEY

Legal descriptions should not be altered or combined without adequate information from a surveyor or title attorney. A licensed surveyor is trained and authorized to locate and determine the legal description of any parcel of land. The surveyor does this by preparing two documents: a survey and a survey sketch. The *survey* states the property's legal description. The *survey sketch* shows the location and dimensions of the parcel. When a survey also shows the location, size and shape of buildings on the lot, it is referred to as a *spot survey*.

---

**In Practice**

When filling in the blanks of a sales contract, an agent should exercise great care to ensure that a proper and accurate legal description is used. However, any positive identification of the property is sufficient, including an accurate address.

In real estate sales contracts permanent parcel identification numbers in counties where they are assigned may be added to further identify that parcel of real estate being sold. If the property has more than one lot, all of the permanent parcel numbers (if available) and sublot numbers should be used.

If a property described by metes and bounds is purchased for a designated price and it is estimated to contain a certain quantity of land, the buyer will not be allowed an abatement (decrease) in the price if the number of acres is less than that estimated. If, however, the seller intentionally misrepresents or conceals facts, the purchaser may claim an abatement.

Customarily, legal descriptions of urban property refer to the recorded subdivision plat and the city and county in which the land is located and give the size of the lot by frontage and depth.

For example, consider this legal description of a property in Cleveland:

"Situated in the City of Cleveland, County of Cuyahoga, and State of Ohio, and known as being Sublot No. 14 in The Ohio Land and Building Company's Re-Subdivision of part of Original Brooklyn Township Lot No. 9, as shown by the recorded plat in Volume 26 of Maps, Page 1 of Cuyahoga County Records and being 40 feet front on the westerly side of West 116th Street (formerly Fruitland Avenue) and extending back of equal width 140 feet, as appears by said plat, be the same more or less, but subject to all legal highways."

Because legal descriptions of newly subdivided land, once recorded, affect title to real estate, they should be prepared only by a registered surveyor. Real estate licensees who attempt to draft legal descriptions create potential risks for themselves and their clients and customers. Further, when entered on a document of conveyance, legal descriptions should be copied with care. For example, an incorrectly worded or improperly punctuated legal description in a sales contract may obligate the seller to convey or the buyer to purchase more or less land than either one intended. Title problems can arise for the buyer who seeks to convey the property at a future date.

## MEASURING ELEVATIONS

Just as surface rights must be identified, surveyed, and described, so must rights to the property above the earth's surface. Recall from Chapter 2 that land includes the space above the ground. In the same way land may be measured and divided into parcels, the air itself may be divided. An owner may subdivide the air above his or her land into air lots. Air lots are composed of the airspace within specific boundaries located over a parcel of land.

The *condominium laws* passed in all states (see Chapter 9) require that a registered land surveyor prepare a plat map that shows the elevations of floor and ceiling surfaces and the vertical boundaries of each unit with reference to an official datum (discussed later in this chapter). A unit's floor, for instance, might be 60 feet above the datum, and its ceiling, 69 feet. Typically, a separate plat is prepared for each floor in the condominium building.

Subsurface rights can be legally described in the same manner as air rights. However, they are measured *below* the datum rather than above it. Subsurface rights are used not only for coal mining, petroleum drilling, and utility line location but also for multistory condominiums—both residential and commercial—that have several floors below ground level.

**Datum**  A **datum** *is a point, line, or surface from which elevations are measured or indicated.* For the purpose of the United States Geological Survey (USGS), datum is defined as the mean sea level at New York Harbor. A surveyor would use a datum in determining the height of a structure or establishing the grade of a street.

**Bench marks.**  Monuments are traditionally used to mark surface measurements between points. A monument could be a marker set in concrete, a piece of steel-reinforcing bar (rebar), a metal pipe driven into the soil, or simply a wooden stake stuck in the dirt. Because such items are subject to the whims of nature and vandals, their accuracy is sometimes suspect. As a result, surveyors rely most heavily on bench marks to mark their work accurately and permanently.

**Land Acquisition Costs**
To calculate the cost of purchasing land, use the same unit in which the cost is given. Costs quoted per square foot must be multiplied by the proper number of square feet; costs quoted per acre must be multiplied by the proper number of acres; and so on.

To calculate the cost of a parcel of land of three acres at $1.10 per square foot, convert the acreage to square feet before multiplying:

> 43,560 square feet per acre × 3 acres = 130,680 square feet
> 130,680 square feet × $1.10 per square foot = $143,748

To calculate the cost of a parcel of land of 17,500 square feet at $60,000 per acre, convert the cost per acre into the cost per square foot before multiplying by the number of square feet in the parcel:

$60,000 per acre ÷ 43,560 square feet per acre = $1.38 (rounded) per square foot
> 17,500 square feet × $1.38 per square foot = $24,150

| Table 10.1 | Units of Land Measurement |
|---|---|
| **Unit** | **Measurement** |
| mile | 5,280 feet; 1,760 yards; 320 rods |
| rod | 16.5 feet; 5.50 yards |
| sq. mile | 640 acres (5,280 × 5,280 = 27,878,400 ÷ 43,560) |
| acre | 43,560 sq. feet; 160 sq. rods |
| cu. yard | 27 cu. ft. |
| sq. yard | 9 sq. feet |
| sq. foot | 144 sq. inches |
| chain | 66 feet; 4 rods; 160 links |

*[handwritten notes: "Test", "Test", "Length, width"]*

Bench marks are permanent reference points that have been established throughout the United States. They are usually embossed brass markers set into solid concrete or asphalt bases. While used to some degree for surface measurements, their principal reference use is for marking datums.

## LAND UNITS AND MEASUREMENTS

It is important to understand land units and measurements because they are integral parts of legal descriptions. Some commonly used measurements are listed in Table 10.1.

### KEY TERMS

| | | |
|---|---|---|
| air lot | lot-and-block system | range |
| base line | metes-and-bounds | rectangular |
| bench mark | description | (government) survey |
| correction line | monument | system |
| datum | plat map | section |
| fractional section | point of beginning | township |
| government check | (POB) | township line |
| government lot | principal meridian | township tier |
| legal description | | |

### SUMMARY

- A legal description is a precise method of identifying a parcel of land. Three methods of legal description can be used:
  - metes-and-bounds system,
  - rectangular (government) survey system, and
  - lot-and-block (recorded plat) system.
- A property s description should always be noted by the same method as the one used in previous documents.
- A metes-and-bounds description uses direction and distance measurement to establish precise boundaries for a parcel.
  - Monuments are fixed objects that establish these boundaries. Their actual location takes precedence over the written linear measurement in a document.
  - When property is being described by metes and bounds, the description must always enclose a tract of land; that is, the boundary line must end at the point at which it started, the point of beginning of land.
- The rectangular (government) survey system is used in 30 states. It involves surveys based on 35 principal meridians. Under this system,

each principal meridian and its corresponding base line are specifically located. Land is surveyed from only one principal meridian and its base line.

- East and west lines parallel with the base line form six-mile-wide strips called *township tiers* or *strips.* North and south lines parallel with the principal meridian form range strips. The resulting squares are 36 square miles in area and are called *townships.* Townships are designated by their township and range numbers and their principal meridians—for example, Township 3 North, Range 4 East of the Meridian. Townships are divided into 36 *sections* of one square mile each.

- When a tract is irregular or its boundaries do not coincide with a section, regular fractions of a section, or a boundary of a lot or block in a subdivision, a surveyor can prepare a combination rectangular survey and metes-and-bounds description.

- Land in every state can be subdivided into lots and blocks by means of a plat map.
  - An approved plat of survey showing the division into blocks, giving the size, location and designation of lots, and specifying the location and size of streets to be dedicated for public use is filed for record in the recorder's office of the county in which the land is located.
  - A subdivision plat gives the legal description of a building site in a town or city by lot, block and subdivision in a section, township, and range of a principal meridian in a county and state.

- Air lots, condominium descriptions, and other measurements of vertical elevations may be computed from the United States Geological Survey datum, which is the mean sea level in New York Harbor. Most large cities have established local survey datums for surveying within the areas. The elevations from these datums are further supplemented by reference points, called bench marks, placed at fixed intervals from the datums.

---

**Real-Life**
**Real Estate**

1. Compare and contrast the uses of a survey, spot survey, and survey sketch.
2. If you had your choice of legal description, which one would you choose for your property?  Why?

# QUESTIONS

1. What is the proper description of this shaded area of a section?

*WORK BACKWARD*

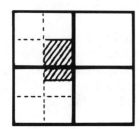

   a. SW¼ of the NE¼ and the N½ of the SE¼ of the SW¼
   b. N½ of the NE¼ of the SW¼ and the SE¼ of the NW¼
   c. SW¼ of the SE¼ of the NW¼ and the N½ of the NE¼ of the SW¼
   d. S½ of the SW¼ of the NE¼ and the NE¼ of the NW¼ of the SE¼

2. When surveying land, a surveyor refers to the principal meridian that is
   a. nearest the land being surveyed.
   b. in the same state as the land being surveyed.
   c. not more than 40 townships or 15 ranges distant from the land being surveyed.
   d. within the rectangular survey system area in which the land being surveyed is located.

*640 × .5 = 320 × .25 = 80*

3. The N½ of the SW¼ of a section contains how many acres?
   a. 20              c. 60
   b. 40              d. 80

4. In describing real estate, the system that uses feet, degrees, and natural and artificial markers as monuments is
   a. rectangular survey.
   b. metes and bounds.
   c. government survey.
   d. lot and block.

*Questions 5 through 8 refer to the following illustration of a whole township and parts of the adjacent townships.*

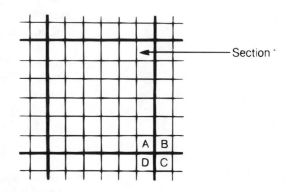

5. The section marked A is which of the following?
   a. School section
   b. Section 31
   c. Section 36
   d. Government lot

6. Which of the following is Section 6?
   a. A              c. C
   b. B              d. D

7. The section directly below C is
   a. Section 7.         c. Section 25.
   b. Section 12.        d. Section 30.

8. Which of the following is Section D?
   a. Section 1          c. Section 31
   b. Section 6          d. Section 36

9. Which of these shaded areas of a section depicts the NE¼ of the SE¼ of the SW¼?

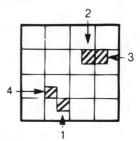

   a. Area 1          c. Area 3
   b. Area 2          d. Area 4

10. *J* purchases a one-acre parcel from *S* for $2.15 per square foot. What is the selling price of the parcel?
    a. $344
    c. $1,376
    b. $774
    d. $93,654

11. How many acres are contained in the tract described as "beginning at the NW corner of the SW¼, then south along the west line to the SW corner of the section, then east along the south line of the section 2,640 feet, more or less, to the SE corner of the said SW¼, then in a straight line to the POB"?
    a. 80 acres
    c. 100 acres
    b. 90 acres
    d. 160 acres

12. The proper description of the shaded township area in this illustration is

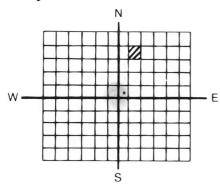

    a. T7N R7W.
    c. T4N R2E.
    b. T4W R7N.
    d. T4N R7E.

13. If a farm described as "the NW¼ of the SE¼ of Section 10, Township 2 North, Range 3 West of the 6th P.M." sold for $1,500 an acre, what would the total sales price be?
    a. $15,000
    c. $45,000
    b. $30,000
    d. $60,000

14. The legal description "the northwest ¼ of the southwest ¼ of Section 6, Township 4 North, Range 7 West" is defective because it contains no reference to
    a. lot numbers.
    b. boundary lines.
    c. a principal meridian.
    d. a record of survey.

15. To keep the principal meridian and range lines as near to six miles apart as possible, a correction known as a government check is made every
    a. 1 mile square.
    b. 3 miles square.
    c. 6 miles square.
    d. 24 miles square.

16. In the rectangular survey system fractional sections along the northern or western border of a check that are less than a quarter-section in area are known as
    a. fractional parcels.
    b. government lots.
    c. hiatus.
    d. fractional townships.

17. *T* purchased 4.5 acres of land for $78,400. An adjoining owner wants to purchase a strip of *T*'s land measuring 150 feet by 100 feet. What should this strip cost the adjoining owner if *T* sells it for the same price per square foot she originally paid for it?
    a. $3,000
    c. $7,800
    b. $6,000
    d. $9,400

18. How many acres are contained in the parcel described as "beginning at the NE corner of the SW¼ of Section 23; then one mile, more or less, in a northerly direction to the NW corner of the SE¼ of Section 14; then one mile, more or less, in a southeasterly direction to the NW corner of the SE¼ of Section 24; then one mile, more or less, in a westerly direction to the point of beginning"?
    a. 160
    c. 640
    b. 320
    d. 1,280

19. A property contains ten acres. How many 50-foot-by-100-foot lots could be subdivided from the property if 26,000 square feet were dedicated for roads?
    a. 80
    c. 82
    b. 81
    d. 83

20. A parcel of land is 400 feet by 640 feet. The parcel is cut in half diagonally by a stream. How many acres are there in each half of the parcel?
    a. 2.75          c. 5.51
    b. 2.94          d. 5.88

21. What is the shortest distance between Section 4 and Section 32 in the same township?
    a. 3 miles       c. 5 miles
    b. 4 miles       d. 6 miles

22. *H* owns the NW¼ and the SW¼ of Section 17, and *J* owns the NE¼ and the SE¼ of Section 18. If they agree that each will install one-half of a common fence, how many rods of fence will each install?
    a. 0             c. 320
    b. 160           d. 440

23. The section due west of Section 18, Township 5 North, Range 8 West, is Section
    a. 12, T5N, R7W.
    b. 13, T5N, R9W.
    c. 17, T5N, R8W.
    d. 19, T5N, R8W.

24. In any township, what is the number of the section designated as the school section?
    a. 1             c. 25
    b. 16            d. 36

25. The least specific method for identifying real property is
    a. rectangular survey.
    b. metes and bounds.
    c. street address.
    d. lot and block.

26. What is the minimum number of acres a landowner can sell without needing to survey and subdivide the land?
    a. Two           c. Four
    b. Three         d. Five

27. In a sales contract, which of the following is an acceptable description of property?
    a. Plat name
    b. The "Johnson" property
    c. A legal description
    d. Lot number

28. Urban real estate in Ohio may be described by
    a. metes and bounds and/or recorded subdivision plat of city and county.
    b. reference to the nearest house.
    c. lot size only.
    d. no particular method; everybody knows the lot lines, so it need not be described.

# Real Estate Taxes and Other Liens

## LIENS

> All liens are encumbrances, but not all encumbrances are liens

A **lien** is a charge or claim against a person's property, made to enforce the payment of money. Whenever someone borrows money, the lender generally requires some form of *security*. Security (also referred to as *collateral*) is something of value that the borrower promises to give the lender if the borrower fails to repay the debt. When the lender's security is in the form of real estate, the security is called a *lien*.

Of course, liens are not limited to security for borrowed money (such as *mortgage liens*). Liens can be enforced against property by a government agency to recover taxes owed by the owner (*tax liens*). A lien can be used to compel the payment of an assessment or other special charge as well. A *mechanic's lien* represents an effort to recover payment for work performed. In all these ways, a person or an entity can use another's property to ensure payment for work performed, services rendered, or debts incurred.

A lien represents only an interest in ownership; it does not constitute actual ownership of the property. It is an encumbrance on the owner's title. An *encumbrance* is any charge or claim that attaches to real property and lessens its value or impairs its use. An encumbrance does not necessarily prevent the transfer or conveyance of the property, but it conveys along with the property. Liens differ from other encumbrances, however, because they are financial or monetary in nature and attach to the property because of a debt. Other encumbrances may be physical in nature (such as the easements and encroachments discussed in Chapter 8).

Generally, a lienholder must institute a legal action to force the sale of the property or acquire title. The debt is then paid out of the proceeds.

There are many different types of liens. (See Figure 11.1.) One way liens are classified is by how they are created. A **voluntary lien** is created *intentionally* by the property owner's action, such as when someone takes out a mortgage loan. An **involuntary lien,** on the other hand, is not a matter of choice: it is created by law. It may be either statutory or equitable. A **statutory lien** is created by statute. A real estate **tax lien,** for example, is an involuntary,

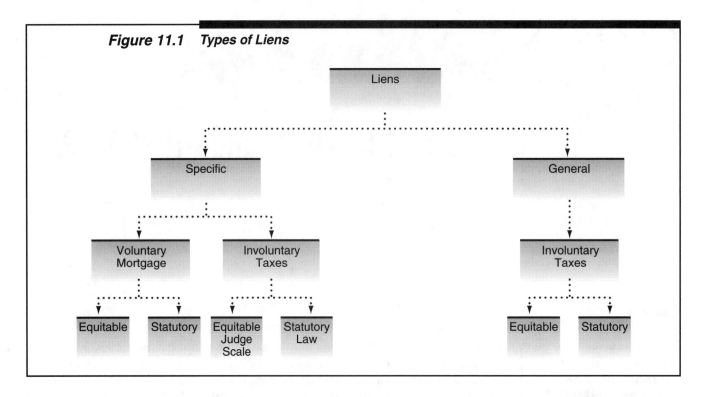

**Figure 11.1   Types of Liens**

statutory lien. It is created by statute without any action by the property owner. An **equitable lien** arises out of common law. It is created by a court based on fairness. A court-ordered judgment that requires a debtor to pay the balance on a delinquent charge account, for instance, would be an involuntary, equitable lien on the debtor's real estate.

> **Memory Tip**
>
> The four ways of creating a lien may be remembered by the acronym **VISE:** *Voluntary, Involuntary, Statutory* and *Equitable.*

Liens also may be classified according to the type of property involved. **General liens** affect all the property, both real and personal, of a debtor. This includes judgments, estate and inheritance taxes, decedent's debts, corporate franchise taxes and Internal Revenue Service (IRS) taxes. A lien on real estate differs from a lien on personal property, however. A lien attaches to real property *at the moment it is filed.* In contrast, a lien does not attach to personal property *until the personal property is seized.* **Specific liens** are secured by specific property and affect only that particular property. Specific liens on real estate include mechanics' liens, mortgage liens, real estate tax liens and liens for special assessments and utilities. (Specific liens can also secure personal property, such as when a lien is placed on a car to secure payment of a car loan.)

**Effects of Liens on Title**

The existence of a lien does not necessarily prevent a property owner from conveying title to someone else. The lien might reduce the value of the real estate, however, because few buyers will take on the risk of a burdened property. Because the lien attaches to the property, not the property owner, a new owner could lose the property if the creditors take court action to enforce payment. Once properly established, a lien *runs with the land* and will bind all successive owners until the lien is cleared. Future resales also could be jeopardized if the debt is not satisfied.

**In Ohio...**

**Priority of liens.** *Priority of liens* refers to the order in which claims against the property will be satisfied. In general, the rule for priority of liens is "first come, first served." Liens take priority from the date they are recorded in the public records of the county in which the property is located. Ohio is a "race" state; first in time is first in right. ◆

**In Ohio...** There are some notable exceptions to this rule. For instance, real estate taxes and special assessments generally take priority over all other liens, regardless of the order in which the liens are recorded. This means that outstanding real estate taxes and special assessments are paid from the proceeds of a court-ordered sale *first*. The remainder of the proceeds is used to pay other outstanding liens *in the order of their priority*. In Ohio, while mechanics' liens and purchase money mortgages may take priority over previously recorded liens, they may never take priority over real estate tax and general assessment liens. ◆

**F**OR EXAMPLE Mottley Mansion is ordered sold by the court to satisfy *B*'s debts. The property is subject to a $25,000 judgment lien, incurred as a result of a suit to recover a mechanic's lien. A total of $295,000 in interest and principal remains to be paid on Mottley Mansion's mortgage. This year's unpaid real estate taxes amount to $50,000. The judgment lien was entered in the public record on February 7, 1996, and the mortgage lien was recorded January 22, 1992. If Mottley Mansion is sold at the tax sale for $390,000, the proceeds of the sale will be distributed in the following order:

1. $50,000 to the taxing bodies for this year's real estate taxes *are alway #1*
2. $295,000 to the mortgage lender (the entire amount of the mortgage loan outstanding as of the date of sale)
3. $25,000 to the creditor named in the judgment lien
4. $20,000 to *B* (the proceeds remaining after paying the first three items)

However, if Mottley Mansion sold for $350,000, the proceeds would be distributed as follows:

1. $50,000 to the taxing bodies for this year's real estate taxes
2. $295,000 to the mortgage lender (the entire amount of the mortgage loan outstanding as of the date of sale)
3. $5,000 to the creditor named in the judgment lien
4. $0 to *B*

Although the creditor is not repaid in full, this outcome is considered fair for two reasons:

1. The creditor's interest arose later than the others, so the others' interests took priority.
2. The creditor knew (or should have known) about the creditors ahead of it when it extended credit to *B*, so it was aware (or should have been aware) of the risk involved.

**Subordination agreements** are written agreements between lienholders to change the priority of mortgage, judgment, and other liens. Under a subordination agreement, the holder of a superior or prior lien agrees to permit a junior lienholder's interest to move ahead of his or her lien. Priority and recording of liens are discussed further in Chapter 14.

## REAL ESTATE TAX LIENS

As discussed in Chapter 8, the ownership of real estate is subject to certain government powers. One of these is the right of state and local governments to impose (levy) taxes to pay for their functions. Because the location of real estate is permanently fixed, the government can levy taxes with a high degree of certainty that the taxes will be collected. The annual taxes levied on real estate usually have priority over previously recorded liens, so they may be enforced by a court-ordered sale.

*Sewers* ←

There are two types of real estate taxes, general real estate taxes (also called *ad valorem taxes*) and special assessments or improvement taxes. Both are levied against specific parcels of property and automatically become liens on those properties.

## General Tax (Ad Valorem Tax)

The **general real estate tax,** or **ad valorem tax,** is made up of the taxes levied on real estate by various governmental agencies and municipalities. These taxing bodies include

- states;
- counties;
- cities, towns, and villages;
- school districts (local elementary and high schools, publicly funded junior colleges, and community colleges);
- drainage districts;
- water districts;
- sanitary districts; and
- parks, forest preserves, and recreation districts.

*Ad valorem* is Latin for "according to value." Ad valorem taxes are based on the *value of the property being taxed.* They are specific, involuntary, statutory liens. General real estate taxes are levied to fund the operation of the governmental agency that imposes the taxes.

**In Ohio...** In Ohio, general taxes are levied annually for a full calendar year and are payable twice a year. Each county establishes it own dates by which the tax payments are due. Nonreceipt of a tax bill does not relieve the property owner from the obligation to pay taxes on time. A penalty of 10 percent is added to any unpaid portion of the tax that is not paid by the due dates. ◆

**In Ohio...** **Exemptions from general taxes.** In Ohio, as in most states, certain property is exempt from real estate taxation. For example, property owned by cities, various municipal organizations (such as schools, parks, and playgrounds), the state and federal governments, religious corporations, nonprofit hospitals, or educational institutions is tax-exempt, if used for tax-exempt purposes. Ohio also allows special exemptions to reduce real estate tax bills for senior citizens, who are granted reductions in the assessed value of their homes, provided they meet specific income qualifications. Real estate tax reductions are also available for certain Ohio agricultural and forest land. ◆

**In Ohio...** **Assessment.** Ohio law provides that the county auditor appraise each lot or parcel of real estate at least once every six years, with a three-year update. The auditor has the right to revalue and assess at any time all or any part of the real estate when he or she finds that it has changed in value or is not on the tax list at its taxable value. The State Board of Tax Appeals or the county court of common pleas has the authority to correct any inequities in the auditor's appraisal and assessed valuations. A taxpayer who believes the tax assessment valuation of his or her property is excessive may file a written complaint with the county board of revision within a certain time period.

All real property in the state of Ohio is appraised at its market value, the best evidence of which is an actual, recent sale of the property in an arm's-length transaction. ◆

**In Ohio...**     **Determining Assessed Value**

The common level of assessment (assessed value) in Ohio is *35 percent of the auditor's appraised value of the property:*

Appraised Value × 35% = Assessed Value

In the case of a home appraised at $100,000, the assessed value would be

$100,000 Appraised Value × 35% = $35,000 Assessed Value

The auditor's appraised value is used to determine the property's assessed value, which, as is discussed below, is the figure used to determine the amount of tax owed. ◆

**In Ohio...**    **Permanent parcel numbers.** In Ohio, county officials have the option of instituting a system of permanent tax numbers for real estate tax bills. These numbers are used to identify the property being taxed, so a very abbreviated description of the land may be used on the bill. These numbers also are often added to the legal description used on a real estate sales contract for further identification of the parcel being sold. This numbering system makes the taxpayer responsible for ascertaining that the tax bill he or she is paying is for the right parcel of land. The taxpayer is responsible for paying taxes on the land even if a tax bill is not received. ◆

**In Ohio...**    **Equalization.** In some jurisdictions, when it is necessary to correct general inequalities in statewide tax assessments, uniformity may be achieved by use of an **equalization factor.** Such a factor may be provided for use in counties or districts where the assessments are to be raised or lowered. The assessed value of each property is multiplied by the equalization factor, and the tax rate is then applied to the equalized assessment. For example, the assessments in one county are determined to be 20 percent lower than the average assessments throughout the rest of the state. This underassessment can be corrected by requiring the application of an equalization factor of 120 percent to each assessment in that county. Thus a parcel of land assessed for tax purposes at $98,000 would be taxed on an equalized value of $117,600 ($98,000 × 1.20 = $117,600). ◆

**In Ohio...**    **Tax rates.** The process of arriving at a real estate tax rate begins with the *adoption of a budget* by each taxing district. Each budget covers the financial requirements of the taxing body for the coming fiscal year, which may be the January through December calendar year or some other 12-month period designated by statute. The budget must include an estimate of all expenditures for the year and indicate the amount of income expected from all fees, revenue sharing, and other sources. The net amount remaining to be raised from real estate taxes is then determined from these figures.

The next step is *appropriation*, the action taken by each taxing body that authorizes the expenditure of funds and provides for the sources of such monies. Appropriation generally involves the adoption of an ordinance or the passage of a law setting forth the specifics of the proposed taxation.

The amount to be raised from the general real estate tax is then imposed on property owners through a tax levy, the formal action taken to impose the tax, by a vote of the taxing district's governing body. ◆

**In Ohio...**

### Determining Tax Rates

A taxing district's budget indicates that $300,000 must be raised from real estate tax revenues, and the assessment roll (assessor's record) of all taxable real estate within this district equals $10,000,000. This is how the tax rate is computed:

$$\$300,000 \div \$10,000,000 = .03 \text{ or } 3\%$$

The tax rate may be stated in a number of different ways. In many areas it is expressed in "mills." A mill is *1/1,000 of a dollar or $.001*. The tax rate may be expressed as a mill ratio, in dollars per hundred or in dollars per thousand. The tax rate computed in this example could be expressed as

30 mills or $3 per $100 of assessed value or $30 per $1,000 of assessed value

The *tax rate* for each individual taxing body is computed separately. To arrive at a tax rate, the total monies needed for the coming fiscal year are divided by the total assessments of all real estate located within the jurisdiction of the taxing body. ◆

**In Ohio...**

**Tax bills.** Generally, one tax bill that incorporates all real estate taxes levied by the various taxing districts is prepared for each property. In Ohio, the county auditor determines the tax liability while the county treasurer collects the taxes. In some areas, however, separate bills are prepared by each taxing body. Sometimes the real estate taxing bodies may operate on different budget years so that the taxpayer receives separate bills for various taxes at different times during the year.

Due dates for tax payments are usually set by statute. Taxes may be payable in two installments (semiannually). ◆

**In Ohio...**

**Tax rate limitations.** Ohio has what is known as a *ten-mill limitation*, which means that its citizens cannot be taxed for more than ten mills on each dollar of tax valuation, except for taxes specifically authorized by taxpayers to be levied in excess of that amount. The ten-mill limitation is the equivalent of $.10 tax on each $10 of tax valuation (or $1 per $100). The purpose of the general levy is to provide one general operating fund from which any expenditures for current expenses of any kind may be made. Additional levies may be made if approved by a majority of the voters.

The board of county commissioners of any county also may levy a tax without taxpayer approval. This tax is limited to three mills on each dollar valuation of taxable property within the county and is for county purposes other than roads, bridges, and county buildings. The boards also may levy a tax, not to exceed two mills on each dollar valuation, for the purpose of purchasing sites and erecting county buildings on them. ◆

**In Ohio...**

**Tax sales.** After the due date for the last half-year's tax, each county auditor certifies a list of all the tax-delinquent lands located in the county. The list is published in local newspapers twice during the next 60 days, to give notice that the delinquent lands will be certified for foreclosure by the auditor unless the taxes, assessments and penalties are paid. If the taxes are not paid within one year after having been certified as delinquent, foreclosure proceedings may be brought by the state and the land may be sold at public auction.

The **tax sale** proceeds are applied to the amount due for taxes or assessments, penalties and charges, costs of sale, and taxes and assessments that have accrued after the commencement of foreclosure. The title of the purchaser at the tax sale is incontestable and is considered free and clear of all liens and encumbrances except those easements and covenants created prior to the due and payable dates for the delinquent taxes and assessments. ◆

**In Ohio...**

### Computing Tax Bills

A property is assessed for tax purposes at $90,000. At a tax rate of 3 percent, or 30 mills, the tax will be $2,700:

$$\$90,000 \times .03 = \$2,700 \text{ tax}$$

Another property has an assessed value of $120,000. At a tax rate of 4 percent with an *equalization factor* of 120 percent, the tax would be as follows:

$$\$120,000 \times 1.20 = \$144,000 \text{ equalized assessed value}$$

$$\$144,000 \times .040 = \$5,760 \text{ tax}$$

Land on which taxes have been certified as delinquent may be redeemed by the owner, but only before the tax foreclosure sale is *confirmed* by a court. In making **redemption** the owner must pay the total delinquent tax amount plus all costs and penalties. *There can be no redemption after the foreclosure sale has been confirmed by the court.* ◆

## Special Assessments (Improvement Taxes)

**In Ohio...**

**Special assessments** are taxes levied on real estate that require that property owners pay for improvements such as streets, alleys, street lighting, curbs, and similar items that benefit their real estate. They are enforced in the same manner as general real estate taxes, with the same lien priority after the general real estate tax liens. ◆

The specific improvement funded by a special assessment is recommended either by a local governing body or by the property owners themselves. An ordinance is adopted that defines the nature and cost of the improvement, and that describes the area subject to assessment. The cost of the assessment is shared by all the parcels that will benefit from the improvement, with the specific amount assessed against a particular property determined by the property's size and the estimated benefit it will receive. Finally, a local authority (usually a court) will hold a hearing at which community members may voice support or objections to the assessment. The authority will then either approve or reject the proposal.

Special assessments are listed on the real estate tax bill and are collected at the same time and in the same manner as real estate taxes. A special assessment is treated as a capital improvement, and as such it is not a deductible item for federal income tax purposes. On the other hand, an improvement may ultimately reduce capital gains by increasing the base price of a property when it is sold.

**In Ohio...** Ohio law places limits on special assessments for municipal improvements to real property. In essence, the total of a new special assessment and all other assessments for the previous five years cannot exceed one third of the final actual market value of the property as enhanced by the improvement for which the new special assessment is levied. ◆

## OTHER LIENS ON REAL PROPERTY

In addition to real estate tax and special assessment liens, a variety of other liens may be charged against real property.

**Mortgage Liens (Deed of Trust Liens)**

A **mortgage lien,** or a *deed of trust lien,* is a voluntary lien on real estate given to a lender by a borrower as security for a real estate loan. It becomes a lien on real property when the lender records the documents in the county where the property is located. Lenders generally require a preferred lien, referred to as a *first mortgage lien.* This means that no other liens against the property (aside from real estate taxes) will take priority over the mortgage lien. Subsequent liens are referred to as *junior liens.* (Mortgages and deeds of trust are discussed in detail in Chapter 15.)

**Mechanics' Liens**

*Contractor*

A **mechanic's lien** is a device to give security to those who perform labor or furnish materials to improve real property. A mechanic's lien is available to contractors, subcontractors, architects, equipment lessors, surveyors, laborers, and others. This type of lien is typically filed when the owner has not fully paid for the work or when the general contractor has failed to pay subcontractors or suppliers.

**In Ohio...**

To be entitled to a mechanic's lien, the person who did the work must have had a contract (express or implied) with the owner or the owner's authorized representative. If improvements that were not ordered by the property owner have commenced, the property owner should execute a document called a *notice of nonresponsibility* to relieve himself or herself from possible mechanics' liens. By posting this notice in some conspicuous place on the property and recording a verified copy of it in the public record, the owner gives notice that he or she will not be responsible for the work done.

Mechanics' liens generally continue for six years after an affidavit is filed in the office of the county recorder. A property owner may, however, compel a mechanic's lien claimant to institute a suit to enforce the lien by notifying the claimant to sue within 60 days from receipt of the notice. If the claimant of the lien fails to do so, the lien becomes void and the real estate is wholly discharged from the lien. To clear a lien while a lawsuit is still pending, a property owner may file a surety bond for twice the amount of the lien claimed.

In the case of home construction contracts, the total dollar amount of all liens filed by subcontractors, suppliers and laborers cannot exceed the total unpaid balance that the owner owes the builder or general contractor. Once the general contractor or builder has been paid in full, an affidavit to that effect may be filed with the county recorder. Such a filing cancels any subcontractor, supplier, or laborer liens against the property.

While a mechanic's lien takes priority from the time it attaches, a claimant's notice of lien will not be filed in the public records until some time after that. A prospective purchaser of property that has been recently constructed, altered, or repaired should therefore be cautious about possible unrecorded mechanics' liens against the property. ◆

**Judgments**

A **judgment** is a decree issued by a court. When the decree provides for the awarding of money and sets forth the amount owed by the debtor to the creditor, the judgment is referred to as a *money judgment.*

On the filing of a certificate of judgment with the clerk of the common pleas court of a county, that judgment becomes a lien on all of the real estate owned by the judgment debtor *in that county.* Real estate of the judgment debtor in other counties is not affected unless similar certificates are filed in those counties.

If a creditor fails to have an execution issued on the judgment or to file a certificate of judgment within five years from the date the judgment is entered, the judgment can become *dormant.* A dormant judgment is not a lien on property. However, a dormant judgment may be revived, which is one reason why title searches are made when a property is purchased.

**In Ohio...**

**Lis pendens.** There is often a considerable delay between the time a lawsuit is filed and the time final judgment is rendered. When any suit is filed that affects title to real estate, a special notice, known as a **lis pendens** (Latin for "litigation pending"), is recorded. A lis pendens is not itself a lien, but rather *notice of a possible future lien.* Recording a lis pendens notifies prospective purchasers and lenders that there is a potential claim against the property. It also establishes a priority for the later lien: the lien is backdated to the recording date of the lis pendens. In Ohio, this process is called a "color of title" claim. ◆

**Attachments.** Special rules apply to realty that is not mortgaged or similarly encumbered. To prevent a debtor from conveying title to such previously unsecured real estate while a court suit is being decided, a creditor may seek a writ of **attachment.** By this writ, the court retains custody of the property until the suit concludes. First, the creditor must post a surety bond or deposit with the court. The bond must be sufficient to cover any possible loss or damage the debtor may suffer while the court has custody of the property. In the event the judgment is not awarded to the creditor, the debtor will be reimbursed from the bond.

**Estate and Inheritance Tax Liens**

**In Ohio...**

Federal **estate taxes** and Ohio **inheritance taxes** (as well as the debts of decedents) are general, statutory, involuntary liens that encumber a deceased person's real and personal property. These are normally paid or cleared in probate court proceedings. Probate and issues of inheritance are discussed in Chapter 13. ◆

**Liens for Municipal Utilities**

Municipalities often have the right to impose a specific, equitable, involuntary lien on the property of an owner who refuses to pay bills for municipal utility services.

**Bail Bond Lien**

A real estate owner who is charged with a crime for which he or she must face trial may post bail in the form of real estate rather than cash. The execution and recording of such a bail bond creates a specific, statutory, voluntary lien against the owner's real estate. If the accused fails to appear in court, the lien may be enforced by the sheriff or another court officer.

**Corporation Franchise Tax Lien**

**In Ohio...**

The state of Ohio imposes a corporation franchise tax on corporations as a condition of allowing them to do business in the state. Such a tax is a general, statutory, involuntary lien on all property, real and personal, owned by the corporation. ◆

**Table 11.1    Real Estate Related Liens**

| | General | Specific | Voluntary | | Involuntary |
|---|---|---|---|---|---|
| General Real Estate Tax (Ad Valorem Tax) Lien | | xx | | | xx |
| Special Assessment (Improvement Tax Lien) | | xx | xx | or | xx |
| Mortgage Lien | | xx | xx | | |
| Deed of Trust Lien | | xx | xx | | |
| Mechanic's Lien | xx | xx | | | |
| Judgment Lien | xx | | | | xx |
| Estate Tax Lilen | xx | | | | xx |
| Inheritance Tax Lien | xx | | | | xx |
| Municipal Utilities Lien | | xx | | | xx |
| Bail Bond Lien | | xx | xx | | |
| Corporation Franchise Tax Lien | xx | | | | xx |
| Income Tax Lien | xx | | | | xx |

**IRS Tax Lien**

A federal tax lien, or Internal Revenue Service tax lien, results from a person's failure to pay any portion of federal taxes, such as income and withholding taxes. A federal tax lien is a general, statutory, involuntary lien on all real and personal property held by the delinquent taxpayer. Its priority, however, is based on the date of filing or recording; it does not supersede previously recorded liens.

A summary of the real estate-related liens discussed in this chapter appears in Table 11.1.

**KEY TERMS**

| | | |
|---|---|---|
| ad valorem tax | judgment | special assessment |
| attachment | junior lien | specific lien |
| equalization factor | lien | statutory lien |
| equitable lien | lien priority | subordination |
| estate taxes | lis pendens | agreement |
| general lien | mechanic's lien | tax lien |
| general real estate tax | mill | tax sale |
| inheritance taxes | mortgage lien | voluntary lien |
| involuntary lien | redemption | |

**SUMMARY**

- Liens are claims of creditors or taxing authorities against the real and personal property of a debtor.
  - A lien is a type of encumbrance.
  - Liens are either general, covering all real and personal property of a debtor-owner, or specific, covering only identified property.

- Liens are also either voluntary, arising from an action of the debtor, or involuntary, created by statute (statutory) or based on the concept of fairness (equitable).
- With the exception of real estate tax liens and mechanics' liens, the priority of liens is generally determined by the order in which they are placed in the public record of the county in which the property is located.
- Real estate taxes are levied annually by local taxing authorities and are generally given priority over other liens.
  - Payments are required before stated dates, after which penalties accrue.
  - An owner may lose title to property for nonpayment of taxes because such tax-delinquent property can be sold at a tax sale.
  - Some states allow a time period during which a defaulted owner can redeem his or her real estate from a tax sale.
- Special assessments are levied to allocate the cost of public improvements to the specific parcels of real estate that benefit from them. Assessments are usually payable annually over a five- or ten-year period, together with interest due on the balance of the assessment.
- Mortgage liens (deed of trust liens) are voluntary, specific liens given to lenders to secure payment for real estate loans.
- Mechanics' liens protect general contractors, subcontractors, and material suppliers whose work enhances the value of real estate.
- A judgment is a court decree obtained by a creditor, usually for a monetary award from a debtor. A judgment lien can be enforced by court issuance of a writ of execution and sale by the sheriff to pay the judgment amount and costs.
- Attachment is a means of preventing a defendant from conveying property before completion of a suit in which a judgment is sought.
- Lis pendens is a recorded notice of a lawsuit that is pending in court and that may result in a judgment affecting title to a parcel of real estate.
- Federal estate taxes and state inheritance taxes are general liens against a deceased owner's property.
- Liens for water charges or other municipal utilities and bail bond liens are specific liens, while corporation franchise tax liens are general liens against a corporation's assets.
- IRS tax liens are general liens against the property of a person who is delinquent in paying IRS taxes.

---

**Real-Life Real Estate**

1. After you list a wonderful property for sale, you discover that the amount of the mortgage, second mortgage, IRS lien, a judgment (which was the result of a mechanic's lien), and your commission total more than the listing price. Now what?
2. How would you avoid the situation in question #1 in the future?
3. You write a contract on October 30 for the sale of a property. There is a large school tax levy on the ballot that will be decided in a week or so. How do you estimate prorated taxes?

# QUESTIONS

1. Which of the following best refers to the type of lien that affects all real and personal property of a debtor?
   a. Specific lien
   b. Voluntary lien
   c. Involuntary lien
   d. General lien

2. *Priority of liens* refers to which of the following?
   a. The order in which a debtor assumes responsibility for payment of obligations
   b. The order in which liens will be paid if property is sold to satisfy a debt
   c. The dates liens are filed for record
   d. The fact that specific liens have greater priority than general liens

3. A lien on real estate made to secure payment for specific municipal improvements is which of the following?
   a. Mechanic's lien
   b. Special assessment
   c. Ad valorem
   d. Utility lien

4. Which of the following is classified as a general lien?
   a. Mechanic's lien
   b. Bail bond lien
   c. Judgment
   d. Real estate taxes

5. Which of the following liens usually would be given highest priority?
   a. A mortgage dated last year
   b. Real estate tax
   c. A mechanic's lien for work started before the mortgage was made
   d. A judgment rendered yesterday

6. A specific parcel of real estate has a market value of $80,000 and is assessed for tax purposes at 35 percent of market value. The tax rate for the county in which the property is located is 30 mills. The tax bill will be
   a. $50.　　　　　　c. $840.
   b. $60.　　　　　　d. $720.

7. Which of the following is used to distribute the cost of public services among real estate owners?
   a. Personal property tax
   b. Sales tax
   c. Real property tax
   d. Special assessment

8. A mechanic's lien claim arises when a contractor has performed work or provided material to improve a parcel of real estate on the owner's order and the work has not been paid for. Such a contractor has a right to
   a. tear out his or her work.
   b. record a notice of the lien.
   c. record a notice of the lien and file a court suit within the time required by state law.
   d. have personal property of the owner sold to satisfy the lien.

9. What is the annual real estate tax on a property that is valued at $135,000 and assessed for tax purposes at $47,250 with an equalization factor of 125 percent, when the tax rate is 25 mills?
   a. $1,418　　　　c. $945
   b. $1,477　　　　d. $1,181

10. Which of the following is a voluntary, specific lien?
    a. IRS tax lien
    b. Mechanic's lien
    c. Mortgage lien
    d. Seller's lien

11. A seller sold a buyer a parcel of real estate. Title has passed, but to date the buyer has not paid the purchase price in full as originally agreed on. If the seller does not receive payment, which of the following would she be entitled to enforce?
    a. Attachment　　　c. Lis pendens
    b. Buyer's lien　　　d. Judgment

12.  A general contractor is going to sue a
     homeowner for nonpayment; the suit will be
     filed in two weeks. The contractor just
     learned that the homeowner has listed the
     property for sale with a real estate broker.
     In this situation, which of the following will
     be used by the contractor and his attorneys
     to protect his interest?
     a. Seller's lien        c. Assessment
     b. Buyer's lien         d. Attachment

13.  Special assessment liens
     a. are general liens.
     b. are paid on a monthly basis.
     c. take priority over mechanics' liens.
     d. cannot be prepaid in full without penalty.

14.  Which of the following is a lien on real
     estate?
     a. An easement running with the land
     b. An unpaid mortgage loan
     c. A license
     d. An encroachment

15.  Both a mortgage lien and a judgment lien
     a. must be entered by the court.
     b. involve a debtor-creditor relationship.
     c. are general liens.
     d. are involuntary liens.

16.  A mechanic's lien would be available to all
     of the following *EXCEPT* a
     a. subcontractor.      c. surveyor.
     b. contractor.         d. broker.

17.  The right of a defaulted taxpayer to recover
     his or her property prior to its sale for
     unpaid taxes is the
     a. statutory right of reinstatement.
     b. equitable right of appeal.
     c. statutory right of assessment.
     d. equitable right of redemption.

18.  Which of the following is a specific,
     involuntary lien?
     a. A real estate tax lien
     b. An income tax lien
     c. An estate tax lien
     d. A judgment lien

19.  Taxes levied for the operation of the
     government are called
     a. assessment taxes.
     b. ad valorem taxes.
     c. special taxes.
     d. improvement taxes.

20.  All of the following probably would be
     exempt from real estate taxes *EXCEPT*
     a. a medical research facility.
     b. a public golf course.
     c. a community church.
     d. an apartment building.

21.  In Ohio, assessments
     a. are not regulated as to the amount that
        may be levied against a property owner.
     b. do not exist.
     c. are regulated as to the amount that may
        be levied against a property owner.
     d. are a percentage of the real estate taxes.

22.  In Ohio, a mechanic's lienor must file suit
     within what time period after the owner of
     the real estate notifies him or her to
     commence suit?
     a. 30 days            c. 40 days
     b. 45 days            d. 60 days

23.  In Ohio, a mechanic's lien once filed as a lien
     on real estate may continue as a lien for
     a. one year renewable.
     b. 60 days nonrenewable.
     c. five years renewable.
     d. six years.

24.  In Ohio, the county auditor must reappraise
     all realty in the state every
     a. four years.
     b. six years.
     c. three years.
     d. ten years.

25.  In Ohio, real estate sold for delinquent real
     estate taxes may
     a. not be redeemed by the former owner.
     b. be redeemed by the former owner by
        payment in full within 30 days after the
        sale.
     c. be redeemed by the former owner by
        payment in full before the confirmation
        of sale.
     d. be redeemed by the former owner by
        payment in full within two years after the
        sale.

26. Which of the following tradespeople are entitled to mechanics' liens?
    a. Only mechanics
    b. Any entity that delivers or installs material on real estate and for which the entity has not been paid
    c. Only builders/developers
    d. Only building suppliers

27. In Ohio, real estate taxes are usually payable
    a. twice a year.          c. monthly.
    b. once a year.           d. biannually.

28. The penalty for failure to pay real estate taxes on the due date in Ohio is
    a. 15 percent of the amount due.
    b. 10 percent of the amount due.
    c. 100 percent of the amount due.
    d. 25 percent of the amount due.

29. Special assessments in Ohio are
    a. collected in the same manner as real estate taxes.
    b. deductible on a federal tax return.
    c. not regulated by any governmental agency.
    d. collected on a quarterly basis.

30. The filing in a county of a certificate of judgment issued by an Ohio court
    a. immediately becomes a lien on all of the debtor's real estate in that county.
    b. immediately becomes a lien on the debtor's real estate anywhere in Ohio.
    c. cannot attach the debtor's real estate.
    d. will become a lien within ten days after filing.

31. The common level of real estate tax assessment (assessed value) in Ohio is
    a. equal to the appraised value.
    b. 35 percent of the appraised value.
    c. 35 percent of the selling price.
    d. 10 percent of the appraised value.

32. A home is valued at $95,000. Property in its area is assessed at 35 percent of its value, and the local tax rate is $2.85 per $100. What is the amount of annual tax paid on the home?
    a. $2,451.27          c. $135.38
    b. $1,470.60          d. $947.63

# CHAPTER 12

# Real Estate Contracts

## CONTRACT LAW

> A **contract** is a voluntary, legally enforceable promise between two competent parties to perform some legal act in exchange for consideration.

A contract is a voluntary agreement or promise between legally competent parties, supported by legal consideration, to perform (or refrain from performing) some legal act. That definition may be easier to understand if we consider its various parts separately. A contract must be

- *voluntary*—no one may be forced into a contract;
- an *agreement or a promise*—a contract is essentially a legally enforceable promise;
- made by *legally competent parties*—the parties must be viewed by the law as capable of making a legally binding promise;
- supported by *legal consideration*—a contract must be supported by some valuable thing that induces a party to enter into the contract, and that "thing" must be legally sufficient to support a contract; and
- about a *legal act*—no one may make a legal contract to do something illegal.

**In Ohio...** Essentially, a contract is an enforceable promise—a promise that someone may be compelled by a court to keep. Brokers and salespersons use many types of contracts and agreements to carry out their responsibilities to sellers, buyers and the general public. The general body of law that governs such agreements is known as contract law. In Ohio, contract law is based on both statutory laws and court cases. ◆

**Express and Implied Contracts** A contract may be *express* or *implied*, depending on how it is created. An **express contract** exists when the parties state the terms and show their intentions in *words*. An express contract may be either oral or written. The majority of real estate contracts are express contracts; they have been reduced to writing. Under the **statute of frauds**, certain types of contracts must be in writing to be enforceable in a court of law. (*Enforceable* means that the parties may be forced to comply with the contract's terms and conditions.) In an **implied contract**, the agreement of the parties is demonstrated by their *acts and conduct*.

**F**OR EXAMPLE  *H* approaches his neighbor, *B*, and says, "I will paint your house today for $50." *B* replies, "If you paint my house today, I will pay you $50." *H* and *B* have entered into an express contract. *K* goes into a restaurant and orders a meal. *K* has entered into an implied contract with the restaurant to pay for the meal, even though payment was not mentioned before the meal was ordered.

**In Ohio...**  The Ohio Statute of Frauds requires that conveyances of interests in real property such as deeds, contracts for sale, mortgages, and certain leases must be in writing and signed by the party to be bound or by his or her legally authorized agent. ◆

*power of attorney* →

**In Practice**

Because a listing agreement is an employment contract, not a conveyance of land, it is not covered by the requirements of the statute of frauds. As a matter of good business practice, however, and to avoid misunderstandings, listing agreements should always be in writing.

**Parol evidence rule.** The *parol evidence rule,* another heritage of the common law, is a rule of evidence that dictates that no prior or contemporaneous oral or written negotiations or agreements that vary or contradict the terms of a written contract may be considered as evidence in a lawsuit based on the written agreement. That is, the written contract is assumed to be the *complete manifestation of the agreement of the parties.* No evidence of what one party may or may not have said or written before the contract was signed may be admitted. There are many exceptions to this rule, however, including evidence that a contract was entered into illegally or evidence intended to clarify an ambiguous contract term.

**Bilateral and Unilateral Contracts**

Contracts may be classified as either bilateral or unilateral. In a **bilateral contract,** both parties promise to do something; one promise is given in exchange for another. A real estate sales contract is a bilateral contract because the seller promises to sell a parcel of real estate and convey title to the property to the buyer, who promises to pay a certain sum of money for the property.

> *bi-* means "two"—a *bilateral contract* must have two promises. *uni-* means "one"—a *unilateral contract* has only one promise.

A **unilateral contract,** on the other hand, is a one-sided agreement. One party makes a promise to induce a second party to do something. The second party is not legally obligated to act. However, if the second party does comply, the first party is obligated to keep the promise. For instance, a law enforcement agency might offer a monetary payment to anyone who can aid in the capture of a criminal. Only if someone does aid in the capture is the reward paid. An option contract, which will be discussed later, is another example of a unilateral contract.

**F**OR EXAMPLE *B* puts up a sign that says, "If you paint my house today, I will pay you $50." If *H* paints *B*'s house, *B* will be legally obligated to pay *H. B* and *H* have a unilateral contract.

**Executed and Executory Contracts**

A contract may be classified as either executed or executory, depending on whether the agreement is performed. An executed contract is one in which all parties have fulfilled their promises: the contract has been performed. This should not be confused with the word *execute,* which refers to the signing of a contract. An **executory contract** exists when one or both parties still have an act to perform. A sales contract is an executory contract from the time it is signed until closing: ownership has not yet changed hands, and the seller has not received the sales price. At closing, the sales contract is executed.

## Validity of Contracts

A contract can be described as valid, void, voidable, or unenforceable, depending on the circumstances.

A **valid contract** meets all the essential elements that make it legally sufficient, or enforceable.

A **void contract** has no legal force or effect because it lacks some or all of the essential elements of a contract.

A **voidable contract** appears on the surface to be valid, but may be rescinded or disaffirmed by one or both parties based on some legal principle. A voidable contract is considered by the courts to be valid if the party who has the option to disaffirm the agreement does not do so within a period of time prescribed by state law. A contract with a minor, for instance, is usually voidable, because minors are generally permitted to disaffirm real estate contracts at any time while under age and for a certain period of time after reaching majority age. (In Ohio, 18 is the age of majority.) A contract entered into by a mentally ill person is usually voidable during the mental illness and for a reasonable period after the person is cured. On the other hand, a contract made by a person who has been adjudicated insane (that is, found to be insane by a court) is void on the theory that the judgment is a matter of public record.

---

**In Practice**   Mental capacity to enter into a contract is not the same as medical sanity. The test is whether the individual in question is capable of understanding what he or she is doing. A party may suffer from a mental illness, but have a clear understanding of the significance of his or her actions. This is a thorny legal and psychological question that requires consultation with experts.

---

A contract may be

- **valid**—has all legal elements: fully enforceable;
- **void**—lacks one or all elements: no legal force or effect;
- **voidable**—has all legal elements: may be rescinded or disaffirmed; or
- **unenforceable**—has all legal elements: enforceable only between the parties.

An **unenforceable contract** also seems on the surface to be valid; however, neither party can sue the other to force performance. For example, an oral agreement for the sale of a parcel of real estate would be unenforceable. Because the statute of frauds requires that real estate sales contracts be in writing, the defaulting party could not be taken to court and forced to perform. There is, however, a distinction between a suit to force performance and a suit for damages, which is permissible in an oral agreement. An unenforceable contract is said to be "valid as between the parties." This means that once the agreement is fully executed and both parties are satisfied, neither has reason to initiate a lawsuit to force performance.

**Reality of consent.** A contract that complies with all of the basic requirements may still be either void or voidable. This is because of the doctrine of *reality of consent*. A contract must be entered into as the free and voluntary act of each party. Each party must be able to make a prudent and knowledgeable decision without undue influence. A mistake, misrepresentation, fraud, undue influence or duress would deprive a person of that ability. If any of these circumstances is present, the contract is voidable by the injured party. If the other party were to sue for breach, the injured party could use lack of voluntary assent as a defense.

**Essential Elements of a Valid Contract**

A contract must meet certain minimum requirements to be considered legally valid. The following are the basic essential elements of a contract.

**Offer and acceptance.** There must be an offer by one party that is accepted by the other. The person who makes the offer is the *offeror*. The person who accepts the offer is the *offeree*. This requirement is also called *mutual assent*. It means that there must be a meeting of the minds, or complete agreement about the purpose and terms of the contract. Courts look to the *objective intent of the parties* to determine whether they intended to enter into a binding agreement. In cases where the statute of frauds applies, the **offer and acceptance** must be delivered to the other party or that party's agent in writing. The wording of the contract must express all the agreed on terms and must be clearly understood by the parties.

*Test*

---

Elements of a contract:

• Offer and acceptance
• Consideration
• Legally competent parties
• Legalilty of object

---

An *offer* is a promise made by one party, requesting something in exchange for that promise. The offer is made with the intention that the offeror will be bound to the terms if the offer is accepted. The terms of the offer must be definite and specific and must be communicated to the offeree.

An *offer may be revoked* by the offeror at any time prior to acceptance if the revocation is communicated directly to the offeree. It also is revoked if the offeree learns of the revocation from a reliable source (such as the listing broker) and observes the offeror acting in a manner that indicates that the offer no longer exists.

An *acceptance* is a promise by the offeree to be bound by the *exact* terms proposed by the offeror. The acceptance must be communicated to the offeror.

**In Ohio...**  Note that the offeree can consider more than one offer at a time. The fact that one offer is pending does not prevent other offers from being presented for consideration. In fact, the license laws of most states, including Ohio, provide that a licensee must present all offers to the parties immediately, regardless of whether another offer is pending or has even been accepted. ◆

*Test*

Proposing any deviation from the terms of the offer constitutes a *rejection—or termination—of the original offer* and becomes a new offer. This is known as a **counteroffer,** and it must be communicated to the original offering party. The counteroffer must be accepted for a contract to exist. Counteroffers are made during negotiations between the buyer and the seller. It is important for licensees to realize that the fact that the offeree made a counteroffer does not prevent the licensee from presenting other offers. *During this process, real estate agents must remember that it is up to the principal to decide which offer to accept or reject. It is an agent's task to offer advice and work on behalf of the client's best interest.*

Besides being terminated by a counteroffer, an offer may be terminated by the offeree's outright rejection of it. Alternatively, an offeree may fail to accept the offer before it expires, in which case it also expires. The offeror may revoke the offer at any time before receiving the acceptance. This *revocation* must be communicated to the offeree by the offeror, either directly or through the parties' agents. The offer is also revoked if the offeree learns of the revocation and observes the offeror acting in a manner that indicates that the offer no longer exists.

**Consideration.** The contract must be based on consideration. **Consideration** is something of legal value offered by one party and accepted by another as an inducement to perform or to refrain from some act. There must be a definite statement of consideration in a contract to show that something of value was given in exchange for the promise.

Consideration must be "good and valuable" between the parties. The courts do not inquire into the adequacy of consideration. Adequate consideration ranges from as little as a promise of "love and affection" to a substantial sum of money. Anything that has been bargained for and exchanged is legally sufficient to satisfy the requirement for consideration. The only requirements are that the parties agree and that no undue influence or fraud has occurred. (Note that the earnest money deposit is not the consideration for a purchase and sale agreement; the purchase price is.)

**Legally competent parties.** Both parties to the contract must be of legal age and have sufficient *mental capacity* to understand the consequences of their actions.

**In Ohio...** As mentioned previously, 18 is the age of contractual capacity in Ohio. A minor's contract is voidable or may be canceled before or within a reasonable time after the minor reaches age 18. A salesperson or broker should carefully inquire into the ages of both the purchaser and the seller of real estate. ◆

Advanced age, in contrast, may (in some cases) be an indication of incapacity to contract as a result of senility, weakness, or other disabilities. In questions of legal competency it may be desirable to refer to the client's attorney. A party who understands the nature and effect of the contract has sufficient mental capacity. Note that mental capacity is not the same as medical sanity.

**Legality of object.** To be valid, a contract must not contemplate a purpose that is illegal or against public policy.

**Absence of undue influence, duress and misrepresentation.** To be valid, every contract must be signed as the free and voluntary act of each party. Contracts signed by a person under duress or undue influence are voidable (may be canceled). Extreme care should be taken when one or more of the parties to a contract is elderly, suffering from physical or mental illness, in emotional distress, or under the influence of alcohol or drugs. Misrepresentation or fraud also may render a contract voidable by the injured party.

**Accurate description of the property.** A *real estate sales contract* must contain an accurate description of the property being conveyed. The test that most courts use is whether the subject property can be identified with reasonable certainty. This may require a legal description, but in many cases a street address is sufficient.

**In Ohio...** In Ohio, when the street address and lot dimensions are used, the permanent tax parcel number or the recording data (page and volume) of the owner's deed may be added for further identification. ◆

# DISCHARGE OF CONTRACTS

A contract is *discharged* when the agreement is terminated. Obviously, the most desirable case is when a contract terminates because it has been completely performed, with all its terms carried out. However, a contract may be terminated for other reasons, such as a party's breach or default.

**Performance of a Contract**

Each party has certain rights and duties to fulfill. The question of *when* a contract must be performed is an important factor. Many contracts call for a specific time by which the agreed-on acts must be completely performed. In addition, many contracts provide that **"time is of the essence."** This means that the contract must be performed within the time limit specified. A party who fails to perform on time is liable for breach of contract.

When a contract does not specify a date for performance, the acts it requires should be performed within a reasonable time. The interpretation of what constitutes a reasonable time depends on the situation. Generally, unless the parties agree otherwise, if the act can be done immediately, it should be performed immediately. Courts have sometimes declared contracts to be invalid because they did not contain a time or date for performance.

**Assignment**

**Assignment** is a transfer of rights or duties under a contract. Rights may be assigned to a third party (called the *assignee*) unless the contract forbids it. Obligations also may be assigned (or *delegated*), but the original party remains primarily liable unless specifically released. Many contracts include a clause that either permits or forbids assignment.

> *Assignment* = substitution of *parties*
>
> *Novation* = substitution of *contracts*

*Test*

**F**OR EXAMPLE   *X* enters into a contract to paint *Y*'s toolshed. Under the terms of the contract, *X* will be paid $1,000 when the job is finished. *X* owes $1,000 to *W*, and so *X* assigns to *W* the right to receive the payment. When the job is done, *Y* will pay $1,000 to *W*.

On the other hand, suppose that the day after *X* contracts to paint *Y*'s toolshed for $1,000, *Z* offers *X* $3,000 to paint a gazebo. *X* wants to take the better-paying job, but doesn't want to breach the contract with *Y*. If the contract with *Y* permits it, *X* may assign both the right to be paid and the duty to paint the toolshed to *P*, another painter. If *P* fails to paint the toolshed, however, *X* will be liable to *Y* for breach of contract.

**Novation**

A contract may be performed by **novation**—that is, the substitution of a new contract in place of the original. The new agreement may be between the same parties, or a new party may be substituted for either (this is *novation of the parties*). The parties' intent must be to discharge the old obligation. For instance, when a real estate purchaser assumes the seller's existing mortgage loan, the lender may choose to release the seller and substitute the buyer as the party primarily liable for the mortgage debt.

**Breach of Contract**

A contract may be terminated if it is breached by one of the parties. A **breach of contract** is a violation of any of the terms or conditions of a contract without legal excuse. For instance, a seller who fails to deliver title to the buyer breaches a sales contract. The breaching or defaulting party assumes certain burdens, and the nondefaulting party has certain remedies.

If the seller breaches a real estate sales contract, the buyer may sue for *specific performance* unless the contract specifically states otherwise. In a **suit for**

**specific performance,** the buyer asks the court to force the seller to go through with the sale and convey the property as previously agreed. The buyer may choose to sue for *damages*, however, in which case he or she asks that the seller pay for any costs and hardships suffered by the buyer as a result of the seller's breach.

If the buyer defaults, the seller can sue for damages or sue for the purchase price. A suit for the purchase price is essentially a suit for specific performance: the seller tenders the deed and asks that the buyer be compelled to pay the agreed price.

The contract may limit the remedies available to the parties, however. A *liquidated damages* clause permits the seller to keep the earnest money deposit and any other payments received from the buyer as the seller's sole remedy. The clause may limit the buyer's remedy to a return of the earnest money and other payments should the seller default.

**In Ohio...**   **Statute of limitations.** Ohio law allows a specific time limit during which parties to a contract may sue to enforce their rights. The statute of limitations varies for different legal actions, and any rights not enforced within the applicable time period will be lost. For written contracts in Ohio the statute of limitations is 15 years. ✓ Test

Contracts also may be discharged or terminated when any of the following occurs:

- *Partial performance* of the terms, along with a written acceptance by the other party.
- *Substantial performance,* in which one party has substantially performed on the contract, but does not complete all the details exactly as the contract requires. (Such performance may be enough to force payment, with certain adjustments for any damages suffered by the other party.) For instance, where a newly constructed addition to a home is finished except for polishing the brass doorknobs, the contractor is entitled to the final payment.
- *Impossibility of performance,* in which an act required by the contract cannot be legally accomplished.
- *Mutual agreement* of the parties to cancel.
- *Operation of law*—such as in the voiding of a contract by a minor—as a result of fraud, due to the expiration of the statute of limitations, or because a contract was altered without the written consent of all parties involved.

# CONTRACTS USED IN THE REAL ESTATE BUSINESS

The written agreements most commonly used by brokers and salespersons are

*Real Estate Agent only*
*Estate*
- listing agreements and buyer agency agreements,
- real estate sales contracts,
- options, — done By attorney
- land contracts or contracts for deed, and — Attorney —
- leases and escrow agreements. — Contract —

**In Ohio...**    Many states have specific guidelines for when and how real estate licensees may prepare contracts for their clients and customers. These guidelines are created by state real estate officials, court decisions, or statutes. *In Ohio, as in most states, a real estate licensee who is not a licensed attorney may not practice law.* The practice of law includes preparing legal documents such as deeds, land contracts, options, leases and mortgages, and offering advice on legal matters. A broker or salesperson may, however, be permitted to fill in the blanks on certain approved preprinted documents (such as sales contracts and leases). No separate fee may be charged for completing the forms. ◆

**Contract forms.** Because so many real estate transactions are similar in nature, preprinted forms are available for most kinds of contracts. The use of preprinted forms raises three problems: (1) what to write in the blanks, (2) what words and phrases should be ruled out by drawing lines through them because they don't apply, and (3) what additional clauses or agreements (called riders or *addenda*) should be added. All changes and additions are usually initialed in the margin or on the rider by both parties when a contract is signed.

**In Ohio...**    There is no common, statewide form of offer to purchase used throughout Ohio. Ohio brokers may fill in the blanks of most form purchase and sale contracts, but brokers should not discourage their buyers and sellers from consulting attorneys. ◆

The Ohio license law requires that licensees furnish all parties involved in a real estate transaction with true copies (originals) of all listings and other agreements to which they are a party at the time each party signs. This requirement helps avoid the problem of changes being made to a contract without the other parties' knowledge or permission. The failure to comply with this rule is one of the major reasons for revocation or suspension of real estate licenses. ◆

**In Practice**    It is essential that both parties to a contract understand exactly what they are agreeing to. Poorly drafted documents, especially those containing extensive legal language, may be subject to various interpretations and lead to litigation. The parties to a real estate transaction should be advised to have sales contracts and other legal documents examined by their lawyers before they sign to ensure that the agreements accurately reflect their intentions. When preprinted forms do not sufficiently cover special provisions in a transaction, the parties should have an attorney draft an appropriate contract.

**Listing and Buyer Agency Agreements**    A *listing agreement* is an employment contract. It establishes the rights and obligations of the broker as agent and the seller as principal. A buyer agency contract establishes the relationship between a buyer and his or her agent. Refer to Chapter 7 for a complete discussion of the various types of listing agreements and buyer agency agreements and for sample contracts.

**In Practice**
**In Ohio...**    If a contract contains any ambiguity, Ohio courts generally interpret the agreement against the party who prepared it. ◆

**Sales Contracts**   A real estate sales contract contains the complete agreement between the buyer of a parcel of real estate and the seller. Depending on the area, this agreement may be known as an *offer to purchase,* a *contract of purchase and sale*, a *purchase agreement*, an *earnest money agreement*, or a *deposit receipt*.

Whatever the contract is called, it is an offer to purchase real estate as soon as it has been prepared and signed by the purchaser. If the document is accepted and signed by the seller, it becomes a contract of sale. This transformation is referred to as *ripening*.

*The contract of sale is the most important document in the sale of real estate.* It establishes the legal rights and obligations of the buyer and seller. In effect, it dictates the contents of the deed.

Several details frequently appear in a sales contract in addition to the essential elements of a contract. These include

- the sales price and terms;
- a legal description of the land;
- a statement of the kind and condition of the title, and the form of deed to be delivered by the seller;
- the kind of title evidence required, who will provide it, and how many defects in the title will be eliminated; and
- statements of all the terms and conditions of the agreement between the parties and any contingencies (discussed later in this chapter).

The following paragraphs discuss some of the issues that often arise as an offer to purchase ripens into a contract of sale.

**Offer.** A broker lists an owner's real estate for sale at whatever price and conditions the owner sets. When a prospective buyer is found, the broker helps him or her prepare an offer to purchase. The offer is signed by the prospective buyer and presented by the licensee to the seller. This is an *offer*.

**Counteroffer.** As discussed earlier, any change to the terms proposed by the buyer creates a *counteroffer*. The original offer ceases to exist because the seller has rejected it. The buyer may accept or reject the seller's counteroffer. If the buyer wishes, he or she may continue the process by making another counteroffer. Any change in the last offer made results in a counteroffer until either the parties reach agreement or one of them walks away.

> A *counteroffer* is a *new offer*; it voids the original offer.

An offer or counteroffer may be *revoked at any time before it has been accepted,* even if the person making the offer or counteroffer agreed to keep the offer open for a set period of time.

**Acceptance.** If the seller agrees to the original offer or a later counteroffer *exactly as it was made* and signs the document, the offer has been *accepted*. Acceptance of the offer means that a contract is *formed*. The licensee must advise the buyer of the seller's acceptance and obtain their lawyers' approval if the contract calls for it. A duplicate original of the contract must be provided to each party.

An offer is not considered accepted until the person making the offer has been *notified of the other party's acceptance.* When the parties communicate through an agent or at a distance, questions may arise regarding whether an acceptance, a rejection, or a counteroffer has occurred. Current technologies make communication faster: a signed agreement that is faxed, for instance, would constitute adequate communication. The licensee must transmit all offers, acceptances, or other responses as soon as possible to avoid questions of proper communication.

**Binder.**  In some states, brokers may prepare a shorter document, known as a *binder,* instead of a complete sales contract. The binder states the essential terms of the offer and acknowledges that the broker has received the purchaser's deposit. The parties have a more formal and complete contract of sale drawn up by an attorney once the seller accepts and signs the binder. A binder also might be used where the details of the transaction are too complex for the standard sales contract form.

**Earnest money deposits.**  It is customary (although not essential) for a purchaser to provide a deposit when making an offer to purchase real estate. This deposit, usually in the form of a check, is referred to as **earnest money.** The earnest money deposit is evidence of the buyer's intention to carry out the terms of the contract in good faith. The check is given to the broker, who usually holds it for the parties in a special account. In some areas, it is common practice for deposits to be held in escrow by the seller's attorney. If the offer is not accepted, the earnest money deposit is immediately returned to the would-be buyer.

The amount of the deposit is a matter to be agreed on by the parties. Under the terms of most listing agreements, a real estate broker is required to accept a "reasonable amount" as earnest money. As a rule, the deposit should be an amount sufficient to

- discourage the buyer from defaulting,
- compensate the seller for taking the property off the market, and
- cover any expenses the seller might incur if the buyer defaults.

Most contracts provide that the deposit becomes the seller's property as liquidated damages if the buyer defaults. The seller also might claim further damages, however, unless the contract limits recovery to the deposit alone.

**In Ohio...**  Earnest money held by a broker must be held in a special trust or *escrow account.* This money cannot be mixed with a broker's own personal funds (called *commingling*). A broker may not use earnest money funds for his or her personal use (called *conversion*). A separate escrow account does not have to be opened for each earnest money deposit received; all deposits may be kept in one account. In Ohio, a broker must maintain full, complete, and accurate records of all earnest money deposits and provide an accounting upon request. ◆

**In Ohio...**  The special account may or may not pay interest, depending on state law. If the account bears interest, there must be some provision in the contract for how the interest earned will be distributed. The broker must provide the parties with an accounting of the amount and dates of interest payments. Usually, a check for the interest amount is given to the buyer at closing. On the other hand, the contract may provide for the interest to be paid to the seller as part of the purchase price. In Ohio, trust accounts must be non-interest bearing accounts. ◆

**In Ohio...**   *Test*   **Equitable title.** When a buyer signs a contract to purchase real estate, he or she does not receive title to the land. Title transfers only on delivery and acceptance of a deed. However, in Ohio, after both buyer and seller have executed a sales contract, the buyer acquires an *interest* in the land. This interest is known as **equitable title.** A person who holds equitable title has rights that vary from state to state. Equitable title may give the buyer an insurable interest in the property. If the parties decide not to go through with the purchase and sale, the buyer may be required to give the seller a *quitclaim deed* to release the equitable interest in the land. ◆

**In Ohio...**   **Destruction of premises.** In many states, including Ohio, once the sales contract is signed by both parties, the buyer bears the risk of any damage to the property that may occur before closing. Of course, the contract may provide otherwise. ◆ Furthermore, the laws and court decisions of a growing number of states have placed the risk of loss on the seller. Many of these states have adopted the *Uniform Vendor and Purchaser Risk Act,* which specifically provides that the seller must bear any loss that occurs before the title passes or the buyer takes possession.

**In Ohio...**   **Liquidated damages.** To avoid a lawsuit if one party breaches the contract, the parties may agree on a certain amount of money that will compensate the nonbreaching party. That money is called **liquidated damages.** If a sales contract specifies that the earnest money deposit is to serve as liquidated damages in case the buyer defaults, the seller will be entitled to keep the deposit if the buyer refuses to perform without good reason. The seller who keeps the deposit as liquidated damages may not sue for any further damages if the contract provides that the deposit is the seller's sole remedy. Many states, including Ohio, provide that liquidated damages must be reasonable and cannot be construed as a penalty. ◆

**Parts of a sales contract.** All real estate sales contracts can be divided into a number of separate parts. Although each form of contract contains these divisions, their location within a particular contract may vary. Most sales contracts include the following information:

- The purchaser's name and a statement of the purchaser's obligation to purchase the property, including how the purchaser intends to take title.
- An adequate description of the property, such as the street address. (Note that while a street address may be adequate for a sales contract, it is not legally sufficient as a description of the real property being conveyed, as discussed in Chapter 10.)
- The seller's name and a statement of the type of deed a seller agrees to give, including any covenants, conditions, and restrictions that apply to the deed.
- The purchase price and how the purchaser intends to pay for the property, including earnest money deposits, additional cash from the purchaser, and the conditions of any mortgage financing the purchaser intends to obtain or assume.
- The amount and form of the down payment or earnest money deposit and whether it will be in the form of a check or promissory note.
- A provision for the closing of the transaction and the transfer of possession of the property to the purchaser by a specific date.
- A provision for title evidence (abstract and legal opinion, certificate, of title, Torrens certificate or title insurance policy).

- The method by which real estate taxes, rents, fuel costs, and other expenses are to be prorated.
- A provision for the completion of the contract should the property be damaged or destroyed between the time of signing and the closing date.
- A liquidated damages clause, a right-to-sue provision, or another statement of remedies available in the event of default.
- Contingency clauses (such as the buyer obtaining financing or selling a currently owned property, or the seller's acquisition of another desired property, or clearing of the title; attorney approval and home inspection are other commonly included contingencies).

**In Ohio...**

- The dated signatures of all parties (the signature of a witness is not essential to a valid contract). In Ohio, the seller's nonowning spouse should also sign to release dower rights. An agent may sign for a principal if the agent has been expressly authorized to do so. When sellers are co-owners, all must sign if the entire ownership is being transferred. ◆

**Additional provisions.** Many sales contracts provide for the following:

- Any personal property to be left with the premises for the purchaser (such as major appliances or lawn and garden equipment)
- Any real property to be removed by the seller before the closing (such as a storage shed)
- The transfer of any applicable warranties on items such as heating and cooling systems or built-in appliances
- The identification of any leased equipment that must be transferred to the purchaser or returned to the lessor (such as security systems, cable television boxes, and water softeners)
- The appointment of a closing or settlement agent
- Closing or settlement instructions
- The transfer of any impound or escrow account funds
- The transfer or payment of any outstanding special assessments
- The purchaser's right to inspect the property shortly before the closing or settlement (often called the *walk-through*)
- The agreement as to what documents will be provided by each party and when and where they will be delivered.

Figure 12.1 shows a typical sales contract.

**Contingencies.** Additional conditions that must be satisfied before a sales contract is fully enforceable are called **contingencies.** A contingency includes the following three elements:

1. The actions necessary to satisfy the contingency
2. The time frame within which the actions must be performed
3. Who is responsible for paying any costs involved

The most common contingencies include

- a *mortgage (financing) contingency.* A mortgage contingency protects the buyer's earnest money until a lender commits the mortgage loan funds.
- an *inspection contingency.* A sales contract may be contingent on the buyer's obtaining certain inspections of the property. Inspections may include those for wood-boring insects, lead-based paint, structural and mechanical systems, sewage facilities, and radon or other toxic materials.

## Figure 12.1   Real Estate Sales Contract

### PURCHASE AGREEMENT

1. PROPERTY PURCHASER: _____
TO BUY PROPERTY LOCATED AT _____
City_____Zip_____,County of_____
State of Ohio, and also known as being Perm. Par. No._____ and further described as_____
The property, which PURCHASER accepts in its present "as is" condition, shall include the land, all appurtenant rights, privileges and easements and all building and fixtures including such of the following as are now on the property: all electrical, heating, plumbing, bathroom fixtures; all window and door shades, blinds, awnings, screens, storm windows, curtain and drapery fixtures; all landscaping, disposal, TV antenna, rotor and control unit, smoke detectors, garage door opener (s) and controls; all permanently attached carpeting. The following items shall remain: range and oven; refrigerator; microwave; dishwasher; washer; dryer; window air conditioner; central air conditioner;

2. PRICE: PURCHASER agrees to pay for said property the sum of . . .                                                              $_____
   (a) Earnest money paid to Broker, to be deposited in a trust account upon acceptance and credited against the purchase price
      ( ) Check      ( ) Note      ( ) Cash . . .                                                           $_____
   (b) Balance of down payment to be deposited in escrow in accordance with section 4 below                                  $_____
   (c) Proceeds of any mortgage to be secured by PURCHASER in the amount of
      ( ) Conventional   ( ) FHA     ( ) VA       Other. . .                              $_____

3. FINANCING: PURCHASER agrees to make signed application, in good faith, for a mortgage loan in an amount not greater than shown in 2C above at a lending institution of PURCHASER's choice within _____ days of acceptance of this offer. If commitment cannot be obtained within_____ days after the acceptance of this offer, this contract shall be null and void and the SELLER and PURCHASER agree to sign a release authorizing the Broker and/or Escrow Agent to return the above mentioned Trust money in full to the PURCHASER.

4. CLOSING: All documents and funds necessary to complete this transaction shall be placed in escrow with PURCHASER'S lending institution or a title company on or before_____19____,and this transaction is to be closed on or about_____,19____, except that if a defect in Title appears, SELLER shall have thirty (30) days after notice to remove such defect and, if unable to do so, PURCHASER may either (1) accept Title subject to such defect without any reduction in the purchase price or (2) terminate this agreement, in which case neither PURCHASER, SELLER nor any REALTOR(s) shall have any further liability to each other, and both PURCHASER and SELLER agree to sign a mutual release, whereupon Broker or Escrow Agent shall return the earnest money to PURCHASER.

5. POSSESSION: Subject to tenants rights, if any, the premises may be occupied rent free _____( ) days after date of title transfer on a rental basis for a maximum period of _____( ) additional days at a rate of $_____per day. Payment and collection of rent after transfer of title are the sole responsibility of SELLER and PURCHASER. On the final day of occupancy, possession shall be no later than 6:00 P.M.

6. CHARGES: SELLER shall pay the following costs through escrow: (a) real estate transfer tax, (b) title exam and one-half the cost of insuring premiums for Owners Fee Policy of Title Insurance, (c) prorations due PURCHASER, (d) broker's commission,and (e) one-half of the escrow fee. SELLER shall pay directly all utility charges to the date of title transfer or the date of possession whichever is later. The escrow agent shall withhold $_____from the proceeds due SELLER for the SELLER's final water and sewer bills. Tenant security deposits, if any, shall be credited in escrow to the PURCHASER. PURCHASER shall secure new insurance. PURCHASER shall pay one-half of the escrow fee, one-half the cost of insuring premiums for Owners Fee Policy of Title Insurance and all recording fees for the deed and any mortgage. PURCHASER acknowledge the availability of a Limited Home Warranty Protection Plan (with deductible paid by PURCHASER) which ( ) will( ) will not be provided at a cost of $_____charged to ____SELLER____PURCHASER from escrow at closing.

7. TITLE: SELLER shall furnish a general warranty deed and/or fiduciary deed, if required, conveying to PURCHASER title to the property with dower rights, if any, released free and clear of all liens and encumbrances whatsoever except (a) any mortgage assumed by PURCHASER, (b) restrictions, reservations, conditions, easements (however created), and oil and gas leases of record, (c) such encroachments as do not materially and adversely affect use or value of property, (d) zoning ordinances, if any, (e) property taxes not yet due and payable for the current half of the taxable year and thereafter. SELLER shall furnish to the PURCHASER an Owners Policy of Title Insurance ("Title Policy") in the amount of the purchase price subject to the above exceptions and any act of PURCHASER. The premium cost shall be shared equally between PURCHASER and SELLER.

8. PRORATIONS: Tenant rents, if any, taxes and assessments, based on the last available tax duplicate, and homeowner's association fees and assessments, if any, shall be prorated by the escrow agent as of the date of recording of deed. The parties hereto agree to adjust directly outside of escrow any change in taxes or assessments resulting from a change in property valuation, tax rate, and/or the construction of improvements occurring before recording of the deed, but not reflected on the last available tax duplicate. SELLER warrants that SELLER has received no notice of pending assessments. In the event the property shall be deemed subject to any agricultural tax recoupment (C.A.U.V.), SELLER agrees to pay the amount of such recoupment.

9. DAMAGES: In the event improvements are damaged in excess of ten percent (10%) of their replacement cost by fire or other hazards prior to the transfer of title, PURCHASER shall have the option of accepting the insurance proceeds for said damage and completing this transaction, or of terminating it and receiving the return of all deposits made hereunder, Risk of loss shall be born by SELLER until transfer of title.

10. CONDITION OF PROPERTY: PURCHASER has examined the property and agrees that the property is being purchased in its "as is" present physical condition including any defects disclosed by the SELLER. PURCHASER has not relied upon any representations warranties or statements about the property (including but not limited to its condition or use) unless otherwise disclosed by the SELLER(s). SELLER shall pay all costs for the repair of any gas line leak found between the street and foundation at the time of transfer of utilities. Where required by law, SELLER shall apply for and obtain any inspections and deposit required permits and/or certificates in escrow.

11. INSPECTION: PURCHASER acknowledges that he has been advised of the availability of a private professional home inspection.
PURCHASER____accepts____waives the option of such inspection (if accepted,see Addendum B). Inspections required by FHA/VA do not eliminate the need for other inspections.

THERE IS NO IMPLIED WARRANTY OF HABITABILITY OR OF GOOD WORKMANLIKE CONSTRUCTION. THERE ARE ABSOLUTELY NO IMPLIED WARRANTIES OF ANY KIND COVERING THIS PROPERTY.

PURCHASER acknowledges receipt of Residential Property Disclosure Form. _____
                                                 Purchaser's's initial(s)

12. BINDING AGREEMENT: Upon written acceptance, this offer and any addendum listed below shall become a LEGALLY BINDING AGREEMENT UPON PURCHASER AND SELLER and their heirs, executors, administrators and assigns and shall represent the entire understanding of the parties regarding this transaction. All counter-offers, amendments, changes or deletions to this Agreement shall be in writing and be signed by both PURCHASER and SELLER. This Agreement shall be used as escrow instructions subject to the Escrow Agent's usual conditions of acceptance.

13. ADDENDUM: The additional terms and conditions in the attached Residential Property Disclosure Form, Agency Disclosure Form, addendum __A,__B,__C,__D,__Other are made a part of this Agreement.

PURCHASER_____ Address & Zip _____ Date _____

PURCHASER_____ Address & Zip _____ Phone _____

DEPOSIT RECEIPT: Receipt is hereby acknowledged, of $_____ ____Check____Note, earnest money, subject to terms of the above offer.
by:_____
ACCEPTANCE: The undersigned SELLER hereby accepts the above offer and agrees to pay to_____ a commission of_____percent (_____%) of the purchase price with a minimum of $3,000, Commission shall be disbursed as follows:_____%to_____ and _____% to_____.

SELLER_____ Address & Zip _____ Date _____ Time _____

SELLER_____ Address & Zip _____ Phone _____

THIS AGREEMENT IS A LEGALLY BINDING CONTRACT. IF YOU HAVE ANY QUESTIONS OF LAW, CONSULT YOUR ATTORNEY.

- a *property sale contingency.* A purchaser may make the sales contract contingent on the sale of his or her current home. This protects the buyer from owning two homes at the same time and also helps ensure the availability of cash for the purchase.

The seller may insist on an escape clause. An escape clause permits the seller to continue to market the property until all the buyer's contingencies have been satisfied or removed. The original buyer should retain the right to eliminate the contingencies if the seller receives a more favorable offer.

**Amendments and addendums.** An *amendment* is a change to the existing content of a contract. Any time words or provisions are *added to or deleted from the body of the contract,* the contract has been amended. For instance, a form contract's provision requiring closing in 90 days might be crossed out and replaced with a 60-day period. Amendments must be initialed by all parties.

On the other hand, an addendum is any provision added to an existing contract *without altering the content of the original.* An addendum is essentially a new contract between the parties that includes the original contract's provisions "by reference"; that is, the addendum mentions the original contract. An addendum must be signed by the parties. For example, an addendum might be an agreement to split the cost of repairing certain flaws discovered in a home inspection.

**In Ohio...** **Disclosures.** As discussed in previous chapters, many states (including Ohio) have enacted mandatory **disclosure** laws. The purpose of these laws is to help consumers make informed decisions. Many brokers have instituted procedures for making disclosures and recommending technical experts to ensure that purchasers have accurate information about real estate. In Ohio, a separate property condition disclosure form is required. ◆

**Options** An **option** is a contract by which an *optionor* (generally an owner) gives an *optionee* (a prospective purchaser or lessee) the right to buy or lease the owner's property at a fixed price within a certain period of time. The optionee pays a fee (the agreed-on consideration) for this option right. The optionee has no other obligation until he or she decides to either exercise the option right or allow the option to expire. An option is enforceable by only one party—the optionee.

An option contract is not a sales contract. At the time the option is signed by the parties, the owner does not sell and the optionee does not buy. The parties merely agree that the optionee has the right to buy and the owner is obligated to sell if the optionee decides to exercise his or her right of option. Options must contain all the terms and provisions required for a valid contract.

The option agreement (which is a unilateral contract) requires the optionor to act only after the optionee gives notice that he or she elects to execute the option. If the option is not exercised within the time specified in the contract, both the optionor's obligation and the optionee's right expire. An option contract may provide for renewal, which often requires additional consideration. The optionee cannot recover the consideration paid for the option right. The contract may state whether the money paid for the option is to be applied to the purchase price of the real estate if the option is exercised.

A common application of an option is a lease that includes an option for the tenant to purchase the property. Options on commercial real estate frequently depend on some specific conditions being fulfilled, such as obtaining a zoning change or a building permit. The optionee may be obligated to exercise the option if the conditions are met. Similar terms could also be included in a sales contract.

**Land Contracts**

**In Ohio...**

A real estate sale can be made under a land contract. A land contract is sometimes called a *contract for deed,* a *bond for title,* an **installment contract,** or *articles of agreement for warranty deed.* Under a typical land contract, the seller (also known as the *vendor*) retains legal title. The buyer (called the *vendee*) takes possession and gets equitable title to the property. The buyer agrees to give the seller a down payment and pay regular periodic installments of principal and interest over a number of years. The buyer also agrees to pay real estate taxes, insurance premiums, repairs, and upkeep on the property. Although the buyer obtains possession under the contract, *the seller is not obligated to execute and deliver a deed to the buyer until the terms of the contract have been satisfied.* This frequently occurs when the buyer has made enough payments to obtain a mortgage loan and pay off the balance due on the contract. Although a land contract is usually assumable by subsequent purchasers, it generally must be approved by the seller. In Ohio, a seller must record the land contract within 20 days of its execution. ◆

---

**In Practice**

Legislatures and courts have not looked favorably on the harsh provisions of some real estate installment contracts. A seller and buyer contemplating such a sale should first consult an attorney to make sure that the agreement meets all legal requirements. The individual concerns of the parties must be addressed.

---

**KEY TERMS**

| | | |
|---|---|---|
| addendum | equitable title | option |
| amendment | executed contract | rectangular |
| assignment | executory contract | (government) survey |
| bilateral contract | express contract | system |
| breach of contract | implied contract | section |
| consideration | installment contract | township |
| contingency | land contract | township line |
| contract | liquidated damages | township tier |
| counteroffer | novation | void contract |
| disclosure | offer and acceptance | voidable contract |
| earnest money | | |

---

**SUMMARY**

- A contract is a legally enforceable promise or set of promises that must be performed; if a breach occurs, the law provides a remedy.
- Contracts may be classified in different ways.
  - They may be classified according to whether the parties' intentions are express or merely implied by their actions.
  - Contracts also may be classified as bilateral (when both parties have obligated themselves to act) or unilateral (when one party is obligated to perform only if the other party acts).
  - In addition, contracts may be classified according to their legal enforceability as valid, void, voidable, or unenforceable.

- Many contracts specify a time for performance. In any case, all contracts must be performed within a reasonable time.
  - An executed contract is one that has been fully performed.
  - An executory contract is one in which some act remains to be performed.
- The essentials of a valid contract are legally competent parties, offer and acceptance, legality of object, and consideration.
  - A valid real estate contract must include a description of the property.
  - A valid real estate contract should also be in writing and signed by all parties to be enforceable in court.
- In many types of contracts, either of the parties may transfer his or her rights and obligations under the agreement by assignment or novation (substitution of a new contract).
- The seller generally has the right to declare a sale canceled if the buyer defaults. If either party suffers a loss because of the other's default, he or she may sue for damages to cover the loss. If one party insists on completing the transaction, he or she may sue the defaulter for specific performance of the terms of the contract; a court can order the other party to comply with the agreement.
- Contracts frequently used in the real estate business include:
  - listing agreements: a contract in which a seller engages a broker to find a buyer for his or her property;
  - sales contracts: in a sales contract the buyer is bound to purchase the property for the amount stated in the agreement and the seller is bound to deliver title, free from liens and encumbrances (except those identified in the contract);
  - options: the optionee purchases from the optionor, for a limited time period, the exclusive right to purchase or lease the optionor's property;
  - land contracts (installment contracts): a sales/financing agreement under which a buyer purchases a seller's real estate on time. The buyer takes possession of and responsibility for the property but does not receive the deed immediately; and
  - leases: a contract that transfers possession of the property from the owner to a tenant for a limited period of time.

---

**Real-Life
Real Estate**

1. You list a "hot" property in the morning and immediately receive the following offerings:
   - a full price offer contingent on the sale of the buyer's house from another broker, which you receive at 2:00 pm;
   - a nearly full price offer at 4:00 pm from a salesperson in your office; and
   - a cash offer at 5:00 pm for $5,000 less than the asking price (which is from your own buyer).

When you meet with the seller at 7:00 pm, how do you present these offers?

2. How do you convince a property owner to respond seriously to a "low ball" offer?

Application #2: Obtain a sample blank "offer to purchase/sales contract" used in your area. Then complete the appropriate segments of the agreement to reflect a typical transaction for the area.

Use the property described below as the subject property being sold by the Sellers to Bill and Betty Buyer.

Lot #258, block A, Hummel Heights Subdivision, Cleveland, Brown Township, Cuyahoga County, Ohio. Known as 57 Summit View Court.

All carpeting and rugs included in the transaction except oriental in the dining room. All drapes and curtains included in the transaction except in the master bedroom. Dining room chandelier goes with the seller. Other features of the house:

> above ground swimming pool
> electronic garage door opener
> range/oven (slide-in)
> 4 ceiling paddle fans
> refrigerator
> 3 window air conditioners

Get the terms of the offer from your instructor or create them yourself.

# QUESTIONS

1. A legally enforceable agreement under which two parties agree to do something for each other is known as a(n)
   a. escrow agreement.
   b. legal promise.
   c. valid contract.
   d. option agreement.

2. *D* approaches *B* and says, "I'd like to buy your house." *B* says, "Sure," and they agree on a price. What kind of contract is this?
   a. Implied
   b. Unenforceable
   c. Void
   d. There is no contract.

3. A contract is said to be bilateral if
   a. one of the parties is a minor.
   b. the contract has yet to be fully performed.
   c. only one party to the agreement is bound to act.
   d. all parties to the contract are bound to act.

4. During the period of time after a real estate sales contract is signed, but before title actually passes, the status of the contract is
   a. voidable.          c. unilateral.
   b. executory.        d. implied.

5. A contract for the sale of real estate that does not state the consideration to be paid for the property and is not signed by the parties is considered to be
   a. voidable.          c. void.
   b. executory.        d. enforceable.

6. *N* and *K* sign a contract under which *N* will convey Blackacre to *K*. *N* changes his mind, and *K* sues for specific performance. What is *K* seeking in this lawsuit?
   a. Money damages
   b. New contract
   c. Deficiency judgment
   d. Conveyance of the property

7. In a standard sales contract, several words were crossed out; others were inserted. To eliminate future controversy as to whether the changes were made before or after the contract was signed, the usual procedure is to
   a. write a letter to each party listing the changes.
   b. have each party write a letter to the other approving the changes.
   c. redraw the entire contract.
   d. have both parties initial or sign in the margin near each change.

8. *M* makes an offer on *Y*'s house, and *Y* accepts. Both parties sign the sales contract. At this point, *M* has what type of title to the property?
   a. Equitable          c. Escrow
   b. Voidable          d. Contract

9. The sales contract says J will purchase only if his wife approves the sale by the following Saturday. Mrs. *J*'s approval is a
   a. contingency.          c. warranty.
   b. reservation.          d. consideration.

10. *C* places an advertisement in the local paper. The ad reads: "I will pay $50,000 for any house, anywhere in town!" What kind of contract is this?
    a. Unilateral
    b. Option
    c. Implied
    d. It is not a contract.

11. An option to purchase binds which of the following parties?
    a. Buyer only
    b. Seller only
    c. Neither buyer nor seller
    d. Both buyer and seller

12. *X* and *H* enter into a real estate sales contract. Under the contract's terms, *X* will pay *H* $500 a month for ten years. *H* will continue to hold legal title to Blueacre. *X* will live on Blueacre and pay all real estate taxes, insurance premiums, and regular upkeep costs. What kind of contract do *X* and *H* have?
    a. Option contract
    b. Contract for mortgage
    c. Unilateral contract
    d. Land or installment contract

13. The purchaser of real estate under an installment contract
    a. generally pays no interest charge.
    b. receives title immediately.
    c. is not required to pay property taxes for the duration of the contract.
    d. is called a vendee.

14. Under the statute of frauds, all contracts for the sale of real estate must be
    a. originated by a real estate broker.
    b. on preprinted forms.
    c. in writing to be enforceable.
    d. accompanied by earnest money deposits.

15. The *F*s offer in writing to purchase a house for $120,000, including its draperies, with the offer to expire on Saturday at noon. The *W*s reply in writing on Thursday, accepting the $120,000 offer, but excluding the draperies. On Friday, while the *F*s consider this counteroffer, the *W*s decide to accept the original offer, draperies included, and state that in writing. At this point, which of the following statements is true?
    a. The *F*s are legally bound to buy the house, although they have the right to insist that the draperies be included.
    b. The *F*s are not bound to buy.
    c. The *F*s must buy the house and are not entitled to the draperies.
    d. The *F*s must buy the house, but may deduct the value of the draperies from the $120,000.

16. A buyer makes an offer to purchase certain property listed with a broker and leaves a deposit with the broker to show good faith. The broker should
    a. immediately apply the deposit to the listing expenses.
    b. put the deposit in an account, as provided by state law.
    c. give the deposit to the seller when the offer is presented.
    d. put the deposit in his or her personal checking account.

17. Between June 5 and September 23, *M* suffered from a mental illness that caused delusions, hallucinations, and loss of memory. On July 1, *M* signed a contract to purchase Blueacre, with the closing set for October 31. On September 24, *M* began psychiatric treatment. *M* was declared completely cured by October 15. Which of the following statements is true regarding *M*'s contract to purchase Blueacre?
    a. The contract is voidable.
    b. The contract is void.
    c. The contract lacks reality of consent.
    d. The contract is fully valid and enforceable.

18. A broker has found a buyer for a seller's home. The buyer has indicated in writing his willingness to buy the property for $1,000 less than the asking price and has deposited $5,000 in earnest money with the broker. The seller is out of town for the weekend, and the broker has been unable to inform him of the signed document. At this point, the buyer has signed a(n)
    a. voidable contract
    b. offer
    c. executory agreement
    d. implied contract.

19. A buyer and seller agree to the purchase of a house for $200,000. The contract contains a clause stating that time is of the essence. Which of the following statements is true?
a. The closing may take place within a reasonable period after the stated date.
b. A "time is of the essence" clause is not binding on either party.
c. The closing date must be stated as a particular calendar date, and not simply as a formula, such as "two weeks after loan approval."
d. If the closing date passes and no closing takes place, the contract may be invalid.

20. C signs a contract under which C may purchase Yellowacre for $30,000 any time in the next three months. C pays Yellowacre's current owner $500 at the time the contract is signed. Which of the following best describes this contract?
a. Contigency
b. Option
c. Installment
d. Sales

21. J has a basis of $30,000 in her primary residence. She sells the house for $45,000. The broker's commission is 6.5 percent, and other selling expenses amounted to $400. What is J's gain on this transaction?
a. $11,450
b. $11,500
c. $11,675
d. $14,025

# CHAPTER 13

# Transfer of Title

## TITLE

*Test*

The term *title* has two meanings. **Title** to real estate means *the right to or ownership of the land;* it represents the owner's bundle of rights, discussed in Chapter 2. Title also serves as *evidence* of that ownership. A person who holds the title would, if challenged in court, be able to recover or retain ownership or possession of a parcel of real estate. "Title" is just a way of referring to ownership; it is *not* an actual printed document. The document that shows who holds title to real property is the deed. The deed must be recorded to give public notice of the holder's ownership.

 **In Ohio...** The laws of Ohio govern real estate transactions for land located within its boundaries. Ohio has the authority to pass legislative acts that affect the methods of transferring title or other interests in real estate. ◆

Real estate may be transferred *voluntarily* by sale or gift. Alternatively, it may be transferred *involuntarily* by operation of law. Real estate may be transferred while the owner lives or by will or descent after the owner dies. In any case, it is the title that is transferred as a symbol of ownership.

## VOLUNTARY ALIENATION

**Voluntary alienation** is the legal term for the voluntary transfer of title. The owner may voluntarily transfer title by either making a gift or selling the property. To transfer during one's lifetime, the owner must use some form of deed of conveyance.

A **deed** is the written instrument by which an owner of real estate intentionally conveys the right, title, or interest in the parcel of real estate to someone else. The statute of frauds requires that all deeds be in writing. The owner who transfers the title is referred to as the **grantor.** The person who acquires the title is called the **grantee.** A deed is executed (that is, signed) only by the grantor.

**Requirements for a Valid Deed**

To be valid in Ohio, a deed must be in writing. The other formal requirements for a valid deed are

*In Ohio...*

- a grantor who has the legal capacity to execute (sign) the deed;
- a grantee named with reasonable certainty to be identified;
- a recital of consideration;
- a granting clause (words of conveyance);
- a habendum clause (to define ownership taken by the grantee);   *-Test- to HAVE + to Hold*
- an accurate legal description of the property conveyed;
- any relevant exceptions or reservations;
- the signature of the grantor, sometimes with a seal, witness, or acknowledgment;
- delivery of the deed and acceptance by the grantee to pass title;
- acknowledgment;
- two witnesses, one of whom may be a notary public; and   *Don't need ✗*
- for the deed to be recorded, the name of the person preparing it. ◆

*In Ohio...*

**Grantor.** A grantor must be of *lawful age,* in Ohio at least 18 years old. A deed executed by a minor is generally voidable. ◆ *Test*

A grantor also must be of *sound mind.* Generally, any grantor who can understand the action is viewed as mentally capable of executing a valid deed. A deed executed by someone who was mentally impaired at the time is voidable, but not void. If, however, the grantor has been judged legally incompetent, the deed will be void. Real estate owned by someone who is legally incompetent can be conveyed only with a court's approval. In Ohio, a grantor's spouse is required to join in and sign any deed of conveyance in order to waive any marital (dower) rights.

The grantor's name must be spelled correctly and consistently throughout the deed. If the grantor's name has been changed since the title was acquired, as when a person changes his or her name by marriage, both names should be shown—for example, "Mary Smith, formerly Mary Jones."

A **grantor** conveys property to a grantee.

A **grantee** receives property from a grantor.

A **deed** is the instrument that conveys property from a grantor to a grantee.

**Grantee.** To be valid, a deed must name a grantee. The grantee must be specifically named so that the person to whom the property is being conveyed can be readily identified from the deed itself.

**FOR EXAMPLE** *O* wanted to convey Whiteacre to *O*'s nephew, Jack Jackson. In the deed, *O* wrote the following words of conveyance: "I, *O*, hereby convey to Jack all my interest in Whiteacre." The only problem was that *O* also had a son named Jack, a cousin Jack, and a neighbor Jack. The grantee's identity could not be discerned from the deed itself. *O* should have conveyed Whiteacre "to my nephew, Jack Jackson."

If more than one grantee is involved, the granting clause should specify their rights in the property. The clause might state, for instance, that the grantees will take title as joint tenants or tenants in common. This is especially important when specific wording is necessary to create a joint tenancy.

*In Ohio...*

**Consideration.** A valid deed must contain a clause acknowledging that the grantor has received consideration. Generally, the amount of consideration is stated in dollars. When a deed conveys real estate as a gift to a relative, love and affection may be sufficient consideration. However, in most states, including Ohio, it is customary to recite a nominal consideration, such as "$10 and other good and valuable consideration." ◆

**Granting clause (words of conveyance).**  A deed must contain a **granting clause** that states the grantor's intention to convey the property. Depending on the type of deed and the obligations agreed to by the grantor, the wording would be similar to one of the following:

- "I, *JKL,* convey and warrant . . ."
- "I, *JKL,* grant . . ."
- "I, *JKL,* grant, bargain, and sell . . ."
- "I, *JKL,* remise, release, and quitclaim . . ."

A deed that conveys the grantor's entire fee simple interest usually contains wording such as "to *ABC* and to her heirs and assigns forever." If the grantor conveys less than his or her complete interest, such as a life estate, the wording must indicate this limitation—for example, "to *ABC* for the duration of her natural life."

**Habendum clause.**  When it is necessary to define or explain the ownership to be enjoyed by the grantee, a **habendum clause** may follow the granting clause. The habendum clause begins with the words to *have and to hold.* Its provisions must agree with those stated in the granting clause. For example, if a grantor conveys a time-share interest or an interest less than fee simple absolute, the habendum clause will specify the owner's rights as well as how those rights are limited (a specific time frame or certain prohibited activities, for instance).

**Legal description of real estate.**  To be valid, a deed must contain an accurate legal description of the real estate conveyed. Land is considered adequately described if a competent surveyor can locate the property using the description.

**Exceptions and reservations.**  A valid deed must specifically note any encumbrances, reservations, or limitations that affect the title being conveyed. This might include such things as restrictions and easements that run with the land. In addition to citing existing encumbrances, a grantor may reserve some right in the land (such as an easement) for his or her own use. A grantor also may place certain restrictions on a grantee's use of the property. Developers often restrict the number of houses that may be built on each lot in a subdivision. Such private restrictions must be stated in the deed or contained in a previously recorded document (such as the subdivider's master deed) that is expressly referred to in the deed. Many of these deed restrictions have time limits and often include renewal clauses.

-giveR

**Signature of grantor.**  To be valid, a deed must be signed by all grantors named in the deed. As discussed earlier, when a grantor is married, the spouse also must sign the deed in order to release dower or other rights.

In Ohio...  In Ohio there must be two identifiable witnesses to the grantor's signature, one of whom may be the notary.

Ohio permits an attorney-in-fact to sign for a grantor. The attorney must act under a *power of attorney*—the specific written authority to execute and sign one or more legal instruments for another person. The power of attorney must be acknowledged, and the power of attorney must give the attorney-in-fact specific authority to act in a real estate transaction. The power of attorney terminates when the person on whose behalf it is exercised dies. As a result, adequate evidence must be submitted that the grantor was alive at the time the attorney-in-fact signed the deed.

In Ohio, it is not necessary for a seal to be affixed (or simply for the word seal to be written or printed) after an individual grantor's signature. ◆

**Acknowledgment.** Often, there is a legal requirement that signatures be acknowledged. An **acknowledgment** is a formal declaration that the person who signs a written document does so *voluntarily* and that his or her signature is genuine. The declaration is made before a *notary public* or an authorized public officer, such as a judge, a justice of the peace, or some other person as prescribed by state law. An acknowledgment usually states that the person signing the deed or other document is known to the officer or has produced sufficient identification to prevent a forgery. The form of acknowledgment required by the state where the property is located should be used even if the party signing is a resident of another ("foreign") state.

An acknowledgment (that is, a formal declaration before a notary public) is not essential to the *validity* of the deed unless it is required by state statute. However, a deed that is not acknowledged is not a completely satisfactory instrument.

**In Ohio...** In most states, including Ohio, an unacknowledged deed is not eligible for recording. While in Ohio the grantor's signature must be notarized, the notary may be one of the two required witnesses. ◆

**Delivery and acceptance.** A title is not considered transferred until the deed is actually *delivered* to and *accepted* by the grantee. The grantor may deliver the deed to the grantee either personally or through a third party. The third party, commonly known as an *escrow agent* (or *settlement agent*), will deliver the deed to the grantee as soon as certain requirements have been satisfied. *Title is said to "pass" only when a deed is delivered and accepted.* The effective date of the transfer of title from the grantor to the grantee is the date of delivery of the deed itself. When a deed is delivered in escrow, the date

> Transfer of title requires both delivery and acceptance of the deed.

**In Ohio...** of delivery generally relates back to the date it was deposited with the escrow agent. (However, under the Torrens system (which is still used in parts of Ohio) title does not pass until the deed has been examined and accepted for registration. The Torrens system is discussed in Chapter 14.) ◆

**In Practice**     All deeds prepared in Ohio must be signed by the grantors in the presence of two persons who attest to the deed and sign as witnesses. While the notary public may be one of the witnesses, neither the grantor nor any grantee may be either a witness or notary. Deeds not acknowledged or not effectively delivered are invalid and pass no legal title. It must be remembered that grantees do not sign the deed; only the grantors.

**In Ohio...** **Recordation.** A deed must be recorded in the office of the county recorder of the county in which the property is located. A deed executed outside Ohio must be acknowledged properly according to the laws of Ohio or of the state in which the deed was prepared and executed. When a deed has been recorded for more than 21 years and there is a defect in the deed, the defect is considered corrected if it is a defect in witnessing or acknowledgment. The name of the person who prepared the deed must be shown at the conclusion. This person is usually a title or escrow officer or an attorney. ◆

## Execution of Corporate Deeds

The laws governing a corporation's right to convey real estate vary from state to state. However, two basic rules must be followed:

1. A corporation can convey real estate only by authority granted in its *bylaws* or on a proper resolution passed by its *board of directors.* If all or a substantial portion of a corporation's real estate is being conveyed, usually a resolution authorizing the sale must be secured from the *shareholders.*
2. Deeds to real estate can be signed only by an authorized officer.

Rules pertaining to religious corporations and not-for-profit corporations vary even more widely. Because the legal requirements must be followed exactly, an attorney should be consulted for all corporate conveyances.

## Types of Deeds

A deed can take several forms, depending on the extent of the grantor's pledges to the grantee. Regardless of any guarantees the deed offers, however, the grantee will want additional assurance that the grantor has the right to offer what the deed conveys. To obtain this protection, grantees commonly seek evidence of title, discussed in Chapter 12.

The most common deed forms are the

- general warranty deed,
- special warranty deed,
- quitclaim deed,
- trustee's deed, and
- deed executed pursuant to a court order.

**General warranty deed.** A **general warranty deed** provides the greatest protection of any deed. It is called a general warranty deed because the grantor is legally bound by certain covenants or warranties. In most states, the warranties are implied by the use of certain words specified by statute. In some states, the grantor's warranties are expressly written into the deed itself.

**In Ohio...** In Ohio, the words "with generally warranty covenants" are sufficient to include the basic warranties in the deed. ◆

The basic warranties are as follows:

- *Covenant of seisin:* The grantor warrants that he or she owns the property and has the right to convey title to it. (*Seisin* simply means "possession.") The grantee may recover damages up to the full purchase price if this covenant is broken.
- *Covenant against encumbrances:* The grantor warrants that the property is free from liens or encumbrances, except for any specifically stated in the deed. Encumbrances generally include mortgages, mechanics' liens, and easements. If this covenant is breached, the grantee may sue for the cost of removing the encumbrances.
- *Covenant of quiet enjoyment:* The grantor guarantees that the grantee's title will be good against third parties who might bring court actions to establish superior title to the property. If the grantee's title is found to be inferior, the grantor is liable for damages.

---

**General Warranty Deed**

*Five covenants:*

1. Covenant of seisin
2. Covenant against encumbrances
3. Covenant of quiet enjoyment
4. Covenant of further assurance
5. Covenant of warranty forever

---

- *Covenant of further assurance:* The grantor promises to obtain and deliver any instrument needed to make the title good. For example, if the grantor's spouse has failed to sign away dower rights, the grantor must deliver a quitclaim deed (discussed later) to clear the title.
- *Covenant of warranty forever:* The grantor promises to compensate the grantee for the loss sustained if the title fails at any time in the future.

These covenants in a general warranty deed are not limited to matters that occurred during the time the grantor owned the property; they extend back to its origins. The grantor defends the title against both himself or herself *and all those who previously held title.*

**Special warranty deed.** A **special warranty deed** contains two basic warranties:

1. That the grantor received title; and
2. That the property was not encumbered during *the time the grantor held title,* except as otherwise noted in the deed

In effect, the grantor defends the title against himself or herself. The granting clause generally contains the words "Grantor remises, releases, alienates, and conveys." The grantor may include additional warranties, but they must be specifically stated in the deed. In areas where a special warranty deed is more commonly used, the purchase of title insurance is viewed as providing adequate protection to the grantee.

---

**Special Warranty Deed**

*Two warranties:*

1. Warranty that grantor received title
2. Warranty that property was unencumbered by grantor

---

A special warranty deed may be used by fiduciaries such as trustees, executors, and corporations. A special warranty deed is appropriate for a fiduciary because he or she lacks the authority to warrant against acts of predecessors in title. A fiduciary may hold title for a limited time without having a personal interest in the proceeds. Sometimes, a special warranty deed may be used by a grantor who has acquired title at a tax sale.

*Also for Divorce*

*Test*

**Quitclaim deed.** A **quitclaim deed** provides the grantee with the least protection of any deed. It carries *no covenants* or *warranties* and generally conveys only whatever interest the grantor may have when the deed is delivered. If the grantor has no interest, the grantee will acquire nothing. Nor will the grantee acquire any right of warranty claim against the grantor. A quitclaim deed can convey title as effectively as a warranty deed if the grantor has good title when he or she delivers the deed, but it provides none of the guarantees that a warranty deed does. Through a quitclaim deed, the grantor only "remises, releases, and quitclaims" his or her interest in the property, if any.

Usually, a quitclaim deed is the only type of deed that may be used to convey less than a fee simple estate. This is because a quitclaim deed conveys only the grantor's right, title, or interest.

---

**Quitclaim Deed**

*No express or implied covenants or warranties*

- Used primarily to convey less than fee simple or to cure a title defect

---

A quitclaim deed is frequently used to cure a defect, called a *cloud on the title.* For example, if the name of the grantee is misspelled on a warranty deed filed in the public record, a quitclaim deed with the correct spelling may be executed to the grantee to perfect the title.

A quitclaim deed is also used when a grantor allegedly *inherits* property but is not certain that the decedent's title was valid. A warranty deed in such an instance could carry with it obligations of warranty, while a quitclaim deed would convey only the grantor's interest, whatever it may be.

*Test*

**In Ohio...**  Finally, in Ohio, a quitclaim deed is commonly utilized to convey any legal interest owned by one spouse to another spouse as part of a divorce decree. ◆

**In Ohio...**  **Deed in trust.**  A **deed in trust** is the means by which a trustor conveys real estate to a *trustee* for the benefit of a *beneficiary*. The real estate is held by the trustee to fulfill the purpose of the trust. The trust deed is not used in Ohio. ◆

---

**Trustee's Deed**

*Conveyance from trustee to third party*

---

**Trustee's deed.**  A deed executed by a trustee is a **trustee's deed.** It is used when a trustee conveys real estate held in the trust to anyone *other than the trustor.* The trustee's deed must state that the trustee is executing the instrument in accordance with the powers and authority granted by the trust instrument.

**Deed executed pursuant to court order.**  Executors' and administrators' deeds, masters' deeds, sheriffs' deeds and many other types are all *deeds executed pursuant to a court order.* These deeds are established by state statute and are used to convey title to property that is transferred by court order or by will. The form of such a deed must conform to the laws of the state in which the property is located.

One common characteristic of deeds executed pursuant to court order is that the *full consideration* is usually stated in the deed. Instead of "$10 and other valuable consideration," for example, the deed would list the actual sales price.

**Transfer Tax**  Most states have enacted laws providing for a tax, usually referred to as the state **transfer tax,** on conveyances of real estate.

**In Ohio...**  The Ohio transfer fee or conveyance fee is usually paid by the seller to the county where the real estate is located. This transfer fee is one mill ($.10 per $100 or fraction thereof) of the total consideration, subject to a $1 minimum fee. For example, the Ohio basic transfer fee on a sales price of $45,550 is $45.60. Counties may add additional transfer taxes to the state tax, not to exceed three mills ($.30 per $100). The additional county transfer taxes are not uniform throughout the state of Ohio. ◆

*#4.00 per thousand*

The law requires that the grantee submit *a transfer declaration form statement* in triplicate, showing the value of the real estate conveyed. The form indicates the grantor's name, the grantee's home address and billing address, whether there are buildings on the land, the type of interest conveyed, the full consideration, and whether an exemption is allowed. The grantee must sign a declaration under penalty of perjury that this is an accurate statement. This form is delivered to the county auditor by the grantee or his or her escrow agent or attorney. The county auditor retains the original statement of value, gives a copy to the board of appeals, and returns one copy to the grantee.

In the case of a conveyance that is not a gift, "value" means the full amount of the consideration and includes all mortgages or possible vendors' liens. In the case of a gift, the value is the estimated price the real estate described would bring in the open market under the existing and prevailing market conditions in a transaction between a willing seller and a willing buyer, both familiar with the property and with prevailing general price levels.

Certain deeds are exempt from the transfer fee, such as those in which the value of interest conveyed does not exceed $100, deeds conveying to or from a government body, deeds that *correct* previous deeds, *gifts* between spouses, deeds by owners creating a survivorship tenancy for themselves, and a transfer to a grantee other than a dealer that is but a step in a sale to others. (A mortgage is also exempt from the tax.) A form listing the reasons for a conveyance's being exempt from the transfer fee is shown in Figure 13.1. Only the grantee or his or her representative signs this form. These forms are public records and may be viewed in the county auditor's office by anyone. They are filed by transfer date.

### Calculating the Transfer Tax

In a county with a total transfer tax of four mills, the total transfer tax on a sales price of $100,000 with an assumed mortgage of $60,000 and a new mortgage is calculated as follows

| | | |
|---|---|---|
| .001 × $100,000 | = $100.00 | (Basic Ohio transfer tax) |
| .003 × $40,000 | = $120.00 | (Additional county transfer tax) |
| Total transfer tax | $220.00 | |

**In Ohio...**

(Conversely, the approximate purchase price may be calculated by dividing the basic transfer tax amount by .001.) ◆

 **In Ohio...**

**County transfer fee (transfer tax, conveyance fee).** Under Ohio law, a county transfer tax may be levied by the county commissioners. This tax is known as the *real property transfer tax.* This tax may not exceed three mills ($.30 per $100) or fraction thereof of the value of the interest assigned, transferred, or conveyed. This tax is computed on a different basis from the state transfer fee. The county transfer tax is based on the purchase price less the balance due on any mortgage being assumed by the buyer (unlike the original one-mill state transfer fee, which is based on the total consideration without deductions for assumed mortgages). A number of counties in Ohio have adopted all or some portion of the additional tax. ◆

## INVOLUNTARY ALIENATION

*Test*

Title to property can be transferred without the owner's consent by **involuntary alienation.** (See Figure 13.2.) Such transfers are usually carried out by operation of law, such as by condemnation or the sale of property to satisfy delinquent tax or mortgage liens. When a person dies intestate and leaves no heirs, the title to the real estate passes to the state by the state's power of escheat.

*Test*

As described in Chapter 8, federal, state, and local governments; school boards; some government agencies; and certain public and quasi-public corporations and utilities (railroads and gas and electric companies) have the right of *eminent domain.* Under this right private property may be taken for public use through *condemnation.* Eminent domain may be exercised only when the use is both necessary and for the benefit of the public, an equitable amount of compensation is paid to the owner, and the rights of the property owner are protected by due process of law. Recent court decisions have affirmed the right of property owners to be compensated when certain actions by the government have been determined to deprive landowners of their private property rights granted under the U.S. Constitution.

## Figure 13.1   *Transfer Fee Conveyance Form*

DTE Form 100 Revised 6/81
O.R.C. 319.202 and 319.54

Craftsman Printing, Inc.—A0005

### REAL PROPERTY CONVEYANCE FEE STATEMENT OF VALUE AND RECEIPT
If exempt by O.R.C. 319.54 (F)(3), Use DTE Form 100 EX

**TYPE OR PRINT ALL INFORMATION**          **SEE INSTRUCTIONS ON REVERSE SIDE**

#### FOR COUNTY AUDITORS USE ONLY

| Type Instrument | Tax List Year | County Number | Tax. Dist. Number | Date |
|---|---|---|---|---|

Property located in _____ Taxing District

Name on _____ Tax Duplicate _____

Acct. or Permanent Parcel No. _____ Map Book _____ Page _____

Description:                                           ☐ Platted    ☐ Unplatted

Front

Depth

**Number**

**No. of Parcels**

**DTE Code No.**

**Neigh. Code**

**Number of Acres**

**Land Value**

**AUDITOR'S COMMENTS**

☐ Split       ☐ New Plat      ☐ New Improvements      ☐ Partial Value

☐ C.A.U.V.   ☐ Other _____

**Bldg Value**

**Total Value**

#### ALL QUESTIONS IN THIS SECTION MUST BE COMPLETED BY GRANTEE OR HIS REPRESENTATIVE

1. Grantors Name _____
2. Grantees Name _____
3. Address of Property _____
4. Tax Billing Address if Other Than Above _____
5. Are there buildings on the land? a) ☐ NO - Intended use _____
   b) ☐ YES - Check Type   ☐ 1, 2 or 3 Family Dwlg.   ☐ Condominium Unit   ☐ Apartment: Number of Units _____
   ☐ House trailer or mobile home   ☐ Farm Buildings   ☐ Other use _____
6. Condition of Sale: Indicate if following conditions prevail: ☐ Not Applicable   ☐ Is Grantor a Relative
   ☐ Part interest — e.g. "Undivided ½"   ☐ Land Contract   ☐ Trade   ☐ Life Estate   ☐ Leased Fee   ☐ Leasehold
   ☐ Mineral and oil rights reserved   ☐ Other: _____
7. a) Full consideration including amount of all mortgages and liens:   ☐ New Mtg.
   ☐ Balance Assumed   Prin. or Bal. Assumed $ _____   Cash $ _____   Total $ _____
   b) Mortgagee _____
   c) Type of Mortgage   ☐ (1) Conv.   ☐ (2) F.H.A.   ☐ (3) V.A.   ☐ (4) Other_____
   d) Enter value of Personal Property or damages included
      in sales agreement, if any, and deduct from Item 7a) ................... $ _____
   e) Consideration of Real Property on which fee is to be paid (7a minus 7d) ......... $ _____
   f) If a gift, in whole or part, the estimated market value ................. $ _____
8. The grantor has indicated that this property (check one box) is (a) ☐   or is not (b) ☐   entitled to receive the senior citizen or disabled persons homestead exemption for the preceding or the current tax year. If box (a) is checked complete DTE Form 101.

9. I DECLARE UNDER PENALTIES OF PERJURY THAT THIS STATEMENT HAS BEEN EXAMINED BY ME AND TO THE BEST OF MY KNOWLEDGE AND BELIEF IS A TRUE AND CORRECT STATEMENT.

_____        _____
Date                    SIGNATURE OF GRANTEE OR REPRESENTATIVE

**DTE Use Only**

**DTE Use Only**

**DTE Use Only**

**Land Only**
1 Yes      2 No

**Valid Sale**
1 Yes      2 No

**Financing**

**Consideration**
$

**Sales Ratio**
%

### RECEIPT FOR PAYMENT OF CONVEYANCE FEE

**Receipt Number**

The Conveyance fee required by section 319.54 (F) (3) R.C., and, if applicable, the fee required by Chapter 322 R.C., in the total amount of

$ _____ has been paid by _____

and received by the _____ County Auditor

DATE _____          _____ COUNTY AUDITOR

SOURCE: Attorney Anthony J. Aveni, Painesville, Ohio.

**Figure 13.1    Transfer Fee Conveyance Form (Continued)**

DTE FORM 100 (EX)    **STATEMENT OF REASON FOR EXEMPTION FROM REAL PROPERTY CONVEYANCE FEE**

(REV 12/98)    Revised Code Sections 319.202 and 319.54(F)(3)

TYPE OR PRINT ALL INFORMATION

| **FOR COUNTY AUDITOR'S USE ONLY** | | | Date | Co. No. | Number |
|---|---|---|---|---|---|
| Instr. | Tax. Dist. No. | Tax List | Land | Bldg. | Tot. |

D.T.E. CODE NO. _____  ☐ Split/New Plat    Remarks: _____

Property Located in _____ Taxing District

Name on Tax Duplicate _____ Tax Duplicate Year _____

Acct. or Permanent Parcel No. _____ Map Book _____ Page _____

Description:

_____

### FOLLOWING MUST BE COMPLETED BY GRANTEE OR HIS REPRESENTATIVE

1. Grantor's Name _____ Phone Number_____
2. Grantee's Name _____ Phone Number_____
   Grantee's Address _____
3. Address of Property _____
4. Tax Billing Address _____
5. No Conveyance fees shall be charged because the real property is transferred:

_____ (a) To or from the United States, this state, or any instrumentality, agency, or political subdivision of the United States or this state;

_____ (b) Solely in order to provide or release security for a debt or obligation;

_____ (c) To confirm or correct a deed previously executed and recorded;

_____ (d) To evidence a gift, in any form, between husband and wife, or parent and child or the spouse of either;

_____ (e) On sale for delinquent taxes or assessments;

_____ (f) Pursuant to court order, to the extent that such transfer is not the result of a sale effected or completed pursuant such order;

_____ (g) Pursuant to a reorganization of corporations or unincorporated associations or pursuant to the dissolution of a corporation, to the extent that the corporation conveys the property to a stockholder as a distribution in kind of the corporation's assets in exchange for the stockholder's shares in the dissolved corporation;

_____ (h) By a subsidiary corporation to its parent corporation for no consideration, nominal consideration, or in sole consideration of the cancellation or surrender of the subsidiary's stock;

_____ (i) By lease, whether or not it extends to mineral or mineral rights, unless the lease is for a term of years renewable forever;

_____ (j) When the value of the real property or interest in real property conveyed does not exceed one hundred dollars;

_____ (k) Of an occupied residential property being transferred to the builder of a new residence when the former residence is traded as part of the consideration for the new residence;

_____ (l) To a grantee other than a dealer in real property, solely for the purpose of and as a step in, its prompt sale to others;

_____ (m) To or from a person when no money or other valuable and tangible consideration readily convertible into money is paid or to be paid for the real estate and the transaction is not a gift;

_____ (n) To an heir or devisee, between spouses or to a surviving spouse, from a person to himself and others, to a surviving tenant, or on the death of a registered owner;

_____ (o) To a trustee acting on behalf of minor children of the deceased;

_____ (p) Of an easement or right-of-way when the value of the interest conveyed does not exceed one thousand dollars;

_____ (q) Of property sold to a surviving spouse pursuant to section 2106.16 of the Revised Code;

_____ (r) To or from an organization exempt from federal income taxation under section 501(c)(3) of the Internal Revenue Code, provided such transfer is without consideration and is in furtherance of the charitable or public purpose of such organization;

_____ (s) Among the heirs at law or devisees, including a surviving spouse of a common decedent, when no consideration in money is paid or to be paid for the real property;

_____ (t) To a trustee of a trust, when the grantor of the trust has reserved an unlimited power to revoke the trust;

_____ (u) To the grantor of a trust by a trustee of the trust, when the transfer is made to the grantor pursuant to the exercise of the grantor's power to revoke the trust or to withdraw trust assets;

_____ (v) To the beneficiaries of a trust if the fee was paid on the transfer from the grantor of the trust to the trustee or pursuant to trust provisions that became irrevocable at the death of the grantor;

_____ (w) To a corporation for incorporation into a sports facility constructed pursuant to section 307.696 [307.69.6] of the Revised Code.

6. Has the grantor indicated that this property is entitled to receive the senior citizen, disabled person, or surviving spouse homestead exemption for the preceding or current tax year? ☐ YES ☐ NO. If yes, complete DTE Form 101.

7. Has the grantor indicated that this property is qualified for current agricultural use valuation for the preceding or current tax year? ☐ YES ☐ NO. If yes, complete DTE Form 102.

8. Application For 2 1/2% Reduction (NOTICE: failure to complete this application prohibits the owner from receiving this reduction until another proper and timely application is filed): Will this property be grantee's principal residence by January 1 of next year? ☐ YES ☐ NO. If yes, is the property a multi-unit dwelling? ☐ YES ☐ NO.

I declare under penalties of perjury that this statement has been examined by me and to the best of my knowledge and belief is a true, correct, and complete statement.

_____    _____
SIGNATURE OF GRANTEE OR REPRESENTATIVE                                 DATE

BARRETT BROTHERS, SPRINGFIELD, OHIO  1-800-322-7711

**Figure 13.2  Involuntary Alienation**

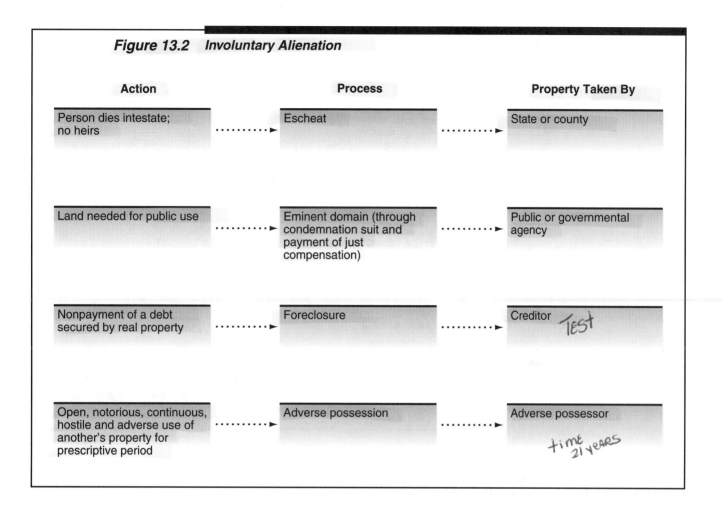

| Action | Process | Property Taken By |
| --- | --- | --- |
| Person dies intestate; no heirs | Escheat | State or county |
| Land needed for public use | Eminent domain (through condemnation suit and payment of just compensation) | Public or governmental agency |
| Nonpayment of a debt secured by real property | Foreclosure | Creditor *Test* |
| Open, notorious, continuous, hostile and adverse use of another's property for prescriptive period | Adverse possession | Adverse possessor *time 21 years* |

Land also may be transferred without an owner's consent to satisfy debts incurred by the owner. In such cases the property is sold and the proceeds of the judicial sale are applied to pay off the debt. Debts that could be foreclosed include mortgage loans, real estate taxes, mechanics' liens, and general judgments against the property owner.

In addition to the involuntary transfer of land by legal processes, land may be transferred by natural forces. As discussed in Chapter 8, owners of land bordering on rivers, lakes, and other bodies of water may acquire additional land through the process of *accretion,* the slow accumulation of soil, rock or other matter deposited by the movement of water on an owner's property. The opposite of accretion is *erosion,* the gradual wearing away of land by the action of water and wind. In addition, property may be lost through *avulsion,* the sudden tearing away of land by such natural means as earthquakes or tidal waves. However, title is not transferred if additional land is created by filling in bodies of water as a result of human efforts.

**Adverse possession** is another means of involuntary transfer. An owner who does not use his or her land or who does not inspect it for a number of years may lose title to another person who makes some claim to the land, takes possession and, most importantly, uses the land. Usually the possession of the claimant must be

**In Ohio...**

- open,
- notorious,
- continuous (uninterrupted for the period of time set by Ohio law— 21 years), ◆
- hostile, and
- adverse to the true owner's possession.

Through the principle of *tacking,* successive periods of different adverse possession by different adverse possessors can be combined, enabling a person who is not in possession for the entire required time to establish a claim of adverse possession. A claimant who does not receive title may acquire an easement by prescription. (See Chapter 8.)

Through adverse possession the law recognizes that the use of land is an important function of its ownership. The subject of adverse possession is extremely technical because the right is statutory, and Ohio's requirements must be followed carefully to establish ownership. Actual record title by adverse possession can be established only by an action in court called a quiet title action. Legal counsel should be consulted in such an instance.

**In Practice**    The right of adverse possession is a statutory right. State requirements must be followed carefully to ensure the successful transfer of title. The parties to a transaction that might involve adverse possession should seek legal counsel.

# TRANSFER OF A DECEASED PERSON'S PROPERTY

A person who dies **testate** has prepared a will indicating how his or her property will be disposed of. In contrast, when a person dies **intestate** (without a will), real estate and personal property pass to the decedent's heirs according to the state's *statute of descent and distribution.* In effect, the state makes a will for an intestate decedent.

Legally, when a person dies, ownership of real estate immediately passes either to the heirs by descent or to the persons named in the will. Before these individuals can take full title and possession of the property, however, the estate must go through a judicial process called *probate,* and all claims against the estate must be satisfied.

**Transfer of Title by Will**
A **will** is an instrument made by an owner to convey title to real or personal property after the owner's death. A will is a testamentary instrument; that is, it takes effect only after death. This differs from a deed, which must be delivered during the lifetime of the grantor, and which conveys a present interest in property. While the **testator** (the person who makes a will) is alive, any property included in the will can still be conveyed by the owner. The parties named in a will have no rights or interests as long as the party who made the will lives; they acquire interest or title only after the owner's death.

Only property owned by the testator at the time of his or her death may be transferred by will. The gift of real property by will is known as a **devise,** and a person who receives property by will is known as a *devisee.*

For title to pass to the devisees, state laws require that on the death of a testator, the will must be filed with the court and *probated.* Probate is a legal procedure for verifying the validity of a will and accounting for the decedent's assets. The process can take several months to complete.

A will cannot supersede the state laws of dower and curtesy, which were enacted to protect the inheritance rights of a surviving spouse. When a will does not provide a spouse with the minimum statutory inheritance, he or she may demand it from the estate.

**In Ohio...**   If the testator died a resident of Ohio, the will should be probated in the county in which he or she lived; otherwise it must be probated in the county in which the real estate is located. The assets as well as the debts of the estate are inventoried by the executor named in the will or, if there is no will, by the administrator appointed by the court. ◆

**Spouse's right of election.** The surviving spouse must elect whether to accept the terms of the will or to take the share allowed by the law of descent. The surviving spouse is given this choice to prevent disinheritance. Prenuptial agreements could have an effect on this option.

This election must be made within one month of the notice from the probate court or within the proper time allowed after the appointment of the executor or administrator.

If the surviving spouse elects to take the share under the law of descent, the will remains effective as to all other provisions, except for as much property as is needed to satisfy the spouse's election under descent and distribution.

The net estate that is distributable is the testator's property remaining after payment of a surviving spouse's statutory allowance, the decedent's debts, funeral expenses, and costs of probate administration.

**Legal requirements for making a will.** Because a will must be valid and admitted to probate to effectively convey title to real estate, it should be executed and prepared in accordance with the laws of the state where the real estate is located. A *testator* must have legal capacity to make a will. Usually a person must be of *legal age* and of *sound mind.*

**In Ohio...**   In Ohio, that means that any person 18 years of age or over who is of sound mind and memory may make a will. There are, however, no rigid tests to determine the capacity to make a will. Generally the courts hold that to make a valid will the testator must have sufficient mental capacity to understand the nature and extent of the property owned and the identity of natural heirs and that at the testator's death the property will go to those named in the will. The drawing of a will must be a voluntary act, free of any undue influence by other people. ◆

The will must be attested and subscribed in the presence of such party by two or more competent witnesses who saw the testator actually sign the will or heard acknowledgment of his or her signature.

The testator may alter the will. A modification of, an amendment of, or an addition to a previously executed will is set forth in a separate document called a *codicil.*

*oral will?*
*yes*

A *holographic will* is one that is in the testator's handwriting and, depending on state laws, need not be further witnessed or acknowledged. A *nuncupative will* is one that is given orally by a testator. Certain states do not permit the use of holographic and/or nuncupative wills to convey title to property.

## Probate Proceedings

**Probate** is the formal judicial process to prove or confirm the validity of a will (if there is one) and to determine the assets of the deceased person (the decedent) and the persons to whom the assets will pass. The purpose of probate is to see that the assets are distributed correctly. They must be properly accounted for, and the debts of the decedent and taxes on the estate must be satisfied prior to the distribution of the assets. The laws of each state govern the probate proceedings and the functions of the individuals who are appointed to administer the decedent's affairs. Assets that are distributed through probate are those that do not otherwise distribute themselves because of the way they are titled, such as in joint tenancy or tenancy by the entirety. Probate proceedings take place in the county in which the decedent resided. If the decedent owned real estate in another county, probate would occur in that county as well.

When an individual dies *testate,* probate is necessary to prove the validity of the will before the assets can be distributed. The person who has possession of the will, normally the individual designated as *executor* or *executrix* in the will, presents it for filing with the court. The court is responsible for determining that the will meets the statutory requirements for its form and execution and, in the event there is a codicil or several wills, how these documents should be probated. To prevent wrongdoing by relatives who would receive more under the laws of descent and distribution than they would under the will, there normally are criminal sanctions for concealing or destroying a will. The court must rule on a challenge if a will is contested. Once the will is upheld, the assets can be distributed according to its provisions. Probate courts will distribute assets according to statute only when no other reasonable alternative exists.

When a person dies *intestate,* the court determines who inherits the assets by reviewing proof from relatives of the decedent and their entitlement under the statute of descent and distribution in that court's state. Once the heirs are determined, the court will appoint an *administrator* or *personal representative* (in lieu of an executor, who would have been named in a will) to administer the affairs of the estate.

The administrator, executor, or executrix has the authority to see that the assets of the estate are appraised and to satisfy all debts owed by the decedent. The estate representative is also responsible for paying federal estate taxes and state inheritance taxes. Once all obligations have been satisfied, the representative distributes the remaining assets of the estate according to the person's will or the state's law of descent.

## Transfer of Title by Descent

By law the title to real estate and personal property of a person who dies intestate passes to the decedent's heirs. Under the statute of descent and distribution the primary **heirs** of the deceased are the spouse and close blood relatives such as children, parents, brothers, sisters, aunts, uncles, and, in some cases, first and second cousins. The right to inherit under laws of descent varies from state to state, and intestate property is distributed according to the laws of the state in which the property is located.

**In Ohio...** In Ohio, the property of a person who dies *intestate* is distributed according to the Statute of Descent and Distribution as follows:

1.  If there is no surviving spouse, and the deceased left one or more children, the children divide the estate equally. The descendants of a deceased child will take the share that their deceased parent would have received if living.
2.  If the deceased left a surviving spouse and only one child or that child's lineal descendants, the surviving spouse inherits a share of cash and one-half of the balance of the estate. If the surviving spouse is the natural or adoptive parent of the child, the surviving spouse's share of the cash is $60,000. If the surviving spouse is not the natural or adoptive parent of the child, the cash amount is $20,000. The remaining half of the estate goes to the child or, if deceased, to the descendants of such child.
3.  If the deceased left a surviving spouse and more than one child or their lineal descendants, the surviving spouse is entitled to a share of cash and one-third of the balance of the estate. The spouse's share of cash is $60,000 if one of the children is the spouse's natural or adopted child; otherwise, it is $20,000. The remaining two-thirds of the estate is shared equally by the children or by the descendants of any deceased child.
4.  If the deceased left a surviving spouse but no children or their lineal descendants, the surviving spouse is entitled to the entire estate.
5.  If the deceased left no spouse and no living children or descendants of a deceased child (as in the case of an unmarried decedent), the decedent's parents share the estate equally. If one parent is deceased, the entire estate goes to the surviving parent. If both parents are deceased, the estate goes equally to the brothers and sisters of the decedent.
6.  If there are no heirs, then maternal or paternal grandparents or their descendants can inherit the property.
7.  If there are no next of kin, then stepchildren or their lineal descendants can inherit the property.
8.  When the deceased leaves no living person to inherit his or her real estate, it escheats, or passes, to the state.

Under the Ohio statute, living children and lineal descendants of the deceased children inherit "per stirpes," which means that if a natural heir dies, his or her portion of the estate goes to that deceased heir's children. ◆

**In Ohio...** **F**OR EXAMPLE  *L* , a widow, has three children, *M, N* and *O. O* dies in a tragic boating accident, leaving two children behind, *V* and *W.* When *L* dies, *L's* estate will be divided into three equal parts. One third will go to *M,* one third to *N,* and *O's* one-third share will be divided equally between *V* and *W.* ◆

**In Practice**     A broker entering into a listing agreement with the executor or administrator of an estate in probate should be aware that the amount of commission is fixed by the court and that the commission is payable only from the proceeds of the sale. The broker will not be able to collect a commission unless the court approves the sale.

**KEY TERMS**

| | | |
|---|---|---|
| acknowledgment | grantor | testate |
| adverse possession | habendum clause | testator |
| deed | heir | title |
| deed in trust | intestate | transfer tax |
| devise | involuntary alienation | trustee's deed |
| general warranty deed | probate | voluntary alienation |
| grantee | quitclaim deed | will |
| granting clause | special warranty deed | |

**SUMMARY**

- Title to real estate is the right to and evidence of ownership of the land. It may be transferred by:
  - voluntary alienation,
  - involuntary alienation,
  - will, and
  - descent.
- The voluntary transfer of an owner's title is made by a deed, executed (signed) by the owner as grantor to the purchaser or grantee.
- Among the most common requirements for a valid deed are a grantor with legal capacity to contract, a readily identifiable grantee, a granting clause, a legal description of the property, a recital of consideration, exceptions, and reservations on the title, and the signature of the grantor.
  - In addition, the deed should be properly witnessed and acknowledged before a notary public or another officer to provide evidence that the signature is genuine and to allow recording.
- Title to property passes when the grantor delivers a deed to the grantee and it is accepted.
- Types of deeds include:
  - a general warranty deed, which provides the greatest protection of any deed by binding the grantor to certain covenants or warranties;
  - a special warranty deed, which warrants only that the real estate is not encumbered except as stated in the deed; and
  - a quitclaim deed, which carries with it no warranties whatsoever and conveys only the interest, if any, the grantor possesses in the property.
- An owner's title may be transferred without his or her permission by a court action, such as a foreclosure or judgment sale, a tax sale, condemnation under the right of eminent domain, adverse possession, or escheat.
- Property may be transferred by the natural forces of water and wind, which either increase property by accretion or decrease it through erosion or avulsion.
- The real estate of an owner who makes a valid will (who dies testate) passes to the devisees through the probating of the will. The title of an owner who dies without a will (intestate) passes according to the provisions of the law of descent and distribution of the state in which the real estate is located.

**Real-Life Real Estate**

1. An estate attorney offers to list a property with you. The owners are five heirs who live in five different states. Three of them are married, one is divorced, and the other is 17 years old. What are some of the challenges you face in this transaction?
2. How many signatures will be on the new deed in question #1.

# QUESTIONS

1. The basic requirements for a valid conveyance are governed by
   a. state law.
   b. local custom.
   c. national law.
   d. the law of descent.

2. *H*, age 15, recently inherited many parcels of real estate from his late father and has decided to sell one of them. If *H* entered into a deed conveying his interest in the property to a purchaser, such a conveyance would be
   a. valid.        c. invalid.
   b. void.         d. voidable.

3. An instrument authorizing one person to act for another is called a(n)
   a. power of attorney.
   b. release deed.
   c. quitclaim deed.
   d. acknowledgment.

4. The grantee receives greatest protection with what type of deed?
   a. Quitclaim
   b. General warranty
   c. Special warranty
   d. Executor's

5. *L* receives a deed from *G*. The granting clause of the deed states, "*I, G*, hereby remise, release, alienate, and convey to *L* the property known as Yellowacre." What type of deed has *L* received?
   a. Special warranty
   b. Quitclaim
   c. General warranty
   d. Executor's

6. Which of the following best describes the covenant of quiet enjoyment?
   a. The grantor promises to obtain and deliver any instrument needed to make the title good.
   b. The grantor guarantees that if the title fails in the future, he or she will compensate the grantee.
   c. The grantor warrants that he or she is the owner and has the right to convey title to the property.
   d. The grantor assures that the title will be good against the title claims of third parties.

7. Which of the following types of deeds merely implies, but does not specifically warrant, that the grantor holds good title to the property?
   a. Special warranty    c. Quitclaim
   b. Executor's          d. Trustee's

8. *Step 1: H* decided to convey Blueacre to *J*. *Step 2: H* signed a deed transferring title to *J*. *Step 3: H* gave the signed deed to *J*, who accepted it. *Step 4: J* took the deed to the county recorder's office and had it recorded. At which step did title to Blueacre actually transfer or pass to *J*?
   a. Step 1        c. Step 3
   b. Step 2        d. Step 4

9. *H* conveys property to *K* by deed. The deed contains the following: (1) *K*'s name, spelled out in full; (2) a statement that *H* has received $10 and *K*'s love and affection; and (3) a statement that the property is conveyed to *K* "to have and to hold." Which of the following correctly identifies, in order, these three elements of the deed?
   a. Grantee; consideration; granting clause
   b. Grantee; consideration; habendum clause
   c. Grantor; habendum clause; legal description
   d. Grantee; acknowledgment; habendum clause

10. *K* signed a deed transferring ownership of Whiteacre to *L*. To provide evidence that *K*'s signature was genuine, *K* executed a declaration before a notary. This declaration is known as an:
    a. affidavit.
    b. acknowledgment.
    c. affirmation.
    d. estoppel.

11. *R* executes a deed to *P* as grantee, has it acknowledged, and receives payment from the buyer. *R* holds the deed, however, and arranges to meet *P* the next morning at the courthouse to give the deed to her. In this situation at this time
    a. *P* owns the property because she has paid for it.
    b. Legal title to the property will not officially pass until *P* has been given the deed the next morning.
    c. Legal title to the property will not pass until *P* has received the deed and records it the next morning.
    d. *P* will own the property when she signs the deed the next morning.

12. Title to real estate may be transferred during a person's lifetime by:
    a. devise.
    b. descent.
    c. involuntary alienation.
    d. escheat.

13. *F* bought acreage in a distant county, never went to see the acreage, and did not use the ground. *H* moved his mobile home onto the land, had a water well drilled, and lived there for 22 years. *H* may become the owner of the land if he has complied with the state law regarding
    a. requirements for a valid conveyance.
    b. adverse possession.
    c. avulsion.
    d. voluntary alienation.

14. Condemnation and escheat are two examples of
    a. voluntary alienation.
    b. adverse possession.
    c. transfers of title by descent.
    d. involuntary alienation.

15. A deed contains a promise that the title conveyed will be good against court actions brought by third parties who seek to establish a superior claim to the property. This is an example of which covenant?
    a. Quiet enjoyment
    b. Seisin
    c. Further assurance
    d. Warranty forever

16. A deed contains a guarantee that the grantor will compensate the grantee for any loss resulting from the title's failure in the future. This is an example of which type of covenant?
    a. Warranty forever
    b. Further assurance
    c. Quiet enjoyment
    d. Seisin

17. A house sells for $89,500; the buyer pays $50,000 in cash and gives the seller a mortgage for the balance. At a rate of 1 percent, what is the amount of state transfer tax that must be paid?
    a. $895          c. $8,950
    b. $3,950         d. $17,900

18. A person who has died leaving a valid will is called a(n)
    a. devisee.       c. legatee.
    b. testator.      d. intestate.

19. Title to real estate can be transferred at death by which of the following documents?
    a. Warranty deed
    b. Special warranty deed
    c. Trustee's deed
    d. Will

20. *J*, a bachelor, died owning real estate that he devised by his will to his niece, *K*. In essence, at what point does title pass to his niece?
    a. Immediately on *J*'s death
    b. After his will has been probated
    c. After *K* has paid all inheritance taxes
    d. When *K* executes a new deed to the property

21. An owner of real estate was declared legally incompetent and was committed to a state mental institution. During his stay, the owner wrote and executed a will. He later died and was survived by a wife and three children. His real estate will pass
    a. to his wife.
    b. to the heirs mentioned in his will.
    c. according to the state laws of descent.
    d. to the state.

22. A spouse dies, leaving a valid will. With regard to real estate, the surviving spouse
    a. must accept the terms of the will.
    b. can contest the will because he or she has dower rights of a one-third interest in the deceased spouse's real estate.
    c. can contest the will because he or she has dower rights of a one-half interest in the deceased spouse's real estate.
    d. can contest the will because he or she has dower rights, which means he or she is the sole heir despite the will.

23. In Ohio, the statutory period for adverse possession is an uninterrupted period of
    a. 30 years.
    b. 7 years.
    c. 3 years.
    d. up to 21 years.

24. Which of the following government entities establishes the Ohio transfer fee rate?
    a. Townships
    b. Villages
    c. Cities
    d. Counties

25. A deed that is signed, witnessed, and acknowledged but not delivered
    a. passes title.
    b. passes no legal title.
    c. is void.
    d. is illegal.

26. The Ohio transfer fee applies to
    a. gifts between spouses.
    b. the conveyance of real estate.
    c. the conveyance of personal property.
    d. the conveyance of residential property only.

27. To be valid, every will executed in Ohio must be signed by
    a. the testator and witnesses.
    b. a notary public.
    c. the grantor.
    d. the mortgagee.

28. The tax levied by the state of Ohio based on the purchase price is known as the
    a. county transfer fee.
    b. state conveyance fee.
    c. federal conveyance fee.
    d. state tax.

29. Deeds conveying Ohio real estate require the signature of the
    a. grantor and grantee.
    b. grantor only.
    c. grantee only.
    d. attorney who prepared the deed.

30. Ohio's transfer fee is
    a. $.10 per $100 of total consideration.
    b. $10 per $100 of total consideration.
    c. $.40 per $100 of total consideration.
    d. $1 per $100 of total consideration.

# Title Records

## PUBLIC RECORDS

Public records contain detailed information about each parcel of real estate in a city or county. These records are crucial in establishing ownership, giving notice of encumbrances, and establishing priority of liens. They protect the interests of real estate owners, taxing bodies, creditors, and the general public. The real estate recording system includes written documents that affect title, such as deeds and mortgages. Public records regarding taxes, judgments, probate, and marriage also may offer important information about the title to a particular property.

Public records are maintained by

- recorders of deeds,
- county clerks,
- county treasurers,
- city clerks,
- collectors, and
- clerks of court.

**In Ohio...**

Public records are just that: open to the public. This means that anyone interested in a particular property can review the records to learn about the documents, claims, and other issues that affect its ownership. A prospective purchaser, for example, needs to be sure that the seller can convey title to the property. If the property is subject to any liens or other encumbrances, a prospective buyer or lender will want to know. (Note that ORC 149 et. seq. mandates that all government records be made public unless protected by one of six statutory exemptions.) ◆

**In Practice**

Although we speak of prospective purchasers conducting title searches, purchasers rarely search the public records for evidence of title or encumbrances themselves. Instead, title companies conduct searches before providing title insurance. An attorney also may search the title. A growing number of lending institutions require title insurance as part of the mortgage loan commitment.

## Recording

In most states, written documents that affect land *must be recorded in the county where the land is located.*

**Recording** is the act of placing documents in the public record. The specific rules for recording documents are a matter of state law. However, although the details may vary, all recording acts essentially provide that any written document that affects any estate, right, title, or interest in land must be recorded in the county where the land is located to serve as public notice. That way, anyone interested in the title to a parcel of property will know where to look to discover the various interests of all other parties. Recording acts also generally give legal priority to those interests recorded first (the "first in time, first in right" or "first come, first served" principle discussed in Chapter 11).

**In Ohio...** In Ohio, a mortgage is not effective as to third persons unless it has been recorded in the county in which the land is located. The public records should reveal the condition of the title, and a purchaser should be able to rely on a search of the public records. ◆

To be recorded by the county recorder, an instrument that conveys, encumbers, or otherwise disposes of title to real estate or personal property must include the name of the individual who prepared the instrument. The preparer must be a licensed Ohio attorney, a grantee or a grantor of the property, and his or her name must be printed, typewritten, stamped, or signed in a legible manner. If the signature on any instrument conveying title to real estate or personal property is illegible, the name must be printed or typed legibly beneath the written signature.

*First in time, First in line,*

When a deed or other instrument is presented for recording, the county recorder notes the date, the time of presentation, and a file number on the document. Until actually recorded, the instrument is kept on file in numerical order for easy reference. When it is actually recorded, the time is endorsed on the instrument and on the page of the book in which it is recorded. After the instrument is recorded, it is returned to the landowner or the person named to receive it.

## Acknowledgment

A deed, mortgage, land contract, or lease for more than three years must be signed by the grantor, mortgagor, or lessor. The signature must be attested by two witnesses and acknowledged before a notary public.

**In Ohio...** The following deficiencies will not invalidate a deed conveying Ohio real estate that has actually been recorded in the office of the appropriate county recorder:

- The dower interest of the spouse of the grantor was not specifically released by the spouse who executed the instrument.
- The officer taking the acknowledgment did not affix the official seal to the certificate of acknowledgment.
- The certificate of acknowledgment was not put on the same sheet of paper as the instrument.
- The executor, administrator, guardian, assignee, or trustee making the instrument signed or acknowledged it individually instead of in his or her representative or official capacity. ◆

## In Practice

**In Ohio...**

An acknowledgment performed in another state that conforms with that state's laws will be considered valid in Ohio if the instrument was executed in that other state. ◆

**Recording of Mortgages**

*In Ohio...*

The statute governing the recording of mortgages in Ohio is different from most recording statutes. In Ohio, prior to recording, a mortgage has no effect in law or in equity as to a third party, even though the third party acquired his or her interest or lien with actual notice of the unrecorded mortgage. ◆

**County Recorder**

*In Ohio...*

A county recorder is elected in each Ohio county every four years. That person keeps several separate sets of records:

1. Deeds and affidavits relating to matters that may affect title to real estate
2. Mortgages and options to purchase real estate, along with all amendments, supplements, and modifications; other instruments by which lands are or may be mortgaged or otherwise conditionally sold or encumbered; and residential installment contracts
3. Powers of attorney
4. Plats and maps of town lots and subdivisions and any center-line highway surveys
5. Leases ◆

The records are kept in two separate sets of books in the recorder's office. The first three items are kept in the recorder's official record books; the leases, plats, maps, and surveys are kept in a separate set of books.

The county recorder also maintains records of miscellaneous matters, such as federal tax liens, mechanics' liens, and judgments.

While it is the county recorder's duty to record all recordable documents presented, he or she is not bound to determine the instruments' validity or to ascertain whether they are genuine or forged.

The county recorder collects fees as provided by law for each document filed. These fees vary with the type and length of the document.

**Notice**

Anyone who has an interest in a parcel of real estate can take certain steps, called *giving notice,* to ensure that the interest is available to the public. This lets others know about the individual's interest. There are two basic types of notice: constructive notice and actual notice.

**Constructive notice** is the legal presumption that information may be obtained by an individual through diligent inquiry. Properly recording documents in the public record serves as constructive notice to the world of an individual's rights or interest. So does the physical possession of a property. Because the information or evidence is readily available to the world, a prospective purchaser or lender is responsible for discovering the interest.

In contrast, **actual notice** means that not only is the information available, but someone has been given the information and actually knows it. An individual who has searched the public records and inspected the property has actual notice. Actual notice is also known as direct knowledge. If an individual can be proved to have had actual notice of information, he or she cannot use a lack of constructive notice (such as an unrecorded deed) to justify a claim.

**Priority. Priority** refers to the order of rights in time. Many complicated situations can affect the priority of rights in a parcel of real estate—who recorded first; which party was in possession first; who had actual or constructure notice. How the courts rule in any situation depends, of course, on the specific facts of the case. These are strictly legal questions that should be referred to the parties' attorneys.

**FOR EXAMPLE** In May, *B* purchased Grayacre from *A* and received a deed. *B* never recorded the deed, but began farming operations on the property in June. In November, *A* (who was forgetful) again sold Grayacre, this time to *C*. *C* accepted the deed and promptly recorded it. However, because *C* never inspected Grayacre to see whether someone was in possession, *B* has the superior right to the property *even though B never recorded the deed.* By taking possession, a purchaser gives constructive notice of his or her interest in the land.

## Foreign-Language Documents

Deeds or mortgages written in a foreign language, although valid between the parties to a transaction, usually do not impart constructive notice when recorded. *All recorded documents must be in English.* An official translation by a consulate of the country in which the language is used, when attached to a foreign-language document, may meet state recording requirements. Both the original document and the translation are then recorded and become part of the public record.

## Unrecorded Documents

Certain types of liens are not recorded. Real estate taxes and special assessments are liens on specific parcels of real estate and are not usually recorded until some time after the taxes or assessments are past due. Inheritance taxes and franchise taxes are statutory liens. They are placed against all real estate owned by a decedent at the time of death or by a corporation at the time the franchise taxes became a lien. Like real estate taxes, they are not recorded.

Notice of these liens must be gained from sources other than the recorder's office. Evidence of the payment of real estate taxes, special assessments, municipal utilities, and other taxes can be gathered from paid tax receipts and letters from municipalities. Creative measures are often required to get information about these "off the record" liens.

## Chain of Title

**Chain of title** is the record of a property's ownership. Beginning with the earliest owner, title may pass to many individuals. Each owner is linked to the next so that a chain is formed. An unbroken chain of title can be traced through linking conveyances from the present owner back to the earliest recorded owner.

*[handwritten note: Quick-claim Deed]*

If ownership cannot be traced through an unbroken chain, it is said that there is a *gap* in the chain. In these cases, the cloud on the title makes it necessary to establish ownership by a court action called a **suit to quiet title.** A suit might be required, for instance, when a grantor acquired title under one name and conveyed it under another. Or there may be a forged deed in the chain, after which no subsequent grantee acquired legal title. All possible claimants are allowed to present evidence during a court proceeding; then the court's judgment is filed. Often, the simple procedure of obtaining any relevant quitclaim deeds (discussed in Chapter 13) is used to establish ownership.

## Title Search and Abstract of Title

*[handwritten note: Test]*

**In Ohio...**

A **title search** is an examination of all of the public records to determine whether any defects exist in the chain of title. The records of the conveyances of ownership are examined beginning with the present owner. Then the title is traced backward to its origin or to 40 years in the past, in accordance with the Ohio Marketable Title Act. This law extinguishes certain interests and cures certain defects arising before the *root of the title*—the conveyance that establishes the source of the chain of title. Normally, the root is considered to be 40 years. Under most circumstances, then, it is necessary to search only from the current owner to the root. ◆

Other public records are examined to identify wills, judicial proceedings, and other encumbrances that may affect title. These include a variety of taxes, special assessments, and other recorded liens.

A title search is usually not ordered until after the major contingencies in a sales contract have been cleared—for instance, after a loan commitment has been secured. Before providing money for a loan, a lender generally orders a title search to ensure that no lien is superior to its mortgage lien. In most cases, the cost of the title search is paid by the buyer.

*Test*

An **abstract of title** is a summary report of what the title search found in the public record. A person who prepares this report is called an abstractor. The abstractor searches all the public records, then summarizes the various events and proceedings that affected the title throughout its history. The report begins with the original grant (or root), then provides a chronological list of recorded instruments. All recorded liens and encumbrances are included, along with their current statuses. A list of all of the public records examined is also provided as evidence of the scope of the search.

*Test*

In a sale of land, the seller's attorney usually orders the abstract continued to cover the current date. When the abstractor has completed the abstract, it is submitted to the buyer's attorney for examination. The attorney must evaluate all the facts and material to prepare a written report for the purchaser, called an **attorney's opinion of title.**

**In Ohio...**  Abstracts of title and attorney's opinion of title are more commonly used in southern Ohio. In northern Ohio, a title guaranty is more common. ◆

---

**In Practice**        An abstract of title is a condensed history of those items that can be found in public records. It does not reveal items such as encroachments or forgeries or any interests or conveyances that have not been recorded.

---

**Title Guaranty**

*Not title Insurance*

**In Ohio...**

In Ohio, a **title guaranty** often is furnished by a title insurance company as evidence of title. This policy is a guaranteed report of the title as shown by the public records, and it lists the liens or encumbrances shown on the records. It does not give extensive coverage, as does a policy of title insurance, which covers unrecorded claims or deficiencies. ◆

**Marketable Title**

Under the terms of the typical real estate sales contract, the seller is required to deliver **marketable title** to the buyer at the closing. To be marketable, a title must

- disclose no serious defects and not depend on doubtful questions of law or fact to prove its validity;
- not expose a purchaser to the hazard of litigation or threaten the quiet enjoyment of the property;
- convince a reasonably well-informed and prudent purchaser, acting on business principles and with knowledge of the facts and their legal

significance, that he or she could sell or mortgage the property at a later time.

Although a title that does not meet these requirements still could be transferred, it contains certain defects that may limit or restrict its ownership. A buyer cannot be forced to accept a conveyance that is materially different from the one bargained for in the sales contract. However, questions of marketable title must be raised by a buyer before acceptance of the deed. Once a buyer has accepted a deed with unmarketable title, the only available legal recourse is to sue the seller under any covenants of warranty contained in the deed.

In some states, a preliminary title search is conducted as soon as an offer to purchase has been accepted. In fact, it may be customary to include a contingency in the sales contract that gives the buyer the right to review and approve the title report before proceeding with the purchase. A preliminary title report also benefits the seller by giving him or her an early opportunity to cure title defects.

## PROOF OF OWNERSHIP

 Proof of ownership is evidence that title is marketable. A deed by itself is not considered sufficient evidence of ownership. Even though a warranty deed conveys the grantor's interest, it contains no proof of the condition of the grantor's title at the time of the conveyance. The grantee needs some assurance that he or she is actually acquiring ownership and that the title is marketable. A certificate of title, title insurance, and a Torrens certificate are commonly used to prove ownership.  —not in Ohio

**Certificate of Title**

A **certificate of title** is a statement of opinion of the title's status on the date the certificate is issued. A *certificate of title is not a guarantee of ownership.* Rather, it certifies the condition of the title based on an examination of the public records—a title search. The certificate may be prepared by a title company, a licensed abstractor, or an attorney. An owner, a mortgage lender, or a buyer may request the certificate.

Although a certificate of title is used as evidence of ownership, it is not perfect. Unrecorded liens or rights of parties in possession cannot be discovered by a search of the public records. Hidden defects, such as transfers involving forged documents, incorrect marital information, incompetent parties, minors, or fraud, cannot be detected. A certificate offers no defense against these defects because they are unknown. The person who prepares the certificate is liable only for negligence in preparing the certificate.

**Title Insurance**

 **WWWeb.Link**
www.ctt.com. The site of Chicago Title Insurance Company. It provides an overview of the company's news, locations, credit services, informative articles, and real estate software.

**Title insurance** is a contract under which the policyholder is protected from losses arising from defects in the title. A title insurance company determines whether the title is insurable, based on a review of the public records. If so, a policy is issued. Unlike other insurance policies that insure against *future* losses, title insurance protects the insured from an event that occurred *before* the policy was issued. Title insurance is considered the best defense of title:

Test

| Table 14.1 | **Owner's Title Insurance Policy** | | |
|---|---|---|---|
| | **Standard Coverage** | **Extended Coverage** | **Not Covered by Either Policy** |
| | 1. Defects found in public records<br>2. Forged documents<br>3. Incompetent grantors<br>4. Incorrect marital statements<br>5. Improperly delivered deeds | Standard coverage plus defects discoverable through the following:<br>1. Property inspection, including unrecorded rights of persons in possession<br>2. Examination of survey<br>3. Unrecorded liens not known of by policy holder | 1. Defects and liens listed in policy<br>2. Defects known to buyer<br>3. Changes in land use brought about by zoning ordinances |

the title insurance company will defend any lawsuit based on an insurable defect and pay claims if the title proves to be defective.

After examining the public records, the title company usually issues what may be called a *preliminary report of title* or a *commitment* to issue a title policy. This describes the type of policy that will be issued and includes

- the name of the insured party;
- the legal description of the real estate;
- the estate or interest covered;
- conditions and stipulations under which the policy is issued; and
- a schedule of all exceptions, including encumbrances and defects found in the public records and any known unrecorded defects.

The *premium* for the policy is paid once, at closing. The maximum loss for which the company may be liable cannot exceed the face amount of the policy (unless the amount of coverage has been extended by use of an *inflation rider*). When a title company makes a payment to settle a claim covered by a policy, the company generally acquires the right to any remedy or damages available to the insured. This right is called *subrogation.*

**Coverage.** Exactly which defects the title company will defend depends on the type of policy. (See Table 14.1.) A *standard coverage policy* normally insures the title as it is known from the public records. In addition, the standard policy insures against such hidden defects as forged documents, conveyances by incompetent grantors, incorrect marital statements and improperly delivered deeds.

*Extended coverage,* as provided by an *American Land Title Association* (ALTA) policy, includes the protections of a standard policy plus additional protections. An extended policy would protect a homeowner against defects that may be discovered by inspection of the property: rights of parties in possession, examination of a survey, and certain unrecorded liens.

Title insurance does not offer guaranteed protection against all defects. A title company will not insure a bad title or offer protection against defects that clearly appear in a title search. The policy generally names certain uninsurable losses, called *exclusions.* These include zoning ordinances, restrictive covenants, easements, certain water rights, and current taxes and special assessments.

**Types of policies.** The different types of policies depend on who is named as the insured. An *owner's policy* is issued for the benefit of the owner and his or her heirs or devisees. A *lender's policy* is issued for the benefit of the mortgage company. The amount of the coverage depends on the amount of the mortgage loan. As the loan balance is reduced, the coverage decreases. Because under a lender's policy only the lender's interest is insured, it is advisable for the owner to obtain a policy as well.

A lessee's interest can be insured with a leasehold policy. *Certificate of sale* policies are available to insure the title to property purchased in a court sale.

*No longer Used in Ohio*
*Test — No!*

**The Torrens System**

**In Ohio...**

The **Torrens system** of land title *registration* was developed in 1857 by an Australian, Sir Robert Torrens, who took the idea from the system of registering title to shipping vessels. Approximately ten states, including Ohio, have adopted the Torrens system; it is also used in Canada.

Ohio is currently phasing out its use of the Torrens system on a county-by-county basis. Each county board of commissioners will consider the merits of abolishing land registration, including such factors as cost, frequency of use, the number of administrators required, the advantages and disadvantages of the system in general, and the level of popular support for retaining or abolishing the system. Such issues as public hearings and the timing of abolition are governed by statute. ◆

If a county elects to abolish land registration, previously registered land in the county is treated as unregistered land, and all instruments for its conveyance or encumbrance will be recorded.

Because the Torrens system is still in use in some counties, we will consider the details of its operation here.

**Torrens land registration.** If a person owns a fee simple estate in a parcel of land, the title may be registered in the Torrens Department in the county in which the land is situated. The title for an interest less than a fee simple (such as a life estate or estate for years) may be registered only if the fee simple estate is registered at the same time. The registration is made by petition and filed in the probate court or court of common pleas of the county in which the land is situated. The clerk of the court files a memorandum in the office of the county recorder that states that the application has been filed, gives the date and place of filing, and includes a copy of the description of the land. This memorandum is recorded and indexed by the recorder. The application must contain the following information:

- Full name, age, residence, and marital status of the owner
- Owner's interest in the land
- An accurate description of the land and the buildings and improvements
- Name of occupant
- Use of premises
- Details of all liens and claims against the land
- Names of owners of adjoining land
- Any other facts regarding title or possession

After the application is filed, the court causes the title to be searched and investigates all facts and allegations of the petitioner. The examination goes back 75 years, if the title record goes back that far. If the examiner concludes that the applicant has good title, the application is published once a week for three consecutive weeks in a general circulation newspaper in the county in which the land is located. Next, if the court finds that the application is proper, a decree of confirmation and registration is entered. This is then given to the recorder, who prepares a certificate of title (see Figure 14.1) and assigns it the next consecutive number. The recorder makes an exact duplicate of the original certificate, called an owner's *duplicate certificate,* and delivers it to the owner.

This Torrens *certificate* signifies that the person named as owner of the land owns it free from all estates and encumbrances except those noted on the certificate and certain federal, state, and local liens, leases, and easements.

The county recorder also obtains a signature card of the registrant (see Figure 14.2), showing his or her place of residence and post office address. This card must be attested by two witnesses and acknowledged, unless it is signed in the recorder's office, in which case it would require witnessing only by the recorder or a deputy.

**In Ohio...**     In Ohio, title to land registered under the Torrens system may be withdrawn from registration by the owner on the filing of a proper affidavit with the county recorder. In some states, land once so registered must remain under the Torrens system. ◆

Title to Torrens-registered property can never be acquired through a claim of adverse possession. This gives an owner of registered land protection against such claims.

## UNIFORM COMMERCIAL CODE

The **Uniform Commercial Code** (UCC) is a commercial law statute that has been adopted, to some extent, in all 50 states. The UCC is concerned with personal property transactions; it does not apply to real estate. The UCC governs the documents when personal property is used as security for a loan.

For a lender to create a security interest in personal property, including personal property that will become fixtures, the UCC requires that the borrower sign a **security agreement.** The agreement must contain a complete description of the items against which the lien applies. A short notice of this agreement (called a **financing statement** or a *UCC-1*) must be filed in the public record. It identifies any real estate involved when personal property is made part of the real estate. Once the financing statement is recorded, subsequent purchasers and lenders are put on notice of the security interest in personal property and fixtures. Many lenders require that a security agreement be signed and a financing statement filed when the real estate includes chattels or readily removable fixtures.

**In Ohio...**     In Ohio, UCC security and financing statements are filed with the Secretary of State, as well as in the county in which the personal property is located. ◆

**Figure 14.1    Torrens Certificate**

*No longer used in Ohio*

Form 86 (Sec. 23)
Revised Code 5309.25

## Transfer Certificate of Title

THE FRED PROCTER CO., CIN'TI. O.

Page No.

| TRANSFERRED FROM | CERTIFICATE No. | DOCUMENT No. | DATE ORIGINALLY REGISTERED | IN BOOK | PAGE | DATE OF THIS CERTIFICATE |
|---|---|---|---|---|---|---|
| | | | | | | Yr. |
| | | | | | | Mo. |
| | | | | | | Day |
| | | | | | | Hr. |

THIS IS TO CERTIFY, That.............................................aged.................years,  under.......................disability................
who resides in the County of...............................................and State of...........................................and whose P. O. Address is
..............................................................and who is....................married......................................................................

.............the owner......in fee.................. ..............................................................lands situated in the
...............................of...........................................County of....................................and State of Ohio, an accurate description
and plat  ⁽¹⁾ of each separate body or parcel of which are as follows, to-wit:
        First Body or Parcel.

¹ Each plat should have stated thereon the scale to which it is drawn.

as will more fully appear by reference to Surveys of Registered Lands, Plat Volume........................page .......................
        Subject to the exceptions mentioned in Section twenty-five of the Act of May 8, 1913, 103 O. L. 914, as amended
August 18, 1937 (Section 5309.28 Revised Code), providing for the registration of land titles, and subject to the lesser
estates and interests, liens, charges and incumbrances mentioned and described in the Memorials indorsed hereon or on
the sheet of Memorials attached hereto.
        In Witness Whereof, I have hereunto set my hand and affixed my Official Seal this................day of.........................,
19.........., at.............o'clock......M.
Entered in Registration Book......................page................
.....................................................Recorder.        (Seal)     Recorder of.....................................County, Ohio
By.................................................Deputy.                   By..................................................................Deputy.

**Figure 14.2 Signature Card of Registrant**

```
Filed -              Date                   Certificate No. -
By Whom              Transferred           Document No. -
                (Do not write above this line)
        SIGNATURE CARD OF OWNERS and of HOLDERS of LESSER
        ESTATES IN and LIENS UPON REGISTERED LANDS (Sec. 27)
Signed in Presence of    )
                         )                          Age
------------------------ )  SAMPLE
                         )                          Age
------------------------ )
Personal signatures
only as signatures       ------------------------------
on future documents               (Full Name)
will be compared
with these               P. O. Address _____

Signed and acknowledged before me this _____ day of _____ 19____

(over)                   ------------------------------
                                        Notary Public

              SAMPLE

NOTE - To guard against POSSIBLE FRAUD BY FORGERY, and for
purposes of FUTURE IDENTIFICATION, the land title registration law
provides that the Recorder must, in all cases where it is practicable to do so,
secure the attested signatures of every owner of and of every holder of any
interest in or lien upon registered lands. If the signature card is not signed
in the presence of the Recorder, it must be ATTESTED BY TWO WIT-
NESSES AND ACKNOWLEDGED before an officer authorized to take
acknowledgments of deeds. The SIGNATURE OF THE HUSBAND OR
WIFE of the registered owner should also be procured.
(Sec. 27.) (Sec. 8)
```

**KEY TERMS**

| | | |
|---|---|---|
| abstract of title | financing statement | title guaranty |
| actual notice | marketable title | title insurance |
| attorney's opinion of title | priority | title search |
| certificate of title | recording | Torrens system |
| chain of title | security agreement | Uniform Commercial Code |
| constructive notice | suit to quiet title | |

**SUMMARY**

- The purpose of the recording acts is to give legal, public, and constructive notice to the world of parties' interests in real estate.
  - The interests and rights of the various parties in a particular parcel of land must be recorded so that such rights are legally effective against third parties who do not have knowledge or notice of the rights.
- Possession of real estate is generally interpreted as constructive notice of the rights of the person in possession. Actual notice is knowledge acquired directly and personally.
- Title evidence shows whether a seller conveys marketable title.
  - A deed of conveyance is evidence that a grantor has conveyed his or her interest in land, but it is not evidence of the title's kind or condition.

- Marketable title is generally one that is so free from significant defects that the purchaser can be insured against having to defend the title.
- Four forms of providing title evidence are commonly used throughout the United States: abstract and attorney's opinion of title, certificate of title, Torrens certificate, and title insurance policy.
- Under the Uniform Commercial Code, the filing of a financing statement gives notice to purchasers and mortgagees of the security interests in personal property and fixtures on the specific parcel of real estate.

---

**Real-Life Real Estate**

1. A property near the county line that you just listed has the deed recorded in the wrong county. Now what?
2. Many brokers require the information files of listed property to contain recording data before the property can be advertised. Why is this good practice?

# QUESTIONS

1. A title search in the public records may be conducted by
   a. anyone.
   b. attorneys and abstractors only.
   c. attorneys, abstractors, and real estate licensees only.
   d. anyone who obtains a court order under the Freedom of Information Act.

2. Which of the following statements best explains why instruments affecting real estate are recorded?
   a. Recording gives constructive notice to the world of the rights and interests of a party in a particular parcel of real estate.
   b. Failing to record will void the transfer.
   c. The instruments must be recorded to comply with the terms of the statute of frauds.
   d. Recording proves the execution of the instrument.

3. A purchaser went to the county building to check the recorder's records. She found that the seller was the grantee in the last recorded deed and that no mortgage was on record against the property. The purchaser may assume which of the following?
   a. All taxes are paid and no judgments are outstanding.
   b. The seller has good title.
   c. The seller did not mortgage the property.
   d. No one else is occupying the property.

4. The date and time a document was recorded establish which of the following?
   a. Priority
   b. Abstract of title
   c. Subrogation
   d. Marketable title

5. *P* bought *L*'s house, received a deed, and moved into the residence, but neglected to record the document. One week later, *L* died, and his heirs in another city, unaware that the property had been sold, conveyed title to *M*, who recorded the deed. Who owns the property?
   a. *P*
   b. *M*
   c. *L*'s heirs
   d. Both *P* and *M*

6. If a property has encumbrances, it:
   a. cannot be sold.
   b. can be sold only if title insurance is provided.
   c. cannot have a deed recorded without a survey.
   d. can still be sold if a buyer agrees to take it subject to the encumbrances.

7. All of the following are acceptable proof of ownership, *EXCEPT* a(n)
   a. Torrens certificate.
   b. title insurance policy.
   c. abstract and attorney's opinion.
   d. deed signed by the last seller.

8. *Chain of title* refers to which of the following?
   a. Summary or history of all documents and legal proceedings affecting a specific parcel of land
   b. Report of the contents of the public record regarding a particular property
   c. Instrument or document that protects the insured parties (subject to specific exceptions) against defects in the examination of the record and hidden risks such as forgeries, undisclosed heirs, errors in the public records, and so forth
   d. Record of a property's ownership

9. *B*, the seller, delivered a title to the buyer at the closing. A title search disclosed no serious defects, and the title did not appear to be based on doubtful questions of law or fact or to expose the buyer to possible litigation. *B*'s title did not appear to present a threat to the buyer's quiet enjoyment, and the title policy was sufficient to convince a reasonably well-informed person that the property could be resold. The title conveyed would commonly be referred to as a(n)
   a. certificate of title.
   b. abstract of title.
   c. marketable title.
   d. attorney's opinion of title.

10. The person who prepares an abstract of title for a parcel of real estate
    a. searches the public records and then summarizes the events and proceedings that affect title.
    b. insures the condition of the title.
    c. inspects the property.
    d. issues a certificate of title.

11. *S* is frantic because she cannot find her deed and now wants to sell the property. She
    a. may need a suit to quiet title.
    b. must buy title insurance.
    c. does not need the deed to sell if it was recorded.
    d. should execute a replacement deed to herself.

12. Mortgagee title policies protect which parties against loss?
    a. Buyers
    b. Sellers
    c. Lenders
    d. Buyers and lenders

13. Which of the following are traditionally covered by a standard title insurance coverage policy?
    a. Unrecorded rights of persons in possession
    b. Improperly delivered deeds
    c. Changes in land use due to zoning ordinances
    d. Unrecorded liens not known of by the policyholder

14. General Title Company settled a claim against its insured, *O*. General Title made a substantial payment to the person who sued *O*. Now, General Title may seek damages from *S*, who originally gave *O* a general warranty deed. Through what right can General Title recover the amount it paid out in the settlement?
    a. Escrow
    b. Encumbrance
    c. Subordination
    d. Subrogation

15. A title insurance policy with standard coverage generally covers all of the following *EXCEPT*
    a. forged documents.
    b. incorrect marital statements.
    c. unrecorded rights of parties in possession.
    d. incompetent grantors.

16. The documents referred to as *title evidence* include
    a. title insurance.
    b. warranty deeds.
    c. security agreements.
    d. a deed.

17. To give notice of a security interest in personal property items, a lienholder must file which of the following?
    a. Security agreement
    b. Financing statement
    c. Chattel agreement
    d. Quitclaim deed

18. *K* sells a portion of her property to *L*. *L* promptly records the deed in the appropriate county office. If *K* tries to sell the same portion of her property to *M*, which of the following statements is true?
    a. *M* has been given constructive notice of the prior sale because *L* promptly recorded it.
    b. *M* has been given actual notice of the prior sale because *L* promptly recorded it.
    c. Because *M*'s purchase of the portion of *K*'s property is the more recent, it will have priority over *L*'s interest, regardless of when *L* recorded the deed.
    d. Because *L* recorded the deed, *M* is presumed by law to have actual knowledge of *L*'s interest.

19. *B* lives in northern Ohio. Which form of title report is *B* most likely to use?
    a. Chain of title
    b. Title guaranty
    c. Torrens certificate
    d. Abstract

20. In Ohio, the county recorder must determine before recording whether the
    a. permanent parcel number is correct.
    b. signature on the instrument is genuine.
    c. form conforms to Ohio statute.
    d. legal description is correct.

21. To be recognized by third parties, a mortgage must be
    a. notarized.
    b. recorded.
    c. witnessed.
    d. registered.

22. It is convenient to record a mortgage on Ohio land
    a. but it is not necessary to create a lien.
    b. so it can be recognized by third parties.
    c. because if it is not recorded, the mortgagor does not have to pay it off.
    d. because if it is not recorded, the mortgagee does not have to pay it off.

23. In Ohio, to be recorded, a deed must bear the signatures of the grantor and the
    a. grantee.
    b. notary public who acknowledged the grantor's signature.
    c. attorney who prepared the deed.
    d. two witnesses and the notary public who acknowledged the grantor's signature.

24. In locations where the abstract system is used, an abstract is usually examined by the
    a. broker.
    b. abstract company.
    c. purchaser.
    d. attorney for the purchaser.

# Real Estate Financing: Principles

## MORTGAGE LAW

> The *mortgagor* is the borrower.
>
> The mortgagee is the lender.

*[handwritten: Test isn't me]*

A mortgage is a voluntary lien on real estate. That is, a person who borrows money to buy a piece of property voluntarily gives the lender the right to take that property if the borrower fails to repay the loan. The borrower, or **mortgagor,** pledges the land to the lender, or **mortgagee,** as security for the debt. Exactly what rights the mortgagor gives the mortgagee, however, vary from state to state.

*[handwritten: No Foreclose in T. the theory States]*

In **title theory** states, the mortgagor actually gives legal title to the mortgagee (or some other designated individual) and retains *equitable title.* Legal title is returned to the mortgagor only when the debt is paid in full (or some other obligation is performed). In theory, the lender actually owns the property until the debt is paid. The lender allows the borrower all the usual rights of ownership, such as possession and use. In effect, because the lender actually holds legal title, the lender has the right to immediate possession of the real estate and rents from the mortgaged property if the mortgagor defaults.

In **lien theory** states, the mortgagor retains both legal and equitable title. The mortgagee simply has a lien on the property as security for the mortgage debt. The mortgage is nothing more than collateral for the loan. If the mortgagor defaults, the mortgagee must go through a formal foreclosure proceeding to obtain legal title. The property is offered for sale, and the funds from the sale are used to pay all or part of the remaining debt. In some states, a defaulting mortgagor may *redeem* (buy back) the property during a certain period *after the sale.* A borrower who fails to redeem the property during that time loses the property irrevocably.

**In Ohio...** A number of states, such as Ohio, have adopted an **intermediate theory** based on the principles of title theory, but requiring the mortgagee to foreclose to obtain legal title. ◆

In reality, the differences between the parties' rights in a lien theory state and those in a title theory state are more technical than actual.

## SECURITY AND DEBT

A basic principle of property law is that no one can convey more than he or she actually owns. This principle also applies to mortgages. The owner of a fee simple estate can mortgage the fee. The owner of a leasehold or sublease-hold can mortgage that leasehold interest. The owner of a condominium unit can mortgage the fee interest in the condominium apartment. Even the owner of a cooperative interest may be able to offer that personal property interest as collateral for a loan.

**Mortgage Loan Instruments**

There are two parts to a mortgage loan: the debt itself and the security for the debt. When a property is to be mortgaged, the owner must *execute* (sign) two separate instruments:

1. The **promissory note,** also referred to simply as the note or *financing instrument,* is the borrower's personal promise to repay a debt according to agreed-on terms. The note exposes all of the borrower's assets to claims by creditors. The mortgagor executes one or more promissory notes to total the amount of the debt.
2. The **mortgage,** also known as the *security instrument,* creates the lien on the property. The mortgage gives the creditor the right to sue for foreclosure in the event the borrower defaults.

Figure 15.1 shows the relationship between mortgagee and mortgagor.

*In Ohio...*  *A mortgage is characterized by Ohio statute as a lien.* Because the mortgage purports to convey property, the courts treat it as a conveyance of the bare legal title to the mortgagee solely for the purpose of enforcing payment. Until a default or breach occurs, the legal and equitable title to the mortgage property is held by the mortgagor. ◆

**Hypothecation** is the term used to describe the pledging of property as security for payment of a loan without actually surrendering possession of the property. A pledge of security—a mortgage or deed of trust—cannot be legally effective unless there is a debt to secure. Both a note and mortgage are executed to create a secured loan.

## PROVISIONS OF THE NOTE

A promissory note executed by a borrower (known as the *maker* or *payor*) generally states the amount of the debt, the time and method of payment and the rate of interest. If a note is used with a mortgage, it names the lender (mortgagee) as the payee. The note may also refer to or repeat several of the clauses that appear in the mortgage document. The note, like the mortgage, should be signed by all parties who have an interest in the property.

*In Ohio...*  In states like Ohio, where dower is in effect or where homestead or community property is involved, both spouses may have interests in the property, and both should sign the note and mortgage. ◆

A **note** is a **negotiable instrument** like a check or bank draft. The individual who holds the note is referred to as the payee. He or she may transfer the right to receive payment to a third party in one of two ways:

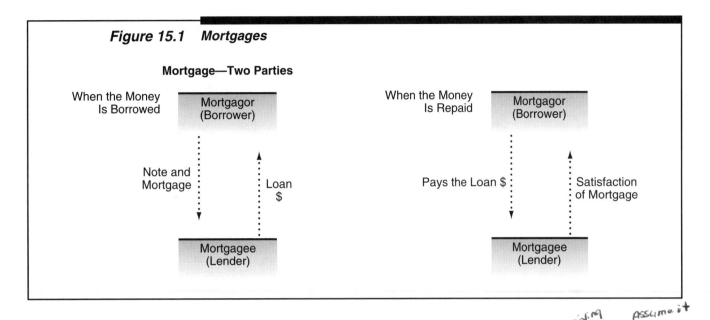

**Figure 15.1 Mortgages**

**Mortgage—Two Parties**

When the Money Is Borrowed — Mortgagor (Borrower) — Note and Mortgage — Loan $ — Mortgagee (Lender)

When the Money Is Repaid — Mortgagor (Borrower) — Pays the Loan $ — Satisfaction of Mortgage — Mortgagee (Lender)

*Test* → *giving* *assume it*

1. By signing the instrument over (that is, by assigning it) to the third party, or
2. By delivering the instrument to the third party

**Interest**    A charge for using money is called **interest.** Interest may be due at either the end or the beginning of each payment period. When payments are made at the end of a period, it is known as payment in arrears. Payments made at the beginning of each period are called *payments in advance.* Whether interest is charged in arrears or in advance is specified in the note. This distinction is important if the property is sold before the debt is repaid in full.

**Usury.** To protect consumers from unscrupulous lenders, many states have enacted laws limiting the interest rate that may be charged on loans. In some states, the legal maximum rate is a fixed amount. In others, it is a floating interest rate, which is adjusted up or down at specific intervals based on a certain economic standard, such as the prime lending rate or the rate of return on government bonds.

**In Ohio...**    Ohio statutes provide for a floating interest ceiling for land installment contracts and certain residential mortgage loans. State law provides for a maximum rate of eight percent higher than the Federal Reserve discount rate on the date of execution of the instrument. (The discount rate is the rate that the Cleveland Fourth Federal Reserve District Bank charges member commercial banks for the use of the Federal Reserve's funds by discounting 90-day commercial paper.) If, for example, the discount rate is seven percent during March, the maximum interest rate that could be charged on new residential mortgage loans made during the month would be 15 percent (the discount rate plus eight percent). ◆

Charging interest in excess of the maximum rate is called **usury,** and lenders are penalized for making usurious loans. While usury laws are state laws, the Depository Institutions Deregulation and Monetary Control Act of 1980, a federal law, specifically exempts all federally related residential first mortgage loans from state interest limitations. "Federally related loans" are those made by federally chartered institutions or insured or guaranteed by a federal agency. The exemption includes loans used to finance manufactured housing (the federal term for mobile homes) and the acquisition of stock in a cooperative housing corporation. All states were given the option of enacting new usury laws within three years of the act.

**MATH CONCEPTS**

### Discount Points and Investor Yield

Depending on the interest rate, it takes between six and eight discount points to change the interest rate 1 percent on a 30-year loan. From the borrower's standpoint, one discount point equals 1 percent of the loan amount.

To calculate the net amount of a $75,000 loan after a three-point discount is taken, multiply the loan amount by 100 percent minus the discount:

$$\$75,000 \times (100\% - 3\%)$$
$$\$75,000 \times 97\%$$
$$\$75,000 \times .97 = \$72,750$$

Or deduct the dollar amount of the discount from the loan:

$$\$75,000 - (\$75,000 \times 3\%)$$
$$\$75,000 - (\$75,000 \times .03)$$
$$\$75,000 - \$2,250 = \$72,750$$

**In Ohio...** Although the federal preemption applies in Ohio, it should be noted that the Ohio usury law still applies to "private" lenders (that is, sellers who hold a first or second mortgage) and others not specifically named in the federal law. ◆

The same federal law also sets a limit of five percentage points above the Federal Reserve discount rate as the ceiling on interest that can be charged by the named lenders on "business and agricultural loans" (including residential real estate loans that are not secured by a first mortgage) exceeding $25,000.

**Loan origination fee.** The processing of a mortgage application is known as *loan origination*. When a mortgage loan is originated, a **loan origination fee,** or transfer fee, is charged by most lenders to cover the expenses involved in generating the loan. These include the loan officer's salary, paperwork, and the lender's other costs of doing business. A loan origination fee is not prepaid interest; rather, it is a charge that must be paid to the lender. The typical loan origination fee is 1 percent of the loan amount.

**Discount points.** A lender may sell a mortgage to investors (as discussed later in this chapter). However, the interest rate that a lender charges for a loan might be less than the yield (true rate of return) an investor demands. To make up the difference, the lender charges the borrower **discount points.** The number of points charged depends on two factors:

> A point is not 1 percent of the purchase price; a point is 1 percent of the *amount being borrowed.*

1. The difference between the interest rate and the required yield
2. How long the lender expects it will take the borrower to pay off the loan

For the borrowers, one discount point equals 1 percent of the loan amount and is charged as prepaid interest at the closing. For instance, three discount points charged on a $100,000 loan would be $3,000 ($100,000 × 3%, or .03). If a house sells for $100,000 and the borrower seeks an $80,000 loan, each point would be $800, not $1,000. In some cases, however, the points in a new acquisition may be paid in cash at closing rather than being financed as part of the total loan amount.

**Prepayment**    Most mortgage loans are paid in installments over a long period of time. As a result, the total interest paid by the borrower can add up to more than the principal amount of the loan. That does not come as a surprise to the lender; the total amount of accrued interest is carefully calculated during the origination phase to determine the profitability of each loan. If the borrower repays the loan before the end of the term, the lender collects less than the anticipated interest. For this reason, some mortgage notes contain a *prepayment clause.* This clause requires that the borrower pay a **prepayment penalty** against the unearned portion of the interest for any payments made ahead of schedule.

The penalty may be as little as 1 percent of the balance due at the time of prepayment or as much as all the interest due for the first ten years of the loan. Some lenders allow the borrower to pay off a certain percentage of the original loan without paying a penalty. However, if the loan is paid off in full, the borrower may be charged a percentage of the principal paid in excess of that allowance. Lenders may not charge prepayment penalties on mortgage loans insured or guaranteed by the federal government.

**In Ohio...**    In the absence of a prepayment privilege granted to the mortgagor by the terms of a mortgage, Ohio law allows a mortgagor to prepay or refinance a residential mortgage without penalty at any time after five years from the execution of the mortgage. Prior to that time, a lender may charge no more than 1 percent of the existing balance as a prepayment penalty. ◆

---

**In Practice**    Interest payments made under a mortgage loan secured by a first or second home are deductible for federal income tax purposes. This deduction in effect reduces the borrower's total cost of housing for the year. Interest deductions are limited, however, to the interest paid on an initial loan amount or refinancing no greater than the purchase price of the home plus capital improvements, unless the loan proceeds are used for qualified medical or educational purposes. Points (prepaid interest) paid at the time of financing a home purchase are fully deductible for the year paid. Points on a loan to finance property improvements are also fully deductible for the year paid. Points paid on a loan refinancing may be deductible (consult with a tax expert). If advance payments of loan principal are made, there is no increase in the deduction. If the entire loan is repaid, however, any undeducted points may be deducted for that year. Tax deductions for the homeowner were discussed in greater detail in Chapter 3.

---

## PROVISIONS OF THE MORTGAGE DOCUMENT

The mortgage document clearly establishes that the property is security for a debt, identifies the lender and the borrower and includes an accurate legal description of the property. Both the mortgage document and deed of trust incorporate the terms of the note by reference. They should be signed by all parties who have an interest in the real estate. Common provisions of both instruments are discussed below.

**Duties of the Mortgagor or Trustor**    The borrower is required to fulfill certain obligations. These usually include the following:

- Payment of the debt in accordance with the terms of the note
- Payment of all real estate taxes on the property given as security

- Maintenance of adequate insurance to protect the lender if the property is destroyed or damaged by fire, windstorm or other hazard
- Maintenance of the property in good repair at all times
- Receipt of lender authorization before making any major alterations on the property

Failure to meet any of these obligations can result in a borrower's default. The loan documents may, however, provide for a grace period (such as 30 days) during which the borrower can meet the obligation and cure the default. If the borrower does not do so, the lender has the right to foreclose the mortgage and collect on the note.

**Provisions for Default**

The mortgage typically includes an **acceleration clause** to assist the lender in foreclosure. If a borrower defaults, the lender has the right to accelerate the maturity of the debt. This means the lender may declare the *entire* debt due and payable *immediately.* Without an acceleration clause, the lender would have to sue the borrower every time a payment was overdue.

Other clauses in a mortgage enable the lender to take care of the property in the event of the borrower's negligence or default. If the borrower does not pay taxes or insurance premiums, or fails to make necessary repairs on the property, the lender may step in and do so. The lender has the power to protect the security (the real estate). Any money advanced by the lender to cure a default may be either added to the unpaid debt or declared immediately due from the borrower.

**Assignment of the Mortgage**

As mentioned previously, a note may be sold to a third party, such as an investor or another mortgage company. The original mortgagee endorses the note to the third party and executes an *assignment of mortgage.* The assignee becomes the new owner of the debt and security instrument. When the debt is paid in full (or satisfied), the assignee is required to execute the satisfaction (or release) of the security instrument.

**Release of the Mortgage Lien**

When all mortgage loan payments have been made and the note has been paid in full, the mortgagor will want the public record to show that the debt has been satisfied and that the mortgagee is divested of all rights conveyed under the mortgage. By the provisions of the **defeasance clause** in most mortgage documents, the mortgagee is required to execute a **satisfaction of mortgage** (also known as a *release of mortgage* or *mortgage discharge*) when the note has been fully paid. This document returns to the mortgagor all interest in the real estate conveyed to the mortgagee by the original recorded mortgage document. Entering this release in the public record shows that the mortgage lien has been removed from the property.

If a mortgage has been assigned by a recorded assignment, the release must be executed by the assignee or mortgagee.

**Tax and Insurance Reserves**

Many lenders require that borrowers provide a reserve fund to meet future real estate taxes and property insurance premiums. This fund is called an *impound,* a *trust* or an *escrow account.* When the mortgage or deed of trust loan is made, the borrower starts the reserve by depositing funds to cover the amount of unpaid real estate taxes. If a new insurance policy has just been purchased, the insurance premium reserve will be started with the deposit of one-twelfth of the insurance premium liability. The borrower's monthly loan payments will include principal, interest, tax and insurance reserves, and other costs, such as flood insurance or homeowners' association dues. RESPA, the federal Real Estate Settlement Procedures Act (discussed in Chapter 25), limits the total amount of reserves that a lender may require.

**Flood insurance reserves.** The *National Flood Insurance Reform Act of 1994* imposes certain mandatory obligations on lenders and loan servicers to set aside (*escrow*) funds for flood insurance on new loans. However, the act also applies to any loan still outstanding on September 23, 1994. This means that if a lender or servicer discovers that a secured property is in a flood hazard area, it must notify the borrower. The borrower then has 45 days to purchase flood insurance. If the borrower fails to procure flood insurance, the lender must purchase the insurance on the borrower's behalf. The cost of the insurance may be charged to the borrower.

The borrower may provide for rents to be assigned to the lender in the event of the borrower's default. The assignment may be included in the mortgage or deed of trust, or it may be a separate document. In either case, the assignment should clearly indicate that the borrower intends to *assign* the rents, not merely pledge them as security for the loan. In title theory states, lenders are automatically entitled to any rents if the borrower defaults.

> The basic recurring components of a borrower's monthly loan payment may be remembered as **PITI:** *P*rincipal, *I*nterest, *T*axes and *I*nsurance.

## Buying Subject to or Assuming a Seller's Mortgage

When a person purchases real estate that is subject to an outstanding mortgage, the buyer may take the property in one of two ways. The property may be purchased subject to the mortgage, or the buyer may *assume* the mortgage and agree to pay the debt. This technical distinction becomes important if the buyer defaults and the mortgage is foreclosed.

When the property is sold subject to the mortgage, the buyer may not be personally obligated to pay the debt in full. The buyer takes title to the real estate knowing that he or she must make payments on the existing loan. On default, the lender forecloses and the property is sold by court order to pay the debt. If the sale does not pay off the entire debt, the purchaser is not liable for the difference. In some circumstances, however, the original seller might continue to be liable.

In contrast, a buyer who purchases the property and *assumes* the seller's debt becomes *personally* obligated for the payment of the *entire debt.* If the mortgage is foreclosed and the court sale does not bring enough money to pay the debt in full, a deficiency judgment against the assumer and the original borrower may be obtained for the unpaid balance of the note. If the original borrower has been released by the assumer, only the assumer is liable.

**F**OR EXAMPLE 1. When *J* bought her house a short time ago, interest rates were very low. Now, *J* has been unexpectedly transferred out of the country and needs to sell the house quickly. Because interest rates have risen dramatically since the time of *J*'s loan, buyers may be attracted by the prospect of *assuming J*'s mortgage. Clearly, if a buyer were to take out a mortgage now, the rate would be higher and the cost of home ownership would be increased. By assuming an existing loan with a more favorable interest rate, a buyer can save money.

2. *B* purchased his house when interest rates were high. In the short time since then, rates have fallen precipitously. If *B* must sell quickly, he may find that buyers are not interested in assuming a high-interest mortgage. A buyer might purchase *B*'s property *subject to* the existing mortgage. That is, the buyer would purchase *B*'s equity; *B* would

still be liable for the mortgage, and the bank could foreclose on the property to recover a default. If the foreclosure sale failed to satisfy the debt, *B* would be liable for the shortfall.

In many cases, a mortgage loan may not be assumed without lender approval. The lending institution would require the assumer to qualify financially, and many lending institutions charge a transfer fee to cover the costs of changing the records. This charge is usually paid by the purchaser.

**Alienation clause.** The lender may want to prevent a future purchaser of the property from being able to assume the loan, particularly if the original interest rate is low. For this reason, some lenders include an **alienation clause** (also known as a *resale clause, due-on-sale clause* or *call clause*) in the note. An alienation clause provides that when the property is sold, the lender may either declare the entire debt due immediately or permit the buyer to assume the loan at the current market interest rate.

### Recording a Mortgage

**In Ohio...**

Ohio's statute governing the recording of mortgages is unlike that of most states. The law provides that mortgages take effect only on delivery to the recorder of the county in which the property is located. Prior to recording, mortgages have no effect in law or in equity as to third parties, even though these third parties acquire their interests (or their liens) with actual notice of the unrecorded mortgages. ◆

This statute applies only to instruments that on their faces are mortgages. A deed or any other instrument that is not a mortgage on its face takes effect from the time it is executed and delivered. Until a nonmortgage deed is recorded, however, it is not enforceable or valid as to subsequent bona fide purchasers without actual or constructive notice.

Ohio law requires that the mortgagee record the satisfaction of a mortgage within 90 days from the date of satisfaction in the appropriate county recorder's office. The mortgagee must pay any fees required for the court recording, unless the parties have provided in the agreement to pass along fees to the mortgagor. This law applies only to mortgages covering one or two dwelling units.

### Priority of a Mortgage

**In Ohio...**

Priority of mortgages and other liens normally is determined by the order in which they were recorded. A mortgage on land that has no prior mortgage lien is a *first mortgage*. If the owner later executes another loan for additional funds, the new loan becomes a *second mortgage* (or a *junior lien*) when it is recorded. The second lien is subject to the first lien; the first has prior claim to the value of the land pledged as security. Because second loans represent greater risk to the lender, they are usually issued at higher interest rates. Ohio's usury laws may limit these rates, however. ◆

The priority of mortgage liens may be changed by a *subordination agreement*, in which the first lender subordinates its lien to that of the second lender. To be valid, such an agreement must be signed by both lenders.

## PROVISIONS OF LAND CONTRACTS

As discussed in Chapter 12, real estate can be purchased under a land contract, also known as a *contract for deed* or an *installment contract*. Real estate is usually sold on contract for specific financial reasons. For instance, mortgage financing may be unavailable to a borrower for some reason. High interest rates may make borrowing too expensive. Or the purchaser may not have a sufficient down payment to cover the difference between a mortgage loan and the selling price.

Under a land contract, the buyer (called the *vendee*) agrees to make a down payment and a periodic loan payment that includes interest and principal. The payment also may include real estate tax and insurance reserves. The seller (called the *vendor*) retains legal title to the property during the contract term, and the buyer is granted equitable title and possession. At the end of the loan term, the seller delivers clear title. The contract usually permits the seller to evict the buyer in the event of default. In that case, the seller may keep any money the buyer has already paid, which is construed as rent.

**In Ohio...** Many states, including Ohio, now offer some legal protection to a defaulting buyer under a land contract. Real estate licensees should consult an attorney for legal guidance in this technical area. ◆

# FORECLOSURE

When a borrower defaults on the payments or fails to fulfill any of the other obligations set forth in the mortgage, the lender's rights can be enforced through foreclosure. **Foreclosure** is a legal procedure in which property pledged as security is sold to satisfy the debt. The foreclosure procedure brings the rights of the parties and all junior lienholders to a conclusion. It passes title to either the person holding the mortgage document or to a third party who purchases the realty at a *foreclosure sale*. The purchaser could be the mortgagee. The property is sold *free of the foreclosing mortgage and all junior liens*.

**In Ohio...** In Ohio, a foreclosure action is filed in the court of common pleas in the county in which the land is located. The mortgagor normally has the right to retain possession of a dwelling during the foreclosure proceedings. However, after default, through a separate court proceeding, the mortgagee may obtain possession. This is one reason why Ohio is sometimes considered an intermediate theory state. ◆

**Methods of Foreclosure**  There are three general types of foreclosure proceedings—judicial, nonjudicial, and strict foreclosure. One, two, or all three may be available. The specific provisions and procedures for each vary from state to state.

**Judicial foreclosure.**  Judicial foreclosure allows the property to be sold by court order after the mortgagee has given sufficient public notice. When a borrower defaults, the lender may accelerate the due date of all remaining monthly payments. The lender's attorney can then file a suit to foreclose the lien. After presentation of the facts in court, the property is ordered sold. A public sale is advertised and held, and the real estate is sold to the highest bidder. This procedure is used in Ohio by means of a *sheriff's sale*. ◆

**Nonjudicial foreclosure.**  Some states allow nonjudicial foreclosure procedures to be used when the security instrument contains a power-of-sale clause. No court action is required. In those states that recognize deed of trust loans, the trustee is generally given the power of sale. Deeds of trust are not used in Ohio.

**Strict foreclosure.** Although judicial foreclosure is the prevalent practice, it is still possible in some states for a lender to acquire mortgaged property through a strict foreclosure process. First, appropriate notice must be given to the delinquent borrower. Once the proper papers have been prepared and recorded, the court establishes a deadline by which time the balance of the defaulted debt must be paid in full. If the borrower does not pay off the loan by that date, the court simply awards full legal title to the lender. No sale takes place. Ohio law, however, prohibits strict foreclosure. ◆

*In Ohio...*

### Deed in Lieu of Foreclosure

As an alternative to foreclosure, a lender may accept a **deed in lieu of foreclosure** from the borrower. This is sometimes known as a *friendly foreclosure* because it is carried out by mutual agreement rather than by lawsuit. The major disadvantage of the deed in lieu of foreclosure is that the mortgagee takes the real estate subject to all junior liens. In a foreclosure action, all junior liens are eliminated. Also, by accepting a deed in lieu of foreclosure, the lender usually loses any rights pertaining to FHA or private mortgage insurance or VA guarantees. This is not a common practice in Ohio, as it is in other states. ◆

*In Ohio...*

### Redemption

Most states give defaulting borrowers a chance to redeem their property through the **equitable right of redemption** (see Chapter 11). If, after default but *before the foreclosure sale*, the borrower (or any other person who has an interest in the real estate, such as another creditor) pays the lender the amount in default, plus costs, the debt will be reinstated. In some cases, the person who redeems may be required to repay the accelerated loan in full. If some person other than the mortgagor or trustor redeems the real estate, the borrower becomes responsible to that person for the amount of the redemption.

Certain states also allow defaulted borrowers a period in which to redeem their real estate after the sale. During this period (which may be as long as one year), the borrower has a **statutory right of redemption.** The mortgagor who can raise the necessary funds to redeem the property within the statutory period pays the redemption money to the court. Because the debt was paid from the proceeds of the sale, the borrower can take possession free and clear of the former defaulted loan. The court may appoint a receiver to take charge of the property, collect rents and pay operating expenses during the redemption period. Redemption is illustrated in Figure 15.2.

*Not in Ohio Test*

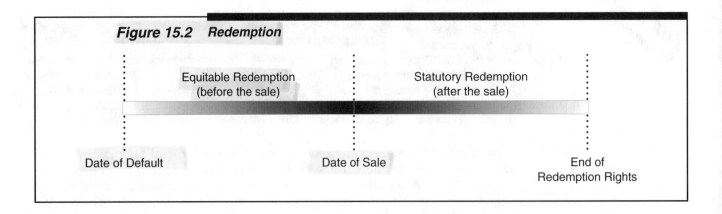

**Figure 15.2    Redemption**

Equitable Redemption (before the sale)          Statutory Redemption (after the sale)

Date of Default                    Date of Sale                    End of Redemption Rights

### Percentage Problems

Percentage problems contain three elements: percentage, total, and part. To determine a specific percentage of a whole, multiply the total by the percentage, as shown in the following formula:

$$\text{total} \times \text{percent} = \text{part}$$
$$200 \times 5\% = 10$$

This formula is used in calculating mortgage loan interest, loan origination fees, and discount points. It is the same formula used to calculate a broker's commission.

To determine the percentage when the amount of the part and the total are known:

$$\text{percent} = (\text{part} \div \text{total})$$

**In Ohio...**   There is no statutory right of redemption in Ohio after a foreclosure sale is completed *and the court has confirmed the sale.* The practice in Ohio is for the court to draw the decree so as to give the mortgagor a certain time within which to redeem before the sale actually takes place. The sale is held in the county in which the land is situated. Then, after the sheriff's sale, the borrower still may redeem the property until the court confirms the sale. However, once the sale is confirmed by the court, there is no right to redeem the property. ◆

**Deed to Purchaser at Sale**

*Test*

If redemption is not made or if state law does not provide for a redemption period, the successful bidder at the sale receives a deed to the real estate. A sheriff or master-in-chancery executes this deed to the purchaser *to convey whatever title the borrower had.* The deed contains no warranties. Title passes as is, but free of the former defaulted debt.

**Deficiency Judgment**

The foreclosure sale may not produce enough cash to pay the loan balance in full after deducting expenses and accrued unpaid interest. In this case, the mortgagee may be entitled to a *personal judgment* against the borrower for the unpaid balance. Such a judgment is a **deficiency judgment.** It also may be obtained against any endorsers or guarantors of the note and against any owners of the mortgaged property who assumed the debt by written agreement. However, if any money remains from the foreclosure sale after paying the debt and any other liens (such as a second mortgage or mechanic's lien), expenses and interest, these proceeds are paid to the borrower.

---

**KEY TERMS**

| | | |
|---|---|---|
| acceleration clause | hypothecation | note |
| alienation clause | interest | prepayment penalty |
| deed in lieu of foreclosure | intermediate theory | promissory note |
| | lien theory | satisfaction of mortgage |
| defeasance clause | loan origination fee | |
| deficiency judgment | mortgage | statutory right of redemption |
| discount points | mortgagee | |
| equitable right of redemption | mortgagor | title theory |
| | negotiable instrument | usury |
| foreclosure | | |

**SUMMARY**

- Some states, known as *title theory states,* recognize the lender as the owner of mortgaged property. Others, known as *lien theory states,* recognize the borrower as the owner of mortgaged property. A few intermediate states, such as Ohio, recognize modified versions of these theories.
- Mortgage loans provide the principal sources of financing for real estate operations. Mortgage loans involve a borrower (the mortgagor) and a lender (the mortgagee).
- After a lending institution has received, investigated, and approved a loan application, it issues a commitment to make the mortgage loan. The borrower is required to execute a note agreeing to repay the debt and a mortgage placing a lien on the real estate to secure the note. The security instrument is recorded to give notice to the world of the lender's interest.
- The mortgage document secures the debt and sets forth the obligations of the borrower and the rights of the lender.
  - Full payment of the note by its terms entitles the borrower to a satisfaction, or release, which is recorded to clear the lien from the public records.
  - Default by the borrower may result in acceleration of payments, a foreclosure sale, and, after the redemption period (if provided by state law), loss of title. In Ohio, the borrower has a right of redemption until the foreclosure sale is confirmed.

**Real-Life Real Estate**

1. Assume you are working with a young couple buying their first house. How would you describe the concept of "points" to them?
2. What are some of the circumstances that make assumption, taking title subject to a mortgage, or a land contract attractive to the parties?

# QUESTIONS

1. Under the law of the State of Ohio, a mortgage takes effect
   a. at the same time as in most other states.
   b. on delivery to the mortgagee.
   c. on delivery to the county recorder.
   d. any time prior to recording.

2. Ohio recognizes the right of redemption
   a. for two years after confirmation of the foreclosure sale.
   b. until the foreclosure sale is confirmed after the successful bidding at the sheriff's sale.
   c. for one year after confirmation of the foreclosure sale.
   d. neither before nor after the foreclosure sale.

3. A prepayment clause in a mortgage instrument
   a. usually penalizes the borrower or mortgagor for early payment of the mortgage.
   b. does not exist in Ohio mortgages.
   c. can never be waived even if the buyer's mortgage is with the same lender as the seller's.
   d. penalizes the lender when the mortgagor pays the loan off early.

4. A charge of three discount points on a $120,000 loan is
   a. $450.               c. $4,500.
   b. $116,400.           d. $3,600.

5. The person who obtains a real estate loan by signing a note and a mortgage is called the
   a. mortgagor.          c. mortgagee.
   b. beneficiary.        d. vendor.

6. Which of the following is true about a second mortgage?
   a. It has priority over a first mortgage.
   b. It cannot be used as a security instrument.
   c. It is not negotiable.
   d. It usually has a higher interest rate than a first mortgage.

7. All of the following would be true for the vendee in a land contract *EXCEPT* that the vendee
   a. is responsible for the real estate taxes on the property.
   b. must pay interest and principal.
   c. obtains possession at closing.
   d. obtains actual title at closing.

8. Laws that limit the amount of interest that can be charged to the borrower are called
   a. truth-in-lending laws.
   b. usury laws.
   c. the statute of frauds.
   d. RESPA.

9. The clause in a note that gives the lender the right to have all future installments become due upon default is the
   a. escalation clause.
   b. defeasance clause.
   c. alienation clause.
   d. acceleration clause.

10. What document is given to the mortgagor when the mortgage debt is completely repaid?
    a. Satisfaction of mortgage
    b. Defeasance certificate
    c. Deed of trust
    d. Mortgage estoppel

11. Under a typical land contract, when does the vendor give the deed to the vendee?
    a. When the contract is fulfilled
    b. At the closing
    c. When the contract for deed is approved by the parties
    d. After the first year's real estate taxes are paid

12. If a borrower must pay $2,700 for points on a $90,000 loan, how many points is the lender charging for this loan?
    a. Two                c. Five
    b. Three              d. Six

13. At the closing of a transaction involving a
    land contract the vendor would not
    a. provide financing for the vendee.
    b. still be liable for any senior financing.
    c. retain actual title.
    d. retain possession of the property.

14. Pledging property for a loan without giving
    up possession is best described as
    a. hypothecation.        c. alienation.
    b. defeasance.           d. novation.

15. Discount points on a mortgage are
    computed as a percentage of the
    a. selling price.
    b. amount borrowed.
    c. closing costs.
    d. down payment.

# CHAPTER 16

# Real Estate Financing: Practice

## INTRODUCTION TO THE REAL ESTATE FINANCING MARKET

Most real estate transactions require some sort of financing. Few people have the cash in hand necessary to buy a house or another large property. Also, as economic conditions change, the forces of supply and demand reshape the real estate market (see Chapter 1). Both of these factors have combined to create a complex and rapidly evolving mortgage market. One of the greatest challenges today's real estate licensees face is how to maintain a working knowledge of all the financing techniques available.

Although it has never been easier to buy a house, it has never been more challenging to keep up with the financing alternatives. By altering the terms of the basic mortgage and note, a borrower and a lender can tailor financing instruments to suit the type of transaction and the financial needs of both parties. Having an overview of current financing techniques and sources of financing can help salespeople direct buyers to the mortgage loans that will help the buyers reach their real estate goals.

## FINANCING TECHNIQUES

As just mentioned, real estate financing comes in a wide variety of forms. While the payment plans described in the following sections are commonly referred to as *mortgages,* they are really *loans* secured by a mortgage.

## STRAIGHT LOANS

A **straight loan** (also known as a *term loan*) essentially divides the loan into two amounts, to be paid off separately. The borrower makes periodic interest payments, followed by the payment of the principal *in full at the end of the term.* Straight loans were once the only form of mortgage available. Today, they are generally used for home improvements and second mortgages rather than for residential first mortgage loans.

## Calculating Simple Interest

To compute simple interest, use the formula $I = P \times R \times T$, where

$I$ = interest
$P$ = principal
$R$ = rate
$T$ = time

Apply this formula to a $30,000 loan *(P)* at 8 percent interest *(I)* to be repaid over 15 years *(T)*:

$$I = \$30,000 \times .08 \times 15$$
$$I = \$36,000$$

The total interest to be paid by the borrower is $36,000. Therefore

$36,000 total interest ÷ 15 years = $2,400 yearly interest payment
$2,400 ÷ 12 months = $200 monthly interest paymen*t*

# AMORTIZED LOANS -first time loan

The word *amortize* literally means "to kill off slowly, over time." Most mortgages and loans are **amortized loans.** That is, they are paid off slowly, over time. Regular periodic payments are made over a term of years. The most common periods are 15 or 30 years, although 20-year and 40-year mortgages are also available. Unlike a straight loan payment, an amortized loan payment partially pays off both principal and interest. Each payment is applied first to the interest owed; the balance is applied to the principal amount.

At the end of the term, the full amount of the principal and all interest due is reduced to zero. Such loans are also called *direct reduction loans.* Most amortized mortgage and deed of trust loans are paid in monthly installments. However, some are payable quarterly (four times a year) or semiannually (twice a year).

Different payment plans tend alternately to gain and lose favor with lenders and borrowers as the cost and availability of mortgage money fluctuate. The

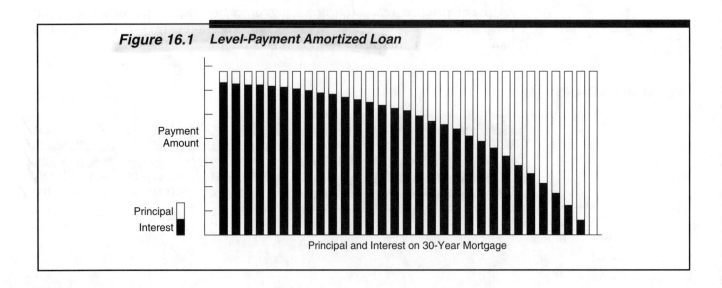

**Figure 16.1    *Level-Payment Amortized Loan***

Payment Amount

Principal
Interest

Principal and Interest on 30-Year Mortgage

most frequently used plan is the *fully amortized loan,* or *level-payment loan.* The mortgagor pays a *constant amount,* usually monthly. The lender credits each payment first to the interest due, then to the principal amount of the loan. As a result, while each payment remains the same, the portion applied to repayment of the principal grows and the interest due declines as the unpaid balance of the loan is reduced. (See Figure 16.1.) If the borrower pays additional amounts that are applied directly to the principal, the loan will amortize more quickly. This benefits the borrower because he or she will pay less interest if the loan is paid off before the end of its term. Of course, lenders are aware of this, too, and may guard against unprofitable loans by including penalties for early payment.

The amount of the constant payment is determined from a prepared mortgage payment book or a mortgage factor chart. (See Table 16.1.) The mortgage factor chart indicates the amount of monthly payment per $1,000 of loan, depending on the term and interest rate. The factor is multiplied by the number of thousands (and fractions of thousands) in the amount borrowed.

## Adjustable-Rate Mortgages (ARMs)

An **adjustable-rate mortgage** (ARM) is generally originated at one rate of interest. That rate then fluctuates up or down during the loan term based on some objective economic indicator. Because the interest rate may change, the mortgagor's loan repayments also may change. Details of how and when the interest rate will change are included in the note. Common components of an ARM include the following:

- The interest rate is tied to the movement of an objective economic indicator called an *index.* Most indexes are tied to U.S. Treasury securities.
- Usually, the interest rate is the index rate plus a premium, called the *margin.* The margin represents the lender's cost of doing business. For example, the loan rate may be two percent over the U.S. Treasury bill rate.
- *Rate caps* limit the amount the interest rate may change. Most ARMs have two types of rate caps—periodic and aggregate. A periodic rate cap limits the amount the rate may increase at any one time. An aggregate rate cap limits the amount the rate may increase over the entire life of the loan.
- The mortgagor is protected from unaffordable individual payments by the *payment cap.* The payment cap sets a maximum amount for payments. Without a cap, a rate increase could result in negative amortization—that is, an increase in the loan balance.
- The *adjustment period* establishes how often the rate may be changed. For instance, the adjustment period may be monthly, quarterly, or annually.
- Lenders may offer a conversion option, which permits the mortgagor to convert from an adjustable-rate to a fixed-rate loan at certain intervals during the life of the mortgage. The option is subject to certain terms and conditions for the conversion.

Figure 16.2 illustrates the effect interest rate fluctuations and periodic caps have on an adjustable-rate mortgage. Obviously, without rate caps and payment caps, a single mortgage's interest rate could fluctuate wildly over several adjustment periods, depending on the behavior of the index to which it is tied. In Figure 16.2, the borrower's rate changes from a low of 5.9 percent to a high of 9.5 percent. Such unpredictability makes personal financial planning difficult. On the other hand, if the loan had a periodic rate cap of 7.5 percent, the borrower's rate would never go above that level, regardless of the

**Table 16.1**  *Mortgage Factor Chart*

### How To Use This Chart

To use this chart, start by finding the appropriate interest rate. Then follow that row over to the column for the appropriate loan term. This number is the *interest rate factor* required each month to amortize a $1,000 loan. To calculate the principal and interest (PI) payment, multiply the interest rate factor by the number of 1,000s in the total loan.

For example, if the interest rate is 10 percent for a term of 30 years, the interest rate factor is 8.78. If the total loan is $100,000, the loan contains 100 1,000s. Therefore

100 × 8.78 = $878 PI

To estimate a mortgage loan amount using the amortization chart, divide the PI payment by the appropriate interest rate factor. Using the same facts as in the first example:

$878 ÷ 8.78 = $100 1,000's, or $100,000

| Term Rate | 10 Years | 15 Years | 20 Years | 25 Years | 30 Years |
|---|---|---|---|---|---|
| 4 | 10.13 | 7.40 | 6.06 | 5.28 | 4.78 |
| 4¼ | 10.19 | 7.46 | 6.13 | 5.35 | 4.85 |
| 4⅛ | 10.25 | 7.53 | 6.20 | 5.42 | 4.92 |
| 4⅜ | 10.31 | 7.59 | 6.26 | 5.49 | 5.00 |
| 4½ | 10.37 | 7.65 | 6.33 | 5.56 | 5.07 |
| 4⅝ | 10.43 | 7.72 | 6.40 | 5.63 | 5.15 |
| 4¾ | 10.49 | 7.78 | 6.47 | 5.71 | 5.22 |
| 4⅞ | 10.55 | 7.85 | 6.54 | 5.78 | 5.30 |
| 5 | 10.61 | 7.91 | 6.60 | 5.85 | 5.37 |
| 5⅛ | 10.67 | 7.98 | 6.67 | 5.92 | 5.45 |
| 5¼ | 10.73 | 8.04 | 6.74 | 6.00 | 5.53 |
| 5⅜ | 10.80 | 8.11 | 6.81 | 6.07 | 5.60 |
| 5½ | 10.86 | 8.18 | 6.88 | 6.15 | 5.68 |
| 5⅝ | 10.92 | 8.24 | 6.95 | 6.22 | 5.76 |
| 5¾ | 10.98 | 8.31 | 7.03 | 6.30 | 5.84 |
| 5⅞ | 11.04 | 8.38 | 7.10 | 6.37 | 5.92 |
| 6 | 11.10 | 8.44 | 7.16 | 6.44 | 6.00 |
| 6⅛ | 11.16 | 8.51 | 7.24 | 6.52 | 6.08 |
| 6¼ | 11.23 | 8.57 | 7.31 | 6.60 | 6.16 |
| 6⅜ | 11.29 | 8.64 | 7.38 | 6.67 | 6.24 |
| 6½ | 11.35 | 8.71 | 7.46 | 6.75 | 6.32 |
| 6⅝ | 11.42 | 8.78 | 7.53 | 6.83 | 6.40 |
| 6¾ | 11.48 | 8.85 | 7.60 | 6.91 | 6.49 |
| 6⅞ | 11.55 | 8.92 | 7.68 | 6.99 | 6.57 |
| 7 | 11.61 | 8.98 | 7.75 | 7.06 | 6.65 |
| 7⅛ | 11.68 | 9.06 | 7.83 | 7.15 | 6.74 |
| 7¼ | 11.74 | 9.12 | 7.90 | 7.22 | 6.82 |
| 7⅜ | 11.81 | 9.20 | 7.98 | 7.31 | 6.91 |
| 7½ | 11.87 | 9.27 | 8.05 | 7.38 | 6.99 |
| 7⅝ | 11.94 | 9.34 | 8.13 | 7.47 | 7.08 |
| 7¾ | 12.00 | 9.41 | 8.20 | 7.55 | 7.16 |
| 7⅞ | 12.07 | 9.48 | 8.29 | 7.64 | 7.25 |
| 8 | 12.14 | 9.56 | 8.37 | 7.72 | 7.34 |
| 8⅛ | 12.20 | 9.63 | 8.45 | 7.81 | 7.43 |
| 8¼ | 12.27 | 9.71 | 8.53 | 7.89 | 7.52 |
| 8⅜ | 12.34 | 9.78 | 8.60 | 7.97 | 7.61 |
| 8½ | 12.40 | 9.85 | 8.68 | 8.06 | 7.69 |
| 8⅝ | 12.47 | 9.93 | 8.76 | 8.14 | 7.78 |
| 8¾ | 12.54 | 10.00 | 8.84 | 8.23 | 7.87 |
| 8⅞ | 12.61 | 10.07 | 8.92 | 8.31 | 7.96 |
| 9 | 12.67 | 10.15 | 9.00 | 8.40 | 8.05 |
| 9⅛ | 12.74 | 10.22 | 9.08 | 8.48 | 8.14 |
| 9¼ | 12.81 | 10.30 | 9.16 | 8.57 | 8.23 |
| 9⅜ | 12.88 | 10.37 | 9.24 | 8.66 | 8.32 |
| 9½ | 12.94 | 10.45 | 9.33 | 8.74 | 8.41 |
| 9⅝ | 13.01 | 10.52 | 9.41 | 8.83 | 8.50 |
| 9¾ | 13.08 | 10.60 | 9.49 | 8.92 | 8.60 |
| 9⅞ | 13.15 | 10.67 | 9.57 | 9.00 | 8.69 |
| 10 | 13.22 | 10.75 | 9.66 | 9.09 | 8.78 |
| 10⅛ | 13.29 | 10.83 | 9.74 | 9.18 | 8.87 |
| 10¼ | 13.36 | 10.90 | 9.82 | 9.27 | 8.97 |
| 10⅜ | 13.43 | 10.98 | 9.90 | 9.36 | 9.06 |
| 10½ | 13.50 | 11.06 | 9.99 | 9.45 | 9.15 |
| 10⅝ | 13.57 | 11.14 | 10.07 | 9.54 | 9.25 |
| 10¾ | 13.64 | 11.21 | 10.16 | 9.63 | 9.34 |

index's behavior. Similarly, a lender would want a floor to keep the rate from falling below a certain rate (here, 6.5 percent). The shaded area in the figure shows how caps and floors protect against dramatic changes in interest rates.

### Interest and Principal Credited from Amortized Payments

Lenders charge borrowers a certain percentage of the principal as interest for each year a debt is outstanding. The amount of interest due on any one payment date is calculated by computing the total yearly interest (based on unpaid balance) and dividing that figure by the number of payments made each year.

For example, assume the current outstanding balance of a loan is $70,000. The interest rate is 7½ percent per year, and the monthly payment is $489.30. Based on these facts, the interest and principal due on the next payment would be computed as shown:

$70,000 loan balance × .075 annual interest rate = $5,250 annual interest

$5,250 annual interest ÷ 12 months = $437.50 monthly interest

$489.30 monthly payment − $437.50 monthly interest = $51.80 monthly principal

$70,000 loan balance − $51.80 monthly principal = $69,948.20

This process is followed with each payment over the term of the loan. The same calculations are made each month, starting with the declining new balance figure from the previous month.

**Balloon Payment Loan**   When the periodic payments are not enough to fully amortize the loan by the time the final payment is due, the final payment is larger than the others. This is called a **balloon payment.** It is a *partially amortized loan* because principal is still owed at the end of the term. It is frequently assumed that if payments are made promptly, the lender will extend the balloon payment for another limited term. The lender, however, is not legally obligated to grant this extension and can require payment in full when the note is due.

**Growing-Equity Mortgage (GEM)**   A **growing-equity mortgage** (GEM) is also known as a rapid-payoff mortgage. The GEM uses a fixed interest rate, but payments of principal are increased according to an index or a schedule. Thus, the total payment increases, and the loan is paid off more quickly. A GEM is most frequently used when the borrower's income is expected to keep pace with the increasing loan payments.

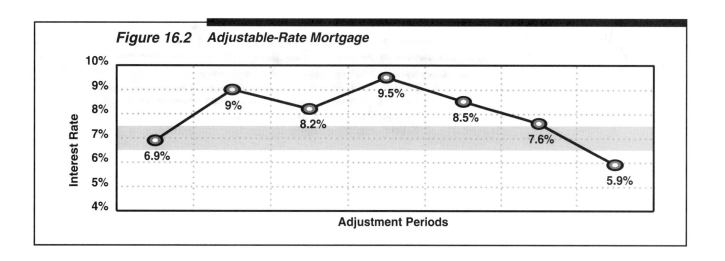

*Figure 16.2*   *Adjustable-Rate Mortgage*

**Reverse-Annuity Mortgage (RAM)**

A reverse-annuity mortgage (RAM) is one in which regular monthly payments are made by the lender *to the borrower.* The payments are based on the equity the homeowner has invested in the property given as security for the loan. This loan allows senior citizens on fixed incomes to realize the equity they have built up in their homes without having to sell. The borrower is charged a fixed rate of interest, and the loan is eventually repaid from the sale of the property or from the borrower's estate upon his or her death.

## LOAN PROGRAMS

 **WWWeb.Link**
www.quickenmortgage.com. Provides information on renting versus buying, credit assessment; and tools to calculate loan payments and refinancing calculations.

Mortgage loans are generally classified based on their **loan-to-value ratios,** or *LTVs.* The LTV is the ratio of debt to value of the property. Value is the sale price or the appraisal value, whichever is less. The *lower* the ratio of debt to value, the *higher* the down payment by the borrower. For the lender, the higher down payment means a more secure loan, which minimizes the lender's risk.

**Conventional #1 Loans**

**Conventional loans** are viewed as the most secure loans because their loan-to-value ratios are lowest. Usually, the ratio is 80 percent of the value of the property or less, because the borrower makes a down payment of at least 20 percent. The security for the loan is provided solely by the mortgage; the payment of the debt rests on the ability of the borrower to pay. In making such a loan, the lender relies primarily on its appraisal of the security (the real estate). Information from credit reports which indicate the reliability of the prospective borrower, is also important. No additional insurance or guarantee on the loan is necessary to protect the lender's interest.

> *Low* LTV = *High* down payment
>
> *High* down payment = *Low* lender risk

Lenders can set criteria by which a borrower and the collateral are evaluated to qualify for a loan. However, in recent years the secondary mortgage market has had a significant impact on borrower qualifications, standards for the collateral, and documentation procedures followed by lenders. Loans must meet strict criteria to be sold to the Federal National Mortgage Association and the Federal Home Loan Mortgage Corporation. Lenders still can be flexible in their lending decisions, but they may not be able to sell unusual loans in the secondary market.

**Private Mortgage Insurance**

*20% - Equity removed*

One way a borrower can obtain a mortgage loan with a lower down payment is under a **private mortgage insurance** (PMI) program. Because the loan-to-value ratio is higher than for other conventional loans, the lender requires additional security to minimize its risk. The borrower purchases insurance from a private mortgage insurance company as additional security to insure the lender against borrower default. LTVs of up to 95 percent of the appraised value of the property are possible with mortgage insurance.

PMI protects a certain percentage of a loan, usually 25 to 30 percent, against borrower default. Normally, the borrower is charged a fee for the first year's premium at closing. The borrower also pays a monthly fee while the insurance is in force. Other methods of payment are available, however: the premium may be financed or the fee at closing may be waived in exchange for slightly higher monthly payments. When a borrower has limited funds for investment, these alternative methods of reducing closing costs are very important. Because only a portion of the loan is insured, once the loan is repaid to a certain level, the lender may agree to allow the borrower to terminate the coverage. Practices for termination vary from lender to lender.

**Balloon Payment Loan**

Consider a loan with the following terms: $80,000 at 8 percent interest, with only interest payable monthly, and the loan fully repayable in 15 years. This is how to calculate the amount of the final balloon payment:

$80,000 × .08 = $6,400 annual interest

$6,400 annual interest ÷ 12 months = $533.33 monthly interest payment

$80,000 principal payment + $533.33 final month's interest
= $80,533.33 final balloon payment

## FHA-Insured Loans

 **WWWeb.Link**

www.hud.gov. The site of the Department of Housing and Urban Development. It provides a description of its housing programs and tips on buying a home, shopping for a mortgage, and finding affordable rental housing.]

 The Federal Housing Administration (FHA), which operates under HUD, neither builds homes nor lends money itself. The common term **FHA loan** refers to a loan that is <u>insured</u> by the agency. These loans must be made by FHA-approved lending institutions. The FHA insurance provides security to the lender in addition to the real estate. As with private mortgage insurance, the FHA insures lenders against loss from borrower default.

The most popular FHA program is Title II, Section 203(b), fixed-interest rate loans for 10 to 30 years on one- to four-family residences. Rates are competitive with other types of loans, even though they are high-LTV loans. Certain technical requirements must be met before the FHA will insure the loans. These requirements include the following:

- The borrower is charged a percentage of the loan as a premium for the FHA insurance. The *upfront premium* is paid at closing by the borrower or some other party. It also may be financed along with the total loan amount. A monthly premium also may be charged. Insurance premiums vary for new loans, refinancing, and condominiums.
- FHA regulations set standards for type and construction of buildings, quality of neighborhood, and credit requirements for borrowers.
- The mortgaged real estate must be appraised by an approved FHA appraiser. The loan amount generally cannot exceed either of the following: (1) 97 percent on the first $25,000 of appraised value or purchase price, whichever is less; 95 percent up to $125,000; and 90 percent of any amount exceeding $125,000 (including the allowable amount for closing costs); or (2) 97.75 percent of the sales price or appraised value, whichever is less. If the purchase price exceeds the FHA-appraised value, the buyer may pay the difference in cash as part of the down payment. In addition, the FHA has set maximum loan amounts for various regions of the country.

Other types of FHA loans are available, including one-year adjustable-rate mortgages; home improvement and rehabilitation loans; and loans for the purchase of condominiums. Specific standards for condominium complexes and the ratio of owner-occupants to renters must be met for a loan on a condominium unit to be financed through the FHA insurance programs.

**Determining LTV**
If a property has an appraised value of $100,000, secured by a $90,000 loan, the LTV is 90 percent:

$$\$90,000 \div \$100,000 = 90\%$$

**In Practice**          The FHA sets lending limits for single-unit and multiple-unit properties. The limits vary significantly, depending on the average cost of housing in different regions of the country. In addition, the FHA changes its regulations for various programs from time to time. Contact your local FHA office or mortgage lender for loan amounts in your area and for specific loan requirements.

**Prepayment privileges.** A borrower may repay an FHA-insured loan on a one- to four-family residence without penalty. For loans made *before* August 2, 1985, the borrower must give the lender written notice of intention to exercise the prepayment privilege at least 30 days before prepayment. If the borrower fails to provide the required notice, the lender has the option of charging up to 30 days' interest. For loans initiated *after* August 2, 1985, no written notice of prepayment is required.

**Assumption rules.** The assumption rules for FHA-insured loans vary, depending on the dates the loans were originated:

- FHA loans originated before December 1986 generally have no restrictions on their assumptions.
- For an FHA loan originated between December 1, 1986, and December 15, 1989, a creditworthiness review of the prospective assumer is required. If the original loan was for the purchase of a principal residence, this review is required during the first 12 months of the loan's existence. If the original loan was for the purchase of an investment property, the review is required during the first 24 months of the loan.
- For FHA loans originated on December 15, 1989, and later, no assumptions are permitted without complete buyer qualification.

*Test*

**Discount points.** The lender of an FHA-insured loan may charge discount points in addition to a loan origination fee. The payment of points is a matter of negotiation between the seller and the buyer. However, if the seller pays more than six percent of the costs normally paid by the buyer (such as discount points, the loan origination fee, the mortgage insurance premium, buydown fees, prepaid items, and impound or escrow amounts), the lender will treat the payments as a reduction in sales price and recalculate the mortgage amount accordingly. Points are tax deductible to the buyer regardless of which party pays them.

**VA-Guaranteed Loans**           **WWWeb.Link**
www.homeloans.va.gov. The site of the Veterans Administration home loan guaranty program. It provides information about the VA loan program and eligibility.

The Department of Veterans Affairs (VA) is authorized to guarantee loans to purchase or construct homes for eligible veterans and their spouses (including unremarried spouses of veterans whose deaths were service-related). The VA also guarantees loans to purchase mobile homes and plots on which to place them. A veteran who meets any of the following time-in-service criteria is eligible for a VA loan:

- 90 days of active service for veterans of World War II, the Korean War, the Viet Nam conflict, and the Persian Gulf War
- A minimum of 181 days of active service during interconflict periods between July 26, 1947, and September 6, 1980
- Two full years of service during any peacetime period after September 7, 1980
- Six or more years of continuous duty as a reservist in the Army, Navy, Air Force, Marine Corps, or Coast Guard or as a member of the Army or Air National Guard

The VA assists veterans in financing the purchase of homes with little or no down payments at comparatively low interest rates. The VA issues rules and regulations that set forth the qualifications, limitations, and conditions under which a loan may be guaranteed.

Like the term *FHA loan, VA loan* is something of a misnomer. The VA does not normally lend money; it guarantees loans made by lending institutions approved by the agency. The term **VA loan** refers to a loan that is not made by the agency, but is guaranteed by it.

There is no VA limit on the amount of the loan a veteran can obtain; this is determined by the lender. The VA limits the amount of the loan it will guarantee. (See Table 16.2.)

To determine what portion of a mortgage loan the VA will guarantee, the veteran must apply for and receive a *certificate of eligibility.* This certificate does not mean that the veteran automatically receives a mortgage. It merely sets forth the maximum guarantee to which the veteran is entitled. For individuals with full eligibility, no down payment is required for a loan up to the maximum guarantee limit.

The VA also issues a *certificate of reasonable value (CRV)* for the property being purchased. The CRV states the property's current market value, based on a VA-approved appraisal. The CRV places a ceiling on the amount of a VA loan allowed for the property. If the purchase price is greater than the amount cited in the CRV, the veteran may pay the difference in cash.

The VA purchaser pays a loan origination fee to the lender, as well as a funding fee (1.25 to 2 percent, depending on the down payment amount) to the Department of Veterans Affairs. Reasonable discount points may be charged on a VA-guaranteed loan, and either the veteran or the seller may pay them.

**Table 16.2** **VA Schedule of Guarantees**

| Loan Amount | Maximum Guarantee Amount |
| --- | --- |
| Up to $45,000 | 50% ($22,500 minimum) |
| $45,001 to $144,000 | The lesser of $36,000 or 40% of loan |
| More than $144,000 to $203,000 | The lesser of $50,750 or 25% of loan |

**Prepayment privileges.** As with an FHA loan, the borrower under a VA loan can prepay the debt at any time without penalty.

**Assumption rules.** VA loans made before March 1, 1988, are freely assumable, although an assumption processing fee will be charged. The fee is ½ percent of the loan balance. For loans made on or after March 1, 1988, the VA must approve the buyer and the assumption agreement. The original veteran borrower remains personally liable for the repayment of the loan unless the VA approves a *release of liability*. The release of liability will be issued by the VA only if

- the buyer assumes all of the veteran's liabilities on the loan and
- the VA or the lender approves both the buyer and the assumption agreement.

A release also would be possible if another veteran used his or her own entitlement in assuming the loan. When the original borrower has been released from liability and another veteran has used his or her own entitlement to assume the loan, the original borrower will be fully eligible for another VA loan.

| | |
|---|---|
| **In Practice** | A release of liability issued by the VA does not release the veteran's liability to the lender. This must be obtained separately from the lender. Real estate licensees should contact their local VA offices or mortgage lenders for specific requirements for obtaining or assuming VA-insured loans. The programs change from time to time. |

**Farm Service Agency**

The **Farm Service Agency** (FSA), formerly the Federal Agricultural Mortgage Corporation (FAMC, or Farmer Mac), is a federal agency of the Department of Agriculture. The FSA offers programs to help families purchase or operate family farms. Through the Rural Housing and Community Development Service, it also provides loans to help families purchase or improve single-family homes in rural areas (generally areas with populations of fewer than 10,000). Loans are made to low- and moderate-income families, and the interest rate charged can be as low as 1 percent, depending on the borrower's income. The FSA provides assistance to rural and agricultural businesses and industry through the Rural Business and Cooperative Development Service.

FSA loan programs fall into two categories: guaranteed loans, made and serviced by private lenders and guaranteed for a specific percentage by the FSA, and loans made directly by the FSA.

## OTHER FINANCING TECHNIQUES

Because borrowers often have different needs, a variety of other financing techniques have been created. Other techniques apply to various types of collateral. The following pages consider some of the loans that do not fit into the categories previously discussed.

**Purchase-Money Mortgages**

A **purchase-money mortgage** is a note and mortgage *created at the time of purchase.* Its purpose is to make the sale possible. The term is used in two ways. First, it may refer to any security instrument that originates at the time of sale. More often, it refers to the instrument given by the purchaser to a seller, who takes back a note for part or all of the purchase price. The mortgage may be a first or a junior lien, depending on whether prior mortgage liens exist.

**FOR EXAMPLE**  *B* wants to buy Brownacre for $200,000. *B* has a $40,000 down payment and agrees to assume an existing mortgage of $80,000. Because *B* might not qualify for a new mortgage under the circumstances, the owner agrees to take back a purchase-money second mortgage in the amount of $80,000. At the closing, *B* will execute a mortgage and note in favor of the owner, who will convey title to *B*.

## Package Loans

A **package loan** includes not only the real estate but also *all personal property and appliances installed on the premises.* In recent years, this kind of loan has been used extensively to finance furnished condominium units. Package loans usually include furniture, drapes, carpets, and the kitchen range, refrigerator, dishwasher, garbage disposal, washer, dryer, food freezer, and other appliances as part of the sales price of the home.

## Blanket Loans

A **blanket loan** covers *more than one parcel or lot.* It usually is used to finance subdivision developments. However, it can be used to finance the purchase of improved properties or to consolidate loans as well. A blanket loan usually includes a provision known as a *partial release clause.* This clause permits the borrower to obtain the release of any one lot or parcel from the lien by repaying a certain amount of the loan. The lender issues a partial release for each parcel released from the mortgage lien. The release form includes a provision that the lien will continue to cover all other unreleased lots.

## Wraparound Loans

A **wraparound loan** enables a borrower with an existing mortgage or deed of trust loan to obtain additional financing from a second lender *without paying off the first loan.* The second lender gives the borrower a new, increased loan at a higher interest rate and assumes payment of the existing loan. The total amount of the new loan includes the existing loan as well as the additional funds needed by the borrower. The borrower makes payments to the new lender on the larger loan. The new lender makes payments on the original loan out of the borrower's payments.

A wraparound mortgage can be used to refinance real property or to finance the purchase of real property when an existing mortgage cannot be prepaid. The buyer executes a wraparound mortgage to the seller, who collects payments on the new loan and continues to make payments on the old loan. The wraparound loan also can finance the sale of real estate when the buyer wishes to invest a minimum amount of initial cash. A wraparound loan is possible only if the original loan permits it. For instance, an acceleration and alienation or a due-on-sale clause in the original loan documents may prevent a sale under a wraparound loan.

## In Practice

To protect themselves against a seller's default on a previous loan, buyers should require that protective clauses be included in any wraparound document to grant buyers the right to make payments directly to the original lender.

## Open-End Loans

An **open-end loan** secures a *note* executed by the borrower to the lender. It also secures any future *advances* of funds made by the lender to the borrower. The interest rate on the initial amount borrowed is fixed, but interest on future advances may be charged at the market rate in effect. An open-end loan is often a less costly alternative to a home improvement loan. It allows the borrower to "open" the mortgage or deed of trust to increase the debt to its original amount, or the amount stated in the note, after the debt has been reduced by payments over a period of time. The mortgage usually states the maximum amount that can be secured, the terms and conditions under which the loan can be opened and the provisions for repayment.

## Construction Loans

A **construction loan** is made to *finance the construction of improvements* on real estate such as homes, apartments, and office buildings. The lender commits to the full amount of the loan, but disburses the funds in payments during construction. These payments are also known as *draws*. Draws are made to the general contractor or the owner for that part of the construction work that has been completed since the previous payment. Before each payment, the lender inspects the work. The general contractor must provide the lender with adequate waivers that release all mechanic's lien rights for the work covered by the payment.

This kind of loan generally bears a higher-than-market interest rate because of the risks assumed by the lender. These risks include the inadequate releasing of mechanics' liens, possible delays in completing the construction, or the financial failure of the contractor or subcontractors. Construction loans are generally *short-term* or *interim financing*. The borrower pays interest only on the monies that have actually been disbursed. The borrower is expected to arrange for a permanent loan, also known as an *end loan* or *take-out loan*, that will repay or "take out" the construction financing lender when the work is completed. Some lenders now offer construction-to-permanent loans that become fixed mortgages on completion. *Participation financing* is when a lender demands an equity position in the project as a requirement for the loan.

## Sale-and-Leaseback

**Sale-and-leaseback** arrangements are used to finance large commercial or industrial properties. The land and building, usually used by the seller for business purposes, are sold to an investor. The real estate is then leased back by the investor to the seller, who continues to conduct business on the property as a tenant. The buyer becomes the lessor, and the original owner becomes the lessee. This enables a business to free money tied up in real estate to be used as working capital.

Sale-and-leaseback arrangements involve complicated legal procedures, and their success is usually related to the effects the transaction has on the firm's tax situation. Legal and tax experts should be involved in this type of transaction.

## Buydowns

A **buydown** is a way to temporarily lower the initial interest rate on a mortgage or deed of trust loan. Perhaps a homebuilder wishes to stimulate sales by offering a lower-than-market rate. Or a first-time residential buyer may have trouble qualifying for a loan at the prevailing rates; relatives or the sellers might want to help the buyer qualify. In any case, a lump sum is paid in cash to the lender at the closing. The payment offsets (and so reduces) the interest rate and monthly payments during the mortgage's first few years. Typical buydown arrangements reduce the interest rate by 1 to 3 percent over the first one to three years of the loan term. After that, the rate rises. The assumption is that the borrower's income will also increase and that the borrower will be more able to absorb the increased monthly payments.

**Home Equity Loans**

Using the equity buildup in a home to finance purchases is an alternative to refinancing. **Home equity loans** are a source of funds for homeowners to use for a variety of financial needs:

- To finance the purchase of expensive items
- To consolidate existing installment loans on credit card debt
- To pay medical, education, home improvement, or other expenses

The original mortgage loan remains in place; the home equity loan is junior to the original lien. If the homeowner refinances, the original mortgage loan is paid off and replaced by a new loan. (This is an alternative way to borrow against the equity; it's not really a home equity loan.)

A home equity loan can be taken out as a fixed loan amount or as an equity line of credit. With the home equity line of credit, the lender extends a line of credit that the borrower can use whenever he or she wants. Borrowers receive their money by checks sent to them, deposits made in checking or savings accounts, or a book of drafts they can use up to their credit limit.

Use of this type of financing has increased in recent years, partly because interest on consumer loans is no longer deductible under IRS rules. Home equity loans are secured by a borrower's residence, and the interest charged is deductible up to a loan limit of $100,000.

---

**In Practice**      The homeowner must consider a number of factors before deciding on a home equity loan. The costs involved in obtaining a new mortgage loan or a home equity loan; current interest rates; total monthly payments; and income tax consequences are all important issues to be examined.

---

**The Federal Reserve System**

The role of the **Federal Reserve System** (also known as the *Fed*) is to maintain sound credit conditions, help counteract inflationary and deflationary trends, and create a favorable economic climate. The Federal Reserve System divides the country into 12 federal reserve districts, each served by a federal reserve bank. All nationally chartered banks must join the Fed and purchase stock in its district reserve banks.

*Controls! Rates*

The Federal Reserve regulates the flow of money and interest rates in the marketplace indirectly through its member banks by controlling their *reserve requirements* and *discount rates.*

**Reserve requirements.** The Federal Reserve requires that each member bank keep a certain amount of assets on hand as reserve funds. These reserves are unavailable for loans or any other use. This requirement not only protects customer deposits but also provides a means of manipulating the flow of cash in the money market.

By increasing its reserve requirements, the Federal Reserve in effect limits the amount of money that member banks can use to make loans. When the amount of money available for lending decreases, interest rates (the amount lenders charge for the use of their money) rise. By causing interest rates to rise, the government can slow down an overactive economy by limiting the number of loans that would have been directed toward major purchases of goods and services. The opposite is also true: by decreasing the reserve requirements, the Fed can encourage more lending. Increased lending causes the amount of money circulated in the marketplace to rise, simultaneously causing interest rates to drop.

**Discount rates.** Federal Reserve member banks are permitted to borrow money from the district reserve banks to expand their lending operations. The interest rate that the district banks charge for the use of this money is called the *discount rate.* This rate is the basis on which the banks determine the percentage rate of interest they will charge their loan customers. The prime rate (the short-term interest rate charged to a bank's largest, most creditworthy customers) is strongly influenced by the Fed's discount rate. In turn, the prime rate is often the basis for determining a bank's interest rate on other loans, including mortgages. In theory, when the Federal Reserve discount rate is high, bank interest rates are high. When bank interest rates are high, fewer loans are made and less money circulates in the marketplace. On the other hand, a lower discount rate results in lower interest rates, more bank loans, and more money in circulation.

## The Primary Mortgage Market

The **primary mortgage market** is made up of the lenders that originate mortgage loans. These lenders make money available directly to borrowers. From a borrower's point of view, a loan is a means of financing an expenditure; from a lender's point of view, a loan is an investment. All investors look for profitable returns on their investments. For a lender, a loan must generate enough income to be attractive as an investment. Income on the loan is realized from two sources:

1. *Finance charges* collected at closing, such as loan origination fees and discount points
2. *Recurring income*—that is, the interest collected during the term of the loan

An increasing number of lenders look at the income generated from the fees charged in originating loans as their primary investment objective. Once the loans are made, they are sold to investors. By selling loans to investors in the secondary mortgage market, lenders generate funds with which to originate additional loans.

In addition to the income directly related to loans, some lenders derive income from servicing loans for other mortgage lenders or the investors who have purchased the loans. Servicing involves such activities as

- collecting payments (including insurance and taxes),
- accounting,
- bookkeeping,
- preparing insurance and tax records,
- processing payments of taxes and insurance, and
- following up on loan payment and delinquency.

The terms of the servicing agreement stipulate the responsibilities and fees for the service.

Some of the major lenders in the primary market include

**Primary Mortgage Market**

- Trusts
- Savings associations
- Commercial banks
- Insurance companies
- Credit unions
- Pension funds
- Endowment funds
- Investment group financing
- Mortgage banking companies
- Mortgage brokers

- *thrifts, savings associations, and commercial banks.* These institutions are known as *fiduciary lenders* because of their fiduciary obligations to protect and preserve their despositors' funds. Mortgage loans are perceived as secure investments for generating income and enable these institutions to pay interest to their depositors. Fiduciary lenders are subject to standards and regulations established by government agencies such as the **Federal Deposit Insurance Corporation** (FDIC). **The Financial Institutions Reform, Recovery, and Enforcement Act of 1989** (FIRREA) created the **Office of Thrift Supervision** (OTS) specifically to govern the practices of fiduciary lenders. The various government regulations (which include reserve fund, reporting, and insurance requirements) are intended to protect depositors against the reckless lending that characterized the savings and loan industry in the 1980s.

- *insurance companies.* Insurance companies accumulate large sums of money from the premiums paid by their policyholders. While part of this money is held in reserve to satisfy claims and cover operating expenses, much of it is free to be invested in profit-earning enterprises, such as long-term real estate loans. Although insurance companies are considered primary lenders, they tend to invest their money in large, long-term loans that finance commercial and industrial properties rather than single-family home purchases.

- *credit unions.* Credit unions are cooperative organizations whose members place money in savings accounts. In the past, credit unions made only short-term consumer and home improvement loans. Recently, however, they have branched out to originating longer-term first and second mortgage and deed of trust loans.

- *pension funds.* Pension funds usually have large amounts of money available for investment. Because of the comparatively high yields and low risks offered by mortgages, pension funds have begun to participate actively in financing real estate projects. Most real estate activity for pension funds is handled through mortgage bankers and mortgage brokers.

- *endowment funds.* Many commercial banks and mortgage bankers handle investments for endowment funds. The endowments of hospitals, universities, colleges, charitable foundations, and other institutions provide a good source of financing for low-risk commercial and industrial properties.

- *investment group financing.* Large real estate projects, such as highrise apartment buildings, office complexes, and shopping centers, are often financed as joint ventures through group financing arrangements like syndicates, limited partnerships, and real estate investment trusts. These complex investment agreements are discussed in Chapter 24.

- *mortgage banking companies.* Mortgage banking companies originate mortgage loans with money belonging to insurance companies, pension funds, individuals and with funds of their own. They make real estate loans with the intention of selling them to investors and receiving a fee for servicing the loans. Mortgage banking companies are generally organized as stock companies. As a source of real estate financing, they are subject to fewer lending restrictions than are commercial banks or savings associations. Mortgage banking companies often are involved in all types of real estate loan activities and often serve as intermediaries between investors and borrowers. They are *not* mortgage brokers.

- *mortgage brokers.* Mortgage brokers are not lenders. They are intermediaries who bring borrowers and lenders together. Mortgage brokers locate potential borrowers, process preliminary loan applications, and submit the applications to lenders for final approval. Frequently, they work with or for mortgage banking companies. They do not service loans once they are made. Mortgage brokers also may be real estate brokers who offer these financing services in addition to their regular brokerage activities. Many state governments are establishing separate licensure requirements for mortgage brokers to regulate their activities.

## The Secondary Mortgage Market

In addition to the primary mortgage market, where loans are originated, there is a **secondary mortgage market.** Here, loans are bought and sold only after they have been funded. Lenders routinely sell loans to avoid interest rate risks and to realize profits on the sales. This secondary market activity helps lenders raise capital to continue making mortgage loans. Secondary market activity is especially desirable when money is in short supply; it stimulates both the housing construction market and the mortgage market by expanding the types of loans available.

When a loan is sold, the original lender may continue to collect the payments from the borrower. The lender then passes the payments along to the investor who purchased the loan. The investor is charged a fee for servicing of the loan.

Warehousing agencies purchase a number of mortgage loans and assemble them into packages (called *pools*). Securities that represent shares in these pooled mortgages then are sold to investors. Loans are eligible for sale to the secondary market only when the collateral, borrower, and documentation meet certain requirements, to provide a degree of safety for the investors. The major warehousing agencies are discussed in the following paragraphs.

### Federal National Mortgage Association.

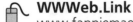 **WWWeb.Link**

www.fanniemae.com. The site for the Federal National Mortgage Association home site: provides information on financing a home which is especially good for first-time buyers. It provides a link to www.homepath.com, a FNMA site that provides a "true cost calculator" for mortgage fees and costs.

The **Federal National Mortgage Association** (*FNMA* or *Fannie Mae*) is a quasi-governmental agency. It is organized as a privately owned corporation that issues its own common stock and provides a secondary market for mortgage loans. FNMA deals in conventional, FHA, and VA loans. FNMA buys a *block* or *pool* of mortgages from a lender in exchange for *mortgage-backed securities,* which the lender may keep or sell. FNMA guarantees payment of all interest and principal to the holder of the securities.

### Government National Mortgage Association.

Unlike FNMA, the **Government National Mortgage Association** (*GNMA,* or *Ginnie Mae*) is entirely a governmental agency. GNMA is a division of the Department of Housing and Urban Development (HUD), organized as a corporation without capital stock. GNMA administers special-assistance programs and works with FNMA in secondary market activities.

In times of tight money and high interest rates, Fannie Mae and Ginnie Mae can join forces through their tandem plan. The tandem plan provides that FNMA can purchase high-risk, low-yield (usually FHA) loans at full market rates, with GNMA guaranteeing payment and absorbing the difference between the low yield and current market prices.

Ginnie Mae also guarantees investment securities issued by private offerors (such as banks, mortgage companies, and savings and loan associations) and backed by pools of FHA and VA mortgage loans. The *Ginnie Mae pass-through certificate* is a security interest in a pool of mortgages that provides for a monthly pass-through of principal and interest payments directly to the certificate holder. Such certificates are guaranteed by Ginnie Mae.

### Federal Home Loan Mortgage Corporation.

The **Federal Home Loan Mortgage Corporation** (*FHLMC*, or *Freddie Mac*) provides a secondary market for mortgage loans, primarily conventional loans. Freddie Mac has the authority to purchase mortgages, pool them, and sell bonds in the open market with the mortgages as security. However, FHLMC does not guarantee payment of Freddie Mac mortgages.

Many lenders use the standardized forms and follow the guidelines issued by Fannie Mae and Freddie Mac. In fact, the use of such forms is mandatory for lenders that wish to sell mortgages in the agencies' secondary mortgage market. The standardized documents include loan applications, credit reports, and appraisal forms.

**In Practice**     Because FNMA's and FHLMC's involvement in the secondary market is so pervasive, many underwriting guidelines are written to comply with their regulations. Bank statements, tax returns, verifications of employment and child support—most of the paperwork a potential borrower must deal with—may be tied to FNMA and FHLMC requirements.

## FINANCING LEGISLATION

The federal government regulates the lending practices of mortgage lenders through the Truth-in-Lending Act, the Equal Credit Opportunity Act, the Community Reinvestment Act of 1977, and the Real Estate Settlement Procedures Act.

**Truth-in-Lending Act and Regulation Z**     **Regulation Z,** which was promulgated pursuant to the **Truth-in-Lending Act,** requires that credit institutions inform borrowers of the true cost of obtaining credit. Its purpose is to permit borrowers to compare the costs of various lenders and avoid the uninformed use of credit. Regulation Z applies when credit is extended to individuals for personal, family, or household uses. The amount of credit sought must be $25,000 or less. Regardless of the amount, however, *Regulation Z always applies when a credit transaction is secured by a residence.* The regulation does not apply to business or commercial loans or to agricultural loans of more than $25,000.

Under Regulation Z, a consumer must be fully informed of all finance charges and the true interest rate before a transaction is completed. The finance charge disclosure must include any loan fees, finder's fees, service charges, and points, as well as interest. In the case of a mortgage loan made to finance the purchase of a dwelling, the lender must compute and disclose the *annual percentage rate (APR).* However, the lender does not have to indicate the total interest payable during the term of the loan. Also, the lender does not have to include actual costs such as title fees, legal fees, appraisal fees, credit reports, survey fees, and closing expenses as part of the finance charge.

**Creditor.** A *creditor,* for purposes of Regulation Z, is any person who extends consumer credit more than 25 times each year or more than 5 times each year if the transactions involve dwellings as security. The credit must be subject to a finance charge or payable in more than four installments by written agreement.

**Three-day right of rescission.** One of the most important consumer protection provisions of Regulation Z is the *three-day right of rescission.* In the case of many consumer credit transactions covered by Regulation Z, the borrower has a three-day period (which begins when the credit documents are signed) in which to rescind the transaction. All the creditor has to do to take advantage of this right of rescission is notify the lender within the time period.

*Note that this right of rescission does not apply to residential purchase-money or first mortgage loans, but it does apply to refinance loans.*

Because of this right to rescission, most refinance lenders will not transfer the loan funds until after the three-day period has passed. In an emergency, the right to rescind may be waived in writing to prevent a delay in funding.

**Advertising.** Regulation Z provides strict regulation of real estate advertisements that include mortgage financing terms. General phrases like "liberal terms available" may be used, but if details are given, they must comply with the act. The annual percentage rate (APR)—which is calculated based on all charges rather than the interest rate alone—must be stated.

Advertisements for buydowns or reduced-interest rate mortgages must show both the limited term to which the interest rate applies and the annual percentage rate. If a variable-rate mortgage is advertised, the advertisement must include

- the number and timing of payments,
- the amount of the largest and smallest payments, and
- a statement of the fact that the actual payments will vary between these two extremes.

Specific credit terms, such as down payment, monthly payment, dollar amount of the finance charge, or term of the loan, may not be advertised unless the advertisement includes the following information:

- Cash price
- Required down payment
- Number, amounts, and due dates of all payments
- Annual percentage rate
- Total of all payments to be made over the term of the mortgage (unless the advertised credit refers to a first mortgage to finance the acquisition of a dwelling)

**Penalties.** Regulation Z provides penalties for noncompliance. The penalty for violation of an administrative order enforcing Regulation Z is $10,000 for each day the violation continues. A fine of up to $10,000 may be imposed for engaging in an unfair or a deceptive practice. In addition, a creditor may be liable to a consumer for twice the amount of the finance charge, for a minimum of $100 and a maximum of $1,000, plus court costs, attorney's fees, and any actual damages. Willful violation is a misdemeanor punishable by a fine of up to $5,000, one year's imprisonment, or both.

**Equal Credit Opportunity Act**

The federal **Equal Credit Opportunity Act** (ECOA) prohibits lenders and others who grant or arrange credit to consumers from discriminating against credit applicants on the basis of

- race,
- color,
- religion,
- national origin,
- sex,
- marital status,
-  age (provided the applicant is of legal age), or
- dependence on public assistance.

*But not on Equal Housing* In addition, lenders and other creditors must inform all rejected credit applicants of the principal reasons for the denial or termination of credit. The notice must be provided in writing, within 30 days. The federal Equal Credit Opportunity Act also provides that a borrower is entitled to a copy of the appraisal report if the borrower paid for the appraisal.

**Community Reinvestment Act of 1977 (CRA)**

*Community reinvestment* refers to the responsibility of financial institutions to help meet their communities' needs for low- and moderate-income housing. In 1977, Congress passed the **Community Reinvestment Act of 1977** (CRA). Under the CRA, financial institutions are expected to meet the deposit and credit needs of their communities; participate and invest in local community development and rehabilitation projects; and participate in loan programs for housing, small businesses, and small farms.

The law requires any federally supervised financial institution to prepare a statement containing

- a definition of the geographical boundaries of its community,
- an identification of the types of community reinvestment credit offered (such as residential housing loans, housing rehabilitation loans, small-business loans, commercial loans, and consumer loans) and
- comments from the public about the institution's performance in meeting its community's needs.

Financial institutions are periodically reviewed by one of four federal financial supervisory agencies: the Comptroller of the Currency; the Federal Reserve's Board of Governors; the Federal Deposit Insurance Corporation; or the Office of Thrift Supervision. The institutions must post a public notice that their community reinvestment activities are subject to federal review, and they must make the results of these reviews public.

**Real Estate Settlement Procedures Act**

The federal **Real Estate Settlement Procedures Act** (RESPA) applies to any residential real estate transaction involving a new first mortgage loan. RESPA is designed to ensure that buyer and seller are both fully informed of all settlement costs. This important federal law is discussed in detail in Chapter 25.

## COMPUTERIZED LOAN ORIGINATION AND AUTOMATED UNDERWRITING

While real estate agents and lenders always had the ability to prequalify buyers—that is, determine how much money buyers could borrow based on their income and debts—giant strides in *computerized loan origination (CLO) systems* now allow quick preapproval as well—that is, the buyer's loan application is actually approved, contingent on the appraisal of the property supporting the loan amount.

A computerized loan origination system is an electronic network for handling loan applications through remote computer terminals linked to several lenders' computers. With a CLO system, a real estate broker or salesperson can call up a menu of mortgage lenders, interest rates, and loan terms, then help a buyer select a lender and apply for a loan right from the brokerage office.

The licensee may assist the applicant in answering the on-screen questions and in understanding the services offered. The broker in whose office the terminal is located may earn fees of up to one half point of the loan amount. The borrower, not the mortgage broker or lender, *must pay the fee*. The fee amount may be financed, however. While multiple lenders may be represented on an office's CLO computer, consumers must be informed that other lenders are available. An applicant's ability to comparison shop for a loan may be enhanced by a CLO system; the range of options may not be limited.

On the lenders' side, new automated underwriting procedures can shorten loan approvals from weeks to minutes. Automated underwriting also tends to lower the cost of loan application and approval by reducing lenders' time spent on the approval process by as much as 60 percent. The Federal Home Loan Mortgage Corporation uses a system called *Loan Prospector*. The Federal National Mortgage Association has a system called *Desktop Underwriter* that reduces approval time to minutes, based on the borrower's credit report (which also may be available instantaneously through computerization), a paycheck stub, and a drive-by appraisal of the property. Complex or difficult mortgages can be processed in less than 72 hours. Through automated underwriting, one of a borrower's biggest headaches in buying a home—waiting for loan approval—is eliminated. In addition, a prospective buyer can strengthen his or her purchase offer by including proof of loan approval.

**KEY TERMS**

adjustable-rate
    mortgage
amortized loan
assumption
balloon payment
blanket loan
buydown
caps
certificate of eligibility
certificate of
    reasonable value
Community
    Reinvestment Act of
    1977
construction loan
conventional loan
discount points
Equal Credit
    Opportunity Act
Farm Service Agency
Federal Deposit
    Insurance
    Corporation
Federal Home Loan
    Mortgage
    Corporation

Federal National
    Mortgage
    Association
Federal Reserve
    System
FHA loan
Financial Institutions
    Reform, Recovery,
    and Enforcement
    Act of 1989
Government National
    Mortgage
    Association
growing-equity
    mortgage
home equity loan
index
loan-to-value ratio
margin
Office of Thrift
    Supervision
open-end loan

package loan
primary mortgage
    market
private mortgage
    insurance
purchase-money
    mortgage
Real Estate Settlement
    Procedures Act
Regulation Z
release of liability
restoration of
    eligibility
reverse-annuity
    mortgage
sale-and-leaseback
secondary mortgage
    market
straight loan
Truth-in-Lending Act
VA loan
wraparound loan

**SUMMARY**

- Types of loans include fully amortized and straight loans as well as adjustable-rate mortgages, growing-equity mortgages, balloon payment mortgages, and reverse-annuity mortgages.
- Many loan programs exist, including:
  - conventional loans,
  - loans insured by the FHA, and
  - loans guaranteed by the VA.
- FHA and VA loans must meet certain requirements for the borrower to obtain the benefits of government backing, which induces the lender to lend its funds. The interest rates for these loans may be lower than those charged for conventional loans.
- Other types of real estate financing include seller-financed purchase-money mortgages or deeds of trust, blanket mortgages, package mortgages, wraparound mortgages, open-end mortgages, construction loans, sale-and-leaseback agreements, and home equity loans.
- The federal government affects real estate financing money and interest rates through the Federal Reserve Board's discount rate and reserve requirements; it also participates in the secondary mortgage market. The secondary market is generally composed of the investors who ultimately purchase and hold the loans as investments. These include insurance companies, investment funds, and pension plans.
- Regulation Z, implementing the federal Truth-in-Lending Act, requires that lenders inform prospective borrowers who use their homes as security for credit of all finance charges involved in such loans.

- The federal Equal Credit Opportunity Act prohibits creditors from discriminating against credit applicants on the basis of race, color, religion, national origin, sex, marital status, age, or dependence on public assistance.
- The Real Estate Settlement Procedures Act requires that lenders inform both buyers and sellers in advance of all fees and charges required for the settlement or closing of residential real estate transactions.

**Real-Life Real Estate**

1. ARMs are more popular as interest rates increase. At what level of interest do you think they make sense? Why?
2. Overall, has FIRREA been good or bad for the real estate business? Why?
3. Where would we be today without the secondary mortgage market?
4. Evaluate the costs versus the benefits of the Truth in lending Act and Regulation Z.

Application #3: Go to a local lender and get a copy of the loan application and the "Good Faith Estimate" required to be completed for all loans.

Complete these documents for the Buyers based on the property description in Chapter 12, Application #2.

# QUESTIONS

1. The buyers purchased a residence for $95,000. They made a down payment of $15,000 and agreed to assume the seller's existing mortgage, which had a current balance of $23,000. The buyers financed the remaining $57,000 of the purchase price by executing a mortgage and note to the seller. This type of loan, by which the seller becomes the mortgagee, is called a
   a. wraparound mortgage.
   b. package mortgage.
   c. balloon note.
   d. purchase-money mortgage.

2. *T* purchased a new residence for $175,000. *T* made a down payment of $15,000 and obtained a $160,000 mortgage loan. The builder of *T*'s house paid the lender 3 percent of the loan balance for the first year and 2 percent for the second year. This represented a total savings for *T* of $8,000. What type of arrangement does this represent?
   a. Wraparound mortgage
   b. Package mortgage
   c. Blanket mortgage
   d. Buydown mortgage

3. Which of the following is not a participant in the secondary market?
   a. FNMA        c. RESPA
   b. GNMA        d. FHLMC

4. *F* purchased her home for cash 30 years ago. Today, *F* receives monthly checks from the bank that supplement her income. *F* most likely has obtained a(n)
   a. shared-appreciation mortgage.
   b. adjustable-rate mortgage.
   c. reverse-annuity mortgage.
   d. overriding deed of trust.

5. If buyers seek a mortgage on a single-family house, they would be likely to obtain the mortgage from any of the following, *EXCEPT* a
   a. mutual savings bank.
   b. life insurance company.
   c. credit union.
   d. commercial bank.

6. A purchaser obtains a fixed-rate loan to finance a home. Which of the following characteristics is true of this type of loan?
   a. The amount of interest to be paid is predetermined.
   b. The loan cannot be sold in the secondary market.
   c. The monthly payment amount will fluctuate each month.
   d. The interest rate change may be based on an index.

7. When the Federal Reserve Board raises its discount rate, all of the following are likely to happen *EXCEPT*
   a. buyer's points will increase.
   b. interest rates will fall.
   c. mortgage money will become scarce.
   d. the percentage of ARMs will increase.

8. In a loan that requires periodic payments that do not fully amortize the loan balance by the final payment, what term best describes the final payment?
   a. Adjustment        c. Balloon
   b. Acceleration      d. Variable

9. A developer received a loan that covers five parcels of real estate and provides for the release of the mortgage lien on each parcel when certain payments are made on the loan. This type of loan arrangement is called a
   a. purchase-money loan.
   b. blanket loan.
   c. package loan.
   d. wraparound loan.

10. Funds for Federal Housing Administration loans are usually provided by
    a. the Federal Housing Administration.
    b. the Federal Reserve.
    c. qualified lenders.
    d. the seller.

11. Under the provisions of the Truth-in-Lending Act (Regulation Z), the annual percentage rate (APR) of a finance charge includes all of the following components *EXCEPT*
    a. discount points.
    b. a broker's commission.
    c. a loan origination fee.
    d. a loan interest rate.

12. A home is purchased using a fixed-rate, fully amortized mortgage loan. Which of the following statements is true regarding this mortgage?
    a. A balloon payment will be made at the end of the loan.
    b. Each payment amount is the same.
    c. Each payment reduces the principal by the same amount.
    d. The principal amount in each payment is greater than the interest amount.

13. Which of the following best defines the secondary market?
    a. Lenders who deal exclusively in second mortgages
    b. Where loans are bought and sold after they have been originated
    c. The major lender of residential mortgages and deeds of trust
    d. The major lender of FHA and VA loans

14. With a fully amortized mortgage loan
    a. interest may be charged in arrears—that is, at the end of each period for which interest is due.
    b. the interest portion of each payment increases throughout the term of the loan.
    c. only interest is paid each period.
    d. a portion of the principal will be owed after the last payment is made.

15. What does Freddie Mac do?
    a. Guarantees mortgages by the full faith and credit of the federal government
    b. Buys and pools blocks of conventional mortgages, selling bonds with such mortgages as security
    c. Acts in tandem with GNMA to provide special assistance in times of tight money
    d. Buys and sells VA and FHA mortgages

16. The federal Equal Credit Opportunity Act prohibits lenders from discriminating against potential borrowers on the basis of all of the following *EXCEPT*
    a. race.
    b. sex.
    c. source of income.
    d. amount of income.

17. A borower obtains a $100,000 mortgage loan for 30 years at 7½ percent interest. If the monthly payments of $902.77 are credited first to interest and then to principal, what will be the balance of the principal after the borrower makes the first payment?
    a. $99,772.00     c. $99,097.32
    b. $99,722.23     d. $100,000.00

18. Using Table 16.1, what is the monthly interest rate factor required to amortize a loan at 8⅛ over a term of 25 years?
    a. 7.72     c. 7.89
    b. 7.81     d. 8.06

19. Using Table 16.1, calculate the principal and interest payment necessary to amortize a loan of $135,000 at 7¾ percent interest over 15 years.
    a. $1,111.85     c. $1,279.80
    b. $1,270.35     d. $1,639.16

20. *H* borrowed $85,000, to be repaid in monthly installments of $823.76 at 11½ percent annual interest. How much of *H*'s first month's payment was applied to reducing the principal amount of the loan?
    a. $8.15          c. $91.80
    b. $9.18          d. $814.58

21. If a lender agrees to make a loan based on an 80 percent LTV, what is the amount of the loan if the property appraises for $114,500 and the sales price is $116,900?
    a. $83,200          c. $91,600
    b. $91,300          d. $92,900

# CHAPTER

# 17

# Leases

## LEASING REAL ESTATE

A lease is a contract between an owner of real estate (the **lessor**) and a tenant (the **lessee**). It is a contract to transfer the lessor's rights to exclusive possession and use of the property to the tenant for a specified period of time. The lease establishes the length of time the contract is to run and the amount the lessee is to pay for use of the property. Other rights and obligations of the parties may be set forth as well.

In effect, the lease agreement combines two contracts. It is a conveyance of an interest in the real estate and a contract to pay rent and assume other obligations. The lessor grants the lessee the right to occupy the real estate and use it for purposes stated in the lease. In return, the landlord receives payment for use of the premises and retains a reversionary right to possession after the lease term expires. The lessor's interest is called a *leased fee estate plus reversionary right.*

The statute of frauds in most states requires lease agreements for more than one year to be in writing to be enforceable. If the lease cannot be performed within one year of being entered into, the statute of frauds also requires a written document. In general, verbal leases for one year or less that can be performed within a year of their making are enforceable. Written leases should be signed by both the lessor and lessee.

---

**In Practice**    Even though a lease that is agreed to orally may be enforceable, such as a lease for one year commencing the day of agreement, it is always better practice to put lease agreements in writing. A written lease provides concrete evidence of the terms and conditions to which the parties have agreed. Any written agreement should be signed by both the landlord and tenant.

---

## LEASEHOLD ESTATES

A tenant's right to possess real estate for the term of the lease is called a **leasehold** (less-than-freehold) **estate.** A leasehold is generally considered

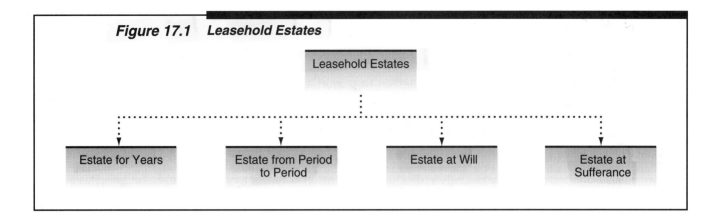

**Figure 17.1   Leasehold Estates**

Leasehold Estates

Estate for Years | Estate from Period to Period | Estate at Will | Estate at Sufferance

personal property. When the tenant assumes many of the landowner's obligations under a lease for life or for more than 99 years, certain states give the tenant some of the benefits and privileges of ownership.

Just as there are several types of freehold (ownership) estates, there are different kinds of leasehold estates. (See Figure 17.1.)

## Estate for Years

An **estate** (tenancy) **for years** is a leasehold estate that continues for a *definite period of time.* That period may be years, months, weeks or even days. An estate for years (sometimes referred to as an *estate for term*) always has specific starting and ending dates. When the estate expires, the lessee is required to vacate the premises and surrender possession to the lessor. *No notice is required to terminate the estate for years.* This is because the lease agreement states a specific expiration date. When the date comes, the lease expires, and the tenant's rights are extinguished.

> **Tenancy for years** = *Any definite period*

If both parties agree, the lease for years may be terminated before the expiration date. Otherwise, neither party may terminate without showing that the lease agreement has been breached. Any extension of the tenancy requires that a new contract be negotiated.

As is characteristic of all leases, a tenancy for years gives the lessee the right to occupy and use the leased property according to the terms and covenants contained in the lease agreement. It must be remembered that a lessee has the right to use the premises for the entire lease term. That right is unaffected by the original lessor's death or sale of the property unless the lease states otherwise. If the original lease provides for an option to renew, no further negotiation is required; the tenant merely exercises his or her option.

## Estate from Period to Period

An **estate from period to period,** or *periodic tenancy,* is created when the landlord and tenant enter into an agreement *for an indefinite time.* That is, the lease does not contain a specific expiration date. Such a tenancy is created initially to run for a definite amount of time—for instance, month to month, week to week, or year to year—but continues indefinitely until proper notice of termination is given. Rent is payable at definite intervals. A periodic tenancy is characterized by *continuity* because it is automatically renewable under the original terms of the agreement until one of the parties gives notice to terminate. In effect, the payment and acceptance of rent extend the lease for another period. A **month-to-month tenancy,** for example, is created when a tenant takes possession with no definite termination date and pays monthly rent. Periodic tenancy is commonly used in residential leases.

> **Periodic Tenancy** = *Indefinite term; automatically renewing*

If the original agreement provides for the conversion from an estate for years to a periodic tenancy, no negotiations are necessary; the tenant simply exercises his or her option.

An estate from period to period also might be created when a tenant with an estate for years remains in possession, or holds over, after the lease term expires. If no new lease agreement has been made, a **holdover tenancy** is created. The landlord may evict the tenant or treat the holdover tenant as one who holds a periodic tenancy. The landlord's acceptance of rent usually is considered conclusive proof of acceptance of the periodic tenancy. The courts customarily rule that a tenant who holds over can do so for a term equal to the term of the original lease, provided the period is for one year or less. For example, a tenant with a lease for six months would be entitled to a new six-month tenancy. However, the holdover tenancy cannot exceed one year, even if the original lease had been for five years. Some leases stipulate that in the absence of a renewal agreement, a tenant who holds over does so as a month-to-month tenant. In Ohio, a holdover tenancy is considered a tenancy at will. ◆

> **Tenancy at will** = *Indefinite term; possession with landlord's consent*

**In Ohio...**

*To terminate* a periodic estate, either the landlord or the tenant must give *proper notice.* The form and timing of the notice are usually established by state statute. Normally, the notice must be given *one period in advance.* That is, to terminate an estate from week to week, one week's notice is required; to terminate an estate from month to month, one month's notice is required. For an estate from year to year, however, the requirements vary from two to six months' notice.

### Estate at Will

An **estate** (tenancy) **at will** gives the tenant the right to possess property with the landlord's consent for an unspecified or uncertain term. An estate at will is a tenancy of indefinite duration. It continues until it is terminated by either party giving proper notice. No definite initial period is specified, as is the case in a periodic tenancy. An estate at will is automatically terminated by the death of either the landlord or the tenant. It may be created by express agreement or by operation of law. During the existence of a tenancy at will, the tenant has all the rights and obligations of a lessor-lessee relationship, including the duty to pay rent at regular intervals.

> **Tenancy at sufferance** = *Tenant's previously lawful possession continued without landlord's consent*

As a practical matter, tenancy at will is rarely used in a written agreement and is viewed skeptically by the courts. It is usually interpreted as a periodic tenancy, with the period being defined by the interval of rental payments.

### Estate at Sufferance

An **estate** (tenancy) **at sufferance** arises when a tenant who lawfully possessed real property continues in possession of the premises *without the landlord's consent* after the rights expire. This estate can arise when a tenant for years fails to surrender possession at the lease's expiration. A tenancy at sufferance can also occur by operation of law when a borrower continues in possession after a foreclosure sale and beyond the redemption period's expiration.

## TYPES OF LEASES

The manner in which rent is determined indicates the type of lease that exists. (See Figure 17.2.)

---

**Figure 17.2   Types of Leases**

| Type of Lease | Lessee | Lessor |
|---|---|---|
| Gross lease | Pays basic rent | Pays property charges (taxes, repairs, insurance, etc.) |
| Net lease | Pays basic rent plus all or most property charges | May pay some property charges |
| Percentage lease (commercial industrial) | Pays basic rent plus percent of gross sales (may pay property costs) | |

---

**Gross Lease**   In a **gross lease,** the tenant pays a fixed rental, and the landlord pays all taxes, insurance, repairs, utilities, and the like connected with the property (usually called *property charges or operating expenses*). This is typically the type of rent structure involved in residential leasing.

**Net Lease**   In a **net lease,** the tenant pays all or *some of the property* charges in addition to the rent. The monthly rental is net income for the landlord after operating costs have been paid. Leases for entire commercial or industrial buildings and the land on which they are located, ground leases, and long-term leases are usually net leases.

In a *triple-net lease,* or *net-net-net lease,* the tenant pays all operating and other expenses in addition to a periodic rent. These expenses include taxes, insurance, assessments, maintenance, utilities, and other charges related to the premises.

**Percentage Lease**   Either a gross lease or a net lease may be a **percentage lease.** The rent is based on a minimum fixed rental fee *plus a percentage of the gross income* received by the tenant doing business on the leased property. This type of lease is usually used for retail businesses. The percentage charged is negotiable and varies depending on the nature of the business, the location of the property, and general economic conditions.

**Other Types of Leases**   **Variable lease.** Several types of leases allow for increases in the rental charges during the lease periods. One of the more common is the *graduated lease.* A graduated lease provides for specified rent increases at set future dates. Another is the *index lease,* which allows rent to be increased or decreased periodically based on changes in the consumer price index or some other indicator.

**Ground lease.** When a landowner leases unimproved land to a tenant who agrees to erect a building on the land, the lease is usually referred to as a **ground lease.** Ground leases usually involve separate ownership of the land and buildings. These leases must be for a long enough term to make the transaction desirable to the tenant investing in the building. They often run for terms of 50 up to 99 years. Ground leases are generally *net leases:* the lessee must pay rent on the ground, as well as real estate taxes, insurance, upkeep, and repairs.

**MATH CONCEPTS**

### Calculating Percentage Lease Rents

Percentage leases usually call for a minimum monthly rent plus a percentage of gross sales income exceeding a stated annual amount. For example, a lease might require minimum rent of $1,300 per month plus 5 percent of the business's sales exceeding $160,000. On an annual sales volume of $250,000, the annual rent would be calculated as follows:

$1,300 per month × 12 months = $15,600
$250,000 − $160,000 = $90,000
$90,000 × .05 (5%) = $4,500
$15,600 base rent + $4,500 percentage rent = $20,100 total rent

**Oil and gas lease.** When an oil company leases land to explore for oil and gas, a special lease agreement must be negotiated. Usually, the landowner receives a cash payment for executing the lease. If no well is drilled within the period stated in the lease, the lease expires. However, most oil and gas leases permit the oil company to continue its rights for another year by paying another flat rental fee. Such rentals may be paid annually until a well is produced. If oil or gas is found, the landowner usually receives a percentage of its value as a royalty. As long as oil or gas is obtained in significant quantities, the lease continues indefinitely.

**Lease purchase.** A **lease purchase** is used when a tenant wants to purchase the property but is unable to do so. Perhaps the tenant cannot obtain favorable financing or clear title; perhaps the tax consequences of a current purchase would be unfavorable. In this arrangement, the purchase agreement is the primary consideration, and the lease is secondary. Part of the periodic rent is applied toward the purchase price of the property until it is reduced to an amount for which the tenant can obtain financing or purchase the property outright, depending on the terms of the lease purchase agreement.

**Agricultural lease.** Agricultural landowners often lease their land to tenant farmers, who provide the labor to produce and bring in the crop. An owner can be paid by a tenant in one of two ways: as an agreed-on rental amount in cash in advance (**cash rents**) or as a percentage of the profits from the sale of the crop when it is sold (**sharecropping**).

## LEASE AGREEMENTS

Most states require no special wording to establish the landlord-tenant relationship. The lease may be written, oral, or implied, depending on the circumstances and the requirements of the statute of frauds. The law of the state where the real estate is located must be followed to ensure the validity of the lease. Figure 17.3 is an example of a typical residential lease.

### Requirements of a Valid Lease

A lease is a form of contract. To be valid, a lease must meet essentially the same requirements as any other contract:

- *Offer and acceptance.* The parties must reach a mutual agreement on all the terms of the contract.
- *Consideration.* The lease must be supported by valid consideration. Rent is the normal consideration given for the right to occupy the leased premises. However, the payment of rent is not essential as long as consideration was granted in creating the lease itself. Sometimes, for

**Figure 17.3    Sample Residential Lease**

## RESIDENTIAL LEASE

| DATE OF LEASE | LEASE TERM | | RENT PER MONTH | SECURITY DEPOSIT |
|---|---|---|---|---|
| | BEGINNING DATE | ENDING DATE | | |
| | | | | |

THIS RESIDENTIAL LEASE AGREEMENT ("Lease") is made between the following parties:

NAME:_____     NAME:_____

ADDRESS OF                                                    BUSINESS
PREMISES:                                                       ADDRESS:
          "LESSEE"                                                         "LESSOR"

### SECTION ONE.  RENT

1. Lessee will pay Lessor (or Lessor's authorized agent) the amount of _____ Dollars ($_____) per month, in advance, as monthly rental for the Premises for the term of this Lease. Total rental for the initial term of this Lease shall be _____ Dollars. Lessee's first monthly rental payment is due on or before _____, 19__, and each subsequent payment will be due on the _____ day of each month following for the term of this Lease. Payments will be made at the Lessor's address as stated in this Lease, or at any other address Lessor may specify in writing to Lessee.

2. Installments of rent that are not received by Lessor as required by this Lease are considered late. Late payment of rent constitutes default under the terms of this lease. If full payment is not received by the Lessor within _____ days of the date of default, Lessee agrees to pay to Lessor an administrative fee of _____ Dollars ($_____). Lessee will pay Lessor a charge of _____ Dollars ($_____) for any check returned to Lessor for insufficient funds. Lessor may require that any rent payment be made in the form of a certified check, money order or cashier's check.

3. Failure by Lessee to make any payment of rent, or any other fee or charge, under this Lease constitutes a default. In the event that Lessee fails to make any payment within _____ days after receiving written notice of Lessor's intention to terminate this Lease, Lessor may terminate this Lease and any and all unpaid rent for the full remaining term of this Lease shall then become due and payable. In the event of termination, Lessor shall be entitled to:
    A.  Immediate possession of the Premises.
    B.  Immediate payment of any unpaid rent or other charges.
    C.  Recovery of any damages incurred due to Lessee's default, including but not limited
        to the cost of reletting the Premises, lost rental under this Lease and the cost of collections.
    D.  Court costs and reasonable attorney's fees as permitted by law, arising due to Lessee's default.
    E.  Any other remedy as provided by the law of the State of _____.

4. Lessor's rights and duties under the terms of this Lease are cumulative, and the exercise of any one or more of them does not prohibit Lessor from the exercise or use of any other right or remedy provided by this Lease or by law.

### SECTION TWO.  SECURITY DEPOSIT

1. Lessee has paid Lessor a Security Deposit in the amount of _____ Dollars ($_____) as set forth above, to secure his or her performance of all the covenants, agreements and terms of this Lease. The Security Deposit is subject to the following conditions:

    A.  Lessor may use, apply or retain any or all of the amount of the Security Deposit for the payment of any rent due from Lessee; for any administrative, maintenance or other charges set forth in this Lease; any damages or expenses incurred by Lessor arising from Lessee's failure to comply with any of the terms of this Lease (including but not limited to expenses incurred in reletting the Premises).

    B.  If, during the term (or any extension of the term ) of this Lease, Lessor is obligated to use all or any part of the Security Deposit in accordance with the terms and conditions of this Lease or any other law or agreement, Lessor shall notify Lessor of the expenditure, in writing, within _____ days of its being incurred, and provide along with such notice an itemized list of the charges and expenses, including the reasonable cost of Lessor's own time and labor. Lessee shall have _____ days in which to deposit with Lessor a sum equal to the amount used, to ensure that the full amount of the Security Deposit is maintained with the Lessor at all times during the term of this Lease.

    C.  The use of all or any part of the Security Deposit by Lessor shall not be Lessor's sole remedy in the event of Lessee's default. If the costs of Lessor's expenses and/or damages incurred exceed the total amount of the Security Deposit, Lessee shall pay any excess. LESSEE MAY NOT APPLY THE SECURITY DEPOSIT AS RENT.

    E.  During the term of this Lease, and during any extensions of this Lease agreement, the Security Deposit shall be held in a/an:☐ interest-bearing ☐ non-interest-bearing [check one] account. Parties initial here: _____ _____

    F.  When Lessee has performed all obligations required under this Lease, has paid all rent and any other charges, and has surrendered the Premises, its keys, passes and any other documents or fixtures in the same condition as they were provided at the beginning of the term of this Lease, reasonable wear and tear excepted, Lessor shall return to Lessee any remaining amount of the Security Deposit, together with a fully itemized list of all charges deducted from it, with documentation, within _____ days of the termination of this Lease and the surrender of the Premises.

    G.  In the event Lessor's interest in the Premises are sold, transferred or assigned, Lessor shall notify Lessee of the change in ownership and the name and business address of the new lessor. Lessor shall transfer the Security Deposit to the new lessor or owner and be released from all liability to Lessee.

**Figure 17.3    Sample Residential Lease (Continued)**

### SECTION THREE. TERM OF LEASE AND EXTENSIONS

The term of this Lease shall be _____ year(s). This Lease will be automatically extended on a month to month basis, on the same terms and conditions as agreed to in this Lease, unless either party gives the other _____ days written notice of his or her intent not to extend the Lease at the end of the term. In the event that this Lease is extended, _____ days prior notice shall be required to terminate it. Such notice must be received by the non-terminating party no later than the _____ day of the month, and Lessee's tenancy shall terminate on the last day of that month.

### SECTION FOUR. CONDITION OF PREMISES

Lessee has examined the condition of the Premises, and acknowledges that the Premises are received in good condition and repair except as otherwise specified in this Lease. Lessee is responsible for all day-to-day maintenance of the Premises as defined in the Rules and Regulations, including maintaining all devices and appliances in working order.

### SECTION FIVE. USE OF PREMISES

1. The Premises are leased to Lessee exclusively, and shall be used strictly as a residence and for no other purpose. The Premises shall be occupied only by Lessee and any children born to, adopted by or placed under Lessee's legal care and/or guardianship. A violation of any condition of this lease by any guest of Lessee shall be construed as a violation by Lessee.

2. The Premises may not be assigned or sublet by Lessee without the prior written consent of Lessor. Lessee shall not undertake any modification or structural change to the Premises without the written consent of Lessor.

3. Lessee shall not use or allow the Premises to be used for any unlawful or disorderly purpose. The Premises may not be used in any way that represents a material detriment to the health or safety of others. Lessee shall comply with all applicable laws and any Rules and Regulations established by Lessor. Lessee shall be provided with a printed copy of the applicable Rules and Regulations at the time this Lease is signed. Lessor has the right to immediately terminate this lease based on any such violation.

### SECTION SIX. ACCESS

Lessee shall permit Lessor, or Lessor's duly authorized agent or representatives, unrestricted access to the Premises at all reasonable times for any necessary purpose, including but not limited to inspection, maintenance and exhibition.

### SECTION SEVEN. PETS

No pets of any kind may be kept in or around the Premises for any purpose. This provision does not apply to companion animals trained and certified to assist a person with a disability.

### SECTION EIGHT. UTILITIES AND MAINTENANCE

1. Lessor will ensure that hot and cold running water are supplied to the Premises for Lessee's use at all times. Lessor will provide reasonable heating of the Premises at all times between the months of _____ and _____, as required by law. Lessor shall provide reasonable air conditioning to the Premises between the months of _____ and _____, or as provided by law. Lessor shall not be responsible to Lessee for any failure to provide water, heat or air conditioning due to causes beyond Lessor's control or for periods when any necessary systems are under repair.

2. Lessor covenants to maintain the Premises and all grounds and public areas appurtenant to the Premises, in good repair and tenantable condition. Lessor certifies that the Premises contains all smoke detectors and other devices required by law, and that all such detectors or other devices are in good working order. Lessee is responsible for maintaining such systems.

4. Should the Premises be damaged by fire or other casualty, Lessor may either (A) repair the damage within a reasonable time, not to exceed _____ days from the date Lessor is notified in writing of such damage, or (B) terminate this Lease by providing Lessee with written notice. Should such fire or other casualty impair Lessee's occupancy, Lessee may vacate the premises and provide Lessor with written notice, within _____ days of so vacating, of the intent to terminate this Lease. Such termination will be without penalty to Lessee. If such damage is caused by Lessee's own fault or negligence, or that of Lessee's agents, guests, visitors, servants or licensees, Lessee shall continue to be liable for all rent and charges during the remaining unexpired term of this Lease unless specifically released by Lessor.

### SECTION NINE. SUBORDINATION, SEVERABILITY AND LAW

1. This Lease is subordinate to all mortgages, deeds of trust or other instruments now or later affecting the Premises.

2. If any provision of this Lease is or should become prohibited under any law, that provision shall be made ineffective, without invalidating any remaining provisions. The governing law of the jurisdiction in which the Premises are located is incorporated into and supersedes this Lease by reference, and the parties agree to be bound by such law.

### SECTION TEN. MISCELLANEOUS

The words "Lessor" and "Lessee," as used in this Lease, are construed as including more than one lessor. All terms and conditions of this Lease are binding on and may be enforced by the parties, their heirs, assigns, executors, administrators and successors. This Lease represents the entire agreement between Lessor and Lessee. Neither party is bound by any representations made by any party that are not included in this Lease, except that the Rules and Regulations of the Premises and Lessee's Application are included by reference.

**ADDITIONAL COVENANTS, TERMS, CONDITIONS AND AGREEMENTS:** [*if none, write "NONE"*]

LESSEE:_____(SEAL)          LESSOR:_____(SEAL)

Date: _____                                                    Date: _____

The elements of a **valid lease** can be remembered by the acronym *CLOAC: Capacity, Legal objective, Offer and Acceptance,* and **Consideration**.

instance, this consideration is labor performed on the property. Because a lease is a contract, it is not subject to subsequent changes in the rent or other terms unless these changes are in writing and executed in the same manner as the original lease.

- *Capacity to contract.* The parties must have the legal capacity to contract.
- *Legal objectives.* The objectives of the lease must be legal.

The leased premises should be clearly described. The legal description of the real estate should be used if the lease covers land, such as a ground lease. If the lease is for a part of a building, such as an apartment, the space itself or the apartment designation should be described specifically. If supplemental space is to be included, the lease should clearly identify it.

## In Practice

Preprinted lease agreements are usually better suited to residential leases. Commercial leases are generally more complex, have different legal requirements, and may include complicated calculations of rent and maintenance costs. Drafting a commercial lease—or a complex residential lease, for that matter—may constitute the practice of law. Unless the real estate licensee is also a licensed attorney, legal counsel should be sought.

## Possession of Premises

The lessor, as the owner of the real estate, is usually bound by the implied covenant of quiet enjoyment. Quiet enjoyment does not have anything to do with barking dogs or late-night motorcycles. The covenant of quiet enjoyment is a presumed promise by the lessor that the lessee may take possession of the premises. The landlord further guarantees that he or she will not interfere in the tenant's possession or use of the property.

The lease may allow the landlord to enter the property to perform maintenance, to make repairs, or for other stated purposes. The tenant's permission is usually required.

If the premises are occupied by a holdover tenant or an adverse claimant at the beginning of the new lease period, most states require that the landlord take whatever measures are necessary to recover actual possession. In a few states, however, the landlord is bound only to give the tenant the right of possession; it is the tenant who must bring a court action to secure actual possession.

## Use of Premises

A lessor may restrict a lessee's use of the premises through provisions included in the lease.

Use restrictions are particularly common in leases for stores or commercial space. For example, a lease may provide that the leased premises are to be used "only as a real estate office *and for no other purpose.*" In the absence of such clear limitations, a lessee may use the premises for any *lawful* purpose.

## Term of Lease

The term of a lease is the period for which the lease will run. It should be stated precisely, including the beginning and ending dates, together with a statement of the total period of the lease. For instance, a lease might run "for a term of 30 years beginning June 1, 1996, and ending May 31, 2026." A perpetual lease for an inordinate amount of time or an indefinite term usually will be ruled invalid. However, if the language of the lease and the surrounding circumstances clearly indicate that the parties intended such a term, the lease will be binding on the parties. Some states prohibit leases that run for 100 years or more.

**Security Deposit**

Most leases require that the tenant provide some form of **security deposit** to be held by the landlord during the lease term. If the tenant defaults on payment of rent or destroys the premises, the lessor may keep all or part of the deposit to compensate for the loss. Some state laws set maximum amounts for security deposits and specify how they must be handled. Some prohibit security deposits from being used for both nonpayment of rent and property damage. Some require that lessees receive annual interest on their security deposits.

Other safeguards against nonpayment of rent may include an advance rental payment, contracting for a lien on the tenant's property, or requiring the tenant to have a third person guarantee payment.

**In Practice**    A lease should specify whether a payment is a security deposit or an advance rental. If it is a security deposit, the tenant usually is not entitled to apply it to the final month's rent. If it is an advance rental, the landlord must treat it as income for tax purposes.

**Improvements**

Neither the landlord nor the tenant is required to make any improvements to the leased property. The tenant may, however, make improvements with the landlord's permission. Any alterations generally become the landlord's property; that is, they become fixtures. However, the lease may give the tenant the right to install trade fixtures. Trade fixtures may be removed before the lease expires, provided the tenant restores the premises to their previous condition, with allowance for the wear and tear of normal use.

**Accessibility.** The federal Fair Housing Act (discussed in Chapter 22) makes it illegal to discriminate against prospective tenants on the basis of physical disability. Tenants with disabilities must be permitted to make reasonable modifications to a property at their own expense. However, if the modifications would interfere with a future tenant's use, the landlord may require that the premises be restored to their original condition at the end of the lease term.

**In Practice**    The *Americans with Disabilities Act (ADA),* discussed in more detail in Chapter 18, applies to commercial, nonresidential property in which public goods or services are provided. The ADA requires that such properties either be free of architectural barriers or provide reasonable accommodations for people with disabilities.

**Maintenance of Premises**

In Ohio...

Ohio law requires that a residential lessor maintain dwelling units in a habitable condition. Landlords must make any necessary repairs to common areas such as hallways, stairs, and elevators and maintain safety features such as fire sprinklers and smoke alarms. The tenant does not have to make any repairs, but must return the premises in the same condition they were received, with allowances for ordinary wear and tear. ◆

**Destruction of Premises**     In leases involving *agricultural land,* the courts have held that when improvements are damaged or destroyed, the tenant is obligated to pay rent to the end of the term. The tenant's liability does not depend on whether the damage was his or her fault. This ruling has been extended in most states to include *ground leases* for land on which the tenant has constructed a building. In many instances, it also includes leases that give possession of an entire building to the tenant. In this case, the tenant leases the land on which that building is located, as well as the structure itself. Insurance is available to cover such contingencies.

A tenant who leases only part of a building, such as office or commercial space or a residential apartment, however, is not required to continue to pay rent after the leased premises are destroyed.

**In Ohio...**     In Ohio, if the property was destroyed as a result of the landlord's negligence, the tenant can recover damages. ◆

**Assignment and Subleasing**     When a tenant transfers all his or her leasehold interests to another person, the lease has been assigned. On the other hand, when a tenant transfers less than all the leasehold interests by leasing them to a new tenant, he or she has **subleased** (or *sublet*) the property. **Assignment** and subleasing are permitted whenever a lease does not prohibit them.

In most cases, the sublease or assignment of a lease does not relieve the original lessee of the obligation to pay rent. The landlord may, however, agree to waive the former tenant's liability. Most leases prohibit a lessee from assigning or subletting without the lessor's consent. This permits the lessor to retain control over the occupancy of the leased premises. As a rule, the lessor must not unreasonably withhold consent. The sublessor's (original lessee's) interest in the real estate is known as a *sandwich lease.*

**Recording a Lease**     Possession of leased premises is considered constructive notice to the world of the lessee's leasehold interests. Anyone who inspects the property receives actual notice. For these reasons, it is usually considered unnecessary to record a lease. However, most states do allow a lease to be recorded in the county in which the property is located. Furthermore, leases of three years or longer often are recorded as a matter of course.

**In Ohio...**     Some states, including Ohio, *require* that long-term leases be recorded, especially when the lessees intend to mortgage the leasehold interests. Generally, commercial leases for more than one year are also recorded. ◆

In some states, only a memorandum of lease is filed. A memorandum of lease gives notice of the interest but does not disclose the terms of the lease. Only the names of the parties and a description of the property are included.

**Options**     A lease may contain an option that grants the lessee the privilege of renewing the lease. The lessee must, however, give notice of his or her intention to exercise the option. Some leases grant the lessees the option to purchase the leased premises. This option normally allows the tenant the right to purchase the property at a predetermined price within a certain time period, possibly the lease term. Although it is not required, the owner may give the tenant credit toward the purchase price for some percentage of the rent paid. The lease agreement is a primary contract over the option to purchase.

| In Practice | All of these general statements concerning provisions of a lease are controlled largely by the terms of the agreement and state law. Great care must be exercised in reading the entire lease document before signing it because every clause in the lease has an economic and a legal impact on either the landlord or the tenant. While preprinted lease forms are available, there is no such thing as a standard lease. When complicated lease situations arise, legal counsel should be sought. |
|---|---|

## DISCHARGE OF LEASES

As with any contract, a lease is discharged when the contract terminates. Termination can occur when all parties have fully performed their obligations under the agreement. In addition, the parties may agree to cancel the lease. If the tenant, for instance, offers to surrender the leasehold interest, and if the landlord accepts the tenant's offer, the lease is terminated. A tenant who simply abandons leased property, however, remains liable for the terms of the lease—including the rent. The terms of the lease will usually indicate whether the landlord is obligated to try to rerent the space. If the landlord intends to sue for unpaid rent, however, most states require an attempt to mitigate damages by rerenting the premises to limit the amount owed.

The lease *does not terminate* if the parties to a lease die or the property is sold. There are two exceptions: a lease from the owner of a life estate ends on the death of that person, and the death of either party terminates a tenancy at will. Otherwise the heirs of a deceased landlord are bound by the terms of existing valid leases. *In addition, if a landlord conveys leased real estate, the new landlord takes the property subject to the rights of the tenants.* A lease agreement may, however, require that a new landlord, after taking title, give some period of notice to the tenant to terminate an existing lease. This is commonly known as a *sale clause.* Because the new owner has taken title subject to the rights of the tenant, the sale clause enables the new landlord to claim possession and/or negotiate new leases under his or her own terms and conditions.

A tenancy may be terminated by operation of law, as in a bankruptcy or condemnation proceeding.

**In Ohio...** In Ohio, a tenancy from year to year terminates at the end of the year without notice, unless the parties extend it. If there is a holdover and there is no protest on the part of the landlord, the period continues, and neither party can terminate the tenancy before the end of the period without the consent of the other.

Ohio law provides that a week-to-week tenancy requires seven days' notice for either party to terminate or fail to renew. Similarly, a month-to-month tenancy requires at least 30 days' notice. ◆

A lease also may be terminated if the building occupied by the lessee is destroyed or damaged to the extent that it is unfit for occupancy, as long as the damage occurred through no fault of or neglect by the tenant.

**Breach of Lease**  When a tenant breaches any lease provision, the landlord may sue the tenant to obtain a judgment to cover past-due rent, damages to the premises, or other defaults. Likewise, when a landlord breaches any lease provision, the tenant is entitled to certain remedies.

*Test*  **In Ohio...**  The rights and responsibilities of the landlord-tenant relationship are governed by the Ohio Landlord-Tenant Act. ◆

# OHIO LANDLORD-TENANT ACT

**In Ohio...**  In Ohio, the rights of landlords and tenants are defined by statute (Ohio Revised Code section 5321). Here, we will examine some of the provisions of that law.

**Landlord Obligations**  A residential landlord has certain minimum obligations under the law. A landlord must

- comply with all building codes affecting health and safety;
- make all repairs to keep the building in habitable condition;
- keep the common areas in a safe and sanitary condition;
- maintain building facilities (such as heating and cooling systems, plumbing, appliances, and sanitary systems) in good and safe condition;
- provide trash containers and pickup service in buildings of four or more apartments;
- supply or provide a source of heat, hot water, and running water, regardless of who pays for the utilities under the lease;
- not abuse his or her right of access to the premises and not harass the tenant by repeated and unreasonable demands for entry;
- give the tenant 24 hours' notice of intent to enter the premises; and
- promptly commence an eviction action against a tenant whom the landlord knows or reasonably believes to be violating Ohio's laws against the manufacture, possession, use, or trafficking of controlled substances (tenants are entitled to three days' notice and the opportunity to vacate the premises prior to the commencement of an eviction action).

**Tenant Obligations**  A residential tenant also has obligations toward his or her landlord. The tenant must

- keep the premises in a safe and sanitary condition;
- dispose of all garbage and rubbish in a sanitary manner;
- keep plumbing fixtures as clean as their condition permits;
- use all electrical and plumbing fixtures properly;
- comply with all applicable state and local housing, health, and safety codes;
- not destroy or damage the premises or allow guests to do so;
- maintain appliances in working order when required by the written lease; and
- not disturb the neighbors' peaceful enjoyment.
- If a tenant violates these obligations, the landlord may evict the tenant and recover actual damages and attorney fees. ◆

**Retaliatory Actions Prohibited**  If a tenant complains to the authorities about a building, housing, health or safety code violation that materially affects health and safety, or about the landlord's violation of the landlord-tenant law, or if the tenant joins a tenants' union, the landlord may not retaliate by increasing the rent, decreasing

**In Ohio...**     services, or threatening eviction. If the landlord does retaliate, the tenant may recover possession, terminate the lease, or seek actual damages and attorney fees, as well as damages for emotional injury. In a legal action, the tenant must prove that the landlord's action was retaliatory. ◆

The landlord is entitled to possession of the premises, however, if the tenant is in default of the payment of rent or if the tenant's own actions caused the code violation. Similarly, if the tenant is in default of payment of rent, the landlord may take what might otherwise be considered "retaliatory" measures. If compliance with a housing code would require major alterations and deprive the tenant of the use of the premises, or if the tenant is holding over his or her term, the landlord's actions may not be considered retaliatory. The landlord may raise the rent to cover improvements made or increases in operating costs.

The rules against retaliatory conduct do not apply to rental agreements between a college or university acting as landlord and a student tenant in student housing. If the student violates a term of the rental agreement or the institution's policies, procedures, or rules of conduct, the rental agreement may be terminated and the student required to vacate the premises. The student is entitled to written notice of the alleged violation and to a formal hearing on the issue prior to eviction.

**Rent Withholding**

**In Ohio...**     If a landlord violates any obligation imposed by Ohio law or any provision of the lease, or if a government agency finds a violation, or if the tenant reasonably believes the landlord has committed a legal or lease violation, the tenant is entitled to withhold rent. First, however, the tenant must give the landlord written notice of the violation. The landlord then has 30 days to remedy the condition. (By law, the landlord must immediately remedy a condition that keeps the premises from being habitable.) Only then, and only if the condition is not remedied and the tenant is current in rent payments, may the tenant withhold rent from the landlord. ◆

"Withholding rent," however, does not mean that the tenant may live on the premises rent-free. Rather, he or she may

- deposit all rent that is due and subsequently becomes due with the clerk of the local court as they become due, or
- apply for a court order to reduce the rent until the condition is remedied, or
- apply for a court order to use the rental payments to remedy the condition, or
- terminate the lease.

**In Practice**     Rent withholding does not apply to a landlord who rents out three or fewer dwelling units and who has provided tenants with written notice that withholding rent is not an option.

A student tenant occupying premises leased by a college or university is not entitled to withhold rent.

A landlord who fails to provide his or her name and address to the tenant, in writing, waives the right to receive written notice prior to the tenant's withholding of rent.

The landlord may apply to the court for release of the withheld rent after repairing the conditions and obtaining the tenant's written approval. Alternatively, the landlord may seek release of the rent on the grounds that the tenant failed to give the required written notice, was not current in rent payments, or that there was no violation of the lease, law, or code.

---

**Illegal Lease Terms**

No obligations imposed by the landlord-tenant law may be modified or waived in the lease, although the landlord may assume any tenant's obligations. In addition, the following terms or conditions are barred by law:

- Any confession of judgment for rent or damages
- Any agreement to pay attorney fees for landlord or tenant
- Any limitation of the landlord's liability or any agreement to indemnify the landlord
- Any modification of the landlord's obligations imposed by law

In addition, a landlord may not terminate services or take any action to regain possession, except as provided by law. No landlord may seize a tenant's furnishings or possessions, except under a court order.

The court may refuse to enforce unconscionable clauses or agreements in any rental agreement.

**Security Deposits**

Any security deposit in excess of the greater of $50 or one month's rent must bear interest on the excess at five percent if the tenant remains in possession for six months or more. Interest is payable annually to the tenant.

**In Ohio...**

When a rental agreement terminates, the landlord must, within 30 days of delivery of possession, return the deposit or amount due, after deductions, to the tenant. The tenant is entitled to an itemized list of deductions for past-due rent and damages suffered under the terms of the lease. The tenant must provide the landlord with his or her new address.

If the landlord fails to return the deposit and itemization of deductions and the tenant has provided the landlord, with his or her new address, the tenant may recover

- the amount due and any property held,
- damages equal to the amount wrongfully withheld by the landlord, and
- reasonable attorney's fees. ◆

# CIVIL RIGHTS LAWS

The fair housing laws affect landlords and tenants just as they do sellers and purchasers. All persons must have access to housing of their choice without any differentiation in the terms and conditions because of their race, color, religion, national origin, sex, handicap, or familial status. State and local municipalities may have their own fair housing laws that add protected classes such as age and sexual orientation. Withholding an apartment that is available for rent, segregating certain persons in separate sections of an apartment complex or parts of a building, and charging different amounts for rent or security deposits to persons in the protected classes all constitute violations of the law. The fair housing laws, including the Ohio Fair Housing Law, are discussed in greater detail in Chapter 22.

It is important that landlords realize that changes in the laws stemming from the federal Fair Housing Amendments Act of 1988 significantly alter past practices, particularly as they affect individuals with disabilities (discussed previously) and families with children. The fair housing laws require that the same tenant criteria be applied to families with children that are applied to adults. A landlord cannot charge a different amount of rent or security deposit because one of the tenants is a child. While landlords have historically argued that children are noisy and destructive, the fact is that many adults are noisy and destructive as well.

## KEY TERMS

| | | |
|---|---|---|
| assignment | ground lease | month-to-month |
| cash rent | holdover tenancy | tenancy |
| estate at sufferance | lease | net lease |
| estate at will | leasehold estate | percentage lease |
| estate for years | lease purchase | reversionary right |
| estate from period to | lessee | security deposit |
| period | lessor | sharecropping |
| gross lease | | sublease |

## SUMMARY

- A lease is an agreement that grants one person the right to use the property of another in return for consideration.
- There are four basic types of leasehold estates:
  - one that runs for a specific length of time creates an estate for years;
  - one that runs for an indefinite period creates an estate from period to period (year to year, month to month);
  - one that runs as long as the landlord permits is an estate at will; and
  - an estate at sufferance is possession without the consent of the landlord.
- A leasehold estate is classified as personal property.
- The requirements of a valid lease include:
  - offer and acceptance,
  - consideration,
  - capacity to contract,
  - legal objectives, and
  - it must be in writing if it will not be completed within one year of the date of its making.
- Most leases include clauses relating to rights and obligations of the landlord and tenant, such as the use of the premises, subletting, judgments, maintenance of the premises, and termination of the lease period.
- A lease may be terminated by:
  - the expiration of the lease period,
  - the mutual agreement of the parties, or
  - a breach of the lease by either the landlord or tenant.
- In most cases, neither the death of the tenant nor the landlord's sale of the rental property terminates a lease.
- The fair housing laws prohibit discrimination based on race, color, religion, familial status, national origin, and sex; and the laws address the rights of individuals with disabilities and families with children.

- The Americans with Disabilities Act provides for access to goods and services by people with disabilities.
- There are several basic types of leases, including:
  - net leases,
  - gross leases, and
  - percentage leases.

**Real-Life
Real Estate**

1. Is the Ohio Landlord-Tenant Act more favorable to landlords or tenants? Justify your position.
2. Rent withholding and the incorrect disposition of deposits account for a significant portion of disagreements between landlords and tenants. How would you advise a landlord to approach these matters?

# QUESTIONS

1. A ground lease is usually
   a. short term.
   b. for 100 years or longer.
   c. long term.
   d. a gross lease.

2. *J* and *Y* enter into a commercial lease that requires a monthly rent based on a minimum set amount plus an additional amount determined by the tenant's gross receipts exceeding $5,000. This type of lease is called a
   a. standard lease.
   b. gross lease.
   c. percentage lease.
   d. net lease.

3. If a tenant moved out of a rented store building because access to the building was blocked as a result of the landlord's negligence, the
   a. tenant would have no legal recourse against the landlord.
   b. landlord would be liable for the rent until the expiration date of the lease.
   c. landlord would have to provide substitute space.
   d. tenant would be entitled to recover damages from the landlord.

4. In June, *V* signs a one-year lease and moves into Streetview Apartments. *V* deposits the required security deposit with the landlord. Six months later, *V* pays the January rent and mysteriously moves out. *V* does not arrange for a sublease or an assignment and makes no further rent payments. The apartment is still in good condition. What is *V*'s liability to the landlord in these circumstances?
   a. Because half the rental amount has been paid and the apartment is in good condition, *V* has no further liability.
   b. *V* is liable for the balance of the rent, plus forfeiture of the security deposit.
   c. *V* is liable for the balance of the rent only.
   d. *V* is liable for the balance of the rent, plus the security deposit, and any marketing costs the landlord incurred.

5. *K* still has five months remaining on a one-year apartment lease. When *K* moves to another city, he transfers possession of the apartment to *L* for the entire remaining term of the lease. *L* pays rent directly to *K*. Under these facts, *K* is a(n)
   a. assignor.     c. sublessee.
   b. sublessor.     d. lessor.

6. A tenant's lease has expired. The tenant has neither vacated nor negotiated a renewal lease, and the landlord has declared that she does not want the tenant to remain in the building. This form of possession is called a(n)
   a. estate for years.
   b. periodic estate.
   c. estate at will.
   d. estate at sufferance.

7. *P*'s tenancy for years will expire in two weeks. *P* plans to move to a larger apartment across town when the current tenancy expires. What must *P* do to terminate this agreement?
   a. *P* must give the landlord two weeks' prior notice.
   b. *P* must give the landlord one week's prior notice.
   c. *P* needs to do nothing; the agreement will terminate automatically.
   d. The agreement will terminate only after *P* signs a lease for the new apartment.

8. When a tenant holds possession of a landlord's property without a current lease agreement and without the landlord's approval, the
   a. tenant is maintaining a gross lease.
   b. landlord can file suit for possession.
   c. tenant has no obligation to pay rent.
   d. landlord may be subject to a constructive eviction.

9. Under the terms of a residential lease, the landlord is required to maintain the water heater. If a tenant is unable to get hot water because of a faulty water heater that the landlord has failed to repair, all of the following remedies would be available to the tenant *EXCEPT*
   a. suing the landlord for damages.
   b. suing the landlord for back rent.
   c. abandoning the premises under constructive eviction.
   d. terminating the lease agreement.

10. *J* has a one-year leasehold interest in Blackacre. The interest automatically renews itself at the end of each year. *J*'s interest is referred to as a tenancy
    a. for years.
    b. from period to period.
    c. at will.
    d. at sufferance.

11. *M* has assigned her apartment lease to *B*, and the landlord has agreed to the assignment. If *B* fails to pay the rent, who is liable?
    a. *B* is primarily liable; *M* is secondarily liable.
    b. *M* is primarily liable; *B* is secondarily liable.
    c. Only *M* is liable.
    d. Only *B* is liable.

12. Which of the following automatically terminates a lease?
    a. Total destruction of the property
    b. Sale of the property
    c. Failure of the tenant to pay rent
    d. Constructive eviction

13. Which of the following describes a net lease?
    a. An agreement in which the tenant pays a fixed rent and the landlord pays all taxes, insurance, and so forth on the property
    b. A lease in which the tenant pays rent plus maintenance and property charges
    c. A lease in which the tenant pays the landlord a percentage of the monthly income derived from the property
    d. An agreement granting an individual a leasehold interest in fishing rights for shoreline properties

14. A tenancy in which the tenant continues in possession after the lease has expired, without the landlord's permission, is a
    a. tenancy for years.
    b. periodic tenancy.
    c. tenancy at will.
    d. tenancy at sufferance.

15. A commercial lease calls for a minimum rent of $1,200 per month plus 4 percent of the annual gross business exceeding $150,000. If the total rent paid at the end of one year was $19,200, how much business did the tenant do during the year?
    a. $159,800        c. $270,000
    b. $250,200        d. $279,200

16. If an Ohio lease is executed properly, the lessee is in possession and the term is for two years, then the lease
    a. is invalid.
    b. must be recorded.
    c. need not be recorded.
    d. is considered a commercial lease.

17. An Ohio landlord may enter leased premises to make repairs if he or she
    a. knocks first to give notice of intent to enter.
    b. gives 24 hours' notice of intent to enter.
    c. gives 48 hours' notice of intent to enter.
    d. enters without knocking.

18. In Ohio, on termination of a residential rental agreement the landlord must return the tenant's security deposit and provide an itemized list of any deductions for damages
    a. within 30 days after the tenant has vacated the premises; however, the tenant must provide the landlord with the new address to which the deposit may be sent.
    b. within ten days after the tenant has vacated the premises.
    c. even if the landlord does not know where to send the returned deposit.
    d. within 45 days after the tenant has vacated the premises.

19. If after notice a landlord fails to remedy a violation of the Ohio Landlord-Tenant Act, the tenant may
    a. withhold rent after giving written notice of the violation.
    b. deposit the withheld rent with the clerk of courts.
    c. deposit the withheld rent in escrow at a bank.
    d. withhold rent until the violation is corrected.

# CHAPTER 18

# Property Management

## THE PROPERTY MANAGER

Property management is a real estate specialization. It involves the leasing, managing, marketing, and overall maintenance of real estate owned by others, usually rental property. The **property manager** has three principal responsibilities:

1. Financial management
2. Physical management (structure and grounds)
3. Administrative management (files and records)

> A *property manager*
>
> - maintains the owner's investment and
> - ensures that the property produces income.

The property manager is responsible for maintaining the owner's investment and making sure the property earns income. This can be done in several ways. The physical property must be maintained in good condition. Suitable tenants must be found, rent must be collected, and employees must be hired and supervised. The property manager is responsible for budgeting and controlling expenses, keeping proper accounts, and making periodic reports to the owner. In all of these activities, the manager's primary goal is to operate and maintain the physical property in such a way as to preserve and enhance the owner's capital investment.

Some property managers work for property management companies. These firms manage properties for a number of owners under management agreements (discussed later). Other property managers are independent. The property manager has an agency relationship with the owner, which involves greater authority and discretion over management decisions than an employee would have. A property manager or an owner may employ building managers to supervise the daily operations of a building. In some cases, these individuals may be residents of the building.

In Ohio... In Ohio, only a licensed real estate broker or salesperson may legally manage or lease real estate for others for a fee. *A real estate salesperson must manage property under the broker he or she is affiliated with, not another broker.* A real estate license also is needed to attempt to lease property or to procure tenants, to negotiate leases, or to advertise that one is in the business of property management. However, neither the regularly salaried employees of property owners nor property owners themselves are required to have real estate licenses to perform their property management duties. ◆

**Securing Management Business**

Possible sources of property management business include

- corporate owners,
- apartment developers and landlords,
- condominium associations,
- homeowners' associations,
- investment syndicates,
- trusts, and
- absentee owners.

When a property manager secures business from any of these sources, a good reputation is often the manager's best advertising. A manager who consistently demonstrates the ability to increase property income over previous levels should have little difficulty finding new business.

Before contracting to manage any property, however, the professional property manager should be certain that the building owner has realistic income expectations. Necessary maintenance, unexpected repairs, and effective marketing all take time and money. If the owner has unreasonable expectations, the manager's time will be wasted.

**The Management Agreement**

The first step in taking over the management of any property is to enter into a **management agreement** with the owner. This agreement creates an agency relationship between the owner and the property manager. The property manager usually is considered to be a *general agent.* As an agent, the property manager is charged with the fiduciary responsibilities of care, obedience, accounting, loyalty, and disclosure. After entering into an agreement with a property owner, a manager handles the property the same way the owner would. In all activities, the manager's first responsibility is to realize the highest return on the property in a manner consistent with the owner's instructions.

Like any other contract involving real estate, the management agreement should be in writing. It should include the following points:

- *Description* of the property.
- *Time period* the agreement covers.
- *Definition of the management's responsibilities.* All the manager's duties should be specifically stated in the contract. Any limitations or restrictions on what the manager may do should be included.
- *Statement of the owner's purpose.* The owner should clearly state what he or she wants the manager to accomplish. One owner may want to maximize net income, while another will want to increase the capital value of the investment. What the manager does depends on the owner's long-term goals for the property.
- *Extent of the manager's authority.* This provision should state what authority the manager is to have in matters such as hiring, firing, and supervising employees; fixing rental rates for space; and making expenditures and authorizing repairs. Repairs that exceed a certain expense limit may require the owner's written approval.
- Reporting. The frequency and detail of the manager's periodic reports on operations and financial position should be agreed on. These reports

**In Ohio...**

serve as a means for the owner to monitor the manager's work. They also form a basis for both the owner and manager to spot trends that are important in shaping management policy.

- *Management fee.* The fee may be based on a percentage of gross or net income, a fixed fee, or some combination of these and other factors. (In Ohio, the typical management fee is 10 percent of the property's gross rental income.) Management fees are subject to the same antitrust considerations as sales commissions. That is, they cannot be standardized in the marketplace; standardization would be viewed as price fixing. The fee *must* be negotiated between the agent and the principal. In addition, the property manager may be entitled to a commission on new rentals and renewed leases. ◆

- *Allocation of costs.* The agreement should state which of the property manager's expenses—such as office rent, office help, telephone, advertising, and association fees—will be paid by the manager. Other costs will be paid by the owner.

**MATH CONCEPTS**

### Rental Commissions

Residential property managers often earn commissions when they find tenants for a property. Rental commissions are usually based on the annual rent from a property. For example, if an apartment unit rents for $475 per month and the commission payable is 8 percent, the commission is calculated as follows:

$$\$475 \text{ per month} \times 12 \text{ months} = \$5,700$$
$$\$5,700 \times .08 \ (8\%) = \$456$$

## MANAGEMENT FUNCTIONS

A property manager's specific responsibilities are determined by the management agreement. Certain duties, however, are found in most agreements. These include budgeting, capital expenditures, setting rental rates, selecting tenants, collecting rent, maintaining the property, and complying with legal requirements.

**Budgeting Expenses**

Before attempting to rent any property, the property manager should develop an o*perating budget.* The budget should be based on anticipated revenues and expenses. In addition, it must reflect the owner's long-term goals. In preparing a budget, the manager should allocate money for *continuous, fixed expenses* such as employees' salaries, property taxes, and insurance premims.

Next, the manager should establish a *cash reserve fund* for variable expenses such as repairs, decorating, and supplies. The amount allocated for the reserve fund can be computed from the previous yearly costs of the variable expenses.

**Capital expenditures.** The owner and the property manager may decide that modernization or renovation of a property will enhance its value. In this case, the manager should budget money to cover the costs of remodeling. The property manager should either be thoroughly familiar with the *principle of contribution* (discussed in Chapter 19) or seek expert advice when estimating any expected increase in value. In the case of large-scale construction, the expenses charged against the property's income should be spread over several years.

The cost of equipment to be installed in a modernization or renovation must be evaluated over its entire useful life. This is called **life cycle costing.** This term simply means that both the *initial* and the *operating* costs of equipment over its expected life must be measured to compare the total cost of one type of equipment with that of another.

## Renting the Property

Effective rental of the property is essential. However, the role of the property manager in managing a property should not be confused with that of a broker who acts as a leasing agent. The manager must be concerned with the long-term financial health of the property; the broker is concerned solely with renting space. The property manager may use the services of a leasing agent, but that agent does not undertake the full responsibility of maintaining and managing the property.

**Setting rental rates.** Rental rates are influenced primarily by supply and demand. The property manager should conduct a detailed survey of the competitive space available in the neighborhood, emphasizing similar properties. In establishing rental rates, the property manager has four long-term considerations:

1. The rental income must be sufficient to cover the property's fixed charges and operating expenses.
2. The rental income must provide a fair return on the owner's investment.
3. The rental rate should be in line with prevailing rates in comparable buildings. It may be slightly higher or slightly lower, depending on the strength of the property.
4. The current vacancy rate in the property is a good indicator of how much of a rent increase is advisable. A building with a low vacancy rate (that is, few vacant units) is a better candidate for an increase than one with a high vacancy rate.

A rental rate for residential space is usually stated as the monthly rate *per unit.* Commercial leases—including office, retail, and industrial space rentals—are usually stated according to either annual or monthly rates *per square foot.*

If the vacancy level is high, the manager should attempt to determine why. An elevated level of vacancy does not necessarily indicate that rents are too high. Instead, the problem may be poor management or a defective or an undesirable property. The manager should attempt to identify and correct the problems first rather than immediately lower rents. On the other hand, a high occupancy rate may mean that rental rates are too low. Whenever the occupancy level of an apartment house or office building exceeds 95 percent, serious consideration should be given to raising rents. First, however, the manager should investigate the rental market to determine whether a rent increase is warranted.

## Selecting Tenants

A building manager's success depends on establishing and maintaining sound, long-term relationships with his or her tenants. The first and most important step is selection. The manager should be sure that the premises are suitable for a tenant in size, location, and amenities. Most important, the manager should be sure that the tenant is able to pay for the space.

**Calculating Monthly Rent per Square Foot**

1. Determine the total square footage of the rental premises (generally floorspace only).

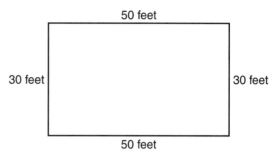

50 feet × 30 feet = 1,500 square feet

2. Find the total annual rent.

$1,850 per month × 12 months = $22,200 per year

3. Divide the total annual rent by the total square feet to determine the annual rate per square foot.

$22,200 ÷ 1,500 square feet = $14.80 per square foot

4. Convert the annual rate to a monthly rate.

$14.80 ÷ 12 months = $1.23 per square foot

A commercial tenant's business should be compatible with the building *and the other tenants.* The manager must consider the business interests of his or her current tenants as well as the interests of the potential tenant. The types of businesses or services should be complementary, and the introduction of competitors into the same property should be undertaken with care. This not only pleases existing tenants but helps diversify the owner's investment and makes profitability more likely. Some commercial leases bar the introduction of similar businesses.

If a commercial tenant is likely to expand in the future, the manager should consider the property's potential for expansion.

The residential property manager must be sure to comply with all federal, state, and local fair housing laws in selecting tenants. (See Chapters 17 and 22.) Although fair housing laws do not apply to commercial properties, commercial property managers need to be aware of federal, state, and local antidiscrimination and equal opportunity laws that may govern industrial or retail properties.

**Collecting rents.** A property manager should accept only those tenants who can be expected to meet their financial obligations. The manager should investigate financial references, check with local credit bureaus, and, when possible, interview a prospective tenant's former landlord.

The terms of rental payment should be spelled out in the lease agreement, including

- time and place of payment,
- provisions and penalties for late payment, and
- provisions for cancellation and damages in case of nonpayment.

The property manager should establish a firm and consistent collection plan. The plan should include a system of notices and records that complies with state and local law.

Every attempt must be made to collect rent without resorting to legal action. Legal action is costly and time consuming and does not contribute to good tenant relations. In some cases, however, legal action is unavoidable. In these instances, a property manager must be prepared to initiate and follow through with the necessary legal steps. Obviously, legal action must be taken in cooperation with the property owner's or management firm's legal counsel.

**In Ohio...** In Ohio, all monies received in a fiduciary capacity by brokers or salespersons must be deposited and maintained in the broker's *separate property management account*. This includes rental monies that are collected on behalf of the owner until they are paid over to the owner. ◆

## Maintaining Good Relations with Tenants

The ultimate success of a property manager depends on the ability to maintain good relations with tenants. Dissatisfied tenants eventually vacate the property. A high tenant turnover rate results in greater expenses for advertising and redecorating. It also means less profit for the owner due to uncollected rents.

An effective property manager establishes a good communication system with tenants. Regular newsletters or posted memoranda help keep tenants informed and involved. Maintenance and service requests must be attended to promptly, and all lease terms and building rules must be enforced consistently and fairly. A good manager is tactful and decisive and acts to the benefit of both owner and occupants.

The property manager must be able to handle residents who do not pay their rents on time or who break building regulations. When one tenant fails to follow the rules, the other tenants often become frustrated and dissatisfied. Careful record keeping shows whether rent is remitted promptly and in the proper amount. Records of all lease renewal dates should be kept so that the manager can anticipate expiration and retain good tenants who might otherwise move when their leases end.

## Maintaining the Property

One of the most important functions of a property manager is the supervision of property maintenance. A manager must learn to balance the services provided with their costs—that is, to satisfy tenants' needs while minimizing operating expenses.

To maintain the property efficiently, the manager must be able to assess the building's needs and how best to meet them. Staffing and scheduling requirements vary with the type, size, and geographic location of the property, so the owner and manager usually agree in advance on maintenance objectives. In some cases, the best plan may be to operate a low-rental property, with minimal expenditures for services and maintenance. Another property may be more lucrative if kept in top condition and operated with all possible tenant services. A well-maintained, high-service property can command premium rental rates.

A primary maintenance objective is to *protect the physical integrity of the property over the long term.* For example, preserving the property by repainting the exterior or replacing the heating system helps decrease long-term maintenance costs. Keeping the property in good condition involves four types of maintenance:

1. Preventive maintenance
2. Repair or corrective maintenance
3. Routine maintenance
4. Construction

**Preventive** maintenance helps prevent problems and expenses.

**Corrective** maintenance corrects problems after they've occurred.

**Routine** maintenance keeps up with everyday wear and tear.

*Preventive maintenance* includes regularly scheduled activities such as painting and seasonal servicing of appliances and systems. Preventive maintenance preserves the long-range value and physical integrity of the building. This is both the most critical and the most neglected maintenance responsibility. Failure to perform preventive maintenance invariably leads to greater expense in other areas of maintenance.

*Repair or corrective maintenance* involves the actual repairs that keep the building's equipment, utilities, and amenities functioning. Repairing a boiler, fixing a leaky faucet, and mending a broken air-conditioning unit are acts of corrective maintenance.

A property manager must also supervise the *routine maintenance* of the building. Routine maintenance includes such day-to-day duties as cleaning common areas, performing minor carpentry and plumbing adjustments, and providing regularly scheduled upkeep of heating, air-conditioning, and landscaping. Good routine maintenance is similar to good preventive maintenance. Both head off problems before they become expensive.

**In Practice**

One of the major decisions a property manager faces is whether to contract for maintenance services from an outside firm or hire on-site employees to perform such tasks. This decision should be based on a number of factors, including the

- size of the building,
- complexity of the tenants' requirements, and
- availability of suitable labor.

**Construction** involves making a property meet a tenant's needs.

A commercial or an industrial property manager often is called on to make **tenant improvements.** These are alterations to the interior of the building to meet a tenant's particular space needs. Such *construction alterations* range from simply repainting or recarpeting to completely gutting the interior and redesigning the space by erecting new walls, partitions, and electrical systems. Tenant improvements are especially important when renting new buildings. In new construction, the interiors are usually left incomplete so that they can be adapted to the needs of individual tenants. One matter that must be clarified is which improvements will be considered trade fixtures (personal property belonging to the tenant) and which will belong to the owner of the real estate. Trade fixtures are discussed in Chapter 2.

Modernization or renovation of buildings that have become functionally obsolete and thus unsuited to today's building needs also is important. (See Chapter 19 for a definition of *functional obsolescence*.) The renovation of a building often enhances the building's marketability and increases its potential income.

## Handling Environmental Concerns

The environment is an increasingly important property management issue. A variety of environmental issues, from waste disposal to air quality, must be addressed by the property manager. Tenant concerns, as well as federal, state, and local regulations, determine the extent of the manager's environmental responsibilities. While property managers are not expected to be experts in all of the disciplines necessary to operate a modern building, they are expected to be knowledgeable in many diverse subjects, most of which are technical in nature. Environmental concerns are one such subject.

The property manager must be able to respond to a variety of environmental problems. He or she may manage structures containing asbestos or radon or be called on to arrange an environmental audit of a property. Managers must see that any hazardous wastes produced by their employers or tenants are properly disposed of. Even the normally nonhazardous waste of an office building must be controlled to avoid violation of laws requiring segregation and recycling of types of wastes. Of course, a property manager may want to provide recycling facilities for tenants even if he or she is not required by law to do so. On-site recycling creates an image of good citizenship that enhances the reputation (and value) of a commercial or residential property. Environmental issues are discussed in detail in Chapter 23.

## The Americans with Disabilities Act

The *Americans with Disabilities Act (ADA)* has had a significant impact on the responsibilities of the property manager, both in building amenities and in employment issues.

Title I of the ADA provides for the employment of qualified job applicants regardless of their disability. Any employer with 15 or more employees must adopt nondiscriminatory employment procedures. In addition, employers must make reasonable accommodations to enable individuals with disabilities to perform essential job functions.

Property managers also must be familiar with Title III of the ADA, which prohibits discrimination in commercial properties. The ADA requires that managers ensure that people with disabilities have full and equal access to facilities and services. The property manager typically is responsible for determining whether a building meets the ADA's accessibility requirements. The property manager also must prepare and execute a plan for restructuring or retrofitting a building that is not in compliance. ADA experts may be consulted, as may architectural designers who specialize in accessibility issues.

To protect owners of existing structures from the massive expense of extensive remodeling, the ADA recommends *reasonably achievable accommodations* to provide access to the facilities and services. New construction and remodeling, however, must meet higher standards of accessibility and usability because it costs less to incorporate accessible features in the design than to retrofit. Though the law intends to provide for people with disabilities, many of the accessible design features and accommodations benefit everyone.

**In Practice**    The U.S. Department of Justice has ADA specialists available to answer general information questions about compliance issues. The ADA Information Line is at 1-800-514-0301 (TDD 1-800-514-0383).

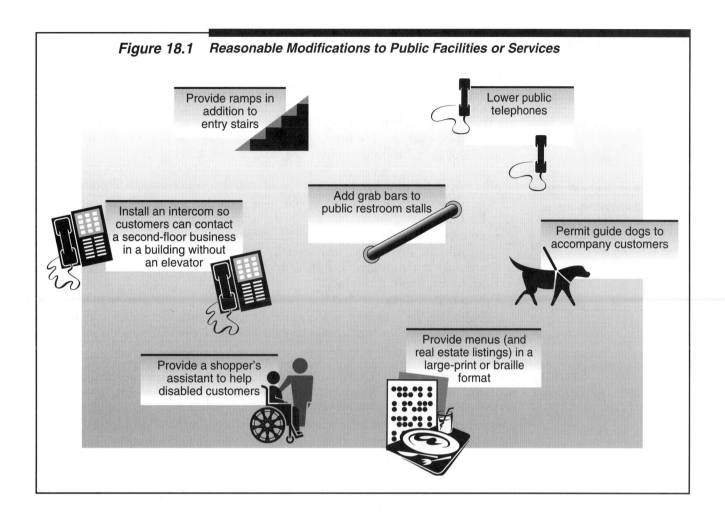

**Figure 18.1   Reasonable Modifications to Public Facilities or Services**

Provide ramps in addition to entry stairs

Lower public telephones

Install an intercom so customers can contact a second-floor business in a building without an elevator

Add grab bars to public restroom stalls

Permit guide dogs to accompany customers

Provide a shopper's assistant to help disabled customers

Provide menus (and real estate listings) in a large-print or braille format

Existing barriers must be removed when this can be accomplished in a readily achievable manner—that is, with little difficulty and at low cost. (See Figure 18.1.) The following are typical examples of readily achievable modifications:

- Ramping or removing an obstacle from an otherwise accessible entrance
- Lowering wall-mounted public telephones
- Adding raised letters and braille markings on elevator buttons
- Installing auditory signals in elevators

Alternative methods can be used to provide reasonable accommodations if extensive restructuring is impractical or if retrofitting is unduly expensive. For instance, installing a cup dispenser at a water fountain that is too high for an individual in a wheelchair may be more practical than installing a lower unit.

**In Practice**   Federal, state, and local laws may provide additional requirements for accommodating people with disabilities. Licensees should be aware of the full range of laws to ensure that their practices are in compliance.

## RISK MANAGEMENT

Enormous monetary losses can result from certain unexpected or catastrophic events. As a result, one of the most critical areas of responsibility for a property manager is risk management. Risk management involves answering the question, "What happens if something goes wrong?" The perils of any risk must be evaluated in terms of options. In considering the possibility of a loss, the property manager must decide whether it is better to

> The four alternative risk management techniques may be remembered by the acronym **ACTOR**: *Avoid, Control, Transfer or Retain.*

- *avoid it,* by removing the source of risk (for instance, a swimming pool may pose an unacceptable risk if a day-care center is located in the building);
- *control it,* by preparing for an emergency before it happens (by installing sprinklers, fire doors, and security systems, for example);
- *transfer it,* by shifting the risk onto another party (that is, by taking out an insurance policy); or
- *retain it,* by deciding that the chances of the event occurring are too small to justify the expense of any other response (an alternative might be to take out an insurance policy with a large *deductible,* which is usually considerably less expensive).

### Security of Tenants

The physical safety of tenants of the leased premises is an important issue for property managers and owners. Recent court decisions in several parts of the country have held owners and their agents responsible for physical harm that was inflicted on tenants by intruders. These decisions have prompted property managers and owners to think about how to protect tenants and secure apartments from intruders.

### Types of Insurance

Insurance is one way to protect against losses. Many types of insurance are available. An *insurance audit* should be performed by a competent, reliable insurance agent who is familiar with insurance issues for the type of property involved. The audit will indicate areas in which greater or lesser coverage is recommended and will highlight particular risks. The final decision, however, must be made by the property owner.

Some common types of coverage available to income property owners and managers follow:

- *Fire and hazard.* Fire insurance policies provide coverage against direct loss or damage to property from a fire on the premises. Standard fire coverage can be extended to include other hazards such as windstorm, hail, smoke damage, or civil insurrection.
- *Consequential loss, use, and occupancy.* Consequential loss insurance covers the results, or consequences, of a disaster. Consequential loss can include the loss of rent or revenue to a business that occurs if the business's property cannot be used.
- *Contents and personal property.* This type of insurance covers building contents and personal property during periods when they are not actually located on the business premises.
- *Liability.* Public liability insurance covers the risks an owner assumes whenever the public enters the building. A claim paid under this coverage is used for medical expenses by a person who is injured in the building

as a result of the owner's negligence. Claims for medical or hospital payments for injuries sustained by building employees hurt in the course of their employment are covered by state laws known as **workers' compensation acts.** These laws require that a building owner who is an employer obtain a workers' compensation policy from a private insurance company.

- *Casualty.* Casualty insurance policies include coverage against theft, burglary, vandalism, and machinery damage as well as health and accident insurance. Casualty policies are usually written on specific risks, such as theft, rather than being all-inclusive.
- *Surety bonds.* **Surety bonds** cover an owner against financial losses resulting from an employee's criminal acts or negligence while performing assigned duties.

Many insurance companies offer **multiperil policies** for apartment and commercial buildings. Such a policy offers the property manager an insurance package that includes standard types of commercial coverage, such as fire, hazard, public liability, and casualty. Special coverage for earthquakes and floods is also available.

**Claims**  Two possible methods can be used to determine the amount of a claim under an insurance policy. One is the *depreciated* or *actual cash value* of the damaged property. That is, the property is not insured for what it would cost to replace it, but rather for what it was originally worth, less the depreciation in value that results from use and the passage of time. The other method is *current replacement cost.* In this sort of policy, the building or property is insured for what it would cost to rebuild or replace it today.

When purchasing insurance, a manager must decide whether a property should be insured at full replacement cost or at a depreciated cost. Full replacement cost coverage is generally more expensive than depreciated cost. As with the homeowner's policies discussed in Chapter 3, commercial policies include *coinsurance clauses* that require that the insured carry fire coverage, usually in an amount equal to 80 percent of a building's replacement value.

## THE MANAGEMENT PROFESSION

Most metropolitan areas have local associations of building and property owners and managers that are affiliates of regional and national associations. The Institute of Real Estate Management (IREM) is one of the affiliates of the National Association of REALTORS®. It awards the Certified Property Manager (CPM) designation. The Building Owners and Managers Association (BOMA) International is a federation of local associations of building owners and managers. The Building Owners and Managers Institute (BOMI) International, an independent institute affiliated with BOMA, offers training courses leading to several designations: Real Property Administrator (RPA), Systems Maintenance Administrator (SMA), and Facilities Management Administrator (FMA). In addition, many specialized professional organizations provide information and contacts for apartment and condominium association managers, shopping center managers, and others.

**KEY TERMS**

| casualty insurance | management | risk management |
|---|---|---|
| consequential loss | agreement | surety bond |
| insurance | multiperil policy | tenant improvement |
| fire and hazard | property management | workers' |
| insurance | property manager | compensation act |
| life cycle costing | public liability insurance | |

**SUMMARY**

- *Property management* is a specialized service provided to owners of income-producing properties. The manager, as agent of the owner, becomes the administrator of the project and assumes the executive functions required for the care and operation of the property.
- A *management agreement* establishes the agency relationship between owner and manager. It must be prepared carefully to define and authorize the manager's duties and responsibilities.
- A primary function of the property manager is setting and collecting rents.
  - Rental rates are determined by projected expenses, the manager's analysis of the building's condition, and local rent patterns.
  - Once a rent schedule is established, the property manager is responsible for soliciting tenants whose needs are suited to the available space. The tenants must be financially capable of meeting the proposed rents.
  - The manager collects rents, maintains the building, hires necessary employees, pays taxes for the building, and deals with tenant problems.
- Maintenance is another important property management function. It includes:
  - safeguarding the physical integrity of the property and performing routine cleaning and repairs, and
  - making tenant improvements, such as adapting the interior space and overall design of the property to suit tenants' needs.
- The manager is expected to secure adequate insurance coverage for the premises.
  - *Fire and hazard insurance* covers the property and fixtures against catastrophes.
  - *Consequential loss, use, and occupancy insurance* protects the owner against revenue losses.
  - *Casualty insurance* provides coverage against losses such as theft, vandalism, and destruction of machinery.
  - *Public liability insurance* insures the owner against claims made by people injured on the premises.
  - *Workers' compensation* policies cover the claims of employees injured on the job.

**Real-Life Real Estate**

1. As the manager of an apartment complex, how do you balance providing services to the tenants with meeting the needs of the property owner?
2. Discuss examples of "reasonably achievable accommodations" (as required by the ADA) that you have observed. What other methods might be used in similar situations?

# QUESTIONS

1.  *K* is an employee who is injured on the job. Which of the following types of insurance coverage insures *K*'s employer against most claims for job-related injuries?
    a. Consequential loss
    b. Workers' compensation
    c. Casualty
    d. Surety bond

2.  Apartment rental rates are usually expressed in what way?
    a. In monthly amounts
    b. On a per-room basis
    c. In square feet per month
    d. In square feet per year

3.  From a management point of view, apartment building occupancy that reaches as high as 98 percent would tend to indicate that
    a. the building is poorly managed.
    b. the building has reached its maximum potential.
    c. the building is a desirable place to live.
    d. rents could be raised.

4.  A guest slips on an icy apartment building stair and is hospitalized. A claim against the building owner for medical expenses may be paid under which of the following policies held by the owner?
    a. Workers' compensation
    b. Casualty
    c. Liability
    d. Fire and hazard

5.  When a property manager is establishing a budget for the building, all of the following should be included as an operating expense *EXCEPT*
    a. heating oil.
    b. cleaning supplies.
    c. foundation repairs.
    d. management fees.

6.  A property manager is offered a choice of three insurance policies: one has a $500 deductible, one has a $1,000 deductible, and the third has a $5,000 deductible. If the property manager selects the policy with the highest deductible, which risk management technique is he or she using?
    a. Avoiding risk
    b. Retaining risk
    c. Controlling risk
    d. Transferring risk

7.  Contaminated groundwater, toxic fumes from paint and carpeting, and lack of proper ventilation are all examples of
    a. issues beyond the scope of a property manager's job description.
    b. problems faced only by newly constructed properties.
    c. issues that arise under the ADA.
    d. environmental concerns that a property manager may have to address.

8.  Tenant improvements are
    a. always construed to be fixtures.
    b. adaptations of space to suit tenants' needs.
    c. removable by the tenant.
    d. paid for by the landlord.

9.  In preparing a budget, a property manager should set up which of the following for variable expenses?
    a. Control account
    b. Floating allocation
    c. Cash reserve fund
    d. Asset account

10. Rents should be determined by
    a. supply and demand factors.
    b. the local apartment owners' association.
    c. HUD.
    d. a tenants' union.

11. Whittaker Towers, a highrise apartment building, burns to the ground. What type of insurance covers the landlord against the resulting loss of rent?
    a. Fire and hazard
    b. Liability
    c. Consequential loss, use, and occupancy
    d. Casualty

12. Property manager *J* hires *W* as the full-time maintenance person for one of the buildings she manages. While repairing a faucet in one of the apartments, *W* steals a television set. *J* could protect the owner against this type of loss by purchasing
    a. liability insurance.
    b. workers' compensation insurance.
    c. a surety bond.
    d. casualty insurance.

13. Which of the following might indicate rents are too low?
    a. Poorly maintained building
    b. Many "for lease" signs in the area
    c. High building occupancy
    d. High tenant turnover rates

14. *P* repairs a malfunctioning boiler in the building she manages. This is classified as which type of maintenance?
    a. Preventive        c. Routine
    b. Corrective        d. Construction

15. A property manager who enters into a management agreement with an owner is usually a
    a. special agent.
    b. general agent.
    c. universal agent.
    d. designated agent.

# CHAPTER 19

# Real Estate Appraisal

## APPRAISING

An **appraisal** is an estimate or opinion of value based on supportable evidence and approved methods. (The term "appraisal" may also refer to the act of appraising property and the actual report of the estimate of value.) An **appraiser** is an independent person trained to provide an *unbiased* estimate of value. Appraising is a professional service performed for a fee.

In Ohio...

### WWWeb.Link
www.appraisalinstitute.org. The site for the Appraisal Institute. It provides a search engine for appraisers, informative articles on appraisal, and links related to appraisal issues. **www.com.state.oh.us** is a site that contains downloaded forms needed by professional appraisers in Ohio. ◆

### Regulation of Appraisal Activities

*Each State*

Title XI of the Financial Institutions Reform, Recovery, and Enforcement Act of 1989 (FIRREA) requires that any appraisal used in connection with a federally related transaction must be performed by a competent individual whose professional conduct is subject to supervision and regulation. Appraisers must be licensed or certified according to state law. Each state adopts its own appraiser regulations. These laws must conform to the federal requirements, which in turn follow the criteria for certification established by the Appraiser Qualifications Board of the Appraisal Foundation. The Appraisal Foundation is a national body composed of representatives of the major appraisal and related organizations. Appraisers are also expected to follow the Uniform Standards of Professional Appraisal Practice (USPAP) established by the foundation's Appraisal Standards Board.

A *federally related transaction* is any real estate-related financial transaction in which a federal financial institution or regulatory agency engages. This includes transactions involving the sale, lease, purchase, or exchange of or investment in real property. It also includes the financing, refinancing, or use of real property as security for a loan or an investment, including mortgage-backed securities. Appraisals of residential property valued at $250,000 or less and of commercial property valued at $1 million or less in federally related transactions are exempt and need not be performed by licensed or certified appraisers.

**Ohio's Appraiser** ✳ **Licensing and Certification Law**

*In Ohio...*

*Test*

While Ohio does not require that appraisers be licensed—either as appraisers or real estate brokers or sales agents—the state has instituted a voluntary licensing and certification system. In Ohio, any person may appraise real estate for compensation, whether or not he or she has chosen to submit to the state's regulatory system. However, an appraiser's compliance with the voluntary procedures assures consumers that he or she has demonstrated professional competence and is subject to the state's standards of professional behavior. It also permits the appraiser to participate in federally regulated transactions. ◆

The law creates a three-tier certification system. In Ohio, an appraiser may be a state-certified general real estate appraiser, a state-certified residential real estate appraiser, or a state-licensed residential real estate appraiser. A **state-certified general real estate appraiser** can appraise all types of real property. A **state-certified residential real estate appraiser** can appraise one to four units of single-family residential real estate regardless of transaction value or complexity. A **state-licensed residential real estate appraiser** can appraise noncomplex one-to-four unit single-family residential real estate having a transaction value of less than $1 million, and complex one-to-four unit single-family residential real estate having a transaction value of less than $250,000.

To be licensed or certified, an appraiser must be:

- at least eighteen years of age,
- honest,
- truthful, and
- of good reputation.

In addition, education and experience requirement's must be met:

- An applicant for a general real estate appraiser certificate must complete:
  - at least 30 months of experience in real estate appraisal, or any equivalent experience the board prescribes, and
  - at least 165 classroom hours of courses in subjects related to real estate appraisal, plus 15 classroom hours related to standards of professional practice and appraisal regulations.
- An applicant for a residential real estate appraiser certificate must complete:
  - at least two years experience in real estate appraisal, or any equivalent experience the board prescribes, and
  - at least 105 classroom hours of courses in subjects related to real estate appraisal, plus 15 classroom hours related to standards of professional practice and appraisal regulations.
- An applicant for a residential real estate appraiser license must complete:
  - at least two years experience in real estate appraisal, or any equivalent experience the board prescribes, and
  - at least 75 classroom hours of courses in subjects related to real estate appraisal, plus 15 classroom hours related to standards of professional practice and appraisal regulations.

Appraisers must pass an extensive written examination covering all aspects of appraisal theory, practice, and law to be licensed or certified.

The written examination requires that applicants demonstrate

- appropriate knowledge of technical terms commonly used in or related to real estate appraising, appraisal report writing, and the economic concepts applicable to real estate;

- understanding of the principles of land economics, real estate appraisal processes, and problems likely to be encountered in gathering, interpreting, and processing of data in carrying out appraisal disciplines;
- understanding of the standards for the development and communication of real estate appraisals;
- knowledge of theories of depreciation, cost estimating, methods of capitalization, direct sales comparison, and the mathematics of real estate appraisal that are appropriate for the certification or licensure for which the applicant has applied;
- knowledge of other principles and procedures as appropriate for the certification or license;
- basic understanding of real estate law; and
- understanding of the types of misconduct for which disciplinary proceedings may be initiated against a certificate holder and licensee.

**In Ohio...**   Appraisers must also meet continuing education requirements. To renew an appraisal license or certificate appraisers must complete at least 14 classroom hours of continuing education instruction in courses or seminars approved by the real estate appraiser board. An appraisal license or certificate must be renewed annually. ◆

A certificate holder or licensee may be reprimanded or have his or her license or certificate suspended or revoked for any of the following violations:

- Procuring or attempting to procure a license or certificate by means of false statement, fraud, deception, or bribery
- Being convicted of a felony or crime involving moral turpitude or being found guilty of fraud, deceit, misrepresentation, or gross negligence in appraising real estate
- Dishonesty, fraud, or misrepresentation intended to benefit or injure any person
- Violation of any of the standards for developing or communicating real estate appraisals, failing or refusing to exercise reasonable diligence in developing or communicating an appraisal, or negligence or incompetence in developing or preparing a report or in communicating an appraisal
- Willfully disregarding or violating the statutory rules and requirements
- Accepting an appraisal assignment contingent on a predetermined estimate, opinion, or valuation
- Violating the confidential nature of government records
- Violating any federal or state civil rights law
- Using misleading or inaccurate advertising
- Failing to maintain records of each appraisal job for five years

*Fraud*
*Civil Rights*
*Felony*

The voluntary appraiser licensing and certification law does not prevent brokers and salespersons from preparing a competitive market analysis (CMA) for their clients (see Chapter 7).

---

**In Practice**

**In Ohio...**

Licensed appraisers may also hold real estate licenses as brokers or salespersons. Although there is no inherent conflict in possessing both, there is a need to be cautious in all activities: Appraisers are expected to be impartial, objective, and independent, making no accommodation for their personal interests. Specifically, brokerage activities should not influence (or even appear to influence) appraisal activities in a single transaction. ◆

**Competitive Market Analysis**

*Opinion*

Not all estimates of *value* are made by professional appraisers. As discussed in Chapter 7, a salesperson often must help a seller arrive at a listing price or a buyer determine an offering price for property without the aid of a formal appraisal report. In such a case, the salesperson prepares a report compiled from research of the marketplace, primarily similar properties that have been sold, known as a *competitive market analysis* (CMA). The salesperson must be knowledgeable about the fundamentals of valuation to compile the market data. The competitive market analysis is not as comprehensive or technical as an appraisal and may be biased by a salesperson s anticipated agency relationship. A competitive market analysis should *not* be represented as an appraisal.

**In Practice**

Today, many CMAs and appraisals are prepared via computer. While someone must still visit the property to make sure it actually exists in an undamaged condition, most of the information used to complete a CMA or appraisal comes directly from computerized data banks.

 **WWWeb.Link**
www.homegain.com allows you to search neighborhoods for recent sales.

# VALUE

 *Test*

> The four characteristics of value may be remembered by the acronym *DUST: **D**emand, **U**tility, **S**carcity,* and ***T**ransferability.*

To have value in the real estate market—that is, to have monetary worth based on desirability—a property must have the following characteristics:

- *Demand:* The need or desire for possession or ownership backed by the financial means to satisfy that need
- *Utility:* The property's usefulness for its intended purposes
- *Scarcity:* A finite supply
- *Transferability:* The relative ease with which ownership rights are transferred from one person to another

**Market Value**

Generally, the goal of an appraiser is to estimate market value.

The **market value** of real estate is *the most probable price that a property should bring in a fair sale.* This definition makes three assumptions. First, it presumes a competitive and open market. Second, the buyer and seller are both assumed to be acting prudently and knowledgeably. Finally, market value depends on the price not being affected by unusual circumstances.

The following are essential to estimating market value:

- The *most probable* price is not the average or highest price.
- The buyer and seller must be unrelated and acting without *undue pressure.*
- Both buyer and seller must be *well informed* about the property's use and potential, including both its defects and its advantages.
- A *reasonable time* must be allowed for exposure in the open market.
- Payment must be made in cash or its equivalent.
- The price must represent a normal consideration for the property sold, unaffected by special financing amounts or terms, services, fees, costs, or credits incurred in the market transaction.

*Market value* is a reasonable opinion of a property's value; *market price* is the actual selling price of a property; *cost* may not equal market value or market price.

**Market value versus market price.** Market value is an opinion of value based on an analysis of data. The data may include not only an analysis of comparable sales but also an analysis of potential income, expenses, and replacement costs (less any depreciation). Market price, on the other hand, is what a property actually sells for—its sales price. In theory, market price should be the same as market value. Market price can be taken as accurate evidence of current market value, however, only if the conditions essential to market value exist. Sometimes, property may be sold below market valueó for instance, when the seller is forced to sell quickly or when a sale is arranged between relatives.

**Market value versus cost.** An important distinction can be made between market value and cost. One of the most common misconceptions about valuing property is the belief that cost represents market value. Cost and market value *may* be the same. In fact, when the improvements on a property are new, cost and value are likely to be equal. But more often, cost does *not* equal market value. For example, a homeowner may install a swimming pool for $15,000; however, the cost of the improvement may not add $15,000 to the value of the property.

**Basic Principles of Value**

A number of economic principles can affect the value of real estate. The most important are defined in the text that follows.

**Anticipation.** According to the principle of **anticipation,** value is created by the expectation that certain events will occur. Value can increase or decrease in anticipation of some future benefit or detriment. For instance, the value of a house may be affected if rumors circulate that an adjacent property may be converted to commercial use in the near future. If the property has been a vacant eyesore, it is possible that the neighboring home's value will increase. On the other hand, if the vacant property is perceived as a park or playlot that added to the neighborhood's quiet atmosphere, the news might cause the house's value to decline.

**Change.** No physical or economic condition remains constant. This is the principle of **change.** Real estate is subject to natural phenomena such as tornadoes, fires, and routine wear and tear. The real estate business is subject to market demands, like any other business. An appraiser must be knowledgeable about both the past, perhaps predictable, effects of natural phenomena, and the behavior of the marketplace.

**Competition.** **Competition** is the interaction of supply and demand. Excess profits tend to attract competition. For example, the success of a retail store may cause investors to open similar stores in the area. This tends to mean less profit for all stores concerned unless the purchasing power in the area increases substantially.

**Conformity.** The principle of **conformity** says that value is created when a property is in harmony with its surroundings. Maximum value is realized if the use of land conforms to existing neighborhood standards. In single-family residential neighborhoods, for instance, buildings should be similar in design, construction, size, and age.

**Contribution.** Under the principle of **contribution,** the value of any part of a property is measured by its effect on the value of the whole. Installing a swimming pool, greenhouse, or private bowling alley may not add value to the property equal to the cost of the addition. On the other hand, remodeling an outdated kitchen or bathroom probably would.

*1st consideration*

**Highest and best use.** The most profitable single use to which a property may be put, or the use that is most likely to be in demand in the near future, is the property s **highest and best use.** The use must be

- legally permitted,
- financially feasible,
- physically possible, and
- maximally productive.

The highest and best use of a site can change with social, political, and economic forces. For instance, a parking lot in a busy downtown area may not maximize the land's profitability to the same extent an office building might. Highest and best use is noted in every appraisal.

**Increasing and diminishing returns.** The addition of more improvements to land and structures increases value only to the property's maximum value. Beyond that point, additional improvements no longer affect a property's value. As long as money spent on improvements produces an increase in income or value, the law of increasing returns applies. At the point where additional improvements do not increase income or value, the *law of diminishing returns* applies. No matter how much money is spent on the property, the property's value does not keep pace with the expenditures.

> *Plottage:* the individual value of two adjacent properties may be greater if they are combined than if each is sold separately.

**Plottage.** The principle of **plottage** holds that merging or consolidating adjacent lots into a single larger one produces a greater total land value than the sum of the two sites valued separately. For example, two adjacent lots valued at $35,000 each might have a combined value of $90,000 if consolidated. The process of merging two separately owned lots under one owner is known as **assemblage.**

> *Regression:* the lowering of a property's value due to its neighbors
>
> *Progression:* the increasing of a property's value due to its neighbors

**Regression and progression.** In general, the worth of a better-quality property is adversely affected by the presence of a lesser-quality property. This is known as the principle of **regression.** Thus, in a neighborhood of modest homes, a structure that is larger, better maintained, or more luxurious would tend to be valued in the same range as the less lavish homes. Conversely, under the principle of **progression,** the value of a modest home would be higher if it were located among larger, fancier properties.

**Substitution.** The principle of **substitution** says that the maximum value of a property tends to be set by how much it would cost to purchase an equally desirable and valuable substitute property.

**Supply and demand.** The principle of **supply and demand** says that the value of a property depends on the number of properties available in the marketplace—the supply of the product. Other factors include the prices of other properties, the number of prospective purchasers, and the price buyers will pay.

## THE THREE APPROACHES TO VALUE

To arrive at an accurate estimate of value, appraisers traditionally use three basic valuation techniques: the sales comparison approach, the cost approach, and the income approach. The three methods serve as checks against each other. Using them narrows the range within which the final estimate of value falls. Each method is generally considered most reliable for specific types of property.

### The Sales Comparison Approach

In the **sales comparison approach** (also referred to as the market approach), an estimate of value is obtained by comparing the property being appraised (the *subject property*) with recently sold *comparable properties* (properties similar to the subject). Because no two parcels of real estate are exactly alike, each comparable property must be analyzed for differences and similarities between it and the subject property. This approach is a good example of the principle of substitution, discussed above. The sales prices of the comparables must be adjusted for any dissimilarities. The principal factors for which adjustments must be made include the following:

- *Property rights.* An adjustment must be made when less than fee simple, the full legal bundle of rights, is involved. This includes land leases, ground rents, life estates, easements, deed restrictions, and encroachments.
- *Financing concessions.* The financing terms must be considered, including adjustments for differences such as mortgage loan terms and owner financing.
- *Conditions of sale.* Adjustments must be made for motivational factors that would affect the sale, such as foreclosure, a sale between family members, or some nonmonetary incentive.
- *Date of sale.* An adjustment must be made if economic changes occur between the date of sale of the comparable property and the date of the appraisal.
- *Location.* Similar properties might differ in price from neighborhood to neighborhood or even between locations within the same neighborhood.
- *Physical features and amenities.* Physical features, such as the structure's age, size, and condition, may require adjustments. Generally, an appraiser is more interested in the outside dimensions of the property than the number of rooms or their dimensions.

The sales comparison approach is essential in almost every appraisal of real estate. It is the preferred method of appraising single-family homes, because it is considered the most reliable. The intangible benefits of home-ownership are difficult to measure unless the sales comparison approach is used. Most appraisals include a minimum of three comparable sales reflective of the subject property. An example of the sales comparison approach is shown in Table 19.1.

### The Cost Approach

The **cost approach** to value also is based on the principle of substitution. The cost approach consists of five steps:

1. Estimate the *value of the land* as if it were vacant and available to be put to its highest and best use.
2. Estimate the *current cost* of constructing buildings and improvements.

3. Estimate the *amount of accrued depreciation* resulting from the property's physical deterioration, functional obsolescence, and external depreciation.
4. *Deduct* the accrued depreciation (Step 3) from the construction cost (Step 2).
5. *Add* the estimated land value (Step 1) to the depreciated cost of the building and site improvements (Step 4) to arrive at the total property value.

The formula for calculating value using the cost approach is

$$\text{Reconstruction cost} - \text{depreciation} + \text{site value} =$$
$$\text{value of the subject property}$$

**FOR EXAMPLE**

| | | |
|---|---|---|
| Current cost of construction | = | $ 85,000 |
| Accrued depreciation | = | –$ 10,000 |
| Value of the land | = | $ 25,000 |
| Value of subject property | = | $100,000 |

In this example, the *total property value* is $100,000.

There are two ways to look at the construction cost of a building for appraisal purposes: reproduction cost and replacement cost. **Reproduction cost** is the construction cost at current prices of an *exact duplicate* of the subject improvement, including both the benefits and the drawbacks of the property. **Replacement cost new** is the cost to construct an improvement similar to the subject property using current construction methods and materials, but not necessarily an exact duplicate. Replacement cost new is more frequently used in appraising older structures because it eliminates obsolete features and takes advantage of current construction materials and techniques.

An example of the cost approach to value, applied to the same property as in Table 19.1, is shown in Table 19.2.

**Determining reproduction or replacement cost new.** An appraiser using the cost approach computes the reproduction or replacement cost of a building using one of the following four methods:

1. **Square-foot method.** The cost per square foot of a recently built comparable structure is multiplied by the number of square feet (using exterior dimensions) in the subject building. This is the most common and easiest method of cost estimation. Table 19.2 uses the square-foot method, which is also referred to as the *comparison method.* For some properties, the cost per *cubic foot* of a recently built comparable structure is multiplied by the number of cubic feet in the subject structure.
2. **Unit-in-place method.** In the unit-in-place method, the replacement cost of a structure is estimated based on the construction cost per unit of measure of individual building components, including material, labor, overhead, and builder's profit. Most components are measured in square feet, although items such as plumbing fixtures are estimated by cost. The sum of the components is the cost of the new structure.
3. **Quantity-survey method.** The quantity and quality of all materials (such as lumber, brick, and plaster), and the labor are estimated on a unit cost basis. These factors are added to indirect costs (for example,

**Table 19.1    Sales Comparison Approach to Value**

| | Subject Property: 155 Potter Dr. | Comparables | | | | |
| --- | --- | --- | --- | --- | --- | --- |
| | | **A** | **B** | **C** | **D** | **E** |
| Sales price | | $118,000 | $112,000 | $121,000 | $116,500 | $110,000 |
| Financing concessions | | none | none | none | none | none |
| Date of sale | none | current | current | current | current | current |
| Location | good | same | poorer +6,500 | same | same | same |
| Age | 6 years | same | same | same | same | same |
| Size of lot | 60′ × 135′ | same | same | larger –5,000 | same | larger –5,000 |
| Landscaping | good | same | same | same | same | same |
| Construction | brick | same | same | same | same | same |
| Style | ranch | same | same | same | same | same |
| No. of rooms | 6 | same | same | same | same | same |
| No. of bedrooms | 3 | same | same | same | same | same |
| No. of baths | 1½ | same | same | same | same | same |
| Sq. ft. of living space | 1,500 | same | same | same | same | same |
| Other space (basement) | full basement | same | same | same | same | same |
| Condition—exterior | average | better –1,500 | poorer +1,000 | better –1,500 | same | poorer +2,000 |
| Condition—interior | good | same | same | better –500 | same | same |
| Garage | 2-car attached | same | same | same | same | none +5,000 |
| Other improvements | none | none | none | none | none | none |
| Net Adjustments | | –1,500 | +7,500 | –7,000 | -0- | +2,000 |
| Adjusted Value | | $116,500 | $119,500 | $114,000 | $116,500 | $112,000 |

**Note:** The value of a feature that is present in the subject but not in the comparable property is *added* to the sales price of the comparable. Likewise, the value of a feature that is present in the comparable but not in the subject property is *subtracted*. The adjusted sales prices of the comparables represent the probable range of value of the subject property. From this range, a single market value estimate can be selected. Because the value range of the properties in the comparison chart (excluding comparables B and E) is close, and comparable D required no adjustment, an appraiser might conclude that the indicated market value of the subject is $116,500. However, appraisers use a complex process of evaluating adjustment percentages and may consider other objective factors or subjective judgments based on research.

building permit, survey, payroll, taxes, and builder's profit) to arrive at the total cost of the structure. Because it is so detailed and time consuming, this method is usually used only in appraising historical properties. It is, however, the most accurate method of appraising new construction.

4. **Index method.** A factor representing the percentage increase of construction costs up to the present time is applied to the original cost of the subject property. Because it fails to take into account individual property variables, this method is useful only as a check of the estimate reached by one of the other methods.

**Depreciation.** In a real estate appraisal, **depreciation** is a loss in value due to any cause. It refers to a condition that adversely affects the value of an improvement to real property. Land does not depreciate—it retains its value indefinitely, except in such rare cases as downzoned urban parcels, improperly developed land, or misused farmland.

Depreciation is considered to be *curable* or *incurable*, depending on the contribution of the expenditure to the value of the property. For appraisal purposes (as opposed to depreciation for tax purposes, discussed in the appendix), depreciation is divided into three classes, according to its cause:

---

**Table 19.2  Cost Approach to Value**

**Subject Property:** 155 Potter Dr.

| | | |
|---|---|---|
| **Land Valuation:** Size 60′ × 135′ @ $450 per front foot | = | $ 27,000 |
| Plus site improvements: driveway, walks, landscaping, etc. | = | 8,000 |
| Total | | $ 35,000 |

**Building Valuation:** Replacement Cost  
  1,500 sq. ft. @ $65 per sq. ft.  =  $97,500

**Less Depreciation:**

| | | |
|---|---|---|
| Physical depreciation | | |
|   Curable | | |
|     (items of deferred maintenance) | | |
|     exterior painting | $4,000 | |
|   Incurable (structural deterioration) | 9,750 | |
| Functional obsolescence | 2,000 | |
| External depreciation | -0- | |
|   Total | | −15,750 |

| | |
|---|---|
| **Depreciated Value of Building** | $ 81,750 |
| **Indicated Value by Cost Approach** | $116,750 |

1. **Physical deterioration.** *Curable:* an item in need of repair, such as painting (deferred maintenance), that is economically feasible and would result in an increase in value equal to or exceeding the cost. *Incurable:* a defect caused by physical wear and tear if its correction would not be economically feasible or contribute a comparable value to the building. The cost of a major repair may not warrant the financial investment.

2. **Functional obsolescence.** *Curable:* outmoded or unacceptable physical or design features that are no longer considered desirable by purchasers. Such features, however, could be replaced or redesigned at a cost that would be offset by the anticipated increase in ultimate value. Outmoded plumbing, for instance, is usually easily replaced. Room function may be redefined at no cost if the basic room layout allows for it. A bedroom adjacent to a kitchen, for example, may be converted to a family room. *Incurable:* currently undesirable physical or design features that could not be easily remedied because the cost of cure would be greater than its resulting increase in value. An office building that cannot be economically air-conditioned, for example, suffers from incurable functional obsolescence if the cost of adding air-conditioning is greater than its contribution to the building s value.

   *Plumbing*

3. **External obsolescence.** *Incurable:* caused by negative factors not on the subject property, such as environmental, social, or economic forces. This type of depreciation is always incurable. The loss in value cannot be reversed by spending money on the property. For example, proximity to a nuisance, such as a polluting factory or a deteriorating neighborhood, is one factor that could not be cured by the owner of the subject property.

The easiest but least precise way to determine depreciation is the **straight-line method,** also called the *economic age-life method.* Depreciation is assumed to occur at an even rate over a structure s **economic life,** the period

***Table 19.3*** *Income Capitalization Approach to Value*

| | |
|---|---|
| Potential Gross Annual Income | $60,000 |
| Market rent (100% capacity) | |
| Income from other sources | + 600 |
| (vending machines and pay phones) | $60,600 |
| | |
| Less vacancy and collection losses (estimated) @4% | −2,424 |
| Effective Gross Income | $58,176 |

**Expenses:**

| | | |
|---|---|---|
| Real estate taxes | $9,000 | |
| Insurance | 1,000 | |
| Heat | 2,800 | |
| Maintenance | 6,400 | |
| Utilities, electricity, water, gas | 800 | |
| Repairs | 1,200 | |
| Decorating | 1,400 | |
| Replacement of equipment | 800 | |
| Legal and accounting | 600 | |
| Management | 3,000 | |
| **Total** | | $27,000 |
| **Annual Net Operating Income** | | $31,176 |

Capitalization rate = 10% (overall rate)

Capitalization of annual net income: $\dfrac{\$31.176}{.10}$

Indicated Value by Income Approach = $311,760

---

during which it is expected to remain useful for its original intended purpose. The property's cost is divided by the number of years of its expected economic life to derive the amount of annual depreciation.

For instance, a $120,000 property may have a land value of $30,000 and an improvement value of $90,000. If the improvement is expected to last 60 years, the annual straight-line depreciation would be $1,500 ($90,000 divided by 60 years). Such depreciation can be calculated as an annual dollar amount or as a percentage of a property's improvements.

The cost approach is most helpful in the appraisal of newer or special-purpose buildings such as schools, churches, and public buildings. Such properties are difficult to appraise using other methods because there are seldom enough local sales to use as comparables and because the properties do not ordinarily generate income.

Much of the functional obsolescence and all of the external depreciation can be evaluated only by considering the actions of buyers in the marketplace.

## The Income Approach

The **income approach** to value is based on the present value of the rights to future income. It assumes that the income generated by a property will determine the property's value. The income approach is used for valuation of income-producing properties such as apartment buildings, office buildings and shopping centers. In estimating value using the income approach, an appraiser must take five steps, illustrated in Table 19.3.

1. Estimate annual *potential gross income.* An estimate of economic rental income must be made based on market studies. Current rental income may not reflect the current market rental rates, especially in the case of short-term leases or leases about to terminate. Potential income includes other income to the property from such sources as vending machines, parking fees, and laundry machines.

2. Deduct an appropriate allowance for vacancy and rent loss, based on the appraiser's experience, and arrive at *effective gross income.*

3. Deduct the annual *operating expenses,* enumerated in Table 19.3, from the effective gross income to arrive at the annual *net operating income* (NOI). Management costs are always included, even if the current owner manages the property. Mortgage payments (principal and interest) are *debt service* and not considered operating expenses.

4. Estimate the price a typical investor would pay for the income produced by this particular type and class of property. This is done by estimating the rate of return (or yield) that an investor will demand for the investment of capital in this type of building. This rate of return is called the **capitalization** (or "cap") **rate** and is determined by comparing the relationship of net operating income to the sales prices of similar properties that have sold in the current market. For example, a comparable property that is producing an annual net income of $15,000 is sold for $187,500. The capitalization rate is $15,000 divided by $187,500, or eight percent. If other comparable properties sold at prices that yielded substantially the same rate, it may be concluded that eight percent is the rate that the appraiser should apply to the subject property.

5. Apply the capitalization rate to the property's annual net operating income to arrive at the estimate of the property's value.

*[handwritten margin notes: "Most Important", "Multi Units or Apartments"]*

With the appropriate capitalization rate and the projected annual net operating income, the appraiser can obtain an indication of value by the income approach.

This formula and its variations are important in dealing with income property:

Income ÷ Rate = Value    Income ÷ Value = Rate    Value × Rate = Income

These formulas may be illustrated graphically as

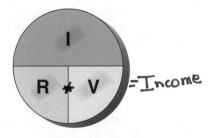

*[handwritten note: "=Income"]*

Net operating income ÷ Capitalization rate = Value

Example: $18,000 income ÷ 9% cap rate = $200,000 value or
$18,000 income ÷ 8% cap rate = $225,000 value

Note the relationship between the rate and value. As the rate goes down, the value increases.

A very simplified version of the computations used in applying the income approach is illustrated in Table 19.3.

| Table 19.4 | *Gross Rent Multiplier* - single | | | |
|---|---|---|---|---|
| | **Comparable No.** | **Sales Price** | **Monthly Rent** | **GRM** |
| | 1 | $93,600 | $650 | 144 |
| | 2 | 78,500 | 450 | 174 |
| | 3 | 95,500 | 675 | 141 |
| | 4 | 82,000 | 565 | 145 |
| | Subject | ? | 625 | ? |

Note: Based on an analysis of these comparisons, a GRM of 145 seems reasonable for homes in this area. In the opinion of an appraiser, then, the estimated value of the subject property would be $625 × 145, or $90,625.

**Gross rent or gross income multipliers.** Certain properties, such as single-family homes and two-unit buildings, are not purchased primarily for income. As a substitute for a more elaborate income capitalization analysis, the **gross rent multiplier** (GRM) and **gross income multiplier** (GIM) are often used in the appraisal process. Each relates the sales price of a property to its rental income.

Because single-family residences usually produce only rental incomes, the gross rent multiplier is used. This relates a sales price to *monthly* rental income. However, commercial and industrial properties generate income from many other sources (rent, concessions, escalator clause income and so forth), and they are valued using their *annual* income from all sources.

The formulas are as follows:

1. For five or more residential units, commercial, or industrial property:
   Sales price ÷ Gross Income = Gross Income (Multiplier) (GIM)

or

2. For one to four residential units:
   Sales price ÷ Gross Rent = Gross Rent Multiplier (GRM)

For example, if a home recently sold for $82,000 and its monthly rental income was $650, the GRM for the property would be computed as follows:

$82,000 ÷ $650 = 126.2 GRM

To establish an accurate GRM, an appraiser must have recent sales and rental data from at least four properties that are similar to the subject property. The resulting GRM then can be applied to the estimated fair market rental of the subject property to arrive at its market value. The formula would be

Rental income × GRM = Estimated market value

Table 19.4 shows some examples of GRM comparisons.

**Reconciliation** When the three approaches to value are applied to the same property, they normally produce three separate indications of value. (For instance, compare Table 19.1 with Table 19.2.) **Reconciliation** is the art of analyzing and effectively weighing the findings from the three approaches.

The process of reconciliation is more complicated than simply taking the average of the three estimates of value. An average implies that the data and logic applied to each of the approaches are equally valid and reliable and should therefore be given equal weight. In fact, however, certain approaches are more valid and reliable with some kinds of properties than with others.

For example, in appraising a home, the income approach is rarely valid, and the cost approach is of limited value unless the home is relatively new. Therefore, the sales comparison approach is usually given greatest weight in valuing single-family residences. In the appraisal of income or investment property, the income approach normally is given the greatest weight. In the appraisal of churches, libraries, museums, schools, and other special-use properties where little or no income or sales revenue is generated, the cost approach usually is assigned the greatest weight. From this analysis, or reconciliation, a single estimate of market value is produced.

## THE APPRAISAL PROCESS

Although appraising is not an exact or a precise science, the key to an accurate appraisal lies in the methodical collection and analysis of data. The appraisal process is an orderly set of procedures used to collect and analyze data to arrive at an ultimate value conclusion. The data are divided into two basic classes:

1. *General data,* covering the nation, region, city and neighborhood. Of particular importance is the neighborhood, where an appraiser finds the physical, economic, social and political influences that directly affect the value and potential of the subject property.
2. *Specific data,* covering details of the subject property as well as comparative data relating to costs, sales, and income and expenses of properties similar to and competitive with the subject property.

Figure 19.1 outlines the steps an appraiser takes in carrying out an appraisal assignment.

Once the approaches have been reconciled and an opinion of value has been reached, the appraiser prepares a report for the client. Note that the appraisal is valid only for the day it is prepared. The report should

- identify the real estate and real property interest being appraised;
- state the purpose and intended use of the appraisal;
- define the value to be estimated;
- state the effective date of the value and the date of the report;
- state the extent of the process of collecting, confirming, and reporting the data;
- list all assumptions and limiting conditions that affect the analysis, opinion and conclusions of value;
- describe the information considered, the appraisal procedures followed, and the reasoning that supports the report's conclusions (if an approach was excluded, the report should explain why);
- describe (if necessary or appropriate) the appraiser's opinion of the highest and best use of the real estate;
- describe any additional information that may be appropriate to show compliance with the specific guidelines established in the Uniform Standards of Professional Appraisal Practice (USPAP) or to clearly identify and explain any departures from these guidelines; and
- include a signed certification, as required by the Uniform Standards.

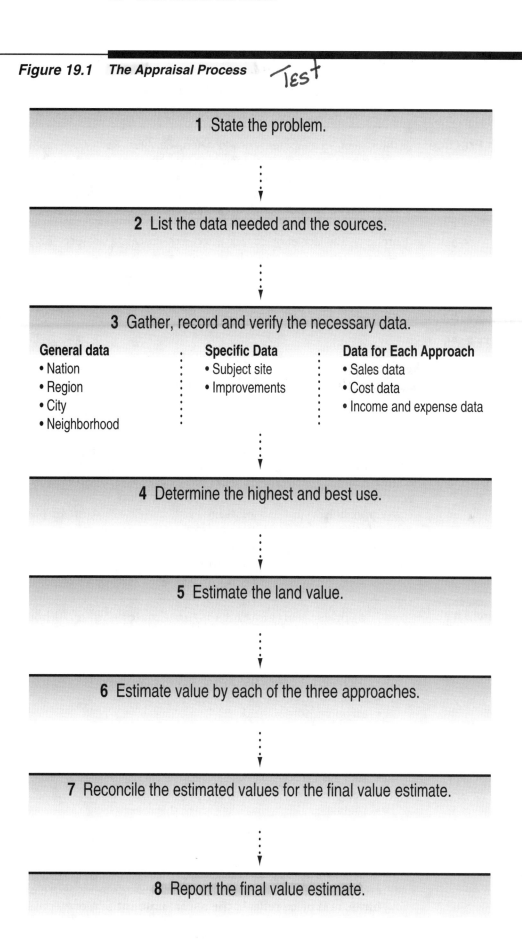

**Figure 19.1    The Appraisal Process**    Test

**1** State the problem.

**2** List the data needed and the sources.

**3** Gather, record and verify the necessary data.

**General data**
- Nation
- Region
- City
- Neighborhood

**Specific Data**
- Subject site
- Improvements

**Data for Each Approach**
- Sales data
- Cost data
- Income and expense data

**4** Determine the highest and best use.

**5** Estimate the land value.

**6** Estimate value by each of the three approaches.

**7** Reconcile the estimated values for the final value estimate.

**8** Report the final value estimate.

Figure 19.2 shows the *Uniform Residential Appraisal Report*, the form required by many government agencies. It illustrates the types of detailed information required of an appraisal of residential property.

**In Practice**     The role of an appraiser is not to determine value. Rather, an appraiser develops a supportable and objective report about the value of the subject property. The appraiser relies on experience and expertise in valuation theories to evaluate market data. The appraiser does not establish the property's worth; instead, he or she verifies what the market indicates. This is important to remember, particularly when dealing with a property owner who may lack objectivity about the realistic value of his or her property. The lack of objectivity also can complicate a salesperson's ability to list the property within the most probable range of market value.

**KEY TERMS**

| | | |
|---|---|---|
| anticipation | functional | reconciliation |
| appraisal | obsolescence | regression |
| appraiser | gross income | replacement cost |
| assemblage | multiplier | reproduction cost |
| capitalization rate | gross rent multiplier | sales comparison |
| change | highest and best use | approach |
| comparable | income approach | square-foot method |
| competition | index method | straight-line method |
| conformity | market value | substitution |
| contribution | physical deterioration | supply and demand |
| cost approach | plottage | unit-in-place method |
| depreciation | progression | value |
| economic life | quantity-survey | |
| external obsolescence | method | |

**SUMMARY**

- To appraise real estate means to estimate its value. Although many types of value exist, the most common objective of an appraisal is to estimate market value—the most probable sales price of a property.
- Basic to appraising are certain underlying economic principles, such as:
  - highest and best use,
  - substitution,
  - supply and demand,
  - conformity,
  - anticipation,
  - increasing and diminishing returns,
  - regression,
  - progression,
  - plottage,
  - contribution,
  - competition, and
  - change.
- Appraisals are concerned with values, prices, and costs. Value is an estimate of future benefits, cost represents a measure of past expenditures, and price reflects the actual amount of money paid for a property.

- A professional appraiser analyzes a property through three approaches to value:
  - the sales comparison approach: the value of the subject property is compared with the values of others like it that have sold recently. Because no two properties are exactly alike, adjustments must be made to account for any differences;
  - the cost approach: an appraiser calculates the cost of building a similar structure on a similar site. The appraiser then subtracts depreciation (losses in value), which reflects the differences between new properties of this type and the present condition of the subject property; and
  - the income approach: an analysis based on the relationship between the rate of return that an investor requires and the net income that a property produces.
- An informal version of the income approach, called the *gross rent multiplier* (GRM), may be used to estimate the value of single-family residential properties that are not usually rented, but could be.
  - The GRM is computed by dividing the sales price of a property by its gross monthly rent.
  - For commercial or industrial property, a gross income multiplier (GIM), based on annual income from all sources, may be used.
- Normally, the application of the three approaches results in three different estimates of value. In the process of reconciliation, the validity and reliability of each approach are weighed objectively to arrive at the single best and most supportable estimate of value.

**Real-Life Real Estate**

1. Assume you are appraising your house (or one you have access to). How would you define the market area where the best comparables are found?
2. "Value" normally means "market value." What other "values" might be the purpose of an appraisal and what impact might those other purposes have on the appraisal process?

Application #4: Complete the Uniform Residential Appraisal Report for the Seller's property based on the description from Application #1 (found in Chapter 7) and the contract terms developed in Application #2 (found in Chapter 12) for the lender used in Application #3 (found in Chapter 16).

### Figure 19.2 Uniform Residential Appraisal Report

**Property Description**

## UNIFORM RESIDENTIAL APPRAISAL REPORT  File No. _____

**SUBJECT**

| Property Address | City | State | Zip Code |
|---|---|---|---|

Legal Description _____ County _____

Assessor's Parcel No. _____ Tax Year ___ R.E. Taxes $ ___ Special Assessments $ ___

Borrower ___ Current Owner ___ Occupant: ☐ Owner ☐ Tenant ☐ Vacant

Property rights appraised ☐ Fee Simple ☐ Leasehold  Project Type ☐ PUD ☐ Condominium (HUD/VA only)  HOA$ ___ /Mo.

Neighborhood or Project Name ___ Map Reference ___ Census Tract ___

Sale Price $ ___ Date of Sale ___ Description and $ amount of loan charges/concessions to be paid by seller ___

Lender/Client ___ Address ___

Appraiser ___ Address ___

**NEIGHBORHOOD**

| Location | ☐ Urban | ☐ Suburban | ☐ Rural | Predominant occupancy | Single family housing | Present land use % | Land use change |
|---|---|---|---|---|---|---|---|

| | | | | | PRICE $(000) | AGE (yrs) | | |
| Built up | ☐ Over 75% | ☐ 25-75% | ☐ Under 25% | | | | One family | ☐ Not likely ☐ Likely |
| Growth rate | ☐ Rapid | ☐ Stable | ☐ Slow | ☐ Owner | Low | | 2-4 family | ☐ In process |
| Property values | ☐ Increasing | ☐ Stable | ☐ Declining | ☐ Tenant | High | | Multi-family | To: ___ |
| Demand/supply | ☐ Shortage | ☐ In balance | ☐ Over supply | ☐ Vacant (0-5%) | Predominant | | Commercial | |
| Marketing time | ☐ Under 3 mos. | ☐ 3-6 mos. | ☐ Over 6 mos. | ☐ Vacant (over 5%) | | | | |

**Note: Race and the racial composition of the neighborhood are not appraisal factors.**

Neighborhood boundaries and characteristics: ___

Factors that affect the marketability of the properties in the neighborhood (proximity to employment and amenities, employment stability, appeal to market, etc.): ___

Market conditions in the subject neighborhood (including support for the above conclusions related to the trend of property values, demand/supply, and marketing time - - such as data on competitive properties for sale in the neighborhood, description of the prevalence of sales and financing concessions, etc.): ___

**PUD**

Project Information for PUDs (If applicable) - - Is the developer/builder in control of the Home Owners' Association (HOA)? ☐ Yes ☐ No

Approximate total number of units in the subject project ___ Approximate total number of units for sale in the subject project ___

Describe common elements and recreational facilities: ___

**SITE**

Dimensions ___ Topography ___

Site area ___ Corner Lot ☐ Yes ☐ No  Size ___

Specific zoning classification and description ___ Shape ___

Zoning compliance ☐ Legal ☐ Legal nonconforming (Grandfathered use) ☐ Illegal ☐ No zoning  Drainage ___

Highest & best use as improved: ☐ Present use ☐ Other use (explain)  View ___

| Utilities | Public | Other | Off-site Improvements | Type | Public | Private | Landscaping ___ |
|---|---|---|---|---|---|---|---|
| Electricity | | | Street | | | | Driveway Surface ___ |
| Gas | | | Curb/gutter | | | | Apparent easements ___ |
| Water | | | Sidewalk | | | | FEMA Special Flood Hazard Area ☐ Yes ☐ No |
| Sanitary sewer | | | Street lights | | | | FEMA Zone ___ Map Date ___ |
| Storm sewer | | | Alley | | | | FEMA Map No. ___ |

Comments (apparent adverse easements, encroachments, special assessments, slide areas, illegal or legal nonconforming zoning use, etc.): ___

**DESCRIPTION OF IMPROVEMENTS**

| GENERAL DESCRIPTION | EXTERIOR DESCRIPTION | FOUNDATION | BASEMENT | INSULATION |
|---|---|---|---|---|
| No. of Units ___ | Foundation ___ | Slab ___ | Area Sq. Ft. ___ | Roof ___ |
| No. of Stories ___ | Exterior Walls ___ | Crawl Space ___ | % Finished ___ | Ceiling ___ |
| Type (Det./Att.) ___ | Roof Surface ___ | Basement ___ | Ceiling ___ | Walls ___ |
| Design (Style) ___ | Gutters & Dwnspts. ___ | Sump Pump ___ | Walls ___ | Floor ___ |
| Existing/Proposed ___ | Window Type ___ | Dampness ___ | Floor ___ | None ___ |
| Age (Yrs.) ___ | Storm/Screens ___ | Settlement ___ | Outside Entry ___ | Unknown ___ |
| Effective Age (Yrs.) ___ | Manufactured House ___ | Infestation ___ | | |

| ROOMS | Foyer | Living | Dining | Kitchen | Den | Family Rm. | Rec. Rm. | Bedrooms | # Baths | Laundry | Other | Area Sq. Ft. |
|---|---|---|---|---|---|---|---|---|---|---|---|---|
| Basement | | | | | | | | | | | | |
| Level 1 | | | | | | | | | | | | |
| Level 2 | | | | | | | | | | | | |

Finished area **above** grade contains: ___ Rooms; ___ Bedroom(s); ___ Bath(s); ___ Square Feet of Gross Living Area

| INTERIOR | Materials/Condition | HEATING | KITCHEN EQUIP. | ATTIC | AMENITIES | CAR STORAGE: |
|---|---|---|---|---|---|---|
| Floors | | Type | Refrigerator ☐ | None ☐ | Fireplace(s) # ☐ | None ☐ |
| Walls | | Fuel | Range/Oven ☐ | Stairs ☐ | Patio ☐ | Garage ☐ # of cars ___ |
| Trim/Finish | | Condition | Disposal ☐ | Drop Stair ☐ | Deck ☐ | Attached ___ |
| Bath Floor | | COOLING | Dishwasher ☐ | Scuttle ☐ | Porch ☐ | Detached ___ |
| Bath Wainscot | | Central | Fan/Hood ☐ | Floor ☐ | Fence ☐ | Built-In ___ |
| Doors | | Other | Microwave ☐ | Heated ☐ | Pool ☐ | Carport ___ |
| | | Condition | Washer/Dryer ☐ | Finished ☐ | | Driveway ___ |

**COMMENTS**

Additional features (special energy efficient items, etc.): ___

Condition of the improvements, depreciation (physical, functional, and external), repairs needed, quality of construction, remodeling/additions, etc.: ___

Adverse environmental conditions (such as, but not limited to, hazardous wastes, toxic substances, etc.) present in the improvements, on the site, or in the immediate vicinity of the subject property.: ___

**Figure 19.2   Uniform Residential Appraisal Report (Continued)**

Valuation Section

**UNIFORM RESIDENTIAL APPRAISAL REPORT**   File No.

**COST APPROACH**

ESTIMATED SITE VALUE . . . . . . . . . . . . . . . . . . . . = $ _____
ESTIMATED REPRODUCTION COST-NEW-OF IMPROVEMENTS:
Dwelling _____ Sq. Ft @ $ _____ = $ _____
_____ Sq. Ft @ $ _____ = _____
= _____
Garage/Carport _____ Sq. Ft @ $ _____ = _____
Total Estimated Cost New . . . . . . . . . . . = $ _____
Less       Physical      Functional      External
Depreciation _____ | _____ | _____ = $ _____
Depreciated Value of Improvements . . . . . . . . . . . . . . . = $ _____
"As-is" Value of Site Improvements . . . . . . . . = $ _____
INDICATED VALUE BY COST APPROACH . . . . . . . . . . . = $

Comments on Cost Approach (such as, source of cost estimate, site value, square foot calculation and for HUD, VA and FmHA, the estimated remaining economic life of the property): _____

**SALES COMPARISON ANALYSIS**

| ITEM | SUBJECT | COMPARABLE NO. 1 | | COMPARABLE NO. 2 | | COMPARABLE NO. 3 | |
|---|---|---|---|---|---|---|---|
| Address | | | | | | | |
| Proximity to Subject | | | | | | | |
| Sales Price | $ | $ | | $ | | $ | |
| Price/Gross Liv. Area | $ ☑ | $ ☑ | | $ ☑ | | $ ☑ | |
| Data and/or Verification Source | | | | | | | |
| VALUE ADJUSTMENTS | DESCRIPTION | DESCRIPTION | + (-) $ Adjustment | DESCRIPTION | + (-) $ Adjustment | DESCRIPTION | + (-) $ Adjustment |
| Sales or Financing Concessions | | | | | | | |
| Date of Sale/Time | | | | | | | |
| Location | | | | | | | |
| Leasehold/Fee Simple | | | | | | | |
| Site | | | | | | | |
| View | | | | | | | |
| Design and Appeal | | | | | | | |
| Quality of Construction | | | | | | | |
| Age | | | | | | | |
| Condition | | | | | | | |
| Above Grade Room Count | Total Bdrms Baths | Total Bdrms Baths | | Total Bdrms Baths | | Total Bdrms Baths | |
| Gross Living Area | Sq. Ft. | Sq. Ft. | | Sq. Ft. | | Sq. Ft. | |
| Basement & Finished Rooms Below Grade | | | | | | | |
| Functional Utility | | | | | | | |
| Heating/Cooling | | | | | | | |
| Energy Efficient Items | | | | | | | |
| Garage/Carport | | | | | | | |
| Porch, Patio, Deck, Fireplace(s), etc. | | | | | | | |
| Fence, Pool, etc. | | | | | | | |
| Net Adj. (total) | | + - $ | | + - $ | | + - $ | |
| Adjusted Sales Price of Comparable | | | $ | | $ | | $ |

Comments on Sales Comparison (including the subject property's compatibility to the neighborhood, etc.): _____

| ITEM | SUBJECT | COMPARABLE NO. 1 | COMPARABLE NO. 2 | COMPARABLE NO. 3 |
|---|---|---|---|---|
| Date, Price and Data Source, for prior sales within year of appraisal | | | | |

Analysis of any current agreement of sale, option, or listing of the subject property and analysis of any prior sales of subject and comparables within one year of the date of appraisal:

**RECONCILIATION**

INDICATED VALUE BY SALES COMPARISON APPROACH . . . . . . . . . . . . . . . . . . . . . . . . . . . . . . . . . . . . . . . . . $_____
INDICATED VALUE BY INCOME APPROACH  (If Applicable) Estimated Market Rent $_____ /Mo. x Gross Rent Multiplier _____ = $
This appraisal is made ☐ "as is" ☐ subject to the repairs, alterations, inspections or conditions listed below ☐ subject to completion per plans and specifications.
Conditions of Appraisal: _____

Final Reconciliation: _____

The purpose of this appraisal is to estimate the market value of the real property that is the subject of this report, based on the above conditions and the certification, contingent and limiting conditions, and market value definition that are stated in the attached Freddie Mac Form 439/Fannie Mae Form 1004B (Revised _____).
I (WE) ESTIMATE THE MARKET VALUE, AS DEFINED, OF THE REAL PROPERTY THAT IS THE SUBJECT OF THIS REPORT, AS OF _____
(WHICH IS THE DATE OF INSPECTION AND THE EFFECTIVE DATE OF THIS REPORT) TO BE $ _____

| APPRAISER: | SUPERVISORY APPRAISER (ONLY IF REQUIRED): | |
|---|---|---|
| Signature | Signature | ☐ Did ☐ Did Not |
| Name | Name | Inspect Property |
| Date Report Signed | Date Report Signed | |
| State Certification # ___ State | State Certification # ___ State | |
| Or State License # ___ State | Or State License # ___ State | |

Freddie Mac Form 70  6-93        10 CH.        PAGE 2 OF 2        Fannie Mae Form 1004 6-93

# QUESTIONS

1. In Ohio, a real estate appraiser
   a. must be licensed by the state.
   b. must pass a written examination and be certified.
   c. may or may not be licensed or certified.
   d. may be licensed or certified without taking an examination.

2. A state-licensed residential real estate appraiser may appraise which of the following types of property?
   a. All types of real property located in the state of Ohio
   b. Noncomplex one- to four-unit single-family residential real estate valued under $1 million
   c. Complex one- to four-unit single-family residential real estate valued over $250,000
   d. Any residential real property located in the county in which he or she resides

3. *L* is a certified real estate appraiser. She is convicted of fraudulently reporting a low appraised value on certain property so that the loan would be denied and her friend *S* could step in and buy the property for less money. She is also convicted of robbing a bank. *L*'s license will
   a. not be revoked if she takes and passes the licensing examination.
   b. be revoked because of the fraud conviction, but not because of the robbery conviction.
   c. not be revoked; *L* did not personally benefit from the fraud, and bank robbery is not an appraisal-related felony.
   d. be revoked because of both the fraud and robbery convictions.

4. Which of the following appraisal methods uses a rate of investment return?
   a. Sales comparison approach
   b. Cost approach
   c. Income approach
   d. Gross income multiplier method

5. The elements of value include which of the following?
   a. Competition
   b. Scarcity
   c. Anticipation
   d. Balance

6. 457 and 459 Tarpepper Street are adjacent vacant lots, each worth approximately $50,000. If their owner sells them as a single lot, however, the combined parcel will be worth $120,000. What principle does this illustrate?
   a. Substitution
   b. Plottage
   c. Regression
   d. Progression

7. The amount of money a property commands in the marketplace is its
   a. intrinsic value.
   b. market value.
   c. subjective value.
   d. book value.

8. *H* constructs an eight-bedroom brick house with a tennis court, a greenhouse, and an indoor pool in a neighborhood of modest two-bedroom and three-bedroom frame houses on narrow lots. The value of *H*'s house is likely to be affected by what principle?
   a. Progression
   b. Assemblage
   c. Change
   d. Regression

9. In Question 8, the owners of the lesser-valued houses in *H*'s immediate area may find that the values of their homes are affected by what principle?
   a. Progression
   b. Increasing returns
   c. Competition
   d. Regression

10. For appraisal purposes, accrued depreciation is caused by all of the following *EXCEPT*
    a. functional obsolescence.
    b. physical deterioration.
    c. external obsolescence.
    d. accelerated depreciation.

11. Reconciliation refers to which of the following?
    a. Loss of value due to any cause
    b. Separating the value of the land from the total value of the property to compute depreciation
    c. Analyzing the results obtained by the different approaches to value to determine a final estimate of value
    d. Process by which an appraiser determines the highest and best use for a parcel of land

12. One method an appraiser can use to determine a building's cost as new construction involves the estimated cost of the materials needed to build the structure, plus labor and indirect costs. This is called the
    a. square-foot method.
    b. quantity-survey method.
    c. cubic-foot method.
    d. unit-in-place method.

13. If a property's annual net income is $24,000 and it is valued at $300,000, what is its capitalization rate?
    a. 8 percent           c. 12.5 percent
    b. 10.5 percent        d. 15 percent

14. Certain figures must be determined by an appraiser before value can be computed by the income approach. All of the following are required for this process *EXCEPT*
    a. annual net operating income.
    b. capitalization rate.
    c. accrued depreciation.
    d. annual gross income.

15. *J*, an appraiser, is asked to determine the value of an existing strip shopping center. *J* probably will give the most weight to which approach to value?
    a. Cost approach
    b. Sales comparison approach
    c. Income approach
    d. Index method

16. The market value of a parcel of real estate is
    a. an estimate of its future benefits.
    b. the amount of money paid for the property.
    c. an estimate of the most probable price it should bring.
    d. its value without improvements.

17. Capitalization is the process by which annual net operating income is used to
    a. determine cost.
    b. estimate value.
    c. establish depreciation.
    d. determine potential tax value.

18. From the reproduction or replacement cost of a building, the appraiser deducts depreciation, which represents
    a. the remaining economic life of the building.
    b. remodeling costs to increase rentals.
    c. loss of value due to any cause.
    d. costs to modernize the building.

19. The effective gross annual income from a property is $112,000. Total expenses for this year are $53,700. What capitalization rate was used to obtain a valuation of $542,325?
    a. 9.75 percent        c. 10.50 percent
    b. 10.25 percent       d. 10.75 percent

20. All of the following factors would be important in comparing properties under the sales comparison approach to value *EXCEPT* differences in
    a. dates of sale.
    b. financing terms.
    c. appearance and condition.
    d. original cost.

21. The selling price of Trendsetter Terrace was $240,000. The building is currently five years old and has an estimated remaining useful life of 60 years. What is the property's total depreciation to date?
    a. $14,364             c. $48,000
    b. $20,000             d. $54,000

22. In Question 21, what is the current value of Trendsetter Terrace?
    a. $235,636            c. $192,000
    b. $220,000            d. $186,000

23. The appraised value of a residence with four bedrooms and one bathroom would probably be reduced because of
    a. external obsolescence.
    b. functional obsolescence.
    c. curable physical deterioration.
    d. incurable physical deterioration.

24. *R*, an appraiser, estimates that it would require 4,000 square feet of concrete, 10,000 square feet of lumber, and $15,000 worth of copper pipe to replace a structure. *R* also estimates other factors, such as material, labor, overhead, and builder's profit. Which method of determining reproduction or replacement cost is *R* using?
    a. Square-foot method
    b. Quantity-survey method
    c. Index method
    d. Unit-in-place method

25. An appraisal is valid
    a. for 60 days.
    b. on the day it is made.
    c. for six months.
    d. for one year.

26. An appraiser is most concerned with the
    a. number of rooms in a house.
    b. size of the rooms in a house.
    c. height of the ceilings.
    d. outside dimensions of the property.

# CHAPTER 20

# Land-Use Controls

## LAND-USE CONTROLS

Broad though they may be, the rights of real estate ownership are not absolute. Land use is controlled and regulated through public and private restrictions and through the public ownership of land by federal, state, and local governments.

Over the years, the government's policy has been to encourage private ownership of land. Home ownership is often referred to as the *American Dream.* It is necessary, however, for a certain amount of land to be owned by the government for such uses as municipal buildings, state legislative houses, schools, and military stations. Government ownership may also serve the public interest through urban renewal efforts, public housing, and streets and highways. Often, the only way to ensure that enough land is set aside for recreational and conservation purposes is through direct government ownership in the form of national and state parks and forest preserves. Beyond this sort of direct ownership of land, however, most government controls on property occur at the local level.

The states' *police power* is their inherent authority to create regulations needed to protect the public health, safety, and welfare. The states delegate to counties and local municipalities the authority to enact ordinances in keeping with general laws. The increasing demands placed on finite natural resources have made it necessary for cities, towns, and villages to increase their limitations on the private use of real estate. There are now controls over noise, air, and water pollution as well as population density.

## THE COMPREHENSIVE PLAN

Local governments establish development goals by creating a **comprehensive plan.** This is also referred to as a *master plan.* Municipalities and counties develop plans to control growth and development. The plan includes the municipality's objectives for the future and the strategies and timing for those objectives to be implemented. For instance, a community may want to ensure that social and economic needs are balanced with environmental and aesthetic concerns. The comprehensive plan usually includes the following basic elements:

- *Land use*—that is, a determination of how much land may be proposed for residence, industry, business, agriculture, traffic and transit facilities, utilities, community facilities, parks and recreational facilities, floodplains, and areas of special hazards
- *Housing needs* of present and anticipated residents, including rehabilitation of declining neighborhoods as well as new residential developments
- *Movement of people and goods*, including highways and public transit, parking facilities, and pedestrian and bikeway systems
- *Community facilities and utilities*, such as schools, libraries, hospitals, recreational facilities, fire and police stations, water resources, sewerage and waste treatment and disposal, storm drainage, and flood management
- *Energy conservation* to reduce energy consumption and promote the use of renewable energy sources

The preparation of a comprehensive plan involves surveys, studies, and analyses of housing, demographic, and economic characteristics and trends. The municipality's planning activities may be coordinated with other government bodies and private interests to achieve orderly growth and development.

**FOR EXAMPLE** After the Great Chicago Fire of 1871 reduced most of the city's downtown to rubble and ash, the city engaged planner Daniel Burnham to lay out a design for Chicago's future. The resulting Burnham Plan of orderly boulevards linking a park along Lake Michigan with other large parks and public spaces throughout the city established an ideal urban space. The plan is still being implemented today.

## ZONING

Zoning ordinances are local laws that implement the comprehensive plan and regulate and control the use of land and structures within designated land-use districts. If the comprehensive plan is the big picture, zoning is the details. Zoning affects such things as

- permitted uses of each parcel of land,
- lot sizes,
- types of structures,
- building heights,
- setbacks (the minimum distance away from streets or sidewalks that structures may be built),
- style and appearance of structures,
- density (the ratio of land area to structure area), and
- protection of natural resources.

Zoning ordinances cannot be static; they must remain flexible to meet the changing needs of society.

**FOR EXAMPLE** In many large cities, factories and warehouses sit empty. Some cities have begun changing the zoning ordinances for such properties to permit new residential or commercial developments in areas once zoned strictly for heavy industrial use. Coupled with tax incentives, the changes lure developers back into the cities. The resulting housing is modern, conveniently located, and affordable. Simple zoning changes can help revitalize whole neighborhoods in big cities.

No nationwide or statewide zoning ordinances exist. Rather, zoning powers are conferred on municipal governments by state **enabling acts.** State and federal governments may, however, regulate land use through special legislation such as scenic easement, coastal management, and environmental laws.

## Zoning Objectives

Zoning ordinances have traditionally divided land use into residential, commercial, industrial, and agricultural classifications. These land-use areas are further divided into subclasses. For example, residential areas may be subdivided to provide for detached single-family dwellings, semidetached structures containing not more than four dwelling units, walkup apartments, highrise apartments, and so forth.

To meet both the growing demand for a variety of housing types and the need for innovative residential and nonresidential development, municipalities are adopting ordinances for subdivisions and planned residential developments. Some municipalities also use **buffer zones,** such as landscaped parks and playgrounds, to screen residential areas from nonresidential zones. Certain types of zoning that focus on special land-use objectives are used in some areas. These include

- *bulk zoning* to control density and avoid overcrowding by imposing restrictions such as setbacks, building heights, and percentage of open area or by restricting new construction projects;
- *aesthetic zoning* to specify certain types of architecture for new buildings; and
- *incentive zoning* to ensure that certain uses are incorporated into developments, such as requiring the street floor of an office building to house retail establishments.

**Constitutional issues and zoning ordinances.** Zoning can be a highly controversial issue. Among other things, it often raises questions of constitutional law. The preamble of the U.S. Constitution provides for the promotion of the general welfare, but the Fourteenth Amendment prevents the states from depriving "any person of life, liberty, or *property,* without due process of law." How is a local government to enact zoning ordinances that protect public safety and welfare without violating the constitutional rights of property owners?

Any land-use legislation that is destructive, unreasonable, arbitrary, or confiscatory usually is considered void. Furthermore, zoning ordinances must not violate the various provisions of the constitution of the state in which the real estate is located. Tests commonly applied in determining the validity of ordinances require that the

- power be exercised in a *reasonable manner;*
- provisions be *clear and specific;*
- ordinances be *nondiscriminatory;*
- ordinances *promote public health, safety and general welfare* under the police power concept; and
- ordinances *apply to all property in a similar manner.*

**Taking.** The concept of **taking** comes from the takings clause of the Fifth Amendment to the U.S. Constitution. The clause reads, "*nor shall private property be taken for public use, without just compensation.*" This means that when land is taken for public use through the government's power of eminent domain or condemnation, the owner must be compensated. In general, no land is exempt from government seizure. The rule, however, is that the government cannot seize land without paying for it. This payment is referred to as *just compensation*—compensation that is just, or fair.

Of course, it is sometimes very difficult to determine what level of compensation is fair in any particular situation. The compensation may be negotiated between the owner and the government, or the owner may seek a court judgment setting the amount.

**In Practice**    One method used to determine just compensation is the *before-and-after method*. This method is used primarily where a portion of an owner's property is seized for public use. The value of the owner's remaining property after the taking is subtracted from the value of the whole parcel before the taking. The result is the total amount of compensation due to the owner.

## Zoning Permits

Zoning laws are generally enforced through the use of permits. Compliance with zoning can be monitored by requiring that property owners obtain permits before they begin any development. A permit will not be issued unless a proposed development conforms to the permitted zoning, among other requirements. Zoning permits usually are required before building permits can be issued.

**Zoning hearing board.** Zoning hearing boards (or zoning boards of appeal) have been established in most communities to hear complaints about the effects a zoning ordinance may have on specific parcels of property. Petitions for variances or exceptions to the zoning law may be presented to an appeal board.

**Nonconforming use.** Frequently, a lot or an improvement does not conform to the zoning use because it existed before the enactment or amendment of the zoning ordinance. Such a **nonconforming use** may be allowed to continue legally as long as it complies with the regulations governing nonconformities in the local ordinance or until the improvement is destroyed or torn down or the current use is abandoned. If the nonconforming use is allowed to continue indefinitely, it is considered to be grandfathered into the new zoning.

**F**OR EXAMPLE Under Pleasantville's old zoning ordinances, the C&E Store was well within a commercial zone. When the zoning map was changed to accommodate an increased need for residential housing in Pleasantville, C&E was grandfathered into the new zoning; that is, it was allowed to continue its successful operations, even though it did not fit the new zoning rules.

**Variances and conditional-use permits.** Each time a plan or zoning ordinance is enacted, some property owners are inconvenienced and want to change the use of their property. Generally, these owners may appeal for either a conditional-use permit or a variance to allow a use that does not meet current zoning requirements.

A **conditional-use permit** (also known as a *special-use permit*) is usually granted to a property owner to allow a special use of property that is defined as an *allowable conditional use within that zone*, such as a house of worship or day-care center in a residential district. For a conditional-use permit to be appropriate, the intended use must meet certain standards set by the municipality.

A **variance,** on the other hand, permits a landowner to use his or her property in a manner that is *strictly prohibited by the existing zoning.* Variances provide relief if zoning regulations deprive an owner of the reasonable use of his or her property. To qualify for a variance, the owner must demonstrate the unique circumstances that make the variance necessary. In addition, the owner must prove that he or she is harmed and burdened by the regulations. A variance might also be sought to provide relief if existing zoning regulations create a physical hardship for the development of a specific property. For example, if an owner's lot is level next to a road, but slopes steeply 30 feet away from the road, the zoning board may allow a variance so the owner can build closer to the road than the setback allows.

> *Conditional-use* permits allow nonconforming but related land uses.
>
> *Variances* permit prohibited land uses to avoid undue hardship.

Both variances and conditional-use permits are issued by zoning boards only after public hearings. The neighbors of a proposed use must be given an opportunity to voice their opinions.

A property owner also can seek a change in the zoning classification of a parcel of real estate by obtaining an *amendment* to the district map or the zoning ordinance for that area. That is, the owner can attempt to have the zoning changed to accommodate his or her intended use of the property. The proposed amendment must be brought before a public hearing on the matter and approved by the governing body of the community.

## Subdivision and Land Development Ordinances

Most communities have adopted *subdivision and land development ordinances* as part of their comprehensive plan. An ordinance will include provisions for submitting and processing subdivision plats, including the charging of fees and review of plats and surveys that are submitted for approval. (See Chapter 21.) A major advantage of subdivision ordinances is that they encourage flexibility, economy, and ingenuity in the use of land. The layout and arrangement of a subdivision or land development usually provide for

- location, grading, alignment, surfacing, and widths of streets and walkways;
- location and design of curbs, gutters, streetlights, and water and sewerage facilities;
- easements or rights-of-way for drainage and utilities;
- minimum setback lines and lot sizes;
- renewable energy systems and energy-conserving building design; and
- areas to be reserved or dedicated for public use, such as parks or recreation facilities.

# BUILDING CODES

Most municipalities have enacted ordinances to specify construction standards that must be met when repairing or erecting buildings. These are called **building codes,** and they set the requirements for kinds of materials and standards of workmanship, sanitary equipment, electrical wiring, fire prevention, and the like.

A property owner who wants to build a structure or alter or repair an existing building usually must obtain a building permit. Through the permit requirement, municipal officials are made aware of new construction or alterations and can verify compliance with building codes and zoning ordinances. Inspectors closely examine the plans and conduct periodic inspections of the work. Once the completed structure has been inspected and found satisfactory, the municipal inspector issues a *certificate of occupancy* or *occupancy permit.*

If the construction of a building or an alteration violates a deed restriction (discussed later in the chapter), the issuance of a building permit will not cure this violation. A building permit is merely evidence of the applicant's compliance with municipal regulations.

Similarly, communities with historic districts, or those that are interested in maintaining a particular "look" or character, may have *aesthetic ordinances.* These laws require that all new construction or restorations be approved by a special board. The board ensures that the new structures will blend in with existing building styles. Owners of existing properties may need to obtain approval to have their homes painted or remodeled.

**In Practice**    The subject of planning, zoning, and restricting of the use of real estate is extremely technical, and the interpretation of the law is not always clear. Questions concerning any of these subjects in relation to real estate transactions should be referred to legal counsel. Furthermore, the landowner should be aware of the costs for various permits.

## PRIVATE LAND-USE CONTROLS

Not all restrictions on the use of land are imposed by government bodies. Certain restrictions to control and to maintain the desirable quality and character of a property or subdivision may be created by private entities, including the property owners themselves. These restrictions are separate from, and in addition to, the land-use controls exercised by the government. No private restriction can violate a local, state, or federal law.

**In Ohio...**

**Restrictive covenants** set standards for all the parcels within a defined subdivision. They usually govern the type, height, and size of buildings that individual owners can erect, as well as land use, architectural style, construction methods, setbacks, and square footage. The deed conveying a particular lot in the subdivision will refer to the plat or declaration of restrictions, thus limiting the title conveyed and binding all grantees. This is known as a *deed restriction.* Restrictions may have *time limitations.* A restriction might state that it is "effective for a period of 25 years from this date." After this time, it becomes inoperative. A time-limited covenant, however, may be extended by agreement. Restrictive covenants are generally enforceable in Ohio. ◆

Restrictive covenants are usually considered valid if they are reasonable restraints that benefit all property owners in the subdivision—for instance, to protect property values or safety. If, however, the terms of the restrictions are too broad, they will be construed as preventing the free transfer of property. If any restrictive covenant or condition is judged unenforceable by a court, the estate will stand free from the invalid covenant or condition. Restrictive covenants cannot be for illegal purposes, such as for the exclusion of members of certain races, nationalities, or religions.

Private land-use controls may be more restrictive of an owner's use than the local zoning ordinances. The rule is that the more restrictive of the two takes precedence.

Private restrictions can be enforced in court when one lot owner applies to the court for an injunction to prevent a neighboring lot owner from violating the recorded restrictions. The court injunction will direct the violator to stop or remove the violation. The court retains the power to punish the violator for failing to obey. If adjoining lot owners stand idly by while a violation is committed, they can lose the right to an injunction by their inaction. The court might claim their right was lost through *laches*—that is, the legal principle that a right may be lost through undue delay or failure to assert it.

## KEY TERMS

| | | |
|---|---|---|
| buffer zone | enabling act | taking |
| building code | nonconforming use | variance |
| comprehensive plan | restrictive covenant | zoning ordinance |
| conditional-use permit | | |

## SUMMARY

- The control of land use is exercised through public controls, private (or nongovernment) controls, and direct public ownership of land.
- Through power conferred by state enabling acts, local governments exercise public controls based on the states' police powers to protect the public health, safety, and welfare.
- A comprehensive plan sets forth the development goals and objectives for the community.
  - Zoning ordinances carrying out the provisions of the plan control the use of land and structures within designated land-use districts.
  - Subdivision and land development regulations are adopted to maintain control of the development of expanding community areas so that growth is harmonious with community standards.
  - Building codes specify standards for construction, plumbing, sewers, electrical wiring, and equipment.
- Public ownership is a means of land-use control that provides land for such public benefits as parks, highways, schools, and municipal buildings.
- Private land-use controls are exercised by owners through deed restrictions and restrictive covenants.
  - Private restrictions may be enforced by obtaining a court injunction to stop a violator.

## Real-Life Real Estate

1. Are planning and zoning activities really worth all the trouble? Justify your response.
2. Should variances be easy or hard to obtain? Explain.

# QUESTIONS

1. A provision in a subdivision declaration used to force the grantee to live up to the terms under which he or she holds title to the land is a
   a. restrictive covenant.
   b. reverter.
   c. laches.
   d. conditional-use clause.

2. A landowner who wants to use property in a manner that is prohibited by a local zoning ordinance but that would benefit the community can apply for which of the following?
   a. Conditional-use permit
   b. Downzoning
   c. Occupancy permit
   d. Dezoning

3. Public land-use controls include all of the following *EXCEPT*
   a. subdivision regulations.
   b. restrictive covenants.
   c. environmental protection laws.
   d. comprehensive plan specifications.

4. Under its police powers, the town of New Pompeii may legally regulate all of the following EXCEPT
   a. the number of buildings.
   b. the size of buildings.
   c. building ownership.
   d. building occupancy.

5. The police power allows regulation of all of the following EXCEPT
   a. the number of buildings.
   b. the size of buildings.
   c. building ownership.
   d. building occupancy.

6. The purpose of a building permit is to
   a. override a deed's restrictive covenant.
   b. maintain municipal control over the volume of building.
   c. provide evidence of compliance with municipal regulations.
   d. show compliance with restrictive covenants.

7. Zoning laws are generally enforced by
   a. zoning boards of appeal.
   b. ordinances limiting the issuance of building permits.
   c. the Ohio Division of Real Estate.
   d. restrictive covenants.

8. Zoning powers are conferred on municipal governments in which of the following ways?
   a. By state enabling acts
   b. Through the master plan
   c. By eminent domain
   d. Through escheat

9. The town of East Westchester enacts a new zoning code. Under the new code, commercial buildings are not permitted within 1,000 feet of Lake Westchester. A commercial building that is permitted to continue in its former use, even though it is built on the lakeshore, is an example of
   a. a nonconforming use.
   b. a variance.
   c. a special use.
   d. inverse condemnation.

10. To determine whether a location can be put to future use as a retail store, one would examine the
    a. building code.
    b. list of permitted nonconforming uses.
    c. housing code.
    d. zoning ordinance.

# Property Development and Subdivision

## LAND DEVELOPMENT

As cities grow, additional land is required for their expansion. Land in large tracts must receive special attention before it can be successfully converted into sites for homes, stores, or other uses. Competent subdividers and land developers are required for new areas to develop soundly. A **subdivider** buys undeveloped acreage and divides it into smaller lots for sale to individuals or developers or for the subdivider's own use. A **developer** (who may also be a subdivider) improves the land, constructs homes or other buildings on the lots, and sells them. Developing is generally a much more extensive activity than subdividing.

**Regulation of Land Development**

There is *no uniform planning and land development legislation that affects the entire country.* Laws governing subdividing and land planning are controlled by the state and local governing bodies where the land is located. Rules and regulations developed by government agencies have, however, provided certain minimum standards that serve as guides. Local regulations reflect customs and local climate, health, and hazard conditions. Many local governments have established standards that are higher than the minimum standards.

Before the actual subdividing can begin, the subdivider/developer must go through the process of land planning. The resulting land development plan must comply with the municipality's *comprehensive plan.* (See Chapter 20.) Although comprehensive plans and zoning ordinances are not necessarily inflexible, a land development plan that relies on alterations often will require long, expensive, and frequently complicated hearings to get the needed authorizations.

From the land development and subdivision plans the subdivider/developer must then draw *plats*—detailed maps that illustrate not only geographic boundaries of the individual lots but also blocks, sections, streets, public easements, and monuments in the prospective subdivision. A plat also may include engineering data and restrictive covenants. The plats must be approved by the municipality before they can be recorded.

Approval is usually obtained in two stages. *Preliminary approval* will be granted on the basis of the plats, often after a public hearing has been held so that the community is involved in the process. *Final approval* is normally conditioned on the subdivider/developer providing some form of financial security or bonding to guarantee completion of certain improvements required by the municipality. The installation of improvements such as streets, curbs, gutters, fire hydrants, water mains, and sanitary and storm sewers involves a major financial commitment from the subdivider/developer.

Providing an adequate supply of water and environmentally sound sewage disposal are major considerations in the development of land. Ordinances frequently require that water be supplied by a certified public utility unless the individual lots within a subdivision can be properly served by private wells. Sewage disposal that does not pollute streams, rivers, and underground water supplies is another major concern. Many states regulate the planning of community and individual sewerage systems. These regulations may not permit septic systems where the soil's absorption or drainage capacity, as determined by a *percolation test,* precludes their use. With the growing emphasis on environmental concerns, a developer may be required to submit an *environmental impact report (EIR)* with the application for subdivision approval.

With increasing development there is a corresponding demand for municipal capital improvements. Municipalities must develop revenue sources to provide adequate transportation routes via municipal highways, roads, and streets to accommodate increased traffic flow. Although the developer is responsible for installation of streets within a subdivision (an "on-site" improvement), the municipality is responsible for these "off-site" improvements. Some states have authorized the local governing body to establish a program to collect *impact fees* at the time of approval of a new subdivision or development to fund these off-site public transportation improvements.

## SUBDIVISION

The process of **subdivision** normally involves three distinct stages of development: the initial planning stage, the final planning stage, and the disposition, or start-up.

During the *initial planning stage* the subdivider seeks out raw land in a suitable area. Once the land is located, the property is analyzed for its highest and best use, and preliminary subdivision plans are drawn up accordingly. Close contact between the subdivider and local planning and zoning officials is initiated. If the project requires zoning variances, negotiations begin. The subdivider also locates financial backers and initiates marketing strategies.

The *final planning stage* is basically a follow-up of the initial stage. Final plans are prepared, approval is sought from local officials, permanent financing is obtained, the land is purchased, final budgets are prepared, and marketing programs are designed.

The *disposition,* or *start-up,* carries the subdividing process to a conclusion. Subdivision plans are recorded with local officials. Once the plat is filed, all areas that have been accepted by the municipality for streets or parks and recreation are considered to be *dedicated,* which is the transfer of privately owned land to the public that is accepted to be used for public purposes. Streets, sewers and utilities are installed. Buildings, open parks, and recreational areas are constructed and landscaped if they are part of the subdivision plan. Marketing programs are then initiated, and title to the individual parcels of subdivided land is transferred as the lots are sold.

**Subdivision Plans**

In plotting out a subdivision according to local planning and zoning controls, a subdivider usually determines the size as well as the location of the individual lots. The maximum or minimum size of a lot is generally regulated by local ordinances and must be considered carefully.

The land itself must be studied, usually in cooperation with a surveyor, so that the subdivision takes advantage of natural drainage and land contours. A subdivider should provide for *utility easements* as well as easements for water and sewer mains.

Most subdivisions are laid out by use of lots and blocks. An area of land is designated as a block, and the area making up this block is divided into lots.

One negative aspect of subdivision development is the potential for increased tax burdens on all residents, both inside and outside the subdivision. To protect local taxpayers against the costs of a heightened demand for public services, many local governments strictly regulate nearly all aspects of subdivision development.

Although subdividers customarily designate areas reserved for schools, parks, and future church sites, this is usually not considered good practice. Once a subdivision has been recorded, the purchasers of the lots have a vested interest in those areas reserved for schools, parks, and churches. If for any reason in the future any such purpose is not appropriate, it will become difficult for the developer to abandon the original plan and use that property for residential purposes. To get around this situation many developers designate such areas as *out-lot A, out-lot B,* and so forth. Such a designation does not vest any rights in these out-lots in the purchasers of the homesites. If one of these areas is to be used for church purposes, it can be so conveyed and so used. If, on the other hand, the out-lot is not to be used for such a purpose, it can be resubdivided into residential properties without the burden of securing the consent of the lot owners in the area.

**Subdivision plat.** The subdivider's completed plat of subdivision must contain all necessary approvals of public officials and must be recorded in the county where the land is located.

Because the plat will be the basis for future conveyances, the subdivided land should be measured carefully, with all lot sizes and streets noted by the surveyor and entered accurately on the document. Survey monuments should be established, and measurements should be made from these monuments, with the location of all lots carefully marked.

**Covenants and restrictions.** Restrictive covenants are originated and recorded by a subdivider as a means of *controlling and maintaining the desirable quality and character of the subdivision.* These restrictions can be included in the subdivision plat, or they may be set forth in a separate recorded instrument, commonly referred to as a *declaration of restrictions.* A copy of the declaration of restrictions must be provided to the buyer prior to closing. ◆

**In Ohio...**

**Subdivision Density**

Zoning ordinances control land use. Such control often includes minimum lot sizes and population density requirements for subdivisions and land developments. For example, a typical zoning restriction may set the minimum lot

**Figure 21.1    Street Patterns**

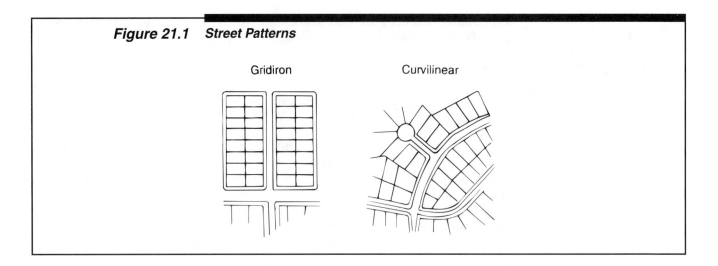

Gridiron                    Curvilinear

area on which a subdivider can build a single-family housing unit at 10,000 square feet. This means that the subdivider can build four houses per acre. Many zoning authorities now establish special density zoning standards for certain subdivisions. **Density zoning** ordinances restrict the *average maximum number of houses per acre* that may be built within a particular subdivision. If the area is density zoned at an average maximum of four houses per acre, for instance, the subdivider may choose to *cluster* building lots to achieve an open effect. Regardless of lot size or number of units, the subdivider will be consistent with the ordinance as long as the average number of units in the development remains at or below the maximum density. This average is called *gross density.*

**Street patterns.**  By varying street patterns and clustering housing units, a subdivider can dramatically increase the amount of open or recreational space in a development. Two of these patterns are the *gridiron* and *curvilinear* patterns. (See Figure 21.1.)

The gridiron pattern evolved out of the government rectangular survey system. This pattern features large lots, wide streets, and limited-use service alleys. Sidewalks are usually adjacent to the streets or separated by narrow grassy areas. While the gridiron pattern provides for little open space and many lots may front on busy streets, it is an easy system to navigate.

The curvilinear system integrates major arteries of travel with smaller secondary and cul-de-sac streets carrying minor traffic. (A *cul-de-sac* is a street that is open only on one end.) Curvilinear developments avoid the uniformity of the gridiron, but often lack service alleys. The absence of straight-line travel and the lack of easy access tend to make curvilinear developments quieter and more secure. However, getting from place to place may be more challenging.

**Clustering for open space.**  By slightly reducing lot sizes and **clustering** them around varying street patterns, a subdivider can house as many people in the same area as could be done using traditional subdividing plans, but with substantially increased tracts of open space.

For example, compare the two subdivisions illustrated in Figure 21.2. Conventional Gardens is a conventionally designed subdivision containing 368 housing units. It uses 23,200 linear feet of street and leaves only 1.6 acres open for parkland. Contrast this with Cluster Estates. Both subdivisions are

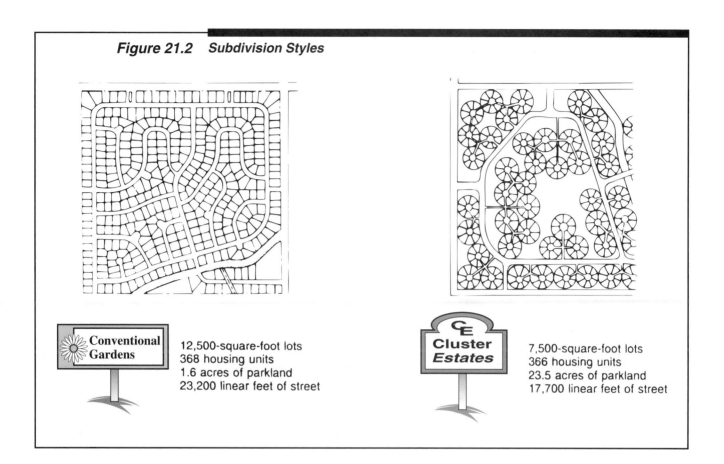

**Figure 21.2   Subdivision Styles**

Conventional Gardens
12,500-square-foot lots
368 housing units
1.6 acres of parkland
23,200 linear feet of street

Cluster Estates
7,500-square-foot lots
366 housing units
23.5 acres of parkland
17,700 linear feet of street

equal in size and terrain. But when lots are reduced in size and clustered around limited-access cul-de-sacs, the number of housing units remains nearly the same (366), with less street area (17,700 linear feet) and dramatically increased open space (23.5 acres). In addition, with modern building designs this clustered plan could be modified to accommodate more than a thousand town houses while retaining the attractive open spaces.

## REGULATION OF LAND SALES

Just as the sale and use of property within a state are controlled by state and local governments, the sale of property in one state to buyers in another is subject to strict federal and state regulations.

**Interstate Land Sales Full Disclosure Act**

The federal **Interstate Land Sales Full Disclosure Act** regulates the interstate sale of unimproved lots. The act is administered by the Secretary of Housing and Urban Development (HUD), through the office of Interstate Land Sales Registration. It is designed to prevent fraudulent marketing schemes that may arise when land is sold without being seen by the purchasers. (You may be familiar with stories about gullible buyers whose land purchases were based on glossy brochures shown by smooth-talking salespersons. When the buyers finally went to visit the "little pieces of paradise" they'd bought, they frequently found worthless swampland or barren desert.)

The act requires that developers file statements of record with HUD before they can offer unimproved lots in interstate commerce by telephone or through the mail. The statements of record must contain numerous disclosures about the properties.

Developers also are required to provide each purchaser or lessee of property with a printed property report before the purchaser or lessee signs a purchase contract or lease. The report must disclose specific information about the land, including

- the type of title being transferred to the buyer,
- the number of homes currently occupied on the site,
- the availability of recreation facilities,
- the distance to nearby communities,
- utility services and charges, and
- soil conditions and foundation or construction problems.

If the purchaser or lessee does not receive a copy of the report before signing the purchase contract or lease, he or she may have grounds to void the contract.

The act provides a number of exemptions. For instance, it does not apply to subdivisions consisting of fewer than 25 lots or to those in which the lots are of 20 acres or more. Lots offered for sale solely to developers also are exempt from the act's requirements, as are lots on which buildings exist or where a seller is obligated to construct a building within two years.

## KEY TERMS

| | | |
|---|---|---|
| clustering | gridiron | property report |
| curvilinear | gross density | restrictive covenant |
| density zoning | Interstate Land Sales | subdivider |
| developer |    Full Disclosure Act | subdivision |
| environmental impact | percolator test | |
|    report (EIR) | | |

## SUMMARY

- Subdividers, developers, and city planners all have a role in developing land:
  - A subdivider buys undeveloped acreage, divides it into smaller parcels, and develops it or sells it.
  - A developer builds homes on the lots and sells them, through the developer's own sales organization or through local real estate brokerage firms.
  - City planners plan whole communities that are later incorporated into cities, towns, or villages.
- Land development must comply with the master plans adopted by counties, cities, villages, or towns. This may entail approval of land-use plans by local planning committees or commissioners.
- The process of subdivision includes dividing the tract of land into lots and blocks and providing for utility easements, as well as laying out street patterns and widths.
  - A subdivider generally records a completed plat of subdivision, with all necessary approvals of public officials, in the county where the land is located.
  - Subdividers usually place restrictions on the use of all lots in a subdivision as a general plan for the benefit of all lot owners.

- By varying street patterns and housing density and clustering housing units, a subdivider can dramatically increase the amount of open and recreational space within a development.
- Subdivided land sales are regulated on the federal level by the Interstate Land Sales Full Disclosure Act.
  - This law requires that developers engaged in interstate land sales or the leasing of 100 or more units register the details of the land with HUD.
  - At least three business days before any sales contract is signed, developers must also provide prospective purchasers with a property report containing all essential information about the property in any development that exceeds 25 lots.

**Real-Life
Real Estate**

1. Property development is a key to increasing value. Discuss the need for balance as development relates to the principle of highest and best use.
2. Subdivision feasibility depends on many things; density is a primary consideration. Explain how zoning density restrictions impact feasibility and whether or not you see this as good for the community.

# QUESTIONS

1. To control and maintain the quality and character of a subdivision, a developer will establish which of the following?
   a. Easements
   b. Restrictive covenants
   c. Buffer zones
   d. Building codes

2. An owner of a large tract of land who, after adequate study of all facts, legally divides the land into lots of suitable size and location for the construction of residences, is known as a(n)
   a. subdivider.
   b. developer
   c. land planner.
   d. urban planner.

3. A map illustrating the sizes and locations of streets and lots in a subdivision is called a
   a. gridiron pattern.
   b. survey.
   c. plat of subdivision.
   d. property report.

4. *Gross density* refers to which of the following?
   a. The maximum number of residents that may, by law, occupy a subdivision
   b. The average maximum number of houses per acre that may, by law, be built in a subdivision
   c. The maximum-size lot that may, by law, be built in a subdivision
   d. The minimum number of houses that may, by law, be built in a subdivision

5. In Glendale, subdivision developers are limited by law to constructing no more than an average of three houses per acre in any subdivision. To what does this restriction refer?
   a. Clustering
   b. Gross density
   c. Out-lots
   d. Covenants

6. The city of Northbend is laid out in a pattern of intersecting streets and avenues. All streets run north and south; all avenues run east and west. Northbend is an example of which street pattern style?
   a. Block plan
   b. Gridiron system
   c. Radial streets plan
   d. Intersecting system

7. All of the following items are usually designated on the plat for a new subdivision *EXCEPT*
   a. easements for sewer and water mains.
   b. land to be used for streets.
   c. numbered lots and blocks.
   d. prices of residential and commercial lots.

8. Acorn Acres is a subdivision featuring spacious homes grouped on large cul-de-sac blocks connected to a central, winding road and surrounded by large, landscaped common areas. This is an example of which type of subdivision plan?
   a. Cluster plan
   b. Curvilinear system
   c. Rectangular street system
   d. Gridiron system

9. A subdivider can increase the amount of open or recreational space in a development by
   a. varying street patterns.
   b. meeting local housing standards.
   c. scattering housing units.
   d. eliminating multistory dwellings.

10. To protect the public from fraudulent interstate land sales, a developer involved in interstate land sales of 25 or more lots must
    a. provide each purchaser with a printed report disclosing details of the property.
    b. pay the prospective buyer's expenses to see the property involved.
    c. provide preferential financing.
    d. allow a 30-day cancellation period.

11. Soil absorption and drainage are measured by a
    a. land survey.
    b. plat of subdivision.
    c. density test
    d. percolation test.

# CHAPTER 22

# Fair Housing Practices

## EQUAL OPPORTUNITY IN HOUSING

The purpose of civil rights laws that affect the real estate industry is to create a marketplace in which all persons of similar financial means have a similar range of housing choices. The goal is to ensure that everyone has the opportunity to live where he or she chooses. Owners, real estate licensees, apartment management companies, real estate organizations, lending agencies, builders, and developers must all take a part in creating this single housing market. Federal, state, and local fair housing or equal opportunity laws affect every phase of a real estate transaction, from listing to closing.

> "All citizens of the United States shall have the same right in every state and territory as is enjoyed by white citizens thereof to inherit, purchase, lease, sell, hold, and convey real and personal property."— *Civil Rights Act of 1866*

The U.S. Congress and the Supreme Court have created a legal framework that preserves the constitutional rights of all citizens. However, while the passage of laws may establish a code for public conduct, centuries of discriminatory practices and attitudes are not so easily changed. Real estate licensees cannot allow their own prejudices to interfere with the ethical and legal conduct of their profession. Similarly, the discriminatory attitudes of property owners or property seekers must not be allowed to affect compliance with the fair housing laws. This is not always easy, and the pressure to avoid offending the person who pays the commission can be intense. However, just remember: *Failure to comply with fair housing laws is both a civil and a criminal violation, and such failure is grounds for disciplinary action against a licensee.*

**In Practice**    Licensees must have a thorough knowledge of both state and federal fair housing laws. State laws may be stricter than the federal requirements and may provide protection for more classes of persons. State rules may provide for fines as well as the suspension or revocation of an offender's license.

The federal government's effort to guarantee equal housing opportunities to all U.S. citizens began with the passage of the **Civil Rights Act of 1866,** an outgrowth of the Thirteenth Amendment to the Constitution. This law prohibits any type of discrimination based on race.

The U.S. Supreme Court's 1896 decision in *Plessy v. Ferguson* established the "separate but equal" doctrine of legalized racial segregation. A series of court decisions and federal laws in the 20 years between 1948 and 1968 attempted to address the inequities in housing that were the results of *Plessy.* Those efforts, however, tended to address only certain aspects of the housing market (such as federally funded housing programs). As a result, their impact was limited. Title VIII of the Civil Rights Act of 1968, however, prohibited specific discriminatory practices throughout the real estate industry.

# FAIR HOUSING ACT

> The *Fair Housing Act* prohibits discrimination based on
>
> • Race,
> • Color,
> • Religion,
> • sex,
> • handicap,
> • familial status, or
> • national origin.

**Title VIII of the Civil Rights Act of 1968** prohibited discrimination in housing based on race, color, religion, or national origin. In 1974, the *Housing and Community Development Act* added sex to the list of protected classes. In 1988, the *Fair Housing Amendments Act* included disability and familial status (that is, the presence of children). Today, these laws are known as the federal **Fair Housing Act.** (See Figure 22.1.) The Fair Housing Act prohibits discrimination on the basis of race, color, religion, sex, handicap, familial status, or national origin.

The act also prohibits discrimination against individuals because of their association with persons in the protected classes. This law is administered by the **Department of Housing and Urban Development** (HUD). HUD has established rules and regulations that further interpret the practices affected by the law. In addition, HUD distributes an *equal housing opportunity poster.* (See Figure 22.2.) The poster declares that the office in which it is displayed promises to adhere to the Fair Housing Act and pledges support for affirmative

**In Ohio...** marketing and advertising programs. Ohio statutes also require the display of this Equal Housing Opportunity poster in a prominent location in each broker's office. Table 22.1 describes the activities prohibited by the Fair Housing Act. ◆

**In Practice**   The HUD poster must be displayed in the same immediate area as the broker's license. When HUD investigates a broker for discriminatory practices, it may consider failure to prominently display the equal housing opportunity poster in the broker's place of business as evidence of discrimination.

**Definitions**   HUD's regulations provide specific definitions that clarify the scope of the Fair Housing Act.

**Housing.**  The regulations define housing as a "dwelling," which includes any building or part of a building designed for occupancy as a residence by one or more families. This includes a single-family house, condominium, cooperative, or mobile home, as well as vacant land on which any of these structures will be built.

**Familial status.**  *Familial status* refers to the presence of one or more individuals who have not reached the age of 18 and who live with either a parent or guardian. The term includes a woman who is pregnant. In effect, it means that the Fair Housing Act's protections extend to families with children. Unless a property qualifies as housing for older persons, all properties must be made available to families with children under the same terms and conditions as to anyone else. It is illegal to advertise properties as being for adults only or to indicate a preference for a certain number of children. The number of persons permitted to reside in a property (the occupancy standards) must be based on objective factors such as sanitation or safety. Landlords cannot restrict the number of occupants to eliminate families with children.

*Figure 22.1*   **Federal Fair Housing Laws**

| Legislation | Race | Color | Religion | National Origin | Sex | Age | Marital Status | Disability | Discrimination | Familial Status | Public Assistance Income |
|---|---|---|---|---|---|---|---|---|---|---|---|
| *Civil Rights Act of 1866* | ● | | | | | | | | | | |
| *Fair Housing Act of 1968 (Title VIII)* | ● | ● | ● | ● | | | | | ● | | |
| *Housing and Community Development Act of 1974* | | | | | ● | | | | ● | | |
| *Fair Housing Amendments Act of 1988* | | | | | | | | ● | ● | ● | |
| *Equal Credit Opportunity Act of 1974 (lending)* | ● | ● | ● | ● | ● | ● | ● | | ● | | ● |

**Figure 22.2** *Equal Housing Opportunity Poster*

U.S. Department of Housing and Urban Development

**EQUAL HOUSING
OPPORTUNITY**

## We Do Business in Accordance With the Federal Fair Housing Law
(The Fair Housing Amendments Act of 1988)

## It is Illegal to Discriminate Against Any Person Because of Race, Color, Religion, Sex, Handicap, Familial Status, or National Origin

*Test*

- In the sale or rental of housing or residential lots

- In advertising the sale or rental of housing

- In the financing of housing

- In the provision of real estate brokerage services

- In the appraisal of housing

- Blockbusting is also illegal

Anyone who feels he or she has been discriminated against may file a complaint of housing discrimination with the:
1-800-669-9777 (Toll Free)
1-800-927-9275 (TDD)

**U.S. Department of Housing and
Urban Development
Assistant Secretary for Fair Housing and
Equal Opportunity
Washington, D.C. 20410**

Previous editions are obsolete

form **HUD-928.1** (8-93)

| Prohibited by Federal Fair Housing Act | Example |
|---|---|
| • Refusing to sell, rent, or negotiate the sale or rental of housing | K owns an apartment building with several vacant units. When an Asian family asks to see one of the units, K tells them to go away. |
| • Changing terms, conditions, or services for different individuals as a means of discriminating | S, a Roman Catholic, calls on a duplex, and the landlord tells her the rent is $400 per month. When she talks to the other tenants, she learns that all the Lutherans in the complex pay only $325 per month. |
| • Advertising any discriminatory preference or limitation in housing or making any inquiry or reference that is discriminatory in nature | A real estate agent places the following advertisement in a newspaper: "Just Listed! Perfect home for white family, near excellent parochial school!"<br><br>A developer places this ad in an urban newspaper: "Sunset River Hollow—Dream Homes Just For You!" The ad is accompanied by a photo of several African-American families. |
| • Representing that a property is not available for sale or rent when in fact it is | J, who uses a wheelchair, is told that the house J wants to rent is no longer available. The next day, however, the For Rent sign is still in the window. |
| • Profiting by inducing property owners to sell or rent on the basis of the prospective entry into the neighborhood of persons of a protected class | N, a real estate agent, sends brochures to home-owners in the predominantly white Ridgewood neighborhood. The brochures, which feature N's past success selling homes, include photos of racial minorities, population statistics, and the caption, "The Changing Face of Ridgewood." |
| • Altering the terms or conditions of a home loan, or denying a loan, as a means of discrimination | A lender requires M, a divorced mother of two young children, to pay for a credit report. In addition, her father must cosign her application. After talking to a single male friend, M learns that he was not required to do either of those things, despite his lower income and poor credit history. |
| • Denying membership or participation in a multiple-listing service, a real estate organization, or another facility related to the sale or rental of housing as a means of discrimination | The Topper County Real Estate Practitioners' Association meets every week to discuss available properties and buyers. None of Topper County's black or female agents is allowed to be a member of the association. |

**F**OR EXAMPLE *G* owned an apartment building. One of his elderly tenants, *P*, was terminally ill. *P* requested that no children be allowed in the vacant apartment next door because the noise would be difficult for *P* to bear. *G* agreed and refused to rent to families with children. Even though *G* only wanted to make things easier for a dying tenant, *G* nonetheless was found to have violated the Fair Housing Act by discriminating on the basis of familial status.

**Disability.** A *disability* is a physical or mental impairment. The term includes having a history of, or being regarded as having, an impairment that substantially limits one or more of an individual's major life activities. Persons who have AIDS are protected by the fair housing laws under this classification.

**In Practice**   The federal Fair Housing Act's protection of disabled persons does not include those who are current users of illegal or controlled substances. Nor are individuals who have been convicted of the illegal manufacture or distribution of a controlled substance protected under this law. However, the law does prohibit discrimination against those who are participating in addiction recovery programs. For instance, a landlord could lawfully discriminate against a cocaine addict but not against a member of Alcoholics Anonymous.

It is unlawful to discriminate against prospective buyers or tenants on the basis of disability. Landlords must make reasonable accommodations to existing policies, practices, or services to permit persons with disabilities to have equal enjoyment of the premises. For instance, it would be reasonable for a landlord to permit support animals (such as guide dogs) in a normally no-pets building or to provide a designated handicapped parking space in a generally unreserved lot.

People with disabilities must be permitted to make reasonable modifications to the premises at their own expense. Such modifications might include lowering door handles or installing bath rails to accommodate a person in a wheelchair. Failure to permit reasonable modification constitutes discrimination. However, the law recognizes that some reasonable modifications might make a rental property undesirable to the general population. In such a case, the landlord is allowed to require that the property be restored to its previous condition when the lease period ends.

The law does not prohibit restricting occupancy exclusively to persons with handicaps in dwellings that are designed specifically for their accommodation.

For new construction of certain multifamily properties, a number of accessibility and usability requirements must be met under federal law. Access is specified for public and common-use portions of the buildings, and adaptive and accessible design must be implemented for the interior of the dwelling units. Some states have their own laws as well.

**Exemptions to the Fair Housing Act**   The federal Fair Housing Act provides for certain exemptions. It is important for licensees to know in what situations the exemptions apply. However, licensees should be aware that *no exemptions involve race* and that *no exemptions apply when a real estate licensee is involved in a transaction.*

The sale or rental of a single-family home is exempt when

- the home is owned by an individual who does not own more than three such homes at one time
- a real estate broker or salesperson is not involved in the transaction, and
- discriminatory advertising is not used.

*—FSBO— Church, clubs, Senior Citizen*

The rental of rooms or units is exempted in an owner-occupied one- to four-family dwelling.

Dwelling units owned by religious organizations may be restricted to people of the same religion if membership in the organization is not restricted on the basis of race, color, or national origin. A private club that is not open to the public may restrict the rental or occupancy of lodgings that it owns to its members as long as the lodgings are not operated commercially.

The Fair Housing Act does not require that housing be made available to any individual whose tenancy would constitute a direct threat to the health or safety of other individuals or that would result in substantial physical damage to the property of others.

Only one such sale by an owner who does not live in the dwelling at the time of the transaction or who is not the most recent occupant is exempt from the law within any 24-month period.

**Housing for older persons.** While the Fair Housing Act protects families with children, certain properties can be restricted to occupancy by elderly persons. Housing intended for persons age 62 or older or housing occupied by at least one person 55 years of age or older per unit (where 80 percent of the units are occupied by individuals 55 or older) is exempt from the familial status protection.

*Test*

| The *Equal Credit Opportunity Act* prohibits discrimination in granting credit based on |
| --- |
| - race, |
| - color, |
| - religion, |
| - national origin, |
| - sex, |
| - marital status, |
| - age, or |
| - public assistance. |

*Test*

**Jones v. Mayer.** In 1968, the Supreme Court heard the case of *Jones v. Alfred H. Mayer Company*, 392 U.S. 409 (1968). In its decision, the Court upheld the Civil Rights Act of 1866. This decision is important because although the federal law exempts individual homeowners and certain groups, the 1866 law *prohibits all racial discrimination without exception.* A person who is discriminated against on the basis of race may still recover damages under the 1866 law. *Where race is involved, no exceptions apply.*

The U.S. Supreme Court has expanded the definition of the term race to include ancestral and ethnic characteristics, including certain physical, cultural, or linguistic characteristics that are commonly shared by a national origin group. These rulings are significant because discrimination on the basis of race, as it is now defined, affords due process of complaints under the provisions of the Civil Rights Act of 1866.

### Equal Credit Opportunity Act

The federal **Equal Credit Opportunity Act** (ECOA) prohibits discrimination based on race, color, religion, national origin, sex, marital status or age in the granting of credit. Note that the ECOA protects more classes of persons than the Fair Housing Act. The ECOA bars discrimination on the basis of marital status and age. It also prevents lenders from discriminating against recipients of public assistance programs such as food stamps and Social Security. As in the Fair Housing Act, the ECOA requires that credit applications be considered only on the bases of income, net worth, job stability, and credit rating.

**Americans with Disabilities Act**

Although the **Americans with Disabilities Act** (ADA) is not a housing or credit law, it still has a significant effect on the real estate industry. The ADA is important to licensees because it addresses the rights of individuals with disabilities in employment and public accommodations. Real estate brokers are often employers, and real estate brokerage offices are public spaces. The ADA's goal is to enable individuals with disabilities to become part of the economic and social mainstream of society.

> The *Americans with Disabilities Act* requires **reasonable accommodations** in employment and access to goods, services and public buildings.

The ADA requires that employers (including real estate licensees) make *reasonable accommodations* that enable an individual with a disability to perform essential job functions. Reasonable accommodations include making the work site accessible, restructuring a job, providing part-time or flexible work schedules, and modifying equipment that is used on the job. The provisions of the ADA apply to any employer with 15 or more employees.

Title III of the ADA provides for accessibility to goods and services for individuals with disabilities. While the federal civil rights laws have traditionally been viewed in the real estate industry as housing-related, the practices of licensees who deal with nonresidential property are significantly affected by the ADA. Because people with disabilities have the right to full and equal access to businesses and public services under the ADA, building owners and managers must ensure that any obstacle restricting this right is eliminated. The Americans with Disabilities Act Accessibility Guidelines (ADAAG) contain detailed specifications for designing parking spaces, curb ramps, elevators, drinking fountains, toilet facilities, and directional signs to ensure maximum accessibility.

**In Practice**

Real estate agents need a general knowledge of the ADA's provisions. It is necessary for a broker's workplace and employment policies to comply with the law. Also, licensees who are building managers must ensure that the properties are legally accessible. However, ADA compliance questions may arise with regard to a client's property, too. Unless the agent is a qualified ADA expert, it is best to advise commercial clients to seek the services of an attorney, an architect, or a consultant who specializes in ADA issues. It is possible that an appraiser may be liable for failing to identify and account for a property's noncompliance.

## OHIO FAIR HOUSING LAW

**In Ohio...**

The Ohio Fair Housing Law is substantially the same as the federal version. It bars discrimination in any type of housing that may be offered for sale or lease. Interestingly, Ohio's law included protections for persons with disabilities long before either the 1988 federal law or the ADA. The law applies to owners and lessors; real estate brokers, agents, and salespersons; trustees; lending institutions; and the state itself. ◆

The law is clear in its intent to do away with discriminatory housing practices. The following acts are illegal if based on considerations of race, color, religion, sex, familial status, disability, ancestry, or national origin:

- Refusal to sell, rent, transfer, assign, sublease, lease, or finance any form of housing accommodation to any person

- Representing to any person that housing is not available for inspection, sale, or rental when it is in fact available
- Discriminating against any person in making or purchasing a loan or providing other financial assistance for the purchase, construction, repair, maintenance, or rehabilitation of housing, if the lender is in the business of making loans, or discriminating on the basis of the neighborhood in which the residence is located (see "Redlining" later in this chapter)
- Discriminating against any person in the sale of fire, extended coverage, or homeowners' insurance because of the race, color, religion, sex, family status, ancestry, disability, or national origin of the person seeking insurance, or because of the racial composition of the neighborhood in which the residence is located
- Refusing to consider the combined income of both husband and wife for the purpose of extending a mortgage loan to a married couple or to one spouse
- Printing, publishing, or circulating any statement or advertisement relating to the sale or lease of housing or the lending of money for the purchase, construction, or rehabilitation of housing that indicates a discriminatory preference, limitation, specification, or limitation
- Making any inquiry, seeking any information, keeping any records, or using any form of application that would inquire into the applicant's race, color, religion, sex, ancestry, or national origin, other than for the purpose of monitoring compliance with the law
- Including or attempting to honor any form of restrictive covenant in any transfer, lease, or rental of housing
- Soliciting or encouraging listings or sales by making representations that the anticipated or actual presence of persons of any race, color, religion, sex, familial status, ancestry, disability, or national origin may or will
  a. lower property values;
  b. change the neighborhood's racial, religious, sexual, family, or ethnic character;
  c. increase criminal or antisocial behavior; or
  d. cause a decline in the quality of the schools serving the area (see "Blockbusting" and "Steering" later in this chapter)
- Denying access to or discriminating against any person with regard to any multiple-listing service, real estate organization, or other service, organization, or facility related to the business of selling or renting housing accommodations
- Coercing, intimidating, threatening, or interfering with any person for exercising his or her rights under the law, or threatening or interfering with anyone who wants to help someone exercise his or her rights
- Discouraging or attempting to discourage a prospective purchaser from buying housing by representing that the religious, racial, sexual, familial status, or ethnic composition of a block, neighborhood, or area has changed or might change (see "Blockbusting" and "Steering" later in this chapter)
- Refusing to sell a burial lot
- Discriminating in the sale or rental or otherwise denying housing accommodations to any buyer or renter, because of a disability of the buyer, renter, or any person who is residing or intends to reside in the housing accommodations or associate with the buyer or renter
- Making inquiries regarding a potential buyer or renter's disability status or the nature or severity of the disability

- Refusing to permit reasonable modifications, at the expense of a person with a disability, of existing housing accommodations necessary to afford that person full enjoyment of the housing, or conditioning permission on the payment of a security deposit greater than that normally required of tenants
- Refusing to make reasonable and necessary accommodations in a residence's rules, policies, practices, or services to afford a person with a disability equal opportunity to use and enjoy the accommodations
- Discriminating against any person in the selling, brokering, or appraising of real estate
- Failing to design and construct multifamily dwellings in accordance with the requirements of the law regarding accessibility to persons with disabilities

## Ohio Civil Rights Commission

### In Ohio...

The provisions of the Ohio Fair Housing Law are enforced by the Ohio Civil Rights Commission. The commission consists of five members appointed by the governor, with the advice and consent of the state senate. No more than three members can be of the same political party. ◆

A person who is discriminated against in housing has one year after the incident to file a written complaint with the commission. On finding probable discrimination, the commission can seek temporary injunctions or restraining orders to prevent the housing from being rented or sold to another party. The commission is required to attempt to resolve the issue outside the courts, through informal and confidential methods of conference, conciliation, and persuasion. Should those methods fail, the commission may initiate a formal hearing. The Ohio attorney general represents the commission at hearings.

The hearing takes place in the county in which the alleged unlawful discriminatory practice took place or in which the respondent resides or transacts business. Although testimony is taken under oath, the commission is not bound by the normal rules of evidence followed in Ohio courts.

If unlawful discrimination is found to have occurred, the offender may be ordered to stop the discriminatory practice, to pay the complaining party's actual damages and attorney's fees, and to pay the following punitive damages:

- Up to $10,000 for a first offense, or where any previous violation occurred more than seven years before
- Up to $25,000 if the offender committed a previous violation within the past five years
- Up to $50,000 if the offender has committed two or more violations within the past seven years

Either the complainant or the alleged offender may appeal the commission's ruling in the court of common pleas of the county in which the discriminatory practice is alleged to have occurred.

---

### In Practice

### In Ohio...

As discussed in Chapter 6, a real estate broker or salesperson may have his or her license suspended or revoked for engaging in repeated unlawful discriminatory practices in violation of the Ohio Fair Housing Law. ◆

**Civil Actions**

A person who has been discriminated against in violation of the Fair Housing Law may elect to enforce his or her rights through a civil action in a court of common pleas. A civil action must be commenced within one year after the alleged practice occurred. The court remedies are injunctive relief, actual damages, and court costs. The court may appoint an attorney for the complainant and may allow the commencement of a civil action without advance payment of court costs.

**In Practice**

**In Ohio...**

In Ohio a person who has been discriminated against in violation of the Fair Housing Law may pursue his or her legal remedies either through the Ohio Civil Rights Commission or through the courts. However, the choice is a final one: the choice of one precludes the other. ◆

**Exceptions to the Fair Housing Law**

**In Ohio...**

While real estate licensees need to be more concerned with complying with the Fair Housing Law than with avoiding its mandates, there are a number of limited exceptions to the law with which you should be familiar.

For instance, the ban against discrimination in the making or purchasing of residential real estate loans does not apply to persons who are not in the business of lending money or who do not lend money as an incidental part of their business. The ban also does not apply to loans that are given only as part of the purchase price of an owner-occupied residence being sold by the owner or to loans made casually or occasionally to relatives or friends. ◆

The prohibition against making inquiries into an applicant's disability does not apply when the inquiry has a legitimate bearing on

- the applicant's ability to fulfill the responsibilities of ownership or tenancy;
- the applicant's qualification for special housing accommodations or priorities; or
- determining whether the applicant uses or has a history of using controlled substances or has been convicted or found guilty of the sale, production, or distribution of controlled substances.

While a lessor may not require a tenant with a disability to pay a greater security deposit than other tenants when he or she wishes to make modifications to the unit, the landlord may condition the modification on

- a reasonable description of the nature and quality of the intended construction;
- an agreement to restore the unit to its original condition at the end of the tenancy; and
- payment of an amount approximating the cost of restoring the unit to its original condition into an interest-bearing escrow account, with the payments made over time and the interest payable to the tenant.

The Fair Housing Law does not bar religious or fraternal organizations from limiting the sale, rental, or occupancy of their housing accommodations to members. Neither does the law prevent the local, state, or federal government from establishing reasonable occupancy restrictions limiting the number of persons permitted in a housing accommodation or imposing regulations regarding the size and number of rooms permissible in a housing accommo

**In Ohio...** dation. The U.S. Supreme Court has ruled that municipalities may not impose restrictions on the number of nonrelated persons permitted to live in a housing unit if similar restrictions are not imposed on related individuals. ◆

Discrimination on the basis of family status is permitted if the housing accommodations are specifically designed and operated to assist elderly persons or are intended for and solely occupied by persons over the age of 62. Similarly, if an accommodation is intended and operated for occupancy by at least one person aged 55 or older per unit, the owner or landlord may discriminate against persons under the age of 18, their parents or custodians, and pregnant women.

**In Ohio...** **Listing agreements.** Ohio fair housing laws require that the following statement be included in all written listing agreements:

> It is illegal, pursuant to the Ohio fair housing law, Division (H) of Section 4112.02 of the revised code and the federal housing law, 42 U.S.C.A. 3601, to refuse to sell, transfer, assign, rent, lease, sublease, or finance housing accommodations, refuse to negotiate for the sale or rental of housing accommodations, or otherwise deny or make unavailable housing accommodations because of race, color, religion, sex, familial status, ancestry, handicap, or national origin; or to so discriminate in advertising the sale or rental of housing, in the financing of housing, or in the provision of real estate brokerage services; it is also illegal for profit to induce or attempt to induce a person to sell or rent a dwelling by representations regarding the entry into the neighborhood of a person or persons belonging to one of the protected classes. ◆

# FAIR HOUSING PRACTICES

For the civil rights laws to accomplish their goal of eliminating discrimination, licensees must apply them routinely. Of course, compliance also means that licensees must avoid violating both the laws and the ethical standards of the profession. The following discussion examines the ethical and legal issues that confront real estate licensees.

## Blockbusting

_Panic Selling_

| |
|---|
| _Blockbusting:_ encouraging the sale or renting of property by claiming that the entry of a protected class of people into the neighborhood will negatively affect property values. |

**Blockbusting** is the act of encouraging people to sell or rent their homes by claiming that the entry of a protected class of people into the neighborhood will have some sort of negative impact on property values. Blockbusting was a common practice during the 1950s and 1960s, as unscrupulous real estate agents profited by fueling "white flight" from cities to suburbs. Any message, however subtle, that property should be sold or rented because the neighborhood is "undergoing changes" is considered blockbusting. It is illegal to assert that the presence of certain persons will cause property values to decline, crime or antisocial behavior to increase, and the quality of schools to suffer.

A critical element in blockbusting, according to HUD, is the profit motive. A property owner may be intimidated into selling his or her property at a depressed price to the blockbuster, who in turn sells the property to another person at a higher price. Another term for this activity is panic selling. To avoid accusations of blockbusting, licensees should use good judgment when choosing locations and methods for marketing their services and soliciting listings.

| | Figure 22.3 | HUD's Advertising Guidelines | | |
|---|---|---|---|---|
| **CATEGORY** | **RULE** | **PERMITTED** | **NOT PERMITTED** | |
| Race<br>Color<br>National Origin | No discriminatory limitation/preference may be expressed | "master bedroom"<br>"good neighborhood" | "white neighborhood"<br>"no French" | |
| Religion | No religious preference/limitation | "chapel on premises"<br>"kosher meals available"<br>"Merry Christmas" | "no Muslims"<br>"nice Christian family"<br>"near great Catholic school" | |
| Sex | No explicit preference based on sex | "mother-in-law suite"<br>"master bedroom"<br>"female roommate sought" | "great house for a man"<br>"wife's dream kitchen" | |
| Handicap | No exclusions or limitations based on handicap | "wheelchair ramp"<br>"walk to shopping" | "no wheelchairs"<br>"able-bodied tenants only" | |
| Familial Status | No preference or limitation based on family size or nature | "two-bedroom"<br>"family room"<br>"quiet neighborhood" | "married couple only"<br>"no more than two children"<br>"retiree's dream house" | |
| Photographs or Illustrations of People | People should be clearly representative and nonexclusive | Illustrations showing ethnic races, family groups, singles, etc. | Illustrations showing only singles, African-American families, elderly white adults, etc. | |

**Steering**

Steering is the channeling of home seekers to particular neighborhoods. It also includes discouraging potential buyers from considering some areas. In either case, it is an illegal limitation of a purchaser's options.

> *Steering*: channeling home seekers to particular neighborhoods based on race, religion, national origin, or some other consideration.

Steering may be done either to preserve the character of a neighborhood or to change its character intentionally. Many cases of steering are subtle, motivated by assumptions or perceptions about a home seeker's preferences, based on some stereotype. Assumptions are not only dangerous—they are often wrong. The licensee cannot assume that a prospective home seeker expects to be directed to certain neighborhoods or properties. Steering anyone is illegal.

**Advertising**

No advertisement of property for sale or rent may include language indicating a preference or limitation. No exception to this rule exists, regardless of how subtle the choice of words. HUD's regulations cite examples that are considered discriminatory. (See Figure 22.3.) The media used for promoting property or real estate services cannot target one population to the exclusion of others. The selective use of media, whether by language or geography, may have discriminatory impact. For instance, advertising property only in a Korean-language newspaper tends to discriminate against non-Koreans. Similarly, limiting advertising to a cable television channel available only to white suburbanites may be construed as a discriminatory act. However, if an advertisement appears in general-circulation media as well, it may be legal.

**Appraising**

*Same Fair Housing Law*

Those who prepare appraisals or any statements of valuation, whether they are formal or informal, oral or written (including a competitive market analysis), may consider any factors that affect value. However, race, color, religion, national origin, sex, handicap, and familial status are not factors that may be considered.

**Redlining**

*Test*

The practice of refusing to make mortgage loans or issue insurance policies in specific areas for reasons other than the economic qualifications of the applicants is known as **redlining.** Redlining refers to literally drawing a line around particular areas. This practice is often a major contributor to the deterioration of older neighborhoods. Redlining is frequently based on racial grounds rather than on any real objection to an applicant's creditworthiness. That is, the lender makes a policy decision that no property in a certain area is qualified for a loan, no matter who wants to buy it, because of the neighborhood's ethnic character. The federal Fair Housing Act prohibits discrimination in mortgage lending and covers not only the actions of primary lenders but also activities in the secondary mortgage market. A lending institution, however, can refuse a loan solely on sound economic grounds.

The *Home Mortgage Disclosure Act* requires that all institutional mortgage lenders with assets in excess of $10 million and one or more offices in a given geographic area make annual reports. The reports must detail all mortgage loans the institution has made or purchased, broken down by census tract. This law enables the government to detect patterns of lending behavior that might constitute redlining.

**Intent and Effect**

If an owner or real estate licensee *purposely* sets out to engage in blockbusting, steering, or other unfair activities, the intent to discriminate is obvious. However, owners and licensees must examine their activities and policies carefully to determine whether they have unintentional discriminatory *effects.* Whenever policies or practices result in unequal treatment of persons in the protected classes, they are considered discriminatory, regardless of any innocent intent. This *effects test* is applied by regulatory agencies to determine whether an individual has been discriminated against.

## ENFORCEMENT OF THE FAIR HOUSING ACT

The federal Fair Housing Act is administered by the Office of Fair Housing and Equal Opportunity (OFHEO) under the direction of the secretary of HUD. Any aggrieved person who believes illegal discrimination has occurred may file a complaint with HUD within one year of the alleged act. HUD may also initiate its own complaint. Complaints may be reported to the Office of Fair Housing and Equal Opportunity, Department of Housing and Urban Development, Washington, DC 20410, or to the Office of Fair Housing and Equal Opportunity in care of the nearest HUD regional office.

On receiving a complaint, HUD initiates an investigation. Within 100 days of the filing of the complaint, HUD either determines that reasonable cause exists to bring a charge of illegal discrimination or dismisses the complaint. During this investigation period, HUD can attempt to resolve the dispute informally through conciliation. *Conciliation* is the resolution of a complaint by obtaining assurance that the person against whom the complaint was filed (the respondent) will remedy any violation that may have occurred. The respondent further agrees to take steps to eliminate or prevent discriminatory practices in the future. If necessary, these agreements can be enforced through civil action.

The aggrieved person has the right to seek relief through administrative proceedings. *Administrative proceedings* are hearings held before administrative law judges (ALJs). An ALJ has the authority to award actual damages to the aggrieved person or persons and, if it is believed the public interest will be served, to impose monetary penalties. The penalties range from up to $10,000 for the first offense to $25,000 for a second violation within five years and $50,000 for further violations within seven years. The ALJ also has the authority to issue an injunction to order the offender to either do something (such as rent an apartment to the complaining party) or refrain from doing something (such as acting in a discriminatory manner).

The parties may elect civil action in federal court at any time within two years of the discriminatory act. For cases heard in federal court, unlimited punitive damages can be awarded in addition to actual damages. The court can also issue injunctions. As noted in Chapter 5, errors and omissions insurance carried by licensees normally does not pay for violations of the fair housing laws.

Whenever the attorney general has reasonable cause to believe that any person or group is engaged in a pattern or practice of resistance to the full enjoyment of any of the rights granted by the federal fair housing laws, he or she may file a civil action in any federal district court. Civil penalties may result in an amount not to exceed $50,000 for a first violation and an amount not to exceed $100,000 for second and subsequent violations.

*Complaints brought under the Civil Rights Act of 1866 are taken directly to federal courts.* The only time limit for action is a state's statute of limitations for *torts*—injuries one individual inflicts on another.

## State and Local Enforcement Agencies

Many states and municipalities have their own fair housing laws. If a state or local law is *substantially equivalent* to the federal law, all complaints filed with HUD are referred to the local enforcement agencies. To be considered substantially equivalent, the local law and its related regulations must contain prohibitions comparable to those in the federal law. In addition, the state or locality must show that its local enforcement agency takes sufficient affirmative action in processing and investigating complaints and in finding remedies for discriminatory practices. Ohio's Fair Housing Law has been found to be substantially equivalent to its federal counterpart. ◆

**In Ohio...**

## Threats or Acts of Violence

Being a real estate agent is not generally considered a dangerous occupation. However, some licensees may find themselves the targets of threats or violence merely for complying with fair housing laws. The federal *Fair Housing Act of 1968* protects the rights of those who seek the benefits of the open housing law. It also protects owners, brokers, and salespersons who aid or encourage the enjoyment of open housing rights. Threats, coercion, and intimidation are punishable by criminal action. In such a case, the victim should report the incident immediately to the local police and to the nearest office of the Federal Bureau of Investigation.

## IMPLICATIONS FOR BROKERS AND SALESPEOPLE

The real estate industry is largely responsible for creating and maintaining an open housing market. Brokers and salespersons are a community's real estate experts. Along with the privilege of profiting from real estate transactions come the social and legal responsibilities to ensure that everyone's civil rights are protected. The reputation of the industry cannot afford any appearance that its licensees are not committed to the principles of fair housing. Licensees and the industry must be publicly conspicuous in their equal opportunity efforts. Establishing relationships with community and fair housing groups to discuss common concerns and develop solutions to problems is a constructive activity. What's more, a licensee who is active in helping to improve his or her community will earn a reputation for being a concerned citizen that may well translate into a larger client base.

Fair housing *is* the law. The consequences for anyone who violates the law are serious. In addition to the financial penalties, a real estate broker's or salesperson's livelihood will be in danger if his or her license is suspended or revoked. That the offense was unintentional is no defense. Licensees must scrutinize their practices and be particularly careful not to fall victim to clients or customers who expect to discriminate.

---

**In Practice**    If a potential buyer asks a licensee about minorities in the neighborhood or whether a person in the house died of AIDS, it is appropriate to respond by saying, "I am sorry but that is a question I am not permitted by law to answer." The licensee can then offer the prospect a pamphlet on Equal Opportunity.

---

All parties deserve the same standard of service. Everyone has the right to expect equal treatment, within his or her property requirements, financial ability, and experience in the marketplace. A good test is to answer the question, "Are we doing this for everyone?" If an act is not performed consistently, or if an act affects some individuals differently from others, it could be construed as discriminatory. Standardized inventories of property listings, standardized criteria for financial qualification, and written documentation of all conversations are three effective means of self-protection for licensees.

HUD requires that its fair housing posters be displayed in any place of business where real estate is offered for sale or rent. Following HUD's advertising procedures and using the fair housing slogan and logo keep the public aware of the broker's commitment to equal opportunity.

Beyond being the law, fair housing is good business. It ensures the greatest number of properties available for sale and rent and the largest possible pool of potential purchasers and tenants.

**KEY TERMS**

| | | |
|---|---|---|
| administrative hearings | conciliator | Ohio Civil Rights Commission |
| Americans with Disabilities Act | Department of Housing and Urban Development | Ohio Fair Housing Law redlining |
| blockbusting | discriminatory actions | steering |
| Civil Rights Act of 1866 | Equal Credit Opportunity Act | Title VIII of the Civil Rights Act of 1968 |
| conciliation | Fair Housing Act | |

**SUMMARY**

- The federal regulations regarding equal opportunity in housing are contained principally in two laws.
  - The Civil Rights Act of 1866 prohibits all racial discrimination.
  - The Fair Housing Act (Title VII of the Civil Rights Act of 1968), as amended, prohibits discrimination on the basis of race, color, religion, sex, handicap, familial status, or national origin in the sale, rental, or financing of residential property.
- Discriminatory actions include refusing to deal with an individual or a specific group, changing any terms of a real estate or loan transaction, changing the services offered for any individual or group, creating statements or advertisements that indicate discriminatory restrictions, or otherwise attempting to make a dwelling unavailable to any person or group because of race, color, religion, sex, handicap, familial status, or national origin.
- The law also prohibits steering, blockbusting, and redlining.
- Complaints under the Fair Housing Act may be reported to and investigated by the Department of Housing and Urban Development (HUD).
  - Such complaints also may be taken directly to U.S. district courts.
  - In states and localities that have enacted fair housing legislation that is substantially equivalent to the federal law (including Ohio), complaints are handled by state and local agencies and state courts.
  - Complaints under the Civil Rights Act of 1866 must be taken to federal courts.

**Real-Life Real Estate**

1. Fair Housing is the "law of the land." Explain your position as a practicing salesperson regarding equal opportunity in housing.
2. Discrimination is a term that is widely used and frequently misunderstood because some discrimination is legal and appropriate. Describe your understanding of the role of real estate salespeople and brokers in educating themselves and the public about discrimination as it applies in the real estate business. (Hint: it's a lot more than just hanging a sign on the wall!)

# QUESTIONS

1. Which of the following actions is legally permitted?
   a. Advertising property for sale only to a special group
   b. Altering the terms of a loan for a member of a minority group
   c. Refusing to make a mortgage loan to a minority individual because of a poor credit history
   d. Telling an individual that an apartment has been rented when in fact it has not

2. Which of the following statements is true of complaints relating to the Civil Rights Act of 1866?
   a. They must be taken directly to federal courts.
   b. They are no longer reviewed in the courts.
   c. They are handled by HUD.
   d. They are handled by state enforcement agencies.

3. Why is the Civil Rights Act of 1866 unique?
   a. It has been broadened to protect the aged.
   b. It adds welfare recipients as a protected class.
   c. It contains "choose your neighbor" provisions.
   d. It provides no exceptions that would permit racial discrimination.

4. "I hear they're moving in. There goes the neighborhood! Better put your house on the market before values drop!" This is an example of
   a. steering.
   b. blockbusting.
   c. redlining.
   d. testing the market.

5. The act of channeling home seekers to particular areas either to maintain or to change the character of the neighborhood is
   a. blockbusting.
   b. redlining.
   c. steering.
   d. permitted under the Fair Housing Act of 1968.

6. A lender's refusal to lend money to potential homeowners attempting to purchase properties located in predominantly African American neighborhoods is known as
   a. redlining.          c. steering.
   b. blockbusting.       d. qualifying.

7. Which of the following would not be permitted under the federal Fair Housing Act?
   a. The Harvard Club in New York rents rooms only to graduates of Harvard who belong to the club.
   b. The owner of a 20-unit residential apartment building rents to men only.
   c. A Catholic convent refuses to furnish housing for a Jewish man.
   d. An owner refuses to rent the other side of her duplex to a family with children.

8. *N*, a real estate broker, wants to end racial segregation. As an office policy, *N* requires that salespersons show prospective buyers from racial or ethnic minority groups only properties that are in certain areas of town where few members of their groups currently live. *N* prepares a map illustrating the appropriate neighborhoods for each racial or ethnic group. Through this policy, *N* hopes to achieve racial balance in residential housing. Which of the following statements is true regarding *N*'s policy?
   a. While *N*'s policy may appear to constitute blockbusting, application of the effects test proves its legality.
   b. Because the effect of *N*'s policy is discriminatory, it constitutes illegal steering, regardless of *N*'s intentions.
   c. *N*'s policy clearly shows the intent to discriminate.
   d. While *N*'s policy may appear to constitute steering, application of the intent test proves its legality.

9. If a mortgage lender discriminates against a loan applicant on the basis of marital status, it violates what law?
   a. ADA
   b. Civil Rights Act of 1866
   c. ECOA
   d. Fair Housing Act

10. A Lithuanian American real estate broker offers a special discount to Lithuanian American clients. This practice is
   a. legal in certain circumstances.
   b. illegal.
   c. legal, but ill-advised.
   d. an example of steering.

11. Which of the following statements describes the Supreme Court's decision in the case of *Jones v. Alfred H. Mayer Company?*
   a. Racial discrimination is prohibited by any party in the sale or rental of real estate.
   b. Sales by individual residential homeowners are exempted, provided the owners do not use brokers.
   c. Laws against discrimination apply only to federally related transactions.
   d. Persons with disabilities are a protected class.

12. After a broker takes a sale listing of a residence, the owner specifies that he will not sell his home to any Asian family. The broker should do which of the following?
   a. Advertise the property exclusively in Asian-language newspapers
   b. Explain to the owner that the instruction violates federal law and that the broker cannot comply with it
   c. Abide by the principal's directions despite the fact that they conflict with the fair housing laws
   d. Require that the owner sign a separate legal document stating the additional instruction as an amendment to the listing agreement

13. The fine for a first violation of the federal Fair Housing Act could be as much as
   a. $500.      c. $5,000.
   b. $1,000.     d. $10,000.

14. A single man with two small children has been told by a real estate salesperson that homes for sale in a condominium complex are available only to married couples with no children. Which of the following statements is true?
   a. Because a single-parent family can be disruptive if the parent provides little supervision of the children, the condominium is permitted to discriminate against the family under the principal of rational basis.
   b. Condominium complexes are exempt from the fair housing laws and can therefore restrict children.
   c. The man may file a complaint alleging discrimination on the basis of familial status.
   d. Restrictive covenants in a condominium take precedence over the fair housing laws.

15. The following ad appeared in the newspaper: "For sale: 4 BR brick home; Redwood School District; excellent Elm Street location; next door to St. John's Church and right on the bus line. Move-in condition; priced to sell." Which of the following statements is true?
   a. The ad describes the property for sale and is very appropriate.
   b. The fair housing laws do not apply to newspaper advertising.
   c. The ad should state that the property is available to families with children.
   d. The ad should not mention St. John's Church.

16. All of the following are true regarding the Ohio Civil Rights Commission *EXCEPT* that it
   a. comprises five members appointed by the governor.
   b. has no more than three members of the same political party.
   c. hears complaints filed before it of events that occurred within the 12-month period preceding filing for the complaint.
   d. attempts to induce compliance with the law.

# CHAPTER

## 23

# Environmental Issues and the Real Estate Transaction

## ENVIRONMENTAL ISSUES

Most states have recognized the need to balance the legitimate commercial use of land with the need to preserve vital resources and protect the quality of the states' air, water, and soil. A growing number of homebuyers base their decisions in part on the desire for fresh air, clean water, and outdoor recreational opportunities. Preservation of a state's environment both enhances the quality of life and helps strengthen property values. The prevention and cleanup of pollutants and toxic wastes not only revitalize the land but create greater opportunities for responsible development.

Environmental issues have become an important factor in the practice of real estate. Consumers are becoming more health-conscious and safety-concerned and are enforcing their rights to make informed decisions. Scientists are learning more about our environment, and consumers are reacting by demanding that their surroundings be free of chemical hazards. These developments affect not only sales transactions, but also appraisers, developers, lending institutions, and property managers.

Real estate licensees must be alert to the existence of environmental hazards. Although it is important to ensure the health and safety of a property's user, the burden for disclosure or elimination of hazards seems to arise at the time the ownership of property transfers. This creates added liability for real estate practitioners if the presence of a toxic substance causes a health problem. If a property buyer suffers physical harm because of the substance, the licensee can be vulnerable to a personal injury suit in addition to other legal liability. Environmental issues are health issues, and health issues based on environmental hazards have become real estate issues. For this reason, it is extremely important that licensees not only make property disclosures but also see that prospective purchasers get authoritative information about hazardous substances so that they can make informed decisions.

Licensees should be familiar with state and federal environmental laws and the regulatory agencies that enforce them. Licensees are not expected to have the technical expertise necessary to determine whether a hazardous substance is present. However, they must be aware of environmental issues and

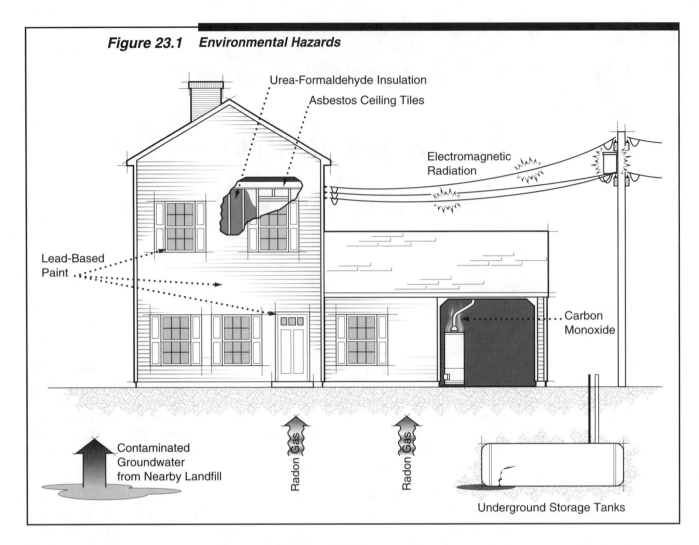

**Figure 23.1   Environmental Hazards**

take steps to ensure that the interests of all parties involved in real estate transactions are protected.

## HAZARDOUS SUBSTANCES

Pollution and hazardous substances in the environment are of interest to real estate licensees because they affect the attractiveness, desirability, and market value of cities, neighborhoods, and backyards. A toxic environment is not a place where anyone would want to live. (See Figure 23.1.)

**Asbestos**   **Asbestos** is a mineral that was once used as insulation because it was resistant to fire and contained heat effectively. Before 1978 (the year when the use of asbestos insulation was banned), asbestos was found in most residential construction. It was a component of more than 3,000 types of building materials. The Environmental Protection Agency (EPA) estimates that about 20 percent of the nation's commercial and public buildings contain asbestos.

Today, we know that inhaling microscopic asbestos fibers can result in a variety of respiratory diseases. The presence of asbestos insulation alone is not necessarily a health hazard. Asbestos is harmful only if it is disturbed or exposed, as often occurs during renovation or remodeling. Asbestos is highly friable. This means that as it ages, asbestos fibers break down easily into tiny filaments and particles. When these particles become airborne, [...] risk to humans. Airborne asbestos contamination is most prevalen[...] and commercial buildings, including schools. If the asbestos fibe[...] indoor air of a building reach a dangerous level, the building becomes d[...] to lease, finance, or insure. No safe level of asbestos exposure has [...] determined.

> *Asbestos* insulation can create airborne contaminants that may result in respiratory diseases.

Asbestos contamination also can be found in residential properties. It was used to cover pipes, ducts, and heating and hot water units. Its fire-resistant properties made it a popular material for use in floor tile, exterior siding, and roofing products. Though it may be easy to identify asbestos when it is visible (for instance, when it is wrapped around heating and water pipes), identification may be more difficult when it is behind walls or under floors.

Asbestos is costly to remove because the process requires state-licensed technicians and specially sealed environments. In addition, removal itself may be dangerous: improper removal procedures may further contaminate the air within the structure. The waste generated should be disposed of at a licensed facility, which further adds to the cost of removal. **Encapsulation,** or the sealing off of disintegrating asbestos, is an alternate method of asbestos control that may be preferable to removal in certain circumstances. However, an owner must periodically monitor the condition of the encapsulated asbestos to make sure it is not disintegrating.

Tests can be conducted to determine the level of airborne asbestos to provide an accurate disclosure in a sales transaction. A more thorough analysis of a building can be performed by an engineer skilled in identifying the presence of materials that contain asbestos. Either of these approaches can satisfy the concerns of a consumer. Appraisers also should be aware of the possible presence of asbestos.

More information on asbestos-related issues is available from the EPA at 202-554-1404. In addition, the EPA has numerous publications that provide guidance, information, and assistance with asbestos issues.

**In Ohio...** In Ohio, the cleanup and removal of asbestos is strictly governed by the Asbestos Hazard Abatement Act, which also sets the standards for licensing asbestos abatement contractors and regulates the procedures used to ensure worker safety during removals. Asbestos cleanup is regulated by the Department of Health. ◆

### Lead-Based Paint and Other Lead Hazards

**Lead** was used as a pigment and drying agent in alkyd oil-based paint. Lead-based paint may be on any interior or exterior surface, but it is particularly common on doors, windows, and other woodwork. The federal government estimates that lead is present in about 75 percent of all private housing built before 1978; that's approximately 57 million homes, ranging from low-income apartments to million-dollar mansions.

An elevated level of lead in the body can cause serious damage to the brain, kidneys, nervous system, and red blood cells. The degree of harm is related to the amount of exposure and the age at which a person is exposed. As many as one in six children may have dangerously high blood levels of lead. In Ohio, **In Ohio...** the screening, diagnosis and treatment services for children under the age of six who have been exposed to lead are coordinated by the state. ◆

Lead dust can be ingested from the hands by a crawling infant, inhaled by any occupant of a structure, or ingested from the water supply because of lead

*Lead* from paint or other sources can result in damage to the brain, nervous system, kidneys, and blood.

pipes or lead solder. In fact, lead particles can be present elsewhere, too. Soil and groundwater may be contaminated by everything from lead plumbing in leaking landfills to discarded skeet shot and bullets from an old shooting range. High levels of lead have been found in the soil near waste-to-energy incinerators. The air may be contaminated by leaded gasoline fumes from gas stations or automobile exhausts.

The use of lead-based paint was banned in 1978. Licensees who are involved in the sale, management, financing or appraisal of properties constructed before 1978 face potential liability for any personal injury that might be suffered by an occupant. Numerous legislative efforts affect licensees, sellers and landlords. There is considerable controversy about practical approaches for handling the presence of lead-based paint. Some suggest that it should be removed; others argue that it should be encapsulated; still others advocate testing to determine the amount of lead present, which then would be disclosed to a prospective owner or resident.

**In Ohio...** In Ohio, only licensed lead inspectors, abatement contractors, risk assessors, abatement project designers, and abatement workers may deal with the removal or encapsulation of lead in a structure. ◆

*No federal law requires that homeowners test for the presence of lead-based paint.* However, *known* lead-based paint hazards must be disclosed. In 1996, the EPA and the Department of Housing and Urban Development (HUD) issued final regulations requiring disclosure of the presence of any known lead-based paint hazards to potential buyers or renters. Under the Lead-Based Paint Hazard Reduction Act, persons selling or leasing residential housing constructed before 1978 must disclose the presence of known lead-based paint and provide purchasers or lessees with any relevant records or reports. A lead-based paint disclosure statement must be attached to all sales contracts and leases regarding residential properties built before 1978, and a lead hazard pamphlet must be distributed to all buyers and tenants. (See Figure 23.2.) Purchasers must be given ten days in which to conduct risk assessments or inspections for lead-based paint or lead-based paint hazards. Purchasers are not bound by any real estate contract until the ten-day period has expired. The regulations specifically require real estate agents to ensure that all parties comply with the law.

EPA guidance pamphlets and other information about lead-based hazards are available from the National Lead Information Center at 800-424-5323.

 **WWWeb.Link**
www.hud.gov/lea/leadsale. The HUD site for information about lead-based paint.

**Radon** **Radon** is a radioactive gas produced by the natural decay of other radioactive substances. Although radon can occur anywhere, some areas are known to have abnormally high amounts. The eastern United States is especially rich in radon. If radon dissipates into the atmosphere, it is not likely to cause harm. However, when radon enters buildings and is trapped in high concentrations (usually in basements with inadequate ventilation), it can cause health problems.

Opinions differ as to minimum safe levels. But growing evidence suggests that radon may be the most underestimated cause of lung cancer, particularly for children, individuals who smoke, and those who spend considerable time indoors.

**Figure 23.2** *Disclosure of Lead-Based Paint and Lead-Based Paint Hazards*

## LEAD-BASED PAINT OR LEAD-BASED PAINT HAZARD ADDENDUM

It is a condition of this contract that, until midnight of _____, Buyer shall have the right to obtain a risk assessment or inspection of the Property for the presence of lead-based paint and/or lead-based paint hazards* at Buyer's expense. This contingency will terminate at that time unless Buyer or Buyer's agent delivers to the Seller or Seller's agent a written inspection and/or risk assessment report listing the specific existing deficiencies and corrections needed, if any. If any corrections are necessary, Seller shall have the option of (i) completing them, (ii) providing for their completion, or (iii) refusing to complete them. If Seller elects not to complete or provide for completion of the corrections, then Buyer shall have the option of (iv) accepting the Property in its present condition, or (v) terminating this contract, in which case all earnest monies shall be refunded to Buyer. Buyer may waive the right to obtain a risk assessment or inspection of the Property for the presence of lead-based paint and/or lead-based paint hazards at any time without cause.

*Intact lead-based paint that is in good condition is not necessarily a hazard. See EPA pamphlet "Protect Your Family From Lead in Your Home" for more information.

### Disclosure of Information on Lead-Based Paint and Lead-Based Paint Hazards

**Lead Warning Statement**
Every Buyer of any interest in residential real property on which a residential dwelling was built prior to 1978 is notified that such property may present exposure to lead from lead-based paint that may place young children at risk of developing lead poisoning. Lead poisoning in young children may produce permanent neurological damage, including learning disabilities, reduced intelligence quotient, behavioral problems, and impaired memory. Lead poisoning also poses a particular risk to pregnant women. The Seller of any interest in residential real property is required to provide the Buyer with any information on lead-based paint hazards from risk assessments or inspections in the Seller's possession and notify the Buyer of any known lead-based paint hazards. A risk assessment or inspection for possible lead-based paint hazards is recommended prior to purchase.

**Seller's Disclosure (initial)**
_____ (a) Presence of lead-based paint and/or lead-based paint hazards (check one below):
 ❑ Known lead-based paint and/or lead-based paint hazards are present in the housing (explain).

 _____
 _____

 ❑ Seller has no knowledge of lead-based paint and/or lead-based paint hazards in the housing.
_____ (b) Records and reports available to the Seller (check one below):
 ❑ Seller has provided the Buyer with all available records and reports pertaining to lead-based paint and/or lead-based paint hazards in the housing (list documents below).

 _____
 _____

 ❑ Seller has no reports or records pertaining to lead-based paint and/or lead-based paint hazards in the housing.

**Buyer's Acknowledgment (initial)**
_____ (c) Buyer has received copies of all information listed above.
_____ (d) Buyer has received the pamphlet *Protect Your Family from Lead in Your Home.*
_____ (e) Buyer has (check one below):
 ❑ Received a 10-day opportunity (or mutually agreed upon period) to conduct a risk assessment or inspection for the presence of lead-based paint and/or lead-based paint hazards; or
 ❑ Waived the opportunity to conduct a risk assessment or inspection for the presence of lead-based paint and/or lead-based paint hazards.

**Agent's Acknowledgment (initial)**
_____ (f) Agent has informed the Seller of the Seller's obligations under 42 U.S.C. 4582(d) and is aware of his/her responsibility to ensure compliance.

**Certification of Accuracy**
The following parties have reviewed the information above and certify, to the best of their knowledge, that the information provided by the signatory is true and accurate.
Buyer: _____ (SEAL) Date _____
Buyer: _____ (SEAL) Date _____
Agent: _____ Date _____
Seller: _____ (SEAL) Date _____
Seller: _____ (SEAL) Date _____
Agent: _____ Date _____

Because radon is odorless and tasteless, it is impossible to detect without testing. Care should be exercised in the manner in which tests are conducted to ensure that the results are accurate. Radon levels vary, depending on the amount of fresh air that circulates through a house, the weather conditions, and the time of year. It is relatively easy to reduce levels of radon by installing ventilation systems or exhaust fans.

Interestingly, the modern practice of creating energy-efficient homes and buildings with practically airtight walls and windows may increase the potential for radon gas accumulation. Once radon accumulates in a basement, efficient heating and ventilation systems can rapidly spread the gas throughout the building.

Home radon-detection kits are available, although more accurate testing can be conducted by radon-detection professionals. The EPA's pamphlet "A Citizen's Guide to Radon" is available from your local EPA office.

**In Ohio...**    In Ohio no one may perform radon testing or provide professional or expert advice on radon testing, exposure, health risks, or mitigation without a valid radon tester or mitigation specialist license. ◆

## Urea-Formaldehyde

**Urea-formaldehyde** was first used in building materials, particularly insulation, in the 1970s. Gases leak out of the urea-formaldehyde foam insulation (**UFFI**) as it hardens and becomes trapped in the interior of a building. In 1982, the Consumer Product Safety Commission banned the use of UFFI. The ban was reduced to a warning after courts determined that there was insufficient evidence to support a ban. Urea-formaldehyde is known to cause cancer in animals, though the evidence of its effect on humans is inconclusive.

Formaldehyde does cause some individuals to suffer respiratory problems as well as eye and skin irritations. Consumers are becoming increasingly wary of the presence of formaldehyde, particularly if they are sensitive to it.

> *UFFI* is an insulating foam that can release harmful formaldehyde gases.

Because UFFI has received considerable adverse publicity, many buyers express concern about purchasing properties in which it was installed. Tests can be conducted to determine the level of formaldehyde gas in a house. Again, however, care should be exercised to ensure that the results of the tests are accurate and that the source of the gases is properly identified. Elevated levels could be due to a source other than the insulation.

Licensees should take care to ensure that any conditions in an agreement of sale that require tests for formaldehyde are worded properly so as to identify the purpose for which the tests are being conducted, such as to determine the presence of the insulation or some other source. Appraisers also should be aware of the presence of UFFI.

## Carbon Monoxide

**Carbon monoxide** (CO) is a colorless, odorless gas that occurs as a by-product of burning such fuels as wood, oil, and natural gas due to incomplete combustion. Furnaces, water heaters, space heaters, fireplaces, and wood stoves all produce CO as a natural result of their combustion of fuel. However, when these appliances function properly and are properly vented, their CO emissions are not a problem. When improper ventilation or equipment malfunctions permit large quantities of CO to be released into a residence or commercial structure, it poses a significant health hazard. Its effects are compounded by the fact that CO is so difficult to detect. CO is quickly absorbed by the body. It inhibits the blood's ability to transport oxygen and

*Carbon monoxide* is a by-product of fuel combustion that may result in death in poorly ventilated areas.

results in dizziness and nausea. As the concentrations of CO increase, the symptoms become more severe. More than 200 deaths from carbon monoxide poisoning occur each year.

Carbon monoxide detectors are available, and their use is mandatory in some areas. Annual maintenance of heating systems also helps avoid CO exposure.

## Electromagnetic Fields

*EMFs* are produced by electrical currents and may be related to a variety of health complaints.

**Electromagnetic fields** (EMFs) are generated by the movement of electrical currents. The use of any electrical appliance creates a small field of electromagnetic radiation: clock radios, blow-dryers, televisions, and computers all produce EMFs. The major concern regarding electromagnetic fields involves high-tension power lines. The EMFs produced by these high-voltage lines, as well as by secondary distribution lines and transformers, are suspected of causing cancer, hormonal changes, and behavioral abnormalities. There is considerable controversy (and much conflicting evidence) about whether EMFs pose a health hazard. Buyers who are aware of the controversy may, however, be unwilling to purchase property near power lines or transformers. As research into EMFs continues, real estate licensees should stay informed about current findings.

# GROUNDWATER CONTAMINATION

**Groundwater** is the water that exists under the earth's surface within the tiny spaces or crevices in geological formations. Groundwater forms the **water table,** the natural level at which the ground is saturated. This may be near the surface (in areas where the water table is very high) or several hundred feet underground. Surface water also can be absorbed into the groundwater.

Any contamination of the underground water can threaten the supply of pure, clean water for private wells or public water systems. If groundwater is not protected from contamination, the earth's natural filtering systems may be inadequate to ensure the availability of pure water. Numerous state and federal laws have been enacted to preserve and protect the water supply.

Water can be contaminated from a number of sources. Run-off from waste disposal sites, leaking underground storage tanks, and pesticides and herbicides are some of the main culprits. Because water flows from one place to another, contamination can spread far from its source. Numerous regulations are designed to protect against water contamination.

**In Ohio...** For example, there are strict limits on the riparian rights of property owners (see Chapter 8), and the state of Ohio has signed the Ohio River Sanitation Compact, along with Illinois, Indiana, Kentucky, New York, Pennsylvania, Tennessee, and West Virginia, to regulate and enforce the responsible treatment and disposal of sewage and industrial waste. Once contamination has been identified, its source can be eliminated. The water may eventually become clean. However, the process can be time consuming and extremely expensive. ◆

**In Practice**   Real estate agents need to be aware of potential groundwater contamination sources both on and off a property. These include underground storage tanks, septic systems, holding ponds, drywells, buried materials, and surface spills. Remember, because groundwater flows over wide areas, the source of contamination may not be nearby.

## UNDERGROUND STORAGE TANKS

Approximately 3 million to 5 million **underground storage tanks** (USTs) exist in the United States. Underground storage tanks are commonly found on sites where petroleum products are used or where gas stations and auto repair shops are located. They also may be found in a number of other commercial and industrial establishments—including printing and chemical plants, wood treatment plants, paper mills, paint manufacturers, dry cleaners, and food processing plants—for storing chemical or other process waste. Military bases and airports are also common sites for underground tanks. In residential areas, they are used to store heating oil.

Some tanks are currently in use, but many are long forgotten. It is an unfortunate fact that it was once common to dispose of toxic wastes by simple burial: out of sight, out of mind. Over time, however, neglected tanks may leak hazardous substances into the environment. This permits contaminants to pollute not only the soil around the tank but also adjacent parcels and groundwater. Licensees should be particularly alert to the presence of fill pipes, vent lines, stained soil, and fumes or odors, any of which may indicate the presence of a UST. Detection, removal, and clean-up of surrounding contaminated soil can be an expensive operation.

**FOR EXAMPLE** In the 1940s, a gas station in a rural Ohio town went out of business. The building fell into disrepair and was torn down. The site was vacant for several years, and its former use was forgotten. A series of commercial ventures were built on the land: a grocery store, a drive-in restaurant, a convenience store. In the late 1980s, residents of the town began noticing strong gasoline fumes in their basements, particularly after a rainstorm. Government investigators concluded that the gasoline tanks buried beneath the former gas station had broken down with age and leaked their contents into the soil. Because the town was located over a large subsurface rock slab, the gasoline could not leach down into the soil, but rather was forced to spread out under the entire town and surrounding farmland. Because the water table floated on the rock slab and the gasoline floated on the water, rains that raised the water table forced the gasoline into the soil near the residents' basements and crawlspaces, resulting in the unpleasant and potentially unhealthy fumes. When the gasoline fumes ignited and destroyed a local manufacturing plant, the residents learned that the problem was not only unpleasant but dangerous as well.

Recent state and federal laws impose very strict requirements on landowners where underground storage tanks are located to detect and correct leaks in an effort to protect the groundwater. The federal UST program is regulated by the EPA. The regulations apply to tanks that contain hazardous substances or liquid petroleum products and that store at least 10 percent of their volume underground. UST owners are required to register their tanks and adhere to strict technical and administrative requirements that govern

- installation,
- maintenance,
- corrosion prevention,
- overspill prevention,
- monitoring, and
- record keeping.

Owners are also required to demonstrate that they have sufficient financial resources to cover any damage that might result from leaks.

The following types of tanks are among those that are exempt from the federal regulations:

- Tanks that hold less than 110 gallons
- Farm and residential tanks that hold 1,100 gallons or less of motor fuel used for noncommercial purposes
- Tanks that store heating oil burned on the premises
- Tanks on or above the floor of underground areas, such as basements or tunnels
- Septic tanks and systems for collecting stormwater and wastewater

Some states have adopted laws regulating USTs that are more stringent than the federal laws.

**In Ohio...** In Ohio the Petroleum Underground Storage Tank Act gives the fire marshal primary responsibility for implementing the state's UST program and for taking corrective action regarding the containment of underground petroleum and the detection of releases. ◆

In addition to being aware of possible noncompliance with state and federal regulations, the parties to a real estate transaction should be aware that many older tanks never were registered. There may be no visible sign of their presence.

## WASTE DISPOSAL SITES

Americans produce vast quantities of garbage every day. Despite public and private recycling and composting efforts, huge piles of waste materials—from beer cans, junk mail, and diapers to food, paint, and toxic chemicals—must be disposed of. Landfill operations have become the main receptacles for garbage and refuse. Special hazardous waste disposal sites have been established to contain radioactive waste from nuclear power plants, toxic chemicals, and waste materials produced by medical, scientific, and industrial processes.

Perhaps the most prevalent method of common waste disposal is simply to bury it. A **landfill** is an enormous hole, either excavated for the purpose of waste disposal or left over from surface mining operations. The hole is lined with clay or a synthetic liner to prevent leakage of waste material into the water supply. A system of underground drainage pipes permits monitoring of leaks and leaching. Waste is laid on the liner at the bottom of the excavation, and a layer of topsoil is then compacted onto the waste. The layering procedure is repeated again and again until the landfill is full, the layers mounded up sometimes as high as several hundred feet over the surrounding landscape. **Capping** is the process of laying two to four feet of soil over the top of the site and then planting grass or some other vegetation to enhance the landfill's aesthetic value and to prevent erosion. A ventilation pipe runs from the landfill's base through the cap to vent off accumulated natural gases created by the decomposing waste.

Federal, state, and local regulations govern the location, construction, content, and maintenance of landfill sites. Test wells around landfill operations are installed to constantly monitor the groundwater in the surrounding area, and soil analyses can be used to test for contamination. Completed landfills have been used for such purposes as parks and golf courses. Rapid suburban growth has resulted in many housing developments and office campuses being built on landfill sites. However, be aware that a poorly constructed landfill can give rise to serious problems.

**FOR EXAMPLE** A suburban office building constructed on an old landfill site was very popular until its parking lot began to sink. While the structure itself was supported by pylons driven deep into the ground, the parking lot was unsupported. As the landfill beneath it compacted, the wide concrete lot sank lower and lower around the building. Each year, the building's management had to relandscape to cover the exposed foundations. The sinking parking lot eventually severed underground phone and power lines and water mains, causing the tenants considerable inconvenience. Computers were offline for hours, and flooding was frequent on the ground floor. Finally, leaking gases from the landfill began causing unpleasant odors. The tenants moved out, and the building was left vacant, a victim of poorly conceived landfill design.

Hazardous and radioactive waste disposal sites are subject to strict state and federal regulation to prevent the escape of toxic substances into the surrounding environment. Some materials, such as radioactive waste, are sealed in containers and placed in "tombs" buried deep underground. The tombs are designed to last thousands of years, built according to strict federal and state regulations. These disposal sites are usually limited to extremely remote locations, well away from populated areas or farmland.

The *Midwest Interstate Compact on Low-Level Radioactive Waste* is one example of a regional approach to the disposal of hazardous materials.

**In Ohio...** The states of Delaware, Illinois, Indiana, Iowa, Kansas, Kentucky, Maryland, Michigan, Minnesota, Missouri, Nebraska, North Dakota, Ohio, South Dakota, Virginia, and Wisconsin have agreed to cooperate in establishing and managing regional low-level radioactive waste sites. This approach allows the participants to share the costs, benefits, obligations, and inconveniences of radioactive waste disposal in a fair and reasonable way. ◆

**In Practice**

**In Ohio...** Environmental issues have a significant impact on the real estate industry. In 1995, a jury in Ohio awarded $6.7 million to homeowners whose property values had been lowered because of the defendant tire company's negligent operation and maintenance of a hazardous waste dump site. The 1,713 plaintiffs relied on testimony from economists and a real estate appraiser to demonstrate how news stories about the site had lowered the market values of their homes. Nationwide, some landfill operators now offer price guarantees to purchasers of homes near waste disposal sites. A recent university study found that a home's value increases by more than $6,000 for each mile of its distance from a garbage incinerator. ◆

**In Ohio...** The policy of the state of Ohio is to reduce reliance on the use of landfills for solid waste disposal, to restrict the types of solid wastes disposed of by landfilling, and to establish objectives for solid waste reduction, recycling and reuse. ◆

## CERCLA AND ENVIRONMENTAL PROTECTION

The majority of legislation dealing with environmental problems has been instituted within the past two decades. Although the EPA was created at the federal level to oversee such problems, several other federal agencies' areas of concern generally overlap. The federal laws were created to encourage state and local governments to enact their own legislation.

**In Ohio...** At the state level the Ohio Environmental Protection Agency has been created to administer such diverse environmental issues as chemical emergency planning; prevention and cleanup of air and water pollution; protection of the public water supply; comprehensive water resource management; and the disposal and treatment of solid, infectious, industrial, and hazardous waste materials. The Ohio EPA is also empowered to ensure state-level compliance with federal regulations. ◆

## Comprehensive Environmental Response, Compensation, and Liability Act

The **Comprehensive Environmental Response, Compensation, and Liability Act** (CERCLA) was created in 1980. It established a fund of $9 billion, called the *Superfund,* to clean up uncontrolled hazardous waste sites and to respond to spills. It created a process for identifying *potential responsible parties* (*PRPs*) and ordering them to take responsibility for the cleanup action. CERCLA is administered and enforced by the EPA.

**Liability.** A landowner is liable under CERCLA when a release or a threat of release of a hazardous substance has occurred on his or her property. Regardless of whether the contamination is the result of the landowner's actions or those of others, the owner can be held responsible for the cleanup. This liability includes the cleanup not only of the landowner's property, but also of any neighboring property that has been contaminated. A landowner who is not responsible for the contamination can seek recovery reimbursement for the cleanup cost from previous landowners, any other responsible party, or the Superfund. However, if other parties are not available, even a landowner who did not cause the problem could be solely responsible for the costs.

Once the EPA determines that hazardous material has been released into the environment, it is authorized to begin remedial action. First, it attempts to identify the potentially responsible parties (PRPs). If the PRPs agree to cooperate in the cleanup, they must agree about how to divide the cost. If the PRPs do not voluntarily undertake the cleanup, the EPA may hire its own contractors to do the necessary work. The EPA then bills the PRPs for the cost. If the PRPs refuse to pay, the EPA can seek damages in court for up to three times the actual cost of the cleanup.

Liability under the Superfund is considered to be strict, joint and several, and retroactive. **Strict liability** means that the owner is responsible to the injured party without excuse. **Joint and several liability** means that each of the individual owners is personally responsible for the total damages. If only one of the owners is financially able to handle the total damages, that owner must pay the total and collect the proportionate shares from the other owners whenever possible. **Retroactive liability** means that the liability is not limited to the current owner but includes people who have owned the site in the past.

## Superfund Amendments and Reauthorization Act

In 1986, the U.S. Congress reauthorized the Superfund. The amended statute contains stronger cleanup standards for contaminated sites and five times the funding of the original Superfund, which expired in September 1985.

The amended act also sought to clarify the obligations of lenders. As mentioned, liability under the Superfund extends to both the present and all previous owners of the contaminated site. Real estate lenders found themselves either as present owners or somewhere in the chain of ownership through foreclosure proceedings.

The amendments created a concept called innocent landowner immunity. It was recognized that in certain cases, a landowner in the chain of ownership was completely innocent of all wrongdoing and therefore should not be held liable. The innocent landowner immunity clause established the criteria by which to judge whether a person or business could be exempted from liability. The criteria included the following:

- The pollution was caused by a third party.
- The property was acquired after the fact.
- The landowner had no actual or constructive knowledge of the damage.
- Due care was exercised when the property was purchased (the landowner made a reasonable search, called an environmental site assessment) to determine that no damage to the property existed.
- Reasonable precautions were taken in the exercise of ownership rights.

**In Ohio...**   In Ohio a person or organization who is found to have created a hazardous waste site may avoid legal liability by entering into a voluntary agreement with the state to clean the site and to monitor further operations to ensure no additional pollution occurs. In exchange, the state agrees not to seek civil damages or to prosecute the polluter as long as the offender complies with the terms of the agreement. The state is thus saved the expense of legal proceedings, the offender is permitted to continue its commercial operations, and the environment is improved. ◆

## LIABILITY OF REAL ESTATE PROFESSIONALS

Environmental law is a relatively new phenomenon. Although federal and state laws have defined many of the liabilities involved, common law is being used for further interpretation. The real estate professional and all others involved in a real estate transaction must be aware of both actual and potential liability.

Sellers, as mentioned earlier, often carry the most exposure. Innocent landowners might be held responsible, even though they did not know about the presence of environmental hazards. Purchasers may be held liable, even if they didn't cause the contamination. Lenders may end up owning worthless assets if owners default on the loans rather than undertaking expensive cleanup efforts. Real estate licensees could be held liable for improper disclosure; therefore, it is necessary to be aware of the potential environmental risks from properties such as gas stations, manufacturing plants, or even funeral homes that abut their listings.

Additional exposure is created for individuals involved in other aspects of real estate transactions. For example, real estate appraisers must identify and adjust for environmental problems. Adjustments to market value typically reflect the cleanup cost plus a factor of the degree of panic and suspicion that exist in the current market. Although the sales price can be affected dramatically, it is possible that the underlying market value would remain relatively equal to others in the neighborhood. The real estate appraiser's greatest responsibility is to the lender, which depends on the appraiser to identify environmental hazards. Although the lender may be protected under certain conditions through the 1986 amendments to the Superfund Act, the lender must be aware of any potential problems and may require additional environmental reports.

Insurance carriers also might be affected in the transactions. Mortgage insurance companies protect lenders' mortgage investments and might be required to carry part of the ultimate responsibility in cases of loss. More important, hazard insurance carriers might be directly responsible for damages if such coverage was included in the initial policy.

## Discovery of Environmental Hazards

*Real estate licensees are not expected to have the technical expertise necessary to discover the presence of environmental hazards.* However, because they are presumed by the public to have special knowledge about real estate, licensees must be aware both of possible hazards and of where to seek professional help.

Obviously, the first step for a licensee is to ask the owner. He or she may already have conducted tests for carbon monoxide or radon. The owner also may be aware of a potential hazardous condition. An environmental hazard can actually be turned into a marketing plus if the owner has already done the detection and abatement work. Potential buyers can be assured that an older home is no longer a lead paint or an asbestos risk.

The most appropriate people on whom a licensee can rely for sound environmental information are scientific or technical experts. *Environmental auditors* can provide the most comprehensive studies. Their services are usually relied on by developers and purchasers of commercial and industrial properties. An environmental audit includes the property's history of use and the results of extensive and complex tests of the soil, water, air and structures. Trained *inspectors* can conduct air-sampling tests to detect radon, asbestos or EMFs. They can test soil and water quality and can inspect for lead-based paints. (Lead inspections required by the Residential Lead-Based Paint Hazard Reduction Act must be conducted by certified inspectors.) While environmental auditors may be called on at any stage in a transaction, they are most frequently brought in as a condition of closing. Not only can such experts detect environmental problems but they can usually offer guidance about how best to resolve the conditions.

## Disclosure of Environmental Hazards

State laws address the issue of disclosure of known material facts regarding a property's condition. These same rules apply to the presence of environmental hazards. A real estate licensee may be liable if he or she should have known of a condition, even if the seller neglected to disclose it. Property condition disclosures are discussed in Chapter 5.

## KEY TERMS

| | | |
|---|---|---|
| asbestos | electromagnetic field | retroactive liability |
| capping | encapsulation | strict liability |
| carbon monoxide | groundwater | UFFI |
| Comprehensive | joint and several | underground storage |
| Environmental | liability | tank |
| Response, | landfill | urea-formaldehyde |
| Compensation, and | lead | water table |
| Liability Act | radon | |

**SUMMARY**

- Environmental issues are important to real estate licensees because they may affect real estate transactions by raising issues of health risk or cleanup costs.
  - Some of the principal environmental toxins include asbestos, lead, radon, and urea-formaldehyde insulation.
- Licensees who are involved with the sale, management, financing, or appraisal of properties constructed before 1978 should be aware of potential lead-based paint in the structures.
- Ohio regulates and licenses professionals to test for or remove asbestos, lead, and radon.
- Landfills are the most common method of disposing of solid waste materials by layering them between several feet of soil. Improperly constructed or maintained landfills may present a danger to groundwater.
- CERCLA established the Superfund to finance the cleanup of hazardous waste disposal sites.
  - Under the Superfund, liability for those found to have created unlawful hazardous waste sites is strict, joint and several, and retroactive.

**Real-Life
Real Estate**

1. Explain why considering environmental impacts of all land use is "the right thing to do."
2. Assume you are a real estate salesperson about to close a BIG deal when you discover that the intended use is environmentally damaging. What do you do?

# QUESTIONS

1. Asbestos is most dangerous when it
   a. is used as insulation.
   b. crumbles and becomes airborne.
   c. gets wet.
   d. is wrapped around heating and water pipes.

2. *Encapsulation* refers to the
   a. process of sealing a landfill with three to four feet of topsoil.
   b. way in which asbestos insulation is applied to pipes and wiring systems.
   c. method of sealing disintegrating asbestos.
   d. way in which asbestos becomes airborne.

3. *J* is a real estate salesman. He shows a pre-World War I house to *T*, a prospective buyer. *T* has two toddlers and is worried about potential health hazards. Which of the following is true?
   a. There is a risk that urea-foam insulation was used in the original construction.
   b. Because *J* is a licensed real estate salesman, he can offer to inspect for lead and remove any lead risks.
   c. Because the house was built before 1978, there is a good likelihood of the presence of lead-based paint.
   d. Lead poisoning may occur only when lead paint chips are chewed and swallowed.

4. Which of the following is true regarding asbestos?
   a. The removal of asbestos can cause further contamination of a building.
   b. Asbestos causes health problems only when it is eaten.
   c. The level of asbestos in a building is affected by weather conditions.
   d. HUD requires all asbestos-containing materials to be removed from all residential buildings.

5. Which of the following best describes the water table?
   a. Natural level at which the ground is saturated
   b. Level at which underground storage tanks may be safely buried
   c. Measuring device used by specialists to measure groundwater contamination
   d. Always underground

6. All of the following are true of electromagnetic fields *EXCEPT* that electromagnetic fields are
   a. a suspected but unproven cause of cancer, hormonal abnormalities, and behavioral disorders.
   b. generated by all electrical appliances.
   c. present only near high-tension wires or large electrical transformers.
   d. caused by the movement of electricity.

7. Which of the following describes the process of creating a landfill site?
   a. Waste is liquefied, treated, and pumped through pipes to "tombs" under the water table.
   b. Waste and topsoil are layered in a pit, mounded up, then covered with dirt and plants.
   c. Waste is compacted and sealed into a container, then placed in a "tomb" designed to last several thousand years.
   d. Waste is buried in an underground concrete vault.

8. Liability under the Superfund is
   a. limited to the owner of record.
   b. joint and several and retroactive, but not strict.
   c. voluntary in Ohio.
   d. strict, joint and several, and retroactive.

9. All of the following have been proven to pose health hazards, *EXCEPT*
   a. asbestos fibers.
   b. carbon monoxide.
   c. radon.
   d. lead-based paint.

10. Which of the following environmental hazards poses a risk due to particles or fibers in the air?
   a. Carbon monoxide
   b. Radon
   c. UFFI
   d. Asbestos

11. In Ohio, radon testing may be performed only by
   a. licensed real estate professionals.
   b. the state Environmental Protection Agency.
   c. the appropriate county inspector.
   d. a licensed radon tester or mitigation specialist.

12. The primary party responsible for regulating and monitoring underground petroleum storage under Ohio's Petroleum Underground Storage Tank Act is the
   a. federal government.
   b. director of the Ohio Environmental Protection Agency.
   c. fire marshal.
   d. landowner.

# CHAPTER 24

# Introduction to Real Estate Investment

## INVESTING IN REAL ESTATE

Real estate is a popular investment. Even though changes in the economy have increased risk or lowered returns, the investment market continues to devise innovative and attractive investment strategies. These developments make it important for real estate licensees to have an elementary and up-to-date knowledge of real estate investment. Even the average homebuyer will want assurance that a residential purchase is a good investment. Of course, this does not mean that licensees should act as investment counselors. *They should always refer investors to competent tax accountants, attorneys, or investment specialists.* These are the professionals who can give expert advice on an investor's specific needs.

**Advantages of Real Estate Investment**

In recent years, real estate values have fluctuated widely in various regions of the country. This results in some investments failing to produce returns greater than the rate of inflation (that is, serving as inflation hedges). Yet many real estate investments have shown above-average *rates of return,* generally greater than the prevailing interest rates charged by mortgage lenders. In theory, this means an investor can use the *leverage* of borrowed money to finance a real estate purchase and feel relatively sure that, if held long enough, the asset will yield more money than it cost to finance the purchase.

Real estate offers investors greater control over their investments than do other options, such as stocks, bonds, or other securities. Real estate investors also receive certain tax benefits. Both leveraging and taxes are discussed in full later in this chapter.

**Disadvantages of Real Estate Investment**

Unlike stocks and bonds, real estate is not highly liquid over a short period of time. *Liquidity* refers to how quickly an asset may be converted into cash. For instance, an investor in listed stocks has only to call a stockbroker when funds are needed. The stockbroker sells the stock, and the investor receives the cash. In contrast, a real estate investor may have to sell the property at a substantially lower price than desired to ensure a quick sale. Of course, a real estate investor may be able to raise a limited amount of cash by refinancing the property.

Real estate investment is expensive. Large amounts of capital are usually required.

It is difficult to invest in real estate without expert advice. Investment decisions must be based on careful studies of all the facts, reinforced by a thorough knowledge of real estate and the manner in which it is affected by the marketplace.

Real estate requires active management. A real estate investor can rarely sit idly by and watch his or her money grow. Management decisions must be made. How much rent should be charged? How should repairs and tenant grievances be handled? The investor may want to manage the property personally. On the other hand, it may be preferable to hire a professional property manager. *Sweat equity* (physical improvements accomplished by the investor personally) may be required to make the asset profitable. Many good investments fail because of poor management.

Finally, despite its popularity, real estate investment is far from a sure thing. In fact, it involves a high degree of risk. The possibility always exists that an investor's property will decrease in value during the period it is held or that it will not generate enough income to make it profitable.

## THE INVESTMENT

Real estate investors hope to achieve various investment objectives. Their effectiveness in reaching their goals depends on the type of property and manner of ownership chosen. The most prevalent form of real estate investment is *direct ownership.* Both individuals and corporations may own real estate directly and manage it for appreciation or cash flow (income). Property held for appreciation is generally expected to increase in value while it's owned and to show a profit when it's sold. *Income property* is just that: property held for current income as well as a potential profit on its sale.

### Appreciation

Real estate is an avenue of investment open to those interested in holding property *primarily* for **appreciation.**

Two main factors affect appreciation: inflation and intrinsic value. **Inflation** is the increase in the amount of money in circulation. When more money is available, its value declines. When the value of money declines, wholesale and retail prices rise. This is essentially an operation of supply and demand, as discussed in Chapter 1. The **intrinsic value** of real estate is the result of a person's individual choices and preferences for a given geographic area. For example, property located in a pleasant neighborhood near attractive business and shopping areas has a greater intrinsic value to most people than similar property in a more isolated location. As a rule, the greater the intrinsic value, the more money a property commands on its sale.

**Unimproved land.** Quite often, investors speculate in purchases of either agricultural land or undeveloped land located in what is expected to be a major path of growth. In these cases, however, the property's intrinsic value and potential for appreciation are not easy to determine. This type of investment carries with it many inherent risks. How fast will the area develop? Will it grow sufficiently for the investor to make a good profit? Will the expected growth occur? More important, will the profits eventually realized from the property be great enough to offset the costs of holding it, such as property taxes? Because these questions often cannot be answered with any degree of certainty, lending institutions may be reluctant to lend money for the purchase of raw land.

Income tax laws do not allow the depreciation (cost recovery) of land. Also, such land may not be liquid (salable) at certain times under certain circumstances because few people will purchase raw or agricultural land on short notice. Despite all the risks, however, land has historically been a good inflation hedge if held long term. It can also be a source of income to offset some of the holding costs. For example, agricultural land can be leased out for crops, timber production, or grazing.

Investment in land ultimately is best left to experts, and even they frequently make bad land investment decisions.

**FOR EXAMPLE** *M*, a real estate investor, learns from her friends in the state capital that the governor is about to announce that a major new international airport will be built at a rural site currently occupied by farm and pasture land. *M* immediately buys several large tracts near the proposed airport site. Once the airport is in place, *M* expects to sell the land to developers for the hotels, restaurants, and office buildings that are likely to be in demand. The governor announces the airport, and the value of *M*'s investment soars. In an election before construction begins, however, the governor is defeated. The newly elected governor thinks the proposed airport would be a waste of taxpayer money, and the project dies. *M*'s investment does not turn out to be profitable after all.

**Income**  The wisest initial investment for a person who wishes to buy and personally manage real estate may be the purchase of rental income property.

**Cash flow.** The object of directing funds into income property is to generate spendable income, usually called **cash flow.** Cash flow is the total amount of money remaining after all expenditures have been paid. These expenses include taxes, operating costs and mortgage payments. The cash flow produced by any given parcel of real estate is determined by at least three factors: amount of rent received, operating expenses, and method of debt repayment.

Generally the amount of rent (income) that a property may command depends on a number of factors, including the property's location, physical appearance, and amenities. If the cash flow from rents is not enough to cover all expenses, *negative cash flow* will result.

To keep cash flow high, an investor should attempt to keep operating expenses reasonably low. Such operating expenses include general maintenance of the building, repairs, utilities, taxes, and tenant services (switchboard facilities, security systems, and so forth).

**In Practice**  With many of the tax advantages of real estate investment being reduced or withdrawn by Congress, licensees should advise investors to analyze each proposed purchase carefully with an accountant. It is more important than ever to be sure an investment will cover its own expenses. Where negative cash flow is anticipated, the investor's tax bracket may be the deciding factor. (Income tax calculations are usually figured at the investor's marginal tax rate—that is, the rate at which his or her top dollar of income is taxed.)

An investor often stands to make more money by investing with borrowed money, usually obtained through a mortgage loan or deed of trust loan. Low mortgage payments spread over a long period of time result in a higher cash flow because they allow the investor to retain more income each month; conversely, high mortgage payments contribute to a lower cash flow.

**Investment opportunities.** Traditional income-producing property includes apartment and office buildings, hotels, motels, shopping centers, and industrial properties. Historically, investors have found well-located, one- to four-family dwellings to be favorable investments. However, in recent years many communities have seen severe overbuilding of office space and shopping centers. The result has been high vacancy rates.

## LEVERAGE

**Leverage** is the use of borrowed money to finance an investment. As a rule, an investor can receive a maximum return from the initial investment (the down payment and closing and other costs) by making a small down payment, paying a low interest rate, and spreading mortgage payments over as long a period as possible.

The effect of leveraging is to provide a return that reflects the result of market forces on the entire original purchase price, but that is measured against only the actual cash invested. For example, if an investor spends $100,000 for rental property and makes a $20,000 down payment, then sells the property five years later for $125,000, the return over five years is $25,000. Disregarding ownership expenses, the return is not 25 percent ($25,000 compared with $100,000), but 125 percent of the original amount invested ($25,000 compared with $20,000).

*Risks are directly proportionate to leverage.* A high degree of leverage translates into greater risk for the investor and lender because of the high ratio of borrowed money to the value of the real estate. Lower leverage results in less risk. When values drop in an area or vacancy rates rise, the highly leveraged investor may be unable to pay even the financing costs of the property.

### Equity Buildup

*Equity buildup* is that portion of the loan payment directed toward the principal rather than the interest, *plus* any gain in property value due to appreciation. In a sense, equity buildup is like money in the investor's bank account. This accumulated equity is not realized as cash unless the property is sold or refinanced. However, the equity interest may be sold, exchanged, or mortgaged (refinanced) to be used as leverage for other investments.

### Pyramiding Through Refinancing

An effective method for a real estate investor to increase his or her holdings without investing additional capital is through pyramiding. **Pyramiding** is simply the process of using one property to drive the acquisition of additional properties. Two methods of pyramiding can be used: *pyramiding through sale* and *pyramiding through refinance.*

In pyramiding through selling, an investor first acquires a property. He or she then improves the property for resale at a substantially higher price. The profit from the sale of the first property is used to purchase additional properties. Thus, the proceeds from a single investment (the point of the pyramid) provide the means for acquiring other properties. These properties are also improved and sold, and the proceeds are reinvested, until the investor is satisfied with his or her return. Of course, the disadvantage is that the proceeds from each sale are subject to capital gains taxation, as discussed below.

The goal of pyramiding through refinancing, on the other hand, is to use the value of the original property to drive the acquisition of additional properties while retaining all the properties acquired. The investor refinances the original property and uses the proceeds of the refinance to purchase additional properties. These properties are refinanced in turn to enable the investor to acquire further properties, and so on. By holding on to the properties, the investor increases his or her income-producing property holdings while simultaneously delaying the capital gains taxes that would result from a sale.

# TAX BENEFITS

One of the main reasons real estate investments were popular and profitable in the past is that tax laws allowed investors to use losses generated by such investments to shelter income from other sources. Although laws have changed and some tax advantages of owning investment real estate are altered periodically by Congress, with professional tax advice, an investor still can make a wise real estate purchase.

**Capital Gains**

The tax law no longer favors long-term investments by reducing taxable gain (profit) on their sale or exchange. This federal policy is subject to change in response to various political and economic factors. Capital gain is defined as the difference between the adjusted basis of property and its net selling price. At various times, the tax law has excluded a portion of capital gains from income tax. The exclusions have ranged from 0 to 60 percent.

**Basis.** A property's cost basis determines the amount of gain to be taxed. The **basis** of the property is the investor's initial cost of the real estate. The investor adds to the basis the cost of any physical improvements subsequently made to the property. The amount of any depreciation claimed as a tax deduction (explained later) is subtracted from the basis. The result is the property's **adjusted basis.** When the investor sells the property, the amount by which the sales price exceeds the property's adjusted basis is the *capital gain.*

**FOR EXAMPLE** Some time ago, an investor purchased a single-family home for use as a rental property. The purchase price was $45,000. The investor now sells the property for $100,000. Shortly before the sale date, the investor makes $3,000 worth of capital improvements to the home. Depreciation of $10,000 on the property improvements has been taken during the term of the investor's ownership. The investor will pay a broker's commission of 7 percent of the sales price. The investor's closing costs will be $600. The capital gain is computed as follows:

| | | |
|---|---:|---:|
| Selling price: | | $100,000 |
| Less: | | |
| 7% commission | $7,000 | |
| closing costs | + 600 | |
| | $7,600 | −7,600 |
| Net sales price: | | $ 92,400 |
| Basis: | | |
| original cost | $45,000 | |
| improvements | +3,000 | |
| | $48,000 | |
| Less: | | |
| depreciation | (10,000) | |
| Adjusted basis: | $38,000 | −38,000 |
| Total capital gain: | | $ 54,400 |

Current tax law specifies what percentage of capital gains is taxable as income. To determine the taxable amount, an investor multiplies the total capital gain by the current percentage (in decimal form).

**Exchanges**

Real estate investors can defer taxation of capital gains by making property **exchanges.** Even if property has appreciated greatly since its initial purchase, it may be exchanged for other property. A property owner will incur tax liability on a sale only if additional capital or property is also received. Note, however, that the tax is *deferred,* not *eliminated.* Whenever the investor sells the property, the capital gain will be taxed.

To qualify as a tax-deferred exchange, the properties involved must be of *like kind*—that is, real estate for real estate of equal value. Any additional capital or personal property included with the transaction to even out the value of the exchange is called **boot.** The IRS requires that tax on the boot be paid at the time of the exchange by the party who receives it. The value of the boot is added to the basis of the property for which it is given. Tax-deferred exchanges are governed by strict federal requirements, and competent guidance from a tax professional is essential.

**FOR EXAMPLE** A owns an apartment building with an adjusted basis of $225,000 and a market value of $375,000. *A* exchanges the building plus $75,000 in cash for another apartment building having a market value of $450,000. That building, owned by *B,* has an adjusted basis of $175,000. *A*'s basis in the new building is $300,000 (the $225,000 basis of the building exchanged plus the $75,000 cash boot paid), and *A* has no tax liability on the exchange. *B* must pay tax on the $75,000 boot received and has a basis of $175,000 (the same as the previous building) in the building now owned.

**Depreciation (Cost Recovery)**

**Depreciation,** or **cost recovery,** allows an investor to recover the cost of an income-producing asset through tax deductions over the asset's useful life. While investors rarely purchase property without expecting it to appreciate over time, the tax laws maintain that all physical structures deteriorate (and lose value) over time. Cost recovery deductions may be taken only on personal property and improvements to land. Furthermore, they can be taken only if the property is used in a trade or business or for the production of income. Thus, a cost recovery deduction cannot be claimed on an individual's personal residence, and *land cannot be depreciated.* Technically, land never wears out or becomes obsolete.

Depreciation taken periodically in equal amounts over an asset's useful life is called *straight-line depreciation.* For certain property purchased before 1987 it was also possible to use the *accelerated cost recovery system (ACRS)* to claim greater deductions in the early years of ownership, gradually reducing the amount deducted in each year of useful life.

**Deductions**

In addition to tax deductions for depreciation, investors may be able to deduct losses from their real estate investments. The tax laws are very complex. The amount of loss that may be deducted depends on whether an investor actively participates in the day-to-day management of the rental property or makes management decisions. Other factors are the amount of the loss and the source of the income against which the loss is to be deducted. Investors who do not actively participate in the management or operation of the real estate are considered *passive investors.* Passive investors may not use losses to offset active income derived from active participation in real estate management, wages, or income from stocks, bonds, and the like. The tax code cites specific rules for active and passive income and losses and is subject to changes.

Certain tax credits are allowed for renovation of older buildings, low-income housing projects, and historic property. A *tax credit* is a direct reduction in the tax due rather than a deduction from income before tax is computed. Tax credits encourage the revitalization of older properties and the creation of low-income housing. The tax laws governing these issues also are complex.

Real estate must be analyzed in conjunction with an investor's other investments and overall financial goals and objectives. Income tax consequences also have a significant bearing on an investor's decisions. *Competent tax advice should be sought to help an investor carefully evaluate the ramifications of an investment decision.*

**Installment Sales**

A taxpayer who sells real property and receives payment on an installment basis pays tax only on the profit portion of each payment received. Interest received is taxable as ordinary income. *Many complex laws apply to installment sales, and a competent tax adviser should be consulted.*

## REAL ESTATE INVESTMENT SYNDICATES

A real estate investment **syndicate** is a business venture in which people pool their resources to own or develop a particular piece of property. This structure permits people with only modest capital to invest in large-scale operations. Typical syndicate projects include highrise apartment buildings and shopping centers. Syndicate members realize some profit from rents collected on the investment. The main return usually comes when the syndicate sells the property.

Syndicate participation can take many legal forms. For instance, syndicate members may hold property as tenants in common or joint tenants. Various kinds of partnership, corporate, and trust ownership options are possible. Private syndication generally involves a small group of closely associated or experienced investors. Public syndication, on the other hand, involves a much larger group of investors who may or may not be knowledgeable about real estate as an investment. Any pooling of individuals' funds raises questions of securities registration under federal and state securities laws. These are commonly referred to as *blue-sky laws.*

To protect members of the public who are not sophisticated investors but who still may be solicited to participate in syndicates, securities laws govern the offer and sale of securities. Real estate securities that fall under the definition of a public offering must be registered with state officials and the federal Securities and Exchange Commission (SEC). Pertinent factors include the number of prospects solicited, the total number of investors, the financial background and sophistication of the investors, and the value or price per unit of investment. Salespersons of real estate securities may be required to obtain special licenses and state registration.

**Forms of Syndicates**

A *general partnership* is organized so that all members of the group share equally in the managerial decisions, profits, and losses involved with the investment. A certain member (or members) of the syndicate is designated to act as *trustee* for the group. The trustee holds title to the property and maintains it in the syndicate's name.

Under a *limited partnership* agreement, one party (or parties), usually a developer or real estate broker, organizes, operates, and holds responsibility for the entire syndicate. This person is called the *general partner*. The other members of the partnership are merely investors; they have no voice in the organization and direction of the operation. These passive investors are called *limited partners*.

The limited partners share in the profits, and the general partner is compensated out of the profits. The limited partners stand to lose only as much as they invest—nothing more. Like their level of participation, their risk of loss is limited. The general partner is totally responsible for any excess losses incurred by the investment.

The sale of a limited partnership interest involves the sale of an *investment security* as defined by the SEC. As a result, the sale is subject to state and federal laws concerning the sale of securities. Unless exempt, the securities must be registered with the SEC and the appropriate state authorities.

## REAL ESTATE INVESTMENT TRUSTS

By directing their funds into **real estate investment trusts** (REITs), real estate investors take advantage of the same tax benefits as do mutual fund investors. A real estate investment trust does not have to pay corporate income tax as long as 95 percent of its income is distributed to its shareholders. Certain other conditions also must be met. To qualify as a REIT, at least 75 percent of the trust's income must come from real estate. Investors purchase certificates in the trust, which in turn invests in real estate or mortgages (or both). Profits are distributed to investors.

REITs are subject to complex restrictions and regulations. A competent attorney should be involved at all stages of a REIT's development.

## REAL ESTATE MORTGAGE INVESTMENT CONDUITS

A **real estate mortgage investment conduit** (REMIC) has complex qualification, transfer and liquidation rules. For instance, the REMIC must satisfy the asset test. The asset test requires that after a startup period, almost all assets must be qualified mortgages and permitted investments. Furthermore, investors' interests may consist of only one or more classes of *regular interests* and a single class of *residual interests*. Holders of regular interests receive interest or similar payments based on either a fixed rate or a variable rate. Holders of residual interests receive distributions (if any) on a pro-rata basis.

---

**KEY TERMS**

| | | |
|---|---|---|
| adjusted basis | depreciation | real estate investment |
| appreciation | exchange | trust |
| basis | inflation | real estate mortgage |
| boot | intrinsic value | investment conduit |
| cash flow | leverage | syndicate |
| cost recovery | pyramiding | |

**SUMMARY**

- Traditionally, real estate investment has offered an above-average rate of return while acting as an effective hedge against inflation.
  - Real estate investments allow an investor to use other people's money through leverage.
  - There also may be tax advantages to owning real estate.
- Real estate is not a highly liquid investment and often carries a high degree of risk. Expert advice is often necessary.
- Investment property held for appreciation purposes is generally expected to increase in value to a point at which its selling price covers holding costs and permits a profit.
  - The two main factors that affect appreciation are inflation and the property's present and future intrinsic value.
  - Real estate held for income purposes is generally expected to generate a steady flow of income, called cash flow, and to show a profit at the time of sale.
- An investor who hopes to use maximum leverage in financing an investment should make a small down payment, pay low interest rates, and spread mortgage payments over as long a period as possible.
  - By holding and refinancing properties, a practice known as *pyramiding,* an investor may substantially increase investment holdings without contributing additional capital.
  - The highly leveraged investor has correspondingly high risk.
- By exchanging one property for another with an equal or a greater selling value, an investor can defer paying tax on the gain realized until a sale is made.
  - A total tax deferment is possible only if the investor receives no cash or other incentive to even out the exchange.
  - If such cash or property is received, it is called *boot,* and it is taxed.
- Depreciation (cost recovery) is a concept that allows an investor to recover in tax deductions the basis of an asset over its useful life.
  - Only costs of improvements to land may be recovered, not costs for the land itself. The Tax Reform Act of 1986 greatly limited the potential for investment losses to shelter other income. But tax credits are still allowed for projects involving low-income housing and older buildings.
- An investor may defer federal income taxes on a gain realized from the sale of an investment property through an installment sale of property.
- Individuals may also invest in real estate through an investment syndicate. These usually consist of general and limited partnerships.
  - Other forms of real estate investment include real estate investment trusts (REITs) and real estate mortgage investment conduits (REMICs).
- Real estate brokers and salespersons should be familiar with the rudimentary tax implications of real property ownership, but should refer clients to competent tax advisers for answers to specific questions.

**Real-Life Real Estate**

1. Compare and contrast *inflation* and *appreciation* as they apply in real estate investing.
2. Describe the impact of *depreciation* on the value of a real estate investment.

# QUESTIONS

1. The advantages of real estate investment include the
   a. illiquidity of the investment.
   b. need for expert advice.
   c. fact that the investment can be an inflation hedge.
   d. degree of risk involved.

2. Vacant land can be a good investment because
   a. it must appreciate enough to cover expenses.
   b. it can have intrinsic value.
   c. bank financing is easily arranged.
   d. it may not be depreciated.

3. The increase of money in circulation, resulting in a sharp rise in prices and an equally sharp decline in the value of money, is called
   a. appreciation.
   b. inflation.
   c. negative cash flow.
   d. recapture.

4. A small multifamily property generates $50,000 in rental income with expenses of $45,000 annually, including $35,000 in debt service. The property appreciates about $25,000 a year. On this property the cash flow is
   a. $5,000.          c. $25,000.
   b. $15,000.          d. $35,000.

5. Leverage involves the use of
   a. cost recovery.
   b. borrowed money.
   c. government subsidies.
   d. alternative taxes.

6. A property's equity represents its current value less
   a. depreciation.
   b. mortgage indebtedness.
   c. physical improvements.
   d. selling costs and depreciation.

7. An investor's marginal tax rate is the
   a. total tax bill divided by net taxable income.
   b. extra tax if he has too many tax shelters.
   c. top applicable income tax bracket.
   d. percentage taxable on an installment sale.

8. The primary source of tax shelter in real estate investments comes from the accounting concept known as
   a. recapture.
   b. boot.
   c. net operating income.
   d. depreciation.

9. For tax purposes the initial cost of an investment property plus the cost of any subsequent improvements to the property, less depreciation, represents the investment's
   a. adjusted basis.          c. basis.
   b. capital gains.          d. salvage value.

10. The money left in an investor's pocket after expenses, including debt service, have been paid is known as
    a. net operating income.
    b. gross income.
    c. cash flow.
    d. internal rate of return.

11. An investment syndicate in which all members share equally in the managerial decisions, profits, and losses involved in the venture is an example of a
    a. real estate investment trust.
    b. limited partnership.
    c. real estate mortgage trust.
    d. general partnership.

12. Shareholders in a real estate trust generally
    a. receive most of the trust's income each year.
    b. take an active part in management.
    c. find it difficult to sell their shares.
    d. realize their main profit through sales of property.

13. In an installment sale of one's own home taxable gain is received and may be reported as income by the seller
    a. in the year the sale is initiated.
    b. in the year the final installment payment is made.
    c. in each year that installment payments are received.
    d. at any one time during the period installment payments are received.

14. A separate license or registration may be required for the sale of
    a. all investment property.
    b. real estate securities.
    c. installment property.
    d. boot.

15. A new tax entity that issues securities backed by a pool of mortgages is a
    a. REIT.
    b. REMIC.
    c. TRA.
    d. general partnership.

# CHAPTER 25

# Closing the Real Estate Transaction

## PRECLOSING PROCEDURES

*Closing* is the point at which ownership of a property is transferred in exchange for the selling price.

Everything a licensee does in the course of a real estate transaction, from soliciting clients to presenting offers, and coordinating inspections, leads to one final event—closing. **Closing** is the consummation of the real estate transaction. Closing actually involves two events: the promises made in the sales contract are fulfilled and the mortgage loan funds (if any) are distributed to the buyer. It is the time when the title to the real estate is transferred in exchange for payment of the purchase price. Closing marks the end of any real estate transaction. Before the property changes hands, however, important issues must be resolved.

**Buyer's Issues**

The buyer will want to be sure that the seller delivers title. The buyer should also ensure that the property is in the promised condition. This involves inspecting

- the title evidence;
- the seller's deed;
- any documents demonstrating the removal of undesired liens and encumbrances;
- the survey;
- the results of any required inspections, such as termite or structural inspections, or required repairs; and
- any leases if tenants reside on the premises.

**In Practice**

One of the most frequent causes of lawsuits against licensees is inaccurate lot lines. Buyers want to be confident that the properties they purchase are in fact what they believe they are paying for. Relying on old surveys is not necessarily a good idea; the property should be resurveyed by a competent surveyor, whether or not the title company or lender requires it.

**Final property inspection.** Shortly before the closing takes place, the buyer usually makes a *final inspection* of the property with the broker (often called the *walk-through*). Through this inspection, the buyer makes sure that necessary repairs have been made, that the property has been well maintained, that all fixtures are in place, and that there has been no unauthorized removal or alteration of any part of the improvements.

**Survey.** A *survey* gives information about the exact location and size of the property. The sales contract specifies who will pay for the survey. It is usual for the survey to "spot" the location of all buildings, driveways, fences, and other improvements located primarily on the premises being purchased. Any improvements located on adjoining property that may encroach on the premises being bought also will be noted. The survey should set out, in full, any existing easements and encroachments. Whether or not the sales contract calls for a survey, lenders frequently require one.

**Seller's Issues**
Obviously, the seller's main interest is in receiving payment for the property. He or she wants to be sure that the buyer has obtained the necessary financing and has sufficient funds to complete the sale. The seller also wants to be certain that he or she has complied with all the buyer's requirements so the transaction will be completed.

Both parties need to inspect the closing statement to make sure that all monies involved in the transaction have been accounted for properly. The parties may be accompanied by their attorneys.

---

**In Practice**
Licensees often assist in preclosing arrangements as part of their service to clients. In some states, licensees are required to advise the parties of the approximate expenses involved in closing when a sales contract is signed. In other states, it is the licensees' statutory duty to coordinate and supervise closing activities.

---

## CONDUCTING THE CLOSING

Closing is known by many names. For instance, in some areas closing is called *settlement and transfer.* In other parts of the country, the parties to the transaction sit around a single table and exchange copies of documents, a process known as *passing papers.* ("We passed papers on the new house Wednesday morning.")

**In Ohio...**
In still other regions (such as the northern areas of Ohio), the buyer and seller may never meet at all; the paperwork is handled by an escrow agent. This process is known as *closing escrow.* ("We'll close escrow on our house next week.") ◆

Whether the closing occurs face to face or through escrow, the main concerns are that the buyer receives marketable title, the seller receives the purchase price, and certain other items are adjusted properly between the two.

 **WWWeb.Link**
www.argosylegal.com. A site that provides free real estate closing software.

**Face-to-Face Closing**
A face-to-face closing (often referred to as a "roundtable closing") involves the resolution of two issues. First, the promises made in the sales contract are fulfilled. Second, the buyer's loan is finalized, and the mortgage lender

disburses the loan funds. The difference between a face-to-face closing and an escrow closing is that in a face-to-face closing, these two issues are resolved during a single meeting of all the parties and their attorneys. As discussed earlier, the parties in an escrow closing may never meet. The phrase *passing papers* vividly describes a face-to-face closing. In southern Ohio, a face-to-face closing is commonly practiced. ◆

**In Ohio...**

Face-to-face closings may be held at a number of locations, including the office of the title company, the lending institution, one of the parties' attorneys, the broker, the county recorder, or the escrow company. Those attending a closing may include

In a *face-to-face closing*, the parties meet face to face.

- the buyer;
- the seller;
- the real estate salespersons or brokers (both the buyer's and the seller's agents);
- the seller's and the buyer's attorneys;
- representatives of the lending institutions involved with the buyer's new mortgage loan, the buyer's assumption of the seller's existing loan, or the seller's payoff of an existing loan; and
- a representative of the title insurance company.

**Closing agent or closing officer.** One person usually conducts the proceedings at a closing and calculates the division of income and expenses between the parties (called *settlement*). In some areas, real estate brokers preside. In others, the closing agent is the buyer's or seller's attorney, a representative of the lender, or a representative of the title company. Some title companies and law firms employ paralegal assistants who conduct closings for their firms.

Preparation for closing involves ordering and reviewing an array of documents, such as the title insurance policy or title certificate, surveys, property insurance policies, and other items. Arrangements must be made with the parties for the time and place of closing. Closing statements and other documents must be prepared.

**The exchange.** When the parties are satisfied that everything is in order, the exchange is made. All pertinent documents are then recorded in the correct order to ensure continuity of title. For instance, if the seller pays off an existing loan and the buyer obtains a new loan, the seller's satisfaction of mortgage must be recorded before the seller's deed to the buyer. The buyer's new mortgage or deed of trust then must be recorded after the deed because the buyer cannot pledge the property as security for the loan until he or she owns it.

**Closing in Escrow**

**In Ohio...**

Although a few states allow transactions that are never closed in escrow, escrow closings are used to some extent in most states. Escrow closings are particularly common in the northern areas of Ohio. ◆

An **escrow** is a method of closing in which a disinterested third party is authorized to act as escrow agent and to coordinate the closing activities. The escrow agent also may be called the *escrow holder*. The escrow agent may be an attorney, a title company, a trust company, an escrow company, or the escrow department of a lending institution. Many real estate firms offer escrow services. However, a broker cannot be a disinterested party in a transaction from which he or she expects to collect a commission. Because the escrow agent is placed in a position of great trust, many states have laws regulating escrow agents and limiting who may serve in this capacity.

**Escrow procedure.** When a transaction will close in escrow, the buyer and seller execute escrow instructions to the escrow agent after the sales contract is signed. One of the parties selects an escrow agent. Which party selects the agent is determined either by negotiation or by state law. Once the contract is signed, the broker turns over the earnest money to the escrow agent, who deposits it in a special trust, or escrow, account.

> In an *escrow closing,* a third party coordinates the closing activities on behalf of the buyer and seller.

Buyer and seller deposit all pertinent documents and other items with the escrow agent before the specified date of closing. The seller usually deposits

- the deed conveying the property to the buyer;
- title evidence (abstract and attorney's opinion, certificate of title, title insurance, or Torrens certificate);
- existing hazard insurance policies;
- a letter or mortgage reduction certificate from the lender stating the exact principal remaining (if the buyer assumes the seller's loan);
- affidavits of title (if required);
- a reduction certificate, or payoff statement (if the seller's loan is to be paid off); and
- other instruments or documents necessary to clear the title or to complete the transaction.

The buyer deposits

- the balance of the cash needed to complete the purchase, usually in the form of a certified check;
- loan documents (if the buyer secures a new loan);
- proof of hazard insurance, including (where required) flood insurance; and
- other necessary documents.

The escrow agent has the authority to examine the title evidence. When marketable title is shown in the name of the buyer and all other conditions of the escrow agreement have been met, the agent is authorized to disburse the purchase price to the seller, minus all charges and expenses. The agent then records the deed and mortgage (if a new loan has been obtained by the purchaser).

If the escrow agent's examination of the title discloses liens, a portion of the purchase price can be withheld from the seller. The withheld portion is used to pay the liens to clear the title.

If the seller cannot clear the title, or if for any reason the sale cannot be consummated, the escrow instructions usually provide that the parties be returned to their former statuses, as if no sale occurred. The escrow agent reconveys title to the seller and returns the purchase money to the buyer.

**IRS Reporting Requirements** Many real estate transactions must be reported to the IRS by the closing agent on a Form 1099-S. Information includes the sales price, the amount of property tax reimbursement credited to the seller, and the seller's Social Security number. If the closing agent does not notify the IRS, the responsibility for filing the form falls on the mortgage lender, although the brokers or the parties to the transaction ultimately could be held liable.

Even for those transactions that are exempt from reporting requirements, the agent must still fill out a 1099-S and keep it on file.

**Broker's Role at Closing**

Depending on local practice, the broker's role at closing can vary from simply collecting the commission to conducting the proceedings. Real estate brokers are not authorized to give legal advice or otherwise engage in the practice of law. This means that in some states, a broker's job is essentially finished as soon as the sales contract is signed. After the contract is signed, the attorneys take over. Even so, a broker's service generally continues all the way through closing. The broker makes sure all the details are taken care of so that the closing can proceed smoothly. This means making arrangements for title evidence, surveys and appraisals, inspections or repairs for structural conditions, water supplies, sewage facilities, or toxic substances.

Though real estate licensees do not always conduct closing proceedings, they usually attend. Often, the parties look to their agents for guidance, assistance, and information during what can be a stressful experience. Licensees need to be thoroughly familiar with the process and procedures involved in preparing a closing statement, which includes the expenses and prorations of costs to close the transaction. It is also in the brokers' best interests that the transactions they worked so hard to bring about move successfully and smoothly to a conclusion. Of course, a broker's (and a salesperson's) commission is generally paid out of the proceeds at closing.

---

**In Practice**

*Licensees should avoid recommending* sources for any inspection or testing services. If a buyer suffers any injury as a result of a provider's negligence, the licensee also may be liable. The better practice is to give clients the names of several professionals who offer high-quality services.

---

**Lender's Interest in Closing**

Whether a buyer obtains new financing or assumes the seller's existing loan, the lender wants to protect its security interest in the property. The lender has an interest in making sure the buyer gets good, marketable title and that tax and insurance payments are maintained. Lenders want their mortgage lien to have priority over other liens. They also want to ensure that insurance is kept up to date in case property is damaged or destroyed. For this reason, a lender generally requires a title insurance policy and a fire and hazard insurance policy (along with a receipt for the premium). In addition, a lender may require other information: a survey, a termite or another inspection report, or a certificate of occupancy (for a newly constructed building). A lender may also request that a reserve account be established for tax and insurance payments. Lenders sometimes even require representation by their own attorneys at closings.

## RESPA REQUIREMENTS

The federal **Real Estate Settlement Procedures Act** (RESPA) was enacted to protect consumers from abusive lending practices. RESPA also aids consumers during the mortgage loan settlement process. It ensures that consumers are provided with important, accurate, and timely information about the actual costs of settling or closing a transaction. It also eliminates kickbacks and other referral fees that tend to inflate the costs of settlement unnecessarily. RESPA prohibits lenders from requiring excessive escrow account deposits.

RESPA requirements apply when a purchase is financed by a federally related mortgage loan. *Federally related loans* means loans made by banks, savings and loan associations, or other lenders whose deposits are insured by federal agencies. It also includes loans insured by the FHA and guaranteed by the VA; loans administered by HUD; and loans intended to be sold by the lenders to Fannie Mae, Ginnie Mae, or Freddie Mac. RESPA is administered by HUD.

RESPA regulations apply to first-lien residential mortgage loans made to finance the purchases of one-family to four-family homes, cooperatives, and condominiums, for either investment or occupancy. RESPA also governs second or subordinate liens for home equity loans. A transaction financed solely by a purchase-money mortgage taken back by the seller, an installment contract (contract for deed), and a buyer's assumption of a seller's existing loan are not covered by RESPA. However, if the terms of the assumed loan are modified or if the lender charges more than $50 for the assumption, the transaction is subject to RESPA regulations.

---

**In Practice**
While RESPA's requirements are aimed primarily at lenders, some provisions of the act affect real estate brokers and agents as well. Real estate licensees fall under RESPA when they refer buyers to particular lenders, title companies, attorneys, or other providers of settlement services. Licensees who offer computerized loan origination (CLO) services also are subject to regulation. Remember: Buyers have the right to select their own providers of settlement services.

---

**Controlled Business Arrangements**
A service that is increasing in popularity is one-stop shopping for consumers of real estate services. A real estate firm, title insurance company, mortgage broker, home inspection company, or even moving company may agree to offer a package of services to consumers. RESPA permits such a **controlled business arrangement** (CBA) *as long as a consumer is clearly informed of the relationship among the service providers and that other providers are available.* Fees may not be exchanged among the affiliated companies simply for referring business to one another. This may be a particularly important issue for licensees who offer **computerized loan origination** (CLO) services to their clients and customers. While a borrower's ability to comparison shop for a loan may be enhanced by a CLO system, his or her range of choices must not be limited. Consumers must be informed of the availability of other lenders.

**Disclosure Requirements**
Lenders and settlement agents have certain *disclosure* obligations at the time of loan application and loan closing:

- *Special information booklet.* Lenders must provide a copy of a special informational HUD booklet to every person from whom they receive or for whom they prepare a loan application (except for refinancing). The HUD booklet must be given at the time the application is received or within three days afterward. The booklet provides the borrower with general information about settlement (closing) costs. It also explains the various provisions of RESPA, including a line-by-line description of the Uniform Settlement Statement.
- *Good-faith estimate of settlement costs.* No later than three business days after receiving a loan application, the lender must provide to the

borrower a good-faith estimate of the settlement costs the borrower is likely to incur. This estimate may be either a specific figure or a range of costs based on comparable past transactions in the area. In addition, if the lender requires use of a particular attorney or title company to conduct the closing, the lender must state whether it has any business relationship with that firm and must estimate the charges for this service.

- *Uniform Settlement Statement (HUD Form 1).* RESPA requires that a special HUD form be completed to itemize all charges to be paid by a borrower and seller in connection with settlement. The **Uniform Settlement Statement (HUD-1)** includes all charges that will be collected at closing, whether required by the lender or by a third party. Items paid by the borrower and seller outside closing, not required by the lender, are not included on HUD-1. Charges required by the lender that are paid before closing are indicated as "paid outside of closing" (POC). RESPA prohibits lenders from requiring that borrowers deposit amounts in escrow accounts for taxes and insurance that exceed certain limits, thus preventing the lenders from taking advantage of the borrowers. *Sellers* are also prohibited from requiring, as a condition of a sale, that the buyer purchase title insurance from a particular company. A copy of the HUD-1 form is illustrated later in this chapter. (See Figure 25.3.)

**RESPA's Consumer Protections**

- CLO regulation
- CBA disclosure
- Settlement cost booklet
- Good-faith estimate of settlement costs
- Uniform Settlement Statement
- Prohibition of kickbacks and unearned fees

The settlement statement must be made available for inspection by the borrower *at or before* settlement. Borrowers have the right to inspect a completed HUD-1, to the extent that the figures are available, *one business day before the closing.* (Sellers are not entitled to this privilege.)

Lenders must retain these statements for two years after the dates of closing. In addition, state laws generally require that licensees retain all records of a transaction for a specific period. The Uniform Settlement Statement may be altered to allow for local custom, and certain lines may be deleted if they do not apply in an area.

**Kickbacks and referral fees.** RESPA prohibits the payment of kickbacks, or unearned fees, in any real estate settlement service. It prohibits referral fees *when no services are actually rendered.* The *payment* or *receipt* of a fee, a kickback, or anything of value for referrals for settlement services includes activities such as mortgage loans, title searches, title insurance, attorney services, surveys, credit reports, and appraisals.

**Title Procedures**

Both the buyer and the buyer's lender want assurance that the seller's title complies with the requirements of the sales contract. The seller is usually required to produce a current *abstract of title* or *title commitment* from the title insurance company. When an abstract of title is used, the purchaser's attorney examines it and issues an opinion of title. This opinion, like the title commitment, is a statement of the status of the seller's title. It discloses all liens, encumbrances, easements, conditions, or restrictions that appear on the record and to which the seller's title is subject.

On the date when the sale is actually completed (the date of delivery of the deed), the buyer has a title commitment or an abstract that was issued several days or weeks before the closing. For this reason, there are usually two searches of the public records. The first shows the status of the seller's title on the date of the first search. Usually, the seller pays for this search. The second search, known as a *bring down,* is made after the closing and generally is paid for by the purchaser. The abstract should be reviewed before closing to resolve any problems that might cause delays or threaten the transaction.

When the purchaser pays cash or obtains a new loan to purchase the property, the seller's existing loan is paid in full and satisfied on record. The exact amount required to pay the existing loan is provided in a current payoff statement from the lender, effective as of the date of closing. This *payoff statement* notes the unpaid amount of principal, the interest due through the date of payment, the fee for issuing the certificate of satisfaction or release deed, credits (if any) for tax and insurance reserves, and the amount of any prepayment penalties. The same procedure is followed for any other liens that must be released before the buyer takes title.

In a transaction in which the buyer assumes the seller's existing mortgage loan, the buyer wants to know the exact balance of the loan as of the closing date. In some areas, it is customary for the buyer to obtain a *mortgage reduction certificate* from the lender that certifies the amount owed on the mortgage loan, the interest rate, and the last interest payment made.

As part of this later search, the seller may be required to execute an *affidavit of title.* This is a sworn statement in which the seller assures the title insurance company (and the buyer) that there have been no judgments, bankruptcies, or divorces involving the seller since the date of the title examination. The affidavit promises that no unrecorded deeds or contracts have been made, no repairs or improvements have gone unpaid, and no defects in the title have arisen that the seller knows of. The seller also affirms that he or she is in possession of the premises. In some areas, this form is required before the title insurance company will issue an owner's policy to the buyer. The affidavit gives the title insurance company the right to sue the seller if his or her statements in the affidavit are incorrect.

In some areas, real estate sales transactions are customarily closed through an escrow (discussed below). In these areas, the escrow instructions usually provide for an extended coverage policy to be issued to the buyer as of the date of closing. The seller has no need to execute an affidavit of title.

## PREPARATION OF CLOSING STATEMENTS

A typical real estate transaction involves, in addition to the purchase price, expenses for both parties. These include items prepaid by the seller for which he or she must be reimbursed (such as taxes) and items of expense the seller has incurred but for which the buyer will be billed (such as mortgage interest paid in arrears when a loan is assumed). The financial responsibility for these items must be prorated (or divided) between the buyer and the seller. All expenses and prorated items are accounted for on the settlement statement. This is how the exact amount of cash required from the buyer and the net proceeds to the seller are determined. (See Figure 25.1.)

**How the Closing Statement Works**

The completion of a **closing statement** involves an accounting of the parties' debits and credits. A **debit** is a charge. That is, it is an amount that a party owes and must pay at closing. A **credit** is an amount entered in a person's favor—an amount that has already been paid, an amount being reimbursed or an amount the buyer promises to pay in the form of a loan.

Test

| Figure 25.1 | Allocation of Expenses | |
|---|---|---|
| **Item** | **Paid by Seller** | **Paid by Buyer** |
| Broker's commission | ✗ by agreement | ✗ by agreement |
| Attorney's fees | ✗ by agreement | ✗ by agreement |
| Recording expenses | ✗ to clear title | ✗ transfer charges |
| Transfer tax | ✗ | |
| Title expenses | ✗ title search | ✗ attorney inspection, title insurance |
| Loan fees | ✗ prepayment penalty | ✗ origination fee |
| Tax and insurance reserves (escrow or impound accounts) | | ✗ |
| Appraisal fees | | ✗ if required by lender |
| Survey fees | ✗ if required to pay by sales contract | ✗ new mortgage financing |

A *debit* is an amount *to be paid by* the buyer or seller; a *credit* is an amount *payable to* the buyer or seller.

To determine the amount a buyer needs at closing, the buyer's debits are totaled. Any expenses and prorated amounts for items prepaid by the seller are added to the purchase price. Then the buyer's credits are totaled. These include the earnest money (already paid), the balance of the loan the buyer obtains or assumes, and the seller's share of any prorated items the buyer will pay in the future. (See Figure 25.2.) Finally, the total of the buyer's credits is subtracted from the total debits to arrive at the actual amount of cash the buyer must bring to closing. Usually, the buyer brings a cashier's or certified check.

A similar procedure is followed to determine how much money the seller actually will receive. The seller's debits and credits are each totaled. The credits include the purchase price plus the buyer's share of any prorated items that the seller has prepaid. The seller's debits include expenses, the seller's share of prorated items to be paid later by the buyer and the balance of any mortgage loan or other lien that the seller pays off. Finally, the total of the seller's debits is subtracted from the total credits to arrive at the amount the seller will receive.

**Broker's commission.** The responsibility for paying the broker's commission will have been determined by previous agreement. If the broker is the agent for the seller, the seller is normally responsible for paying the commission. If an agency agreement exists between a broker and the buyer, or if two agents are involved, one for the seller and one for the buyer, the commission may be apportioned as an expense between both parties or according to some other arrangement.

**Attorney's fees.** If either of the parties' attorneys will be paid from the closing proceeds, that party is charged with the expense in the closing

| Figure 25.2 | Credits and Debits | Test | | | |
|---|---|---|---|---|---|
| **Item** | **Credit to Buyer** | **Debit to Buyer** | **Credit to Seller** | **Debit to Seller** | **Prorated** |
| Principal amount of new mortgage | X | | | | |
| Payoff of existing mortgage | | | | X | |
| Unpaid principal balance if assumed mortgage | X | | | X | |
| Accrued interest on existing assumed mortgage | X | | | X | X |
| Tenants' security deposit | X | | | X | |
| Purchase-money mortgage | X | | | X | |
| Unpaid water and other utility bills | X | | | X | X |
| Buyer's earnest money | X | | | | |
| Selling price of property | | X | X | | |
| Fuel oil on hand (valued at current market price) | | X | X | | X |
| Prepaid insurance and tax reserve for mortgage assumed by buyer | | X | X | | X |
| Refund to seller of prepaid water charges and similar utility expenses | | X | X | | X |
| Prepaid general real estate taxes | | X | X | | X |

statement. This expense may include fees for the preparation or review of documents or for representing the parties at settlement.

**Recording expenses.** *The seller* usually pays for recording charges (filing fees) necessary to clear all defects and furnish the purchaser with a marketable title. Items customarily charged to the seller include the recording of release deeds or satisfaction of mortgages, quitclaim deeds, affidavits, and satisfaction of mechanics' liens. The *purchaser* pays for recording charges that arise from the actual transfer of title. Usually, such items include recording the deed that conveys title to the purchaser and a mortgage or deed of trust executed by the purchaser.

**In Ohio...** **Transfer tax.** Ohio requires a transfer tax on real estate conveyances. This expense is borne by the seller. ◆

**In Ohio...** **Title expenses.** Custom varies through Ohio in handling title matters. In some areas, the seller is required to furnish evidence of good title and pay for the title search. If the buyer's attorney inspects the evidence or if the buyer purchases title insurance policies, the buyer is charged for the expense. In other areas, custom follows the caveat emptor principal, and the buyer must obtain and pay for his or her own title examination. ◆

**Loan fees.** When the buyer secures a new loan to finance the purchase, the lender ordinarily charges a loan origination fee of one to two percent of the loan. The fee usually is paid by the purchaser at the time the transaction closes. The lender also may charge discount points. If the buyer assumes the seller's existing financing, the buyer may pay an assumption fee. Also, under the terms of some mortgage loans, the seller may be required to pay a prepayment charge or penalty for paying off the mortgage loan before its due date.

**Tax reserves and insurance reserves (escrow or impound accounts).** Most mortgage lenders require that borrowers provide reserve funds or escrow accounts to pay future real estate taxes and insurance premiums. A borrower starts the account at closing by depositing funds to cover at least the amount of unpaid real estate taxes from the date of lien to the end of the current month. (The buyer receives a credit from the seller at closing for any unpaid taxes.) Afterward, an amount equal to one month's portion of the estimated taxes is included in the borrower's monthly mortgage payment.

The borrower is responsible for maintaining adequate fire or hazard insurance as a condition of the mortgage loan. Generally, the first year's premium is paid in full at closing. An amount equal to one month's premium is paid each month after that. The borrower's monthly loan payment includes the principal and interest on the loan, plus one-twelfth of the estimated taxes and insurance (PITI). The taxes and insurance are held by the lender in the escrow or impound account until the bills are due.

**Appraisal fees.** Either the seller or the purchaser pays the appraisal fees, depending on who orders the appraisal. When the buyer obtains a mortgage, it is customary for the lender to require an appraisal. In this case, the buyer bears the cost. If the fee is paid at the time of the loan application, it is reflected on the closing statement as already having been paid.

**Survey fees.** The purchaser who obtains new mortgage financing customarily pays the survey fees. The sales contract may require that the seller furnish a survey.

**Additional fees.** An FHA borrower owes a lump sum for payment of the mortgage insurance premium (MIP) if it is not financed as part of the loan. A VA mortgagor pays a funding fee directly to the VA at closing. If a conventional loan carries private mortgage insurance, the buyer prepays one year's insurance premium at closing.

## Accounting for Expenses

Expenses paid out of the closing proceeds are debited only to the party making the payment. Occasionally, an expense item, such as an escrow fee, a settlement fee, or a transfer tax, may be shared by the buyer and the seller. In this case, each party is debited for their share of the expense.

# PRORATIONS

Most closings involve the division of financial responsibility between the buyer and seller for such items as loan interest, taxes, rents, fuel, and utility bills. These allowances are called **prorations.** Prorations are necessary to ensure that expenses are divided fairly between the seller and the buyer. For example, the seller may owe current taxes that have not been billed; the buyer will want this settled at the closing. Where taxes must be paid in advance, the seller is entitled to a rebate at the closing. If the buyer assumes the seller's existing mortgage or deed of trust, the seller usually owes the buyer an allowance for accrued interest through the date of closing.

**Accrued items** are expenses to be prorated (such as water bills and interest on an assumed mortgage) that are owed by the seller, but later will be paid by the buyer. The seller therefore pays for these items by giving the buyer credits for them at closing.

> Accrued items = buyer credits
>
> Prepaid items = seller credits

**Prepaid items** are expenses to be prorated, such as fuel oil in a tank, that have been prepaid by the seller but not fully used up. They are therefore credits to the seller.

## The Arithmetic of Prorating

Accurate prorating involves four considerations:

1. Nature of the item being prorated
2. Whether it is an accrued item that requires the determination of an earned amount
3. Whether it is a prepaid item that requires the determination of an unearned amount (that is, a refund to the seller)
4. What arithmetic processes must be used

The computation of a proration involves identifying a yearly charge for the item to be prorated, then dividing by 12 to determine a monthly charge for the item. Usually, it also is necessary to identify a daily charge for the item by dividing the monthly charge by the number of days in the month. These smaller portions then are multiplied by the number of months or days in the prorated time period to determine the accrued or unearned amount that will be figured in the settlement.

Using this general principle, there are two methods of calculating prorations:

**In Ohio...**

1. The yearly charge is divided by a *360-day year* (commonly called a *banking year*), or 12 months of 30 days each. (For the Ohio exam, you should use this method.) ◆
2. The yearly charge is divided by 365 (366 in a leap year) to determine the daily charge. Then the actual number of days in the proration period is determined, and this number is multiplied by the daily charge.

The final proration figure varies slightly, depending on which computation method is used. The final figure also varies according to the number of decimal places to which the division is carried. *All of the computations in this chapter are computed by carrying the division to three decimal places.* The third decimal place is rounded off to cents only after the final proration figure is determined.

**Accrued Items**

When the real estate tax is levied for the calendar year and is payable during that year or in the following year, the accrued portion is for the period from January 1 to the date of closing (or to the day before the closing in states where the sale date is excluded). If the current tax bill has not yet been issued, the parties must agree on an estimated amount based on the previous year's bill and any known changes in assessment or tax levy for the current year.

**Sample proration calculation.** Assume a sale is to be closed on September 17. Current real estate taxes of $1,200 are to be prorated. A 360-day year is used. The accrued period, then, is 8 months and 17 days. First determine the prorated cost of the real estate tax per month and day:

$$\frac{\$100 \text{ per month}}{12)\overline{\$1,200}} \qquad \frac{\$3.333 \text{ per day}}{30)\overline{\$100.000}}$$
$$\text{months} \qquad\qquad \text{days}$$

Next, multiply these figures by the accrued period, and add the totals to determine the prorated real estate tax:

$$
\begin{array}{lll}
\$100 & \$\ 3.333 & \$800.000 \\
\underline{\times\ \ 8 \text{ months}} & \underline{\times\ \ \ \ 17 \text{ days}} & \underline{+\ 56.661} \\
\$800 & \$56.661 & \$856.661
\end{array}
$$

Thus, the accrued real estate tax for 8 months and 17 days is $856.66 (rounded off to two decimal places after the final computation). This amount represents the seller's accrued earned tax. It will be a credit to the buyer and *a debit to the seller on the closing statement.*

To compute this proration using the actual number of days in the accrued period, the following method is used: The accrued period from January 1 to September 17 runs 260 days (January's 31 days plus February's 28 days and so on, plus the 17 days of September).

$$\$1,200 \text{ tax bill} \div 365 \text{ days} = \$3.288 \text{ per day}$$
$$\$3.288 \times 260 \text{ days} = \$854.880, \text{ or } \$854.88$$

While these examples show proration as of the date of settlement, the agreement of sale may require otherwise. For instance, a buyer's possession date may not coincide with the settlement date. In this case, the parties could prorate according to the date of possession.

**In Practice**

On state licensing examinations, tax prorations are usually based on a 30-day month (360-day year) unless specified otherwise. This may differ with local customs regarding tax prorations. Many title insurance companies provide proration charts that detail tax factors for each day in the year. To determine a tax proration using one of these charts, multiply the factor given for the closing date by the annual real estate tax.

**Prepaid Items**

A tax proration could be a prepaid item. Because real estate tax may be paid in the early part of the year, a tax proration calculated for a closing taking place later in the year must reflect the fact that the seller has already paid the tax. For example, in the preceding problem, suppose that all taxes had been paid. The buyer, then, would have to reimburse the seller; the proration would be *credited to the seller* and *debited to the buyer.*

In figuring the tax proration, it is necessary to ascertain the number of future days, months, and years for which taxes have been paid. The process commonly used for this purpose is as follows:

|  | **Years** | **Months** | **Days** |
|---|---|---|---|
| Taxes paid to (Dec. 31, end of tax year) | 199– | 12 | 30 |
| Date of closing (Sept. 17, 199–) | 1999 | –9 | 17 |
| Period for which tax must be paid |  | 3 | 13 |

With this process, we can find the amount the buyer will reimburse the seller for the *unearned* portion of the real estate tax. The prepaid period, as determined using the procedure for prepaid items, is three months and 13 days. Three months at $100 per month equals $300, and 13 days at $3.333 per day equals $43.33. Add this to determine that the proration is $343.33 *credited to the seller* and *debited to the buyer.*

**Sample prepaid item calculation.** One example of a prepaid item is a water bill. Assume that the water is billed in advance by the city without using a meter. The six months' billing is $60 for the period ending October 31. The sale is to be closed on August 3. Because the water bill is paid to October 31, the prepaid time must be computed. Using a 30-day basis, the time period is the 27 days left in August plus 2 full months: $60 ÷ 6 = $10 per month. For one day, divide $10 by 30, which equals $0.333 per day. The prepaid period is 2 months and 27 days, so:

$$\begin{array}{ll} 27 \text{ days} \quad \times \$ \ 0.333 \text{ per day} & = \$ \ 8.991 \\ 2 \text{ months} \quad \times \$10 & = \$20 \\ \hline & \$28.991, \text{ or } \$28.99 \end{array}$$

This is a prepaid item; it is *credited to the seller and debited to the buyer on the closing statement.*

To figure this based on the actual days in the month of closing, the following process would be used:

| | |
|---|---|
| $10 per month ÷ 31 days in August | = $0.323 per day |
| August 4 through August 31 | = 28 days |
| 28 days × $0.323 | = $9.044 |
| 2 months × $10 | = $20 |
| $9.044 + $20 | = $29.044, or $29.04 |

**General Rules for Prorating**

The rules or customs governing the computation of prorations for the closing of a real estate sale vary widely from state to state. The following are some general guidelines for preparing the closing statement:

**In Ohio...**

- In Ohio, as in most states, the seller owns the property on the day of closing, and prorations or apportionments are usually made *to and including the day of closing.* ◆ In a few states, however, it is provided specifically that the buyer owns the property on the closing date. In that case, adjustments are made as of the day preceding the day on which title is closed.

- Mortgage interest, general real estate taxes, water taxes, insurance premiums, and similar expenses are usually computed by using *360 days in a year and 30 days in a month.* However, the rules in some areas provide for computing prorations on the basis of the *actual number of days* in the calendar month of closing. The agreement of sale should specify which method will be used.

- Accrued or prepaid *general real estate taxes* are usually prorated at the closing. When the amount of the current real estate tax cannot be determined definitely, the proration is usually based on the last obtainable tax bill.

- *Special assessments* for municipal improvements such as sewers, water mains, or streets are usually paid in annual installments over several years, with annual interest charged on the outstanding balance of future installments. The seller normally pays the current installment, and the buyer assumes all future installments. *The special assessment installment generally is not prorated at the closing.* A buyer may insist that the seller allow the buyer a credit for the seller's share of the interest to the closing date. The agreement of sale may address the manner in which special assessments will be handled at settlement.

- *Rents* are usually adjusted on the basis of the *actual number of days* in the month of closing. It is customary for the seller to receive the rents for the day of closing and to pay all expenses for that day. If any rents for the current month are uncollected when the sale is closed, the buyer often agrees by a separate letter to collect the rents if possible and remit the pro-rata share to the seller.

- *Security deposits* made by tenants to cover the last month's rent of the lease or to cover the cost of repairing damage caused by the tenant are generally transferred by the seller to the buyer.

- The seller usually maintains *insurance* on the building against loss by fire or other hazards until the sale is closed and the deed is delivered or possession surrendered.

**In Ohio...**
- Under Ohio law, risk of loss falls on the purchaser from the contract date, unless there is a protecting clause in the purchase agreement. When the buyer takes over the seller's fire and extended-coverage insurance policy, the unearned premium usually is prorated. ◆

**Real estate taxes.** Proration of real estate taxes varies widely, depending on how the taxes are paid in the area where the real estate is located. In some states, real estate taxes are paid *in advance;* that is, if the tax year runs from January 1 to December 31, taxes for the coming year are due on January 1. In this case, the seller, who has prepaid a year's taxes, should be reimbursed for the portion of the year remaining after the buyer takes ownership of the property. In other areas, taxes are paid *in arrears,* on December 31 for the year just ended. In this case, the buyer should be credited by the seller for the time the seller occupied the property. Sometimes, taxes are due during the tax year, partly in arrears and partly in advance; sometimes they are payable in installments. It gets even more complicated: city, state, school, and other property taxes may start their tax years in different months. Whatever the case may be in a particular transaction, the licensee should understand how the taxes will be prorated.

**In Ohio...**     Local custom varies throughout counties in Ohio, but generally taxes are billed and collected six months at a time, six months in arrears. Ohio law permits delinquent unpaid water and sewer bills to be added to the real estate taxes and become a lien on the property. ◆

**Mortgage loan interest.** On almost every mortgage loan the interest is paid *in arrears,* so buyer and seller must understand that the mortgage payment due on June 1, for example, includes interest due for the month of May. Thus, the buyer who assumes a mortgage on May 31 and makes the June payment pays for the time the seller occupied the property and should be credited with a month's interest. On the other hand, the buyer who places a new mortgage loan on May 31 may be pleasantly surprised to hear that he or she will not need to make a mortgage payment until a month later.

**In Practice**

**In Ohio...**

On Ohio's licensing examinations, tax prorations are usually based on the number of days in each month, unless specified otherwise in the problem. Note that this may differ with your local custom regarding tax prorations. Many title insurance companies provide proration charts that detail tax factors for each day in the year. To determine a tax proration using one of these charts, multiply the factor given for the closing date by the annual real estate tax. ◆

**Accounting for Credits and Charges**

The items that must be accounted for in the closing statement fall into two general categories: prorations or other amounts due to either the buyer or seller (credit to) and paid for by the other party (debit to) and expenses or items paid by the seller or buyer (debit only). In the following lists the items marked by an asterisk (*) are not prorated; they are entered in full as listed.

**Items credited to the buyer and debited to the seller.** These closing statement items include

- the buyer's earnest money,*
- the principal amount of a new mortgage loan or unpaid principal balance of an outstanding mortgage loan being assumed by the buyer,*
- interest on an existing assumed mortgage not yet paid (accrued),
- the unearned portion of current rent collected in advance,
- tenants' security deposits,*
- a purchase-money mortgage*, and
- unpaid water and other utility bills.

The *buyer's earnest money,* while credited to the buyer, *is not usually debited to the seller.* The buyer receives a credit because he or she has already paid that amount toward the purchase price. Under the usual sales contract the money is held by the broker or attorney until the settlement, when it will be included as part of the total amount due the seller. If the seller is paying off an existing loan and the buyer is obtaining a new one, these two items are accounted for with a debit only to the seller for the amount of the payoff and a credit only to the buyer for the amount of the new loan.

**Items credited to the seller and debited to the buyer.** These items include

- the sales price;*
- any fuel oil on hand, usually figured at current market price (prepaid);

- an insurance and tax reserve (if any) when an outstanding mortgage loan is being assumed by the buyer (prepaid);
- a refund to the seller of prepaid water charges and similar expenses; and
- any portion of general real estate tax paid in advance.

**Accounting for expenses.** Expenses paid out of the closing proceeds are debited only to the party making the payment. Occasionally an expense item—such as an escrow fee, a settlement fee, or a transfer tax—may be shared by the buyer and the seller, and each party will be debited for his or her share of the expense.

## SAMPLE CLOSING STATEMENT

Settlement computations take many possible formats. The remaining portion of this chapter illustrates a sample transaction using the RESPA Uniform Settlement Statement in Figure 25.3. Because customs differ in various parts of the country, the way certain expenses are charged in some locations may be different from the illustration.

**Basic Information of Offer and Sale**

John and Joanne Iuro list their home at 3045 North Racine Avenue in Dayton, Ohio, with the Open Door Real Estate Company. The listing price is $118,500, and possession can be given within two weeks after all parties have signed the contract. Under the terms of the listing agreement, the sellers agree to pay the broker a commission of six percent of the sales price.

On May 18, the Open Door Real Estate Company submits a contract offer to the Iuros from Brook Redemann, a bachelor residing at 22 King Court, Riverdale. Redemann offers $115,000, with earnest money and down payment of $23,000 and the remaining $92,000 of the purchase price to be obtained through a new conventional loan. No private mortgage insurance is necessary because the loan-to-value ratio does not exceed 80 percent. The Iuros sign the contract on May 29. Closing is set for June 15 at the office of the Open Door Real Estate Company, 720 Main Street, Dayton.

The unpaid balance of the Iuros' mortgage as of June 1, will be $57,700. Payments are $680 per month, with interest at 11 percent per annum on the unpaid balance.

The sellers submit evidence of title in the form of a title insurance binder at a cost of $10. The title insurance policy, to be paid by the sellers at the time of closing, costs an additional $540, including $395 for lender's coverage and $145 for homeowner's coverage. Recording charges of $20 are paid for the recording of two instruments to clear defects in the sellers' title. State transfer tax stamps in the amount of $115 ($.50 per $500 of the sales price or fraction thereof) are affixed to the deed. In addition, the sellers must pay an attorney's fee of $400 for preparing the deed and for legal representation. This amount will be paid from the closing proceeds.

The buyer must pay an attorney's fee of $300 for examining the title evidence and for legal representation. He also must pay $10 to record the deed. These amounts also will be paid from the closing proceeds.

Real estate taxes in Ohio are paid in arrears. Taxes for this year, estimated at last year's figure of $1,725, have not been paid. According to the contract, prorations will be made on the basis of 30 days in a month.

## Figure 25.3    RESPA Uniform Settlement Statement

*Test*

U.S. DEPARTMENT OF HOUSING AND URBAN DEVELOPMENT

OMB No. 2502-0265(Exp. 12-31-86)

| A. Settlement Statement | B. Type of Loan |
|---|---|
| | 1. ☐ FHA   2. ☐ FMHA   3. ☐ CONV. UNINS. |
| | 4. ☐ VA   5. ☒ CONV. INS. |
| | 6. File Number |
| | 7. Loan Number |
| | 8. Mortgage Insurance Case Number |

**C. Note:** This form is furnished to give you a statement of actual settlement costs. Amounts paid to and by the settlement agent are shown. Items marked '(p.o.c)' were paid outside the closing; they are shown here for informational purposes and are not included in the totals.

**D. Name of Borrower:** Brook Redemann

**E. Name of Seller:** John and Joanne Iuro

**F. Name of Lender:** Thrift Federal Savings

**G. Property Location:** 3045 North Racine Avenue

**H. Settlement Agent:** Open Door Real Estate Company
**Address:**

**Place of Settlement:**
**Address:**

**I. Settlement Date:** June 15, 2000

| J. Summary of Borrower's Transaction | | K. Summary of Seller's Transaction | |
|---|---|---|---|
| **100. Gross Amount Due From Borrower** | | **400. Gross Amount Due To Seller** | |
| 101. Contract Sales Price | $115,000.00 | 401. Contract Sales Price | $115,000.00 |
| 102. Personal Property | | 402. Personal Property | |
| 103. Settlement charges to borrower (line 1400) | 5,070.58 | 403. | |
| 104. | | 404. | |
| 105. | | 405. | |
| *Adjustments for items paid by seller in advance* | | *Adjustments for items paid by seller in advance* | |
| 106. City/town taxes          to | | 406. City/town taxes          to | |
| 107. County taxes          to | | 407. County taxes          to | |
| 108. Assessments          to | | 408. Assessments          to | |
| 109. | | 409. | |
| 110. | | 410. | |
| 111. | | 411. | |
| 112. | | 412. | |
| 113. | | 413. | |
| 114. | | 414. | |
| 115. | | 415. | |
| **120. Gross Amount Due From Borrower** | $120,070.58 | **420. Gross Amount Due To Seller** | $115,000.00 |
| **200. Amounts Paid By Or In Behalf Of Borrower** | | **500. Reductions In Amount Due To Seller** | |
| 201. Deposit or earnest money | $ 23,000.00 | 501. Excess deposit (see instructions) | |
| 202. Principal amount of new loan(s) | 92,000.00 | 502. Settlement charges (line 1400) | $ 8,080.00 |
| 203. Existing loan(s) taken subject to | | 503. Existing loan(s) taken subject to | |
| 204. | | 504. Payoff of first mortgage loan | 57,960.84 |
| 205. | | 505. Payoff of second mortgage loan | |
| 206. | | 506. | |
| 207. | | 507. | |
| 208. | | 508. | |
| 209. | | 509. | |
| *Adjustments for Items unpaid by seller* | | *Adjustments for Items unpaid by seller* | |
| 210. City/town taxes          to | | 510. City/town taxes          to | |
| 211. County taxes  1/1/00  to 6/15/00 | $ 790.63 | 511. County taxes  1/1/00  to 6/15/00 | $ 790.63 |
| 212. Assessments          to | | 512. Assessments          to | |
| 213. | | 513. | |
| 214. | | 514. | |
| 215. | | 515. | |
| 216. | | 516. | |
| 217. | | 517. | |
| 218. | | 518. | |
| 219. | | 519. | |
| **220. Total Paid By/For Borrower** | $115,790.63 | **520. Total Reductions Amount Due Seller** | $ 66,831.47 |
| **300. Cash At Settlement From/To Borrower** | | **600. Cash At Settlement To/From Seller** | |
| 301 Gross amount due from borrower (line 120) | $120,070.58 | 601 Gross amount due to seller (line 420) | $115,000.00 |
| 302. Less amounts paid by/for borrower (line 220) | ($115,790.63) | 602. Less reductions in amount due to seller (line 520) | ($ 66,831.47) |
| 303. Cash  (☒ From)  (☐ To) Borrower | $ 4,279.95 | 603. Cash  (☐ To)  (☐ From) Seller | $ 48,168.53 |

HUD-1 Rev (3/86)

## Figure 25.3 RESPA Uniform Settlement Statement (Continued)

OBM No. 2502-0265 (Exp. 12-31-86)

| L. Settlement Charges | Paid From Borrower's Funds at Settlement | Paid From Seller's Funds at Settlement |
|---|---|---|
| 700. Total Sales/Broker's Commission based on price $ 115,000 @ 6 % = $6,900 | | |
| Division of Commission (line 700) as follows | | |
| 701. $ to | | |
| 702. $ to | | |
| 703. Commission paid at Settlement | | $ 6,900.00 |
| 704. | | |
| **800. Items Payable In Connection With Loan** | | |
| 801. Loan Origination Fee % | $ 920.00 | |
| 802. Loan Discount 2 % | 1,840.00 | |
| 803. Appraisal Fee to Swift Appraisal in the amount of $125.00 | POC | |
| 804. Credit Report to Acme Credit Bureau in the amount of $60.00 | POC | |
| 805. Lender's Inspection Fee | | |
| 806. Mortgage Insurance Application Fee to | | |
| 807. Assumption Fee | | |
| 808. | | |
| 809. | | |
| 810. | | |
| 811. | | |
| **900. Items Required By Lender To Be Paid In Advance** | | |
| 901. Interest from 6/16/00 to 6/30/00 @ $ 25.205 /day | $ 378.08 | |
| 902. Mortgage Insurance Premium for months to | | |
| 903. Hazard Insurance Premium for 1 years to Hite Insurance Company | 345.00 | |
| 904. | | |
| 905. | | |
| **1000. Reserves Deposited With Lender** | | |
| 1001. Hazard Insurance 3 months @ $ 28.75 per month | $ 86.25 | |
| 1002. Mortgage Insurance months @ $ per month | | |
| 1003. City property taxes months @ $ per month | | |
| 1004. County property taxes 7 months @ $143.75 per month | 1,006.25 | |
| 1005. Annual assessments months @ $ per month | | |
| 1006. months @ $ per month | | |
| 1007. months @ $ per month | | |
| 1008. months @ $ per month | | |
| **1100. Title Charges** | | |
| 1101. Settlement or closing fee to FIRST AMERICAN TITLE INSURANCE COMPANY | | |
| 1102. Abstract or title search to | | |
| 1103. Title examination to | | |
| 1104. Title insurance binder to | | $ 10.00 |
| 1105. Document preparation to | | |
| 1106. Notary fees to | | |
| 1107. Attorney's fee to | $ 300.00 | 400.00 |
| (includes above items numbers: ) | | |
| 1108. Title insurance to | | 540.00 |
| (includes above items numbers: 1102-1103-1104 ) | | |
| 1109. Lender's coverage $ 395.00 | | |
| 1110. Owner's coverage $ 145.00 | | |
| 1111. | | |
| 1112. | | |
| 1113. | | |
| **1200. Government Recording And Transfer Charges** | | |
| 1201. Recording fees: Deed $ 10.00 Mortgage $ 10.00 Release $ 10.00 | $ 20.00 | $ 10.00 |
| 1202. City/county tax/stamps: Deed $ ;Mortgage $ | | |
| 1203. State tax/stamps: Deed $ 115.00 ;Mortgage $ | | 115.00 |
| 1204. Record two documents to clear title | | 20.00 |
| 1205. | | |
| **1300. Additional Settlement Charges** | | |
| 1301. Survey to | $ 175.00 | |
| 1302. Pest inspection to | | $ 85.00 |
| 1303. | | |
| 1304. | | |
| 1305. | | |
| **1400. Total Settlement Charges** (enter on lines 103, Section J and 502, Section K) | $ 5,070.58 | $ 8,080.00 |

I have carefully reviewed the HUD-1 Settlement Statement and to the best of my knowledge and belief, it is a true and accurate statement of all receipts and distributions made on my account or by me in this transaction. I further certify that I have received a copy of HUD-1 Settlement Statement.

_____     _____

Borrowers                           Sellers

The HUD-1 Settlement Statement which I have prepared is a true and accurate account of this transaction. I have caused or will cause the funds to be disbursed in accordance with this statement.

_____     _____

Settlement Agent                    Date

**WARNING:** It is a crime to knowingly make false statements to the United States on this or any other similar form. Penalties upon conviction can include a fine or imprisonment. For details see Title 18 U.S. Code Section 1001 and Section 1010.

**Computing the prorations and charges.** The following list illustrates the various steps in computing the prorations and other amounts to be included in the settlement to this point:

- Closing date: June 15
- Commission: 6% (.06) × $115,000 sales price = $6,900
- Seller's mortgage interest: 11% (.11) × $57,700 principal due after June 1 payment = $6,347 interest per year; $6,347 ÷ 360 days = $17.631 interest per day; 15 days of accrued interest to be paid by the seller × $17.631 = $264.465 interest owed by the seller; $57,700 + $264.465 = $57,964.465, or $57,964.47 payoff of seller's mortgage
- Real estate taxes (estimated at $1,725): $1,725 ÷ 12 months = $143.75 per month; $143.75 ÷ 30 days = $4.792 per day
- The earned period, from January 1 to and including June 15, equals five months and 15 days: $143.75 × 5 months = $718.75; $4.792 × 15 days = $71.88; $718.75 + $71.88 = $790.63 seller owes buyer
- Transfer tax ($.50 per $500 of consideration or fraction thereof): $115,000 ÷ $500 = 230; 230 × $.50 = $115 transfer tax owed by seller

The sellers' loan payoff is $57,964.47. They must pay an additional $10 to record the mortgage release, as well as $85 for a pest inspection and $175 for a survey, as negotiated between the parties. The buyer's new loan is from Thrift Federal Savings, 1100 Fountain Plaza, Dayton, in the amount of $92,000 at ten percent interest. In connection with this loan, Redemann will be charged $125 to have the property appraised by Swift Appraisal. Acme Credit Bureau will charge $60 for a credit report. (Because appraisal and credit reports are performed before loan approval, they are paid at the time of loan application, whether or not the transaction eventually closes. These items are noted as POC—paid outside closing—on the settlement statement.) In addition, Redemann will pay for interest on his loan for the remainder of the month of closing: 15 days at $25.556 per day, or $383.34. His first full payment (including July's interest) will be due on August 1. He must deposit $1,006.25 into a tax reserve account. That's 7/12 of the anticipated county real estate tax of $1,725. A one-year hazard insurance premium at $3 per $1,000 of appraised value ($115,000 ÷ 1,000 × 3 = $345) is paid in advance to Hite Insurance Company. An insurance reserve to cover the premium for three months is deposited with the lender. Redemann will have to pay an additional $10 to record the mortgage. He will also pay a loan origination fee of $920 and two discount points. The sellers agree to pay the survey fee.

**The Uniform Settlement Statement**

The Uniform Settlement Statement is divided into 12 sections. Sections J, K, and L contain particularly important information. The borrower's and seller's summaries (J and K) are very similar. In Section J, the buyer-borrower's debits are listed on lines 100 through 112. They are totaled on line 120 (gross amount due from borrower). The total of the settlement costs itemized in Section L of the statement is entered on line 103 as one of the buyer's charges. The buyer's credits are listed on lines 201 through 219 and totaled on line 220 (total paid by or for borrower). Then the buyer's credits are subtracted from the charges to arrive at the cash due from the borrower to close (line 303).

In Section K, the seller's credits are entered on lines 400 through 412 and totaled on line 420 (gross amount due to seller). The seller's debits are entered on lines 501 through 519 and totaled on line 520 (total reduction amount due seller). The total of the seller's settlement charges is on line 502. Then the debits are subtracted from the credits to arrive at the cash due to the seller to close (line 603).

Section L summarizes all the settlement charges for the transaction; the buyer's expenses are listed in one column and the seller's expenses in the other. If an attorney's fee is listed as a lump sum in line 1107, the settlement should list by line number the services that are included in that total fee.

## KEY TERMS

| | | |
|---|---|---|
| accrued item | credit | Real Estate Settlement |
| closing | debit | Procedures Act |
| closing statement | escrow | Uniform Settlement |
| computerized loan | prepaid item | Statement (HUD-1) |
| origination | proration | |
| controlled business | | |
| arrangement | | |

## SUMMARY

- Closing a real estate sale involves both title procedures and financial matters.
- The real estate salesperson or broker is often present at the closing to see that the sale is actually concluded and to account for the earnest money deposit.
- Closings must be reported to the IRS on Form 1099.
- The federal Real Estate Settlement Procedures Act (RESPA) requires disclosure of all settlement costs when a residential real estate purchase is financed by a federally related mortgage loan.
  - RESPA requires lenders to use a Uniform Settlement Statement to detail the financial particulars of a transaction.
- The actual amount to be paid by a buyer at closing is computed on a closing, or settlement, statement. This lists the sales price, earnest money deposit and all adjustments and prorations due between buyer and seller.
  - The purpose of the closing statement is to determine the net amount due the seller at closing.

## Real-Life Real Estate

1. Closing means "payday" for real estate practitioners. What are some pre-closing activities taken to ensure closings proceed smoothly?
2. Talk to a real estate practitioner in your area about the customary closing procedures. Are they typically escrow or round table? Do the practitioners in your community like the way closings are conducted? What would they change?

Application #5: Prepare a RESPA Uniform Settlement Statement for the transaction from the Sellers to the Buyers based on information developed in prior applications (found in Chapters 7, 12, 16, 19).

# QUESTIONS

1. Which of the following statements is true of real estate closings in Ohio and most states?
   a. Closings are generally conducted by real estate salespersons.
   b. The buyer usually receives the rents for the day of closing.
   c. The buyer must reimburse the seller for any title evidence provided by the seller.
   d. The seller usually pays the expenses for the day of closing.

2. All encumbrances and liens shown on the report of title other than those waived or agreed to by the purchaser and listed in the contract must be removed so that the title can be delivered free and clear. The removal of such encumbrances is the duty of the
   a. buyer.              c. broker.
   b. seller.             d. title company.

3. Legal title always passes from seller to buyer
   a. on the date of execution of the deed.
   b. when the closing statement has been signed.
   c. when the deed is placed in escrow.
   d. when the deed is delivered and accepted.

4. Which of the following would a lender generally require at the closing?
   a. Title insurance binder
   b. Market value appraisal
   c. Application
   d. Credit report

5. *W* is buying a house. In *W*'s area, closings are traditionally conducted in escrow. Which of the following items will *W* deposit with the escrow agent before the closing date?
   a. Deed to the property
   b. Title evidence
   c. Estoppel certificate
   d. Cash needed to complete the purchase

6. The RESPA Uniform Settlement Statement must be used to illustrate all settlement charges for
   a. every real estate transaction.
   b. transactions financed by VA and FHA loans only.
   c. residential transactions financed by federally related mortgage loans.
   d. all transactions involving commercial property.

7. A mortgage reduction certificate is executed by a(n)
   a. abstract company.
   b. attorney.
   c. lending institution.
   d. grantor.

8. The principal amount of a purchaser's new mortgage loan is a
   a. credit to the seller.
   b. credit to the buyer.
   c. debit to the seller.
   d. debit to the buyer.

9. The earnest money left on deposit with the broker is a
   a. credit to the seller.
   b. credit to the buyer.
   c. balancing factor.
   d. debit to the buyer.

10. The annual real estate taxes on a property amount to $1,800. The seller has paid the taxes in advance for the calendar year. If closing is set for June 15, which of the following is true?
    a. Credit seller $825; debit buyer $975
    b. Credit seller $1,800; debit buyer $825
    c. Credit buyer $975; debit seller $975
    d. Credit seller $975; debit buyer $975

11. If a seller collected rent of $400, payable in advance, from an attic tenant on August 1, which of the following is true at the closing on August 15?
    a. Seller owes buyer $400
    b. Buyer owes seller $400
    c. Seller owes buyer $200
    d. Buyer owes seller $200

12. Security deposits should be listed on a closing statement as a credit to the
    a. buyer.
    b. seller.
    c. lender.
    d. broker.

13. A building was purchased for $85,000, with 10 percent down and a loan for the balance. If the lender charged the buyer two discount points, how much cash did the buyer need to come up with at closing if the buyer incurred no other costs?
    a. $1,700
    b. $8,500
    c. $10,030
    d. $10,200

14. A buyer of a $100,000 home has paid $12,000 as earnest money and has a loan commitment for 70 percent of the purchase price. How much more cash does the buyer need to bring to the closing, provided the buyer has no closing costs?
    a. $18,000
    b. $30,000
    c. $58,000
    d. $61,600

15. At closing, the listing broker's commission usually is shown as a
    a. credit to the seller.
    b. credit to the buyer.
    c. debit to the seller.
    d. debit to the buyer.

16. In Ohio, water bills
    a. are not collectible with real estate taxes.
    b. may become a lien on the property and should be collected from the seller.
    c. are "forgiven" when title transfers; this is a gift from the city.
    d. do not have to be paid.

17. At the closing of a real estate transaction, the seller's attorney gave the buyer a credit for certain accrued items. These items were
    a. bills relating to the property that have already been paid by the seller.
    b. bills relating to the property that will have to be paid by the buyer.
    c. all of the seller's real estate bills.
    d. all of the buyer's real estate bills.

18. The Real Estate Settlement Procedures Act applies to the activities of
    a. brokers selling commercial and office buildings.
    b. security salespersons selling limited partnerships.
    c. Ginnie Mae or Fannie Mae when purchasing mortgages.
    d. lenders financing the purchases of borrowers' residences.

19. The purpose of RESPA (Real Estate Settlement Procedures Act) is to
    a. make sure buyers do not borrow more than they can repay.
    b. make real estate brokers more responsive to buyers' needs.
    c. help buyers know how much money is required.
    d. see that buyers know all settlement costs.

20. The document that provides borrowers with general information about settlement costs, RESPA provisions, and the Uniform Settlement Statement is the
    a. HUD Form 1.
    b. special information booklet.
    c. good-faith estimate of settlement costs.
    d. closing statement.

21. Which of the following statements is true of a computerized loan origination (CLO) system?
    a. The mortgage broker or lender may pay any fee charged by the real estate broker in whose office the CLO terminal is located.
    b. The borrower must pay any fee charged by the real estate broker in whose office the CLO terminal is located.
    c. The real estate broker in whose office the CLO terminal is located may charge a fee of up to two points for the use of the system.
    d. The fee charged by the real estate broker for using the CLO terminal may not be financed as part of the loan.

# Math FAQs

ANSWERS TO YOUR MOST
FREQUENTLY ASKED
REAL ESTATE MATH QUESTIONs

# ? MATH APPENDIX

## Introduction

If you are a person who would rather have teeth pulled than do math, you're in luck! This math appendix is designed for those of you who are getting started in real estate and who might benefit from a little math refresher.

If truth be told, real estate math is not so much about performing calculations as performing the *right* calculation. These days, calculators and computers can regurgitate numbers galore with little effort. All you need to do is input the numbers correctly, and before you have a chance to blink, the right answer will appear.

The goal of this appendix is to try to ensure that you are punching the correct numbers into the calculator (or computer). It is designed for various levels of learners. For those of you who need a refresher on the basics, you should start with Part I, "Fractions, Decimals, and Percentages," and work through to the end. If you feel you are already proficient in math, then you may wish to browse the opening sections and skip ahead to Parts II and III, "Percentage Problems" and "Measurement Problems," respectively. Whatever your needs, this appendix will walk you through some of the math you will need in order to be successful on the real estate exam.

### Calculators

For any job, you have to have the proper tools. Carpenters need hammers, baseball players need bats, and a real estate agent needs a good financial calculator. Since there are so many calculators available, with various "key strokes" to perform the operations, it would not be helpful to discuss the workings of any individual calculator. What works for one calculator

might not work for another. However, here are a few basic guidelines that you should follow before and after purchasing your calculator.

- Buy a calculator that has the ability to calculate loan payments and has a "future value" function.
- Be well acquainted with the functions of your calculator and know which "key strokes" yield the proper results.
- Make sure to practice on your calculator as much as possible before the licensing exam. You do not want to waste time on the exam fumbling with your calculator, nor do you want to be unsure of the results the calculator yields.

While having the right calculator and knowing how to use it will certainly help with basic math calculations, an understanding of certain math concepts is also necessary.

## Part I: Fractions, Decimals, and Percentages

### Fractions

A **fraction** is a relationship between two numbers. The number on top is called the *numerator,* the one on the bottom, the *denominator.*

$$\frac{7}{8} \qquad \begin{array}{l}\text{Numerator}\\\text{Denominator}\end{array}$$

It is helpful to think of fractions in terms of a pie.

- The **bottom** number divides the pie into pieces.
- In the fraction ⅞, there are 8 pieces in the pie.

- The **top** number tells you how many pieces of the pie you are going to take.
- In the fraction ⅞, you are going to take 7 pieces (denoted by the shaded area).

At times you will have to work with **improper fractions**.

- An improper fraction is a fraction where the top number is larger than the bottom, such as ¹¹⁄₆.
- The bottom number works exactly as it does above. With ¹¹⁄₆ divide the pie into 6 pieces.

- However, when you turn to the top number, you notice that 11 is larger than 6.
- So first, you take 6 pieces of the pie.

- Yet you still need 5 more to get to eleven. So you must have another 6-piece pie, and take 5 pieces from that.

$$\bigcirc \quad + \quad \bigcirc \quad = \text{\textonesuperior}\!/\!_6 + \text{\textfiveoldstyle}\!/\!_6 = {}^{11}\!/\!_6.$$

You also might have to work with a **mixed fraction.**

- A mixed fraction is a fraction that contains a whole number plus a fraction, such as 2½.
- 2½ = 2 + ½. So you have 2 whole pies, plus one half pie.

$$2\text{½} = \quad \bigcirc \quad + \quad \bigcirc \quad + \quad \bigcirc$$

It is important to understand that fractions also can be represented as decimals. Although long division would yield results, using a calculator would be simpler.

$$\begin{aligned}
\text{\textsevenoldstyle}\!/\!_8 &= .875 \\
{}^{11}\!/\!_6 &= 1.8333 \\
2\text{½} &= 2 + \text{½} = 2 + .5 = 2.5
\end{aligned}$$

## Decimals

Because of calculators and computers, the addition, subtraction, multiplication, and division of decimals has become simplified. However, below you will find a few reminders and hints to help guide you through the process.

*Adding (or Subtracting) Decimals.* Simply line up the decimal points and add down as you normally would.

$$\begin{array}{r} 3.45 \\ + \ 12.789 \\ \hline 16.239 \end{array} \qquad \begin{array}{r} 6.789 \\ - \ 4.1 \\ \hline 2.689 \end{array}$$

A calculator will figure out the correct decimal place for you, but this means you must input the decimal points correctly when performing calculations.

*Multiplying (or Dividing) Decimals.* When multiplying or dividing decimals, again we recommend you use a calculator. As with addition and subtraction, when multiplying and dividing decimals it is important to input the decimals in the correct place.

$$83.22$$
$$\times\ 4.26$$
$$\overline{35.45172}$$

$$83.22$$
$$\times\ 4.26$$
$$\overline{354.5172}$$

As you can see, misplacing a decimal point vastly changes your answer.

### Converting Decimals to Fractions

Since the use of certain decimals recurs in real estate and real estate math, below is a table of common decimal-to-fraction conversions.

| Decimal | Fraction | Decimal | Fraction |
|---------|----------|---------|----------|
| .125 | ⅛ | .5 | ½ |
| .1666 | ⅙ | .6 | ⅗ |
| .20 (or .2) | ⅕ | .625 | ⅝ |
| .250 (or .25) | ¼ | .666 | ⅔ |
| .333 | ⅓ | .75 | ¾ |
| .375 | ⅜ | .8 | ⅘ |
| .40 (or .4) | ⅖ | .875 | ⅞ |

If a decimal is preceded by a whole number, such as 2.25, simply tack the leading whole number (2) onto the converted fraction. So 2.25 becomes 2¼, and 125.625 becomes 125⅝.

### Percentages and Decimals

A percentage is a simplified, and often more understandable, way of expressing a decimal. The number .25 may not mean much to some people, though 25% is clearer. In reality .25 and 25% are expressing the same value. There are two simple rules for converting decimals to percentages and percentages to decimals.

***Percentage to Decimal (←).*** Move the decimal point to the LEFT (←) two places and drop the percentage sign.

$$35.2\% = .352 = 0.352$$
$$12\% = .12 = 0.12$$
$$123.56\% = 1.2356$$

---

**MATH TIP:** Always convert percentages to decimals before performing calculations.

---

***Decimal to Percentage (→).*** Move the decimal point to the RIGHT (→) two places and add a % sign.

$$0.23 = 23\%$$
$$13.56 = 1356\%$$
$$0.0025 = 0.25\%$$
$$0.7834 = 78.34\%$$
$$1.575 = 157.5\%$$

# Part II: Percentage Problems

Some of the problems you will encounter in real estate math are percentage problems. For example, a question may ask, "An owner lists a house at $125,000 and tells his agent he will not accept less than 90% of the asking price. What is the lowest offer the owner will accept?" When solving problems such as these, there are three formulas that will aid you.

$$\text{Part} = \text{Total} \times \text{Paid Rate}$$
$$\text{Paid Rate} = \text{Part/Total}$$
$$\text{Total} = \text{Part/Paid Rate}$$

In the above example,

$$\text{Total} = \$125,000$$
$$\text{Paid Rate} = 90\%$$
$$\text{Part} = ?$$

So the lowest price the owner will accept for the house is,

$$\text{Part} = \$125,000 \times .9 = \$112,500$$

## Total, Part, and Paid Rate: What are these?

**Total & Part.** •*Total* is always the *larger* number in these problems (above, the asking price of the house).
   • *Part* is always the *smaller* number (above, the lowest sale price that the owner will accept).
   • *Part* is often a percentage of the *Total*.

**Paid Rate.** •This is the percentage *paid* for a particular item.
   • **Be Careful!** Many problems will present a Discounted Rate.

   **For Example:** If you buy a coat 30% off of its original price of $100, how much was the coat?

   30% is the Discounted Rate.
   Paid Rate = 100% - Discounted Rate
   Paid Rate = 100% - 30% = 70% (you are actually paying only 70% of the original price of the coat).

Although you can memorize the above formulas for Total/Part/Paid Rate and get the correct answers, some people prefer a visual aid to memorization. In this book, the focus will be on the visual aid called the T-Bar.

### What is the T-Bar?

$$\frac{\text{PART}}{\text{TOTAL} \mid \text{RATE}}$$

Notice that you still have the same elements as in the formulas; however, when using this method, every problem begins exactly the same way. The T-Bar method provides a nice continuity when solving these types of problems.

### How Does the T-Bar Work?

The procedure works as follows:

1. Enter the two known items in the correct places.
2. If the line separating the two known items is *horizontal*, you divide to equal the missing item. (Total = Part/Paid Rate)
3. If the line separating the two known items is *vertical*, you multiply to equal the missing item. (Part = Total × Paid Rate)

Here are some examples to get you acquainted with how the T-Bar works.

### Problem #1:

Convert percentages to decimals before performing calculations.

$$\frac{\text{Part} = 100}{\text{Total} = ? \mid \text{Paid Rate} = 20\%}$$

Total = Part/Paid Rate = 100/20% = 100/.20 = 500

### Problem #2:

$$\frac{\text{Part} = ?}{\text{Total} = 65 \parallel \text{Paid Rate} = .12}$$

Part = Total × Paid Rate = 65 × .12 = 7.80

### Problem #3:

$$\frac{\text{Part} = 30}{\text{Total} = 90 \mid \text{Paid Rate} = ?}$$

Paid Rate = Part/Total = 30/90 = .333333 = 33.33%

## Before Going On!

Using the T-Bar is easy enough, but you must be certain you are plugging in the correct values for Total, Part, and Paid Rate. Here is one last quick review before a few more examples.

- Total – The larger of the two numbers.
- Part – The smaller of the two numbers.
- Paid Rate – The percentage you pay for an item (if a coat is marked 20% off, the Paid Rate is 80%).

## Examples

**Problem #1:** Chris bought a coat originally priced at $150. If it is on sale for 20% off, how much does Chris pay for the coat?

**Step 1:** Identify Total, Paid Rate, and Part.

*Total* = larger value = full price of the coat = $150
*Paid Rate* = Discounted Rate is 20%, the Paid Rate = 80%
  (100%-20%)
*Part* = the smaller value = the discounted price of the coat = ?

Total = $150
Paid Rate = 80% = .80
Part = ?

**Step 2:** Set up the T-Bar.

$$\frac{\text{Part} = ?}{\text{Total} = 150 \quad \| \quad \text{Paid Rate} = .8}$$

Part = Total × Paid Rate (the line dividing Total and Paid Rate
                is vertical, so multiply)

Part = 150 × .8 = **$120**.

**Problem #2:** Gina paid $112.50 for a dress that was reduced 25 percent. How much was the dress originally marked?

**Step 1:** Identify Total, Paid Rate, and Part.

*Total* = the bigger value = ? (since $112.50 is the reduced
  price or smaller number)
*Paid Rate* = The Discounted Rate is 25% so the Paid Rate
  = 75%
*Part* = the smaller value = $112.50 (the reduced or smaller
  price)

Total = ?
Paid Rate = 75% = .75
Part = $112.50

**Step 2:** Set up the T-Bar.

$$\begin{array}{c|c} & \text{Part} = 112.50 \\ \hline \text{Total} = ? & \text{Paid Rate} = .75 \end{array}$$

*Total* = 112.5/.75 (the line separating Part and Paid Rate is horizontal) = **$150**.

**Problem #3:** Charlie paid $127.50 for a coat that was marked down from the original price of $150. What percent discount did Charlie receive?

**Step 1:** Identify Total, Paid Rate, and Part.

*Paid Rate* = the percentage Paid = ?
*Total* = the larger value = $150
*Part* = the smaller value = $127.50

Paid Rate = ? (Since the question is asking for the Discounted Rate, when you use the T-Bar, you will get the Paid Rate. To get the correct answer perform the calculation, 100% – Paid Rate.)
Total = $150
Part = $127.50

**Step 2:** Set up the T-Bar.

$$\begin{array}{c|c} & \text{Part} = 127.50 \\ \hline \text{Total} = 150 & \text{Paid Rate} = ? \end{array}$$

Paid Rate = 127.50 ÷ 150 = .85 = 85%

DON'T FORGET: The Discounted Rate = 100% - 85% = **15%**

**Problem #4:**

A) Tony bought a house for $124,000. He paid 93% of the original asking price. How much was the house originally?

B) How much did Tony save from the original asking price? (Just a small twist.)

**Step 1:** Identify Total, Paid Rate, and Part.

*Total* = the original price of the house before it was discounted = ?
*Paid Rate* = 93%, since 93% is the amount Paid, not a Discount.
*Part* = the smaller number = $124,000.

Total = ?
Paid Rate = 93% = .93
Part = $124,000

**Step 2:** Set up the T-Bar.

$$\frac{\text{Part} = \$124,000}{\text{Total} = ? \quad | \quad \text{Paid Rate} = .93}$$

Total = $124,000 ÷ .93 = **$133,333**

C) Since the original price was $133,333 and the sale price was $124,000, subtract the two numbers to get the amount saved.

$133,333
− $124,000
$   **9,333** is the amount saved off the original price.

## Further Examples of the T-Bar

There will be other types of real estate problems that require the use of the T-Bar. Oftentimes, the *terms* used might be a little different, but the methods will be the same.

***Commission Problems.*** Problems on commission will certainly arise as you enter the field of real estate. Many different terms will pop up in the problems. Sales Price, Commission Rate, Full Commission, Brokerage Commission, Brokerage Rate. All these terms may seem a bit daunting, but in many cases, an understanding of the T-Bar will make these problems manageable.

So we can formulate a T-Bar that works exactly the same way regardless of our terms.

$$\frac{\text{Part}}{\text{Total} \quad | \quad \text{Paid Rate}}$$

$$\frac{\text{Smaller Number}}{\text{Larger Number} \quad | \quad \text{Paid Rate}}$$

So the key to these problems, and the T-Bar, is finding the Larger Number, Smaller Number, and Paid Rate, and although the terms may be slightly different, you should be able to use the T-Bar as you did above.

### Problem #1:

**Part A**—A seller listed a home for $200,000 and agreed to pay a full commission rate of 5%. The home sold 4 weeks later for $180,000. What was the full commission?

> **REMINDER!**
>
> - Total – The larger of the two numbers.
> - Part – The smaller of the two numbers.
> - Paid Rate – The percentage you pay for an item (if a coat is 20% off, the Paid Rate is 80%).

**Step 1**: Identify the Larger Number, Smaller Number, and Paid Rate.

*Larger Number* = Sales Price (Total) = $180,000 (Note that although $200,000 is the largest number in this problem, since the house did not sell at that price, this number is a decoy.)

*Smaller Number* = Full Commission (Part) = ? (A commission must be smaller than the price paid for the house!)

*Paid Rate* = Commission Rate = 5% = .05

**Step 2**: Set up the T-Bar.

Full Commission = ?

| Sales Price = $180,000 | Commission Rate = .05 |

Full Commission = Sales Price × Commission Rate =
180,000 × .05 = $9,000

**Part B**—If the selling broker was to receive 50% of her share of the commission, how much would she receive?

**Step 1**: This problem is the same as above, only we're using different *terms*. So find the Larger Number, Smaller Number, and Paid Rate.

Full Commission (Larger Number) = $9,000
Broker's Commission (Smaller Number) = ?
Broker Rate (Paid Rate) = 50% = .5

**Step 2**: Set up the T-Bar.

Broker's Commission = ?

| Full Commission = $9,000 | Commission Rate = 50% |

Broker's Commission = Full Commission × Commission Rate =
9,000 × .50 = $4,500

**Part C**—If the selling broker paid the salesperson $2,700 for her commission, what percentage of the broker's commission did the salesperson receive?

**Step 1**: Once more, we have a Total/Part/Paid Rate problem (which you already know how to do quite well) only different terms are used.

Broker's Commission (Largest Number) = $4,500
Salesperson's Commission (Smaller Number) = $2,700
Salesperson's Paid Rate = ?

**Step 2**: Set up the T-Bar.

$$\begin{array}{c|c} \text{Salesperson's Commission} = \$2,700 \\ \hline \text{Broker's Commission} = & \text{Commission} \\ \$4,500 & \text{Rate} = ? \end{array}$$

Salesperson's Paid Rate = Salesperson's Commission/Broker's
Commission = $2,700 ÷ $4,500 = .6 = 60%

### Conclusion

Hopefully you're getting the hang of these T-Bar problems. As you encounter more and more, you will begin to get quite comfortable with them. Also, you will see that while it might appear that there are many formulas you have to memorize, in actuality a clear understanding of the T-Bar will eliminate most of those.

## Measurement Problems

### What are linear measurements?

**Linear measurement** is line measurement. When the terms

- *per foot*,
- *per linear foot*,
- *per running foot* or
- *per front foot*

are used, you are being asked to determine the *total length* of the object whether measured in a straight line, crooked line, or curved line.

***What does the phrase "front foot" refer to?*** When the term *per front foot* is used, you are dealing with the number of units on the **frontage** of a lot. The frontage is normally the street frontage, but it could be the water frontage if the lot is on a river, lake, or ocean. If two dimensions are given for a tract of land, the first dimension given is the frontage if the dimensions are not labeled.

***How do I convert one kind of linear measurement to another?***

12 inches = 1 foot
Inches ÷ 12 = Feet
Feet × 12 = Inches

36 inches = 1 yard
Inches ÷ 36 = Yards
Yards × 36 = Feet

3 feet = 1 yard

Feet ÷ 3 = Yards

Yards × 3 = Feet

5,280 feet = 1 mile

Feet ÷ 5,280 = Miles

Miles × 5,280 = Feet

16½ feet = 1 rod

Feet ÷ 16.5 = Rods

Rods × 16.5 = Feet

320 rods = 1 mile

Rods ÷ 320 = Miles

Miles × 320 = Rods

**For Example:** A rectangular lot is 50 feet × 150 feet. The cost to fence this lot is priced per linear/running foot. How many linear/running feet will be used to calculate the price of the fence?

| | 150′ | |
|---|---|---|
| 50′ | | 50′ |
| | 150′ | |

50 Feet + 150 Feet + 50 Feet + 150 Feet = 400 Linear/Running Feet

**400 Linear/Running Feet** is the answer.

**For Example:** A parcel of land that fronts on Interstate 45 in Houston, Texas, is for sale at $5,000 per front foot. What will it cost to purchase this parcel of land if the dimensions are 150′ by 100¢?

150′ is the frontage because it is the first dimension given.

150 Front Feet × $5,000 = $750,000 Cost

**$750,000 Cost** is the answer.

### How do I solve for area measurement?

**Area** is the two-dimensional surface of an object. Area is quoted in *square units* or in *acres*. We will look at calculating the area of squares,

When two dimensions are given, we assume it to be a rectangle unless told otherwise.

rectangles and triangles. Squares and rectangles are four-sided objects. All four sides of a square are the same. Opposite sides of a rectangle are the same. A triangle is a three-sided object. The three sides of a triangle can be the same dimension or three different dimensions.

### How do I convert one kind of area measurement to another?

144 square inches = 1 square foot
Square Inches ÷ 144 = Square Feet
Square Feet × 144 = Square Inches

1,296 square inches = 1 square yard
Square Inches ÷ 1,296 = Square Yards
Square Yards × 1,296 = Square Inches

9 square feet = 1 square yard
Square Feet ÷ 9 = Square Yards
Square Yards × 9 = Square Feet

43,560 square feet = 1 acre
Square Feet ÷ 43,560 = Acres
Acres × 43,560 = Square Feet

640 acres = 1 section = 1 square mile
Acres ÷ 640 = Sections (Square Miles)
Sections (Square Miles) × 640 = Acres

### How do I determine the area of a square or rectangle?

FORMULA: LENGTH ¥ WIDTH = AREA OF A SQUARE OR RECTANGLE

**For Example:** How many square feet are in a room 15′6″ × 30′9″?

6″ ÷ 12 = 0.5′ + 15′ = 15.5′ wide

9″ ÷ 12 = 0.75′ + 30′ = 30.75′ long

30.75′ × 15.5′ = 476.625 Square Feet

**476.625 Square Feet** is the answer.

**For Example:** If carpet costs $63 per square yard to install, what would it cost to carpet the room in the previous example?

476.625 Square Feet ÷ 9 = 52.958333 Square Yards × $63 per Square Yard = $3,336.375 or $3,336.38 rounded

**$3,336.38 Carpet Cost** is the answer.

**For Example:** How many acres are there in a parcel of land that measures 450′ × 484′?

$$484' \times 450' = 217,800 \text{ Square Feet} \div 43,560 = 5 \text{ Acres}$$

**5 Acres of Land** is the answer.

### How do I determine the area of a triangle?

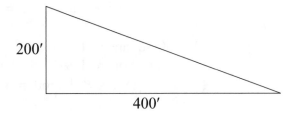

FORMULA:   ½ Base × Height =   Area of a Triangle

or

Base   × Height ³ 2 =   Area of a Triangle

**For Example:** How many square feet are contained in a triangular parcel of land that is 400 feet on the base and 200 feet high?

200′

400′

$$400' \times 200' \div 2 = 40,000 \text{ Square Feet}$$

**40,000 Square Feet** is the answer.

**For Example:** How many acres are in a three-sided tract of land that is 300′ on the base and 400′ high?

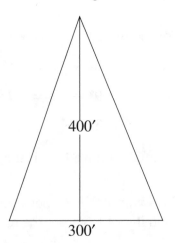

400′

300′

$$300' \times 400' \div 2 = 60,000 \text{ Square Feet} \div 43,560 = 1.377 \text{ Acres}$$

**1.377 Acres** is the answer.

## How do I solve for volume?

**Volume** is the space inside a three-dimensional object. Volume is quoted in *cubic units*. We will look at calculating the volume of boxes and triangular prisms.

### How do I convert from one kind of volume measurement to another?

1,728 cubic inches = 1 cubic foot
Cubic Inches ÷ 1,728 = Cubic Feet
Cubic Feet × 1,728 = Cubic Inches

46,656 cubic inches = 1 cubic yard
Cubic Inches ÷ 46,656 = Cubic Yards
Cubic Yards × 46,656 = Cubic Inches

27 cubic feet = 1 cubic yard
Cubic Feet ÷ 27 = Cubic Yards
Cubic Yards × 27 = Cubic Feet

### How do I determine the volume of a room?
For purposes of determining volume, think of a room as if it were a box.

FORMULA: Length × Width × Height = Volume of a Box

**For Example:** A building is 500 feet long, 400 feet wide and 25 feet high. How many cubic feet of space are in this building?

500′ × 400′ × 25′ = 5,000,000 Cubic Feet

**5,000,000 Cubic Feet** is the answer.

**For Example:** How many cubic yards of concrete would it take to build a sidewalk measuring 120 feet long; 2 feet, 6 inches wide; and 3 inches thick?

6″ ÷ 12 = .5′ + 2′ = 2.5′ Wide

3″ ÷ 12 = .25′ Thick

120′ × 2.5′ × .25′ = 75 Cubic Feet ÷ 27 = 2.778 Cubic Yards (rounded)

**2.778 Cubic Yards** is the answer.

### How do I determine the volume of a triangular prism?
The terms *A-frame*, *A-shaped* or *gable roof* on an exam describe a triangular prism.

FORMULA:   ½ Base× Height × Width  =  Volume of a Triangular Prism

or

Base  × Height × Width ³ 2 =  Volume of a Triangular Prism

**For Example:** An A-frame cabin in the mountains is 50 feet long and 30 feet wide. The cabin is 25 feet high from the base to the highest point. How many cubic feet of space does this A-frame cabin contain?

$$50\,' \times 30' \times 25' \div 2 = 18{,}750 \text{ Cubic Feet}$$

**18,750 Cubic Feet** is the answer.

**For Example:** A building is 40 feet by 25 feet with a 10-foot-high ceiling. The building has a gable roof that is 8 feet high at the tallest point. How many cubic feet are in this structure, including the roof?

$$40' \times 25' \times 10' = 10{,}000 \text{ Cubic Feet in the Building}$$

$$40' \times 25' \times 8' \div 2 = 4{,}000 \text{ Cubic Feet in the Gable Roof}$$

$$10{,}000 \text{ Cubic Feet} + 4{,}000 \text{ Cubic Feet} = 14{,}000 \text{ Total Cubic Feet}$$

**14,000 Cubic Feet** is the answer.

# REAL ESTATE MATH PRACTICE PROBLEMS

1. What was the price per front foot for a 100′ × 125′ lot that sold for $125,000?
   a. $1,250
   b. $1,000
   c. $556
   d. $10

2. If the savings and loan gives you a 90 percent loan on a house valued at $88,500, how much additional cash must you produce as a down payment if you have already paid $4,500 in earnest money?
   a. $3,500
   b. $4,000
   c. $4,350
   d. $8,850

3. What is the total cost of a driveway 15′ wide, 40′ long and 4″ thick if the concrete costs $60.00 per cubic yard and the labor costs $1.25 per square foot?
   a. $527.25
   b. $693.75
   c. $1,194.00
   d. $1,581.75

4. An owner agrees to list his property on the condition that he will receive at least $47,300 after paying a 5 percent broker's commission and paying $1,150 in closing costs. At what price must it sell?
   a. $48,450
   b. $50,815
   c. $50,875
   d. $51,000

5. Two brokers split the 6 percent commission equally on a $73,000 home. The selling salesperson, Joe, was paid 70 percent of his broker's share. The listing salesperson, Janice, was paid 30 percent of her broker's share. How much did Janice receive?
   a. $657
   b. $4,380
   c. $1,533
   d. $1,314

6. Find the number of square feet in a lot with a frontage of 75 feet, 6 inches, and a depth of 140 feet, 9 inches.
   a. 10,626.63
   b. 10,652.04
   c. 216.25
   d. 25,510.81

7. A 100-acre farm is divided into lots for homes. The streets require 1/8 of the whole farm, and there are 140 lots. How many square feet are in each lot?
   a. 43,560
   b. 35,004
   c. 31,114
   d. 27,225

8. A salesperson sells a property for $58,500. The contract he has with his broker is 40% of the full commission earned. The commission due the broker is 6 percent. What is the salesperson's share of the commission?
   a. $2,106
   b. $1,404
   c. $3,510
   d. $2,340

9. A warehouse is 80′ wide and 120′ long with ceilings 14′ high. If 1,200 square feet of floor surface has been partitioned off, floor to ceiling, for an office, how many cubic feet of space will be left in the warehouse?
   a. 151,200
   b. 134,400
   c. 133,200
   d. 117,600

10. There is a tract of land that is 1.25 acres. The lot is 150 feet deep. How much will the lot sell for at $65 per front foot?
    a. $9,750
    b. $8,125
    c. $23,595
    d. $8,125

11. If the broker received a 6.5 percent commission that was $5,200, what was the sales price of the house?
    a. $80,400
    b. $80,000
    c. $77,200
    d. $86,600

12. The seller received a $121,600 check at closing after paying a 7 percent commission, $31,000 in other closing costs and the $135,700 loan payoff. What was the total sales price?
    a. $288,300
    b. $306,300
    c. $308,500
    d. $310,000

# Glossary

**abstract of title** The condensed history of a title to a particular parcel of real estate, consisting of a summary of the original grant and all subsequent conveyances and encumbrances affecting the property and a certification by the abstractor that the history is complete and accurate.

**acceleration clause** The clause in a mortgage or trust deed that can be enforced to make the entire debt due immediately if the mortgagor defaults on an installment payment or other covenant.

**accession** Acquiring title to additions or improvements to real property as a result of the annexation of fixtures or the accretion of alluvial deposits along the banks of streams.

**accretion** The increase or addition of land by the deposit of sand or soil washed up naturally from a river, lake, or sea.

**accrued interest** The amount of interest that is due for the period of time since interest was last paid.

**accrued items** On a closing statement, expense items that are incurred but not yet payable, such as interest on a mortgage loan or taxes on real property.

**acknowledgment** A formal declaration made before a duly authorized officer, usually a notary public, by a person who has signed a document.

**acre** A measure of land equal to 43,560 square feet, 4,840 square yards, 4,047 square meters, 160 square rods, or 0.4047 hectares.

**actual eviction** The result of legal action, originated by a lessor, whereby a defaulted tenant is physically ousted from the rented property pursuant to a court order. *See also* eviction.

**actual notice** Express information or fact; that which is known; direct knowledge.

**adjustable-rate mortgage (ARM)** A loan characterized by a fluctuating interest rate, usually one tied to a bank or savings and loan association cost-of-funds index.

**adjusted basis** *See* basis.

**ad valorem tax** A tax levied according to value; generally used to refer to real estate tax. Also called the *general tax.*

**adverse possession** The actual, visible, hostile, notorious, exclusive, and continuous possession of another's land under a claim of title. Possession for a statutory period may be a means of acquiring title.

**agency** The relationship between a principal and an agent, wherein the agent is authorized to represent the principal in certain transactions.

**agency coupled with an interest** An agency relationship in which the agent is given an estate or interest in the subject of the agency (the property).

**agent** One who acts or has the power to act for another. A fiduciary relationship is created under the *law of agency* when a principal authorizes a licensed real estate broker to be his or her agent.

**agreement of sale** An offer to purchase that has been accepted by the seller and has become a binding contract.

**air lot** A designated airspace over a piece of land. An air lot, just as surface property, may be transferred.

**air rights** The right to use the open space above a property, generally allowing the surface to be used for another purpose.

**alienation** The act of transferring property to another. Alienation may be voluntary, such as by gift or sale, or involuntary, such as through eminent domain or adverse possession.

**alienation clause** The clause in a mortgage that states that the balance of the secured debt becomes immediately due and payable at the mortgagee's option if the property is sold by the mortgagor. In effect, this clause prevents the mortgagor from assigning the debt without the mortgagee's approval.

**allodial system** A system of land ownership in which land is held free and clear of any rent or service due to the government; commonly contrasted with the feudal system. Land is held under the allodial system in the United States.

**amenities** Features, tangible and intangible, that enhance the value or desirability of real estate.

**American Land Title Association (ALTA) policy** A title insurance policy that protects the interest in a collateral property of a mortgage lender who originates a new real estate loan.

**Americans with Disabilities Act** Federal legislation mandating architectural standards that facilitate accessibility and mobility by disabled persons.

**amortized loan** A loan in which the principal as well as the interest is payable in monthly or other periodic installments over the term of the loan.

**annual percentage rate** The relationship of the total finance charges associated with a loan. This must be disclosed to borrowers by lenders under the Truth-in-Lending Act.

**anticipation** The appraisal principle that holds that value can increase or decrease based on the expectation of some future benefit or detriment produced by the property.

**antitrust laws** Laws designed to preserve the free enterprise of the open marketplace by making illegal certain private conspiracies and combinations formed to minimize competition. Violations of antitrust laws in the real estate business generally involve either *price fixing* (brokers conspiring to set fixed compensation rates) or *allocation of customers or markets* (brokers agreeing to limit their areas of trade or dealing to certain areas or properties).

**apportionment clause** Clause in an insurance policy providing that if the insured is covered by more than one policy, any payments will be apportioned according to the amount of coverage.

**appraisal** An estimate of the quantity, quality, or value of something. The process through which conclusions of property value are obtained; also refers to the report that sets forth the process of estimation and conclusion of value.

**appreciation** An increase in the worth or value of a property due to economic or related causes, which may prove to be either temporary or permanent; opposite of *depreciation.*

**appurtenance** A right, privilege, or improvement belonging to, and passing with, the land.

**ARELLO** Association of Real Estate License Law Officials.

**assemblage** The combining of two or more adjoining lots into one larger tract to increase their total value.

**assessment** The imposition of a tax, charge, or levy, usually according to established rates.

**assignment** The transfer in writing of interest in a bond, mortgage, lease, or other instrument.

**associate broker** A person licensed as a real estate broker who chooses to work under the supervision of another broker.

**assumption of mortgage** Acquiring title to property on which there is an existing mortgage and agreeing to be personally liable for the terms and conditions of the mortgage, including payments.

**attachment** The act of taking a person's property into legal custody by writ or other judicial order to hold it available for application to that person's debt to a creditor.

**attorney's opinion of title** An abstract of title that an attorney has examined and has certified to be, in his or her opinion, an accurate statement of the facts concerning the property ownership.

**automatic renewal** A clause in a listing agreement that states that the agreement will continue automatically for a certain period of time after its expiration date. In many states, use of this clause is discouraged.

**avulsion** The sudden tearing away of land, as by earthquake, flood, volcanic action, or a sudden change in the course of a stream.

**balance** The appraisal principle that states that the greatest value of a property will occur when the type and size of the improvements are proportional to each other as well as to the land.

**balloon payment** A final payment of a mortgage loan that is considerably larger than the required periodic payments because the loan amount was not fully amortized.

**base line** One of a set of imaginary lines running east and west and crossing a principal meridian at a definite point, used by surveyors for reference in locating and describing land under the rectangular survey (or government survey) system of property description.

**basis** The financial interest that the Internal Revenue Service attributes to an owner of an investment property for the purpose of determining annual depreciation and gain or loss on the sale of the asset. If a property was acquired by purchase, the owner's basis is the cost of the property plus the value of any capital expenditures for improvements to the property, minus any depreciation allowable or actually taken. This new basis is called the *adjusted basis.*

**bench mark** A permanent reference mark or point established for use by surveyors in measuring differences in elevation.

**beneficiary** (1) The person for whom a trust operates or in whose behalf the income from a trust estate is drawn. (2) A lender who lends money on real estate and takes back a note and trust deed from the borrower.

**bilateral contract** *See* contract.

**binder** An agreement that may accompany an earnest money deposit for the purchase of real property as evidence of the purchaser's good faith and intent to complete the transaction.

**blanket loan (mortgage)** A mortgage covering more than one parcel of real estate, providing for each parcel's partial release from the mortgage lien on repayment of a definite portion of the debt.

**blockbusting** The illegal practice of inducing homeowners to sell their properties by making representations regarding the entry or prospective entry of minority persons into the neighborhood.

**blue-sky laws** Common name for those state and federal laws that regulate the registration and sale of investment securities.

**boot** Money or property given to make up any difference in value or equity between two properties in an *exchange.*

**branch office** A secondary place of business apart from the principal or main office from which real estate business is conducted. A branch office generally must be run by a licensed real estate broker working on behalf of the broker who operates the principal office.

**breach of contract** Violation of any terms or conditions in a contract without legal excuse; for example, failure to make a payment when it is due.

**broker** One who buys and sells for another for a commission. *See also* real estate broker.

**brokerage** The business of bringing together parties interested in making a real estate transaction for a fee or commission.

**broker of record** The individual broker responsible for the real estate transactions and activities of licensees in a partnership or corporation.

**broker protection clause** A provision of a listing agreement that provides for the payment of a broker's commission if within a certain period after the listing expires, the owner transacts business with a contact made through the broker.

**buffer zone** A strip of land, usually used as a park or designated for a similar use, separating land dedicated to one use from land dedicated to another use (e.g., residential from commercial).

**builder-owner salesperson** An individual who is a full-time employee of the owner or builder of single-family or multifamily residences who is licensed to perform certain acts on behalf of the builder-owner.

**building code** An ordinance that specifies minimum standards of construction for buildings to protect public safety and health.

**building permit** Written governmental permission for the construction, alteration, or demolition of an improvement, showing compliance with building codes and zoning ordinances.

**bulk transfer** *See* Uniform Commercial Code.

**bundle of legal rights** The concept of land ownership that means *ownership of all legal rights to the land*—for example, possession, control within the law, and enjoyment.

**business name** The name in which the broker's license is issued. Any time the name of the business appears, it must be represented exactly as it appears on the broker's license.

**buydown** A financing technique used to reduce the monthly payments for the first few years of a loan. Funds in the form of discount points are given to the lender to buy down or lower the effective interest rate paid by the buyer, thus reducing the monthly payments for a set time.

**buyer-agency agreement** A principal/agent relationship in which the broker is the agent for the buyer, with fiduciary responsibilities to the buyer. The broker represents the buyer under the law of agency.

**campground membership** An interest, other than in fee simple or by lease, that gives the purchaser the right to use a unit of real property for the purpose of locating a recreational vehicle, trailer, tent, camper or other similar device on a periodic basis pursuant to a membership contract.

**campground membership salesperson** A licensee who, either as an employee or independent contractor, sells campground memberships under the supervision of a broker.

**capital gain** Profit earned from the sale of an asset.

**capitalization** A mathematical process for estimating the value of a property using a proper rate of return on the investment and the annual net income expected to be produced by the property. The formula is expressed as

$$\frac{\text{Income}}{\text{Rate}} = \text{Value}$$

**capitalization rate** The rate of return a property will produce on the owner's investment.

**cash flow** The net spendable income from an investment, determined by deducting all operating and fixed expenses from the gross income. If expenses exceed income, a *negative cash flow* is the result.

**cash rent** In an agricultural lease, the amount of money given as rent to the landowner at the outset of the lease, as opposed to share-cropping.

**caveat emptor** A Latin phrase meaning "Let the buyer beware."

**cemetery associate broker** A licensed cemetery broker who is employed by another cemetery broker or broker.

**cemetery broker** An individual or entity licensed to engage exclusively in the sale of cemetery lots, plots, and mausoleum spaces or openings.

**cemetery salesperson** A licensee employed by a broker or cemetery broker to sell cemetery lots exclusively.

**certificate of reasonable value** A form indicating the appraised value of a property being financed with a VA loan.

**certificate of sale** The document generally given to the purchaser at a tax foreclosure sale. A certificate of sale does not convey title; generally it is an instrument certifying that the holder received title to the property after the redemption period had passed and that the holder paid the property taxes for that interim period.

**certificate of title** A statement of opinion on the status of the title to a parcel of real property based on an examination of specified public records.

**certified general real estate appraiser** An individual who is certified under the state Certified Appraisers Act to perform appraisals of any type or value of property for federally related real estate transactions.

**certified residential real estate appraiser** An individual who is certified under the state Certified Appraisers Act to perform residential (one-unit to four-unit dwellings) appraisals for federally related real estate transactions.

**chain of title** The succession of conveyances, from some accepted starting point, whereby the present holder of real property derives his or her title.

**chattel** *See* personal property.

**Civil Rights Act of 1866** An act that prohibits racial discrimination in the sale and rental of housing.

**closing statement** A detailed cash accounting of a real estate transaction showing all cash received, all charges and credits made, and all cash paid out in the transaction.

**cloud on title** Any document, claim, unreleased lien, or encumbrance that may impair the title to real property or make the title doubtful; usually revealed by a title search and removed by either a quitclaim deed or suit to quiet title.

**clustering** The grouping of homesites within a subdivision on smaller lots than normal, with the remaining land used as common areas.

**Code of Ethics** NAR-suggested standards of conduct for compliance with fair housing laws.

**codicil** A supplement or addition to a will, executed with the same formalities as a will, that normally does not revoke the entire will.

**coinsurance clause** A clause in insurance policies covering real property that requires that the policyholder maintain fire insurance coverage generally equal to at least 80 percent of the property's actual replacement cost.

**commingling** The illegal act of a real estate broker of placing client or customer funds with personal funds. By law, brokers are required to maintain a separate *trust account* for other parties' funds held temporarily by the broker.

**commission** Payment to a broker for services rendered, such as in the sale or purchase of real property; usually a percentage of the selling price of the property.

**common elements** Parts of a property that are necessary or convenient to the existence, maintenance, and safety of a condominium or are normally in common use by all of the condominium residents. Each condominium owner has an undivided ownership interest in the common elements.

**common law** The body of law based on custom, usage, and court decisions.

**community property** A system of property ownership based on the theory that each spouse has an equal interest in the property acquired by the efforts of either spouse during marriage. This system stemmed from Germanic tribes and, through Spain, came to the Spanish colonies of North and South America. The system was unknown under English common law.

**comparables** Properties listed in an appraisal report that are substantially equivalent to the subject property.

**competition** The appraisal principle that states that excess profits generate competition.

**competitive market analysis (CMA)** A comparison of the prices of recently sold homes that are similar to a listing seller's home in terms of location, style, and amenities. Also called *comparative market analysis.*

**comprehensive plan** *See* master plan.

**condemnation** A judicial or administrative proceeding to exercise the right of eminent domain, through which a government agency takes private property for public use and compensates the owner.

**conditional-use permit** Written governmental permission allowing a use inconsistent with zoning but necessary for the common good, such as locating an emergency medical facility in a predominantly residential area.

**condition subsequent** A clause that returns property to the previous owner should the new owner fail to perform a condition upon which the sale was based.

**condominium** The absolute ownership of a unit in a multiunit building based on a legal description of the airspace the unit actually occupies, plus an undivided interest in the ownership of the common elements, which are owned jointly with the other condominium unit owners.

**confession of judgment clause** Permits judgment to be entered against a debtor without a creditor's having to institute legal proceedings.

**conformity** The appraisal principle that holds that the greater the similarity among properties in an area, the better they will hold their value.

**consideration** (1) That received by the grantor in exchange for his or her deed. (2) Something of value that induces a person to enter into a contract.

**construction loan** *See* interim financing.

**constructive eviction** Actions of a landlord that so materially disturb or impair the tenant's enjoyment of the leased premises that the tenant is effectively forced to move out and terminate the lease without liability for any further rent.

**constructive notice** Notice given to the world by recorded documents. All people are charged with knowledge of such documents and their contents, regardless of whether they have actually examined them. Possession of property is also considered constructive notice that the person in possession has an interest in the property.

**contingency** A provision in a contract that requires that a certain act be done or a certain event occur before the contract becomes binding.

**contract** A legally enforceable promise or set of promises that must be performed and for which, if a breach of the promise occurs, the law provides a remedy. A contract may be either *unilateral,* where only one party is bound to act, or *bilateral,* where all parties to the instrument are legally bound to act as prescribed.

**contribution** The appraisal principle that states that the value of any component of a property is what it gives to the value of the whole or what its absence detracts from that value.

**conventional loan** A loan that is not insured or guaranteed by a government or private source.

**conveyance** A term used to refer to any document that transfers title to real property. The term also is used in describing the act of transferring.

**cooperating brokers** *See* listing brokers.

**cooperative** A residential multiunit building whose title is held by a trust or corporation that is owned by and operated for the benefit of persons living within the building, who are the beneficial owners of the trust or stockholders of the corporation, each possessing a proprietary lease.

**co-ownership** Title ownership held by two or more persons.

**corporation** An entity or organization created by operation of law, whose rights of doing business are essentially the same as those of an individual. The entity has continuous existence until it is dissolved according to legal procedures.

**correction lines** Provisions in the rectangular survey (government survey) system made to compensate for the curvature of the earth's surface. Every fourth township line (at 24-mile intervals) is used as a correction line on which the intervals between the north and south range lines are remeasured and corrected to a full 6 miles.

**cost approach** The process of estimating the value of a property by adding to the estimated land value the appraiser's estimate of the reproduction or replacement cost of the building, less depreciation.

**cost recovery** An Internal Revenue Service term for *depreciation.*

**counteroffer** A new offer made as a reply to an offer received. It has the effect of rejecting the original offer, which cannot be accepted thereafter unless revived by the offeror.

**covenant** A written agreement between two or more parties in which a party or parties pledges to perform or not perform specified acts with regard to property; usually found in such real estate documents as deeds, mortgages, leases, and contracts for deed.

**covenant of quiet enjoyment** The covenant implied by law by which a landlord guarantees that a tenant may take possession of leased premises and that the landlord will not interfere in the tenant's possession or use of the property.

**credit** On a closing statement, an amount entered in a person's favor—either an amount the party has paid or an amount for which the party must be reimbursed.

**creditor** A person to whom a debt is owed.

**cul-de-sac** A street that has an opening on one end only; the other end is usually a turnaround.

**curtesy** A life estate, usually a fractional interest, given by some states to the surviving husband in real estate owned by his deceased wife. Most states have abolished curtesy.

**datum** A horizontal plane from which heights and depths are measured.

**debit** On a closing statement, an amount charged; that is, an amount that the debited party must pay.

**debtor** A person who owes money.

**decedent** A person who has died.

**dedication** The voluntary transfer of private property by its owner to the public for some public use, such as for streets or schools.

**deed** A written instrument that, when executed and delivered, conveys title to or an interest in real estate.

**deed in lieu of foreclosure** A deed given by the mortgagor to the mortgagee when the mortgagor is in default under the terms of the mortgage.

This is a way for the mortgagor to avoid foreclosure.

**deed in trust** An instrument that grants a trustee full powers to sell, mortgage, and subdivide a parcel of real estate. The beneficiary controls the trustee's use of these powers under the provisions of the trust agreement.

**deed of trust** *See* trust deed.

**deed restrictions** Clauses in a deed limiting the future uses of the property. Deed restrictions may impose a vast variety of limitations and conditions—for example, they may limit the density of buildings, dictate the types of structures that can be erected, or prevent buildings from being used for specific purposes or even from being used at all.

**default** The nonperformance of a duty, whether arising under a contract or otherwise; failure to meet an obligation when due.

**defeasance clause** A clause used in leases and mortgages that cancels a specified right on the occurrence of a certain condition, such as cancellation of a mortgage on repayment of the mortgage loan.

**defeasible fee estate** An estate in which the holder has a fee simple title that may be divested on the occurrence or nonoccurrence of a specified event. There are two categories of defeasible fee estates: fee simple determinable and fee simple subject to a condition subsequent.

**deficiency judgment** A personal judgment levied against the mortgagor when a foreclosure sale does not produce sufficient funds to pay the mortgage debt in full.

**demand** The amount of goods people are willing and able to buy at a given price; often coupled with *supply.*

**denial, suspension, or revocation of license** The potential penalties for licensees who violate real estate statutes or rules and regulations.

**density zoning** Zoning ordinances that restrict the average maximum number of houses per acre that may be built within a particular area, generally a subdivision.

**depreciation** (1) In appraisal, a loss of value in property due to any cause, including *physical deterioration, functional obsolescence,* and *external obsolescence.* (2) In real estate investment, an expense deduction for tax purposes taken over the period of ownership of income property.

**descent** Acquisition of an estate by inheritance in which an heir succeeds to the property by operation of law.

**developer** One who attempts to put land to its most profitable use through the construction of improvements.

**devise** A gift of real property by will. The donor is the devisor and the recipient is the devisee.

**direct public ownership** The system under which government owns land used for public use, such as schools, highways, parks, etc.

**discount point** A unit of measurement used for various loan charges; one point equals 1 percent of the amount of the loan.

**doctrine of prior appropriation** *See* prior appropriation.

**dominant tenement** A property that includes in its ownership the appurtenant right to use an easement over another person's property for a specific purpose.

**dower** The legal right or interest, recognized in some states, that a wife acquires in the property her husband held or acquired during their marriage. During the husband's lifetime, the right is only a possibility of an interest; upon his death it can become an interest in land.

**dual agency** Representing both parties to a transaction. This is unethical unless both parties agree to it, and it is illegal in many states.

**due-on-sale clause** A provision in the mortgage that states that the entire balance of the note is immediately due and payable if the mortgagor transfers (sells) the property.

**duress** Unlawful constraint or action exercised on a person whereby the person is forced to perform an act against his or her will. A contract entered into under duress is voidable.

**earnest money** Money deposited by a buyer under the terms of a contract, to be forfeited if the buyer defaults but applied to the purchase price if the sale is closed.

**easement** A right to use the land of another for a specific purpose, such as for a right-of-way or utilities; an incorporeal interest in land.

**easement appurtenant** An easement that is annexed to the ownership of one parcel and allows the owner the use of the neighbor's land.

**easement by condemnation** An easement created by the government or government agency that has exercised its right under eminent domain.

**easement by necessity** An easement allowed by law as necessary for the full enjoyment of a parcel of real estate; for example, a right of ingress and egress over a grantor's land.

**easement by prescription** An easement acquired by continuous, open, and hostile use of the property for the period of time prescribed by state law.

**easement in gross** An easement that is not created for the benefit of any *land* owned by the owner of the easement but that attaches *personally to the easement owner.* For example, a right granted by Eleanor Franks to Joe Fish to use a portion of her property for the rest of his life would be an easement in gross.

**economic life** The number of years during which an improvement will add value to the land.

**egress** A way to exit a property.

**emblements** Growing crops, such as grapes and corn, that are produced annually through labor and industry; also called *fructus industriales.*

**eminent domain** The right of a government or municipal quasi-public body to acquire property for public use through a court action called *condemnation.*

**employee** Someone who works as a direct employee of an employer and has employee status. The employer is obligated to withhold income taxes and social security taxes from the compensation of employees. *See also* independent contractor.

**employment contract** A document evidencing formal employment between employer and employee or between principal and agent. In the real estate business, this generally takes the form of a listing agreement or management agreement.

**enabling acts** State legislation that confers zoning powers on municipal governments.

**encroachment** A building or some portion of it— a wall or fence, for instance—that extends beyond the land of the owner and illegally intrudes on some land of an adjoining owner or a street or alley.

**encumbrance** Anything—such as a mortgage, tax, or judgment lien, an easement, a restriction on the use of the land, or an outstanding dower right—that may diminish the value of a property.

**Equal Credit Opportunity Act (ECOA)** The federal law that prohibits discrimination in the extension of credit because of race, color, religion, national origin, sex, age, or marital status.

**equalization** The raising or lowering of assessed values for tax purposes in a particular county or taxing district to make them equal to assessments in other counties or districts.

**equalization factor** A factor (number) by which the assessed value of a property is multiplied to arrive at a value for the property that is in line with statewide tax assessments. The *ad valorem tax* would be based on this adjusted value.

**equitable lien** *See* statutory lien.

**equitable right of redemption** The right of a defaulted property owner to recover the property prior to its sale by paying the appropriate fees and charges.

**equitable title** The interest held by a vendee under an installment contract or agreement of sale; the equitable right to obtain absolute ownership to property when legal title is held in another's name.

**equity** The interest or value that an owner has in the property over and above any mortgage indebtedness.

**erosion** The gradual wearing away of land by water, wind, and general weather conditions; the diminishing of property caused by the elements.

**escheat** The reversion of property to the state or county, as provided by state law, in cases where a decedent dies intestate without heirs capable of inheriting or when the property is abandoned.

**escrow** The closing of a transaction through a third party called an *escrow agent,* or *escrowee,* who receives certain funds and documents to be delivered on the performance of certain conditions outlined in the escrow agreement.

**escrow account** The trust account established by a broker under the provisions of the license law for the purpose of holding funds on behalf of the broker's principal or some other person until the consummation or termination of a transaction.

**estate (tenancy) at sufferance** The tenancy of a lessee who lawfully comes into possession of a landlord's real estate but who continues to occupy the premises improperly after his or her lease rights have expired.

**estate (tenancy) at will** An estate that gives the lessee the right to possession until the estate is terminated by either party; the term of this estate is indefinite.

**estate (tenancy) for years** An interest for a certain, exact period of time in property leased for a specified consideration.

**estate (tenancy) from period to period** An interest in leased property that continues from period to period—week to week, month, to month or year to year.

**estate in land** The degree, quantity, nature, and extent of interest that a person has in real property.

**estate taxes** Federal taxes on a decedent's real and personal property.

**estoppel** Method of creating an agency relationship in which someone states incorrectly that another person is his or her agent, and a third person relies on that representation.

**estoppel certificate** A document in which a borrower certifies the amount owed on a mortgage loan and the rate of interest.

**ethics** The system of moral principles and rules that become standards for professional conduct.

**eviction** A legal process to oust a person from possession of real estate.

**evidence of title** Proof of ownership of property; commonly a certificate of title or title insurance.

**exchange** A transaction in which all or part of the consideration is the transfer of *like-kind* property (such as real estate for real estate).

**exclusive-agency listing** A listing contract under which the owner appoints a real estate broker as his or her exclusive agent for a designated period of time to sell the property, on the owner's stated terms, for a commission. The owner reserves the right to sell without paying anyone a commission if he or she sells to a prospect who has not been introduced or claimed by the broker.

**exclusive-right-to-sell listing** A listing contract under which the owner appoints a real estate broker as his or her exclusive agent for a designated period of time, to sell the property on the owner's stated terms, and agrees to pay the broker a commission when the property is sold, whether by the broker, the owner, or another broker.

**executed contract** A contract in which all parties have fulfilled their promises and thus performed the contract.

**execution** The signing and delivery of an instrument. Also, a legal order directing an official to enforce a judgment against the property of a debtor.

**executory contract** A contract under which something remains to be done by one or more of the parties.

**express agreement** An oral or written contract in which the parties state the contract's terms and express their intentions in words.

**express contract** *See* express agreement.

**external obsolescence** Reduction in a property's value caused by outside factors (those that are off the property). Also called *environmental* or *economic* obsolescence.

**Fair Housing Act** The federal law that prohibits discrimination in housing based on race, color, religion, sex, handicap, familial status, and national origin.

**Fannie Mae** *See* Federal National Mortgage Association (FNMA).

**Farmers Home Administration (FmHA)** An agency of the federal government that provides credit assistance to farmers and other individuals who live in rural areas.

**Federal Deposit Insurance Corporation (FDIC)** An independent federal agency that insures the deposits in commercial banks.

**Federal Home Loan Mortgage Corporation (FHLMC)** A corporation established to purchase primarily conventional mortgage loans on the secondary mortgage market.

**Federal National Mortgage Association (FNMA)** A quasi-government agency established to purchase any kind of mortgage loans in the secondary mortgage market from the primary lenders.

**Federal Reserve System** The country's central banking system, which is responsible for the nation's monetary policy by regulating the supply of money and interest rates.

**fee simple absolute** The maximum possible estate or right of ownership of real property, continuing forever. Also known as *fee simple.*

**fee simple defeasible** *See* defeasible fee estate.

**feudal system** A system of ownership usually associated with precolonial England, in which the king or other sovereign is the source of all rights. The right to possess real property was granted by the sovereign to an individual as a life estate only. On the death of the individual title passed back to the sovereign, not to the decedent's heirs.

**FHA loan** A loan insured by the Federal Housing Administration and made by an approved lender in accordance with the FHA's regulations.

**fiduciary** One in whom trust and confidence is placed; usually a reference to a broker employed under the terms of a listing contract.

**fiduciary relationship** A relationship of trust and confidence, as between trustee and beneficiary, attorney and client, or principal and agent.

**Financial Institutions Reform, Recovery, and Enforcement Act (FIRREA)** This act restructured the savings and loan association regulatory system; enacted in response to the savings and loan crisis of the 1980s.

**financing statement** *See* Uniform Commercial Code.

**FIRREA** *See* Financial Institutions Reform, Recovery, and Enforcement Act (FIRREA).

**first mortgage** The mortgage loan that takes first lien position by being recorded first.

**fiscal policy** The government's policy in regard to taxation and spending programs. The balance between these two areas determines the amount of money the government will withdraw from or feed into the economy, which can counter economic peaks and slumps.

**fixture** An item of personal property that has been converted to real property by being permanently affixed to the realty.

**foreclosure** A legal procedure whereby property used as security for a debt is sold to satisfy the debt in the event of default in payment of the mortgage note or default of other terms in the mortgage document. The foreclosure procedure brings the rights of all parties to a conclusion and passes the title in the mortgaged property to either the holder of the mortgage or a third party who may purchase the realty at the foreclosure sale, free of all encumbrances affecting the property subsequent to the mortgage.

**fractional section** A parcel of land less than 160 acres, usually found at the end of a rectangular survey.

**fraud** Deception intended to cause a person to give up property or a lawful right.

**Freddie Mac** *See* Federal Home Loan Mortgage Corporation (FHLMC).

**freehold estate** An estate in land in which ownership is for an indeterminate length of time, in contrast to a *leasehold estate.*

**front footage** The measurement of a parcel of land by the number of feet of street or road frontage.

**functional obsolescence** A loss of value to an improvement to real estate arising from functional problems, often caused by age or poor design.

**future interest** A person's present right to an interest in real property that will not result in possession or enjoyment until some time in the future, such as a reversion or right of reentry.

**gap** A defect in the chain of title of a particular parcel of real estate; a missing document or conveyance that raises doubt as to the present ownership of the land.

**general agent** One who is authorized by his or her principal to represent the principal in a specific range of matters.

**general contractor** A construction specialist who enters into a formal construction contract with a landowner or master lessee to construct a real estate building or project. The general contractor often contracts with several *subcontractors* specializing in various aspects of the building process to perform individual jobs.

**general lien** The right of a creditor to have all of a debtor's property—both real and personal—sold to satisfy a debt.

**general partnership** *See* partnership.

**general warranty deed** A deed in which the grantor fully warrants good clear title to the premises. Used in most real estate transfers, a general warranty deed offers the greatest protection of any deed.

**Ginnie Mae** *See* Government National Mortgage Association (GNMA).

**government lot** Fractional sections in the rectangular survey (government survey) system that are less than one quarter-section in area.

**Government National Mortgage Association (GNMA)** A government agency that plays an important role in the secondary mortgage market. It sells mortgage-backed securities that are backed by pools of FHA and VA loans.

**government survey system** *See* rectangular (government) survey system.

**graduated payment mortgage (GPM)** A loan in which the monthly principal and interest payments increase by a certain percentage each year for a certain number of years and then level off for the remaining loan term.

**grantee** A person who receives a conveyance of real property from the grantor.

**granting clause** Words in a deed of conveyance that state the grantor's intention to convey the property at the present time. This clause is generally worded as "convey and warrant," "grant," "grant, bargain, and sell," or the like.

**grantor** The person transferring title to or an interest in real property to a grantee.

**gross income multiplier** A figure used as a multiplier of the gross annual income of a property to produce an estimate of the property's value.

**gross lease** A lease of property under which a landlord pays all property charges regularly incurred through ownership, such as repairs, taxes, insurance, and operating expenses. Most residential leases are gross leases.

**gross rent multiplier (GRM)** A figure used as a multiplier of the gross monthly income of a property to produce an estimate of the property's value.

**ground lease** A lease of land only, on which the tenant usually owns a building or is required to build his or her own building as specified in the lease. Such leases are usually long-term net leases; the tenant's rights and obligations continue until the lease expires or is terminated through default.

**growing-equity mortgage (GEM)** A loan in which the monthly payments increase annually, with the increased amount being used to reduce directly the principal balance outstanding and thus shorten the overall term of the loan.

**habendum clause** That part of a deed beginning with the words "to have and to hold," following the granting clause and defining the extent of ownership the grantor is conveying.

**heir** One who might inherit or succeed to an interest in land under the state law of descent if the owner dies without leaving a valid will.

**highest and best use** That possible use of land that would produce the greatest net income and thereby develop the highest land value.

**holdover tenancy** A tenancy whereby a lessee retains possession of leased property after the lease has expired and the landlord, by continuing to accept rent, agrees to the tenant's continued occupancy as defined by state law.

**holographic will** A will that is written, dated, and signed in the testator's handwriting.

**home equity loan** A loan (sometimes called a *line of credit*) under which a property owner uses the equity in his or her residence as collateral and can then draw funds up to a prearranged amount against the property.

**homeowner's insurance policy** A standardized package insurance policy that covers a residential real estate owner against financial loss from fire, theft, public liability, and other common risks.

**homestead** Land that is owned and occupied as the family home. In many states, a portion of the area or value of this land is protected or exempt from judgments for debts.

**hypothecation** The pledge of property as security for a loan.

**impact fees** Charges assessed developers by a municipality that relate to expenses incurred by the municipality for additional improvements necessitated by increased development.

**implied agreement** A contract under which the agreement of the parties is demonstrated by their acts and conduct.

**implied contract** *See* implied agreement.

**implied warranty of habitability** A theory in landlord/tenant law in which the landlord renting residential property implies that the property is habitable and fit for its intended use.

**improvement** (1) Any structure, usually privately owned, erected on a site to enhance the value of the property—for example, building a fence or a driveway. (2) A publicly owned structure added to or benefiting land, such as a curb, sidewalk, street, or sewer.

**income approach** The process of estimating the value of an income-producing property by capitalization of the annual net income expected to be produced by the property during its remaining useful life.

**incorporeal right** A nonpossessory right in real estate; for example, an easement or right-of-way.

**independent contractor** Someone who is retained to perform a certain act but who is subject to the control and direction of another only as to the end result and not as to the way in which he or she performs the act. Unlike an employee, an independent contractor pays for all his or her expenses and Social Security and income taxes and receives no employee benefits. Many real estate salespeople are independent contractors.

**index method** The appraisal method of estimating building costs by multiplying the original cost of the property by a percentage factor to adjust for current construction costs.

**inflation** The gradual reduction of the purchasing power of the dollar, usually related directly to the increases in the money supply by the federal government.

**ingress** A way to enter a property.

**inheritance taxes** State-imposed taxes on a decedent's real and personal property.

**installment contract** A contract for the sale of real estate whereby the purchase price is paid in periodic installments by the purchaser, who is in possession of the property even though title is retained by the seller until a future date, which may be not until final payment. Also called a *contract for deed* or *articles of agreement for warranty deed.*

**installment sale** A transaction in which the sales price is paid in two or more installments over two or more years. If the sale meets certain requirements, a taxpayer can postpone reporting such income until future years by paying tax each year only on the proceeds received that year.

**interest** A charge made by a lender for the use of money.

**interim financing** A short-term loan usually made during the construction phase of a building project (in this case, often referred to as a *construction loan*).

**Interstate Land Sales Full Disclosure Act** A federal law that regulates the sale of certain real estate in interstate commerce.

**intestate** The condition of a property owner who dies without leaving a valid will. Title to the property will pass to the decedent's heirs as provided in the state law of descent.

**intrinsic value** An appraisal term referring to the value created by a person's personal preferences for a particular type of property.

**investment** Money directed toward the purchase, improvement, and development of an asset in expectation of income or profits.

**involuntary alienation** *See* alienation.

**involuntary lien** Lien placed on property without the consent of the property owner.

**IRS tax lien** A general, involuntary lien placed by the taxing authority on the property of a delinquent taxpayer.

**joint venture** The joining of two or more people to conduct a specific business enterprise. A joint venture is similar to a partnership in that it must be created by agreement between the parties to share in the losses and profits of the venture. It is unlike a partnership in that the venture is for one specific project only, rather than for a continuing business relationship.

**judgment** The formal decision of a court on the respective rights and claims of the parties to an action or suit. After a judgment has been entered and recorded with the county recorder, it usually becomes a general lien on the property of the defendant.

**judicial deed** A deed that is delivered pursuant to court order.

**judicial precedent** In law, the requirements established by prior court decisions.

**junior lien** An obligation, such as a second mortgage, that is subordinate in right or lien priority to an existing lien on the same realty.

**laches** An equitable doctrine used by courts to bar a legal claim or prevent the assertion of a right because of undue delay or failure to assert the claim or right.

**land** The earth's surface, extending downward to the center of the earth and upward infinitely into space, including things permanently attached by nature, such as trees and water.

**land contract** *See* installment contract.

**law of agency** *See* agency.

**lease** A written or oral contract between a landlord (the *lessor*) and a tenant (the *lessee*) that transfers the right to exclusive possession and use of the landlord's real property to the lessee for a specified period of time and for a stated consideration (*rent*). By state law, leases for longer than a certain period of time must be in writing to be enforceable.

**leasehold estate** A tenant's right to occupy real estate during the term of a lease; generally considered to be a personal property interest.

**lease option** A lease under which the tenant has the right to purchase the property either during the lease term or at its end.

**lease purchase** The purchase of real property, the consummation of which is preceded by a lease, usually long-term. Typically done for tax or financing purposes.

**legacy** A disposition of money or personal property by will.

**legal description** A description of a specific parcel of real estate complete enough for an independent surveyor to locate and identify it.

**legally competent parties** People who are recognized by law as being able to contract with others; those of legal age and sound mind.

**lessee** *See* lease.

**lessor** *See* lease.

**leverage** The use of borrowed money to finance the bulk of an investment.

**levy** To assess; to seize or collect. To levy a tax is to assess a property and set the rate of taxation. To levy an execution is to officially seize the property of a person to satisfy an obligation.

**liability coverage** Insurance that indemnifies a property owner who is found liable for damage in the event of an individual's being injured on the insured's property.

**license** (1) A privilege or right granted to a person by a state to operate as a real estate broker or salesperson. (2) The revocable permission for a temporary use of land—a personal right that cannot be sold.

**lien** A right given by law to certain creditors to have their debt paid out of the property of a defaulting debtor, usually by means of a court sale.

**lien theory** Some states interpret a mortgage as being purely a lien on real property. The mortgagee thus has no right of possession but must foreclose the lien and sell the property if the mortgagor defaults.

**life cycle costing** In property management, comparing one type of equipment to another based on both purchase cost and operating cost over its expected useful lifetime.

**life estate** An interest in real or personal property that is limited in duration to the lifetime of its owner or some other designated person or persons.

**life tenant** A person in possession of a life estate.

**limited partnership** *See* partnership.

**liquidated damages** An amount predetermined by the parties to a contract as the total compensation to an injured party should the other party breach the contract.

**liquidity** The ability to sell an asset and convert it into cash, at a price close to its true value, in a short period of time.

**lis pendens** A recorded legal document giving constructive notice that an action affecting a particular property has been filed in either a state or a federal court.

**listing agreement** A contract between an owner (as principal) and a real estate broker (as agent) by which the broker is employed as agent to find a buyer for the owner's real estate on the owner's terms, for which service the owner agrees to pay a commission.

**listing broker** The broker in a multiple-listing situation from whose office a listing agreement is initiated, as opposed to the *cooperating broker,* from whose office negotiations leading up to a sale are initiated. The listing broker and the cooperating broker may be the same person.

**littoral rights** (1) A landowner's claim to use water in large navigable lakes and oceans adjacent to his or her property. (2) The ownership rights to land bordering these bodies of water up to the high-water mark.

**loan origination fee** A fee charged to the borrower by the lender for making a mortgage loan. The fee is usually computed as a percentage of the loan amount.

**loan-to-value ratio** The relationship between the amount of the mortgage loan and the value of the real estate being pledged as collateral.

**lot-and-block system** A method of describing real property that identifies a parcel of land by reference to lot and block numbers within a subdivision, as specified on a recorded subdivision plat. Sometimes called *recorded plat system.*

**management agreement** A contract between the owner of income property and a management firm or individual property manager that outlines the scope of the manager's authority.

**market** A place where goods can be bought and sold and a price established.

**marketable title** Good or clear title reasonably free from the risk of litigation over possible defects.

**market value** The most probable price property would bring in an arm's-length transaction under normal conditions on the open market.

**master plan** A comprehensive plan to guide the long-term physical development of a particular area.

**mechanic's lien** A statutory lien created in favor of contractors, laborers, and materialmen who have performed work or furnished materials in the erection or repair of a building.

**metes-and-bounds description** A legal description of a parcel of land that begins at a well-marked point and follows the boundaries, using directions and distances around the tract, back to the place of beginning.

**mill** One-tenth of one cent. Some states use a mill rate to compute real estate taxes; for example, a rate of 52 mills would be $.052 tax for each dollar of assessed valuation of a property.

**minor** Someone who has not reached the age of majority and therefore does not have legal capacity to transfer title to real property.

**monetary policy** Governmental regulation of the amount of money in circulation through such institutions as the Federal Reserve Board.

**money judgment** A court judgment ordering payment of money rather than specific performance of a certain action. *See also* judgment.

**month-to-month tenancy** A periodic tenancy under which the tenant rents for one month at a time. In the absence of a rental agreement (oral or written), a tenancy is generally considered to be month to month.

**monument** A fixed natural or artificial object used to establish real estate boundaries for a metes-and-bounds description.

**mortgage** A conditional transfer or pledge of real estate as security for the payment of a debt. Also the document creating a mortgage lien.

**mortgage banker** Mortgage loan companies that originate, service, and sell loans to investors.

**mortgage broker** An agent of a lender who brings the lender and borrower together. The broker receives a fee for this service.

**mortgagee** A lender in a mortgage loan transaction.

**mortgage lien** A lien or charge on the property of a mortgagor that secures the underlying debt obligations.

**mortgagor** A borrower in a mortgage loan transaction.

**multiperil policies** Insurance policies that offer protection from a range of potential perils, such as those of a fire, hazard, public liability, and casualty.

**multiple-listing clause** A provision in an exclusive listing for the additional authority and obligation on the part of the listing broker to distribute the listing to other brokers in the multiple-listing organization.

**multiple-listing service (MLS)** A marketing organization composed of member brokers who agree to share their listing agreements with one another in the hope of procuring ready, willing, and able buyers for their properties more quickly than they could on their own. Most multiple-listing services accept only exclusive-right-to-sell listings or exclusive agency listings from their member brokers, although any broker can sell a property listed in an MLS.

**negotiable instrument** A written promise or order to pay a specific sum of money that may be transferred by endorsement or delivery. The transferee then has the original payee's right to payment.

**net lease** A lease requiring the tenant to pay not only rent but also costs incurred in maintaining the property, including taxes, insurance, utilities, and repairs.

**net listing** A listing based on the net price the seller will receive if the property is sold. Under a net listing the broker can offer the property for sale at the highest price obtainable to increase the commission. This type of listing is illegal in many states.

**net operating income (NOI)** The income projected for an income-producing property after deducting losses for vacancy and collection and operating expenses.

**nonconforming use** A use of property that is permitted to continue after a zoning ordinance prohibiting it has been established for the area.

**nonhomogeneity** A lack of uniformity; dissimilarity. Because no two parcels of land are exactly alike, real estate is said to be nonhomogeneous.

**note** *See* promissory note.

**novation** Substituting a new obligation for an old one or substituting new parties to an existing obligation.

**nuncupative will** An oral will declared by the testator in his or her final illness, made before witnesses and afterward reduced to writing.

**obsolescence** The loss of value due to factors that are outmoded or less useful. It may be functional or economic.

**offer and acceptance** Two essential components of a valid contract; a "meeting of the minds."

**offeror/offeree** The person who makes the offer is the *offeror*. The person to whom the offer is made is the *offeree*.

**Office of Thrift Supervision (OTS)** Monitors and regulates the savings and loan industry. OTS was created by FIRREA.

**open-end loan** A mortgage loan that is expandable by increments up to a maximum dollar amount, the full loan being secured by the same original mortgage.

**open listing** A listing contract under which the broker's commission is contingent on the broker's producing a ready, willing, and able buyer before the property is sold by the seller or another broker.

**option** An agreement to keep open for a set period an offer to sell or purchase property.

**option listing** Listing with a provision that gives the listing broker the right to purchase the listed property.

**ostensible agency** A form of implied agency relationship created by the actions of the parties involved rather than by written agreement or document.

**package loan** A real estate loan used to finance the purchase of both real property and personal property, such as in the purchase of a new home that includes carpeting, window coverings, and major appliances.

**parol evidence rule** A rule of evidence providing that a written agreement is the final expression of the agreement of the parties, not to be varied or contradicted by prior or contemporaneous oral or written negotiations.

**participation mortgage** A mortgage loan wherein the lender has a partial equity interest in the property or receives a portion of the income from the property.

**partition** The division of cotenants' interests in real property when the parties do not all voluntarily agree to terminate the co-ownership; takes place through court procedures.

**partnership** An association of two or more individuals who carry on a continuing business for profit as co-owners. Under the law a partnership is regarded as a group of individuals rather than as a single entity. A *general partnership* is a typical form of joint venture, in which each general partner shares in the administration, profits, and losses of the operation. A *limited partnership* is a business arrangement whereby the operation is administered by one or more general partners and

funded, by and large, by limited or silent partners, who are by law responsible for losses only to the extent of their investments.

**party wall** A wall that is located on or at a boundary line between two adjoining parcels of land and is used or is intended to be used by the owners of both properties.

**patent** A grant or franchise of land from the United States government.

**payment cap** The limit on the amount the monthly payment can be increased on an adjustable rate mortgage when the interest rate is adjusted.

**payoff statement** *See* reduction certificate.

**percentage lease** A lease, commonly used for commercial property, whose rental is based on the tenant's gross sales at the premises; it usually stipulates a base monthly rental plus a percentage of any gross sales above a certain amount.

**percolation test** A test of the soil to determine if it will absorb and drain water adequately to use a septic system for sewage disposal.

**periodic tenancy** *See* estate from period to period.

**personal property** Items, called *chattels*, that do not fit into the definition of real property; movable objects.

**physical deterioration** A reduction in a property's value resulting from a decline in physical condition; can be caused by action of the elements or by ordinary wear and tear.

**planned unit development (PUD)** A planned combination of diverse land uses, such as housing, recreation, and shopping, in one contained development or subdivision.

**plat map** A map of a town, section, or subdivision indicating the location and boundaries of individual properties.

**plottage** The increase in value or utility resulting from the consolidation *(assemblage)* of two or more adjacent lots into one larger lot.

**point of beginning (POB)** In a metes-and-bounds legal description, the starting point of the survey, situated in one corner of the parcel; all metes-and-bounds descriptions must follow the boundaries of the parcel back to the point of beginning.

**police power** The government's right to impose laws, statutes, and ordinances, including zoning ordinances and building codes, to protect the public health, safety, and welfare.

**power of attorney** A written instrument authorizing a person, the *attorney-in-fact*, to act as agent on behalf of another person to the extent indicated in the instrument.

**prepaid items** On a closing statement, items that have been paid in advance by the seller, such as insurance premiums and some real estate taxes, for which he or she must be reimbursed by the buyer.

**prepayment penalty** A charge imposed on a borrower who pays off the loan principal early. This penalty compensates the lender for interest and other charges that would otherwise be lost.

**price fixing** *See* antitrust laws.

**primary mortgage market** The mortgage market in which loans are originated. The primary mortgage market consists of such lenders as commercial banks, savings and loan associations, and mutual savings banks.

**principal** (1) A sum loaned or employed as a fund or investment, as distinguished from its income or profits. (2) The original amount (as in a loan) of the total due and payable at a certain date. (3) A main party to a transaction—the person for whom the agent works.

**principal meridian** The main imaginary line running north and south and crossing a base line at a definite point, used by surveyors for reference in locating and describing land under the rectangular (government) survey system of legal description.

**prior appropriation** A concept of water ownership in which the landowner's right to use available water is based on a government-administered permit system.

**priority** The order of position or time. The priority of liens is generally determined by the chronological order in which the lien documents are recorded; tax liens, however, have priority even over previously recorded liens.

**private mortgage insurance (PMI)** Insurance provided by any private carrier that protects a lender against a loss in the event of a foreclosure and deficiency.

**probate** A legal process by which a court determines who will inherit a decedent's property and what the estate's assets are.

**procuring cause of sale** The effort that brings about the desired result. Under an open listing the broker who is the procuring cause of the sale receives the commission.

**progression** An appraisal principle that states that, between dissimilar properties, the value of the lesser-quality property is favorably affected by the presence of the better-quality property.

**promissory note** A financing instrument that states the terms of the underlying obligation, is signed by its maker, and is negotiable (transferable to a third party).

**property manager** Someone who manages real estate for another person for compensation. Duties include collecting rents, maintaining the property, and keeping up all accounting.

**property reports** The mandatory federal and state documents compiled by subdividers and developers to provide potential purchasers with facts about a property prior to its purchase.

**proprietary lease** A lease given by the corporation that owns a cooperative apartment building to the shareholder for the shareholder's right as a tenant to an individual apartment.

**prorations** Expenses, either prepaid or paid in arrears, that are divided or distributed between buyer and seller at the closing.

**protected class** Any group of people designated as such by the Department of Housing and Urban Development (HUD) in consideration of federal and state civil rights legislation. Currently includes ethnic minorities, women, religious groups, the handicapped, and others.

**public offering statement** A disclosure document given to a prospective purchaser under applicable federal and state laws. It contains the material facts about the property to allow the consumer to make an informed decision.

**puffing** Exaggerated or superlative comments or opinions.

**pur autre vie** "For the life of another." A life estate pur autre vie is a life estate that is measured by the life of a person other than the grantee.

**purchase-money mortgage (PMM)** A note secured by a mortgage or trust deed given by a buyer, as borrower, to a seller, as lender, as part of the purchase price of the real estate.

**pyramiding** The process of acquiring additional properties by refinancing properties already owned and investing the loan proceeds in additional properties.

**quantity-survey method** The appraisal method of estimating building costs by calculating the cost of all of the physical components in the improvements, adding the cost to assemble them, and then including the indirect costs associated with such construction.

**quiet title** A court action to remove a cloud on the title.

**quitclaim deed** A conveyance by which the grantor transfers whatever interest he or she has in the real estate, without warranties or obligations.

**range** A strip of land six miles wide, extending north and south and numbered east and west according to its distance from the principal meridian in the rectangular (government) survey system of legal description.

**rate cap** The limit on the amount the interest rate can be increased at each adjustment period in an adjustable-rate loan. The cap also may set the maximum interest rate that can be charged during the life of the loan.

**ratification** Method of creating an agency relationship in which the principal accepts the conduct of someone who acted without prior authorization as the principal's agent.

**ready, willing, and able buyer** One who is prepared to buy property on the seller's terms and is ready to take positive steps to consummate the transaction.

**real estate** Land; a portion of the earth's surface extending downward to the center of the earth and upward infinitely into space, including all things permanently attached to it, whether naturally or artificially.

**Real Estate Commission** The agency established to administer real estate laws and supervise the activities of licensees.

**real estate investment syndicate** *See* syndicate.

**real estate investment trust (REIT)** Trust ownership of real estate by a group of individuals who purchase certificates of ownership in the trust, which in turn invests the money in real property and distributes the profits back to the investors free of corporate income tax.

**real estate license laws** State laws enacted to protect the public from fraud, dishonesty, and incompetence in the purchase and sale of real estate.

**real estate mortgage investment conduit (REMIC)** A tax entity that issues multiple classes of investor interests (securities) backed by a pool of mortgages.

**real estate recovery fund** A fund established for aggrieved parties who have obtained uncollectible judgments against real estate licensees for fraud, deceit, or misrepresentation.

**Real Estate Settlement Procedures Act (RESPA)** The federal law that requires certain disclosures to consumers about mortgage loan settlements. The law also prohibits the payment or receipt of kickbacks and certain kinds of referral fees.

**real property** The interests, benefits, and rights inherent in real estate ownership.

**REALTOR®** A registered trademark term reserved for the sole use of active members of local REALTOR® boards affiliated with the National Association of REALTORS®.

**reconciliation** The final step in the appraisal process, in which the appraiser reconciles the estimates of value received from the sales comparison, cost, and income approaches to arrive at a final estimate of market value for the subject property.

**recorder of deeds** The county office in which matters relating to the real estate located within that county are filed.

**recording** The act of entering or recording documents affecting or conveying interests in real estate in the recorder's office established in each county. Until it is recorded, a deed or mortgage ordinarily is not effective against subsequent purchasers or mortgagees.

**rectangular (government) survey system** A system established in 1785 by the federal government, providing for surveying and describing land by reference to principal meridians and base lines.

**redemption** The right of a defaulted property owner to recover his or her property by curing the default.

**redemption period** A period of time established by state law during which a property owner has the right to redeem his or her real estate from a foreclosure or tax sale by paying the sales price, interest, and costs. Many states do not have mortgage redemption laws.

**redlining** The illegal practice of a lending institution's denying loans or restricting their number for certain areas of a community.

**reduction certificate (payoff statement)** The document signed by a lender indicating the amount required to pay a loan balance in full and satisfy the debt; used in the settlement process to protect both the seller's and the buyer's interests.

**regression** An appraisal principle that states that between dissimilar properties, the value of the better-quality property is adversely affected by the presence of the lesser-quality property.

**Regulation Z** Implements the Truth-in-Lending Act requiring that credit institutions inform borrowers of the true cost of obtaining credit.

**remainder interest** The remnant of an estate that has been conveyed to take effect and be enjoyed after the termination of a prior estate, such as when an owner conveys a life estate to one party and the remainder to another.

**rent** A fixed, periodic payment made by a tenant of a property to the owner for possession and use, usually by prior agreement of the parties.

**rental listing referral agent** A licensee who owns or manages a business that collects rental information for the purpose of referring prospective tenants to rental units or locations.

**rent schedule** A statement of proposed rental rates, determined by the owner or the property manager or both, based on a building's estimated expenses, market supply and demand, and the owner's long-range goals for the property.

**replacement cost** The construction cost at current prices of a property that is not necessarily an exact duplicate of the subject property but serves the same purpose or function as the original.

**reproduction cost** The construction cost at current prices of an exact duplicate of the subject property.

**rescission** The complete cancellation of a contract for the purchase of some types of personal property; does not apply to the purchase of real estate.

**restrictive covenants** A clause in a deed that limits the way the real estate ownership may be used.

**Resolution Trust Corporation** The organization created by FIRREA to liquidate the assets of failed savings and loan associations.

**reverse annuity mortgage (RAM)** A loan under which the homeowner receives monthly payments based on his or her accumulated equity rather than a lump sum. The loan must be repaid at a prearranged date or on the death of the owner or the sale of the property.

**reversionary interest** The remnant of an estate that the grantor holds after granting a life estate to another person.

**reversionary right** The return of the rights of possession and quiet enjoyment to the owner at the expiration of a lease or life estate.

**right of survivorship** *See* joint tenancy.

**right-of-way** The right given by one landowner to another to pass over the land, construct a roadway, or use as a pathway, without actually transferring ownership.

**riparian rights** An owner's rights in land that borders on or includes a stream, river, or lake. These rights include access to and use of the water.

**risk management** Evaluation and selection of appropriate property and other insurance.

**rules and regulations** Real estate licensing authority orders that govern licensees' activities; they usually have the same force and effect as statutory law.

**sale and leaseback** A transaction in which an owner sells his or her improved property and, as part of the same transaction, signs a long-term lease to remain in possession of the premises.

**sales comparison approach** The process of estimating the value of a property by examining and comparing actual sales of comparable properties.

**salesperson** A person who performs real estate activities while employed by or associated with a licensed real estate broker.

**sandwich lease** A lease under which the original tenant leases property and then sublets it for more money.

**satisfaction of mortgage** A document acknowledging the payment of a mortgage debt.

**secondary mortgage market** A market for the purchase and sale of existing mortgages, designed to provide greater liquidity for mortgages; also called the *secondary money market*. Mortgages are first originated in the *primary mortgage market*.

**section** A portion of a township under the rectangular (government) survey system. A township is divided into 36 sections, numbered 1 through 36. A section is a square with mile-long sides and an area of 1 square mile or 640 acres.

**security agreement** *See* Uniform Commercial Code.

**security deposit** A payment by a tenant, held by the landlord during the lease term and kept (wholly or partially) on default or destruction of the premises by the tenant.

**separate property** Under community property law, property owned solely by either spouse before the marriage, acquired by gift or inheritance after the marriage, or purchased with separate funds after the marriage.

**servient tenement** Land on which an easement exists in favor of an adjacent property (called a *dominant estate*); also called *servient estate*.

**setback** The amount of space local zoning regulations require between a lot line and a building line.

**severalty** Ownership of real property by one person only, also called *sole ownership*.

**severance** Changing an item of real estate to personal property by detaching it from the land; for example, cutting down a tree.

**sharecropping** In an agricultural lease, the agreement between the landowner and the tenant farmer to split the crop or the profit from its sale, actually sharing the crop.

**shared-appreciation mortgage (SAM)** A mortgage loan in which the lender, in exchange for a loan with a favorable interest rate, participates in the profits (if any) the borrower receives when the property eventually is sold.

**situs** The personal preference of people for one area over another, not necessarily based on objective facts and knowledge.

**special agent** One who is authorized by a principal to perform a single act or transaction; a real estate broker is usually a special agent authorized to find a ready, willing, and able buyer for a particular property.

**special assessment** A tax or levy customarily imposed against only those specific parcels of real estate that will benefit from a proposed public improvement such as a street or sewer.

**special limited warranty deed** A deed in which the grantor warrants, or guarantees, the title only against defects arising during the period of his or her ownership of the property and not against defects existing before that time, generally using the language, "by, through, or under the grantor but not otherwise."

**specific lien** A lien affecting or attaching only to a certain, specific parcel of land or piece of property.

**specific performance** A legal action to compel a party to carry out the terms of a contract.

**square-foot method** The appraisal method of estimating building costs by multiplying the number of square feet in the improvements being appraised by the cost per square foot for recently constructed similar improvements.

**statute of frauds** That part of a state law that requires that certain instruments, such as deeds, real estate sales contracts, and certain leases, be in writing to be legally enforceable.

**statute of limitations** That law pertaining to the period of time within which certain actions must be brought to court.

**statutory lien** A lien imposed on property by statute—a tax lien, for example—in contrast to an *equitable lien*, which arises out of common law.

**statutory right of redemption** The right of a defaulted property owner to recover the property after its sale by paying the appropriate fees and charges.

**steering** The illegal practice of channeling home seekers to particular areas to maintain the homogeneity of an area or to change the character of an area in order to create a speculative situation.

**straight-line method** A method of calculating depreciation for tax purposes, computed by dividing the adjusted basis of a property by the estimated number of years of remaining useful life.

**straight (term) loan** A loan in which only interest is paid during the term of the loan, with the entire principal amount due with the final interest payment.

**subagent** One who is employed by a person already acting as an agent. Typically a reference to a salesperson licensed under a broker (agent) who is employed under the terms of a listing agreement.

**subdivider** One who buys undeveloped land, divides it into smaller, usable lots, and sells the lots to potential users.

**subdivision** A tract of land divided by the owner, known as the *subdivider,* into blocks, building lots, and streets according to a recorded subdivision plat, which must comply with local ordinances and regulations.

**subdivision and development ordinances** Municipal ordinances that establish requirements for subdivisions and development.

**subdivision plat** *See* plat map.

**sublease** *See* subletting.

**subletting** The leasing of premises by a lessee to a third party for part of the lessee's remaining term. *See also* assignment.

**subordination** Relegation to a lesser position, usually in respect to a right or security.

**subordination agreement** A written agreement between holders of liens on a property that changes the priority of mortgage, judgment, and other liens under certain circumstances.

**subrogation** The substitution of one creditor for another, with the substituted person succeeding to the legal rights and claims of the original claimant. Subrogation is used by title insurers to acquire from the injured party rights to sue in order to recover any claims they have paid.

**substitution** An appraisal principle that states that the maximum value of a property tends to be set by the cost of purchasing an equally desirable and valuable substitute property, assuming that no costly delay is encountered in making the substitution.

**subsurface rights** Ownership rights in a parcel of real estate to the water, minerals, gas, oil, and so forth that lie beneath the surface of the property.

**suit for possession** A court suit initiated by a landlord to evict a tenant from leased premises after the tenant has breached one of the terms of the lease or has held possession of the property after the lease's expiration.

**suit for specific performance** *See* specific performance.

**suit to quiet title** A court action intended to establish or settle the title to a particular property, especially when there is a cloud on the title.

**supply** The amount of goods available in the market to be sold at a given price. The term is often coupled with *demand.*

**supply and demand** The appraisal principle that follows the interrelationship of the supply of and demand for real estate. As appraising is based on economic concepts, this principle recognizes that real property is subject to the influences of the marketplace just as is any other commodity.

**surety bond** An agreement by an insurance or bonding company to be responsible for certain possible defaults, debts, or obligations contracted for by an insured party; in essence, a policy insuring one's personal and/or financial integrity. In the real estate business, a surety bond is generally used to ensure that a particular project will be completed at a certain date or that a contract will be performed as stated.

**surface rights** Ownership rights in a parcel of real estate that are limited to the surface of the property and do not include the air above it (*air rights*) or the minerals below the surface (*subsurface rights*).

**survey** The process by which boundaries are measured and land areas are determined; the on-site measurement of lot lines, dimensions, and position of a house on a lot, including the determination of any existing encroachments or easements.

**syndicate** A combination of people or firms formed to accomplish a business venture of mutual interest by pooling resources. In a *real estate investment syndicate,* the parties own and/or develop property, with the main profit generally arising from the sale of the property.

**tacking** Adding or combining successive periods of continuous occupation of real property by adverse possessors. This concept enables someone who has not been in possession for the entire statutory period to establish a claim of adverse possession.

**taxation** The process by which a government or municipal quasi-public body raises monies to fund its operation.

**tax credit** An amount by which tax owed is reduced directly.

**tax deed** An instrument, similar to a certificate of sale, given to a purchaser at a tax sale. *See also* certificate of sale.

**tax lien** A charge against property created by operation of law. Tax liens and assessments take priority over all other liens.

**tax sale** A court-ordered sale of real property to raise money to cover delinquent taxes.

**tenancy (estate) by the entirety** The joint ownership, recognized in some states, of property acquired by husband and wife during marriage. Upon the death of one spouse the survivor becomes the owner of the property.

**tenancy in common** A form of co-ownership by which each owner holds an undivided interest in real property as if he or she were sole owner. Each individual owner has the right to partition. Unlike joint tenants, tenants in common have right of inheritance.

**tenant** One who holds or possesses lands or tenements by any kind of right or title.

**tenant improvements** Alterations to the interior of a building to meet the functional demands of the tenant.

**testate** Having made and left a valid will.

**testator** A person who has made a valid will. A woman often is referred to as a *testatrix,* although testator can be used for either gender.

**time is of the essence** A phrase in a contract that requires the performance of a certain act within a stated period of time.

**time-share ownership** A form of ownership interest that may include an estate interest in property or a contract for use, which allows use of the property for a fixed or variable time period.

**time-share salesperson** A licensee who, either as an employee or independent contractor, sells time-shares under the supervision of a broker.

**title** (1) The right to or ownership of land. (2) The evidence of ownership of land.

**title insurance** A policy insuring the owner or mortgagee against loss by reason of defects in the title to a parcel of real estate, other than encumbrances, defects, and matters specifically excluded by the policy.

**title search** The examination of public records relating to real estate to determine the current state of the ownership.

**title theory** Some states interpret a mortgage to mean that the lender is the owner of mortgaged land. On full payment of the mortgage debt the borrower becomes the landowner.

**Torrens system** A method of evidencing title by registration with the proper public authority, generally called the *registrar,* named for its founder, Sir Robert Torrens.

**township** The principal unit of the rectangular (government) survey system. A township is a square with 6-mile sides and an area of 36 square miles.

**trade fixture** An article installed by a tenant under the terms of a lease and removable by the tenant before the lease expires.

**transfer tax** Tax stamps required to be affixed to a deed by state and/or local law; also called *conveyance fee.*

**trust** A fiduciary arrangement whereby property is conveyed to a person or institution, called a *trustee,* to be held and administered on behalf of another person, called a *beneficiary.* The one who conveys the trust is called the *trustor.*

**trust deed** An instrument used to create a mortgage lien by which the borrower conveys title to a trustee, who holds it as security for the benefit of the note holder (the lender); also called a *deed of trust.*

**trustee** The holder of bare legal title in a deed of trust loan transaction.

**trustee's deed** A deed executed by a trustee conveying land held in a trust.

**trustor** A borrower in a deed of trust loan transaction.

**undivided interest** *See* tenancy in common.

**unenforceable contract** A contract that has all the elements of a valid contract, yet neither party can sue the other to force performance of it. For example, an unsigned contract is generally unenforceable.

**Uniform Commercial Code** A codification of commercial law, adopted in most states, that attempts to make uniform all laws relating to commercial transactions, including chattel mortgages and bulk transfers. Security interests in chattels are created by an instrument known as a *security agreement.* To give notice of the security interest, a *financing statement* must be recorded. Article 6 of the code regulates *bulk transfers*—the sale of a business as a whole, including all fixtures, chattels, and merchandise.

**unilateral contract** A one-sided contract wherein one party makes a promise so as to induce a second party to do something. The second party is not legally bound to perform; however, if the second party does comply, the first party is obligated to keep the promise.

**unit-in-place method** The appraisal method of estimating building costs by calculating the costs of all of the physical components in the structure, with the cost of each item including its proper installation, connection, etc.; also called the *segregated cost method.*

**unity of ownership** The four unities that are traditionally needed to create a joint tenancy—unity of title, time, interest, and possession.

**usury** Charging interest at a higher rate than the maximum rate established by state law.

**valid contract** A contract that complies with all the essentials of a contract and is binding and enforceable on all parties to it.

**VA loan** A mortgage loan on approved property made to a qualified veteran by an authorized lender and guaranteed by the Department of Veterans Affairs in order to limit the lender's possible loss.

**value** The power of a good or service to command other goods in exchange for the present worth of future rights to its income or amenities.

**variance** Permission obtained from zoning authorities to build a structure or conduct a use that is expressly prohibited by the current zoning laws; an exception from the zoning ordinances.

**vendee** A buyer, usually under the terms of a land contract.

**vendor** A seller, usually under the terms of a land contract.

**voidable contract** A contract that seems to be valid on the surface but may be rejected or disaffirmed by one or both of the parties.

**void contract** A contract that has no legal force or effect because it does not meet the essential elements of a contract.

**voluntary alienation** *See* alienation.

**voluntary lien** A lien placed on property with the knowledge and consent of the property owner.

**warranty of habitability** *See* implied warranty of habitability.

**waste** An improper use or an abuse of a property by a possessor who holds less than fee ownership, such as a tenant, life tenant, mortgagor, or vendee. Such waste ordinarily impairs the value of the land or the interest of the person holding the title or the reversionary rights.

**will** A written document, properly witnessed, providing for the transfer of title to property owned by the deceased, called the *testator*.

**wraparound loan** A method of refinancing in which the new mortgage is placed in a secondary, or subordinate, position; the new mortgage includes both the unpaid principal balance of the first mortgage and whatever additional sums are advanced by the lender. In essence it is an additional mortgage in which another lender refinances a borrower by lending an amount over the existing first mortgage amount without disturbing the existence of the first mortgage.

**zoning ordinance** An exercise of police power by a municipality to regulate and control the character and use of property.

# Answer Key

**Chapter 1**
**Introduction to the**
**Real Estate Business**

1. b (3)
2. b (4)
3. d (5)
4. c (4–5)
5. b (2)
6. d (3)
7. b (6)
8. a (2)
9. c (4)
10. b (4)
11. d (4)
12. d (5)
13. d (4)
14. d (3)
15. d (4)

**Chapter 2**
**Real Property**
**and the Law**

1. c (10)
2. b (14)
3. c (16)
4. c (14)
5. d (16)
6. b (11)
7. a (13)
8. a (15)
9. a (13)
10. a (13)
11. c (11)
12. b (12)

13. c (13)
14. d (11)
15. a (10)

**Chapter 3**
**Concepts of**
**Home Ownership**

1. d (23–24)
2. b (24)
3. a (22)
4. b (22)
5. b (25)
6. d (25)
7. d (26)
8. b (25)
9. c (24)
10. b (24)
11. c (25–26)
12. c (23–24)

**Chapter 4**
**Real Estate**
**Brokerage**

1. b (36)
2. c (34)
3. b (34)
4. b (33–34)
5. a (36–37)
6. d (34–35)
7. d (39–40)
8. a (39)
9. c (N/A)
10. b (37)
11. d (36)

12. a (37)
13. c (37–38)
14. a (37–38)
15. c (39)

**Chapter 5**
**Agency**

1. d (48)
2. a (46)
3. a (51)
4. b (46)
5. c (57)
6. b (48)
7. d (48)
8. d (51)
9. c (51–52)
10. c (51–52)
11. c (57)
12. c (44)
13. c (46)
14. d (60)
15. d (62)

**Chapter 6**
**Real Estate License**
**Laws**

1. a (91–93)
2. a (70–71)
3. c (90)
4. b (76)
5. a (91–93)
6. a (77)
7. c (92)
8. a (83)

9. a (91)
10. c (87)
11. b (87)
12. b (93)
13. d (71)
14. a (71)
15. a (72)
16. d (72)

**Chapter 7**
**Listing Agreements**
**and Buyer**
**Representation**

1. a (100)
2. c (100–101)
3. c (104)
4. a (101)
5. b (107–108)
6. d (103)
7. a (101)
8. c (105)
9. a (104)
10. d (107)
11. c (101–102)
12. b (101–102)
13. a (101)
14. b (101)
15. b (105–106)
16. a (107)
17. c (107)
18. c (103)
19. b (104)
20. c (114)

**Chapter 8**
**Interests in**
**Real Estate**

1. b (132)
2. a (124)
3. c (124)
4. d (129)
5. c (125)
6. a (125)
7. a (127)
8. d (129)
9. c (134)
10. a (130)
11. d (124)
12. b (128)
13. a (123)
14. b (125)
15. b (131)
16. c (127)
17. d (130)
18. a (129)
19. d (123)
20. b (129)
21. b (126)
22. d (126)
23. a (127)
24. c (N/A)
25. c (N/A)

**Chapter 9**
**Forms of Real Estate**
**Ownership**

1. b (142)
2. b (148)
3. b (145)
4. d (145)
5. b (142)
6. a (145)
7. b (148)
8. c (151)
9. c (147)
10. d (142)
11. d (143)
12. b (141)
13. b (142)
14. c (148)
15. b (148)
16. d (148)
17. a (143)
18. a (142)
19. b (143)
20. c (142)
21. a (147)

22. b (150)
23. d (151)
24. a (150)
25. d (150)
26. b (150)
27. d (N/A)

**Chapter 10**
**Legal Descriptions**

1. b (165)
2. d (165)
3. d (164)
4. b (157–158)
5. c (163–166)
6. c (163–166)
7. a (163–166)
8. a (163–166)
9. a (164–167)
10. d (170)
11. a (162–163)
12. c (162–163)
13. d (164–165)
14. c (163)
15. d (164)
16. b (164)
17. b (169)
18. b (164–165)
19. b (170)
20. b (170)
21. b (164–165)
22. b (164, 170)
23. b (163–165)
24. b (162)
25. c (157)
26. d (167)
27. c (157)
28. a (157–160)

**Chapter 11**
**Real Estate Taxes**
**and Other Liens**

1. d (176)
2. b (176–179)
3. b (181)
4. c (176)
5. b (176–178)
6. c (180–183)
7. c (178)
8. c (182)
9. b (178–181)
10. c (175–178)
11. d (183)
12. d (183)

13. c (181)
14. b (175)
15. b (175)
16. d (183)
17. d (181)
18. a (175–178)
19. b (178)
20. d (178)
21. c (180)
22. d (182)
23. d (180)
24. b (178)
25. c (181)
26. b (182)
27. a (180)
28. b (178)
29. a (181)
30. a (183)
31. b (178–179)
32. d (181)

**Chapter 12**
**Real Estate**
**Contracts**

1. c (189)
2. b (191)
3. d (190)
4. b (190)
5. c (191)
6. d (194)
7. d (197)
8. a (198)
9. a (199)
10. d (193)
11. b (202)
12. d (202)
13. d (202)
14. c (190)
15. b (192)
16. b (198)
17. a (193)
18. b (192)
19. d (193)
20. b (202)

**Chapter 13**
**Transfer of Title**

1. a (209)
2. d (210)
3. a (211)
4. b (213)
5. a (214)
6. d (213)

7. b (214)
8. c (211)
9. b (210–211)
10. b (211)
11. b (212)
12. c (215)
13. b (218–219)
14. d (217)
15. a (213)
16. a (213)
17. a (214)
18. b (219)
19. d (219)
20. b (219)
21. c (221–222)
22. b (221–222)
23. d (218)
24. d (214)
25. b (211)
26. b (214)
27. a (220)
28. b (214)
29. b (210)
30. a (214)

**Chapter 14**
**Title Records**

1. a (228)
2. a (229)
3. c (230–233)
4. a (238)
5. a (229–230)
6. d (232)
7. d (233)
8. d (230)
9. c (231)
10. a (230–231)
11. c (231–232)
12. c (235)
13. b (233)
14. d (233)
15. c (233)
16. a (232)
17. b (235)
18. a (229)
19. b (231)
20. c (229)
21. b (229)
22. b (229)
23. d (229)
24. d (231)

## Chapter 15
## Real Estate Financing: Principles

1. c (250)
2. b (253)
3. a (247)
4. d (246)
5. a (243)
6. d (250)
7. d (251)
8. b (245)
9. d (248)
10. a (248)
11. a (251)
12. b (246)
13. d (251)
14. a (244)
15. b (246)

## Chapter 16
## Real Estate Financing: Practice

1. d (266)
2. d (267)
3. c (272–273)
4. c (261)
5. b (271)
6. a (258)
7. b (271)
8. c (261)
9. b (267)
10. c (263)
11. b (273)
12. b (259)
13. b (272)
14. a (258)
15. b (273)
16. d (275)
17. b (261)
18. b (259)
19. b (259)
20. b (261)
21. c (262)

## Chapter 17
## Leases

1. c (285)
2. c (285)
3. d (293)
4. c (292–293)
5. b (291)
6. d (284)

7. c (283)
8. b (284)
9. b (294)
10. b (283–284)
11. a (291)
12. a (291)
13. b (285)
14. d (284)
15. c (285)
16. c (291)
17. b (293)
18. a (289)
19. b (294)

## Chapter 18
## Property Management

1. b (310)
2. a (304)
3. d (304)
4. c (310)
5. c (303–304)
6. b (310)
7. d (308)
8. b (307)
9. c (303)
10. a (304)
11. c (310)
12. c (311)
13. c (304)
14. b (307)
15. b (302)

## Chapter 19
## Real Estate Appraisal

1. c (315–316)
2. b (316)
3. d (317)
4. c (325–326)
5. b (318)
6. b (320)
7. b (319)
8. d (320)
9. a (320)
10. d (323–325)
11. c (327–328)
12. b (322–323)
13. a (325)
14. c (324–325)
15. c (325–326)
16. c (318)
17. b (326)

18. c (322)
19. d (325)
20. d (325)
21. b (321)
22. b (321)
23. b (324)
24. d (322–323)
25. b (328)
26. d (321)

## Chapter 20
## Land-Use Controls

1. a (342)
2. a (340–341)
3. b (342)
4. c (339)
5. c (339)
6. b (341–342)
7. a (340)
8. b (339)
9. a (340)
10. d (338)

## Chapter 21
## Property Development and Subdivision

1. b (347–348)
2. a (346–347)
3. c (347)
4. b (347–348)
5. b (348)
6. b (348)
7. d (347)
8. d (348)
9. a (348)
10. a (349–350)
11. a (346)

## Chapter 22
## Fair Housing and Ethical Practices

1. c (361–363)
2. a (368)
3. d (360)
4. b (365)
5. c (366)
6. a (367)
7. b (355–356)
8. b (366)
9. c (360)
10. b (363)
11. a (360)

12. b (362–363)
13. d (368)
14. c (355)
15. d (366)
16. c (363)

## Chapter 23
## Environmental Issues and the Real Estate Transaction

1. b (374–375)
2. c (375)
3. c (375–376)
4. a (374–375)
5. a (379)
6. c (379)
7. b (381–382)
8. d (383)
9. c (376–378)
10. d (374–375)
11. d (378)
12. c (381)

## Chapter 24
## Introduction to Real Estate Investment

1. c (389)
2. b (390–391)
3. b (390)
4. a (392)
5. b (392)
6. b (392)
7. c (N/A)
8. d (394)
9. a (393)
10. c (391)
11. d (395–396)
12. a (396)
13. c (395)
14. b (395)
15. b (396)

## Chapter 25
## Closing the Real Estate Transaction

1. d (413–414)
2. b (400)
3. d (402)
4. a (407)
5. d (403)
6. c (404–405)
7. c (407)
8. b (415)

9. b (415)

10. d (416–419)

11. c (416–419)

12. a (415–416)

13. c (411–412)

14. a (416–419)

15. c (408)

16. b (409)

17. b (411)

18. d (405–406)

19. d (405–406)

20. b (406)

21. b (405)

**Math Appendix**

1. a

2. c

3. c

4. d

5. a

6. a

7. d

8. b

9. d

10. c

11. b

12. d

# Index